THE DESTRUCTION OF REASON

THE DESTRUCTION OF REASON

Georg Lukács

Translated by Peter Palmer

HUMANITIES PRESS
ATLANTIC HIGHLANDS, N.J.

First published in the United States of America
in 1981 by
Humanities Press Inc., Atlantic Highlands, N.J.
and in Great Britain by
The Merlin Press Ltd,
3 Manchester Road,
London E14

Library of Congress Cataloging in Publication Data

Lukács, György, 1885-1971.
The destruction of reason.

Translation of: Az ész trónfosztása.
Includes index.
1. Philosophy, German. 2. Sociology--Germany--History. I. Title.
B2743.L7813 1981 193 81-2006
ISBN 0-391-02247-4 (Humanities) AACR2
ISBN 085036 247 4 (Merlin)

Printed in Great Britain by
Whitstable Litho Ltd., Whitstable, Kent

TRANSLATOR'S PREFACE

In Buffon's words, the style is the man. Among the salient features of Georg Lukács's German prose are the occasional rhetorical flourishes, reflecting the public speaker's communicative urge, and a penchant for elaborate sentence-constructions which, in their tracing of complex ideas, aim at illuminating both the wood *and* the trees. Inevitably, such features will undergo some modification in any readable English translation. It is hoped that the following text has not distorted them appreciably.

It is also hoped that the non-academic reader will accept the need for a certain amount of specialist terminology. Philosophy is not the only pursuit to use common words in an uncommon sense or to require some terms not to be found in common use. The esoteric language of a Heidegger, admittedly, comes close to defying translation, and a number of key terms have been rendered with the German in brackets for the benefit of the student of philosophy. For *Lebensphilosophie*, which forms the subject of Chapter IV, I have adopted Claud Sutton's 'Vitalism' in preference to the possibly confusing 'Life-philosophy'.

Unless otherwise indicated, existing translations of the German sources quoted have not been reproduced. Among the pros and cons of re-translation, a decisive factor for this book was the discovery of a post-World War II, 'definitive' Nietzsche translation bowdlerized in precisely the way which Lukács describes in Chapter III. If *The Destruction of Reason* succeeds in conveying its author, 'warts and all', then the present translator will consider his principal duty accomplished.

P.R.P.

CONTENTS

PREFACE

ON IRRATIONALISM AS AN INTERNATIONAL PHENOMENON IN THE IMPERIALIST PERIOD

This book lays no claim whatever to be a history of reactionary philosophy or even a primer of its development. Above all, the author is conscious that the irrationalism, whose growth and expansion into a dominant trend in bourgeois philosophy this book portrays, is only one of the important tendencies in reactionary bourgeois philosophy. Although there is hardly a reactionary philosophy without a definite irrationalist cast to it, the scope of reactionary bourgeois philosophy is nevertheless far broader than that of irrationalist philosophy in the authentic, stricter sense.

But even this qualification will not suffice to circumscribe our task precisely. Even within this narrower subject-range we are not offering a detailed, comprehensive and would-be complete history of irrationalism, but will simply be elaborating its chief line of development and analysing its most important, most typical stages and representatives. We intend to focus attention on this chief line as the most significant and influential kind of reactionary answer to the great topical problems of the past century and a half.

The history of philosophy, like that of art and literature, is never simply a history of philosophical ideas or even personalities, as its bourgeois historians think. Problems, and the directions in which they may be resolved, are posed in philosophy by the evolution of forces of production, by social developments and the development of class struggles. Only the observation of these primary motive forces can serve as a basis for tracing the decisive, fundamental lines of any philosophy. If one tries to posit and to solve the interrelations of philosophical problems starting out from a so-called immanent

philosophical development, an idealist distortion of the most important interrelations will inevitably come about. This is true even where a historian shows the necessary knowledge and, subjectively, an honest desire for objectivity. As against this standpoint, of course, the so-called humanistic (*geisteswissenschaftlich*) attitude is not a step forward but a step backwards: the distorting ideological starting-point remains, but it is even more blurred and ideologically distorting. One has only to compare Dilthey and his followers with the philosophical historiography of such Hegelians as Erdmann.

To argue thus does not by any means entail, as the vulgarizers suppose, a neglect of purely philosophical problems; on the contrary. Only such a context can clearly illustrate the difference between important questions of lasting significance and trivial academic hair-splitting. It is just the road leading away from social life and back again which lends philosophical ideas their real breadth and determines their profundity, even in the narrowly philosophical sense. How far individual thinkers are aware of their position in this respect, of their socio-historical function, is entirely secondary. In philosophy as outside of it, votes are cast not for attitudes but for deeds – for the objectified expression of ideas and for its historically necessary influence. In this sense, every thinker is responsible to history for the objective substance of his philosophizing.

Thus the subject-matter which now presents itself to us is Germany's path to Hitler in the sphere of philosophy. That is to say, we mean to show how this concrete path is reflected in philosophy, and how philosophical formulations, as an intellectual mirroring of Germany's concrete development towards Hitler, helped to speed up the process. That we are therefore confining ourselves to portraying the most abstract part of this development by no means implies an over-estimation of philosophy's importance in the turbulent totality of concrete developments. But we believe it is not superfluous to add that to underestimate the philosophical driving forces would be at least as dangerous and as little in accordance

with reality.

These perspectives will determine our mode of treating the subject-matter. The primary issues, above all with regard to the selection of material, are social genesis and function. It will be our task to bring to light all the intellectual spade-work done on behalf of the 'National Socialist outlook', however far removed (on the face of it) from Hitlerism it may be and however little (subjectively) it may cherish such intentions. It is one of this book's basic theses that there is no such thing as an 'innocent' philosophy. Such a thing has never existed, and especially not in relation to our stated problem. This is so in precisely the philosophical sense: to side either with or against reason decides at the same time the character of a philosophy as such and its role in social developments. Reason itself can never be something politically neutral, suspended above social developments. It always mirrors the concrete rationality – or irrationality – of a social situation and evolving trend, sums it up conceptually and thereby promotes or inhibits it. This social determinant of the contents and forms of reason does not, however, imply a historical relativism. For all the socio-historical conditioning of these contents and forms, the progressiveness of any situation or evolutionary trend is an objective thing operating independently of human consciousness. Now whether this forward thrust is interpreted as rational or irrational, and affirmed or repudiated as one or the other, is a crucially important factor in the taking of sides in philosophy, and in the class struggle.

To reveal this social genesis and function is of the greatest importance, but in itself by no means sufficient. Granted, the objectivity of progress will suffice correctly to condemn as reactionary an individual phenomenon or orientation. But a really Marxist-Leninist critique of reactionary philosophy cannot permit itself to stop at this. Rather it must show in real terms, in the philosophical material itself, the philosophical falsity and the distortion of basic philosophical questions, the negation of philosophy's achievements and so on to be

inevitable, objectively philosophical consequences of such stances. To this extent, an immanent critique is a justified and indeed indispensable element in the portrayal and exposure of reactionary tendencies in philosophy. The classic Marxist authors have constantly used it. Engels, for example, in his *Anti-Dühring* and Lenin in his *Empirio-Criticism*. To reject immanent criticism as one element in an overall survey also embracing social genesis and function, class characteristics, exploration of the true nature of society and so on is bound to lead to a philosophical sectarianism, to the attitude that everything which is axiomatic to a conscious Marxist-Leninist is also immediately obvious to his readers. Lenin wrote of the communists' political attitude: 'But the whole point is that one does *not* regard what is outmoded *for us* as outmoded *for the class* or outmoded *for the masses*.' And this also applies in its entirety to a Marxist presentation of philosophy. The antithesis between the various bourgeois ideologies and the achievements of dialectical and historical materialism is the self-evident foundation of our treatment and critique of the subject-matter. But to prove in factual, philosophical terms the inner incoherence, contradictoriness, etc., of the separate philosophies is also unavoidable if one wants to illustrate their reactionary character in a truly concrete way.

This general truth applies especially to the history of modern irrationalism. For the latter, as our book will undertake to show, arose and became operative in perpetual conflict with materialism and the dialectical method. In that respect, too, this philosophical controversy is a reflection of class struggles. For it is certainly no accident that the final and most advanced form of idealist dialectics developed in connection with the French Revolution and in particular with its social consequences. Only after the Revolution did the historical character of this dialectic, of which Herder and Vico were major forerunners, acquire a methodologically conscious and logically worked-out expression, principally in Hegel's dialectics. We are dealing now with the necessity

of a historical defence and amplification of the idea of progress reaching far beyond the Enlightenment's conception of it. (Of course this does not exhaust the factors encouraging this idealistic dialectic by a long chalk: I refer the reader merely to the new tendencies in the natural sciences which Engels locates in his *Feuerbach*.) Accordingly, the first important period of modern irrationalism has its origin in the struggle against the idealist dialectical-historical concept of progress. It constitutes the road from Schelling to Kierkegaard, and also the road from a feudal reaction against the French Revolution to bourgeois hostility to progress.

With the June massacre of the Parisian proletariat and with the Paris Commune in particular, the situation altered quite radically. From that time onwards the proletariat's world-view, dialectical and historical materialism, was the adversary whose character determined the further development of irrationalism. The new period found its first and most important representative in Nietzsche. Both phases of irrationalism contested the highest philosophical concept of progress obtaining at the time. But it made a qualitative difference – in the purely philosophical sense as well – whether the adversary was a bourgeois-idealist dialectic or the materialist dialectic and proletarian world-view, socialism. In the first phase, a relatively accurate critique based on factual knowledge and pointing out real failings and limitations in the idealist dialectic was still possible. In the second, on the other hand, we can see that the bourgeois philosophies were already unable and downright unwilling really to study the opponent and to refute him in a serious manner. This was already the case with Nietzsche, and the more firmly the new adversary emerged – especially after the October Revolution in 1917 – the weaker the will and capacity to contest the real, and correctly identified, opponent with respectable intellectual tools became. Distortion of the facts, calumny and demagogy increasingly superseded honest scientific polemics. This again clearly reflects an exacerbation of the class struggle. Each phase confirmed more and more strongly

Marx's statement after the 1848 revolution that '*Les capacités de la bourgeoisie s'en vont.*' And the bourgeoisie was losing ground not just in the aforesaid central polemics, but also in the whole construction, the overall working-out of the separate irrationalist philosophies. The apologetic virus was spreading from the question's core to the periphery: arbitrariness, contradictions, unsubstantiated and sophistic arguments, etc., characterized the later irrationalist philosophies more and more acutely. A lowering of the philosophical level is therefore a distinguishing mark of the development of irrationalism. This tendency was to reveal itself most vividly and obviously in the 'National Socialist outlook'.

But in spite of all this, we need to emphasize the unity behind the development of irrationalism. For merely to note the fact of a decline in philosophical standards will by no means suffice to characterize irrationalism's history. Such observations were repeatedly made in the bourgeois struggle – or purported struggle – against Hitler. Their purpose, however, was very often a counter-revolutionary one, indeed even that of an apologia for fascism itself: an exposure of Hitler and Rosenberg in order to salvage on the ideological plane 'the essence', the most reactionary form of German monopoly capitalism and the future of a new and aggressive German imperialism. The retreat from the 'sub-standard' Hitler to the 'eminent' Spengler, Heidegger or Nietzsche is thus, both politically and philosophically, a strategic withdrawal, a withdrawal from the pursuing enemy in order to organize the reactionary ranks and to instigate – under more favourable conditions – a renewed, methodologically 'improved' offensive on the part of reactionary extremism.

With regard to these tendencies, whose beginnings reach far into the past, two points need stressing. Firstly, the decline in philosophical standards was a necessary, socially determined phenomenon. The crucial factor was not the inferiority of Rosenberg's philosophical personality as compared, say, to Nietzsche. On the contrary: it was precisely Rosenberg's moral and intellectual inferiority that made him

the fit ideologist of National Socialism. And should the strategic retreat to Nietzsche or Spengler that we have indicated grow into a philosophical offensive again, its protagonist must – as a matter of historical necessity – represent philosophically an even lower level than Rosenberg, quite irrespective of his personal abilities, knowledge, etc. For what ultimately determines an ideologist's philosophical level is the depth to which he fathoms the questions of his day, his ability to raise these to the peak of philosophical abstraction, and the extent to which the standpoint derived from his class base allows him to explore these questions in their full depth and breadth. (We must always remember that Descartes's *cogito* or Spinoza's *deus sive natura* were highly topical and boldly partisan propositions and answers in their time.) Nietzsche's 'brilliant' arbitrariness and superficiality are, in their inferiority to classical thought, as much dictated by society as his superiority to the even more frivolous and vapid constructions of Spengler and indeed to Rosenberg's hollow demagogy. If we shift an appraisal of modern irrationalism to the plane of abstractly isolated differences in intellectual level, we are trying to evade the politico-social character and effects of its ultimate conclusions. Beside the political character of all such endeavours, we must also strongly emphasize another point which is inseparable from it: the futility of these endeavours, and precisely in the philosophical sense. (How this assumed concrete form in the post-war period we shall discuss in our epilogue.)

This observation has a close connection with our second point. We shall attempt in this book to demonstrate in detail that at no stage does the development of irrationalism evince an 'immanent' character, as though, that is to say, one proposition or answer could give rise to another, driven by the inner dialectic of the philosophical train of thought. We mean to show, on the contrary, that the various stages of irrationalism came about as reactionary answers to problems to do with the class struggle. Thus the content, form, method, tone, etc., of its reaction to progress in society are dictated

not by an intrinsic, inner dialectic of this kind, but rather by the adversary, by the fighting conditions imposed on the reactionary bourgeoisie. This must be borne in mind as the basic principle of the development of irrationalism.

But that does not mean that irrationalism — within the social framework we have defined – has no ideal unity behind it; just the opposite. It follows from its very nature that the problems of content and methodology it raises are closely linked and reveal a striking unity (and a narrow one). The disparagement of understanding and reason, an uncritical glorification of intuition, an aristocratic epistemology, the rejection of socio-historical progress, the creating of myths and so on are motives we can find in virtually any irrationalist. The philosophical reaction by representatives of the remains of feudalism and by the bourgeoisie to social progress may in specific circumstances, in personally talented individual proponents of this direction, receive an ingenious and brilliant form. The philosophical substance pervading the whole development, however, is extremely monochrome and threadbare. And, as we have shown above, the intellectual scope of the polemic, the chance of absorbing within the system of ideas at least some reflections of reality, however distorted, will shrink continually by dint of social necessity. Hence a fall in the philosophical standard while specific crucial intellectual factors remain constant is inevitable. The adherence to these pervasive thought-determinants is a reflection of the uniformly reactionary social foundations of irrationalism, however many qualitative changes can and must be noted in the development from Schelling to Hitler. Thus the contribution of German irrationalist philosophy to Hitlerism is an inevitable thing only insofar as the concrete class struggles produced this result – not without the help, certainly, of this ideological development. From the standpoint of irrationalism's development, therefore, the products of these class struggles are unalterable facts acquiring a matching philosophical reflection to which irrationalism reacts in one way or another. Seen from this angle, though, they are

just that – unalterable. Of course we are far from asserting that they were, from an objective historical angle, predestined.

If, therefore, we are seeking a proper understanding of the development of German irrationalist philosophy, we must always bear in mind the following related factors: the dependence of irrationalism's development on the crucial class struggles in Germany and throughout the world, which naturally implies the denial of an 'immanent' development; the uniformity of the contents and methods, along with a continual narrowing of the scope for real philosophical development, which is bound to encourage a heightening of apologetic and demagogic tendencies; and finally as a sequel to this, a necessary, constant and rapid decline in the philosophical level. Only now can we understand how Hitler contrived a demagogic popularization of all the intellectual motives of entrenched philosophical reaction, the ideological and political 'crowning' of the development of irrationalism.

The aim of clearly elaborating these motives and tendencies in German irrationalism's development will determine our mode of presentation. Hence our concern can be only to present the most important nodal points in their proper light by thorough analysis, not a complete history of irrationalism or even of reactionary thought in general claiming to deal with or at least to enumerate all the basic shapes and tendencies. Thus we are consciously renouncing any claim to comprehensiveness. If, for instance, we discuss Romantic irrationalism at the start of the nineteenth century, we shall demonstrate its most important characteristics in Schelling, the chief proponent of this direction, while Friedrich Schlegel, Baader, Görres, etc., will be mentioned in passing or not at all. We shall also omit a discussion of Schleiermacher, whose particular tendencies attained a broad reactionary significance only through Kierkegaard; we shall omit the irrationalism of Fichte's second period, which gained an influence (episodic in the overall development) only in the Rickert school, with Lask especially; we shall omit Weisse and the

younger Fichte, etc., etc. Thus in the imperialist period, Husserl will take a back seat because the irrational tendencies inherent in his philosophical method from the outset only became really explicit through Scheler and particularly through Heidegger. Leopold Ziegler and Keyserling will play second fiddle to Spengler, Theodor Lessing to Klages, Jaspers to Heidegger, and so on.

Our interpretation of irrationalism as the decisive principal stream of reactionary philosophy in the nineteenth and twentieth centuries dictates a further omission. This is the omission of some important and influential, firmly reactionary thinkers for whom irrationalism did not constitute the centre of their intellectual world. These include the eclectic Eduard von Hartmann, when set beside the entrenched irrationalist Nietzsche; Lagarde, again in relation to Nietzsche; and in the period directly foreshadowing German fascism, Moeller van den Bruck and many others. By thus restricting our subject-matter we hope to bring out the main line of development more clearly. Future historians of German philosophy will, we hope, round out and present in full detail the general line of reactionary philosophy in Germany portrayed in this book.

Our aim and our subject-matter further dictate that the line running from Schelling to Hitler cannot be presented in that unitary form which it had in social reality. Chapters II to IV will attempt to illustrate this development in the sphere of irrationalist thought in the narrower sense. These chapters will expound the aforesaid programme: the line of development from Schelling to Hitler. But this cannot be considered a complete answer. Firstly, we are still obliged to show with at least one significant example how irrationalism, as the epoch's chief reactionary bias, was able to make the whole of bourgeois philosophy subservient to it. This will be demonstrated in detail in Chapter V, on imperialist neo-Hegelianism, with only a brief reference to the most important pioneers. Secondly, Chapter VI will present the same development in the realm of German sociology that we will have already

analysed in philosophy. We believe that by treating so important a topic in isolation rather than divided and scattered over the philosophical sections, we cannot but enhance the clarity and meaning of the overall picture. And thirdly and lastly, the historical forerunners of racial theory will likewise be dealt with in isolation in Chapter VII. Only in this way can we set in its proper light the central importance which so humdrum an eclectic as H.S. Chamberlain attained in German fascism: for he it was who 'synthesized' the philosophical irrationalism of the imperialist age, vitalism, with racial theory and the findings of Social Darwinism. Thus he became a direct precursor of Hitler and Rosenberg, the philosophical 'classic' of National Socialism. Plainly it is in just this context that our summary treatment of the Hitlerian age can be properly made to tell, although of course the findings of Chapters IV and VI must always be taken into consideration. It goes without saying that this mode of presentation has its drawbacks; Simmel, for instance, was an influential sociologist, but we shall analyse his work essentially with regard to imperialist vitalism. And although there exist close connections between Rickert and Max Weber, Dilthey and Freyer, Heidegger and Carl Schmitt, etc., they must still be dealt with separately. These are unavoidable flaws to which we must call attention in advance. We hope, however, that the clear presentation of the principal line will outweigh the negative aspects.

We can hardly look to historical preliminary studies for support in this task. So far there is no Marxist history of philosophy, and the bourgeois accounts are totally useless from the standpoint of our inquiries. Of course this is no accident. The bourgeois historians of German philosophy ignore or chop down the roles of Marx and of Marxism. Hence they cannot adopt a proper stance either to the major crisis of German philosophy in the thirties and forties or to its later phase of decline, not even approximately and in respect of the facts. According to the Hegelians German philosophy ended with Hegel; according to the neo-Kantians

it reached its peak with Kant and the confusion sown by his successors could only be rectified by a return to Kant. Eduard von Hartmann tried to effect a 'synthesis' between Hegel and irrationalism (the irrationalism of the later Schelling and Schopenhauer), and so on. At all events the bourgeois historians regard the decisive crisis in German philosophy, viz., the dissolution of Hegelianism, as lying outside the history of philosophy. Chiefly on the basis of their affirmation of irrationalism, the imperialist historians of philosophy created a harmony between Hegel and Romantic thought on the one hand, and a harmony between Kant and Hegel on the other. They thereby mentally excluded all the important conflicts of orientation, drawing instead a unitary and unproblematic, non-contradictory line of development up to the irrationalism – which they affirmed – of the imperialist period. The sole Marxist historian, Franz Mehring, achieved a great deal in other fields. But as regards this subject, he knew too little of classical German philosophy, Kant excepted, and did not sufficiently perceive the specific features of the imperialist age to offer us any pointers.

The one book in recent times which at least bids fair to examine the problems pertaining to the German development is Karl Löwith's knowledgeable work, *From Hegel to Nietzsche*. It marks the first bourgeois attempt in German history of philosophy to incorporate the dissolution of Hegelianism, the young Marx's philosophy, organically into the development. But the mere fact that Löwith makes this development culminate in Nietzsche and – not in a depreciatory sense – proves that he failed to see the real problems of the period under discussion and turned them firmly on their heads wherever he encountered them. Since he perceives the main direction merely as leading away from Hegel, he sets on the same plane the Right- and the Left-wing critics of Hegel, particularly Kierkegaard and Marx, and presents their opposition on every question as a mere difference of thematic material, assuming them to share an essentially related basic tendency. It goes without saying that, given this attitude,

Löwith sees only shades of difference within a similar bias and no qualitative antitheses between the Hegelians of the time of dissolution (Ruge, Bauer), Feuerbach and Marx. Since his book occupies an almost unique position, with regard to knowledge of the subject, in the more recent bourgeois history of philosophy, we shall quote a crucial passage at some length. This will enable the reader to judge for himself how this method led to the equating of Marx and Kierkegaard, and so on, to the similar conclusions drawn by some 'Leftist' pre-fascists (e.g., H. Fischer in *Marx und Nietzsche*). Löwith writes:

> Shortly before the revolution of 1848, Marx and Kierkegaard lent to the demand for a resolution a language whose words still claim our attention: Marx in the *Communist Manifesto* (1847) and Kierkegaard in *A Literary Review*, (1846). The one manifesto ends 'Proletarians of all countries, unite!' and the other to the effect that each person must work at his own salvation, prophecies about the course of the world being tolerable only as a joking matter. But regarded from the historical angle, this antithesis only signifies two sides of a common destruction of the bourgeois Christian world. For a revolution of the bourgeois *capitalist* world, Marx found support in the proletarian mass, whereas Kierkegaard, in his struggle against the bourgeois *Christian* world, staked everything on the individual. Accordingly, bourgeois society for Marx is a society of 'isolated individuals' where man is alienated from his 'generic character', and Christendom for Kierkegaard is a Christianity disseminated on a mass scale where nobody is an apostle of Christ. But because Hegel reconciled these contradictions of existence in the essence, bourgeois society with the State and the State with Christianity, the resolution of both Marx and Kierkegaard aims at emphasizing the difference and contradiction in precisely those conciliatory acts. Marx is concerned with the kind of self-alienation which capitalism causes in a person, and Kierke-

gaard with the self-alienation which Christianity causes in a Christian.

Thus here again we meet with an obscurity in which all cats look grey. Marxist historians will find no help in such preliminary studies when it comes to mastering this subject.

Finally, we must raise the question of why our account – with a few interpolations like Kierkegaard and Gobineau – confines itself to *German* irrationalism. In Chapter I we shall try and outline the particular conditions which made Germany eminently suitable as a hotbed of irrationalism. But that does not alter the fact that irrationalism is an international phenomenon, both in its campaign against the bourgeois concept of progress and the campaign against the socialist concept of it. And there can be no question that important spokesmen for social and political reaction have appeared in the most diverse countries in both periods. That goes for Burke in England, whilst the French Revolution was still in progress, and for Bonald, De Maistre and others in France later on. To be sure these thinkers were contesting the ideology of the French Revolution without constructing for the purpose a specific and new philosophical method, as happened in Germany. Granted, such attempts were indeed made; let us recall, say, Maine de Biran. But there can be no doubt that even the last-named was far from causing such lasting international repercussions as Schelling or Schopenhauer. He also elaborated the foundations of the new irrationalism far less resolutely and dogmatically. This in turn is linked with the fact that Maine de Biran, in contrast to the German Romantics' firmly reactionary nature, was an ideologist of the *juste milieu* or golden mean. The irrationalist upsurge in imperialist times is a particularly salient example of the leading role that Germany played in this sphere. Here, of course, we are thinking chiefly of Nietzsche, who became the paradigm in content and methodology of irrationalist philosophical reaction from the U.S.A. to Tsarist Russia, and whose influence could not and cannot be rivalled even

approximately by a single other reactionary ideologist. But later on, too, Spengler was still an international model for irrationalist conceptions of the philosophy of history up to Toynbee. Heidegger, the model for French existentialism, who had long previously exerted a decisive influence on Ortega y Gasset, has a profound and dangerous sort of influence on bourgeois thought in the United States, and so on and so forth.

The determining causes of this difference between Germany and elsewhere could, of course, only be worked out on the basis of the concrete history of the separate countries. It would take such a historical study to establish the specific tendencies which, while receiving in Germany their 'classic', most rigorously evolved form, mostly stopped half way in other countries. Naturally there is the case of Mussolini, whose philosophical sources were William James, Pareto, Sorel and Bergson; but even here the international influence does not have anything like the breadth and depth already reached in pre-fascist Germany and, most of all, under Hitler. Thus we can everywhere observe the emergence of all the motive elements of irrationalism. And to that extent it is indeed an international phenomenon, especially in the imperialist period. Only extremely seldom, in isolated episodic cases, however, was irrationalism taken to all its conclusions to become a universally dominant tendency, as it became in Germany. To that extent, the hegemony of the German development remained intact. (The present situation will be discussed in our epilogue.)

One can already discern this tendency before the First World War. In nearly all the leading countries as in Germany, irrationalism achieved highly developed forms in the imperialist period. There was Pragmatism in the English-speaking countries, Boutroux, Bergson and others in France, Croce in Italy. Despite a profound affinity in their ultimate intellectual foundations, the forms display an extremely motley diversity. This was determined primarily by the nature, height and intensity of the class struggle in each country

concerned, and also by the traditional philosophical heritage and the immediate intellectual opposition. In our detailed analyses of the individual stages of the German development we shall adduce these, as already indicated, from concrete historical circumstances. Without thus locating the real socio-historical foundations, no scientific analysis is possible. This, of course, applies also to the following studies. They therefore make no claim whatever to be even the outline of a scientific definition of philosophies or intellectual trends. They will merely suggest that specific highly universal features had their origin in the (general) identity of imperialist economics. To be sure, this is not to overlook the different stages of development achieved in different countries, the uneven character of the development under imperialism, which produced concrete differences notwithstanding the identical foundations.

Here, of course, we can only give a number of swiftly sketched examples to illustrate our conception. Similar ideological needs, deriving this similarity from imperialist economics, produced very different and indeed – superficially considered – apparently opposed versions of irrationalism in differing concrete social circumstances. Let us look now at Croce, and at William James and Pragmatism. Both thinkers, as far as direct philosophical forerunners are concerned, were at odds with specific Hegelian traditions. The fact that this was possible in the imperialist age reflects a difference between the German philosophical development and that in other Western European countries. The 1848 revolution ended, for Germany, the disintegration of Hegelianism; the irrational Schopenhauer became the leading philosopher of post-revolutionary Germany and the time of preparation for the establishment of the Reich under Bismarck. In the English-speaking countries and Italy, on the other hand, Hegelian philosophy still played a leading part during this period, indeed it even gained a greater influence. This rested upon the fact that the bourgeois idea of progress had not yet entered the overt crisis present in Germany; here

the crisis remained latent and out of sight, and the concept of progress merely underwent a liberal ironing-out and watering-down in accordance with the results of 1848. Philosophically the upshot of this was that Hegelian dialectics completely lost their character as the 'algebra of revolution' (Herzen) and that Hegel was brought increasingly in line with Kant and Kantianism. Hence a Hegelianism of this kind, especially in English-speaking countries, could be a parallel phenomenon to the burgeoning sociology which was similarly preaching a liberal evolutionism, primarily that of Herbert Spencer. Here, let us note in passing that a similar retrogression to Kant occurred in the remnants of German Hegelianism, but because of the whole trend's general repression it played a less important role than it did farther West. Suffice it to refer to the development of Rosenkranz and Vischer. The latter played a pioneering role in imperialist philosophy inasmuch as his recourse to Kant already incorporated the irrationalist view of that philosopher.

Although Croce was by no means directly influenced by Vischer, his relation to Hegel (and to Vico whom he 'discovered' and promoted) followed a similar line of irrationalization. He therefore came very close to the later German Hegelianism of the imperialist period, but with the major difference that, whereas this purportedly renewed Hegelian philosophy was seen as a blanket ideology for a reactionary movement (National Socialism included) that needed unifying, Croce halted at an imperialist liberalism – albeit an abundantly reactionary one – and rejected fascism philosophically. (To be sure the other prominent Italian Hegelian, Gentile, temporarily became the ideologist of fascism's 'consolidation period'.) When Croce divorces the 'live' from the 'dead' matter in Hegel, the former is nothing but an irrationalism of a moderate liberal cast, and the latter: dialectics and objectivity. Both tendencies have as their main content the rebuttal of Marxism. What is philosophically crucial about this is the radical subjectifying of history and the radical elimination from it of all laws and principles. 'A historical

law, a historical concept are', wrote Croce, 'a veritable contradiction in terms.' History, Croce expounded elsewhere, is always a history of the present. What is remarkable about this is not only the close affinity with the Windelband-Rickert bias in Germany, with the incipient irrationalizing of history. It is also the way that Croce resolves a real dialectical proposition, viz., that our perception of the present (the highest stage so far in an evolutionary series) provides the key to knowing the less advanced stages of the past, into an irrational subjectivism. History turns into art – art, of course, in Croce's meaning of the term, whereby a purely formal perfection is coupled with intuition, purported to be the sole organ of creativity and an appropriate receptiveness. Except for an area of economic praxis (subordinated to the system) and a preserve of logic and natural sciences (similarly subsumed in the system and conceived in independence of actual reality), reason was banished from every sphere of men's social activity. (Here again we can see the parallel with Windelband and Rickert.) In short: Croce created an irrationalist 'system' for the bourgeois-decadent use of the parasitic elements of the imperialist period. For reactionary extremists, this irrationalism was already ceasing to suffice before the First World War; let us recall the Right-wing opposition to Croce on Papini's part, etc. But it is a notable fact – contrasted with Germany – that Croce's liberal-reactionary irrationalism has managed to survive as one of Italy's leading ideologies to this day.

Of Pragmatism's proponents, we shall now briefly discuss only the most outstanding, William James. Pragmatism is, in its philosophical essence, far more radically irrationalist than Croce's thought, without going decidedly farther in its conclusions as a result. Only, the public to whom James offered his irrationalist substitute for a world-view was of an entirely different nature. Granted, if we take the immediate philosophical background, the direct historical predecessors whose work was taken up by James polemically, the situation appears to exhibit certain similarities. For in both cases we

are dealing with so-called Hegelians who are in fact overt or clandestine Kantians and subjective idealists. However, their attitudes were already diametrically opposed. Whereas Croce professed to be continuing Italy's Hegelian (and Vicoesque) traditions while actually carrying them over into an irrationalism, James was openly at odds with the Hegelian traditions of the English-speaking countries.

This overt polemic displays a very far-reaching affinity with the European development. Mach and Avenarius, while apparently directing the brunt of their attacks against obsolescent idealism, were in fact only offering a real challenge to philosophical materialism, and so was William James. And he is also very close to them in that this combining of the real struggle against materialism with sham attacks on idealism carries with it a presumption that his 'new' philosophy would finally transcend the false antithesis of materialism and idealism and marked the discovery of a 'third road' in philosophy. Since this affinity relates to virtually all the essential philosophical issues, it must form the basis for an appraisal of Pragmatism. The differences between James and the European minds are, however, at least as important from our particular standpoint. The main reason for this is that the irrationalism which is contained implicitly in Machism and only gradually emerges with any firmness was already explicit in James and appears fully fledged. This is seen in the fact that, whereas Mach and Avenarius were striving mainly for an epistemological rationale of the exact natural sciences and professed complete neutrality on questions of world-view, James claimed nothing less than the ability to give a direct answer to these questions with the help of his new philosophy. From the start, therefore, he did not address himself to relatively restricted scholarly circles but endeavoured to satisfy the philosophical needs of everyday life and the man in the street. In appearance, there is only a terminological difference when the Machists set up 'economy of thought' (*Denkökonomie*) as the epistemological criterion of truth, whereas James simply equates truth and utility (for the

individual concerned). On the one hand, James was thereby extending the validity of Machist epistemology to cover the whole of life and lending it a pronounced vitalistic accent. On the other, he was giving it a more universal validity that went beyond the technics of *Denkökonomie*.

Here again, irrationalism's basic attitude to dialectics is clearly visible. It is a fundamental thesis of dialectical materialism that praxis forms the criterion of theoretical truth. The accuracy or inaccuracy of the intellectual reproduction of objective reality existing independently of our consciousness, or rather our degree of approximation to it, is verified only in praxis and through praxis. Now James clearly saw the limitations, the futility of metaphysical idealism and repeatedly pointed it out (e.g., idealism views the world 'as perfect and finished from all eternity', whereas Pragmatism attempts to grasp it in its becoming). Yet he took away from both theory and praxis all relation to objective reality, thereby converting the dialectic into a subjectivistic irrationalism. And James openly admitted as much with his undertaking to meet the philosophical needs of the American 'man in the street'. Reality, in everyday business life, must be scrupulously observed – on pain of bankruptcy (notwithstanding the epistemological denial of its objective truth and its independence of the consciousness). In all other spheres of life, however, irrational arbitrariness has a quite unlimited sway. James wrote: 'The practical world of business is, for its own part, highly rational to the politician, the soldier, the man ruled by the commercial spirit . . . But it is irrational for the moral and artistic temperament.'

Here one very important determining factor of irrationalism becomes clearly evident. For in the eyes of the reactionary bourgeoisie, one of irrationalism's most important tasks is to provide men with a philosophical 'comfort', the semblance of total freedom, the illusion of personal autonomy, moral and intellectual superiority – while maintaining an attitude that continually links them with the reactionary bourgeoisie in their real dealings and renders them absolutely subservient

to it. We shall have a chance to see in detailed analyses later how this 'comfort' underlies even the 'most sublime' asceticism of irrationalist philosophy, as in Schopenhauer or Kierkegaard. James expresses this idea with the naive cynicism of the successful, self-aware American businessman, fulfilling the philosophical needs of persons of Babbitt's type. Babbitt too, as Sinclair Lewis so neatly shows, wants his right confirmed to a highly personal intuition, and he too learns in practice that truth and utility are synonymous terms in the life a true American leads. Intellectually, of course, James's awareness and cynicism are a cut above those of Sinclair Lewis's Babbitt. James, for example, rejects idealism, but he does not neglect to pay pragmatic lip-service to it insofar as it is of use in daily life, since it enhances the philosophical comfort. James wrote of the Absolute in idealism: 'It guarantees us time off from morality. That is also what every religious outlook provides.' But this comfort would have little influence intellectually if it did not contain a sharp repudiation of materialism, an alleged refutation of the scientifically based world-view. James makes cynically light work of this task as well. He does not cite – logically, pragmatically – a single solid argument against materialism; he merely notes that it is no whit 'more useful' than a belief in God as a theoretical explanation for the world. 'If', he states, 'we call the world's first cause matter, we will not be taking away a single component part or adding to its abundance when we call its first cause God . . . God, if He exists, has performed exactly as much as atoms can, and God has earned just as much thanks as the atoms, not more.' So Babbitt is free to believe in God, the god of any religion or sect whatever, without transgressing against the demands which science makes of an up-to-date gentleman.

With James the idea of myth-making never appears with the same clear substantiality it has in Nietzsche, who exhibits many pragmatic features in his epistemology and ethics. But James did create an epistemological rationale and even a moral law for every Babbitt's creation or adoption in all

spheres of life, for his personal use, of those myths that happen to seem useful to him; Pragmatism allows him to do this with a clear conscience intellectually. In its very insubstantiality and shallowness, then, Pragmatism was the storehouse of philosophies that pre-war America needed with her perspective of unlimited prosperity and security.

It is, of course, axiomatic that as far as Pragmatism gained an influence in other lands conditioned by an acuter and more advanced form of the class struggle, its merely implicit elements had quickly to become explicit. Bergson is the best illustration of this. Naturally we are by no means suggesting that Pragmatism influenced Bergson directly; on the contrary, we are now dealing once more with parallel tendencies, and the mutual esteem in which Bergson and James held each other underlines the parallel from the subjective side as well. What they had in common was the rejection of objective reality and its rational observability, the reduction of perception to a merely technical utility, and their recourse to an intuitive apprehension of true reality which they decreed to be irrational in essence. Despite this common underlying bias there are considerable differences of accents and proportions whose causes must be sought in the different societies in which they wrote, and accordingly in the different intellectual traditions which they inherited, whether willingly or the opposite. On the one hand, Bergson developed modern agnosticism into an overt proclaiming of myths far more boldly and firmly than James. On the other hand, his philosophy was aimed far more exclusively – at least at the time he had an internationally crucial influence – at a critique of natural-scientific views, at destroying their right to pronounce objective truths, and at a philosophical replacement of the natural sciences with biological myths, than at tackling problems relating to the life of society. Only very late in his career did his book on morality and religion appear, and it was far from gaining the general influence of his earlier biological myths. Bergsonian intuition was projected outwards as a tendency to destroy the objectivity and truth of

natural scientific knowledge; and it was directed inwards as the introspection of an isolated parasitic individual divorced from the life of society during the imperialist period. (It is no accident that the greatest literary influence Bergson exerted was on Proust.)

Here, the contrast not only to William James but in particular to Bergson's German contemporaries and admirers is quite palpable. Dilthey's equally intuitive 'vision of genius', Simmel's and Gundolf's intuition, Scheler's 'intuitive vision' (*Wesensschau*), etc., were predisposed to be socially oriented. (Not to mention Nietzsche and Spengler.) In such cases, the departure from objectivity and rationality presents itself promptly and directly as a resolute stand against social progress. With Bergson this was only indirectly the case. In this respect his late ethico-religious work, despite a strong reactionary and mystical bias, lagged far behind German irrationalism at the time of its publication. Naturally that is not to say that Bergson's influence in France was not similarly oriented; of Sorel we shall write in more detail shortly. And among other authors, from Péguy's conversion to reactionary Catholicism up to the early works of Raymond Aron, De Gaulle's present ideological agent, the same influence can always be detected.

Bergson's main attack, however, was levelled against the objectivity and scientific character of natural scientific knowledge. The abstract and stark confrontation of rationality and irrationalist intuition reached its climax with Bergson, epistemologically speaking, in pre-war imperialism. What Mach still treated as purely epistemological and James developed into a general argumentation of subjective individual myths, Bergson presents as a coherent mythical and irrational world-picture. And this sets up a mobile and colourful metaphysical tableau in contrast to the picture offered by the natural sciences, whose claim to an objective perception of reality Bergson rejected as firmly as Mach or James and to which, like them, he accorded only a mechanical utility. A world of movement, vitality, time and duration confronts a

lifeless, moribund world ossified in the spatial dimension. With Bergson, Mach's purely agnosticist recourse to the subjective immediacy of apprehension grows into a philosophy based on radically irrationalist intuition.

Here too the basic character of modern irrationalism is clearly discernible. Bergson did not contrast the failure of the metaphysical-mechanical approach in the face of the dialectics of reality – the cause of the natural sciences' universal crisis under imperialism – with perception of the real dialectical movement and principle. Only dialectical materialism could do that. Bergson's achievement lies instead in his invention of a world-picture which, behind the attractive semblance of a vital mobility, actually restored the conservative, reactionary stasis. Let us clarify the situation with just one key problem. Bergson challenged the mechanical, moribund element in evolutionary theories of Spencer's type, but at the same time he rejected the biological inheritability of acquired characteristics. Thus on the very issue where a dialectical extension of Darwin had become necessary and feasible (Michurin and Lysenko have proceeded with this problem on the basis of dialectical materialism), Bergson went against the real theory of evolution. His philosophy thus became linked above all with the international movement to destroy the natural sciences' objectivity which Mach and Avenarius had started, and which also found very important exponents in France during the imperialist age. We need only refer to Poincaré and Duhem.

In France, where the Enlightenment tradition (along with that of materialism and atheism) has far deeper roots than in Germany, these tendencies were of particularly great significance philosophically. But as we have shown, Bergson far exceeded this tendency in creating decidedly irrational myths. Championing an irrationalist world-picture, he levelled his philosophical attacks against objectivity and rationality, against the dominance of reason (another old French tradition). He thereby provided those Right-wing, reactionary critics of capitalist life who had already been active for

decades with a philosophical corner-stone, the semblance of an agreement with the latest findings of the natural sciences. Up to this time most of the reactionary ideologists in France had conducted their attack largely in the name of Royalism and ultramontanism, so that their influence was restricted to circles predisposed to be firmly reactionary. But Bergson's philosophy also addressed itself to an intelligentsia which, dissatisfied with the capitalistically corrupt development of the Third Republic, was also starting to look for a path leading Left in the socialist direction. Like every major irrational vitalist, Bergson 'added depth' to the problem by treating it as a question of the universal philosophical antithesis between the live and the moribund. And without his spelling it out to them, these circles readily grasped that capitalist democracy was meant by the concept of the moribund, and that Bergson was offering their opposition to it a philosophical prop. (We will try and illustrate with Sorel how this took effect in reality.)

In this respect, Bergson enjoyed an influence in France during the crisis at the end of the nineteenth and the start of the twentieth century (the Dreyfus case, etc.) similar to Nietzsche's in Germany at the time the anti-socialist law was revoked. The difference lies once more in the fact that Nietzsche's irrational vitalism was an overt summons to reactionary, anti-democratic, anti-socialist, imperialist activity whereas with Bergson, these aims were not openly stated, only announced in general philosophical terms and even hidden by a veil of neutrality. But Bergson's seeming political neutrality not only had a confusing and misleading effect on the intellectuals landed in an ideological crisis. It confused and misled them in none other than a reactionary direction. (This effect that Bergson had can best be studied in Péguy's development.) Politzer, the communist Resistance fighter murdered by Hitler's fascists, very correctly characterized the reactionary nature of the Bergsonian abstraction as follows: 'To merge with the whole of life, to vibrate with the whole of life means to remain cold and indifferent with regard to life:

genuine emotions perish amid universal sensibility. In duration (*durée*) a pogrom happens in the same way as a revolution: in seeking to apprehend the elements of duration in their individual hues, in admiring the dynamics of their jumbled features, one actually forgets that the one is a pogrom and the other a revolution.' Here the link is plainly evident between the most significant advocate of Western European hostility to reason, Bergson, and the central German figure in this trend in modern times, Nietzsche. And we can see also how far the former, because of the different development of their respective countries, necessarily lagged behind the latter in concreteness and determination when constructing his reactionary-irrationalist world-picture.

This difference is also manifest in the relation to philosophical traditions. In Germany it was already the older Schelling who instigated the attack against the rationalism founded by Descartes. As we shall see in due course, this attack subsequently assumed its supreme form during the time of Hitler with the repudiation of all progressive bourgeois philosophies and the canonization of all out-and-out reactionaries. Bergson and his movement, in contrast, proceeded along the line of a largely unpolemical reinterpretation of the progressive philosophers. Certainly Bergson criticizes the Positivists, even Kant, and harked back to French mystics like Madame Guyon. But with him and his disciples there is no question of a firm rejection of the great French traditions. This did not occur even in the course of later developments; Jean Wahl, who comes very close to existentialism, attempted to preserve Bergson's inner connection with Descartes by finding a Bergsonian parallel for Descartes's *cogito*: '*Je dure, donc je suis*.' Here we have an exact parallel to those German thinkers who sought to reinterpret Kant or Hegel as irrationalists, as did Simmel and Dilthey respectively. In France, not even the existentialist school surpassed this stage; it too stressed its Cartesian 'orthodoxy'.

Now to express concretely how far Bergson goes in extending irrationalism is not at all to say that no militant ideologi-

cal reaction existed in France; on the contrary. The whole imperialist period was full of it (let us recall Bourget, Barrès, Maurras, etc.). In French reaction, however, *philosophical* irrationalism held sway to a far lesser degree than in Germany. In *sociology*, on the other hand, the overtly reactionary offensive was even sharper than on German soil. The retarded development of German capitalism, the establishment of national unity in the reactionary-Junker, Bismarckian form even meant that Germany sociology, as a typical discipline of the period of bourgeois apologetics, could only gain ground with difficulty after overcoming strong resistance on the part of the ideology of the feudal remnants. And as we shall note in the relevant chapter, German sociology frequently regurgitated the products of Western European thinking in its critique of democracy and extended them in accordance with specifically German objectives.

Here, of course, we cannot deal with Western sociology even in outline. It enlarged upon what had been devised by the founders of this new bourgeois science – the careful divorce of social phenomena from their economic basis, and the assigning of economic problems to another discipline completely separate from sociology. This in itself achieved an apologetic purpose. The de-economizing of sociology was at the same time a de-historicizing: the preconditions of capitalist society (presented in an apologetically distorted form) could henceforth be treated as 'perennial' categories of all social life in general. And again, we need not remark on the fact that this methodology sets out to prove directly or indirectly the impossibility of socialism and of any revolution. From the almost immeasurable thematic richness of Western sociology, let us now pick out just two themes of particular importance to philosophical developments. There now arose an autonomous science, the 'psychology of the masses'. Its outstanding exponent Le Bon placed it, to give a bald summary, in contrast to the rational and civilized nature of individual minds, regarding it as the psychology of the merely instinctive and barbaric. Thus the greater the influence

the masses obtain on public life, the greater the threat to the products of mankind's cultural evolution. If this was a summons to stave off democracy and socialism in the name of science, another leading sociologist of the imperialist period, Pareto, struck up a comforting tune in the name of the same scientific discipline. If – to give another very bald summary – the history of all social changes is only the superseding of an old 'élite' by a new one, then the 'perennial' foundations of capitalist society are saved sociologically and there can be no question of a fundamentally new type of society, the socialist type. The German Robert Michels, a later follower of Mussolini, also applied these principles to the labour movement. He exploited the fact of the origin of a labour bureaucracy under imperialist conditions – of which he naturally said nothing – to prove the embourgeoisement of every labour movement as a sociological law.

Sorel occupies a special position in Western philosophy and sociology. On one occasion Lenin called him 'the well-known advocate of confusion', and quite rightly. For the most blatantly contradictory hypotheses and conclusions intermingle in his writings. In his intellectual convictions Sorel was a purely bourgeois thinker, a typical petty-bourgeois intellectual. Both economically and politically he accepted Bernstein's revision of Marx. Like Bernstein he rejected the inner dialectic of economic growth, especially that of capitalism, as leading inevitably to proletarian revolution; accordingly – and again in line with Bernstein – he also dismissed dialectics as a philosophical method. He replaced it with James's Pragmatism and, above all, with Bergson's intuition. He took over from the bourgeois sociology of his time the idea of the anti-rational character of the movement of the masses and also Pareto's conception of the élite. He regarded progress as a typically bourgeois illusion, usually appropriating the arguments of the reactionary ideologists.

With a genuinely irrational intellectual *salto mortale*, Sorel now developed out of all these bourgeois-idealist reactionary hypotheses a theory of 'pure' proletarian revolution, the

myth of the general strike and the myth of the proletarian use of violence. This is a typical illustration of petty-bourgeois rebellion. Sorel hated and despised bourgeois culture, but he was unable on a single concrete point to detach himself from its influence, which determined the whole of his thinking. Thus when his hatred and contempt were striving for expression the result could only be an irrational leap into the totally unknown, into pure nothingness. What Sorel termed proletarian was nothing more than an abstract negation of bourgeois life without any real substance in it. For the moment he started to think, he did so in terms of bourgeois contents and forms. Here, then, Bergsonian intuition and the irrationalism of *durée réelle* are slanted towards a utopia of utter despair. This abstract insubstantiality finds clear expression in the very conception of Sorel's myth, for Sorel dismissed *a priori* all politics and was totally indifferent to the real, concrete ends and means of individual strikes. Irrationalist intuition, along with the insubstantial myth it creates, stands quite apart from concrete social reality and is no more than a delirious leap into nothingness.

But it is just this which explains Sorel's fascination for a particular sector of the intelligentsia in imperialist times. It is precisely why this irrationalism succeeded in heightening discontent with capitalist society emotionally, deflecting it from any real challenge to that society. Sorel's own Royalism may have been only a passing phase, but the same cannot be said of the enthusiasm he summoned up for Lenin, Mussolini and Ebert simultaneously in the major revolutionary crisis at the end of the First World War. With Sorel, the careless lack of direction of which Politzer accused Bergson takes the formal shape of an emotional campaign, without however managing to overcome its disoriented character. And it is certainly far more than a coincidence that Sorel's totally insubstantial theory of myth began to matter to Mussolini, for a while at least. Here, of course, Sorel's spontaneous, irrationalist confusion was converted into conscious demagogy. But – and this is the essential point – the conversion could be effected

without any substantial reconstruction of content and method. Sorel's myth was so exclusively emotional, so empty of meaning that it could pass without difficulty into the demagogically exploited myth of fascism. Mussolini wrote: 'We have created a myth for ourselves. Myth is a faith, a passion. It does not have to be a reality. It is real by virtue of the fact that it is a spur and a faith, and signifies valour.' This is pure Sorel, and in it the epistemology of Pragmatism and Bergsonian intuition has become the vehicle of fascist ideology.

We are still speaking, however, of a fascism which, for all its atrocities, never attained the import of the terror which Hitlerism held for the entire world. (For example, it is typical that Horthy's fascism in Hungary, while very closely related to Italian fascism politically, took its ideology from the still pre-fascist Germany of the time.) Here again, admittedly, Mussolini's ideological connection with Bergson, James and Sorel was much more tenuous and formal than that between Hitler and German irrationalism. But even with all these reservations, this state of affairs in itself illustrates what we are seeking to prove now and in every succeeding chapter: a philosophical stance cannot be 'innocent'. Bergson's own philosophy of morality and history did not lead to fascist conclusions. But, with regard to his human responsibility, that is totally irrelevant beside the fact that without falsifying his philosophy Mussolini was able to develop a fascist ideology out of it. It no more exculpates Bergson than it is an exoneration of Spengler or Stefan George as Hitler's ideological precursors that 'National Socialism' in practice was not altogether to their personal taste. The mere existence of the connecting links we are outlining must be a serious *discite moniti* ('learn from the warning') for every honest Western thinker. It shows that the possibility of a fascist, aggressively reactionary ideology is objectively contained in every philosophical stirring of irrationalism. When, where and how such a – seemingly innocent – possibility turns into a dreadful fascist reality is not decided philosophically, in the philo-

sophical realm. But insight into this connection should heighten the thinking man's sense of responsibility, not blunt it. It would be a dangerous self-deception and sheer hypocrisy to wash one's hands in innocence and – invoking the name of Croce or William James – to look down on the development of German irrationalism with aloof contempt.

And in conclusion we hope our studies have shown that, in spite of the intellectual link between Bergson, Sorel and Mussolini, the leading role played by German irrationalism remains undiminished. Germany in the nineteenth and twentieth centuries is still the 'classic' land of irrationalism, the soil where it evolved in the most diverse and comprehensive ways and can hence be studied to greatest profit, just as England is where Marx investigated capitalism.

This fact, we believe, belongs to the most disgraceful pages of German history. A detailed study is needed precisely in order for the Germans radically to surmount it and to take vigorous steps to prevent its continuance or return. The nation of Dürer and Thomas Münzer, Goethe and Karl Marx has achieved such great things in the past and has such great prospects for the future that there is no need for it to flinch from a merciless coming to terms with a perilous past and its damaging, menacing legacy. In this double sense – German and international – the present book wishes to voice a warning, a lesson for every thinking person of integrity.

BUDAPEST, NOVEMBER 1952

CHAPTER I

ON SOME CHARACTERISTICS OF GERMANY'S HISTORICAL DEVELOPMENT

Generally speaking, the fate, the tragedy of the German people lies in the fact that it entered into the modern bourgeois line of development too late. But this is too much of a generalization and needs to be made historically concrete. For historical processes are extraordinarily complicated and contradictory, and it can be said of neither an early nor a late entry *per se* that one is better than the other. We have only to look at the bourgeois-democratic revolutions. On the one hand, the English and French peoples gained a big lead over the Germans through fighting out their bourgeois-democratic revolutions in the seventeenth century and at the end of the eighteenth respectively. But, on the other hand, it was precisely as a result of its retarded capitalist development that the Russian nation managed to transfer its bourgeois-democratic revolution to the proletarian one, thereby sparing itself sorrows and conflicts which still exist in the German nation today. We must always take into account, therefore, the concrete interaction of socio-historical tendencies; but with these reservations, we shall find that the decisive factor in the (modern) history of Germany to date lies here, in the delayed development of capitalism with all its social, political and ideological consequences.

The major European peoples formed themselves into nations at the start of the modern period. They constructed unified national territories to replace feudal fragmentation, and there sprang up a national economy pervading and uniting the entire people, a national culture that was unified in spite of all class divisions. In the development of the bourgeois class and its struggle with feudalism, it was always absolute

monarchy which came into temporary being as the executive organ of this unification.

It was in this period of transition that Germany began to pursue a different, opposite course. This is by no means to suggest that it was able to withdraw from all the exigencies of the general capitalist line of development in Europe and grow into a nation in a wholly unique manner, as was claimed by reactionary historians and the fascist historians after them. Germany, as the young Marx so vividly put it, 'shared the *sorrows* of this development without sharing in its pleasures, its partial satisfaction'. And to this observation he added the prophetic forecast: 'Hence one fine day, Germany will find herself on the level of the European decline before ever having reached the level of European emancipation.'

To be sure, mining, industry and commerce grew profusely in Germany at the end of the Middle Ages and the start of the modern period, but more slowly than in England, France or Holland. As Engels points out, a major disadvantage of the German development of that period was that the different domains were less strongly linked by unified economic interests than were the different parts of the major civilized countries of the West. For instance, the Hanseatic League's trading interests in the North and Baltic Seas were virtually unrelated to the interests of centres of trade in southern and central Germany. In these circumstances the re-routing of trade passages which followed the discovery of America and the sea-route to India and stopped goods passing through Germany in transit was bound to be particularly disastrous in its effects. Although here too the class struggles were waged with religious slogans, Western Europe was firmly taking the road to capitalism, to the economic underpinning and ideological evolution of bourgeois society. But Germany, at this precise moment, was preserving all the wretchedness associated with the transition from the medieval to the modern epoch. Indeed the misery in which the resulting reaction in Germany was bogged down was further increased by elements absorbed within the country from the social content of this

transition. The causes of this were the conversion of the larger feudal domains into an absolutism (on the duodecimo pattern but without its progressive side, viz., assistance in reinforcing the bourgeois class) and heightened forms of peasant exploitation. For while the latter did create in Germany, as in the original accumulation of the West, a class of vagabonds, a broad stratum of socially deracinated lives, they could not possibly – since no manufactory existed – permit the development of pre-proletarian plebeians. The deracinated remained a *lumpenproletariat*, raw material for mercenary and brigandish activities.

All these factors meant that from the beginning of the sixteenth century, the great class struggles had a completely different character and, above all, quite different consequences in Germany from those they had elsewhere in the West. Ideologically this amounts to saying that the humanist movement contributed far less to the origin of a national consciousness in Germany than elsewhere. It also had far less influence on the development of a uniform national formal or written language. It is altogether typical of Germany's situation at the time that it was just here that the religio-ideological movement of the transitional era gained the greatest preponderance over secular humanism, and did so – an extremely important point – in its socially most backward form. For it is almost a platitude not only among Marxists but also, since Max Weber and Troeltsch, in bourgeois sociology that the origins of the Reformation are linked very closely with those of capitalism. But the Reformation provided a banner for the first major bourgeois revolutions inside Holland and England in its Western, Calvinist form; this became the ruling ideology in the first period of burgeoning capitalism. The Lutheranism which became uppermost in Germany, on the other hand, offered a religious transfiguration of subjection to *Kleinstaat* absolutism and supplied a spiritual background, a moral foundation for Germany's economic, social and cultural backwardness.

Naturally this ideological development is only a reflection

of those class struggles which decided the country's way of life and direction of growth for centuries to come. We are referring to the conflicts which reached their height in the Peasants' War of 1525. The significance which this revolution, and more especially the crushing of it, took on for Germany's destiny illuminates from a fresh angle that general economic state of affairs we have just discussed. All major peasant risings at the close of the Middle Ages were two-sided movements. On the one side, there were the defensive struggles of a peasantry in retreat, still yoked to feudal values and seeking to regain positions of the transitional 'golden age', now lost for ever on the economic plane as a result of the unleashing of capitalist forces of production. And on the other, we have the more or less callow vanguard actions of the imminent bourgeois-democratic revolution. The special situation of Germany as we have portrayed it entailed two things. It meant that both aspects of the peasant revolts received greater prominence in the Peasants' War than otherwise (I refer you, to underline the progressive component, to Wendel Hippler's reform programme for the Reich and to the plebeian movement under Thomas Münzer); it meant also that the loss of that war had irremediably disastrous results. What the Kaiser was incapable of doing, the peasants' revolution sought to accomplish: the unification of Germany and liquidation of the constantly consolidating feudal-absolutist centrifugal tendencies. These very forces were bound to gain strength from the peasants' defeat. A modernized feudalism superseded a purely feudal fragmentation: the petty princes, as victors and profiteers in the class struggles, stabilized Germany's divided condition. And thus, like Italy from other causes, Germany became an impotent complex of petty, formally independent states as a result of the crushing of the first major revolutionary wave (the Reformation and Peasants' War). As such, it was now the object of the politics of the emergent capitalist world, the great absolute monarchies. Mighty nation-states (Spain, France, England), the House of Habsburg in Austria, ephemeral major powers like Sweden

and also, from the eighteenth century, Tsarist Russia were to decide the fate of the German people. And since Germany, as a political pawn of theirs, was at the same time a useful object of exploitation, these countries saw to it that her national fragmentation was preserved for years to come.

In becoming the battleground and victim of the conflicting interests of the major European powers, Germany went to the wall economically and culturally as well as politically. This general decay was manifested not only in the universal impoverishment and ravaging of the country, in the backward development of both agricultural and industrial production, and the regression of once flourishing towns, etc., but also in the cultural physiognomy of the whole German people. It took no part in the great economic and cultural upsurge of the sixteenth and seventeenth centuries; its masses, including the mass of the emergent bourgeois intelligentsia, lagged far behind the development of the major civilized countries. The reasons were primarily material ones. But they were determined by certain ideological characteristics of the German development as well. Firstly, there was the incredible pettiness, narrowness and short-sightedness of life in the small German duchies compared to England or France. Secondly, and closely connected with this, there was the far greater and more tangible dependence of the subjects on the monarch and his bureaucratic machinery, the far more restricted scope for an ideologically hostile or merely critical attitude than elsewhere. A further point is that Lutheranism (and later on, Pietism, etc.) limited this scope in the subjective sense also, converting external subjection into an inner submissiveness and thus breeding that underdog mentality which Engels termed 'servile'. There was, of course, a reciprocal influence in play here, but one which constantly diminished the scope for protest both objectively and subjectively. Accordingly, the Germans could have no hand either in bourgeois-revolutionary movements which aimed at replacing governance through absolute monarchy (not yet realized for a unified Germany) with a higher political form better suited to

capitalism in its more advanced stages. The petty states, whose existence the rival major powers were artificially conserving, could exist only as hirelings of those powers. To resemble their great models outwardly, they could maintain themselves only on the most ruthless and retrograde draining of the working people.

Naturally no rich, independent and powerful bourgeoisie will spring up in such a country, and no progressive revolutionary intelligentsia to match. The bourgeois and petty-bourgeois classes were economically much more dependent on the Courts than elsewhere in Western Europe. Hence there developed among them a servility, a petty, mean and wretched spirit hardly to be found in other European countries at this time. And with economic development stagnant, there was in Germany little or no trace of those plebeian groupings outside the feudal hierarchy of estates which constituted the most important propulsive force in the revolutions of the modern period now dawning. In the Peasants' War they still played a crucial role under Münzer; now they comprised, where they existed at all, a servile and venal social stratum that was declining into a *lumpenproletariat*. Certainly, Germany's bourgeois revolution at the start of the sixteenth century created an ideological foundation for a national culture in the uniform modern written language. But this too underwent a regression, becoming crabbed and barbarized in this period of profound national humiliation.

Not until the eighteenth century, especially in its second half, did an economic recovery set in. And it went hand in hand with an economic and cultural strengthening of the bourgeois class. The bourgeoisie, however, was still far too weak to remove the obstacles to national unity, or indeed even to raise this question in serious political terms. But the backwardness was beginning to be generally sensed, a national feeling was awakening, and the longing for national unity was constantly growing, although there was no chance of political associations with specific programmes on this basis, even on a local scale. Nevertheless the economic necessity of embourg-

eoisement was appearing more and more forcefully in the feudal-absolutist petty states. That class compromise in which Engels saw the social stamp of the status quo in Germany, as late as the 1840s, was starting to take shape between the nobility and the petty bourgeoisie, with the former playing the leading part. Its form was bureaucratization which, here as everywhere else in Europe, became a transitional form of the dissolution of feudalism, of the bourgeoisie's struggle for political power. Granted, this process of German fragmentation into largely helpless petty states again took very lowly forms, and the essence of the compromise between nobility and petty bourgeoisie was that the former occupied the higher and the latter the lower bureaucratic posts. But despite these mean and backward forms of social and political life, the German middle class was starting to arm itself for the power struggle at least in the ideological sense. After having been cut off from progressive movements in the West, it was now making contact with the English and French Enlightenment, digesting it and even in part amplifying it of its own accord.

It was in this state that Germany spent the period of the French and Napoleonic revolutions. From the political angle, the German people was still the object of the rival power blocs, the modern bourgeois world emerging in France and the feudal-absolutist Central and Eastern European powers ranged against it with English support. The great events of the period hastened to a remarkable extent the development and growing consciousness of the bourgeois class, fanning the flames of national unity more strongly than ever. At the same time, however, the politically fateful consequences of fragmentation were emerging more sharply than ever. In Germany there were still – objectively speaking – no unified national politics. Large sections of the avant-garde bourgeois intellectuals welcomed the French Revolution with enthusiasm (Kant, Herder, Bürger, Hegel, Hölderlin, etc.). And contemporary documents such as Goethe's travel reports show that this enthusiasm was by no means limited to the celebrated

top minds of the middle class but had roots in broader sectors of the class itself. All the same, it was impossible for the democratic revolutionary movement to spread even in the more advanced West of Germany. Although Mainz joined the French Republic, it remained totally isolated, and its downfall at the hands of the Austro-Prussian army evoked no echo in the rest of Germany. The leader of the Mainz rising, the important scholar and humanist Georg Forster, died as an exile in Paris, forgotten and neglected.

This fragmentation was repeated on a larger scale in the Napoleonic period. Napoleon succeeded in finding supporters and allies in the West and South of Germany and also, in part, in Central Germany (Saxony). And he was aware that this alliance – the *Rheinbund* – could only be assured of any degree of survival if the dissolution of feudalism was at least embarked on in the states supporting him. This happened to a large extent in the Rhinelands, far less so in the other states of the *Rheinbund*. Even as reactionary, chauvinistic a historian as Treitschke was forced to observe of the Rhineland: 'The old order was abolished without trace, the chance of restoring it went begging; soon even the memory of *Kleinstaat* times evaporated. The history which is a really living memory in the hearts of the rising generation of Rhinelanders only began with the incursion of the French.'

But since Napoleon's power was not sufficient to reduce the whole of Germany to a similar dependence on the French empire, the country's fragmentation was only rendered still deeper and stronger in consequence. Napoleonic rule was felt by broad sectors of the people to be an oppressive foreign domination. To combat it there started, especially in Prussia, a national popular movement which reached a climax in the so-called wars of liberation.

Germany's political fragmentation was matched by her ideological disunion. The leading progressive thinkers of the age, notably Goethe and Hegel, sympathized with a Napoleonic unification of Germany and a liquidation carried out from France of the relics of feudalism. In accordance with

the problematical inner nature of this view, the concept of the nation dwindled in these thinkers to a mere cultural idea, as is best seen in the *Phenomenology of Mind*.

But just as full of contradictions was the thinking of the political and military leaders of the wars of liberation, who sought a release from the yoke of France and the creation of a German nation by way of a Prussian uprising in league with Austria and Russia. Men like Stein, Scharnhorst and Gneisenau wanted to introduce the social and military benefits of the French Revolution because they saw clearly that only an army organized on such lines could take up the contest with Napoleon. But they not only wished to achieve this without a revolution. They also wanted, through continual compromises, to accommodate Prussia – albeit a Prussia reformed by them – to the feudal leftovers and the classes representing the leftovers economically and ideologically. This yielding to Germany's current backwardness was forced upon them, but at the same time the agents of the process transfigured it ideologically. One of the consequences of accommodation was that the longing for national liberation and unity often turned into a narrow chauvinism, a blind and petty Francophobia, and it also failed to produce a real ideology of liberation among the masses now mobilized. This was especially the case in that there was no avoiding an alliance with those circles of reactionary Romanticism which interpreted the anti-Napoleonic struggle as a struggle for the complete restoration of conditions existing before the French Revolution. Naturally such contradictions were also manifest in the philosopher of this trend, Fichte in his later years, although he was much more radical in the political and social sense than many of the national movement's political and military leaders.

There was, then, a profound disunion within the spiritual and political leadership of the German people and a very widespread ideological confusion with regard to the aims and methods of the campaign for national unity. Yet, in spite of it all, national unity became the object demanded by a large

mass movement embracing important sectors of the German people during this period – for the first time since the Peasants' War. Thereupon the issue of national unity became (as Lenin first clearly formulated it) the central question of the German bourgeois revolution.

If we consider German history in the nineteenth century, we can assure ourselves at every stage of the truth and accuracy of Lenin's observation. The struggle for national unity did indeed govern the whole political and ideological development of nineteenth-century Germany. And the particular form in which this question was finally solved left its stamp on the whole of German intellectual life from the 1850s to the present day.

Herein lies the fundamental singularity of Germany's development, and it may be readily seen that this axis around which everything revolves is no more than a consequence of its retarded capitalist development. The other major nations of the West, especially England and France, had already attained to national unity under an absolute monarchy, i.e., in their cases, national unity was one of the first products of the class conflicts between bourgeois and feudal life. In Germany, on the other hand, the bourgeois revolution had first to fight for national unity and lay its corner-stones. (Only Italy experienced a similar development; moreover its intellectual consequences show, despite all the historical differences between the two countries, a certain affinity which has had notorious repercussions in the very recent past.) Particular historical circumstances, into which we cannot go in detail now, also dictated the realization of national unity under an absolute monarch in Russia. And the revolutionary movement's development in Russia, the Russian Revolution show too all the consequences that will arise in such circumstances, consequences basically different from those obtaining in Germany.

Accordingly, in countries where national unity is already a product of earlier class struggles under absolute monarchy, the task of bourgeois-democratic revolution consists *only* of

completing this work, of more or less purging the national State of existing feudal and absolutist bureaucratic leftovers, and of aligning it with the purposes of bourgeois society. This happened in England through a gradual reconstruction of the older national institutions and in France through a revolutionary transformation of the bureaucratic-feudal character of the State machinery. Naturally there were serious relapses here in periods of reaction, but there was no impairing or jeopardizing of the national sense of unity. Class struggles lasting for centuries had laid this foundation, which left bourgeois-democratic revolutions with the advantage that the accomplishment of national unity, its adaptation to the exigencies of modern bourgeois society could form an organic and fruitful link with the revolutionary struggle against feudalism's economic and social institutions (the peasant question as the core of bourgeois revolution in France and Russia).

It may be readily seen that for Germany, the differently shaped central question of bourgeois-democratic revolution created a whole series of unfavourable circumstances. Revolution would have to shatter at one blow institutions whose gradual undermining and demolition had taken centuries of class struggles in, for instance, France. It would have to produce at a stroke those central national institutions and bodies which in England or Russia were the products of a development lasting centuries.

But this not only made the objective task harder to solve. The central revolutionary proposition also had an unfavourable effect on the attitude of the different classes to the problem and created constellations obstructing the radical execution of bourgeois-democratic revolution. We shall just pick out a few of the most important factors. Above all, there was a manifold blurring of the sharp antithesis between the feudal leftovers (the monarchy and its machinery as well as the nobility) and the bourgeois class because the more strongly capitalism develops, the greater the need will become, even for classes interested in preserving the remnants

of feudalism, to realize national unity – their own version of it, that is. Let us take as a prime example Prussia's role in the creation of national unity. Objectively, Prussia's particular constitution was always the greatest hindrance to a real national unity, and yet that unity was attained with Prussian bayonets. And from the wars of liberation to the creation of the German Empire, the bourgeois revolutionaries were always confused and misled by the question of whether national unification was to be reached with the aid of Prussian military power or by crushing it. From the standpoint of Germany's democratic development, the second course would unquestionably have been the commendable one. But for crucial sections of the German middle class, especially in Prussia, there was available a convenient road of class compromise, an escape from the extreme plebeian consequences of bourgeois-democratic revolution, and therefore the possibility of achieving their economic goals without a revolution, albeit on the basis of a surrender of political hegemony in the new State.

But equally unfavourable conditions obtained even within the bourgeois camp. The revolution's central issue was national unity, and this bolstered the hegemony of an upper middle class always inclined towards class compromises. It meant that it was less threatened than in eighteenth-century France and nineteenth-century Russia. To mobilize the petty-bourgeois and plebeian masses against the compromise aims of the upper middle class was much harder in Germany. The prime reason for this was that the bourgeois revolution's central issue of national unity presupposed a far more highly developed awareness and alertness among the plebeian masses than did, for example, the peasant question, where the economic contrasts between different classes were incomparably more obvious and thus more immediately apparent to the plebeian masses. Because of its seemingly purely political nature, the issue of national unity often hid from sight the immediate and directly intelligible economic problems, which remained latent in the various possibilities of

solving the issue. For revolutionary patriotism to turn into counter-revolutionary chauvinism was more likely here than in other bourgeois-democratic upheavals, especially as the upper-middle-class tendencies towards class compromise and the Bismarckian Bonapartism arising after 1848 were consciously veering in this direction. But for the masses, it was harder to have a clear perception of such manoeuvres *before* national unity had been achieved than in states where this had been taken for granted for centuries. This covering-up tendency acquired an objective shape in that the struggle for national unity – so long as the individual states that made up Germany were not elevated into union, and that was naturally the end of the process, not he start – took the form of a problem of foreign affairs. It involved the 'foreign' policy of the separate states in their mutual relations and their foreign policy in relation to the external major powers which, as a result of Germany's development hitherto, were deemed entitled to intervene in her internal affairs. Clearly this supplied apparently plausible pretexts for keeping the masses, sometimes including the democratic revolutionary-minded masses, away from these decisions of 'foreign policy' and for driving them into a blind chauvinism (the Francophobia of 1870).

This situation presupposed in addition a far greater insight into complicated external political relations than the other central questions of bourgeois revolutions. Naturally, there is a connection between foreign and domestic affairs as far as every democratic revolution is concerned. But the insight, for instance, that Court intrigues with feudal-absolutist foreign powers were endangering the revolution was incomparably easier of access to the plebeian masses in the French Revolution than was the real relation between national unity and foreign policy to the German masses at the time of the 1848 revolution. Above all it was hard for the German masses to see that a revolutionary war against Tsarist Russia would be necessary to the achievement of national unity, as Marx

constantly preached with great lucidity in the *Neue Rheinische Zeitung*. This difficulty and the concomitant upper-middle-class hegemony, including that which existed with regard to class compromises and a betrayal of democratic revolution, were further reinforced by the fact that the danger facing any bourgeois revolution, viz., the turning of national wars of liberation into wars of conquest, was more imminent and fraught with still greater domestic consequences here than in bourgeois revolutions of another type.

For all these reasons, the masses were far more quickly and intensively influenced by chauvinistic propaganda in Germany than in other countries. The rapid turning of a justified and revolutionary national enthusiasm into reactionary chauvinism facilitated, on the one hand, the deception of the masses at home by the upper-middle class and the Junkers allied to the monarchy. And on the other hand the democratic revolution was deprived of its most important allies. Thus in 1848, the German bourgeoisie was able to exploit the Polish question in a reactionary chauvinist spirit while the plebeian masses – again, despite timely and accurate warnings from the *Neue Rheinische Zeitung* – failed to put a stop to it and to convert the Poles from revolutionary Germany's natural allies into real partners in the campaign against reactionary powers on both a German and an international scale.

These adverse circumstances were created by the nationally fragmented situation in which Germany found herself at the time when bourgeois-democratic revolution was the issue of the day. As far as the subjective factor in the revolution is concerned, it was a disadvantage for the bourgeoisie, petty bourgeoisie, plebeian masses and proletariat to enter the revolution without political preparation. The fragmentation into petty states was extremely unfortunate for the revolutionary-democratic training of the lower sections of the people, for the development of revolutionary-democratic traditions among the plebeian masses. Their sole political experience consisted merely of minor and trivial local struggles within

the bounds of the *Kleinstaaten*. The collective national interests, being abstractly suspended above those struggles, could thus very easily turn into clichés. And this cliché-making by the leading bourgeois ideologists, expressed in its crudest form in the Frankfurt National Assembly, could – consciously or unconsciously, deliberately or involuntarily – be directed into reactionary channels with the greatest ease.

A fact which helped to exacerbate this situation was that at the start of the nineteenth century, the south German duchies formed the centre of the country's political-democratic movement, so that it was precisely democratic trends which were most afflicted by this pettiness, trifling and cliché-making. To be sure the Rhinelands, the most advanced region of Germany economically and socially, belonged to Prussia, but they formed a kind of enclave within it. They lay far away from the centre of political decision-making, the Berlin of the Court and petty bourgeoisie. And since the remnants of feudalism had been abolished here by Napoleon's régime, they had quite different immediate interests from the backward, still markedly feudal areas of Prussia proper.

Thus a tactical consideration added to the adverse circumstances. As a result of the national fragmentation, the bourgeois-democratic revolution was unable to find a particularly decisive centre such as Paris formed in the eighteenth century. The major reactionary powers, Prussia and Austria, had their concentrated bureaucratic and military power. In the face of this the revolutionary forces were more than divided. The National Assembly sat in Frankfurt; Cologne was the centre of revolutionary democracy. The critical struggles in Berlin and Vienna occurred spontaneously, without clear ideological leadership, and after the defeats in the capital cities it was possible for the movements which flared up in Dresden, the Palatinate, Basle, etc., to be put down one by one.

These factors determined the destiny of democratic revolution in Germany, not only with regard to national unity but in all areas where it became necessary to abolish the feudal leftovers. Not for nothing did Lenin describe this

course as internationally typical, unfavourable to the genesis of modern bourgeois society, and as the 'Prussian' road. This observation must not only be restricted to the agrarian question in the narrower sense, but must be applied to the whole development of capitalism and the political superstructure it acquired in Germany's modern bourgeois society.

Even in Germany, the feudal remnants could only slow down the spontaneous growth of capitalist production, not prevent it. (Napoleon's continental blockade itself called forth a certain capitalist upsurge in Germany.) But this spontaneous development of capitalism did not arise in Germany in the period of artisan labour, as it did in England or France, but in the age of modern capitalism in the real sense. And the feudal-absolutist bureaucracy of Germany's petty states, above all the Prussian bureaucracy, was obliged actively to take the initiative in underpinning the capitalist development.

Certainly, precisely where the crucial questions were concerned this often happened much against its will and nearly always without the least insight into the true dimensions of what was occurring with its assistance and through its initiative. We can see this very clearly in Treitschke's account of the origin of the German Customs Union. Since he always tended to idealize the political foresight and national aims of the Hohenzollern régime, his version is particularly instructive.

> And this development took place largely against the will of the Prussian Crown itself; here we see an inner natural force at work. Nothing was further from the mind of Friedrich Wilhelm III than to pave the way for a separation from Austria through the Customs Union. He regarded dualism as a blessing for the fatherland; it was in the nature of things that this should finally be reached. There thus took shape a true Germany bound by shared economic interests, whereas theory alone held sway in Frankfurt, as previously in Regensburg. Friedrich Wilhelm IV too was

> pro-Austria and enthused over Austria more than his own State; and nevertheless the merging of interests between non-Austrian Germany and Prussia continued inexorably. Although the central states would gladly have crushed Prussia after 1851, none of them dared to disrupt the Customs Union; they could no longer break free of this tie.

The most interesting feature of this account is the irrationalism bordering on mysticism: the development of German capitalism, the process of asserting its elementary interests, the incomprehension and incompetence of the German petty and Prussian monarchies in the face of this process – all this Treitschke presents as a kind of Fate-tragedy. If this attitude were only typical of the historian it would not be all that important. But here Treitschke was giving eminently precise intellectual expression to the general mood in Germany. Whereas nations which had won their present political form through struggle regarded it as their own creation, the Germans looked on nationhood as a mysterious gift from higher irrational powers.

But the 'Prussian course' of Germany's development also had more direct consequences. Because economic unity had come about in this way, we find in capitalist circles a widespread dependence on the Prussian State from the outset, a constant making of deals with the semi-feudal bureaucracy. They entertained the prospect of asserting the bourgeoisie's economic interests in peaceful agreement with the Prussian monarchy. Hence Engels's subsequent comment that 1848 did not present the Prussian bourgeoisie with any cogent need to solve the question of power in the State by revolutionary means.

But the fact that this process was belated in Germany, that it took place not in the artisan period but in that of modern capitalism had another important consequence. Undeveloped though German capitalism was in the mid nineteenth century, it was no longer confronted by socially amorphous masses which could – at least temporarily – be lumped together

with the bourgeoisie as a 'third estate', as the French bourgeoisie had been before the French Revolution. It faced a modern, albeit likewise undeveloped, proletariat. We can best appreciate the difference if we reflect that in France, Gracchus Babeuf instigated a rising with a consciously socialist goal only some years *after* Robespierre's execution, whereas in Germany the revolt of the Silesian spinners broke out four years *before* the 1848 revolution and the first complete formulation of revolutionary proletarian ideology, the *Communist Manifesto*, appeared on the eve of revolution itself.

This situation, derived from Germany's delayed capitalist development, produced a proletariat that was already emerging of its own accord but was as yet unable, however, to exert a decisive influence on events (as did the Russian proletariat of 1917). The effect of international events in the class struggle made the situation acuter still. Granted, on the one hand, the February revolution in Paris helped to spark off the revolution in Berlin and Vienna. But, on the other hand, the class struggle strongly in evidence there between bourgeoisie and proletariat had a discouraging effect on the German bourgeoisie and promoted its inclination, already present for the reasons we have stated, to compromise with the 'old powers' with the greatest determination. In particular the battle of June and its sorry outcome became an event crucial to the development of the German class struggles. From the outset, Germany lacked that irresistible unity of an anti-feudal people which had boosted the French Revolution, while at the same time the German proletariat was still too feeble to make itself the leaders of the whole nation as did the Russian proletariat half a century later. Accordingly the dissolution of the original anti-feudal unity ensued more quickly and went through the opposite process to the French. Admittedly 1848 was the German equivalent of 1789; but the relationship between the bourgeoisie and the lower classes was closer to French conditions in 1830 and 1840 than to those of 1789.

Hence there already appeared in 1848 a feature of the German development which became of moment for the democratic transformation of Germany in later years as well. Firstly, these democratic upheavals began where they usually ended in the classic revolutions of England and France: with the struggle against the radical plebeian-proletarian wing. That, of course, was no mere difference of chronology. In the French Revolution especially we see a development going up to the farthest bounds of purely bourgeois democracy (1793-4); thus the struggle against plebeian Leftist radicalism only signified a rebuttal of the attempt to urge the revolution beyond those bounds. (Similar tendencies are apparent in Cromwell's struggles against the Levellers, albeit at a lower stage corresponding to the class relations of his times.) In the Germany of both 1848 and 1918, on the other hand, the direct struggle which began against proletarian-democratic Left-wing radicalism tended to retain within the democratic forms thrown up by revolution as much as possible of the old order, either intact or with minor external reforms. Thus no revolution in Germany brought about, for example, a real agrarian reform; not one seriously affected the fragmentation into petty states; not one really disturbed Junker rule in Prussia, and so on.

Here, needless to say, it is impossible to relate the history of Germany in the nineteenth century in however abbreviated a form. We can but briefly outline the most essential elements in the development of social trends. Germany's plebeian sectors did not have the power during this period to fight for their interests by way of revolution. Thus the compulsory economic and social advances came about either under the pressure of foreign relations or as a compromise by the ruling classes. No internal class struggle was responsible even for the south German and central German constitutions in the ducal states, the starting-points for democratic movements and parties in Germany after Napoleon's overthrow. They were the product of a need to administer in some kind of uniform manner the heterogeneous feudal

territories swept together in Napoleonic times and confirmed by the Congress of Vienna. Thus the population of Württemberg, for example, increased from 600,000 to 1½ million during the Napoleonic age; no less than seventy-eight provincial domains were tacked on to it. Such territories were heterogeneous in every respect. The administrative unifying of them – Württemberg is a typical example of the period – naturally called for a minimum number of centralized institutions which, in view of conditions in the Napoleonic period and the after-effects of the wars of liberation, were bound to involve a dissolution of the feudal-absolutist, medieval leftovers. Under Napoleon's régime the rulers of the petty German states were already striving to limit these concessions to a minimum; after Napoleon's defeat, even this was further reduced. The character of the central institutions meant that they had no deep roots in the nation and that the people could never regard them as its own personal creations, which was why they were so easy to abrogate both before and after 1848. And, when a serious revolution broke out in that year, it was possible for the effects of economic backwardness and national fragmentation that we have briefly depicted to leave the plebeian masses enfeebled and to lead the bourgeoisie to betray its own revolution, thus sealing the victory of feudal-absolutist reaction.

That defeat was crucial to the whole of Germany's later political and ideological development. In the terminology of the day, the proposition in respect of the central problem of democratic revolution read: 'Unity through Freedom' or 'Unity before Freedom'? Or in respect of the concretely most important problem of revolution and Prussia's future position in Germany: 'Absorption of Prussia by Germany' or 'Prussianization of Germany'? The quelling of the 1848 revolution meant that, in both cases, the second solution was the one adopted.

To be sure, the triumphant reactionaries would have been delighted simply to return to the pre-1848 status quo. That, however, was impossible from an objective economic and

social standpoint. The Prussian monarchy had to change, and had to do so – as Engels stressed time and again – on the lines of creating a 'Bonapartist monarchy'. This apparently gave rise to a parallel between the development of France and Germany. It apparently meant that Germany's development was now catching up politically with France's. But this was only seemingly so. For in France Bonapartism was a reactionary backlash beginning with the June defeat of the French proletariat, and its ignominious collapse led to the glorious Commune of 1871. And with the Third Republic, France reverted to the normal road of bourgeois democratic development. Bismarck's Germany was, as Engels accurately demonstrated, a copy of Bonapartist France in many respects. But Engels pointed out very firmly at the same time that 'Bonapartist monarchy' in Prussia and Germany marked an advance compared to conditions before 1848 – an objective advance in that the bourgeoisie's economic demands were met within this régime's framework and a freer avenue was opened up for the evolution of the forces of production. But these economic advances were realized without a triumphant bourgeois revolution. The national unity that had arisen consisted of a 'Prussianization' of Germany which carefully preserved both the aristocratic bureaucracy and all the machinery to keep its political hegemony intact (three-class suffrage in Prussia, etc.). Given Parliament's total lack of power, universal suffrage for the empire was still just a quasi-constitutional, quasi-democratic facade. Hence Marx, in criticizing the Gotha programme, could rightly describe a nationally united Germany as 'a military despotism embellished with parliamentary forms and with feudal additions thrown in, already influenced by the bourgeoisie, bureaucratically structured and under political surveillance'.

We have located one of the most important weak points of the 1848 revolution in the lack of democratic experience and tradition, in the want of a democratic training of the masses and their ideological spokesmen through major internal class struggles. It is understandable that events after

1848, the conditions of 'Bonapartist monarchy', the creation of Germany unity 'from the top' through Prussian bayonets, again failed to provide any conditions favourable to the origin of revolutionary democratic traditions or a revolutionary democratic training of the masses. As a result of its impotence, the German Parliament was automatically condemned to sterility. And since every single bourgeois party had its basis in a compromise with 'Bonapartist monarchy', the extra-parliamentary struggles of the masses, as far as they could spring up in the first place, were similarly doomed to sterility. The few real democrats left over from the pre-1848 period remained isolated, lacking in influence and unable to educate a succeeding generation of democrats. The fate of Johann Jacobi, who as a convinced petty-bourgeois democrat accepted a Social Democratic mandate out of despair and protest without holding any socialist views at all, and who could subsequently make nothing of his mandate, is typical of the situation of the few strict bourgeois democrats in Germany.

An important ideological obstacle to the origin of democratic traditions in Germany was the ever-increasing, large-scale falsification of German history. Here again we cannot even outline the details. It was – to summarize very briefly – a matter of idealizing and 'Germanizing' the retarded sides of the German development, i.e., of a version of history which extolled precisely the retarded character of Germany's development as particularly glorious and in accord with 'Germany's essence'. It criticized and repudiated all the principles and products of Western bourgeois democratic and revolutionary developments as un-German and contrary to the character of the German 'national spirit'. And the seeds of progressive turns in Germany history – the Peasants' War, Jacobinism in Mainz, specific democratic trends in the era of the wars of liberation, plebeian reactions to the July Revolution in the revolution of 1848 – were either totally hushed up or so falsified as to strike the reader as terrible warnings. From now on, 1848 was called the 'year of madness'

in German bourgeois terminology. The reactionary periods in Germany's history, by contrast, were made to look splendid and illustrious.

This re-writing was not limited however to historical facts, their selection and treatment. It influenced in a significant way the methodology of the social and historical sciences, and indeed, far over and above them, the whole of social and historical thinking in Germany. Briefly summarizing,we may say that after the pre-1848 period's attempts to grasp the rational laws of society and history (here it will suffice to refer to Hegel), there arose a fresh wave of historico-social irrationalism. This was already strongly developed in the Romantic movement and its offshoots, but only became a dominant trend after the crushing of the 1848 revolution. Here we are less concerned with a methodological and scientific characterization of this trend – as we shall see, although irrationalism in the imperialist age found numerous points of connection with it, *that* represented something essentially new – than with its roots in Germany's social and political life.

The most important factor of all is the average German's underdog mentality, a mentality by no means affected by the 1848 revolution, and also that of the intellectual however highly placed. We have noted that the major upheavals at the start of the modern era, which laid the foundations for democratic developments in the West, ended in Germany with the establishment, for centuries to come, of petty tyrants, and that the German Reformation founded an ideology of submission to them. Neither the struggles for liberation from the Napoleonic yoke nor the year 1848 could alter this intrinsically. And since the German nation's unity was created not by way of revolution but from 'the top' and, according to historical legend, through 'blood and iron', the 'mission' of the Hohenzollerns and the 'genius' of Bismarck, this side of the Germans' mentality and morals remained virtually unchanged. There sprang up large cities in place of often semi-medieval small towns; the big capitalist with his agents

replaced the shopkeeper, artisan and small entrepreneur; world politics superseded parish-pump politics – but during this process the German people's subservience to its 'authorities' underwent only the slightest of changes. Hessling in Heinrich Mann's novel *Man of Straw*[1] differs from the bourgeois 'hero' of Gustav Freytag only in his aggressiveness towards inferiors, not in servility to those above him. So the characterization published by Hugo Preuss in 1919 is valid for the German people – with the obvious period variations – throughout the nineteenth and twentieth centuries:

> The most easily governed nation in the world is the German . . . meaning a lively and active nation of average proficiency and intelligence with a developed critical bent for argument; a nation, however, which in public affairs is neither accustomed nor willing to act spontaneously without or against the will of authority; a nation which thus is excellently ordered and acts under official guidance almost as though it were only performing its own common will. This readiness to be organized, along with its efficiency, does indeed provide incomparably fine material for an organization, the purest form of which is of course the military type.

Here we have the immediate, subjective source of pre-imperialist German irrationalism. Whereas the Western democracies – by and large – considered the State, State policies and so on to be largely their own work, expected rationality from them and saw their own rationality reflected therein, the German attitude – again, by and large – was the complete opposite. The German historians' axiom 'History is man-made' was only the historico-methodological reverse side of the Prusso-bureaucratic view of the 'subjects' limited understanding' of the proclamation of the Battle of Jena: 'A citizen's first duty is to keep the peace.' In both instances it is 'authority' alone which acts, and does so on the basis of an intuitive reading of inherently irrational facts. The ordinary

mortal, 'mass man', the subject, is either the unquestioning tool or the object or the open-mouthed observer of actions by those with a special vocation for them. Through its initial successes (up to the founding of the Reich), Bismarck's unscrupulous *Realpolitik* contributed greatly to the development of this irrationalism. The sterility and failures which followed the foundation of the Reich were painted as an irrational 'tragedy' if not passed off as successes, successes achieved by exploiting irrational 'constellations' through a 'brilliant *Realpolitik*'. Admirers of the period of overt and aggressive German imperialism under Wilhelm II explained it as reflecting the Emperor's 'personality of genius', and its detractors with the statement that Bismarck left no successor of the same stature. These widespread tendencies in average German historical studies were reinforced by the journalism of circles who saw a threat to their interests in a parliamentarization of Germany and therefore propagated Hohenzollern 'personal rule' (in reality: the uncurbed reign of a civil and military bureaucracy) as the German people's only road to salvation. Clearly the way in which the German empire was founded substantially strengthened the opportunity for the extensive spread of such views.

Closely connected with this development was the battle of German historical theorists and historians against the concept of a rationally comprehensible progress. As we know, this battle was a universal one which, as we shall note in detail later, springs up inexorably from the soil of a capitalism in decline, indeed a capitalism that has become internally problematic – an international phenomenon therefore. What was specific to the German development was 'merely' that this tendency emerged much earlier and much more firmly than in any other country. This peculiarity in Germany's intellectual development, viz., that it yielded leading thinkers with a radically reactionary attitude to reality – chiefly Schopenhauer and Nietzsche, but also Spengler, Heidegger and others – we shall examine in detail later with regard to its philosophical principles and consequences. For the moment,

however, we are concerned with the primary, elementary, socio-historical basis. This is the curious unity, simultaneous and indivisible in reality, of Germany's seasonable and unseasonable evolutionary trend. For a long time Germany was simply a backward country both economically and socially, although in the intellectual sphere she was growing into the equal partner and indeed in some areas the spiritual leader of the bourgeois world. This situation engendered an ideology paving the way for democratic revolution in Germany (German writers and thinkers from Lessing to Heine, from Kant to Hegel and Feuerbach). Certainly there was already arising at that time – in the Romantic movement and its offshoots – an idealization of German backwardness which, in order to defend this position, was forced to interpret the course of events in a radically irrationalist way and to contest the idea of progress as an allegedly shallow, dim and misleading conception. Schopenhauer went farthest in this respect, and that accounts for both his total lack of influence before 1848 and his world-wide effect after the revolution was defeated.

With the founding of the Reich, indeed already during the time leading up to it, the objective foundations of these problems gained in complexity. Year by year Germany became less backward economically. On the contrary: in the imperialist age German capitalism outstripped English capitalism, hitherto pre-eminent in Europe; Germany became – next to the United States – the most highly developed and most typical capitalist area of the world. But at the same time, as we have seen, there was a consolidating of her democratically retarded social and political structure (agrarian conditions, quasi-parliamentarianism, the Emperor's 'personal rule', remnants of the territorial division into small duchies, and so on).

Thereupon, the contradiction existing in the earlier phases was reproduced at a higher and also qualitatively new stage. Abstractly considered, two ways of surmounting this contradiction presented themselves. One was the call for Germany's

social and political structure to align itself with her economic development. This demand could be put in a revolutionary style; it was possible to propose the task of at last carrying out the completion of democratic revolution in Germany (Friedrich Engels posed the issue thus to the German social democrats in his critique of the Erfurt programme). Alternatively, and from the standpoint of a real and inwardly seasonable German imperialism, the target could be to align (without touching the social structure) the political superstructure with the established and – in relation to Germany – constantly enduring forms of Western parliamentary democracy. (As we shall see, this was the – fairly isolated – position of Max Weber; it bore, *mutatis mutandis*, a certain similarity to the endeavours of Scharnhorst and Gneisenau, who strove to introduce the French Revolution's military achievements into a 'reformed' Old Prussia.)

But the contradictory relationship thus presented between economics and politics in Germany did not impede the evolution of German capitalism – it is here that the 'Prussian road' of capitalist development in Germany is fully tangible. Because of this, there arose as a matter of necessity an ideology constituting the intellectual defence of the contradiction between Germany's economic and political structure as a higher stage of development, with a better potential for development compared to the democratic West.

Clearly, this defence had to look for philosophical support in irrationalism again. Here, of course, it was possible for all kinds of conceptions to originate, and historically and philosophically to analyse them all, indeed just to enumerate them, would burst the bounds of these studies. Hence we shall only indicate some of the typical theories that arose. Capitalism may – in a positive or negative spirit, with enthusiasm, disapproval or resignation – be viewed as 'predestined'; I need only refer to Treitschke's account of the origin of the Customs Union. Germany's highly developed capitalism thereby acquires the rating of an irrational 'destiny', and the vessel of the other principle (also irrational, but differently

rated), the German State, acquires the task of bestowing meaning on the blind 'destiny' of the economy on the basis of the ruler's purely personal (hence again irrational) disposition. Or we impute to the State (in its German form) a salutary – irrational – counterbalance to the sickly, life-destroying rationality represented by the capitalist economy, and so on and so forth. All such conceptions contain a polemic against the universal bourgeois idea of progress in the Western democracies. They imply a repudiation of the notion that the development of State and society out of feudal forms, their increasing adaptation to the demands of capitalism (we recall Herbert Spencer's sociology) signifies a step forward. On the contrary, the German development was rated the higher one precisely because, as a result of the conservation of older (non-rational) forms of governance, it could solve various problems (ethical, cultural, etc.) for which the society and social thinking of the rationally oriented West could never find a solution. It goes without saying that here, the effective combating of socialism played a decisive role.

Irrationalism and a hostility to progress therefore go together. In this very togetherness they formed an effective ideological defence of the social and political backwardness of a Germany rapidly developing in the capitalist sphere. And it is at once clear that the 'philosophical' hypotheses we have outlined of the German reading of history exerted a crucial influence on that fabrication of historical legends which we mentioned earlier.

The weakness of the democratic movement in Germany is also evident in its inability to oppose this ideological campaign of falsification on a grand scale with anything of its own, any real history of Germany or history of the struggles for democratic revolutions. It was also unable to put up an effective challenge to the 'philosophical' foundations of these historical legends. The epistemological-agnosticist, ethico-socially postulative character of the neo-Kantianism now predominant was as incapable of doing so as the sociology

occasionally imported from other Western countries. Thus the whole of German youth grew up lacking a democratic tradition. Franz Mehring was the only German historian to make a vigorous stand against this fabrication of legends, bringing great honour upon himself in the process. But his efforts too remained isolated, and this to a growing degree as a result of the dominance of German social democracy by the reformist movement. So democratic traditions became more and more rootless in Germany. The sporadic democratic campaigners who appeared later had mostly so little real contact with German history that they often took over uncritically and on trust the dichotomy which reaction had created, artificially, between the purportedly ancient German character of their fatherland's stunted development and democracy as 'imported from the West'. They just applied the antithesis in reverse, i.e., siding with the 'un-German West'. Naturally this further increased their ideological and political isolation in Germany.

Here, only the labour movement could have provided a centre of political and ideological resistance, as the *Neue Rheinische Zeitung* did in 1848-9 and as Lenin and the Bolsheviks did on Russia's behalf. But the general trends of Germany's development were operative in the labour movement as well. Before Bismarck rounded off national unity it was a matter of course that the central question of democratic revolution should become the essential cause of a split in the emergent labour movement. On the one hand, Lassalle and Schweitzer after him stood for the Prussian Bonapartist road. Here the unfavourable circumstances of the German development had a momentous effect. Lassalle, with whom the mass movement of the working class began after the 1848 revolution, was far more under the ideological influence of the reigning Bonapartist trend than histories of the German labour movement would have it. His personal and political move towards Bismarck in the last years of his life was by no means a chance aberration, as it is often depicted, but rather the inevitable logical consequence

of his whole philosophical and political position. Lassalle took over from Hegel in a wholly uncritical fashion the reactionary idealist concept of the State's primacy over the economy, which he mechanically applied to the proletarian liberation movement. He was thereby rejecting those forms of the labour movement which, through an independent stand by the proletariat, might have led to a struggle for democratic elbow-room and a democratic confrontation with the bureaucratic State of Bonapartist Prussia. Economically, too, the workers were to expect their liberation to come from the Prussian State, from the State of Bismarck. In this context, the one-sided emphasis on universal suffrage as the central demand likewise acquired a Bonapartist accent, all the stronger in that the internal organization of the 'German General Workers' Union', with its combination of Lassalle's personal dictatorship and occasional referendum polls by the 'sovereign people', similarly exhibited a markedly Bonapartist character. It was possible for Lassalle to send the statutes of his 'empire', as he himself put it, to Bismarck with the comment that the latter might perhaps be envious of them. It is not surprising that on this basis, Lassalle now even proceeded to 'social kingship' and a direct underpinning of Bismarck's unifying policy.

Meanwhile Wilhelm Liebknecht who, under the influence of Marx and Engels, recognized and criticized the errors of Lassalle and his school, was also unable to sustain the proper line. Succumbing very often to the ideological influence of democratic petty-bourgeois trends from Southern Germany, he opposed the Bismarckian solution and Lassalle's defence of it not with the old revolutionary democratic line of the *Neue Rheinische Zeitung*, but with a petty-bourgeois democratic federalism of 'South German' anti-Prussian character.

In the course of the German labour movement's later development, the reinforced reformist movement was also operative in this question. Engels criticized with ruthless venom the opportunistic failings of the Erfurt manifesto in this respect. Above all he stressed what the programme

lacked: the call for a resolute struggle for the real democratization of Germany; for a revolutionary democratic completion of national unity, which in Bismarck's solution was reactionary and therefore remained incomplete. After Engels's death, reformism became stronger and stronger and fell increasingly in step with the compromising liberal bourgeoisie. The real battle for Germany's radical democratization – for the ideological and political underpinning of revolutionary democratic movements – found a diminishing echo in German social democracy; the isolation of Franz Mehring, the sole strict representative of such traditions, may be ascribed not least to this situation. And the reformist distortion of Marxism was not only confined to the overtly opportunistic Right wing, which even went so far as to support colonial imperialism. It also embraced the so-called 'Marxist Centre' which, while using universal revolutionary catchwords, made its peace with Germany's existing state of affairs very much in the spirit of *Realpolitik*. In this way the German labour movement was prevented from becoming a rallying point and cynosure for the democratic forces sporadically in evidence, and from training and leading these. And in opposing reformism's opportunist tendencies, large sections of the dissident Left lapsed into a sectarian attitude to the problems of bourgeois democracy and in particular to the national question. That is a major reason why they – and later on, in the war, the Spartacist League – were unable to radiate any influence of the kind the Bolsheviks had in Russia.

It was in such circumstances that Germany entered the imperialist epoch. As we know, it was accompanied by a major economic boom, an extraordinarily strong concentration of capital, etc.; Germany became the leading imperialist state in Europe and also the most aggressive imperialist state, the one pressing most fiercely for the redivision of the world. Again, the character of German imperialism was a consequence of the belated but very swift development of capitalism. When Germany became a major capitalist power the carving up of the colonial world was already nearly over,

so that imperialist Germany could only create a colonial empire to match her economic weight on the basis of aggression and the takeover of existing colonies. Hence there arose in Germany an especially 'voracious' imperialism, greedy for spoils, aggressive, vehemently and ruthlessly pressing for the reapportioning of the colonies and vested interests.

This economic situation contrasted very remarkably with the German people's great democratic-political immaturity in this period. But its immaturity was not only an extremely important political factor and meant not only that the cavalier and adventurous foreign policy of Wilhelm II could carry the day without major internal friction; it also had ideological consequences of importance to the problem we are studying. No state of affairs is ever stable, it must always go on moving either forwards or backwards. And since no progressive democratic further development of the German people ensued in the imperialist age, for the reasons we have shown, a further retrogression was bound to set in. This was connected with a general politico-ideological trend existing during the imperialist period on an international scale. On the one hand, there reigned a far-reaching general anti-democratic tendency; on the other, where there existed a bourgeois democracy, imperialist conditions inevitably gave rise to a certain disappointment with democracy on the part of the masses and their ideological spokesmen because of its *de facto* meagre power over the bourgeoisie's private executive, and because of certain anti-democratic phenomena necessarily associated with it under capitalism (the election machinery, etc.). Hence it was far from being an accident that precisely in democratic countries, there set in a widespread criticism of democracy extending from overtly reactionary movements to within the labour movement (syndicalism in the Mediterranean countries).

The general drift of this criticism was unquestionably romantic-reactionary. Hence we must bear in mind that it often contained a justified disappointment with bourgeois democracy, a disillusioned and sometimes relatively forward-

looking experience of its social limitations. Let us recall Anatole France's mockery of democratic equality before the law, magisterially prohibiting rich and poor alike from sleeping under the arches. And let it be noted: when Anatole France wrote that, he was still far removed from socialism, which makes his statement typical of the critical attitude towards democracy of progressive intellectual circles in the West. A characteristic mixture of accurate criticism and muddled reactionary tendencies may also be observed in Bernard Shaw. The most complicated and, for a time, most influential assortment of such trends appeared in Georges Sorel, ideologist of syndicalism.

Particularly in their reactionary nuances, these tendencies had an important and far-reaching effect on the German intelligentsia of the imperialist age. When, however, they were taken up in Germany, they underwent a profound social change. For whereas in the other Western countries they expressed a disappointment with the bourgeois democracy already attained, in Germany they became an obstacle to its attainment, a renunciation of persistent struggle on its behalf. These tendencies were mingled, in Germany, with the old official propaganda of the Bismarck period, which located in Germany's backwardness the expression of 'Germany's essence', the specifically German quality which it propagated in history, sociology, and so forth. During the Bismarck period the democratic and indeed, in part, liberal intelligentsia rebutted such a view of society and history (Virchow, Mommsen, etc.), but they were weak internally and lacked influence externally.

Criticism of democracy was now accepted in Germany as an advanced Western intellectual trend. With the aid of different historical and ideological rationales, a capitulation ultimately came about to those ideologists who were enervating the struggle for democracy and sapping it of its ideological and political vigour. Let us take, to cite one characteristic example, the most important bourgeois sociologist and historian of the Wilhelmine age, Max Weber. For patriotic

reasons Weber was against the Wilhelmine system, clearly perceiving its dilettantism and its inability to compete diplomatically with French or English democracy. Accordingly, he became an increasingly firm supporter of the democratizing of Germany. But since his thinking was deeply pervaded by the disillusioned Western criticism of democracy, Weber only regarded this as the 'lesser evil' compared with the existing system. We can observe similar contradictions in other politicians and thinkers of the time – varying, to be sure, from individual to individual – as in Friedrich Naumann. Clearly it was impossible for a radical bourgeois-democratic movement or even party to originate on such an ideological basis. (With Naumann this switch from Left-wing criticism to Right-wing principles and praxis is especially striking.)

There thus appeared among the leading German intellectuals of the Wilhelmine period a repetition of the 'German *Misere*' on a higher scale: ultimately, in the majority of cases, a philistinism without real public concerns. The Western critique of democracy led most of them to see something special in Germany's undemocratic development, a higher stage compared to the problematic undemocratic democracy of the West. There thus arose a climate of narrow pen-pushing capitulation to Germany's existing political system, very often a snobbish, aristocratic attitude which, while criticizing bourgeois life and culture in a sometimes acute, often even witty and telling way, kow-towed to the Wilhelmine system's titled bureaucrats and officers and idealized their undemocratic machinery with its semi-feudal leftovers. (These tendencies are particularly apparent in Sternheim, the witty satirist, and the democratic politician Rathenau.)

Naturally such a Right-wing critique of Western bourgeois democracy too contained certain elements of truth; above all, many facts cited against the essentially undemocratic character of the Western democracies were true in themselves. Precisely regarding this question, however, an accurate critique could only come from the Left. It will suffice to look at

Anatole France. Already in his early output we find sharply satirical observations and comments on the democracy of the Third Republic. But only when he started to develop in a socialist direction as a result of the lessons of the Dreyfus case does this critique become an organic, dynamic part of his shaping of society and history.

Mutatis mutandis, a similar tendency may be traced in Thomas Mann. In his *Reflections of a Non-Political Man*, the German brand of romantic anti-capitalism still obscures and distorts the rightful elements of his critique of bourgeois democracy. But when, in the period of the Weimar Republic, Thomas Mann was really converted to the democratic line, his scepticism with regard to Western bourgeois democracy also began to bear fruit in his writing. An example is the portrait of Settembrini in *The Magic Mountain*, where Mann unites ironic criticism of the typical narrowness of bourgeois democracy, its total inability to resolve the basic social questions of modern society, with a constant emphasis on Settembrini's relative progressiveness compared with Naphta's mystificatory proto-fascism and Hans Castorp's apolitical lethargy.

The idealizing of bureaucracy's 'competence', 'expertise', 'impartiality', etc., in contrast to the 'dilettantism' of party politicians and Parliament was another general trend in the anti-democratic movements of Western Europe. (Faguet is just one example.) It expresses very clearly the reactionary character of the movement as a whole. Sometimes consciously, but mostly unconsciously, the writers who proclaimed such ideas were the hacks of imperialist monetary capital, which sought and very often achieved the continuous assertion of its specific interests through its sub-committees, through stooges rendered independent of elections or ministerial changes. (Consider the internal power structure in the Foreign Ministries, the oft-changing parliamentary leaders and unchanging Secretaries of State, principal spokesmen, etc., in the bourgeois-democratic countries of Western Europe.) Because this tendency cropped up in a Germany

that was not yet democratic, it reinforced ideologically the successful resistance of the Imperial and Prussian civil and military bureaucracy to any attempt at a progressive restructuring of State institutions. Quasi-parliamentarianism degenerated into total impotence; but its obligatory, patent sterility did not motivate an extension of democracy. It led, on the contrary, to its further paralysis and stasis and to a greater powerlessness. Needless to say, German imperialist monetary capital was as much capable of exploiting this situation as that of Western Europe was of exploiting the parliamentary system.

For the German development, however, this constellation signified the growth of remnants of the 'German *Misere*' into a particularly reactionary imperialism unaffected by any kind of democratic controls. This trend had a particularly devastating effect in Germany because it not only helped to preserve the old servility of the average, and even the spiritually and morally highly developed intellectual, but also gave it a new ideological sanction. The absolutist leftovers, which Bismarckian 'Bonapartism' conserved and modernized simultaneously, found a special buttress in the politico-moral intellectual culture of bureaucracy. The bureaucrat considered it his particular 'pride and honour' to carry out the orders of higher authority in a technically perfect way, even if he disagreed with their substance. And this spirit, which was confined to the bureaucrat class in the narrowest sense in lands with old democratic traditions, spread far beyond the bureaucracy in Germany. To submit unreservedly to the decisions of authority was regarded as a special German virtue – in contrast to freer democratic thinking elsewhere – and extolled more and more loudly as the hallmark of a socially higher stage of development. Even Bismarck, who personally and in his institutions greatly promoted this transference of politico-social abasement from the petty States to the united, powerful nation, this perpetuating of the nullity of public opinion, occasionally criticized the German's lack of *Zivilcourage* (individual sense of public

duty). For the reasons we have indicated, this tendency degenerated during the Wilhelmine period into nothing short of a Byzantinism of the intelligentsia, a very widespread middle-class servility that was boastful outwardly and cringing inwardly.

This was, we repeat, a sometimes involuntary intellectual sell-out to the history-fudging propaganda of the glory of German backwardness. Although it had already started in the age of Bismarck, it now embraced even the most advanced and highly developed sections of leading bourgeois intellectuals in a 'more refined', 'higher' form that was sometimes subjectively oppositional, objectively always quasi-oppositional and hence of all the more service to imperialism. Here the social affinity and also the spiritual parallel between 'higher' and 'ordinary' reactionary ideology is quite palpable. Just as Schopenhauer's Buddhist quietism, say, matched petty-bourgeois apathy after the 1848 revolution, and the transformation requested by Nietzsche of the relationship between capitalists and workers into one between officers and soldiers corresponds to specific capitalist-militaristic wishes in the imperialist age, so the same applies here. In establishing these parallels, we are on no account disputing the difference in intellectual level. That, on the contrary, will continue to be a prominent consideration. Not, however, chiefly because of the intellectual standard, but because it enlarged the social scope of the reactionary currents, and because these currents engulfed sectors which they did not reach with 'normal' intellectual methods and which had precious little time for their usual demands. Only in their *ultimate* social consequences – and these were crucial to Germany's fate, intellectually as otherwise – did they lead into the same reactionary stream. When, for instance, Plenge opposed the 'ideas of 1914', as the higher and 'German' ones, to the 1789 ideas at the start of the First World War, it meant that a large portion of the best German intellectuals had already sunk to the level of Treitschke's propagandistic history. This unscrupulousness and loss of intellectual and moral standards can be observed

in a particularly crude form in the pamphlets appearing at the outbreak of war. Take, to select one very characteristic example, Werner Sombart's contrasting of 'heroes' (the Germans) and 'dealers' (English democracy).

The collapse of the Wilhelmine system in the First World War and the setting up of the Weimar Republic also brought no radical change for the better with regard to Germany's democratization and the origin of deep-seated democratic traditions among the broad masses, beyond the class-conscious proletariat. In the first place, this political democratization stemmed less from the inner power of popular forces than from a military collapse. Large circles of the German bourgeoisie accepted the Republic and democracy partly because the situation compelled them to, partly because they expected to gain advantages in foreign affairs, more favourable peace terms with President Wilson's help, etc. (This was a major difference from the democratic republic in the Russia of 1917. There, large petty-bourgeois and peasant masses were firmly democratic from the outset, although a very similar climate to Germany's could be noted among the upper middle class and the leading members of petty-bourgeois and peasant democracy were betrayers of democracy. The schisms among the social revolutionaries, for instance, clearly reflect the democratic mood among the petty-bourgeois and peasant masses.) Secondly, Germany's retarded development had repercussions here as well. Right at the outset of the bourgeois democratic revolution in 1918 the proletariat was waiting as the decisive social power. But owing to the strength of reformism and the current ideological and organizational weakness of the labour movement's Left flank, it was unequal to the problems of Germany's regeneration. Therefore bourgeois democracy was, as Engels had prophesied long before, essentially a union of all bourgeois forces against the impending danger of a proletarian revolution. Here the experiences just undergone of the Russian Revolution of 1917 had an enormous effect not only on the bourgeoisie itself but also on the reformist wing of the

labour movement. Accordingly, this wing in fact supported unreservedly the democratic coalition of all bourgeois forces against the proletariat – indeed it formed its real centre, its dynamo.

Hence the Weimar Republic was essentially a republic without republicans, a democracy without democrats, just as the French Republic was – in historically totally different circumstances, of course – between 1848 and 1851. The Leftist bourgeois parties allied with the reformists did not serve the cause of revolutionary democracy. While parading the republican and democratic banners, they were in essence 'parties standing for order', which meant in practice that as few changes as possible were made to the Wilhelmine social structure (preservation of the Junker officer corps, the old bureaucracy and most of the petty states, no agrarian reform, etc.). In these circumstances it is not surprising that there very soon arose a deep disappointment with democracy among the popular masses who, as we have seen, had never received a democratic training and fostered no live democratic traditions, and that they turned away from democracy relatively quickly. This process gained in speed and depth for the particular reason that the Weimar democracy was forced to implement and engender the greatest national humiliation experienced by Germany since the time of Napoleon, the imperialist peace of Versailles. To the democratically uneducated popular masses, therefore, the Weimar Republic signified the executive organ of this national humiliation in contrast to the times of national greatness and expansion associated with Friedrich II of Prussia, Blücher and Moltke, i.e., with monarchist, undemocratic memories. Here again we can observe the big contrast between the German and the Franco-English development, where revolutionary democratic periods (Cromwell, the Great Revolution, etc.) were the periods of greatest national upsurge. The circumstances of the Weimar Republic's origin supported the old view of an anti-democratic development that was 'specifically German' and uniquely suited to 'Germany's essence'. They supplied a

seemingly obvious pretext for the tale that German national greatness could come about only on anti-democratic foundations. Reactionary philosophy, history and journalism richly exploited this situation, and the Left wing of the bourgeoisie and bourgeois intelligentsia could find no effective countermeasures.

So among broad sections of the bourgeoisie and petty bourgeoisie, the old prejudice gained ground in the course of the Weimar Republic that democracy in Germany was a 'Western import', a harmful foreign body which the nation had to expel for its own good. An indication of the lack of tradition in many subjectively convinced democrats is that for their part, they made the allegedly exclusively 'Western' character of democracy the basis for their propaganda. By tactlessly and untactically placing in the forefront their anti-German sentiments, their enthusiasm for Western democracy, they were involuntarily helping the reactionaries in their anti-democratic yarn-spinning. (This ideology is seen at its clearest in the ambit of the *Weltbühne*.) A further point was the nihilistic attitude of large sections of the radical bourgeois intelligentsia to the national humiliation (abstract pacifism), a nihilism which also found its way into the labour movement, although in different forms. (This tendency was particularly marked in the German Independent Socialist camp, but under the influence of Rosa Luxemburg's ideological errors even the German Communist Party was not untouched by national nihilism at the start of its development.)

Nevertheless the overt attempts to restore the Hohenzollern monarchy came to nothing (the Kapp *Putsch* of 1920). The party propounding this restoration, the 'German National', was never able to grow into a really major and decisive mass party, although its representatives retained most of their positions of power in the civil and military machinery because of the Weimar Republic's anti-proletarian, anti-revolutionary tendencies. Only when the disappointment of enormous masses reached a climax, as a result of the major crisis which set in from 1929, did the reactionaries succeed in gaining a

foothold among the masses: in the 'National Socialist German Workers' Party', in Hitlerian fascism.

Our concern in these introductory studies is therefore briefly to outline the socio-ideological features which made possible in Germany this disgracefully swift and even more disgracefully long-term triumph of fascism. While briefly showing how it derived from Germany's previous development, we shall indicate at the same time the substance of its specifically new attributes, and also the reason why this new element should only signify a qualitative heightening of tendencies already present before.

We have seen that the Weimar Republic, owing to the manner of its origin, its social methods of defence (against the Left), its establishment and consolidation, was, on the one hand, a republic without republicans, a democracy without democrats. The initial enthusiasm of the masses quickly evaporated: it did so with the crumbling of hopes of a 'Wilsonian' peace for a German democracy and the dashing of the expectations linked with 'socialization'. In the revolutionary-minded, Leftist section of the labour movement especially, a hostile attitude to the Weimar system took root, a system which became fully established with the murder of the greatest heroes of Germany's new revolutionary labour movement, Karl Liebknecht and Rosa Luxemburg. On the other hand the supporters of a Hohenzollern restoration, entrenched reaction at the beginning of the era were, as we have also seen, far too weak to effect a permanent overthrow; it is also significant that their followers never grew into a real mass movement. It was now apparent that the Hohenzollern régime never possessed a real footing in the masses. And that was far from accidental. As long as Hohenzollern rule was or at least seemed to be undisturbed, the overtly and strictly 'authoritative' character of the old form of reaction was able to keep the majority of the population in a mood of loyal enthusiasm. But after the collapse, when there appeared a new and less popular 'authority' and a restoration could only be implemented by means of an

armed rising, or, in the preliminary period, by way of a resolute political opposition, the quantitative and qualitative weakness of the mass basis of the old reaction came to light.

So as a result of the weakness of its adversaries on the Left and Right, the Weimar Republic acquired a chance of survival – inwardly very shaky and obtained through continual concessions to reaction. As long as Germany was in no position openly to renounce the peace of Versailles, this was also underpinned by the pressure of foreign affairs and the German imperialists' corresponding deliberations on foreign policy. For a proper overthrow to occur, new conditions had to come into being.

Prominent among such conditions was the shift of class power within the reactionary camp: after the war, the monopoly capitalists became the leading group. This was also the conclusion to a long development, but a conclusion bringing something qualitatively new. In 1848, the Rhine industrial magnates who represented German capitalism at its most advanced at that time already played a major role in quelling the revolution and re-establishing an anti-democratic régime in Germany, although the majority of them were liberal, hence in opposition to the régime. With their 'endeavours for an agreement', they provided the anti-democratic monarchist forces with a breathing space at the time of the mounting revolutionary wave. With their formal parliamentary and always loyal 'opposition' they contributed to the disorganization of the democratic movement to stave off Hohenzollern reaction, then arming itself for reprisals, and so on. Under Bismarck, as also under Wilhelm II, the upper-middle classes had an increasing influence on government policy that corresponded to the rapid development of German capitalism. But this influence was largely exerted via the back stairs: apart from rare exceptions (Dernburg), official political command remained in the old hands, preserving its old 'authoritative' technique – indeed Wilhelm II's style of government resembled an imperialist re-creation of the style of Friedrich Wilhelm IV. After the world war, too, the now decidedly

dominant influence of monopoly capital often operated behind the scenes, preferring the election of executive organs and figureheads legitimized in other ways (Hindenburg, Brüning, Schleicher, etc.). The alliance with the Prussian Junker class, with the 'Junker' patriciate of the military and civil bureaucracy, remained in force, but monopoly capital now assumed the leading role on all matters in this alliance. It was no longer content to assert its aims in economic complexes that were vital to its vested interests.

This development took place, however, in a social milieu in which the anti-capitalist sentiments of the masses were constantly increasing. The vanguard of the German working class keenly followed the Russian events of 1917 and subsequently perceived in them the perspective of German history they needed as well. The hopes pinned on the 1918 promises of socialization, the disappointments stemming from the whole movement's breakdown in the ensuing years, the gradual alienation of broad masses of workers from a Weimar Republic more and more patently under the thumb of monopoly capitalism, the provocative effects of the mass unemployment linked with the crisis after 1929, etc. – all this gave birth to anti-capitalist feelings stretching far beyond the working class in scope. The reactionaries of monopoly capitalism were thus presented with a new task, the task of exploiting just these mass feelings to establish their own command; and using them for support, to found a new type of reactionary régime securing once and for all the absolute predominance of monopoly capitalism in all spheres of political and social life.

Here we cannot make it our business to portray this political development of Germany even in outline. We only needed to indicate these political and social factors so that the tendencies portrayed and analysed in our later philosophical studies may stand in proper relief to their social foundations. Let us just take the task stated above, namely the conversion of anti-capitalist mass drifts, indeed mass movements into the naked absolute dominance of monopoly capitalism (which

set itself the closely related task of converting widespread mass indignation – understandable and rightful in itself – at the imperialist peace of Versailles into an aggressive, imperialist chauvinism). It will be clear that only a radically irrationalist world-view is suited to even a purely demagogic 'reconciliation' of such mutually conflicting tendencies. It will also be apparent at once that the required irrationalism, which was a long time in preparation and found a consummation in the 'National Socialist world-view', must differ qualitatively from the irrationalism of before and after 1848. Of course, given the German bourgeoisie's special receptiveness to irrationalism in the inter-war period, its 'education' by way of the old irrational philosophies plays no mean role. But if we wish to understand from the social angle the forcible propagation on a mass scale of the new, fascist slant, we must look at a couple of new socio-ideological phenomena.

Here the first thing we meet is a transformation in the working class. It is striking that this anti-rational tendency should take hold of broad masses, including considerable parts of the working class, and that the workers should now readily accept arguments which previously rebounded harmlessly off them. For where the masses are concerned, the question of reason or irrationality has more of the impact of a vital question, rather than a mere theoretical problem, than it does for the intelligentsia. The labour movement's great advances, the clear perspective of successful struggles to improve the situation and of a foreseeable overthrow of capitalism led the working class to see something rational and ordered in their own lives, their own historical development. Each successful battle, each rebuttal of the reactionaries (e.g., at the time of the anti-socialist laws) reinforced this outlook and inculcated a sovereign contempt for the then crude religio-irrationalist propaganda put out by the reactionary camp.

With the victory of reformism and the reformists' participation in the Weimar system, this situation changed drastically.

The idea of rationality in itself acquired a fundamentally different accent. Bernstein had already tried to disparage as utopian the revolutionary struggle for a socialist society and a 'final goal', proposing instead the humdrum and philistine '*Realpolitik* reasonableness' of compromise with the liberal bourgeoisie and adjustment to capitalist society. Ever since the social democrats had become the ruling party, this '*Realpolitik* reasonableness' had held sway over its members, in its propaganda and above all its deeds. In the first years of revolution this propaganda was mingled with demagogic promises of imminent socialization, a socialism to be realized in this 'rational' manner as opposed to the 'unreasonable' adventures, the 'unrealistic policy of disaster' pursued by the communists. 'Relative stabilization' in Germany meant the total command of Bernstein's rationality in reformist theory and practice. And in the era of the big economic world crisis, the reformists at the helm maintained this line of '*Realpolitik* reasonableness' with iron vigour. Thus 'reason' signified in practice for the masses: not to go on strike because of a wage reduction but to submit to it; to refrain from any demonstrations, any energetic steps if unemployment benefits were reduced or if larger and larger masses were disqualified from receiving them; to steer clear of the most bloody fascist provocation, to withdraw to safety, not to defend the working class and its right of way but, as Dimitrov accurately characterized this policy, to avoid danger and not to tempt the beast from its lair.

So reformist 'reason' not only rendered the working class practically helpless in the struggles against imperialist capitalism and a fascism which was arming itself for a takeover of power. It also compromised and broke down the old conviction of a rationality in historical developments leading, through properly conducted struggles, to an improvement in the everyday situation of the working class and ultimately to its complete liberation. The reformists' propaganda against the Soviet Union reinforced this development by portraying the heroism of the Russian working class as futile, inappropriate

and fruitless.

This development entailed various consequences among the working class itself. A relatively large vanguard turned away from reformism to extend the old Marxian traditions in the new form appropriate to the imperialist age, that of Leninism. A broad sector remained transfixed on the level of '*Realpolitik* reasonableness' and became incapable in practice of providing an effective challenge to fascism. Hence for a relatively substantial mass of people, especially among the young workers whom the desperate crisis had made impatient, this development shattered their faith in reason in general, in the revolutionary rationality of historical developments and the inner connection and compatibility of reason and revolution. So this sector, precisely as a result of its theoretical and practical training through reformism when the crisis loomed, was ready to assimilate in its outlook the modern tendencies of anti-rationality and the contempt for reason and science, and to indulge in the superstition of myth.

That does not mean, of course, that these embittered young workers became readers and admirers of Nietzsche or Spengler. But since the antithesis of reason and emotion seemed to the masses to have sprung from life itself, they were bound to conceive a receptiveness to this doctrine on the ideological plane as well.

Among the intelligentsia and petty bourgeoisie we find another kind of change, but one that became just as important in its consequences regarding a receptiveness to fascist irrationalism. Here we are dealing with despair as a mass emotion, and, closely connected with it, gullibility and the expectation of saving miracles. Without question, the universal spreading of an ideology of despair in Germany was primarily a sequel to the war, the peace of Versailles and the loss of a national and political perspective, which these groups associated – consciously or not – with a German imperialist victory. Spengler's huge success, which extended far beyond philosophical circles, is a clear reflection of this mood. Disappointments felt during the Weimar period, both

among the Right-wingers, who hoped to restore the monarchy, and among the more Left-oriented, who were hoping for a democratic and indeed socialist regeneration of Germany, were bound to reinforce these sentiments still more, and they subsequently reached a climax in the great economic crisis of 1929. The objective foundations of these moods were therefore of an economic, political and social character. If, however, we examine their vehement, virtually unresisted propagation, we cannot possibly mistake the important role of the ideological development up to the First World War. And this in both a positive and negative respect. Negatively, the social ideology of helplessness and dependence we find in Germans brought up in the atmosphere of the 'authoritarian State' played an exceptionally important role. The average German – however proficient and even outstanding in his own field (including also philosophy, art, and so on) – expected all decisions, even those determining his livelihood, to come from 'upstairs', from 'vocational leaders' in the Army, politics, and economics, and it was completely beyond him to regard his own standpoints as co-determining factors in political and economic life, etc. Thus after the collapse of the Hohenzollern régime he remained helplessly disoriented. He always expected an improvement in his fortune to stem partly from the 'old and tried leaders', partly from a newly created 'leader's outfit', and when it gradually became evident that they had all failed him, he was left in a state of total despair. However, this despair was linked with expectations of a 'new leader'; generally speaking, it produced no intention of an independent appraisal of the situation and of independent action. And on the positive side, the sentiments which made the fascist deception of the masses possible were nurtured by the influence of the agnosticist, pessimistic philosophical trends of which we shall give a detailed analysis later. Their common feature is that pessimism or despair was the standard moral attitude to the problems of the time. Only, of course, for the intellectual 'élite'; the plebs might believe in progress, but its optimism was inferior

or 'infamous', as Schopenhauer already termed it.

In this connection German philosophy in the imperialist age proceeded, as we shall see, from Nietzsche to Spengler and later in the Weimar period from Spengler to fascism. If we stress this spadework by German philosophy from Schopenhauer and Nietzsche onwards, it might be objected that we are dealing with esoteric doctrines circulated only within quite small groups. We believe, on the contrary, that one must not underestimate the indirect, subterranean effect on the masses of the fashionable reactionary ideologies analysed so far. This effect was not limited to the direct influence of those philosophers' actual books, although it should be remembered that editions of the works of Schopenhauer and Nietzsche certainly reached many tens of thousands. But via universities, public lectures, the press, etc., these ideologies also spread to the broadest masses – needless to say in a coarsened form, but that strengthened rather than weakened their reactionary content, their ultimate irrationalism and pessimism, since the central ideas now received greater attention at the expense of qualifying statements. Through such ideologies the masses can be intensively corrupted without ever glimpsing the immediate source of corruption. Nietzsche's barbarizing of the instincts, his vitalism, his 'heroic pessimism', etc., were necessary products of the imperialist age, and Nietzsche's speeding up of the process operated on the minds of tens of thousands of people who had never even heard of Nietzsche.

These factors, however, merely reinforced the readiness for a philosophy of despair. What was new about it in relation to similar past tendencies stemmed from Germany's situation between the two world wars. The most important difference between the pre-war and post-war period was undoubtedly the severe shock to, and later the almost complete loss of 'security' in the social and individual life of the middle classes, above all the intelligentsia. If a person was a pessimist before the First World War, and primarily with regard to culture, this attitude had a placidly contemplative character

without any intention of possible action. Since an individual's own existence seemed secure in material and social, spiritual and human terms, it was possible for his philosophy to remain as good as purely theoretical, without seriously influencing his conduct and inner attitude. The cessation of 'security', the continual threatening of both the inner and outward life caused this irrationalist pessimism to take a practical turn. This is not to say that a person's view of the world was now bound to produce actions in an immediate sense, but merely that – on the one hand – it started out from a personally sensed threat to his existence (and not only from the contemplation of an objective cultural situation), and that, on the other hand, practical claims were made with regard to his philosophy, albeit in the form that the impossibility of action was deduced 'ontologically' from the structure of the world.

At all events, the old forms of irrationalism proved to be unsuitable for answering these questions. And now we can see the need – to which we shall hark back repeatedly – for fascist demagogy, much though it took over from the old type of reactionary ideology in both form and content, to be oriented in method towards the more recent ideologies created under imperialism, stripping them of everything 'private' and 'spiritually high-flying' and converting what was left into a determined and uncouth form of popular corruption. Everything that had been said on irrational pessimism from Nietzsche and Dilthey to Heidegger and Jaspers on lecture platforms and in intellectuals' salons and cafés, Hitler and Rosenberg transferred to the streets. We shall see how much was preserved of the particular methodology of this development, in the basic contents, either in spite or because of demagogic coarsening through 'National Socialist philosophy'. Its starting-point, as regards the psychology of the masses, was precisely this mass despair, the resulting credulity and belief in miracles; and here the masses included the most highly qualified intellectuals. That despair was the sociopsychological connecting link between National Socialism

and the broad masses is evident from the fact that the movement's real impetus, its real penetration of the masses began with the economic crisis of 1929. It began the moment that an initially general philosophical despair, which gradually assumed increasingly concrete social forms, turned into a massive threat to individual existence – the moment, therefore, that the aforestated intentions in a practical direction yielded the possibility of rendering philosophical despair subservient to the politics of desperadoes.

These politics now drew on the old servile instincts of the 'authority-minded' Germans, instincts which the Weimar democracy had hardly affected. But the method of subjection had to be a new one because, for the first time in German history, it was not now a matter of submission to a traditional, legitimate power, nor of the mere restoration of such a power, but of joining a radical coup, a 'revolution' as National Socialism liked to style itself in its early days as well as in later crises. This non-legitimate, 'revolutionary' character of fascist power is one of the reasons why, with regard to methodology, National Socialism needed to associate itself with philosophical models of Nietzsche's kind more than with reactionary ideology of the old school. To be sure fascist demagogy was extremely versatile; simultaneously with the assertion of its 'revolutionary' character it tried to appeal also to potential instincts of legitimacy (e.g., Hindenburg's role in the transitional period, the formally legitimate seizure of power, etc.).

But despair alone would not have sufficed as a socio-psychological connecting link. Precisely in respect of its practical intention, it needed implicitly to contain the elements of gullibility and superstitiousness we have already mentioned. These elements were indeed present, and not by accident. For the greater the personal despair, the more this expresses the sense of a threat to individual existence, the more it will give rise on average – under the social and the spiritual, moral conditions of the German development – to gullibility and superstition. After Schopenhauer, and especially

after Nietzsche, irrationalist pessimism broke down the conviction that there existed an objective external world and that an unrestricted and thorough perception of it would indicate a way out of the problems arousing despair. *Knowledge* of the world was now increasingly converted into a (more and more arbitrary) *interpretation* of the world. Naturally this philosophical tendency heightened this sector's habit of expecting everything to come from the 'authorities', for to their mind life too was not a question of the objective analysis of concrete connections, but of interpreting decisions whose reasons could never be known. And it is also immediately clear that here lay one of the socio-psychological sources of the faith in miracles: however desperate the situation, the 'genius favoured by God' (Bismarck, Wilhelm II, Hitler) would find an answer 'all right' through his 'creative intuition'. It is further plain to see that, the greater the risk to 'security' and the more directly individual existence was itself at stake, the more intensive this credulity and faith in miracles would become. Thus we are dealing with an old, traditional failing of the German middle class, embracing Nietzschean philosophy and the mentality of the average beer-hall philosopher.

We will often be asked in amazement how it was that large masses of the German people could trustingly accept the puerile myth propounded by Hitler and Rosenberg. We may counter with the historical question: how could the best-educated and intellectually most eminent men in Germany believe in Schopenhauer's mythical 'will', the pronouncements of Nietzsche's Zarathustra, or the history-myths of the decline of the West? And it is not good enough to say that the intellectual and artistic level of Schopenhauer and Nietzsche is immeasurably higher than the coarse and contradictory demagogy of Hitler and Rosenberg. For if a person educated in philosophy and literature is able to follow epistemologically the nuances of Nietzsche's reworking of Schopenhauer, and to appreciate with aesthetic and psychological sensitivity the nuances of his critique of decadence,

yet still believes in the Zarathustra myth, the myth of the Superman and 'eternal recurrence', this is at bottom harder to fathom than the despairing belief of a poorly educated working youth – someone who was never or only temporarily a member of a party and was left out in the cold after finishing his apprenticeship – that Hitler would realize 'German socialism'.

The same applies here as what Marx once said about the 'cynical' doctrines of classical economics: that the doctrines did not come out of books into reality, but entered books from reality. The question of whether, at a given time, there reigns a climate of sound and sober criticism or a climate of superstition, faith in miracles and irrationalist credulity in specific sections of society is not a matter of intellectual standards but of the condition of society. Obviously ideologies which have previously exerted an influence will play a considerable part by reinforcing or weakening the tendency towards criticism or credulity. But do not let us forget that the efficacy or inefficacy of an intellectual tendency likewise enters books from reality, and not vice versa.

History tells us that eras of particularly acute credulity, superstition and a faith in miracles must by no means always be eras of notably inferior civilization. The very opposite is true. We see such a tendency at the close of antiquity in the climax of Greco-Roman civilization, at the time when Alexandrian learning was at its most prevalent. And we find that during this period, it was by no means merely uneducated slaves or small craftsmen, the transmitters of Christianity, who were most prone to believe in miracles. Credulity and superstition are just as much to be found in the highly gifted and well educated scholars and artists of the era, in Plutarch or Apuleius, Plotinus or Porphyrios; to be sure with a quite different substance, on a higher literary plane, more subtle intellectually, more educated. And the climax of the witchcraft craze – to cite one more characteristic example – was never the darkest hour of the Middle Ages, but the great critical transitional period between the

medieval and modern epochs, the age of Galileo and Kepler. Once again we find that many of the most important minds of the epoch were not free from various forms of superstition; we have only to think of Francis Bacon, Jacob Boehme, Paracelsus, etc.

The factor common to such ages of social folly, of superstition and a faith in miracles taken to extremes, is that they were always periods of the decline of an old social order and a culture implanted for centuries, and at the same time epochs of fresh birth pangs. In the German crisis years, this general uncertainty of capitalist life saw a heightening which marked a change-over into a qualitatively new and special state of affairs, and the change-over caused this susceptibility to folly to spread on an unprecedented mass scale. This susceptibility fascism exploited in the most ruthless manner possible.

Later we shall describe and analyse the theoretical forms concretely assumed by this demagogic exploitation of the desperate situation in which the broadest sections of the German people found themselves. Only then – in our concrete analysis – can we really drive it home how fascist demagogy and tyranny was only the ultimate culmination of a long process which initially had an 'innocent' look (innocent in a strictly or more generally philosophical sense): the destruction of reason.

The beginnings of this process may be found in the feudal counter-reformist, reactionary-romantic struggle against the French Revolution, and as we have noted it reached its peak in the imperialist age of capitalism. This process was by no means merely restricted to Germany. Its origins, its Hitlerian manifestation, and its survival in the present age all have international roots from the socio-economic standpoint, and irrationalist philosophy is therefore likewise in evidence internationally. However, we have seen in our introduction that it could attain the same fiendish influence nowhere but in Hitler's Germany, that apart from very rare exceptions it nowhere reached the same hegemony it had already reached

in Germany, and not only on the national but also on an international scale. Hence it has been necessary briefly to record and to analyse in this chapter the socio-historical tendencies which turned Germany into such a breeding-ground and centre of hostility to reason.

Hence the following account of philosophico-historical tendencies must – with a few exceptions such as Kierkegaard or Gobineau – be confined to the German development. So far it and it alone has led to a Hitlerian movement. And hence, we believe, to confine ourselves to an account of the history of irrationalism in Germany is not to diminish the internationalism of it, but to heighten that aspect. It is a *Discite moniti*, a 'Learn from this warning!', addressed to the thinking persons of all nations. A warning that no philosophy is 'innocent' or merely academic; that everywhere and always, the danger is objectively at hand that some global fire-raiser will again spark off a devouring conflagration à la Hitler with the philosophical tinder of 'innocent' salon conversations, café discussions, university lectures, literary supplements, essays, and so on. With the altered circumstances of today's world situation and their philosophical consequences, we shall occupy ourselves in the epilogue. They show far-reaching differences between the ideological spadework for the Second and the Third imperialist World War. It seems, for reasons that will be examined in due course, that nowadays irrationalism in general does not play the leading role it had at the time that the second world inferno was organized. But we shall show that irrationalism still forms the philosophical climate, so to speak, of the new war propaganda; at least it plays no small part in it. Therefore present-day circumstances, though different in many respects, have by no means deprived of immediacy our intended caution to learn from the past. This is even less the case if we consider that a whole series of important elements in the 'classical' irrationalism of the Hitler period (agnosticism, relativism, nihilism, proneness to myth-making, uncritical thinking, credulity, faith in miracles, racial prejudices, racial

hatred, etc., etc.) also play an undiminished, sometimes even stronger part in the philosophical propaganda of the 'Cold War'.

So today as well, although the struggles are being fought out with other immediate contents and methods than in Hitler's time, the main controversy – philosophically speaking – between progress and reaction is over the further evolution or destruction of reason. Hence we believe that today the significance of a history of the basic problems of irrationalism still points far beyond the merely historical realm.

From the lesson that Hitler taught the world, each individual and each nation should try and learn something for their own good. And this responsibility exists in a particularly acute form for philosophers, whose duty it should be to supervise the existence and evolution of reason in proportion to their concrete share in social developments. (But we must not overestimate their real significance in the development of society.) They have neglected that duty both within and outside Germany. So far, not every country has seen the realization of Mephistopheles's lines about the desperate Faust:

> Only look down on reason and science,
> The highest faculties of humankind . . .
> And then I have you trapped.[2]

But, unless things take a new turn, this does not mean the slightest guarantee for any other land with an imperialist economy, or any other bourgeois culture which is overshadowed by irrationalism, that it will not be taken over tomorrow by a fascist maniac compared to whom Hitler himself may have been only a clumsy novice. Thus the purpose of confining our analysis to Germany's development and German philosophy is to underline precisely this warning.

NOTES

1 Translator's note. A bourgeois satire published in 1911. Gustav Freytag (1816-95), author of *Soll und Haben*, was a journalist, scholar and bourgeois liberal who rejected a noble title.

2 Translator's note. Goethe: *Faust*, Part I. The German reads: '*Verachte nur Vernunft und Wissenschaft,/Der Menschen allerhöchste Kraft/ . . . So hab ich dich schon unbedingt!*'

CHAPTER II

THE FOUNDING OF IRRATIONALISM IN THE PERIOD BETWEEN TWO REVOLUTIONS (1789-1848)

1. Basic Preliminary Remarks on the History of Modern Irrationalism

Understandably, the irrationalism of our time is much occupied with looking for ancestors. Because it seeks to trace the history of philosophy back to a 'perennial' struggle between rationalism and irrationalism, it finds it necessary to prove the existence of irrationalist world-views in the Orient, antiquity, the Middle Ages, and so on. It is not worth enumerating all the (sometimes grotesque) forms taken by this deliberate distortion of the history of philosophy; for in dealing with the neo-Hegelians, for example, we shall find even Hegel presented as supremely irrationalist. So what comes about is an unprincipled eclectic mish-mash, a totally arbitrary selection of famous or not-so-famous names without definite criteria for the choice. It may be said that only the immediate pre-fascists and fascists possessed a criterion: the degree of reactionary firmness. For that reason Baeumler excluded the early Romantics of Jena from this illustrious gathering. For the same reason Rosenberg recognized only Schopenhauer, Richard Wagner, Lagarde and Nietzsche as 'classics' of fascist irrationalism.

At this point let us just note in passing that the catchword 'irrationalism' is relatively new as a label for a philosophical tendency, school, etc. As far as I know, it first crops up in Kuno Fischer's *Fichte*. Windelband, in his *History of Philosophy*, already deals with Schelling and Schopenhauer in a section headed 'Metaphysics of Irrationalism'. This

terminology predominates even more in Lask. At first this use of the word 'irrationalism' in such an enlarged sense met with critical reservations[1], but between the two world wars in particular it became a generally acknowledged term for the philosophical stream whose history will be the subject of this book.

In classical German philosophy itself, Hegel uses the word 'irrational' only in its mathematical sense; when criticizing the philosophical directions we are discussing, he writes of 'immediate knowing'. Even Schelling[2] still uses the expression in a derogatory sense, as a synonym for 'non-absoluteness'. Only in the later Fichte do we find seeds of the present-day use of the word. In his (fruitless) attempt to come to terms with the triumphantly advancing objective idealism of Schelling and Hegel, Fichte wrote in his *Science of Knowledge* of 1804: 'The absolute projection of an object whose origin cannot be accounted for, where accordingly it is dark and empty in the middle space between projection and *projectum*, the *projectio per hiatum irrationalem* as I expressed it a little scholastically but, I think, very tellingly . . .'[3] This recourse to irrationalism, like the whole of Fichte's later epistemology, had no influence on subsequent developments. Only in Lask can we see the influence of the later Fichte to any profound extent, while isolated fascists have endeavoured to include Fichte's name in their roll of ancestors. Hence we are confining ourselves to indicating the most important terminological facts and will deal in the following pages only with those representatives of philosophical irrationalism who became of historical influence.

Needless to say, this (relative) terminological newness of the expression does not mean that the question of irrationalism did not already arise in classical German philosophy as a major problem; quite the contrary. Our ensuing studies will show that the crucial formulations of the problem belong precisely to the time between the French Revolution and the period of ideological spadework for the revolution of 1848.

Hegel himself did not use the term 'irrationalism', but that

again is not to say that he did not debate the problem of the relation of dialectics and irrationalism. He certainly did so, and not only in his polemic against Friedrich Heinrich Jacobi's 'immediate knowing'. It is perhaps a coincidence, but an illuminating one, that his fundamental coming to terms with this subject begins precisely with geometry and mathematics. At all events he was dealing, in this context, with the limits of the determinants of understanding, their contradictoriness and the urging onwards and higher of the dialectical movement towards reason that now arose. Hegel wrote of geometry: 'In its course, however – and this is most remarkable – it finally meets with *incommensurabilities* and *irrationalities* where, if it wants to take definition farther, it is *driven beyond* the principle of understanding. As frequently occurs with terminology there now appears the inverse proposition that what we call *rational* is the *sensible* thing (*das Verständige*), but what is *irrational* is rather a beginning and sign of *rationality*.'[4]

The starting-point of this statement was a special one, and it was still far from Hegel's mind to make general philosophical use of the terms employed. Yet here he was touching on the central philosophical problem of irrationalism's entire later development, namely those questions with which irrationalism has been always connected philosophically. These, as we shall see in the course of our studies, are the very questions resulting from the limitations and contradictions of thinking governed simply by understanding. If human thought detects in these limitations a problem to be solved and, as Hegel aptly states, 'the beginning and sign of rationality', i.e., of a higher knowledge, then the encounter with them can become the starting-point for the further development of thinking, for dialectics. Irrationalism, on the other hand – we are briefly summarizing in advance what we shall set out in concrete detail later – stops at precisely this point, absolutizes the problem, hardens the limitations of perception governed by understanding into perceptional limitations as a whole, and indeed mysticizes into a 'supra-rational'

answer the problem thus rendered artificially insoluble. The equating of understanding and perception of the limits of understanding with perceptional limitations as a whole, the introduction of 'supra-rationality' (intuition, etc.) when it is possible and necessary to proceed to a rational perception – these are the most universal hallmarks of philosophical irrationalism.

What Hegel is here elucidating with a fundamentally important example is one of the central questions of the dialectical method. He defines 'the realm of laws' as 'the *quiescent* image of the existing or phenomenal world'. So – to take here only the real gist of his line of thought – 'the appearance is the totality as against law, for it contains law but more besides, namely the element of the autonomously moving form'.[5] Here Hegel has elaborated the most general logical elements which constitute the most markedly forward-looking tendency of the dialectical method: the approximating character of dialectical knowledge. And Lenin, who revealed this crucial aspect of the dialectical method – naturally the materialistic one, no longer fettered by Hegel's idealist limitations, vigorously stressed the significance of the statements by Hegel just quoted: 'That is an eminently materialist and (with the word "quiescent") remarkably apt definition. Law takes the quiescent element – and hence law, every law is narrow, incomplete, an approximation.'[6]

Here we cannot examine in greater detail Hegel's increasingly concrete statements on the dialectical reciprocal relations of law (essence) and appearance. It merely remains for us to point out briefly that in the course of these concretizations, Hegel surmounted the barrier of subjective idealism, where the general conditions (essence, etc.) cannot lie in objectivity, in objectiveness itself, and argued philosophically the objectivity of essence: 'Essence still lacks existence; but it *is*, and in a profounder sense than Being'; 'Law is therefore the *essential* appearance'[7], a definition whose fundamental importance Lenin too stresses strongly in the marginal notes we have quoted to Hegel's *Science of Logic*.

With these statements we can already define a little more closely the general, methodological relation of irrationalism to dialectics. Since objective reality is fundamentally richer, more diverse and more intricate than the best developed concepts of our thinking can ever be, clashes of the kind we have depicted between thinking and Being are inevitable. And so in times when the objective development of society and the consequent discovery of new natural phenomena proceed apace, great possibilities emerge for irrationalism to convert this advance into a retrograde movement with the help of mysticizing. Such a situation arose at the turn of the eighteenth-nineteenth centuries, partly as a result of the social upheaval caused by the French Revolution and the Industrial Revolution in England, partly as a result of the crises in natural scientific thinking, the development of chemistry, biology, etc., on the basis of the age's fresh discoveries in geology, palaeontology, etc. Hegel's dialectic, in its attempt to comprehend the problems now raised from the historical angle as well, was the highest stage in bourgeois philosophy, its most energetic attempt to master the difficulties intellectually: to create a method which could guarantee such an approximation (the fullest so far) of thought, the intellectual reflection of reality, to that reality itself. (We are not going to discuss Hegel's well-known idealist limitations, his idealist mystifications or the antithesis between method and system; the critique of them made by the classic Marxist-Leninist authors is generally known and we take it as read.)

Now irrationalism begins with this (necessary, irrevocable, but always relative) discrepancy between the intellectual reflection and the objective original. The source of the discrepancy lies in the fact that the tasks directly presented to thought in a given instance, as long as they are still tasks, still unresolved problems, appear in a form which at first gives the impression that thought, the forming of concepts, breaks down in the face of reality, that the reality confronting thought represents an area beyond reason (the rationality of

the category system of the conceptual method used so far). As we have seen, Hegel analysed this situation correctly. His dialectic of phenomenon and essence, existence and law, and above all his dialectic of the concepts of understanding (*Verstandesbegriffe*), the determinants of reflection, and the bridge from understanding to reason indicate quite distinctly the real road to a resolution of these difficulties.

But what if thought – for reasons to be analysed in concrete detail later – stops short of the difficulties and shies away from them? What if it renders fundamentally irrevocable the constellation inexorably appearing (since this is bound to repeat itself with each decisive step forward)? What if it hypostasizes the inability of *specific* concepts to comprehend a specific reality into the inability of thought, conceptions and rational perception in general to master the essence of reality intellectually? What if a virtue is then made of this necessity and the inability to comprehend the world intellectually is presented as 'higher perception', as faith, intuition, and so on?

Clearly this problem will crop up at every stage of knowledge, i.e., each time that social evolution and hence science and philosophy are forced to make a leap forward in order to master the real questions arising. From this it will be already evident that the choice between *ratio* and *irratio* is never an 'immanent' philosophical question. It is not chiefly intellectual or philosophical considerations which decide a thinker's choice between the new and the old, but class situation and class allegiance. If we take the broad perspectives of centuries, it often seems almost unbelievable how important thinkers have halted at the threshold of a problem nearly resolved, and indeed have turned round and fled in the opposite direction. Only the class character of their stance can illuminate such 'enigmas'.

We should look for this social conditioning of rationalism and irrationalism not only in the mass of social injunctions and prohibitions. The great seventeenth-century English materialist, Thomas Hobbes, aptly characterized the structure

of this conditioning when he wrote: 'For I do not doubt that if it conflicted with somebody's proprietorial rights or (to put it more accurately) with the interests of proprietors for the three angles of a triangle to be equal to two corners of a square; then this thesis, if not disputed, would nonetheless be suppressed through the burning of all geometry books, as far as those involved were able to carry it through.'[8] Accordingly it must be said that on no account is this element of a direct suppression of new truths to be underestimated either. Let us recall the beginnings of modern philosophy, the fate of Bruno, Vanini and Galileo. This situation has undoubtedly exerted a major influence, manifesting itself in many striking ambiguities and finding clear expression in the philosophical 'diplomacy' of Gassendi, Bayle, Leibniz, etc.; similarly connected with this is Lessing's public silence about his Spinozist views. Nor should we underestimate the philosophical importance of such 'diplomacy'. Granted, in the cases of Gassendi or Bayle posterity has obtained a clear picture of their real standpoint. But in the case of Leibniz this question has already become much harder to unravel, and Lessing's silence on Spinoza formed the basis for a totally false interpretation of his outlook.

Despite all this, the social conditioning we mean is connected more deeply and intimately with personality and output. It is not solely external social pressure which creates so many deliberate ambiguities, so much clouding of what is actually meant in philosophy from Descartes to Hegel, particularly where decisive philosophical issues are at stake. Far more important still is the fact that social determinants rule the thinkers concerned down to their most private convictions, their manner of thinking and the way they set out a proposition, etc., unknown to themselves. With this in mind Marx replied to the radical Hegelians who sought to explain Hegel's ambiguities as simply external accommodation and to counter the 'exoteric' Hegel who made compromises with an 'esoteric' Hegel belonging to radicalism: 'There can no longer be any question of Hegel's accommodating himself to

religion, the State, and so on, since this lie is the lie of his progress.'[9]

Internally as well, philosophers are always tied – consciously or unconsciously, deliberately or involuntarily – with their society, a specific class in it, and the forward- or backward-oriented endeavours of that class. This foundation (and its historical destiny) nurtures, defines, forms and guides precisely what is really personal and original about their philosophy. Even where, at first glance, an individual stance going to the point of isolation from one's own class seems to predominate, this stance has the most intimate of links with the class situation and the vicissitudes of the class struggle. Thus Marx shows us how Ricardo's connection with capitalist production and its development of the productive forces determined his stance towards the various classes. 'If Ricardo's views as a whole are in the interest of the *industrial bourgeoisie*, that is only *because* and inasmuch as this sector's interest coincides with that of production or the productive development of human labour. Where his views are antithetical to it he is just as *harsh* towards the bourgeoisie as he otherwise is to the proletariat and the aristocracy.'[10]

The more genuine and significant a thinker is, the more he will be a child of his time, his country and his class. For every fruitful and really philosophical proposition – however strong the effort to place it *sub specie aeternitatis* – is concrete; i.e., in content and form it is determined by the social, scientific, artistic, etc., exigencies and strivings of its age and itself contains (always within the concrete tendencies operating here) a real tendency to go forward or back, towards the new or the old. Whether and how far the philosopher concerned is aware of this connection is a secondary problem.

We have kept these observations on a general plane to start with. They lead us to a second question: each period, and within each period, each class playing a fighting part in the philosophical field poses in a different form the problem initially outlined, a problem out of which an irrationalism

may arise in specific circumstances. Admittedly the dialectical tension between rational conceptualization and its material from reality is a general fact of the perceiving relation to reality. But the manner in which this problem emerges in each instance and in which its resolution is tackled, or, alternatively, evaded and fled from, varies qualitatively in accordance with the historical situation and the historical evolution of the class struggles.

These differences touching the structure of the propositions and solutions manifest themselves very distinctly as differences between philosophy and individual sciences. The sciences are often in a position to resolve directly the problems that life poses, often without bothering very much about the philosophical consequences. Take, for example, the development of mathematics, where important dialectical problems are correctly posed and resolved but the greatest dialectical pioneers are as little aware of their discovery of new dialectical territory as was Molière's *Gentilhomme* of the fact that he was always talking in prose. Philosophy, on the other hand, is compelled to tackle fundamental questions concerned with a world-view, no matter how the answers turn out.

But this difference too is relative and so at the same time *historically* relative as well. For in specific socio-historical circumstances the utterance of a purely scientific truth without any philosophical generalizing or a prompt drawing of philosophical conclusions from it may go directly to the centre of class-based conflicts of world-view. That was once the case with the Copernican theory, and it happened later with Darwinism; today it is happening with the further development of Darwinism by Michurin and Lysenko. On the other hand, there were relatively long-lasting philosophical tendencies which made the avoidance of any proposition related to a world-view the fundamental programme and core of the method. (Here we wish only to suggest that a specific stance in the sense of a class-based world-view, that is, a philosophical partisanship, is of course implicit in all such

evasions. That is so with precisely the most significant manifestation of the type just indicated, neo-Kantianism and Positivism in the second half of the nineteenth century.)

It is, I think, unnecessary to take this general analysis any further. Already it is evident that the specific form of evading a decisive philosophical proposition, bound up in methodology with a world-view in which we have recognized the general basic shape of irrationalism, must manifest itself in qualitatively different forms at different stages of social and, accordingly, philosophical development. From this it also follows that irrationalism cannot possibly have a unified, coherent history like, for instance, materialism or dialectics. And this applies even if irrationalism or something very like it can be established in the most diverse crisis periods of very different social formations. Of course the 'autonomy' of such histories of a development is extremely relative too, just as the entire history of philosophy can be comprehended and portrayed in terms of rational science only as part of the total history of society, only with the history of mankind's socio-economic life for its basis. Marx's statement in the *German Ideology*: 'Not forgetting that right has a history of its own as little as religion does'[11], naturally refers to the history of philosophy as well.

But with irrationalism something else, something more is involved. Irrationalism is merely a form of reaction (reaction in the double sense of the secondary and the retrograde) to the dialectical development of human thought. Its history therefore hinges on that development of science and philosophy, and it reacts to the new questions they pose by designating the mere problem as an answer and declaring the allegedly fundamental insolubility of the problem to be a higher form of comprehension. This styling of the declared insolubility as an answer, along with the claim that this evasion and side-stepping of the answer, this flight from it, contains a positive solution and 'true' achievement of reality is irrationalism's decisive hallmark. Agnosticism too avoids answering such questions; but it confines itself to declaring

them unanswerable and more or less openly rejects the possibility of solving them in the name of an allegedly exact scientific philosophy. (Granted, this is only to characterize two poles; in actual philosophy, especially that of the imperialist period, we find all kinds of links between agnosticism and irrationalism, with the first frequently turning into the second. Not to mention the fact that, for reasons we shall often encounter again, almost every modern irrationalism more or less props itself up on the epistemology of agnosticism.)

Therefore: on the reactionary side, every major crisis in philosophical thinking as a socially conditioned struggle between burgeoning and decaying forces produces tendencies to which we might apply the term 'irrationalism'. Whether the general employment of this term would have any scientific purpose is, we admit, questionable. On the one hand, it could give rise to the false impression of a uniformly irrationalist line in the history of philosophy, such as modern irrationalism has actually tried to give. On the other hand modern irrationalism, for reasons we are about to state, has such specific conditions of existence stemming from the peculiarity of capitalist production that a uniform term would easily blur the specific differences, and would modernize in an unacceptable way old intellectual tendencies that have little in common with those of the nineteenth century. As it is, this latter trend is widely prevalent in the history of philosophy written in the time of the bourgeois decline; we may recall Natorp's 'Kantian' Plato, Petzold's 'Machist' Protagoras, and so on. Modern irrationalism's various streams then proceeded to reduce the entire history of philosophy, from Heraclitus and Aristotle to Descartes, Vico and Hegel, to an impenetrable 'vitalist' or existentialist murkiness.

Now what constitutes the specific quality of modern irrationalism? It is chiefly the fact that it arose on the basis of capitalist production and its specific class struggles – first the progressive battle for power against feudalism and absolute monarchy waged by the bourgeois class, and later the

bourgeoisie's reactionary defensive struggles against the proletariat. Throughout this book we will show in concrete terms the decisive changes which the various stages of those class struggles wrought in the development of irrationalism in both form and content, determining equally the propositions and the solutions, and we will show how they altered its physiognomy.

Now if we wish to sum up the fundamental importance of capitalist production to our philosophical problem, we must emphasize first of all a major difference between capitalist and pre-capitalist development: the problem of the productive forces' development. In slave societies the contradiction between the forces and the conditions of production expresses itself, at that critical point in the system which we find of decisive importance, in the ever-increasing regression and stunting of the productive forces, whereby a process was initiated which made the survival of the slave system as a society's economic and social basis impossible in the long run. In feudal times the same contradiction was already expressed in a markedly altered form: in the lap of feudal society the bourgeois class, originally a mere component of the feudal formation itself, evolved its increasingly superior productive forces, whose constantly growing development was ultimately bound to shatter feudalism. (We cannot now examine the various forms this process evinces in England, France, etc., although precisely these variations profoundly affected the specific nature of the class struggle and the particular character of Anglo-French philosophy, etc.) But the productive forces' development since the rise of capitalist production has differed qualitatively from all earlier social formations. The very pace of their evolution has a qualitatively new accent to it. This, however, is connected also with an unprecedented internal interaction between the development of science and the ascent of the productive forces. The immense upsurge of the natural sciences since the Renaissance can be traced primarily to this interaction. But the further sequel to all this was that, on the one hand, the bourgeoisie's

reactionary development in the political, the social and – our particular concern – the ideological sphere began at a stage in history at which the forces of production were still energetically ascending. Naturally the obstruction of the productive forces' development by the conditions of production also occurred in capitalism. Lenin supplied convincing proof of this with regard to imperialism, and this obstruction already manifested itself at the pre-monopolist stage in every economic crisis. But where capitalism is concerned, even this state of affairs meant only that the productive forces did not evolve to an extent matching their economic organization, the level of technology, etc., and that important existing forces of production remained unexploited (take the industrial exploitation of atomic energy in capitalism). On the other hand, the result of a qualitatively heightened interaction of productive forces and natural science in capitalism was that the bourgeoisie was forced – in order to survive – to pursue the development of the natural sciences to a certain extent even in its age of decline; the technology of modern warfare in itself made this imperative.

A complete change in the character of the class struggles is inseparably linked with this economic development. Recent Soviet historians have pointed out the decisive part played by revolts of slaves and vassals in the dissolution of the slave economy and feudalism. But that does not lessen the qualitative difference between the proletariat and the classes previously exploited. We cannot analyse here the important consequences which this new situation entailed. Let us just point to one factor which will play a crucial role in our subsequent studies: the proletariat is the first oppressed class in history that has been capable of countering the oppressors' philosophy with an independent and higher world-view of its own. We shall note that the whole development of bourgeois philosophy has been dictated by the class struggles which arose in this way; and that the decisive turning-point in the evolution of modern irrationalism, as well, may be located in whether it still opposes bourgeois

progress and the liquidation of feudal leftovers, or already supports the reactionary bourgeoisie's defensive struggle in the philosophical field as bourgeois ideology's ultra-reactionary wing, indeed assumes the ideological command in this struggle.

Such a tendency in the development of the productive forces, then, is bound up with scientific developments – more intimately so the higher the stage. Even in a period of decline, this tendency dictates a different relationship between the governing class and science, above all the natural sciences, than was the case in earlier class societies. Whereas in the latter, the contradiction that emerged between the forces and the conditions of production inevitably meant the end also of the rise of the sciences, and chiefly the natural sciences, these have necessarily sustained a certain further development (admittedly obstructed in many ways) in capitalism even during the period of decline. Here again, of course, the economic restrictions which we have just indicated already played a major part. This tendency expresses itself more distinctly still in the criss-crossing of imperialist warfare and the natural sciences. On the one hand, it caused a precipitous higher development of specific technological questions, while, on the other, the same tendencies added to the general crisis which modern physics was undergoing and led it more and more up a blind alley as a theoretical science. We shall come in a moment to the key question of the relation between science and philosophy, which is a relationship of mutual promotion in a time of upward growth and becomes an obstruction to both in a time of decline. At all events these factors combine to create a particular situation for philosophy in a bourgeois society with regard to our problem: the unscientific character or rather the anti-scientific spirit of philosophy, which overtly opposes reason at critical junctures. This produces an entirely different intellectual climate for two reasons. Firstly, parallel with these tendencies and in constant interaction with them, the conquest of nature through natural science and technology

goes on all the time, albeit at a reduced tempo. And secondly, the stagnation and regression of the productive forces, their withering during the decay of capitalism does not take the form of a forced return to inferior production methods. The new situation for modern bourgeois philosophy which now originated, and which determined the specific features of modern irrationalism, was further heightened and exacerbated to a special degree through the conversion of constantly growing natural scientific and historical knowledge into a new quality, through the irreversible philosophical consequences of this growth, and through the effect which this development had on the issue of religion.

Here, once again, the capitalist development occupies a unique position in history to date. Previously, religious crises always accompanied the critical dissolution of social structures. But in the process – and this includes the genesis of capitalism – one religion was superseded by another each time. The fact that the origin of capitalism manifests itself as a crisis within Christianity makes no difference. Not only did the Reformation create a new religion, although likewise a Christian one: the development of Catholicism in the Counter-Reformation also signifies a qualitative change compared to the Middle Ages.

However, in spite of the intolerance and aggression of the various Churches, which perhaps had never been so strong before, religion during this period was already starting to be forced on the defensive philosophically. The new sciences evolving during the Renaissance, especially the natural sciences, differed from those of all previous stages of evolution in that they were not only hostile to religion in their philosophical (cosmological) foundations and consequences, as was ancient natural philosophy, but undermined the foundations of religion through exact findings precisely in their specialist inquiries; and this still applied where the researchers concerned stood personally on a religious footing and these consequences were thus unintentional. Religion's defensive posture stemmed from the fact that it was no

longer able, as in Aquinas's time, to create a world-picture from a set of religious principles, a world-picture which appeared and presumed to include and embrace the principles, method and findings of science and philosophy. Cardinal Bellarmin was already forced to adopt an agnosticist position with regard to the Copernican theory, i.e., to admit heliocentrism as a useful 'working hypothesis' for scientific praxis, while challenging the competence of science to make a statement about true (religious) reality. (This development, to be sure, already begins in the Middle Ages with the philosophy of nominalism; its argumentation reflects the aforesaid economic state of affairs whereby the growth of the bourgeois class in feudalism started at a specific stage as an element of its internal dissolution.)

This is not the place and hence it cannot be our aim to portray even in mere outline the phases of this development, its crises and struggles. Here we can only make some basic observations. Firstly, it should be remarked that already in nominalism, this development – as a struggling new world-picture of anti-religious tendency and opposing the old religion – began and was perpetuated as a struggle by one religious form against another, as an internal tussle between religions. That was also the case in the bourgeois revolutions and even, partly, in the French Revolution; let us recall Robespierre's cult of the 'supreme being'. That is to say, the bourgeoisie as a collective class was incapable of radically doing away with religious consciousness. When its ideologists, and chiefly the great materialists of the seventeenth and eighteenth centuries, had a will to go that far, the sciences had not yet developed to an extent enabling their world-picture to be really filled out on the basis of a radical immanence. Engels wrote of the period: 'The philosophy of the time deserves the greatest credit for not letting itself be led astray by the age's limited knowledge of nature and for persisting – from Spinoza to the great French materialists – in explaining the world from its own premises, leaving a detailed rationale to the natural science of the future.'[12]

The scientific possibility of explaining the world from its own premises has become greater and greater. In our own day it is in the process of reaching completion with the approach of our knowledge to the concrete transitions between inorganic and organic nature. The astronomical hypotheses of Kant and Laplace, the discoveries of geology, Darwinism, Morgan's analysis of primitive society, Engels's theory of the role of labour in the humanization of the ape, Pavlov's doctrine of unconditioned and conditioned reflexes and of the second signal-system, the further development of Darwinism by Michurin and Lysenko, research into the origin of life by Oparin and Lepeshinskaya, etc., are a number of milestones on this road. However, the further bourgeois society proceeds to develop, the more the bourgeoisie just defends its power against the proletariat, and the more it turns into a reactionary class, the less often bourgeois scholars and philosophers will be prepared to draw the philosophical consequences from the facts already so abundantly present; and bourgeois philosophy will turn more firmly to irrationalist solutions when the development approaches a point calling for a step further in an immanent explanation of the world, an interpretation of it from its own premises and the rational comprehension of the dialectic of its own movement.

Such crises, naturally enough, are by no means of a purely scientific character; on the contrary. The exacerbation of a scientific crisis, the compulsion either to advance dialectically or to take flight into the irrational nearly always coincides – and not by chance – with major social crises. For as much as the development of the natural sciences is determined chiefly by material production, so the philosophical inferences stemming from their new propositions and answers, their problems and attempted solutions depend on the class struggles of the period concerned. Whether the philosophical generalizations of the natural sciences are forward-thrusting in methodology and world-outlook or are restrained from advancing, i.e., the *side which philosophy takes* on this question, is decided – consciously or unconsciously – by their representatives'

position in the class struggles of the relevant period.

This holds good to a heightened extent for the relationship of philosophy to the social sciences, chiefly economics and history. Here the connection between the direction of the philosophical stance, forward or backward looking, and contemporaneous class struggles is more inward and intimate. We see this link at its clearest in Hegel. Although many important philosophers have expressed themselves less directly on the economic and socio-historical questions of their time, we could easily trace the same link between their epistemological standpoint and their socio-historical and economic stance.

Although presented in very general terms, this concretization of our picture, as initially outlined, of irrationalism's philosophical roots already shows the shakiness of that search for ancestors so eagerly pursued by modern representatives of this direction. All in all, the basic philosophical tendency from the sixteenth to the first half of the nineteenth century was a vehement forward thrust, a vigorous urge to master intellectually the whole of reality, nature as well as society. The impetuous development of the sciences, the enlarged horizon in surveying phenomena in both domains therefore raises dialectical problems all the time. Metaphysical thinking – chiefly as the result of this scientific development – dominated this period up to the start of classical German philosophy. But significant, if often only instinctive, dialecticians emerged everywhere, and dialectical problems were raised and solved in the sciences, often without philosophical awareness. Even thinkers whose epistemological approach was a metaphysical one often cast off their shackles when it came to concrete questions and discovered new dialectical realms. Engels presents this situation very clearly:

> Modern philosophy . . . , although it gave rise to some excellent dialecticians (e.g., Descartes and Spinoza), became increasingly rooted – especially through England's

> influence – in the so-called metaphysical mode of thinking, and this also dominated, almost exclusively, the French thinkers of the eighteenth century, at least in their specialist works of philosophy. Outside philosophy proper they were similarly capable of producing dialectical masterpieces; let us mention just Diderot's *Rameau's Nephew* and Rousseau's *Discourse on the Origin of Inequality among Men*.[13]

The main philosophical controversy of this period too was that between materialism and idealism. After materialism (now and then in mystico-religious forms) had already made a start in the Middle Ages, it waged its first major public battle with idealism in the debates on Descartes's meditations, when its most important exponents in that era, Gassendi and Hobbes, spoke out against Descartes. That Spinoza further reinforced these tendencies is a matter requiring no closer analysis. And the eighteenth century, particularly in France, brought with it the greatest flowering of metaphysical materialism, the age of Holbach, Helvétius and Diderot. In English philosophy, as a result of the ideological compromises of the 'Glorious Revolution', the chief official line (the Berkeley-Hume line associated with the superficialities of Locke) was agnosticist-idealist, but the continuing emergence of outstanding and influential materialist thinkers, or thinkers inclining to materialism, must not be overlooked. How strong the conviction was, even among thinkers who were not declared materialists, that consciousness is determined by Being is shown by the famous similes, recurring in various forms, of the human idealist illusion of free will: not only Spinoza's image of the tossed stone or Bayle's weathercock, but also Leibniz's image of the magnet.

It is evident that religious reactionary opposition to this advance by materialism, this immanent trend in cosmology and anthropology, and the possibility of a society functioning without a Beyond and a Christian transcendental morality (Bayle's society of atheists, Mandeville's idea of vice as the

basis of social progress, etc.) was voiced in violent polemics. It is similarly evident that these polemics inevitably expressed some ideas which were later to play an important part in modern irrationalism as well. This was the case, above all, where the thinkers concerned were already more or less guided by the feeling that conventional theological arguments no longer sufficed to rebut materialism, at least in respect of methodology, and that the Christian religion's concrete, substantial world-picture had to be defended with a method which was 'more modern', 'more philosophical', and therefore more in line with irrationalism.

In this sense individual figures from this stage of development, such as Pascal in relation to Cartesianism and F.H. Jacobi in relation to the Enlightenment and classical German philosophy, may be regarded as precursors of modern irrationalism. In both, we can clearly see the flinching from social and scientific progress as dictated by their period's pace of development and against which the pair, Pascal especially, formed a kind of romantic opposition, criticizing its results from a Rightist angle.

In Pascal's case the double line of this critique is distinctly visible. Pascal provides a keen-witted, acute critical description of aristocratic Court society and the nihilistic moral consequences which were the necessary product of the dissolution that was already plainly setting in. He often borders in these descriptions on the writings of La Rochefoucauld and La Bruyère. But whereas these authors bravely faced up to the moral problems now arising, Pascal registered them only in order to gain a seasonable pathos as a springboard for his *salto mortale* into religion. With La Rochefoucauld and La Bruyère there ensued, if only in an aphoristic or descriptive-argumentative fashion, a strong approximation to the dialectic of morality in the nascent capitalist society. With Pascal, on the other hand, these contradictions were presented from the outset as insoluble in human and immanent terms; as symptoms of a hopeless and irremediable isolation and loneliness experienced by the human being

left to his own devices in a God-forsaken world. (It is no accident that Pascal often comes close to Schopenhauer in describing and analysing deadly, disconsolate boredom as the chronic malady of the ruling classes.)

This philosophical description of the forsaken state, which forms the most important connecting-link with the irrationalist philosophy of later periods, was also the basis of his reflections on mankind's relations to Nature. From the 'geometrized' study of Nature now arising, Pascal the important, ingenious mathematician drew philosophical inferences which were diametrically opposed to Descartes, Spinoza or Hobbes alike – for all their other differences. Here, these thinkers perceived inexhaustible possibilities for the intellectual mastery and practical conquest of nature by man. Pascal, on the contrary, saw this as transforming a cosmos hitherto populated with anthropomorphist, mythico-religious figures into an empty infinity, inhuman and alien to man. Man was a lost soul astray in that minutely tiny corner of the universe whither natural scientific discoveries had hurled him; he stood at a loss in the face of the insoluble mysteries of the two abysses: the infinitely small and the infinitely great. Only the experience of religion, the truth of the heart (Christian truth), could restore to him life's meaning and direction. Pascal, therefore, saw both the de-humanizing effects of the capitalist boom – then still occurring in the forms of feudal absolutism – and the necessary and progressive methodological consequences of the new natural sciences which were destroying the preceding world-picture's anthropomorphism, and of the new philosophy they engendered. But while seeing the problems, he made an about-turn precisely where his great contemporaries went on in the direction of a dialectic or at least endeavoured to go on.

This turning back, this retreat when directly faced with the newly posed problems, links Pascal with the new irrationalism. He differed from it otherwise in that the connection with positive, dogmatic religion as regards content was in his case incomparably stronger. The real content of his

philosophy, the goal of his dissolution of the dialectical tendencies into a desperate, basically insoluble paradox requiring his *salto mortale* into the religious sphere was nothing else than dogmatic Christianity, albeit in a post-reformist shape – the shape of Jansenism. Thus Pascal rose to become a forebear of modern irrationalism less through the contents he affirmed than through his method, in consequence of an aphoristic phenomenology of the religious experience of despair. But in this respect only was he to some extent a genuine precursor. His, in some ways, 'modern' phenomenology of despair with its bent towards religious fulfilment led, as indicated, to a dogmatic acknowledgement of Christianity; in just this, through acknowledging the 'rationality' of dogmas, he and modern irrationalism follow entirely different paths. Certainly – and stress was often laid on this – he was now arguably very close to Kierkegaard. But our later analyses of the latter's standpoint and method will show that here, the historical distance of nearly two centuries meant a change into something qualitatively new. For in Kierkegaard's case, the phenomenology of despair was so dominant that against his own will, the tendency towards its religious fulfilment and subliming decisively modified the object of the religious intention. That is to say, it led to a decomposition of the religious contents converting the Christian tendencies very strongly into the merely optative and postulative, and bringing his whole philosophy close to a religious atheism, an existentialist nihilism. Certainly seeds of all this are present in Pascal, but seeds and nothing more.

With Friedrich Heinrich Jacobi, the contemporary of the German Enlightenment and German classicism, the rebuff to materialism and atheism was manifested far more clearly at first; but the positive content of his religious experience was then far emptier. In his case, almost all that remained was the attempt to salvage an abstract religious generality. In this Jacobi came close to and at the same time remained apart from modern irrationalism. His proximity to it lies in the fact that he opposed intuition (which he called 'immediate

knowledge') with the greatest radicalism to conceptual knowing and discursive, i.e., metaphysical thinking, according only a pragmatic-practical meaning to the latter, in order to conserve for religious experience alone the attainment of true reality. (Here, although in a very abstract way, we can see definite outlines of modern irrationalism; we find the same duality, for instance, in Bergson in a far more advanced form.) But at the same time Jacobi stands apart from modern irrationalism because with him, the content of the leap is restricted to a general God in the abstract.

Hence Jacobi halted at that set of problems – in their empty undefined state, to be sure – which modern irrationalism was later to fill with myths: that is, at the experience of that nihility which was growing more and more distinct but very seldom honestly admitted. And this experience was presented as a purported search for true substance, intuitively turning aside from dialectics. The vacuum of Jacobi's 'immediate knowing' still contains the same illusions which pervade the German Enlightenment's theism. On the one hand we note the attempt to reconcile the view then held by mechanical natural science of the 'first impulse' with a God who winds up, as it were, the clock of the universe. Granted, Jacobi was violently opposed to the German exponents of such views (e.g., Moses Mendelssohn), but he could only counter their empty, insubstantial and powerless God of humdrum good sense with an equally empty, insubstantial and powerless God of pure intuition. Hegel aptly characterized this side of Jacobi's world-view: 'In the end immediate knowledge of God is only meant to extend to saying *that* God is, not *what* God is; for the latter would be a perception and refer to mediated knowledge. Hence God as the object of religion is expressly limited to God *in general*, to the indefinite preternatural, and religion is reduced to a minimum in its content.'[14] On the other hand, Jacobi shared with the surviving section of the German Enlightenment a philosophical hostility towards the important thinkers who attempted, in the seventeenth to eighteenth century, to

outline a world-picture aspiring above the current level of the natural sciences, one that was self-contained, dialectically animated and based on the autonomous movement of things themselves (Spinoza, Leibniz, French materialists).

The upshot was, in Jacobi's case, that he faced the dialectical tendencies of his contemporaries (Hamann, Herder, Goethe) as uncomprehendingly as he rejected the pseudo-rational German Enlightenment figures affiliated to Wolff's scholastic metaphysics. Later he criticized classical German philosophy from the same standpoint as the great minds of the seventeenth to eighteenth century. Now incapable even of welcoming the irrationalist tendency emerging with Schelling, a colleague and ally, he also assailed this with the arguments of his Spinoza controversy.

So despite the common feature we have indicated, Jacobi was not a real representative of modern irrationalism either. Only, he came markedly nearer to it in two respects than anybody else at the time. Firstly, he proclaimed intuition in all its nakedness and abstractness to be the sole method of true philosophizing, and did so with far greater candour and honesty than the later irrationalists. For he stated that the arguments of someone like Spinoza were irrefutable, although this meant that they inevitably led to atheism. Thus he said in his famous discussion with Lessing: 'Spinoza is good enough for me: but what a poor salvation we reach in his name!'[15] This position produces a certain affinity between Jacobi and the beginnings of modern irrationalism. For the acuter the social antitheses and the more imperilled the situation of the religious world-view, the more vigorously the irrationalists denied that there was a faculty of rational perception of reality. This line already starts with Schopenhauer.

Hence Jacobi sought his road to 'immediate knowledge'. He said of such 'knowledge' in the same discussion: 'Its ultimate purpose is what cannot be explained: the indissoluble, immediate and simple.'[16] At this point, however, all the methods of philosophical perception are switched to a purely subjectivist track. For Jacobi, it was not the examination

of the world of objects, not the inner nature of objects themselves that determined the philosophical method. Instead the true or false object of philosophy arose in accordance with the thinker's subjective attitude (conceptual deduction or immediate perception, intuition). Hence in the polemical writings of his youth, Hegel already drew a parallel between Jacobi's philosophy and the subjective idealism of Kant and Fichte. This pair endeavoured to develop from their subjectivist standpoint a philosophically objective method of perception, whereas Jacobi aligned himself quite openly with extreme subjectivism.

He did so not only in the epistemological field, but also in that of ethics. Jacobi expressed his standpoint in relation to Fichte in the most vivid terms. His avowal reads as follows:

> Yes, I am the atheist and godless man who, contrary *to the will that wills nothing* – wants to lie, as *Desdemona* lied with her dying breath; wants to lie and dissemble as *Pylades* did for Orestes, wants to murder like *Timoleon*; break the law and oath like *Epaminondas*, like Johann de Wit; commit suicide like *Otho*; commit desecration, like *David* – indeed I want to pluck ears of corn on the *Sabbath* simply because I am *hungry* and *the law is made for man's sake, not man for the law's sake*. I am this godless man and laugh at the philosophy which consequently calls me ungodly, laugh at it and at its supreme being: for I know with the most hallowed certainty that is within me – that the *privilegium aggratiandi* with regard to such crimes against the pure letter of the absolutely general law of reason is the authentic *prerogative* of man, the seal of his dignity, his divine nature.[17]

To make this historically concrete, it will be useful to point out that on the one hand, Jacobi correctly draws attention to certain central flaws in Fichte's subjective idealism, to the 'will that wills nothing' and the abstract generality of his ethics. On the other hand, however, his own ethical

requirements have as their substance only an unprincipled self-adulation, a subjective rhapsodizing over the bourgeois individual, his endeavour to be an 'exception'. Hence he did not want to revoke the general law but only to guarantee the bourgeois individual's right to a special position (*privilegium aggratiandi*): the aristocratic prerogative of the bourgeois intellectual to form an exception to the general rule – at least in Jacobi's imagination, for of course it never occurred to him to commit the aforestated deeds in reality.

So Jacobi turned the epistemological and ethical questions into subjective psychological problems. Now a blurring of the frontiers between epistemology and psychology is one of the most important characteristics of modern irrationalism (and above all so-called phenomenology). It is therefore interesting to establish that this tendency appeared still quite bare-faced in Jacobi himself and that Hegel criticized this characteristic of immediate knowledge from this angle:

> In this respect we have to state that it is the commonest of experiences that truths which we know very well to be products of the most complex highly mediated studies present themselves *directly* in the consciousness of somebody to whom such perception has become second nature . . . The facility we may have acquired in some kind of knowledge, art as well, and technical skill, consists precisely of having such knowledge and types of activity *directly* in the consciousness in such an event, indeed in one's very limbs where the activity is outward going. In all such cases, the immediacy of the knowledge not only does not exclude the mediation of it, but they are so linked that immediate knowledge is even the product and result of mediated knowledge.[18]

In his sober astuteness, Hegel was proving the self-delusion in the belief that something new and unmediated can be found through immediacy. With this he furnished a criticism striking not only at Jacobi but also at all later intuition theories.

The other important point is that with Jacobi 'immediate knowledge' emerges not only as an escape from the atheistic conclusions of the great seventeenth- and eighteenth-century thinkers but also – and this is closely connected – as a defence against materialism. In the extremely interesting aforementioned discussion between Jacobi and Lessing, which actually contains the former's entire philosophy, Jacobi openly expressed this danger, again in contrast to the many later irrationalists who, time and again, obscured the problem with their pseudo-materialist shadow-boxing and their attempts to show a 'third road' beyond the philosophical antithesis of materialism and idealism. To characterize materialism Jacobi said in this discussion: 'Thinking is not the source of the substance; substance is the source of thinking. Therefore something non-thinking must be assumed to take primacy over thinking . . . Leibniz, honestly enough, called souls *automates spirituales* for that reason.'[19] This comment on Leibniz applies, of course, to Spinoza more acutely still.

Jacobi's irrationalism appeared, therefore, on the eve of that major ideological crisis which brought irrationalism's modern forms into being, as a kind of reactionary summation of the spiritual struggles of the seventeenth and eighteenth centuries. It was a public declaration of idealism's bankruptcy, a declaration that even the denial of reason, even the flight into empty absurdity, flimsy paradoxes and a religiously embellished nihilism could offer only the semblance of a rebuttal of materialism. Some of Jacobi's contemporaries already recognized this tendency towards nihilism. In their discussion, which Jacobi himself recorded, Lessing stated candidly that he regarded him as a 'complete sceptic' who had to 'turn his back on all philosophy'[20] in his thinking. And, in his radically republican period, the young Friedrich Schlegel criticized Jacobi's philosophy not only because it had to 'end in unbelief and despair, or in superstition and fanaticism',[21] but also attacked it for its immorality. He said of Jacobi's works: 'There lives, breathes and thrives in

them a seductive spirit of complete spiritual debauchery, a boundless lack of moderation which, despite its noble origin, destroys totally all laws of justice and morality. The objects change; only the idolatry is permanent. – All luxury ends in slavery: even luxuriation in the purest love to the most sacred being. So it is here; and what bondage is more horrible than mystical bondage?'[22] That Friedrich Schlegel similarly ended up as a mystical irrationalist does not affect the accuracy of this critique.

What was most fraught with consequences in Jacobi's stand was his denunciation of Spinoza as an atheist (along with Lessing and later the whole of classical German philosophy). This, naturally, supplied the reactionaries with a weapon at once. For in its principal line, a development of dialectics, this philosophy was necessarily a thorn in the reactionaries' side. Therefore the accusation of atheism could form an effective means of suppressing it. (Accused on that charge, although not directly by Jacobi, Fichte was in fact obliged to vacate his chair at Jena.) But regarded in terms of the history of philosophy, this barbed statement from Jacobi did have the significance that it created an awareness of the basic irreconcilability of rigorously practised philosophy and religion and did much to make it a matter for topical debate. And it did so such that the progressive philosophy declared to be necessarily atheistic was now no longer countered with a reactionary philosophy that was Christian or at least respected Christianity. Instead we find a naked intuitionism, an unadorned irrationalism and a repudiation of conceptual-philosophical and rational thought altogether.

This blunt Either-Or did not exert an immediate influence. Herder and Goethe, who took Spinoza's (and Lessing's) side against Jacobi in the Spinoza controversy, adhered to pantheism and rejected Jacobi's atheistic inferences. As for the natural philosophy of the young Schelling and his followers, as for Hegel's philosophy – however frequent their protestations, and although the charge of atheism was levelled against Schelling by Jacobi himself and against Hegel, later on, by

the Romantic reaction – these too did not go beyond their own interpretation of Spinoza on this question, and even lagged a few steps behind it. Here it was not so much a matter of 'diplomacy', still necessary in this age with regard to temporal Christian power. Of course this motive often played an important part in German classical philosophy as well. But the main issue was that, owing to the necessary incompleteness and inconsequentiality of idealist dialectics, the theological remains of this philosophy could be never really surmounted. Hence Feuerbach rightly said: 'Pantheism is *theological atheism*, *theological materialism*, *the negation of theology*, but itself takes the *standpoint of theology*; for it makes matter, the negation of God *a predicate* or *attribute of the divine being*.'[23] And in this connection he drew a parallel between Hegel and Spinoza: 'Identity philosophy only differs from Spinozist philosophy in that it animates the dead, phlegmatic thing of substantiality with the *spiritus* of idealism. Hegel in particular made autonomous activity, the autonomous power of discrimination and self-consciousness an attribute of substantiality. Hegel's paradoxical statement that "consciousness of God is God's self-consciousness" rests on the same foundation as Spinoza's paradoxical statement: "expansion or matter is an attribute of substantiality" and means nothing else than "self-consciousness is an attribute of substantiality or God, God is I".'[24] Thus there now arose an objective, methodological-philosophical ambiguity reaching its climax in Hegel's philosophy. Feuerbach said correctly of speculative philosophy that it was 'theism and atheism at one and the same time'.[25]

We find these characteristics of German philosophy's development – to be sure with marked variations, the individual motives fluctuating a great deal – in many of the most significant thinkers from Descartes to Hegel. They need stressing at once because it is just in such weak spots that modern irrationalism has sought, and purported to find, a pretext for stamping as irrationalists after the event and fitting into its contrived line of descent some great thinkers

from the past who, in essence, represented the strict opposite of irrationalism, indeed criticized with devastating acuteness the irrationalist tendencies appearing in their age. (We shall see in the chapter on neo-Hegelianism that this fate could befall even Hegel.) A clear-cut confirmation of the ambiguity we are stressing in the works of the important idealists, an ambiguity from which, or course, only the most outstanding materialists could be free, puts us in a position to examine the question of the affirmation or denial of reason not merely on a terminological basis, and never proceeding from individual statements which might sound somewhat irrationalist in isolation from the full context and the general intention of the philosophy concerned. Instead, we can devote all our attention to this basic line.

This question is an important one bcause enormous efforts were made to present such thinkers as Vico or Hamann, Rousseau or Herder as irrationalists. Certainly from the angle of an idealistically contrived 'intellectual history', it is easy to bring such thinkers into the most direct proximity to irrationalism. For starting with Vico's polemic against Descartes, they were very strongly opposed to those philosophical tendencies of their times which we are generally wont (though highly inadequately, highly abstractly) to characterize as rationalist. And if we construe in such an abstract-formal, shallow way the contrast between rational and irrational, these thinkers will 'automatically' turn out on the side of irrationalism, as happened to Rousseau and Hamann in particular a long time ago, even before irrationalism began to become all the rage. (Rousseau as an 'irrationalist Romantic' is a product of polemics against the French Revolution.)

Rather than that, let us consider irrationalism concretely in the ideological struggles of the age concerned as an element and side-taking in the continual dispute, repeatedly born of class conflicts, between the new and old, between concretely historical progress and regression. Then we are equally bound to have a completely different illumination, a picture that comes closer to the truth. Then we will see, above all,

that precisely the thinkers just mentioned were trying – in an epoch whose dominant tendency was the intellectual mastering of mechanical natural phenomena and, correspondingly, a metaphysical thinking – to fight in opposition to *this* direction for the right of the philosophical idea with regard to a constantly changing, constantly developing historical world. To be sure, when we speak of the historical realm, the reader should not be blinkered by that decadent bourgeois theory which automatically interpreted the historical as merely 'singular', 'unique' and contradicting the concept of law, thus irrational by nature to a certain extent. We shall demonstrate shortly that this construction of the historical arose as reactionary-legitimist opposition to the French Revolution and was appropriated by bourgeois economic theory and practice in proportion to the growth of reaction within the bourgeois class itself (Ranke, Rickert).

The thinkers with whom we are now dealing have nothing in common with such tendencies. However much they differed in world-outlook and range of talent (although Goethe, when introduced to Vico in Italy, was involuntarily reminded of Hamann, a native inspiration in his youth), they were united in a single endeavour. This was to fathom the laws governing the course of history and socio-historical progress, to discover and form an idea of the reason behind history, viz., the reason inherent in human history, the reason behind the autonomous movement of collective history. This impulse brought them up against dialectical problems at a time when neither had the actual foundations of these laws been investigated (consider the state of prehistory), nor did the dominant trends of thought even have a mind to produce a conceptual apparatus, a scheme of classification for mastering these problems. Indeed the dominant epistemological tendencies (with geometry as the model) could only inhibit a development in this direction.

So the quest for the reason immanent in the autonomous movement of society and history had to proceed against the current of the dominant epistemology. From the

epistemological angle it was an often very ill-defined search, often filled with purely imaginary anticipations, for the dialectical categories capable of expressing adequately the laws of social and historical development. There was, for example, the young Goethe's distaste for the 'rationalist' philosophy of his age – remarkably, but by no means fortuitously, he always made an exception of Spinoza. And his distaste stemmed from the fact that Goethe was seeking – albeit, for many years, merely instinctively – the dialectical categories in the development of living beings and the historical view of nature. That was why the irrational vitalists advertised and celebrated him as their ancestor throughout the imperialist period, although Goethe developed in reality from methodologically tentative early essays at a radical empiricism into an independent supporter of classical German philosophy, especially its dialectics. We should further remark on Goethe's reservations with regard to important contemporary philosophers. One of the grounds for this was that he came far nearer to philosophical materialism than they did (no matter whether he described his materialism, which was never quite rigorous, as hylozoism or something different). The other reason is that he would never allow his own experimental findings to be trapped within an idealist system.

The example of Goethe demonstrates quite plainly which features matter here: Goethe the adversary of the absolutizing of Linnaeus's system, Goethe the supporter of Geoffroy de Saint-Hilaire and fellow-campaigner against Cuvier, but not the individual statements or even discourses of his in which, or into which – if we interpret them in an unhistorical, *geisteswissenschaftlich* sense – we may read something irrationalist.

It makes no crucial difference that Goethe was chiefly interested in the history of nature, Vico, Rousseau or Herder in the historicity of all social occurrences, and that God plays a far more positive role in the world-picture of most of those thinkers than for Goethe. Take, for example, the historical

function of 'providence' in Vico's work. Vico described this as a spirit 'which produces out of the passions of human beings (who all cling only to personal gain and would therefore live in the wilds like wild beasts) the civil codes through which they can live in human community'.[26] And when Vico lucidly sums up this idea at the conclusion of his book, we almost catch an echo of Hegel: 'For only men themselves have created this world of nations – that was the first undisputed principle of this science, but it has doubtless proceeded from a spirit which often differs from men's particular goals, sometimes opposes them and is always superior to them; these limited goals this spirit has rendered subservient to its higher ones, constantly using them to preserve the human race on the earth.'[27] Here, to be sure, as in the later case of Hegel's 'cunning of reason' (*List der Vernunft*), we are dealing with mystificatory expressions vividly registering a connection not perceived in its ultimate implications but brilliantly surmised, thereby entering new dialectical realms, but also mysticizing these connections idealistically. But it will be evident to any open-minded reader of Vico that he is here referring to an autonomous history made by men themselves, hence knowable and rational. Although Vico introduces the mystificatory term 'providence', he so defines it in his concrete accounts that these definitions eliminate all transcendental power from a dialectical historical framework which is rational, if appearing contradictory, indeed paradoxical to the understanding. And given this basic tendency, it will not surprise us that Vico – the avowed adversary of Descartes's epistemology – comes extremely close to the materialist Spinoza as regards the crucial basic questions of his theory of categories. Vico's statement 'The arrangement of ideas must proceed according to the arrangement of objects'[28] only differs from Spinoza in that Vico, in line with his historical endeavours, interprets this materialist view of categories in a livelier, more dynamic sense than Spinoza. Thus he modified and built on the latter's philosophy in the same direction as was later taken by German idealist dialectics,

principally in the work of Hegel.

Here, it cannot possibly be our aim to provide even an abridged sketch of Vico's philosophy, far less to essay analyses in respect of Herder, Hamann or Rousseau. Our sole purpose was to underline the basic dialectical tendency which, in all these authors, aimed at developing the history of mankind and human society out of its autonomous movement, the deeds and sufferings of men themselves, and at grasping the reason, i.e., the principles behind the movement. It is the same whether we take the human origin of language, which Herder (polemicizing against the theological explanation for it) grasped as a development of reason and a product of man's spiritual powers, or the origin in private property of bourgeois society with its inflammatory inequality as Rousseau presented it. For the purpose of our present studies, it is likewise of secondary importance how far individual perceptions of this kind, and the individual categories in which they are classified, stand up to later developments in knowledge. In the present context the one thing that matters is to elucidate that basic intellectual trend which has evolved in historical dialectics from Vico to Herder. Details which, torn out of their proper overall historical context, may be interpreted as irrationalist signify at most accessory vacillations, obscure mystical presagings, mystificatory formulations of sets of facts or of categories which were then not yet clearly comprehensible dialectically. From Vico to Herder there runs a path which traces the extension, enrichment and consolidation of reason just as surely as the path taken by Descartes or Bacon leads in this direction. This gave rise to some very important differences, indeed antitheses, but all in all they were antitheses *within* a single camp fighting for a philosophy based upon the rationality of the world; nowhere do we find the abstract antithesis of rationalism and irrationalism.

2. Schelling's 'Intellectual Intuition' as the First Manifestation of Irrationalism

Modern irrationalism springs from the major socio-economic, political and philosophical crisis occurring at the turn of the nineteenth-twentieth century. The decisive event sparking off the main elements in the crisis was naturally the French Revolution. Above all, it was a world event in a quite different sense to the great earlier revolutions (the Dutch or the English). These produced transformations only on the national scale, and they had an incomparably slighter effect internationally — as revolutionary tendencies in society and consequently in ideology. Only the French Revolution had important repercussions for the social structure of many European countries, prompting a dissolution of feudalism in the Rhinelands, Upper Italy, etc., albeit on nothing like the scale of 1793. And even where this did not happen, feudal-absolutist society's need of reconstruction remained a permanent item on the agenda. Thus an ideological process of fermentation started up everywhere, even in such countries as England which already had their bourgeois revolution behind them; for the extremely deficient nature of the liquidation of English feudalism was revealed in the light of happenings in France.

This new element emerged with such overwhelming force that it could be neither defended nor attacked in the old manner. Not by accident did the modern historical movement stem from these conflicts: the dialectical view of history in classical German philosophy, the rapid further development of historical studies by the French historians of the restoration period, the historical spirit in the literary works of Walter Scott, Manzoni and Pushkin. Although it was a reactionary fable that the Enlightenment was anti-historically minded, what now sprang up far exceeded the stimuli provided by Herder. But it turned out that even the old elements could no longer be defended in the old manner. Little though Burke himself was a Romantic thinker, it was

from him that romantic pseudo-historicism proceeded: the demolition of historical development and historical progress in the name of a purportedly deepened, irrationalized version of historicity.

But at the same time the French Revolution also pointed beyond bourgeois horizons. It achieved this in a directly political sense in the Gracchus Babeuf revolt. (This too had international echoes such as Thomas Münzer or the Levellers could never have found in earlier eras.) We can discern this more distinctly still in the great utopian socialists, whose systems and methods likewise cannot be divorced from the global shock brought about by the French Revolution. The general ideological crisis, represented by the utopians in its plainest, forward-looking tendency, derived from the contradictions in the French Revolution itself and engendered an essentially new element even where the basic line of the development was still purely bourgeois. Engels vividly formulated the central point of this latter crisis. The Enlightenment, the ideological preliminary to the Revolution, was striving to set up the 'realm of reason' through it and in it. The Revolution triumphed, the sought-after realm of reason was realized, but: 'We now know that this realm of reason was no more than the idealized realm of the bourgeoisie.'[29] But this means that now, through the impact of concrete facts, the contradictions inherent in bourgeois society which cropped up in the presentient criticisms of many a member or contemporary of the Enlightenment – from Mandeville and Ferguson to Linguet and Rousseau – were shifted to the centre of interest. The results of the Industrial Revolution in England further heightened the impact of these experiences, although the first major economic crises best illustrating the contradictions in capitalism did not break out until the second decade of the nineteenth century. All these facts signified for the ideological development chiefly that the contradictory character of bourgeois society, previously barely suspected, was now quite patently its universal central problem. Consequently the philosophy of society became

historical and dialectical in a totally different sense from ever before. What hitherto could only be surmised now became a more and more markedly conscious programme: the historical dialectic as philosophy's central question. That was the basis of the significance of Hegelian philosophy. In its methodology, the question of the historical comprehension of revolution played a crucial part; the solution to its conceivability took on a meaning far outstripping this individual question (conversion of quantity into quality, a new view of the relationship between individual and species). But these new facts also supplied Right-wing criticism with a fresh basis. From the Romantic movement and the 'historical law school' to Carlyle, there sprang up an entirely new line of defence for the old-established and the pre-revolutionary age going back as far as the Middle Ages, one that was inseparable from the general irrationalizing of history.

We can be sure that it was not by chance that the major crisis in natural scientific thinking went hand in hand with the social crisis. With the discovery of a whole series of new phenomena, mainly in the fields of chemistry and biology, the critique of mechanical-metaphysical thinking came more and more firmly to the fore. It was sensed more and more distinctly that the thinking based solely on geometry and mechanics to which physics and astronomy in the seventeenth-eighteenth century owed their successes was bound to fall down with regard to the new tasks and the comprehension of natural phenomena in their totality. This growth crisis in natural-philosophical thought was not limited to problems of mere conceptualization. Here again, the historical mode of contemplation was starting to take hold. Consider the astronomical theories of Kant and Laplace, the discoveries of geology and palaeontology, the beginnings of the theory of evolution, the incipient opposition to great mechanistic systematizers like Linnaeus and Cuvier; consider Goethe, Geoffroy de Saint-Hilaire, Lamarck, and so on.

Only in this context does the significance of German natural philosophy, above all the young Schelling's, become

intelligible. For it was here that the first attempt began to grasp these tendencies in a methodologically, philosophically uniform way. Here again it was the case that the dialectical contradictions appearing more and more clearly in the immense and constantly increasing factual material were no longer repudiated or 'surmounted' in terms of formal logic; instead these very contradictions, their dialectical suspension and synthesis, etc., shifted to the centre of the new, dialectical method. Engels was careful not to appraise these natural-philosophical theories and methods solely from the standpoint of their frequently absurd findings, as did nearly all natural scientists in the second half of the nineteenth century. He himself summarized his judgement as follows: 'The natural philosophers are related to conscious-dialectical natural science as are the utopians to modern communism.'[30]

The great seventeenth-century systems achieved an intellectual grasp of their new findings derived from this period's major discoveries by means of an (essentially) static-geometric method. But now there began an attempt to interpret the pre-human and socio-human world as a uniform historical process. 'Spirit', the idealist central figure in this process, was at the same time viewed as a result of the process. Hence Schelling spoke of the genesis of philosophy as an 'odyssey of the spirit'[31] in which the mind, hitherto working unconsciously at its own achievement of awareness, now took possession of its home, its reality, in full awareness. It was this effort to master intellectually the basic problems of scientific progress after the French Revolution in the age of upheaval in the natural sciences which gave rise to Schelling's dialectical method. It tried to provide this enormous range of problems with philosophical answers and to raise philosophy to the level of the age. Inevitably, Germany's social backwardness meant that this energetic turn to dialectics as the philosophical method's central problem could only be accomplished in idealist terms. And it was no more fortuitous that this development occurred largely in Germany than that France took the lead in bourgeois philosophy in the eighteenth

century, as did Russia from 1840. The pathos and determination behind such propositions and answers only made it a social fact of bourgeois thought that in a time of preparation for democratic revolution, it performed the ideological spadework for this revolution.

But by virtue of the fact that the idealist, historically-oriented dialectic was becoming the philosophical method of the progressive wing, philosophical reaction too now had to use other weapons. The English empiricism in Burke disappointed his German supporters as well in the long run; the need arose to go beyond Burke philosophically and to 'deepen' his theories in an irrationalist fashion. There was a similar attitude towards official restoration thinkers in France. The trend towards dialectics dictated the whole philosophical tempo, determined the propositions and forced the reactionaries to distort the new philosophical principles. Thus, precisely in Germany, the philosophical rationale of modern irrationalism sprang up on the basis of the struggle for the new dialectic, in the counter-struggle.

Initially, to be sure, this hostile relation between dialectics and irrationalism was extremely complicated. For a start, ultimately homogeneous but not quite identical, hence mentally divisible dialectical tendencies are operative in nature or society, as the case may be. It was with the natural process that the young Schelling was largely occupied, although it appeared at first as if, starting thence, he was going to create a general theory of dialectics. The starting-point of Hegel and the main emphasis in his dialectics were social ones, although the system he constructed also marks the philosophical climax of the dialectical method of natural philosophy. But often highly paradoxical complications occur elsewhere during this period. Granted, Oken evinces the most concrete progressiveness of the age in his dialectics of natural philosophy and was at the same time radical in his social, political and philosophical thinking. But Baader, for example, was already one of the chief restoration and reactionary figures in philosophy and history, while sympathizing

with the dialectical view of nature. There were often similar occurrences under Schelling's influence.

The centre of this ambiguity was the young Schelling himself. Its main source was his character. Marx wrote of him to Feuerbach in the 1840s: 'Schelling's *genuine* – to be charitable to our adversary – *youthful idea*, for whose realization he had no tool but imagination, no energy other than vanity, no stimulant but opium, no other organ than the irritability of a feminine receptiveness . . .'[32] This set of characteristics is only apparently paradoxical: it was just this disposition which predestined Schelling to be the initiator – the ambiguous initiator – of objective idealism. He began to tackle the task half unconsciously. Although he shared, in his youth, Hegel's and Hölderlin's enthusiasm for the French Revolution, his awareness of the philosophical extent of the social upheaval was very undeveloped. Later when – as the public leader of the new school of objective idealism – he fitted society and history into his system, the effect on him of the restoration and post-thermidorian reaction was already very considerable.

Schelling's original philosophical interest was focused on the new situation in natural philosophy. This seized his attention, and in a naive incautious way he simply took over the then most advanced form of dialectics, that of Fichte. For the time being he believed that he was just applying it and rounding it out philosophically; a natural philosophy's objective dialectics, he believed, could be reconciled with the principles of the *Science of Knowledge*. At first he did not see that the mere fact of a dialectic in nature already includes a principle of objectivity and is therefore irreconcilable in principle with Fichte's subjective dialectics. Fichte noticed at once that their ways parted at this point, and a correspondence started between Fichte and Schelling; but it was Hegel who drove Schelling further, leading him to break with subjective idealism, and it was Hegel who formulated the principles behind the break philosophically in this exchange. He rendered Schelling's own discoveries – as far as was

possible for him – philosophically conscious to him.

But they were never fully conscious. For even when he was working together with Hegel at Jena, there never dawned in Schelling a real awareness of the new dialectical method. But just this disposition of his, brilliant because it contained many an element of the future in embryo and unconsciously took many a step into the future, was capable of making him the first central figure in the new philosophy, of turning his initial activities into a centre radiating to Goethe, Oken and Treviranus on the Left, Baader and Görres on the Right. (It was clever of Erdmann to derive both Oken and Baader from Schelling.)

Now let us study Schelling's philosophical beginnings rather more closely. Fichte, in removing Kant's 'thing-in-itself' from transcendental idealism, was directly converting his philosophy epistemologically into a subjective idealism on the Berkeley model, thus effecting what Kant called a 'philosophical scandal'. But unlike Berkeley or, at a later date, Schopenhauer, the *Science of Knowledge* did not posit a Christian God or a highly un-Christian 'will' as the ultimate metaphysical principle behind the 'veil of *maya*', a phenomenal world viewed philosophically in purely subjective terms. Instead it sought to infer the whole cosmos of perception as just as self-contained, just as immanently self-motivating and creative from the dialectic of Ego and Non-Ego as Spinoza inferred his world from expansion and thinking. Thus Fichte's Ego acquired a methodologically and systematically new function as well. Not because Fichte was reluctant to identify this Ego with individual consciousness and was trying rather to deduce the latter from the former dialectically, but because this Ego – independently of Fichte's conscious aims, indeed at odds with them – was bound through his system's aforestated inner necessity to take over the function of Spinoza's substance or, more exactly, Hegel's later world-spirit. At first, the young Schelling's natural philosophy could be fitted effortlessly into the gap formed by this internal discrepancy in Fichte's system, whose

latent antitheses were openly to emerge only later, after the crisis in his thinking. Schelling was able to believe that in one-sidedly enlarging this Spinozist element in Fichte's philosophy into the sole corner-stone of his ideas, he was a strict pupil of Fichte and amplifying his work. Objectively speaking, however, he was at the same time exploding the whole artificial and laboured synthesis of the *Science of Knowledge*.

But philosophically this was a major step forwards, and the real flowering of objective idealism and obiective-idealist dialectics could now begin. However, Fichtean ambiguity was surmounted at the cost of an ambiguity on a higher plane. The Ego of the *Science of Knowledge* perpetually hovered between a merely epistemological (and subjectivist) procedure and a principle of objective reality, between Kant's 'consciousness as a whole' and that demiurge of nature and history which the Hegelian mind or spirit was later meant to represent. Schelling chose the latter alternative. Hence he incorporated in his system's foundation something that was at the same time meant to exist objectively, i.e., independently of human consciousness, and yet to have somcthing of consciousness about it. So the whole opalescent ambiguity of objective idealism already arises in the young Schelling. Objective idealism had, on the one hand, to draw a firm line between itself and subjective idealism and to try and answer the latter's insoluble problems (objective reality, the perceptibility of the thing in itself), but was bound time and again to succumb epistemologically to the general weaknesses of subjective idealism. The latter process is particularly evident in Schelling, who did not accomplish his break with Fichte entirely consciously from the philosophical-methodological angle. On the other hand, this philosophy's supreme principle was likewise bound to be ambiguous, fluctuating between an approximation to philosophical materialism (independence of consciousness) and an idealist-pantheistic conception of God which, since it was made concrete by being applied to natural and historical life, had to surpass Spinoza's aloof and abstract generality and come close to theistic ideas of God.

We have already pointed out this ambiguity in objective idealism in its most general features. Now we must study more closely Schelling's specific version of it and in particular the nuances it takes on with the *young* Schelling. Here we should give special emphasis to the rapid fluctuation between the materialist-atheistic version of this Spinozist substance rendered alive, mobile and evolutionary, and its mystical-mythological interpretation. What is important is this universal line, not individual expressions of it. *Heinz Widerporst*[33] shows the young Schelling's extremely materialistic view of natural philosophy, but also the point at which Jacob Boehme, who was becoming increasingly fashionable among Romantic minds, began to exert a strong influence on Schelling with his mysticism.[34] In the philosophizing of the Romantic school, to be sure, the mystical tendencies had the upper hand. That the materialist ones also influenced the young Schelling is a feature peculiar to him. We shall see how inexorably the mystical tendency moved more and more to the centre of Schelling's philosophy as well. But it needs to be remarked that he still made Giordano Bruno the patron saint of his philosophy at the end of his Jena period – although, for reasons we are about to see, in order to argue epistemologically the perceptibility of things in themselves he had to resort with mounting vigour to the Platonic theory of ideas, thereby putting his ambiguousness in an even more advanced form. To be sure, this recourse to the Platonic theory of ideas was likewise fraught with the typical ambiguity of Schelling's objective idealism in his Jena period. On the one hand, in sharp contrast to Kant and Fichte, he introduced the theory of reflection into transcendental philosophy, while on the other he produced a version of this doctrine that was extremely idealistic and spilled over into mysticism. Schelling's Jena period is characterized, therefore, by this intermediate position, always hovering somewhere between progressive and reactionary tendencies in objective idealism. Schelling, while in intimate contact with both Goethe's natural philosophy and the 'magical idealism'

of Novalis, stood between the two.

Schelling's 'genuine youthful idea' was centred upon the discovery and philosophical formulation of the dialectic in the process of natural development. As we have seen, the need to grasp the perception of nature dialectically, and thus to outstrip the mechanical-metaphysical method of the seventeenth and eighteenth centuries, was a universal tendency in this period. In Kant's *Critique of Judgement* this necessity received the formulation which had the greatest influence on German philosophy. Here Kant, in attempting to grasp the problems of life philosophically, hit upon the dialectic of possibility and reality, the whole and the part, the universal and the particular. In Kant, the problem of this dialectical surpassing of metaphysical thought appears in an extremely distorted form. These distortions had such a determining influence on certain propositions in the emergent modern irrationalism, in the young Schelling's case especially, that we are obliged to give a brief indication of them at this point. Above all, Kant identified thinking – he writes of 'our' thinking, human thought – with the thought-forms of metaphysics in the seventeenth and eighteenth centuries. In the case of the dialectic of the general and particular, for example, this led to the following definition:

> Accordingly our understanding is peculiarly circumstanced in respect of judgement. For in cognition by means of understanding the particular is not determined by the universal. Therefore the particular cannot be derived from the universal alone. Yet in the multiplicity of nature, and through the medium of conception and laws, this particular has to accord with the universal in order to be capable of being subsumed under it. But under the circumstances mentioned this accord must be very contingent and must exist without any determinate principle to guide our judgement.[35]

But Kant was not content with this identification of metaphysical thinking with 'human' thought as a whole. Instead he described this too as 'discursive' in rigid contrast to intuitive apprehension. In these circumstances the only solution he could find was to advance the claim of:

> *intuitive* understanding . . . which does not move, as ours does with its conceptions, from the universal to the particular and so to the individual. Such an understanding would not experience the above contingency in the way nature and understanding accord in natural products subject to *particular* laws. But it is just this contingency that makes it so difficult for our understanding to reduce the multiplicity of nature to the unity of knowledge.[36]

So thinking, as Kant saw it, was led to this 'idea' of an '*intellectus archetypus*', an intuitive understanding. This idea, in his view, contained no internal contradiction, but it did however remain only a mere idea where human judgement was concerned.

It is easy to demonstrate the subjective-idealist weaknesses in the Kantian proposition; above all, the weakness in equating dialectics and intuition, especially when combined – as Kant could not avoid doing – with his agnosticist deductions. It was not just that the 'idea' was only propounded for human thought, not given and therefore unattainable; these objects were also detached from the possibilities of practical natural-scientific research. Kant expressly related this to the perceptibility of evolution in nature:

> . . . it is absurd for men even to entertain any thought of so doing or to hope that maybe another Newton may some day arise, to make intelligible to us even the genesis of but a blade of grass from natural laws that no design has ordered.[37]

But the mere raising of this question strongly encouraged

the theoretical and practical formulation of the dialectical problems. Goethe's reaction to this Kantian proposition is very characteristic. He showed his practical wisdom in silently brushing aside both the one-sided orientation to intuitive thinking and Kant's agnosticist-pessimistic deductions with regard to the perspective of human knowledge of nature. All he perceived here was a fresh task, and one that was soluble. With direct regard to Kant's theory, Goethe said of his own praxis: 'If I had ceaselessly hunted after that proto-typical, typical element unconsciously at first and through an inner impulse, and if I had even succeeded in constructing a picture based on natural principles, then nothing could prevent me now from bravely undergoing the *adventure of reason*, as the sage of Königsberg himself calls it.'[38] And both his natural philosophy and his aesthetics are full of concrete propositions and answers in which the dialectics postulated find practical expression without laying any weight on the Kantian antithesis of discursive and intuitive.

With the young Schelling the situation is quite different. For him these famous paragraphs from the *Critique of Judgement* were not, as with Goethe, merely an inducement to go on strictly pursuing a path already taken, but the real, philosophical starting-point in the battle simultaneously to overcome Fichte's subjective idealism and mechanical-metaphysical thinking in natural philosophy to date. That is why the antithesis of discursive and intuitive plays a downright crucial role in Schelling's philosophy. His natural philosophy, whose basic problem was to surpass the mechanical-metaphysical intuition of nature, tried to complete the change to dialectics in the form of an abrupt departure from the Enlightenment's simple categories of understanding; hence it had to seek an 'organon' of philosophical knowledge whose intrinsic nature guaranteed a differently disposed, qualitatively superior, dialectical stance to reality. The antithesis of discursive and intuitive, contrasted even more sharply but differently accented than it was with Kant, therefore shifted to the centre of the young Schelling's epistemology,

acquiring a shape which was effective for a long time in the form of 'intellectual intuition'.

It is perhaps striking, but very characteristic of Schelling, how he introduced and applied this central category of his early system almost without an argumentation. Exactly what caused Kant's doubts about human reality and the possibility of realizing the *intellectus archetypus*, that is to say the very act of surpassing the limits of discursive thinking (metaphysical and governed by understanding), was the evidence for Schelling of intellectual intuition.

The problem of dialectics was in the air in the Germany of the time. Dialectical beginnings were already rife in the transcendental philosophy of Kant and Fichte. Every attempt to make scientific headway with the period's major topical problems was bound to raise dialectical questions and to reveal the limitations of mechanical-metaphysical thought. The young Schelling's best and most positive side was that he was repeatedly confronted with these contradictions in natural phenomena and simultaneously with the objectivity and unity of the process of nature; and that he stated his new insights into these – even if they lacked an adequate scientific and philosophical foundation – with great vigour, intrepidity and forthrightness. So the result was his departure from both Enlightenment philosophy and that of Kant and Fichte. He was divided from the former by the need for a radically new conceptualizing capable of expressing philosophically contradictoriness itself as the foundation of natural phenomena. Let us take as an example the problem of life:

> Life comes about through a contradiction in nature, but it would expire of its own accord if nature did not offer resistance . . . If the outside influence contrary to life serves precisely to support life, then again that which seems *most favourable* to life must become absolutely unreceptive to this influence and the reason for its decline, so paradoxical is the life-phenomenon even as it becomes

> defunct. The product, as long as it is organic, can never lapse into indistinctness ... Death is a return to general indistinctness ... The components extracted from the universal organism now return to it, and since life is nothing else but a heightened condition of ordinary natural forces, the product will succumb to the dominion of *these* forces once that condition has passed. The same forces which sustained life for a while will also finally destroy it. So life is not itself something, but only the manifestation of a transition of certain forces from that heightened condition into the ordinary condition of universality.[39]

Here we can clearly see what distinguishes Schelling's natural philosophy from metaphysical thinking, but also what separates his dialectics from the dialectics of Kant and Fichte. For with these thinkers, the dialectical contradictions always derived solely from the relation of the – subjective – categories of understanding to an objective reality (assumed to be unknowable or subjectified into non-Ego). With the young Schelling, on the contrary, the dialectical contradiction (occasionally coming very close to materialism) is an inherent decisive attribute, a category of objective reality itself. Therefore the philosophical statement of the dialectic does not proceed primarily from the subject of knowledge; it must, as the subjective side of the total context, attain to expression in the subject as a dialectical connection precisely because the essence of objective reality is itself dialectical.

In Schelling's work, to be sure, this dialectical objectivity is, as we already know, idealistic. Its foundation is the theory of the identical subject-object as the ultimate basic principle of reality and hence of philosophy. The 'odyssey of the spirit' to which we referred earlier is just that process whereby – in Schelling's terminology – the unconscious productivity of nature attains in man to consciousness and self-consciousness, a radical self-consciousness in the sense that an adequate philosophical perception of the world expresses its object appropriately for the very reason that it is nothing

but an elevation to consciousness of what the objective natural processes have produced unconsciously, and because this very self-consciousness represents the supreme product of the process of nature.

Here we see how, as Vico had already sought to achieve, Spinoza's epistemology whereby 'the ordering and associating of ideas is the same as the ordering and associating of things'[40] reappears in a dynamic-dialectical, historical continuation of it. Admittedly, this heightening of the dialectical was achieved at the expense of a heightened idealist ambiguity. True, the epistemological relation of the attributes of the single substance, expansion and thought, does not appear fully clarified in Spinoza's work either. But all epistemological clarification is supplanted in the objective idealism of Schelling and Hegel by the myth of the identical subject-object.

Schelling's intellectual intuition was the first version of this dialectic of objective idealism. Since it was two-sided, i.e., both dialectical and irrationalist, the young Schelling's ambiguous position in the history of philosophy clearly emerges in a provisional way that was automatically condemned to be superseded (on both the Right and the Left). His intuition was two-sided because we find, on the one hand, a dialectical surpassing of the contradictions apparent in objective reality as immediately given, a path towards perceiving the essence of things in themselves, and hence an epistemological surpassing of these manifest contradictions, rigidly pinned down, through the categories of pure understanding — those of the Enlightenment's metaphysical thinking, but also those of Kant and Fichte. On the other hand, this same intuition implies an irrationalist flinching in the face of the immense perspectives and logical difficulties inseparably linked with an advance beyond merely sensible thinking to rationality and rigorous dialectics. In my book on the young Hegel[41] I have analysed in detail – from the angle of Hegel's development – the contrast in philosophical method which now arose between Schelling and Hegel, who both built their systems and methods upon the identical

subject-object. Here I shall only recapitulate the philosophically crucial elements.

With Hegel the bridge from understanding (*Verstand*) to reason is a supersession (*Aufhebung*) in its specific triple meaning, as negation, preservation and elevation to a higher plane. Between understanding and reason there prevails a dialectical contradiction which permeates Hegel's whole system and constitutes in particular the core of the logic of essence. Hence logic, for Hegel, had to become the basic science of the new, dialectical philosophy.

With Schelling, on the other hand, a rigid contrast is established between understanding and reason. Here there are no dialectical bridges and mediating links; the transition is now a leap which, once accomplished, negates the categories of understanding from the standpoint of the philosophy reached through this leap and leaves them behind. Schelling repeatedly expressed the contrast as abruptly as he could. He regarded intellectual intuition as something raised above all doubt: 'It is that which can be presupposed straightaway and entirely unsummoned, and in this respect it cannot even be called a postulate of philosophy.'[42] Hence it could not be taught either: 'It is clear that it is not something which can be taught; all attempts to do so are therefore wholly futile in learned philosophy, and approaches to it, since they necessarily form an avenue which precedes philosophy, preliminary expositions and the like, cannot be found in exact learning.'[43] Next Schelling writes of the contrast with understanding: 'And we cannot grasp why philosophy should be obliged to pay special heed to those incapable of it. It is more proper to cut off access to it sharply and to isolate it from ordinary knowledge on all sides such that there is no road or footpath from the one to the other. This is the start of philosophy, and anyone who has not arrived yet or who fears this point can stay away or turn back.'[44] And with strict logic, Schelling contrasts intellectual intuition with all abstraction by defining it as follows: 'This knowledge must be an absolutely free knowledge precisely because all other

knowledge is *not free*. It must therefore be a knowledge not attained through proofs, conclusions or the mediation of any concepts at all, and thus altogether an intuition . . .'[45]

Here we have a model example of how irrationalism arises out of the philosophical evasion of a dialectical question clearly posed by the age. The task, one that was posed equally for natural philosophy and social philosophy, was that of breaking through, in scientific-philosophical terms, the barriers of metaphysical thinking (discursive and governed by understanding, in the terminology of the period), thereby acquiring a philosophical-conceptual, scientifically usable and progressive instrument for solving the major problems of the period. We have noted the importance of the steps which Schelling took in this direction. He surpassed the philosophical subjectivism of Kant and Fichte, albeit tentatively and not with philosophical conviction; in a series of important natural-philosophical questions, he at least presaged those of objective dialectics by posing them in their most general abstract outlines; he recognized and demanded the necessity of a philosophical conceptualizing higher than that of the categories of understanding. At first, to be sure, the escape into irrationalism came about with as little clear awareness of it on the philosophical level as that evinced when Schelling went beyond the subjectivism of the *Science of Knowledge*. And this at the crucial point with regard to the problem of the nature of the new science of dialectics, and of its philosophical relation to the contradictions of the conditions of understanding.

This crucial point was the interpretation of the dialectic itself. Naturally Schelling saw the difference and contrast between formal and dialectical logic, between metaphysical and dialectical thinking relatively clearly. He said of the former: 'Accordingly, it is a quite empirical doctrine which postulates the laws of ordinary understanding as absolute, e.g., that of two concepts which are contradictory opposites, only one accrues to each essential being, which is perfectly correct in the finite sphere but not in speculation, which

begins only in the equating of opposites.'[46] Thus logic itself in its form up to then was something purely empirical to him. He saw, however – obviously under the temporary influence of Hegel, with whom he was still closely collaborating when he penned these considerations – a certain possibility of coherence between dialectical logic and philosophy proper on the basis of intellectual intuition. Hence in the exposition directly preceding the passage just quoted he was able to say of logic: 'If this was intended to be a science of form, a pure aesthetic theory of philosophy, so to speak, it would have to be what we have characterized above under the name of dialectics. Such a theory does not yet exist. Should it be purely an account of finite forms in their relation to the absolute, it would have to be scientific scepticism: and Kant's transcendental logic cannot be taken for that either.'[47] Thus the maximum philosophical role which Schelling concedes to such a logic is to prepare the ground for intellectual intuition and the leap into authentic, intuitive philosophy by analysing the categories of understanding and by proving their immanent contradictoriness.

But philosophy itself has little to do with this preliminary science. Here Schelling was, objectively – as we shall see later on –, the direct forerunner of Kierkegaard's view of dialectics, or rather, of Kierkegaard's repudiation of dialectics as a means of knowing reality.

We see therefore how, already with the young Schelling, just that mode of perception which was supposedly qualified to open the way to dialectics closes this door to scientific, rational dialectics, dialectical logic and rational knowledge, at the same time opening up all the avenues to an irrationalism. It makes no essential difference to this basic fact that the young Schelling was as yet by no means an irrationalist in the present-day sense, indeed not even in Schopenhauer's or Kierkegaard's, or at any rate he did not intend to be. For the world which intellectual intuition was supposed to render accessible was, as Schelling then conceived it, by no means inimical to reason, not even meta-rational. On the contrary:

it was precisely here that the real forward movement and development of the universe was supposed to be revealed in all its rationality.

Certainly, after Schelling abandoned the means of rationally revealing and accounting for it – dialectical logic – at the entrance to the actual sanctuary, there only remained at his disposal the tools of formal logic. These, far from fortuitously, gave the impression of this inspired intuitiveness through a subjectivistic, arbitrary treatment of the problems. It is significant how great a part analogy plays in the young Schelling's practical *Logic of Philosophy*. But this was just how this first, wholly indecisive phase of irrationalism nonetheless became the methodological model for all the later ones: formal logic always constitutes the internal complement, the material's formally ordering principle for any irrationalism claiming to do more than to transform the whole world-picture into an amorphous flux apprehended by a purely intuitive intuition. So this method of Schelling's already defines the propositions for Schopenhauer as later for Nietzsche and, after Nietzsche, for Dilthey's 'descriptive psychology', for 'intuition of the essence' (*Wesenschau*) in phenomenology, ontology in existentialism, etc.

The resultant irrationalist deviation from dialectics at the entrance to its real domain produced in Schelling another motive acquiring a lasting significance for the development of irrationalism: epistemological aristocratism. For every philosophical rationalism, especially the Enlightenment's, which looked upon itself more or less consciously as the ideological preliminary to a democratic upheaval, it was self-evident that knowledge of truth was accessible, in principle, to everybody who obtained the factual prerequisites (pieces of information, etc.). Hegel, in continuing philosophy's great scientific traditions, found it equally self-evident when giving his rationale of dialectical philosophy, dialectical logic, that this was in principle attainable by all. Granted, dialectical thinking always appears to 'sound common sense' to be paradoxical and topsy-turvy, but for

that very reason, Hegel believed, it was the new dialectical philosophy's obvious task to account for philosophically and to render viable the path leading thence from a subjective and pedagogic angle as well. It is generally recognized that the great crowning work of his early period, the *Phenomenology of Mind*, set itself this aim among others, and this aim was not the least of them.

But that was exactly why the *Phenomenology* was levelled in essence against Schelling, the aristocratic nature of his epistemology included. True, Schelling went as far as to concede that 'what cannot be actually learnt from philosophy but can be practised under instruction is the art-side of this discipline, or what we can really call dialectics'.[48] But we already know that dialectics, with Schelling, could form at best a propaedeutic to *authentic* philosophy. Because, however, this – albeit negative – connection existed, Schelling took it as proven 'that the dialectics too has a side from which it cannot be *learnt* and that it rests on the creative faculty no less than what we might term the poetry of philosophy, in the original meaning of the word'.[49] Thus insofar as the dialectic is really philosophical (going beyond Kant), it ceases to be something which may be 'learnt' by everyone. It goes without saying that this impossibility of essential knowing for everybody, the restriction to those 'chosen' from birth, pertains to intellectual intuition itself to an even greater degree.

Thus the new irrationalism was adopting, with bourgeois and secular overtones, an epistemological motive of most religious philosophies: perception of the Deity is only possible for those whom God has chosen. This outlook had already sprung up in pre-historical magic rites as the class prerogative of the priesthood; it dominated the Eastern religions, above all Brahmanism, and it was, with certain modifications, also prevalent in the Middle Ages. To be sure, it is characteristic of the strong influence of the embourgeoisement process from the Renaissance and Reformation onwards that this theme plays hardly any part in Pascal. Even

Jacobi, in spite of his aristocratic individualism, did not consider it important to make much of the aristocratic character of his intuitionism, 'immediate knowing'. Only with the pseudo-historical, pseudo-dialectical philosophy of the restoration period, and the reactionary backlash against Enlightenment philosophy which was the philosophy of the French Revolution, did aristocratism again begin to occupy a central place in epistemology.

In Germany it was Franz von Baader who advocated this tendency with the greatest determination. Its restoration character is far more plainly visible in him than in Schelling. Baader took up arms against the whole of philosophy since Descartes with the exclamation that it was absurd 'without God, to wish to perceive God'.[50] Perception against the will of what is perceived is bound to be an incomplete perception. And he drew this inference: not to begin philosophy with God is tantamount to repudiating God. Here, quite evidently, only a man whom God has chosen can perceive God; philosophical knowledge is, according to Baader, the privilege of aristocratic saviour-figures chosen by God.

Naturally the young Schelling's aristocratism was far less thorough-going, although we shall see how the remorseless logic of his development drove him closer and closer to Baader. Politically and socially too, Schelling in his Jena period did not yet overtly support a restoration, although again we shall see that the logic of his development made him the philosophical inspiration for Stahl's philosophy of right and the champion of Romantic reaction under Friedrich Wilhelm IV in the 1840s. But already in Jena, his aristocratic anti-Enlightenment philosophical tendencies were closely combined with reactionary political ones. His polemic against the Enlightenment philosophy of understanding was quite overtly anti-democratic; it quite openly opposed it for paving the way for the Revolution: 'The elevation of common understanding to an arbiter in rational matters inevitably produces ochlocracy (rule by the mob) in the domain of the sciences and with it, sooner or later, a general uprising by

the mob.'[51] To counter it, philosophy had to use its aristocratic veto: 'If anything is capable of stemming the inrush – whose mixing of higher and lower values has become more and more visible since even the mob has begun to write and every plebeian has promoted himself to the rank of a judge – then it is philosophy, whose natural motto is the phrase *Odi profanum vulgus et arceo*.'[52] The foundations of the completely reactionary turn can therefore already be found in the young Schelling as well.

These early tendencies of his were further heightened by the manner in which – in contrast to Goethe – he anchored intellectual intuition philosophically in his system and method. Given Schelling's declarative manner and the abrupt, clear-cut separation from everything conceptual, we can hardly speak of a philosophical rationale. Goethe interpreted the problem set by the *Critique of Judgement*, the problem of the new association of the universal and particular exceeding the simple laws of understanding, as a practical task for natural science in the light of philosophy. As a spontaneous dialectician he established a whole series of such connections in reality, or began in his natural science at least to fathom them on a presentient basis. He could therefore commit himself with a philosophically clear conscience to the 'adventure of reason'. For Hegel, the dialectic of the categories of understanding, which he called reflection determinants, produced those concrete logical bridges which could lead to solving this task. Here it is important to establish that the dialectical contradictions emerging in this way (spontaneously with Goethe, consciously with Hegel) no longer have anything to do with the Kantian antithesis of discursive and intuitive knowledge; these expressions never play any part in the mature Hegel's terminology.

This was not so with Schelling. He accepted uncritically the Kantian opposition of 'discursive' and 'intuitive', exceeding Kant in this respect only inasmuch as he affirmed, at least for the chosen few, the philosophical geniuses, the realizability of intuitive perception for human consciousness, which

Kant denied. From this position, he was forced into somehow demonstrating the possibility of the reality of intellectual intuition for human consciousness. This demonstration consisted, in essence, of showing forth an unquestionably existing and creatively functioning human procedure in which, he asserted, there was such an intuitive perception, raised above all doubts. This, in Schelling's view, was the aesthetic procedure. The faculty which thereby attained expression and the subject-object structure manifesting itself were proof for him that the human subject can indeed possess the attributes required for intuitive reason.

Kant himself did not contemplate using aesthetics to resolve the new epistemological difficulties. When this problem cropped up, the *Critique of Judgement* had left the whole sphere of aesthetics far behind it, and even in retrospect Kant did not think of resorting to the aesthetic process to resolve this question. To be sure, Kant's diffidence derived from the fact that he did not see in the aesthetic procedure any way at all of perceiving objective reality. With Schelling, on the other hand, it was possible for this procedure to become the 'organon' of world-perception because to his mind, the essence of art was the apprehension and revelation of the cosmos of things-in-themselves, and he therefore viewed art – albeit in an idealist-mysticized form – as reflecting the objective reality of the world of things-in-themselves.

Fichte, on the contrary, already touches on this connection. In his *System of Ethical Theory* (*System der Sittenlehre*) Fichte takes up the relation between the transcendental and aesthetic view of the world and defines the relationship by stating that art 'turns the transcendental viewpoint into the universal one. What the philosopher toils to acquire, the aesthete possesses . . . without definite thoughts on it.'[53] Whether or not Schelling found a stimulus in this Fichtean formulation, written when they were still close collaborators, he went considerably further than Fichte in linking aesthetics and philosophy – a philosophy based on intellectual intuition.

In the *System of Transcendental Idealism*, Schelling's prime concern in this respect appears in the title of the final section, 'Deduction of an Organ of Philosophy'. This deduction Schelling summed up as follows:

> All philosophy proceeds and must proceed from a principle which, as the absolute principle, is at the same time the identical purely and simply. What is absolutely simple and identical cannot be interpreted or communicated through description, nor through concepts at all. It can only be intuited. Such an intuition is the organ of all philosophy. But this intuition, which is an intellectual and not a sensory one, and which has for its object not the objective or the subjective but the absolutely identical, in itself neither subjective nor objective, is itself merely an inner one which cannot become objective again for itself: it can only become objective through a second intuition. This second intuition is aesthetic intuition.[54]

This definition elucidates Schelling's general principle: 'This generally acknowledged and wholly undeniable objectivity of intellectual intuition is art itself. For aesthetic intuition is nothing other than intellectual intuition become objective.'[55]

So art, the creative genius' procedure, becomes the 'organon' of philosophy; and aesthetics become the core of the philosophical method, revealing the real mysteries of the cosmos and the world of things-in-themselves.

> If aesthetic intuition is only intellectual intuition become objective, then it is self-evident that art is the sole organon, both true and permanent, and document of philosophy, constantly verifying afresh what philosophy cannot represent externally, namely the unconscious in action and creativity and its original identity with the conscious. Art, for the philosopher, is supreme precisely because it opens up to him the innermost sanctuary, so to speak, where it is as if a single flame consumes in permanent and original

union that which is divided in nature and history and that which must eternally flee from itself in life and in action, just as in thinking. The view which a philosopher forms of nature artificially is the pristine and natural one for the artist.[56]

Clearly, this linking and indeed identification of aesthetic and intellectual intuition was bound to reinforce Schelling's aforestated tendencies to aristocratism in his epistemology. In Schopenhauer's philosophy this aristocratism becomes still more marked, more overtly reactionary than in the young Schelling's. This trend received a further boost from Nietzsche and the philosophers of the imperialist period whom he influenced, as our later studies will show. True, in order fully to understand the stance taken by Schelling – as yet not an entirely reactionary one – we must bear in mind the fact that even in his aesthetics, there is a prevalent tendency towards objectivism, a mystificatory variant of the interpretation of art as reflecting objective reality, and consequently of a harmonizing of truth and beauty. Such endeavours throw the chief line of his aesthetics in very sharp relief to Schopenhauer's and, even more so, to that pursued in the imperialist period.

Schelling's argumentation of the objectivity of art may have been extremely mystical; we have already mentioned that he repeatedly harks back in this period, in aesthetics especially, to the Platonic theory of ideas. His arguments may often have invoked God and deduced in God's name the objectivity of art, the identity of truth and beauty. Nonetheless an orientation towards the reflection theory is still there and indeed central to his rationale of aesthetics, and so in this area Schelling really did surpass the subjective idealism of Kant and Fichte. Thus he states:

The true construction of art is representation of its forms as forms of things as they are in themselves or as they are in the absolute . . . Accordingly the forms of art too, since

> they are the forms of beautiful things, are forms of things as they are in God or in themselves, and since all construction is representation of things in the absolute, so is the construction of art, and especially *representation of its forms*, as forms of things as they are in the absolute . . . This statement completes the construction of the general idea of art. For art is demonstrated to be a *real* representation of forms of things as they are in themselves – of forms of the archetypes, therefore.[57]

To be sure, this Platonic and mystical version of the reflection of things-in-themselves in art had extremely important consequences for the young Schelling's whole philosophy. We cannot take the mysticizings away from it in order to reach the rational core; here the connection between mysticism and the tendency to concrete perception is far more intimate than in Hegel's logic. Above all, as we have seen in Schelling's expositions, the 'organon' of philosophy which he finally located entailed the method of 'constructing' the universe, that is to say the method of arbitrarily fitting heterogeneous phenomena together with the aid of mere analogies. Indeed this method is visible right from the start of Schelling's career; but the discovery of art as the 'organon' of philosophy led to its becoming heightened, further generalized and completely rigid. Here again Schelling foreshadowed the later irrationalism. After all, intuition as the 'organon' of philosophy can only function and register a substantial pseudo-image of the world if there is a 'methodological' underpinning of the arbitrary fitting together of objects.

Where Schelling's own development is concerned, the methodological construction of philosophy we have outlined, with such an 'organon' as its basis and the foundation and guarantee of intellectual intuition, became of great moment. As long as this 'organon' was aesthetics, he could somehow sustain the general ambiguity of his objective idealism, the bobbing to and fro between a God-saturated mysticism and a

pantheism which occasionally even shows materialist features. Even the term God could fluctuate between its usage in Giordano Bruno or Spinoza and its religious and mystical connotations. For in art, as much as in natural philosophy, one is dealing with objects and the objectiveness of the real world, and however much a philosophical or aesthetic comprehension of it may deteriorate into arbitrary construction, the orientation was still – in part at least – to objective reality itself.

3. Schelling's Later Philosophy

This ambiguity with which all objective idealism is bound to be fraught promptly ceases, however, once a shift occurs in the view of the 'organon'. And there disappears with it all Schelling's relatively progressive, distortedly progressive tendencies, all traces of his 'genuine youthful idea'. This happened almost immediately after he left Jena and moved to Würzburg (1803), when he forfeited the direct influence of intercourse with Goethe and Hegel, and his supporters and pupils, the majority of whom were overt reactionaries, began to exert a direct influence over him. Very soon afterwards he published *Philosophy and Religion* (1804), which marked a decisive change in his career and the start of his second, unequivocally reactionary period. This change consisted 'merely' in the fact that it was now religion and no longer art that was the 'organon' of philosophy.

The immediate cause of it was external and indeed subaltern. A second-rate pupil of Schelling's, C.A. Eschenmayer, wrote an intrinsically wholly unimportant little book (*Philosophy in its Transition to Non-Philosophy*) in which he raised and criticized with great deference, but from a very firm Rightist standpoint, the problems of the ambiguity of Schelling's early philosophy. Eschenmayer fully accepted the schema which Schelling outlined of knowledge, the road to

intellectual intuition as a product of the dialectic of the determinants of understanding. Where his doubts and critical misgivings set in was in that area of reality that intellectual intuition was supposed to master. As we have noted, Schelling's ambiguity lay in the fact that, on the one hand, he attempted to 'purge' the 'organon' of philosophy of all conceptual elements, all traces of reflection and understanding, while on the other, he wanted to lay down this area as one of knowledge. Eschenmayer, in a naive and radical way, thought Schelling's method through to a conclusion: 'Therefore as far as *knowledge* reaches, *speculation* reaches also, but knowledge is only extinguished in the absolute where it becomes identical with what is perceived and this is also the culminating point for speculation. Hence what lies beyond this point can no longer be an act of perception, but a *presaging* or *devotion* (*Andacht*). What lies beyond all imagining, all concepts and ideas, and indeed beyond speculation is something which devotion apprehends – *namely the divinity* – and this power is the quality of bliss, which is infinitely higher than the eternal.'[58]

However primitive Eschenmayer's thinking, it is nonetheless evident that he drew all the consequences from the supra-conceptual nature of Schellingian speculation. If speculation and dialectics form only the threshold, the preamble to intellectual intuition and are extinguished in it, knowledge will thereby come to revoke itself, eliminating itself in order to enter the realm of the Beyond, of faith, devotion and prayer: philosophy is only a preliminary to 'non-philosophy'. And this means the cutting of any ties between speculation and immanent world-systems like Bruno's or Spinoza's: intellectual intuition is no longer the means of knowing *this* world – however mystificatory – but a leap into the Beyond. Eschenmayer wrote: 'It is as little possible to overcome the main antithesis between the *here-and-now* and the *Beyond* as it is true that all antitheses in the sphere of knowledge are revoked in absolute identity . . . The *here-and-now* is the tractional weight of the will, which in knowledge is chained

to the finite . . . The *Beyond*, on the contrary, implies the freedom of all directions and the immortal life of genius.'[59] However much Eschenmayer accepted the terminology of Schelling's early philosophy, what he was formulating here was the unconditional surrender of thought to religion.

Polemically it was not hard for Schelling to refute Eschenmayer's naive and primitive arguments and – outwardly – to defend his earlier positions. But where the philosophical essence is concerned, these polemical fireworks are quite unable to conceal the fact of a total withdrawal. Granted, he constantly asserts that he is only defending his earlier views against misinterpretations. But on the important philosophical issues he was taking up new positions, or alternatively shifting the accents so firmly that the double-edged ambiguity of his early natural philosophy ceased to obtain, along with that of the objective idealism deriving from it, and an association was established with the overtly reactionary philosophy of the restoration thinkers.

As we shall see, almost all the important elements in Schelling's later 'positive philosophy' are already contained, at least in embryo, in this short work. This development is so characteristic of Schelling, and the change now completed so important to his later development, that we must look at the problem now emerging in rather more detail. As regard the nature of Schelling's development, we have already pointed out that his divorce from Fichtean subjective idealism and the transition to objective idealism similarly occurred in an unconscious way. Hegel characterized this peculiarity in Schelling's development with the comment that Schelling 'underwent his philosophical education in public' and that his work contained 'not a sequence of the sectors of philosophy elaborated one after the other, but a series of stages in his training'.[60] This is a vivid description of the outward appearance of Schelling's works but, despite the tacit condemnation implied in the description, it still fails to furnish a real critique of the character of Schelling's development. This is found not only in the often unconscious, spontaneous

change of outlook but, most of all, in the fact that Schelling still maintained there was an (imagined, fictive) uniformity to his philosophy long after abandoning his old views and indeed going over to the opposite. While we may concede his good faith in his youth, when he was passing from subjective to objective idealism, henceforth this 'instinctiveness' turned more and more into mere demagogy.

Let us now consider the most important factual questions discussed in *Philosophy and Religion*. Above all, Schelling, despite his polemics against the 'misunderstanding' of his philosophy on Eschenmayer's part, allowed philosophy to be sharply divided into two areas. Here we already see the first outlines of his later distinction between negative and positive philosophy. He deduced the following from the absolute and the kind of knowledge appropriate to it:

> Hence, too, the intention of philosophy with regard to man is not so much to bestow something on him as to separate him as cleanly as possible from the contingent element provided by the physical body, the phenomenal world and the life of the senses, and to lead him back to the original realm. Hence, furthermore, all reference to philosophy preceding that knowledge can only be negative in that it shows the nullity of all finite antitheses and leads the soul indirectly to an intuition of the infinite. Once that is reached, it automatically leaves behind those expedients of a merely negative describing of absoluteness, disposing of them as soon as they are no longer needed. [61]

It will be clear to everyone how far this view of knowledge – in spite of the peculiarity of Schelling's dialectic as we have analysed it, and its deviation into the irrational at the crucial point – is removed from that of his early period and how near it comes to Eschenmayer's division into philosophy and 'non-philosophy'. Even the term 'negative' is now used for the lower sphere of perception. To be sure the difference remains that Schelling still persisted – and always would

persist – in comprehending his 'positive philosophy' as knowledge, and therefore never formally denied in his epistemology the cognitional character of this positive sphere. As we shall see, it is just here that we find the transitional features in Schelling's whole irrationalism, and they explain why the influence of his later work was so short-lived.

The chief consequence of this sharp dichotomy was that now, in strict contrast to his early period, Schelling no longer viewed the absolute, the object of intellectual intuition, as the cosmos of things-in-themselves, even if this was then thought of as a Platonic world of ideas. Instead he viewed it as something that could be apprehended only directly, as downright singular. Hence he rejected any explanation or description pertaining to this world and wrote: 'For only a combination can be perceived through description, while the singular needs to be intuited.'[62] And in another passage he challenged for this knowledge even the coherence of the universal with the particular, i.e., the very problem for whose resolution intellectual intuition was, as we have noted, devised in the first place. He now said of this: 'That the whole absolute world with all its gradations of beings is reduced to the absolute oneness of God, so that nothing in that world is truly particular . . .'[61] So here a world-knowledge originally founded on natural philosophy goes over to being a purely mystical knowledge of God.

This marks the completion of Schelling's break with the – admittedly always somewhat equivocal – pantheism of his youth. If previously he had striven to verify, to historicize in a dynamic-dialectical way Spinoza's principle of *Deus sive natura*, he now laid down a sharp, unbridgeable duality between the absolute and the real, God and the world, which could only be linked through a leap: 'In short, there is no permanent bridge from the absolute to the real, and the origin of the sensory world can only be conceived as a complete breakaway from absoluteness, through a leap.'[64] And now, significantly, Schelling's speculation promptly entered a wholly mystical channel by imagining the origin

of the sensory world no longer as evolution or even creation, but as a 'fall' from God. In itself, this would affect us no more than the difference, for Lenin, between a green devil and a yellow one, were it not that Schelling's conception also implied a sharp break with the idea of evolution in natural philosophy. At the end of this treatise he denies the evolution of man from the animal to the human state, the great dialectical conjecture by Goethe and Hegel which also played a decisive role in the beginnings of natural philosophy and the 'odyssey of the spirit'. Just as the whole world, in a grotesquely mystical fashion, was deemed to originate in a 'fall' from God, so now 'the extremely crepuscular frontier of known history' already evinces, according to Schelling, 'a culture that had sunk from an earlier height and disfigured remnants of earlier science, symbols whose meaning seems to have been long forgotten'.[65] And the myth of a Golden Age was held to be a proof of this downward-sloping, anti-evolutionist trend in human history.

Thus we see on which crucial philosophical issues Schelling broke with his early period, and how vigorously the irrationalism of intellectual intuition, previously a merely methodological irrationalism up to a point, was increasingly transformed into a substantial world-image belonging to irrationalist mysticism. This change is also expressed in the fact that, whereas in the pre-Jena and Jena period natural philosophy stood at the centre of Schelling's thinking and all other philosophical fields, except for aesthetics, were only included – so to speak – as systematic supplements, the philosophical treatment of the problems of nature now faded right into the background. The aesthetic questions too remained episodic, and the irrationalist interpretation of myth and religion became the hub of Schelling's entire thinking.

It took, however, nearly thirty years, until Schelling came forward, at least in his lectures, with the complete new, positive philosophy, as the official philosophy of the romanticizing Prussian reactionary groups clustered round Friedrich Wilhelm IV, for him to become regarded as a St George

whose mission it was to slay the dragon of Hegelian philosophy, and especially its radical left flank.

Before going any further, let us try and give a brief sketch of these thirty years in at least their main features. Here the stages in the inner development of Schelling's philosophy itself matter far less than the change in the objective social situation in Germany and the change of fronts it evoked in the philosophical conflicts. For on the one hand, as we have just shown, the decisive change in the goal, content and method of Schelling's philosophy had already taken place in 1804, so that both the unchanging basic principles of it and the socially dictated alterations may easily be understood from the historically changing times without an analysis of the intermediate stages. On the other hand the old Schelling, who for decades was totally forgotten and played virtually no further part in the development of German philosophy, owed his (episodic and temporary) central position in the philosophical conflicts to just this change in Germany's objective social evolution.

Philosophy and Religion appeared before the completion of Hegel's *Phenomenology of the Mind*. Without question that book's attack on intellectual intuition also applied to this new version of it – chiefly the association of 'singleness' with the concept of the absolute, and above all the whole conception of intellectual intuition in general and the analogizing method of construction which followed from it. Here Hegel denounced with great vehemence the 'monotony and abstract generality' of the absolute and Schelling's 'abyss of emptiness for the speculative mode of contemplation'; the latter, he wrote, was equivalent to the 'night in which . . . all cats look grey'. And a particular charge he levelled against Schelling was that according to him, 'to be unsatisfied in it (this monotony of the absolute, G.L.) was an inability to master the absolute standpoint and to adhere to it'.[66]

It now becomes patent that Hegel's struggle against Schelling was a struggle between the extension of dialectics and a flight from dialectics into irrationalism. And Hegel posed this

question in a historical form as well. The *Phenomenology of the Mind* proceeds from the thesis that the world had entered upon a new period. I have shown in my book on Hegel that he located this new element in the French Revolution and the transformation of Europe wrought by the Napoleonic Wars, in the liquidation of the feudal remnants, especially in Germany. Now this new element, according to Hegel, necessarily appears in abstract form at first. So 'the first manifestation of the new world is only at first the whole wrapped in its *singleness*, or its universal ground'. Hence it appeared first of all 'to be an esoteric possession of a number of individuals'. Philosophy's historical task, however, was to perceive the new element in its own agitation and its universal determination, i.e., in a concretely dialectical way: 'Only what is perfectly determined is at the same time exoteric, comprehensible and capable of being learnt and the property of all. Scientific understanding is the road to it that is equally available to all, and to reach rational knowledge through understanding is the rightful claim of the consciousness joining science.'[67] Therefore Hegel's polemic against Schelling's aristocratic epistemology – one that was closely linked with the change to irrationalism – can no more be separated from the issue of a concrete and scientific or abstract-irrationalist method than it can be separated from the contrast between the two thinkers' socio-historical perspective in the great crisis of their age – from the question of whether to be forward-oriented in this crisis, towards the dissolution of the feudal remnants, or oriented backwards to restoration.

This marked the first major battle between objective-idealist dialectics and irrationalism. It meant the defeat of the Schelling form of irrationalism – both the first, ambiguous form, which was linked with the historico-evolutionist method in natural philosophy, and the second, already overtly religio-mystical form. The Hegelian form of dialectics began to assume its dominant position. It did so, to be sure, only gradually and not without very important modifications. For with the fall of Napoleon and with the rule of the

Holy Alliance, the young Hegel's energetically forward-pointing, futuristic perspective, which saw in the contemporary period the start of a new era in human history, likewise entered a crisis. The later Hegel's philosophy of history was a resigned one, far more prone to compromises than was the philosophy of his *Phenomenology*.[68] Henceforth the contemporary period was no longer viewed as the start but as the conclusion of a major era of development. Philosophy no longer looked forwards but into the past, and the future ceased to define the contemporary age and its philosophical interpretation. Philosophy, no longer under an obligation to 'welcome and to acknowledge' the new departures of the mind, was presented as the 'owl of Minerva', able to set out on its flights only as dusk began to fall.[69]

In our present examination of the history of irrationalism, we cannot undertake to expound the consequences of this change for Hegel's philosophy. We must confine ourselves to stating that, in spite of it, Hegelian philosophy logically fulfilled the programme of the *Phenomenology*, the scientific exposition of the objective categories of the dialectic, as far as was possible within the bounds of idealism; that its method, again within idealist bounds, took hold of the idea of evolution and tried to implement it concretely in different areas; and that its view of society was oriented to constitutional monarchy, thus outstripping, albeit extremely irresolutely, the political state of affairs then obtaining in Germany and so always polemicizing against the ideological advocates of Romantic reaction (Haller, Savigny).

This form of Hegelian philosophy became dominant in Germany, especially in Prussia. To be sure, its predominance only lasted until the July revolution in France. Thereupon Germany entered a new phase in the class struggles, of which the philosophical reflection was bound to disrupt first the Hegelian system and then Hegel's idealist-dialectical method as well. This process of dissolution in Hegelianism already began during the philosopher's lifetime in his controversy over the July revolution with his hitherto faithful pupil,

Eduard Gans. We cannot discuss the process in detail here, but Heine, David Friedrich Strauss, the *Halle Yearbooks*, the Berlin 'Freethinkers', Feuerbach, etc., signify different stages in this dissolution occurring before the 1848 revolution, and all these intellectual conflicts were part of the ideological spadework for that revolution. Then Marx and Engels founded dialectical and historical materialism, thereby surmounting for good every form of idealist dialectics.

The central philosophical question in this transitional period was the struggle against the ambiguity of the idealist dialectic grounded in its essence. To elaborate and to unmask its backward tendencies, which crossed the line into theology, was one of the main achievements of Ludwig Feuerbach in paving the way for the great – and sudden – changeover to the highest type of dialectics: the materialist type. Therefore the battle over the part of Hegelian philosophy concerned with the philosophy of religion was only partly rooted in the German political backwardness which forced the most important thinkers from Reimarus and Lessing, indeed from Leibniz onwards, to fight out the major philosophical controversies in semi-theological or theological forms. At this stage, the battle was a necessary preliminary to overcoming philosophical idealism in its supreme form, that of Hegelian dialectics. Its ambiguity on the religious issue, the aforestated vacillation of idealist dialectics between official Christian theology and a pantheism sometimes bordering on atheism, had to be openly elaborated and criticized in order to clear the way for the overcoming of idealism. In this process, with Feuerbach for example, there may have been a temporary loss of some valuable dialectical elements whose progressive conjectures only dialectical materialism subsequently raised to a scientific plane. But the surpassing of Hegel in this respect was very closely connected with the social necessity of advancing, politically, beyond Hegelian philosophy of right, philosophy of society and so forth.

So for all the bourgeois limitations, the ideological eccentricities and muddle-headedness of the leading radical Young

Hegelians, the dissolution of Hegelianism still created for Germany an ideological basis for the ultra-Leftist bourgeois democrats' struggle on the eve of the democratic revolution. The campaign against Hegel and Hegelianism as viewed from the democratic angle necessitated the summoning of Schelling to Berlin on the part of the Prussian reactionaries, with Friedrich Wilhelm IV at their head.

Here it makes no difference how far Schelling himself was clear about the situation, and how far he thought that he was only going into battle against Hegel, who had pushed his own philosophy into the background. What matter are the ideological needs he had to fulfil. In the social context we have the following factors to consider. Restoration ideology was striving for a return to the pre-revolutionary *ancien régime*, and indeed many of its spokesmen even envisaged a return to the Middle Ages. Novalis provided the clearest expression of this tendency in Germany with the essay *Christendom or Europe*. But the more lucid and resolute the outward formulation, the more confused it becomes inwardly and intrinsically, because then the gap between ideology and the social reality becomes all the more unbridgeable. For inwardly, the reign of the remnants of feudalism in France before the Revolution was so badly shaken that French society around 1789 was far removed from a genuine feudalism, let alone feudalism as idealized à la Novalis. While it was the feudal leftovers that dictated the necessity of the Revolution, it was at the same time their decomposition and the continual growth of capitalist elements that produced the objective impossibility of a return to the old state of affairs. Despite all the Holy Alliance's desperate efforts to restore or else to preserve pre-revolutionary political conditions, the rapid capitalization of Europe was inexorably advancing with all its ideological and political consequences, and during restoration rule also it came into continual, increasingly acute conflict with that rule's official politics and ideology. Balzac was the great historian in France of this process, in which the power of money triumphed over all

aristocratic facades and the isolated persons who took restoration ideology seriously became tragi-comic 'knights of the doleful countenance'.

This conflict also determined restoration philosophy in Germany, although of course here the capitalization process advanced far more slowly than in France, thus allowing such examples of the fanatical narrow-minded reactionary or unscrupulous corruptible speculator as Görres or Adam Müller a far louder and more effective say. The typical thinkers were however those who endeavoured to harmonize the restoration outlook with the new scientific and philosophical trends, trying to reinterpret the latter to such an extent that they would be acceptable to the official clerical-reactionary world-view. Such efforts can be already noticed in Schelling himself; but the most important such figure in Germany philosophy during that age was Franz von Baader.

From our standpoint, the most important thing about him is that he unmasked from a Rightist angle objective idealism's ambiguity on the question of religion, always bringing to light the latent godless tendencies. Such forms of denunciation we have already observed in Jacobi. But Jacobi countered philosophical atheism not with a concrete religion but only with his own vapid and abstract immediate knowing; so Schelling – under restoration conditions – could easily ward off his attack. Here Baader always had a concrete religiosity as an answer; the essence of his philosophy, as we have previously intimated, was to arrange the results of the development from Kant to Hegel in such a way that their atheistic and revolutionary elements were eliminated and a philosophy arose on this basis that was acceptable both to scholars and the orthodox reactionaries. Thus he accused Fichte of atheism on account of the autonomy of his Ego; thus he saw a materialism in Hegel's view of matter as an externalization of the mind (God).[70] It is particularly important in this context that in specific newly discovered natural phenomena such as galvanism, animal magnetism, etc., Baader saw forces which dealt 'the *coup de grâce*, as it were', to the mechanistic

natural phenomena dominant since Descartes. And since his chief polemic was directed against Enlightenment psychology, ethics and political theory, he so summed up his standpoint as almost to sound like a modern Jeans or Eddington: 'The despiriting (*Entgeistung*) of one's own soul was already thought to be finished and the objective proof and guarantee of this self-derailment to be located in external nature, held moreover in a totally mindless (soulless or godless) state, when nature herself began to utter more distinctly than ever what is of the soul and the mind – something, admittedly, that constantly addresses us through its multivocal sign language.'[71]

Here it is far plainer than with the young Schelling how the contradictions that had appeared in the mechanistic view of nature – which the progressive advocates of German natural philosophy (e.g., Oken) were taking more and more in the direction of dialectics – turned into reactionary irrationalism. In the interests of a reactionary world-view, the failure of mechanistic concept-forming and the fresh problems this was unable to solve were reinterpreted as revelations of a supra-rationality in natural phenomena as well. This was the basis upon which all social progress could be challenged, the Devil could be presented as 'the first revolutionary'[72] and aspersions could be cast on any efforts in the direction of liberty and equality.

It is not worth discussing at length the details of all this wildly irrationalist mysticism. But it is typical of the character of the restoration, as outlined above, that Baader not only sought to support his arguments with the new natural philosophy but tried – just like Schelling – to dissociate himself from the most extreme irrationalism. Granted, with his whole philosophy he sought to secure the ideological and socio-political predominance of religion over every facet of life. But this, although it incorporated all the irrationalist elements in the evasion of dialectics, was still meant to be an (allegedly) higher rationality, not an absence of reason and repudiation of rationality altogether. This tendency was only

fifty per cent a resorting to the old theology – which advanced similar claims – of times preceding the ideological crisis. In its other fifty per cent, however, it was a concession to the restoration period's incipient capitalization and embourgeoisement – a concession, to be sure, which retained the supremacy of the theological-aristocratic elements. Hence Baader objected sharply to German classical philosophy which, in his opinion, established the 'dichotomy between religion and science' more thoroughly than the French and English and was endeavouring 'to instil even in the good young people the *radical error* that *religion* is in essence irrational and that *reason* is in essence irreligious'.[73]

Naturally the exacerbation of the German class struggles had an effect not only on the radicalizing dissolution, on Left-wing Hegelianism, but also on the reactionaries' philosophical strivings. When, one decade after Hegel's death, the old Schelling was summoned to Berlin by the Romanticizing reactionary group to deal with the ideological trends paving the way for revolution, he entered a world where, as a result of capitalism's development, pure Romantic thinking had become much more absurd than at the time of the Holy Alliance. As the Frenchman to perceive this absurdity the most clearly had been the great writer Balzac, so the man who did so in the Germany of the 1840s – apart, of course, from Marx and Engels – was the greatest poet of the age, Heinrich Heine. In his winter tale *Germany* he invented a fantasy-conversation with the Emperor Barbarossa and used it to express his accurate and trenchantly ironic view of the endeavours of Friedrich Wilhelm IV and his circle. In addressing that ideal figure of the Romantic restoration he wrote:

> Restore the old Holy Roman Empire, restore it complete, give us back the mustiest old lumber and all that frippery.
>
> In spite of everything, I will gladly put up with the Middle Ages as they really were – just free us from that mongrel state,

> from that martinetism which is a nauseating mixture of Gothic folly and modern deceit, which is neither fish nor fowl.
>
> Chase away the band of actors and close the theatres where they parody the olden days . . .[74]

Naturally Marx and Engels fathomed this situation even more clearly than was possible for Heine. It was they, during this transitional period, who took the most energetic steps in both theory and practice to marshal all the forces in German society that felt the feudal-absolutist leftovers to be thwarting their development and were seeking a democratic renewal of Germany. This was already the goal of the young Marx's activity as editor of the *Rheinische Zeitung*; his critique of Hegelian philosophy of right set out to criticize Hegel's orientation to constitutional monarchy as historically obsolete and creating universal confusion. The subject of how their stance brought both of them to a clear appreciation of the hegemony of the proletariat in democratic revolution, a clear recognition of the perspectives of socialist revolution and the foundation of dialectical and historical materialism does not belong to this study, especially as the process was not yet entirely complete at the time of Schelling's arrival in Berlin.

But that makes it all the more important to state how clearly they at once perceived the demagogic mendacity in Schelling's so-called positive philosophy. In the letter to Feuerbach from which we quoted earlier, Marx wrote: 'He (Schelling, G.L.) is calling to the French Romantics and mystics: "I, the union of philosophy and theology"; to the French materialists: "I, the union of flesh and idea"; and to the French sceptics: "I, the scourge of dogmatics, in short: I . . . Schelling!" '[75] Engels, for his part, formulated this view as follows in his pamphlet opposing Schelling's Berlin platform, which was first published under the pseudonym of Oswald: 'All philosophy has hitherto set itself

the task of comprehending the world as rational. Now what is rational is, to be sure, also necessary, and what is necessary must be or become real. That is the bridge to the major practical results of modern philosophy. Now if Schelling does not acknowledge these findings, it was logical also to deny the rationality of the world. However, he did not dare to say so outright but preferred to deny the rationality of philosophy. So he proceeds along the most devious possible line between reason and unreason, calling the rational comprehensible *a priori* and the irrational comprehensible *a posteriori* and assigning the former to "pure rational science or negative philosophy", the latter to a freshly argued "positive philosophy". Here is the first major split between Schelling and all other philosophers; the first attempt to smuggle into the liberal science of thought a faith in authority, emotional mysticism and Gnostic fantasizing.'[76] And Engels likewise stresses that Schelling's attack on Hegel was very closely linked with the dissolution of Hegelianism: 'It is an odd fact that precisely at this time he (Hegel, G.L.) is being attacked from two sides, by his predecessor Schlegel and by his latest follower, Feuerbach.'[77] Somewhat earlier Engels takes up the ambiguity of Hegel's philosophy of religion and again stresses the substantially time-conditioned connection between Schelling's Right-wing critique and Left-wing criticism by the radical Young Hegelians: 'The side of the Hegelian system concerned with the philosophy of religion causes him (Schelling, G.L.) to show contradictions between premises and deduction which the Young Hegelian school discovered and acknowledged long ago. Thus he quite rightly says that this philosophy aims to be Christian, yet nothing forces it to be; were it to abide by the first position of a rational science it would have its truth in itself.'[78]

Already it is not difficult to determine from all this the historical situation, both the class content and philosophical content of the later Schelling. The struggle now no longer revolved around the rationale of an objective dialectic in general where, as we have seen, the young Schelling ventured

boldly forwards on individual questions in the direction of a natural dialectic, but halted methodologically with his intellectual intuition at the threshold of dialectics and founded the first form of modern irrationalism. How this philosophical stance is connected with his political attitude to revolution and restoration we have, again, already indicated. At the start of the 1840s the historical situation was far more ripe and acute: the Romanticizing reaction of Friedrich Wilhelm IV and his supporters was, although backed by Prussian State power, far more of a rearguard action than was the original Romantic reaction after the French Revolution and in the restoration period. The capitalization of Germany made rapid strides in these decades. Not only was the pressure of the bourgeois classes on the feudal-absolutist system beginning to grow stronger and stronger. The stark contrasts between bourgeoisie and proletariat, a sure sign of the vigorous advance of capitalism, were manifested more and more firmly; the great revolt of the Silesian weavers (1844) took place only a few years after Schelling came before the public.

Ideologically, the result was not only that Hegelian philosophy, as an expression of undeveloped class conflicts before the July Revolution, inevitably seemed obsolete from now on. It also meant that its adversaries were obliged to look for more timely intellectual tools than were supplied by the Romantic reaction of the restoration period. Schelling now came forward claiming to provide such tools. He was now already an overt opponent of Hegelian dialectics, aiming not only at refuting them critically and hence also at putting a stop to the radical tendencies in Hegel's successors, but at replacing them at the same time with a new philosophy. This philosophy would, on the one hand, fulfil the meanwhile intensified religious needs of Romanticizing reaction, while, on the other, it would not disturb ideologically the rapport between these reactionaries and bourgeois circles that might be prepared to go along with them. We saw this duality in Schelling's efforts in the statement by Engels we quoted, to

the effect that the peak of Schelling's new philosophy, a peak enshrouded in theological mysticism, was pure irrationalism and anti-rationality, but that Schelling still did not declare allegiance to irrationalism openly and resolutely but 'followed devious roads', evading the ultimate consequences.

That alone would not suffice to establish his uniqueness within the bourgeois development. After all, we have shown that every bourgeois philosophy – even if as radically irrationalistic as it was in the imperialist age – must concede as much to understanding and reason as the science serving capitalist production will need at all costs. The demands of the times, however, caused Schelling to go in part too far and in part not far enough in this respect. Hence the powerful effect of his first appearance, but hence also its rapid waning and his total loss of influence after 1848 when the class structure of reaction underwent a change.

That Schelling did not go far enough for the reactionary bourgeoisie in his proclamation of irrationalism is connected, on the one hand, with his link with orthodox religion, which still claimed in this period to represent a higher rationality and not a crass irrationalism.[79] On the other hand, the idea of scientific thinking in the 1840s differed from that of the post-1848 period. Contemporary bourgeois thinkers were influenced by German classical philosophy and its tendencies toward dialectical thought. Therefore irrationalism's universal bourgeois concession to scientific thinking had also to extend to dialectics; it was not yet able to take up a radical-agnosticist position. Thus while Schelling's adherence – a merely nominal one, as we shall see – to the dialectics of his early period of natural philosophy may directly follow, in biographical and psychological terms, from his vanity about his own life-work, ultimately we are nevertheless dealing now with an objectively dominant trend of the age. This may also be discerned from the fact that such Right-wing adversaries of Hegelianism as the younger Fichte and especially Weisse had to make bigger and bigger concessions to dialectics in their theistic, anti-pantheistic strivings; much the same can

even be seen in Baader, Friedrich Schlegel, etc. Only after the defeat of the 1848 revolution did Schopenhauer's radically anti-dialectical tendency come into operation. (Trendelenburg's critique of Hegel we shall discuss in more detail in connection with Kierkegaard.)

But at the same time the older Schelling's irrationalism went further than the development after 1848. This too is connected with the historical situation of his philosophizing. Like all restoration philosophers he sought, with his irrationalism, to save the intellectual respectability of orthodox religion. The methodological consequences of this position we have just discussed. As regards contents, the result was that Schelling was forced to present the entire Christian religion with all its dogmas and myths as the true substance of his irrationalism, and to 'prove' it philosophically. In this he still belonged to irrationalism's first period, the semi-feudal age of restoration. Resolutely bourgeois irrationalism, on the contrary, was inclined to dissociate itself more and more strongly from positive religions and to lay down in irrationalist terms merely a religious content in general: after Schopenhauer and Nietzsche its dominant tendency increasingly became a 'religious atheism'. But even such thinkers as Schleiermacher or Kierkegaard – in whom, especially the latter, we can trace on the surface a religious affiliation perhaps even stronger than the older Schelling's – were far more inclined, in their method and the accenting of the essential content, not only towards abstract religiosity in general but even religious atheism. This tendency is an important reason for Schelling's increasing neglect after the 1848 revolution, as also for Kierkegaard's influence on the atheistic existentialists of our own times.

In his later years, therefore, Schelling was as much a mere transitional figure as he was in his youth, albeit in completely different circumstances and with a different philosophy. To be sure, his earlier activity had marked the transition from the newly arising dialectic to modern irrationalism's beginnings and foundation. But now, during the crisis of objective

idealist dialectics, he was temporarily active as a central figure of irrationalist-reactionary resistance to these dialectics, with the aim of preventing this crisis from giving rise to a higher stage in dialectics.

It follows naturally from this situation that Schelling should level his chief attack against Hegelian philosophy. Philosophically, this attack was now placed in a far more comprehensive context than his similar early endeavours had been. Then, his hatred and contempt had only extended to the Enlightenment since about the time of Locke. Now, the whole development of modern bourgeois philosophy from Descartes to Hegel was stigmatized as a major aberration from the correct road and Hegel himself was treated as the acme of this false tendency. Schelling was thereby setting out in a direction which was to become the dominant one in the interpretation of the history of philosophy during the period of the advanced irrationalism promoted by the immediate pre-fascists and the fascists. At the same time, however – and this expresses that incompleteness, that transitional character we have just mentioned – his own early philosophy was not to be entirely repudiated, although objectively it constituted an important part of the intellectual development he had rejected.

The construction used by Schelling here was – with, to be sure, important modifications – the universal schema of irrationalism: rational philosophy, or so-called negative philosophy, was likewise a means of knowledge, indeed an indispensable one in its total context; only it was not the sole knowledge possible, as philosophy from Descartes to Hegel would have it, and on no account the one capable of grasping true reality. This was the general irrationalist line after Schopenhauer: an agnosticist epistemology rejects all assertions of the perceptibility of objective reality, to which both philosophical materialism and objective idealism laid claim, and grants access to this sphere only to irrationalist intuition. Two facts indicate that the later Schelling's position was more than a little confused epistemologically. On

the one hand, he did not want to be radically agnosticist on the first issue (although objectively his deductions come extraordinarily close to such a standpoint), while on the other hand, he wished to avoid proclaiming a resolute anti-rationality in his new system's culmination in positive philosophy (although his deductions, if thought out to their conclusion, imply a pure irrationalism).

In contrast to Hegel's philosophy, his own early work was supposed to represent the correct negative philosophy. He had, Schelling maintained, already 'declared the true negative philosophy which, in awareness of itself, perfects itself within its limits with noble restraint, to be the greatest benefit which may first of all be bestowed on the human mind at least; for through such a philosophy reason enters its appropriate, unrestricted domain and is installed to grasp and to state the essence, the In-themselves of things.'[80] On the other hand, Schelling stresses: 'The philosophy which Hegel expounds is negative philosophy driven beyond its limits, it does not exclude the positive element but has, in its view, subjugated it in itself, to itself.'[81]

We are now looking briefly at the later Schelling's concrete account of negative philosophy and proving its fundamental antitheses to that of his early period. But we are not concerned with the philological question of whether Schelling was deluding himself by stating (or asserting) that he was incorporating his first philosophy in his later one. We are concerned with illuminating the basic incompatibility of all the early Schelling's progressive contents and tendencies with his later irrationalist stance in matters of philosophical principle. The point at issue is that the basically reactionary character of any irrationalism reveals itself in Schelling's case also. Some of these questions we have already discussed in connection with his *Philosophy and Religion*.

We have already cited the young Schelling's image of the 'odyssey of the spirit' as constituting the main content of his natural philosophy in a nutshell. We have pointed out that it contains the (idealist) formulation of a unitary evolution

of nature in an upward direction; that it views man and human consciousness as the product of this natural evolution (in the form, to be sure, of the identical subject-object); and that it entails the capability of human consciousness adequately to comprehend the natural process of which consciousness itself is a component part and result. Above all the older Schelling made a radical break with this conception of a unity – albeit understood in an idealist sense – of man and nature. 'For our self-consciousness *is* by no means consciousness of that nature which has traversed everything, it is just *our* consciousness and by no means encompasses a knowledge of all becoming; this universal becoming remains as alien and impenetrable to us as if it never had any relation to us.'[82] Thus the natural process, as far as it can be perceived at all as Schelling now interprets it, in no respect illuminates the knowledge of man, any more than its praxis can contribute to making reality comprehensible: 'Man and his doings are therefore far removed from rendering the world comprehensible; man himself is the most incomprehensible thing of all . . .'[83]

But the disruption of this coherence entailed the adoption of a clear anti-evolutionist stance. Schelling now wrote ironically of the idea of a boundless progress, which for him could only be a 'senseless progress.' 'A departing without ceasing and without a pause wherein something truly new and different might begin belongs to the articles of faith of present-day wisdom.'[84] This dismissal of the idea of progress led Schelling likewise to reject evolution in an upward direction, from primitive beginnings to a higher level. Here again he vigorously opposed the theory of historical evolution which had gained strength in Germany chiefly under the influence of the dialectical tendencies of objective idealism. 'One of these axioms is that all human science, art and culture must have derived from the most wretched beginnings.'[85] And since evolution did not move in an upward direction, Schelling did not allow it to be the immanent product of its own forces either, or the evolution of man to be the result of man's own deeds.

Hence he regarded as similarly erroneous the 'prevalent view that man and mankind were left solely to their own devices from the outset, that they groped their way, as it were, blindly, *sine numine*, and exposed to the harshest workings of chance'.[86]

For the older Schelling there is ultimately no evolution at all. Whereas in his youth – in league with Goethe – he helped to inaugurate the evolutionism sharply hostile to the theory of a static nature (or a nature interrupted by catastrophes) as mooted by Linnaeus and Cuvier, he now invoked precisely Cuvier to counter the idea of evolution and, using him for support, repudiated all evolution in principle. To take this *ad absurdum* he stated that 'anyone believing in a real historical course of events would also have to accept real, successive creations'.[87] Of course: if events are not allowed to be the result of the actual forces participating in them, either in nature or in history, then a 'creation' is needed to give rise to something qualitatively new – whereby it is hard to see why this intervention of a transcendental power on *one* occasion would be more credible scientifically than its repeated occurrence. Schelling's demagogy consists in the fact that according to his needs, he sometimes produces pseudo-scientific arguments against dialectics while in other instances, he cites the irrationalist 'grounds' of theology against scientific thinking as a whole.

Granted, Schelling's ensuing statements about history are in strict contrast to the 'genuine youthful idea' of his beginnings. But in substance they are not only repetitions of the Romantic-reactionary philosophy of the Restoration, but also extensions to those reactionary elements in his first period which we have already touched on. For in respect of the history of mankind Schelling stresses: 'For we view the human race by no means as a single whole but as divided into two large masses, and so divided that the human aspect seems to be only on the one side.'[88] The fundamental, qualitative inequalities within the human race are of its essence and irrevocable: 'Differences such as those of *Kaffirs*,

Abyssinians and *Egyptians* go back into the world of ideas.' There follows on from this an apologia, tortuous in its language but quite plain in meaning, for Negro slavery in Africa.[89] (We are now barely a step away from Gobineau and racial theory.)

Needless to say the basis of the new Schellingian political philosophy too was 'the objective reason dwelling in things themselves' which, for instance, 'requires a natural inequality', the 'difference between rulers and ruled originating in the world of ideas'.[90] It is not worth quoting and analysing in detail these views, whose philosophical basis was Romantic 'facticity', i.e., the irrationalism of social and political life with its Haller-Savignyesque inference that statutes and constitutions cannot be 'made'. If we briefly note that according to Schelling a political overthrow 'if intended, is a crime second to none and one which only parricide parallels in importance',[91] we will have a clear enough picture of why Schelling was the appropriate ideologist for Prussian reaction under Friedrich Wilhelm IV.

It is likewise evident from what we have expounded so far why the point of Schelling's polemics had to be levelled against Hegelian philosophy. For all its conservatism, its fluctuations and concessions to the Right, its ideological-theological ambiguities, the essence of the Hegelian dialectical method was nonetheless an autonomous movement of the concept, an inwardly enclosed and ordered state of conditions mundanely obtaining for this world and leaving no scope for the transcendental either in nature or in history. Hence Schelling's great accusation that with Hegel, negative philosophy claimed to voice the truth in itself alone and did not need supplementing with a positive philosophy.

Schelling's critique of this tendency in Hegel, which was aimed against what was genuinely progressive about his philosophy, against the dialectical method, was not content to demonstrate the path to atheism which Hegel himself was held to have taken. It went so far as to state that the then already overtly emerging political radicalism and atheism of

the Left Hegelians was a necessary logical consequence of Hegelian philosophy. Hegel's chief transgression was that he took that which in proper, negative philosophy was only potentially present 'as the proceedings of real Becoming'. 'Presupposing this, since in indifferentism God was only potential in accordance with autonomous or detached Being, and not movement but that which-is-in-being (*das Seiende*) was placed in God, the idea of a process in which God is perennially realized, along with everything that ill-informed and otherwise perhaps unreliable men . . . have further made of it or added to it, was not to be prevented.'[92] In another passage Schelling similarly deplored the confusion between negative and positive philosophy: 'Therein, as has been stated, lies the ground of the confusion and the wild and disorderly state into which men fell by first attempting to present God as involved in a necessary process but thereafter, when they could get no further, taking refuge in downright atheism. This confusion has prevented them from even understanding the distinction (i.e., between negative and positive philosophy, G.L.).'[93] And he did not neglect to point out that Hegel's ideas, after they had 'already lost currency' among the 'more highly educated classes' (in the Prussian bureaucracy) 'subsided in the meantime into the deeper strata of society and still maintain themselves there'.[94]

This denunciation of dialectics in its hitherto highest form as atheistic, revolutionary and plebeian was to gain particular weight precisely by virtue of the fact that it came from Schelling, Hegel's early colleague and co-founder of objective-idealist dialectics, whose early (negative, as he now put it) philosophy Hegel too regarded as the immediate, historical starting-point for the construction of his dialectical method. Schelling believed that the proof that the Hegelian dialectic was a simple misunderstanding of negative philosophy would be a devastating blow for Hegel's supporters and lead them, except for the already hopelessly radicalized and thus more or less staunch liberals, into the reactionary camp of Friedrich Wilhelm IV.

But this exploiting of the by now already historical authority of Schelling's early philosophy does not exhaust the significance of his anti-Hegel polemics. True, he directed the brunt of his attack against the progressive side of Hegelian dialectics. But in the course of the polemic itself, motives crop up which reveal Hegel's weak side very neatly as well. As we shall see, this polemic was demagogic in method and obscurantist in purpose. But it is instructive to observe that in it, real and very important flaws in objective-idealist dialectics are shown forth, flaws which, if pinpointed with philosophical accuracy, could lead to a higher development of dialectics. It is here manifest that the stages in irrationalism's development do not arise out of its own growth tendencies, and that with each kind of irrationalism, content and method are determined by the concrete set of problems associated with the relevant advance in the life of society and correspondingly in ideology. In the 1840s this question related to the transition from idealist to materialist dialectics. Accordingly a Right critique of objective idealism formed, methodologically speaking, the centre of the irrationalist strivings, and it encouraged efforts to steer the development away from these consequences and towards an irrationalist mysticism. We have already shown that these tendencies played a crucial role in Schelling's polemic against Hegel at the time of the dissolution of Hegelianism.

The decisive problem raised by this dissolution was primarily the old principle of philosophical division: idealism or materialism, the priority of Being or consciousness. Here objective idealism found a specious answer in the theory of the identical subject-object and attempted to erect the proud edifice of a dialectical system on this hollow foundation. In all areas of philosophy, the exacerbation of the class struggles in Germany after the July Revolution necessarily brought about the collapse of this inwardly false quasi-solution. We have, too, already pointed out that this trend within bourgeois philosophy reached its climax in Ludwig Feuerbach, around the time of Schelling's appearance in Berlin.

This question now played a crucial part in Schelling's epistemological criticism of Hegel. Our analysis of the self-delusion whereby Schelling thought that his negative philosophy was identical with his early conceptions and that he could merely complement these through a positive philosophy, without reconstructing them, shows us that he had abandoned the standpoint of the identical subject-object. And in now criticizing Hegelian philosophy he saw himself obliged to raise the question of the priority of Being or consciousness. Time and again he did so – as it appears at first sight – with great lucidity and firmness. Writing, for instance, of the supreme antithesis and the supreme unity in philosophy, he arrived at the conclusion: 'But in this unity the priority is not on the side of thought; Being comes first and thought only second or subsequently.'[95] Or in another passage, more clearly still: 'For it is not because there is thought that there is Being, but there is thought because there is Being.'[96]

In what direction Schelling was led by these ideas we can study in closer detail shortly. At this point we must round out the underlying proposition now visible with another one which, although it reappears over and over again in the disintegration of Hegelianism, does not even approach a real answer, which is rather given first in historical materialism: we refer to the question of theory and praxis. The Hegelian system culminates in a perfect contemplation, in a conscious evocation of Aristotle's '*theoria*'; despite the fact that earlier, Hegel's method raised a whole series of important questions about the reciprocity of theory and praxis, especially in the relation of labour (the tool and so on) to teleology. Here, however, the age of the disintegration of Hegelianism moved between two false extremes. The idealist attempts to surmount the contemplative peak in the Hegelian system largely harked back to subjective idealism and such thinkers as Fichte (Bruno Bauer, Moses Hess); Feuerbach, on the contrary, guided by the ambition to go radically beyond subjectivism *and* Hegel's theology, succumbed to an 'intuitive

materialism'. Thus for all that this question occupied the centre of philosophical interest, not even anything like a satisfactory answer existed before the advent of dialectical materialism.

Considering his constantly strong flair for topical relevance, it is not surprising that Schelling also attacked the Hegelian philosophy of reason on the theory-praxis issue. Here, to be sure, it is already evident from the most general formulation what purpose lay behind the Schellingian proposition. In treating the difference between negative and positive philosophy, where he referred to a 'crisis in natural science' (which did in fact exist at this time), he took up the antithesis of theory and praxis, criticizing Hegel, and stated: 'Therefore rational science really leads beyond itself and drives towards revolution (*Umkehr*); but this itself cannot emanate from thought. It is rather a practical impulse which is needed; but there is nothing practical in thought, the concept is only contemplative and has only to do with the necessary, whereas we are dealing with something located outside of necessity, something willed-for.'

If we take these formulations in their straightforward abstract generality it is clear that Schelling had an inkling of the real philosophical crisis of his age. He did suspect that the key to resolving its problems could be found in the priority of Being over thought, in praxis as the criterion of theory. However – and this is characteristic of the origin of any historically influential irrationalist philosophy – Schelling only brought up these assertions, topical in their abstract generality and correctly pinpointing the real idealist flaws in Hegelian philosophy, in order to create a diversion from the step forward which contemporary philosophy was in the process of making. His aim was to neutralize the contemporary struggle for a new social content and for the birth of a dialectical philosophy adequately expressing it, to channel this struggle into an irrationalist mysticism with a seasonable look and fitting the social and political goal of reaction.

This becomes plain as soon as we take even a brief glance at the concretization of the aforestated views of Schelling. In undertaking to define more concretely the intrinsic nature of Being independent of and conditioning thought, he naturally raised the matter of the Kantian thing-in-itself. His critique of the Kantian shortcoming was of course far less fundamental than Hegel's, in spite of the latter's idealist limitations. Schelling stated: 'For this thing-in-itself is either a thing, i.e., it is a being (*ein Seiendes*), and then it is necessarily something perceptible as well and hence not *in itself* – in the Kantian sense –, for by "in itself" he understands precisely what lies outside all determinants of the understanding. Or this thing-in-itself is really In-itself, i.e., something unknowable and unimaginable, in which case it is not a *thing*.'[97] When, however, he continued this concretization and examination of his own views, he arrived at the duality of subjective-idealist agnosticism in the phenomenal world and pure irrationalism in the world of 'noumenon' which constitutes the essence of Schopenhauer's philosophy. (Since Schopenhauer himself was determined by Schellingian influences in this question to a large extent, we emphasize this affinity only as characterizing the irrationalist trend, not as a historical connection – which scarcely existed – between the later Schelling and Schopenhauer.) Schelling stated: 'We say: there may be a first principle, unknowable for itself, Being devoid of measure and definition, but there is no *thing* in itself; everything that is an object for us is already in itself affected by subjectivity, i.e., something which in itself is already, in part, subjectively established.'[98]

But this lapsing into a subjective idealism and also into a bottomless irrationalism was only the necessary result of Schelling's method, not of his conscious intention. On the contrary, as we have shown Schelling sought to efface the epistemologically and scientifically-oriented tendencies in the dialectical method, now in a state of growth crisis, not simply through a radical irrationalism, but through the 'higher rationality' of so-called positive philosophy, through a resolute

turn to theology that was purportedly grounded philosophically. When, therefore, the concrete transition from negative to positive philosophy is sought, the priority of Being over thought, previously stated so firmly, evanesces; or rather, the Being previously expressed abstractly and without definition is suddenly transformed, without any rationale or interposition, into the supra-rational God, a God set above all rationality. 'To be sure,' Schelling wrote,

> I have demonstrated through the whole of evolution to date: if there is or should be a rational Being, I must presuppose that (supreme) mind. But we are still given no *ground* for the Being of this mind. Rationality would only give a ground for the aforesaid if rational Being and reason itself were to be set absolutely. And this is not the case. For speaking in absolute terms, it is just as possible that there is *no* rationality and no rational Being as that there is a rationality and a rational Being. The ground or, more properly, the cause of rationality is therefore itself first given, rather, in that perfect mind. Rationality is not the cause of perfect mind; it is only because there is the latter that there is rationality. And this destroys the basis of all philosophical rationalism, i.e., any system which elevates rationality to a *principle*. Only a perfect mind is a rationality. But this very mind is without ground, simply because it Is.[99]

This 'Is', the later Schelling's version of Being, was represented by him as the ground of rationality and was even supposed to guarantee the rule of reason in the field assigned to it: '*Positive* philosophy proceeds from what is sheerly outside reason, but reason yields to this only in order to enter straight into its rights again.'[100] Thus according to Schelling's assertions, we have only the 'impression' that positive philosophy 'is a science contrary to reason'. But his own terminology already betrays his illogicality, his demagogic ambiguity: the absurd expression 'anti-rational science'

clearly shows how much Schelling wanted to reconcile basically incompatible elements in his positive philosophy, and to revive the insoluble internal contradictions of a scholastic theology with the highly advanced intellectual apparatus of idealist dialectics.

This irrevocable inner conflict stands out in the basic methodological ideas of his later philosophy. The whole famous division of negative and positive philosophy hinges on the fact that Schelling divides sharply and metaphysically the essence of things (their What) from the existence (their That). 'It is two quite different matters to know what a being (*ein Seiendes*) is, *quid sit*, and that it is, *quod sit*. The former – the answer to the question: *what* it is – affords me an insight into the *essence* of the thing, or has the effect that I understand the thing, have an understanding or a concept of it, or have *the thing itself* in my grasp. But the other answer, the insight *that* it is, affords me not merely a concept but something surpassing the mere concept, and that is existence.'[101] Clearly, by stressing that existence is not deducible from the concept, Schelling was once again rightly criticizing a weakness in Hegel's absolute idealism, albeit from a Right standpoint and hence with reactionary distortions. Also it made a strong impression – for that sector of the bourgeoisie that was deterred by Hegelian (and earlier Schellingian) philosophy because it was disposed to scorn empiricism and construe *a priori* – when Schelling countered *a priori* conclusions from pure reason in negative philosophy, with positive philosophy seen as the philosophy of experience. Here again, Schelling's working with so distorted a concept of experience that revelation itself could be presented as its authentic object stamps him as a precursor of modern irrationalism, in which – from Mach via Pragmatism to the trend dominant today – we find the same abuse of the term 'experience'.

But his aforestated critique of Hegel, since it started out from the Right, promptly turned into complete nonsense in that reason, concept, etc., were separated from all reality. Schelling even went so far as to challenge Hegel on the

following lines. He established that according to Hegel, reason was concerned with the In-themselves of things. But what, he asked, is this In-themselves? Is it that they exist, their Being? 'Not at all, for the In-itself, the essence, concept and nature of man, for example, would remain the same even if there were no men in the world, just as the In-itself of a geometric figure remains the same whether the figure exists or not.'[102] Here the invocation of a geometric figure's independence of its existence is pure sophistry, for every such figure is an intellectual image of essential spatial connections, just as the concept of a man is. Schelling's 'experience philosophy' would have faced an insoluble task if it had had to form a concept of man 'independently' of his existence. The flaw in Hegelian idealism was that while always acknowledging this connection from the practical, methodological angle, it acted from the systematic angle as though all concrete determinants were products of the concept's autonomous motivation. Here Schelling's Right-wing critique, instead of establishing the proper epistemological connection between reality and the intellectual image, as Feuerbach's Leftist critique did, repudiated all objectivity of the concept, the essence, and their basis in reality. It turned objective idealism into a subjectivist caricature and removed from it the unconscious and inconsistently still present relation to objective reality (with Hegel, essence as the condition of Being). Schelling's curious position is seen in the fact that his negative philosophy, while deliberately giving the impression of an idealist objectivism, became purely subjectivist-pragmatic without so much as trying at this point to confirm from the angle of the subject the totally non-objective categories thus obtained, as did the philosophical advocates of subjective idealism. But for that very reason, Schellingian existence (his That) was necessarily stripped of all content, all rationality. Essentially Schellingian existence was an abyss of nothingness, again laying grandiloquent claims to a higher, divine rationality.

So precisely this system's basic structure reflects Schelling's

shaky desire to unite the irreconcilable – the typical attitude of one caught between two periods as ideological leader of a movement confused in terms of social class. The close link with the feudal-aristocratic, Romanticizing-absolutist circle of Friedrich Wilhelm IV determined those consciously 'constructive features' of his system which made it a continuation of and conclusion to Restoration thinking and tendencies à la Baader. The bourgeois components of Prussian reaction, on the other hand, produced those subjective-idealist, radical-irrationalist undercurrents which made his philosophy, although quickly outmoded as a whole, an important precursor of modern irrationalism.

The same dichotomy is manifest in Schelling's concretization of praxis. We have shown how far Schelling criticized with some fairness, albeit from the Right, the contemplative character of Hegel's system. But for all its limited fairness as a pure critique, the standpoint that now emerged in Schelling was a severe reactionary regression compared with classical German philosophy. This, within its idealist confines, had also tried to elaborate the objectivity of human praxis in economic, historical and social terms. On the one hand, the decisive role of species in Hegel's philosophy was admittedly a sign that he failed to understand the real class structure of bourgeois society, mysticizing it and its development as the development of the species. But, on the other hand, there was still a tendency in Hegel to comprehend objective sociality philosophically as an essential and inseparable feature of human life and human praxis. The irrevocable antitheses we have traced in the later Schelling's cardinal tendencies also appear in the fact that, on the one hand, it was the aim of his philosophy to create a rationale for reactionary feudal-absolutist conservatism. (It is no accident that Friedrich Stahl, a philosopher of law and politician proceeding from Schelling's philosophy, became the ideological leader of Prussian conservatism in this phase.)

But on the other hand, it is likewise no accident that the praxis concept of Schelling's positive philosophy is radically

anti-social and confirms an individualism as extreme as we find somewhat later in Kierkegaard and then, in the imperialist period, in the existentialists. Schelling wrote:

> It has therefore been shown how the Ego's need for a God outside of rationality (not just in thought or in the idea of God) arises in a thoroughly practical fashion. This willing is not contingent, it is a willing by the mind which, in conformity with inner necessity and in its longing for its own liberation, cannot stop at that which is contained in thought. Just as this demand cannot have its starting-point in thought, it is not a postulate of practical reason either. It is not the latter, as Kant would have it, but only the individual that leads to God. For it is not the universal element in man which hankers after blessedness but the individual. If man is restricted (through conscience or practical reason) to gauging his relationship to other individuals according to their relationship in the world of ideas, only the universal, the rationality in him can be satisfied, not the individual man. The individual for himself can demand nothing but blessedness.[103]

Here too the aforestated central conflict between the basic ideas in Schelling's later philosophy finds clear expression, and here too it indicates its social foundation, the dichotomy in its class basis. This concludes our study of the irrationalist characteristics of Schelling's second period. It is not worth examining in detail the separate questions of his construction of mythology and revelation. As a whole, as a system-model this philosophy exerted, after all, only a very fleeting influence on irrationalism's development. On the other hand, it has been possible to observe so far that individual motives – directly or sometimes through manifold agencies – have become important components of the later irrationalism. Hence we deem it necessary to touch briefly on several more of these motives, without analysing in too much detail the place they occupy in Schelling's system.

It will suffice to note once again that Schelling, contrary to his assertions, abandoned the progressive trends of his youth on all important questions and indeed reversed those trends. But wherever he had already set out in a reactionary direction in his youth, he continued to pursue it and developed it further. That goes, above all, for the aristocratism in his epistemology. Earlier, it was artistic genius that provided the specious basis for this aristocratism; now it was Christian revealed wisdom which became the 'organon' of the chosen state of a few, marking this theory's open return to the magic world which, historically, formed its origin. Revelation, wrote Schelling, 'is neither a *primal* relationship nor a *universal* one extending to all men, nor an *eternal*, *lasting* one'.[104]

Schelling's view of time points even more noticeably towards the later irrationalism. We have dealt already with the universally reactionary trend in his theory of history, and above all the complete dropping of the idea of evolution entertained in his youth. Epistemologically, this change was to be now underpinned by repudiating the objectivity of time, by completely subjectifying it and by identifying it with the experience of time. Here, once again, it needs to be stated that an elaboration of the objectivity of space and time is among the most progressive elements in the development from Kant to Hegel (to which the young Schelling's philosophy belongs, at least in part) – within, to be sure, the limits inside which this could be performed idealistically.

Now if Schelling reverts to subjectifying time in his later works, there are two points that need to be stressed. Firstly, this subjectivity of time was no straightforward return to the Kantian *a priori*. It was, in its basic tendency – Schelling thrashed the problem out far less than Schopenhauer before him or Kierkegaard after him – a dissolving of all objectivity of time in its subjectively experienced state. Secondly, Schelling, in contrast to Schopenhauer who subjectified space and time equally thereby harking back from Kant to Berkeley, wanted to ensure for time a privileged place in the system of

philosophical knowledge. We must lay special emphasis on this tendency because here, again, Schelling became a precursor of the later irrationalism. For it was an essential part of this irrationalism that intuition, as the 'organon' for grasping true reality, inflated its own experiential nature and hence experienced time into the essence of this reality. And the vitalist trend in imperialist irrationalism reinforced the movement towards interpreting space as the principle of the lifeless, dead or ossified; experienced time as the principle of life, and towards placing the two principles in opposition. With Schelling, naturally, such vitalist motives appear only in isolation; for instance he occasionally states that negative philosophy 'will remain the preferred philosophy for *schooling*, positive philosophy the one for *life*'.[105] But in his case this was a passing phase. This renders the favoured position of subjectified experienced time all the more important with regard to the subjectifying of history and the denial of the objectivity of evolution. Schelling amplified: 'Now since we know of no real time other than that which is set with the here-and-now (*Jetztwelt*) . . . , we will be most certain of avoiding absurdity if we say: In reality ultimate time is the first that is set, and the earlier ones . . . only come after in that they only appear as *past* . . . in ultimate time, each according to its degree of precedence . . .'[106]

The immediate gist of this was to render the whole of pre-human evolution inessential, to deprive it of its objectivity. Its events, Schelling wrote, 'are without meaning or purpose if they do not relate to man'.[107] This interpretation of time, however, leaves its mark on his whole construction of history. Schelling interpreted history as a 'system of times' consisting of 'absolutely prehistorical, relatively prehistorical and historical time'. These times, according to Schelling, differ from one another qualitatively, corresponding to the state of completion or genesis in which mythology is found in each. Of the time of the first period Schelling wrote that it was 'no *true* succession of times'; it was 'sheerly *identical*, and therefore, at bottom, *timeless* time'. And from

this he inferred: 'Hence with it, not just one particular time but *time as a whole* is delimited, and it is itself the ultimate to which we can return in time. No further step can be taken beyond it except into the *preterhistorical*. It is a time, but one which is already no longer a time *in itself*, only in relation to what follows; *in itself* it is not a time because there is no true *Before* and *After* in it, because it is a kind of eternity . . .'[108]

This wild mysticism, the logical consequence of a fanatical denial of evolution in natural and human history, takes us to the core of Schelling's world-construction. For the philosophical 'proof' of revelation was, after all, supposed to form the climax to the system. Its aristocratic character we have just discussed. Schelling – who, as we have shown repeatedly, always wanted to underpin his irrationalist pronouncements with pseudo-rational arguments or ones purportedly 'in line with experience' – explained in that context that revelation must be proved by a *fact* independent of revelation. 'But this fact independent of revelation is nothing else than the appearance of mythology.'[109] We see therefore that the 'timeless time' of the genesis of mythology furnishes 'proof' of the truth of Christian revelation.

This mystical construction is of little interest as regards the history of philosophy; after 1848 it virtually ceased to play any part at all. A brief outline of it was needed here not so much to round off the later Schelling's characteristics, but rather because this underpinning of latter-day myth construction with the 'primeval' productiveness of an 'absolutely prehistorical' time became an important element in directly pre-fascist irrationalism (Klages, Heidegger) and in fascist irrationalism itself (Baeumler). How far Schellingian influences – direct or indirect ones – entered into the process is a secondary issue. It matters more that we should see how such myths and the theorems 'confirming' them are logically bound to spring up on the basis of a radical denial of evolution, and how the destruction of the reason active in history drives thought into the nothingness of a bottomless mysticism.

And it further matters that we should clearly see that no intellectual or aesthetic cultivation and no concretely extant knowledge offers a critical safeguard against this abyss of nonsense if the class struggle impels a particular social stratum, its ideologists and their public to deny and to contest the most important facts of social reality.

4. Schopenhauer

The road from Schelling to Schopenhauer appears to lead backwards; chronologically it certainly does. Schopenhauer's *chef d'oeuvre*, *The World as Will and Idea* (1819), after all, came out long before Schelling's late emergence. Historically, however, Schopenhauer's philosophy still signifies – all things considered – a more highly developed stage of irrationalism than Schelling's. The following studies are intended to justify this assertion.

Why is Schopenhauer's philosophy a more advanced stage of irrationalism than Schelling's? In fine: because it is in Schopenhauer that the purely bourgeois version of irrationalism crops up for the first time – not only within German philosophy but also on an international scale. With Schelling, it was possible to trace a whole set of ideas which acquired great importance for irrationalism's later forms. Directly, however, as regards his system-type in its entirety, his historical influence on the irrationalism of the imperialist age was by no means decisive. The influence of his later period died out after 1848; only Eduard von Hartmann and his school carried on, with marked modifications, part of what Schelling had begun. And when a reactionary 'renaissance' of classical German philosophy commenced in the imperialist period, Hegel's influence – Hegel in an appropriately irrationalist reinterpretation – blotted out that of Schelling. The young Schelling exerted an influence only inasmuch as he provided mental tools with which to bring Hegel closer to Romantic

thought. And when ultra-reactionary Romanticism became the heritage that most mattered in pre-fascism and in fascism, Schelling played a subordinate role beside Görres and Adam Müller.[110]

It was quite different where Schopenhauer's influence is concerned. As long as German reactionary philosophy pursued a restoration line, albeit one transformed in many respects in the 1840s, he was a wholly forgotten outsider. When the defeat of the 1848 revolution created in Germany a situation that was basically altered in ideological terms as well, Schopenhauer acquired instantaneous fame, dislodging Feuerbach as ideological leader of the bourgeois classes. Richard Wagner's development before and after 1848 is highly typical.

In various writings Engels gives a precise description of this German transformation resulting from the suppression of the 1848 revolution. He wrote:

> The monarchy that had been slowly rotting away since 1840 had had as its basic determinant the struggle between nobility and bourgeoisie, in which it preserved a balance; the moment that it was no longer a case of protecting the nobility against the inroads of the bourgeoisie but of protecting all classes of proprietors against the inroads of the working class, the old absolute monarchy had to go over completely to the political form specially devised for this purpose: *Bonapartist monarchy*. I have already examined elsewhere this Prussian transition to Bonapartism . . . What I did not need to stress then, but is now very important, is that this transition was the *greatest advance* that Prussia made in 1848; such was the extent to which Prussia had lagged behind modern developments. It was still a semi-feudal state, and Bonapartism is at all events a modern form of government whose precondition is the elimination of feudalism. The Prussians had therefore to make up their minds to clear away their many feudal remnants and to sacrifice the Junker class as such. Naturally this occurred

> in the mildest of forms and according to the old saying: Gently does it! . . . The cause remained, and was simply translated from the feudal to the bourgeois dialect . . . Thus it was the peculiar destiny of Prussia, at the end of this century, to complete in the agreeable form of Bonapartism the bourgeois revolution it had initiated in 1808-13 and taken a stage further in 1848 . . . The abolition of feudalism, put in positive terms, meant the establishing of bourgeois conditions. Legislation took on a bourgeois character to the same extent as the aristocratic privileges lapsed. And here we reach the core of the German bourgeoisie's relationship to the government. We saw that the government was *forced* to introduce these slow and petty reforms. But it presented each of these small concessions to the bourgeois as a *sacrifice* made to his class, a concession wrung with difficulty from the Crown for which they, the bourgeoisie, had now to concede something in return to the government . . . The bourgeoisie purchased its gradual social emancipation at the price of the prompt renunciation of political power of its own. Naturally the main reason inducing the bourgeoisie to accept such a bargain was not fear of the government but fear of the proletariat.[111]

Here Engels is characterizing not only the embourgeoisement of Germany after 1848 but also the crucial specific features of that process: the using of the German bourgeoisie's renunciation, Germany's capitalization and the constantly growing prominence of capitalist production in Germany to attain to political power. Capitalist production, bourgeois life-styles in a country which continued to be ruled by the Hohenzollerns and the Prussian Junkers: that is the quintessence of the change occasioned by the quelling of democratic revolution. And since it was not only the bourgeoisie itself which adopted this course but also – with few and, we may state, ever-fewer exceptions – the bourgeois intellectuals, it is not surprising that the ideological consequences of this change were

necessarily very far-reaching.

I have dealt in detail elsewhere with the change in German literary tendencies.[112] Philosophically, it reflected the leading part which Schopenhauerian philosophy played among the German bourgeois intelligentsia, especially its so-called élite; a pre-eminence challenged partly by the vulgarizing representatives of the old materialism (Büchner, Moleschott, etc.) and partly, later on, by neo-Kantianism. The philosophically decisive trends of the pre-revolutionary age, such as Hegelianism, Feuerbach and – on the Right – Schelling, fell increasingly into oblivion.

In the process Schopenhauer's emergence took on more and more of an international character. For this too there were social reasons. Much as the development of the most important European nations differed from Germany's, there still existed in this very respect, during this period, related features of some importance. Not for nothing did Engels call this phase of the Prussian development a Bonapartist one: the position of the French bourgeoisie and bourgeois intellectuals after June 1848 and their surrender to Napoleon III created a situation which displays a set of related features, for all the natural differences obtaining. (To be sure, the French intellectuals' capitulation to Napoleon III was far less unconditional than that of the Germans to the Hohenzollerns, exhibiting far more serious examples of at least an ideological opposition.) The founding of Italian national unity, again 'from above' (taking into account once more the manifold differences), the forms of embourgeoisement in the Austro-Hungarian monarchy, indeed even the 'Victorian era' in England resulting from the defeat of the Chartists – all this indicates that, for all its specific national peculiarities, the German development after 1848 still only represents an extreme instance of what was then a universally European development in bourgeois society. Engels draw attention to these common features when analysing the bourgeoisie's stance to questions of State power under the threat of the working class.[113]

That gives us the social basis for the international influence of Schopenhauerian philosophy: the social basis for an irrationalism founded in the social Being of the bourgeoisie. In this second major crisis of bourgeois society German philosophy assumed the leading role internationally, just as it had done in the first major crisis at the time of the French Revolution and afterwards. But there was an immense difference. Then, the forward-looking dialectical problems of the epoch were formulated in German philosophy, and chiefly by Hegel. As we have noted, the corresponding irrationalist backlash with Schelling, Baader and the Romantics was naturally part and parcel of this. And here we can also say that German philosophy at that time was the leading philosophy even in a reactionary sense, in that it captured intellectually certain basic elements of the later irrationalism, whereas most of the counter-revolutionary French and English ideologists, from Burke to Bonald and de Maistre, expressed the legitimist-reactionary content essentially in old concepts. (There were, of course, precursors of irrationalism as well, such as Maine de Biran in France and Coleridge in England.) German philosophy of this period gained a really international significance, however, through its progressive dialectical evolutionist tendencies. Not for nothing did Cuvier tax his evolutionist adversaries with trying to introduce into science the 'mystical' trends of German natural philosophy.

The second crisis, around and after 1848, has an essentially different character. Admittedly, it was just at this time that there arose the most towering peak of German thought, the dialectical and historical materialism of Marx and Engels. But this was a departure from the bourgeois foundation; it marked the final close of the progressive era of bourgeois thought, the working out of the problems of mechanical materialism and idealist dialectics. Bourgeois philosophy's settlement with this lethal instrument, its attempts to go on creating reactionary types of irrationalism on the new ontological basis, and in the new ideological situation, belong to a

later period. Granted, the philosophy of the later Schelling and still more that of Kierkegaard, as we shall see shortly, was closely linked to the dissolution of Hegelianism, but Kierkegaard's international influence likewise belongs in the imperialist age. Like Schopenhauer's and Nietzsche's philosophy, Kierkegaard's is a kind of anticipation of decadent trends which later became universal. And let us remark here that it was not until Nietzsche that bourgeois irrationalism began its real defensive struggle against the ideas of socialism.

Schopenhauer wrote his most important books at a time when Hegelian philosophy was still enjoying its growth and dominance. His achievement in the history of irrationalism anticipated developments insofar as tendencies found expression in his work which, because of the socio-historical situation just depicted, only became universally dominant after the defeat of the 1848 revolution. Thus it is with Schopenhauer that German philosophy starts to play its fateful role as the ideological leader of reactionary extremism.

Naturally such an ability to anticipate events indicates a certain intellectual stature. And without doubt Schopenhauer, Kierkegaard and Nietzsche possessed considerable philosophical gifts: for instance a high capacity for abstraction, and not in a formalistic sense, but a flair for conceptualizing living phenomena, for building a mental bridge between immediate life and the most abstract idea and taking with philosophic seriousness phenomena of Being which only existed in embryo, as trends which had scarcely begun at the time and did not become the universal symptoms of an era until decades later. To be sure – and this distinguishes Schopenhauer, Kierkegaard and Nietzsche from the truly great philosophers – the vital movement to which they devoted themselves as thinkers, and whose future sweeping power they anticipated, was the rise of bourgeois reaction. For its advent and its growth, as for its crucial symptoms, they had a decided flair, the faculty of intellectual clairvoyance and anticipatory abstraction.

If we have called Schopenhauer the first irrationalist

standing on a purely bourgeois foundation, it is not too difficult to perceive the associated personal traits in his social being. His biography distinguishes him quite sharply from all his German predecessors and contemporaries. He was a '*grand bourgeois*' in contrast to the others' petty-bourgeois status, which in Fichte's case was even semi-proletarian. Accordingly Schopenhauer did not experience the normal straits of petty-bourgeois German intellectuals (private tutoring, etc.) but spent a large part of his youth on journeys all over Europe. After a brief transitional period as a business trainee he lived a peaceful existence on private means, an existence in which even his university link – the teaching post in Berlin – played a merely episodic role.

Thus he was the first major instance in Germany of a writer with private means, a breed which had become important to the bourgeois literature of capitalistically advanced countries long before. (It is significant that Kierkegaard and Nietzsche also enjoyed an independence stemming from a private income which much resembled Schopenhauer's.) This material freedom from all daily cares provided the basis of Schopenhauer's independence not only from semi-feudal, State-determined conditions of existence (a university career, etc.) but also from the intellectual movements connected with them. Thus it was possible for him to occupy a stubbornly personal position on all questions without having to make any sacrifices. In this respect he became a model for Germany's later 'rebel' bourgeois intellectuals. Nietzsche said of him: 'What he *taught* is accomplished;/What he *lived* will stand:/Just look at him –/He was a slave to no one!'

Naturally this independence was an illusion, and one typical of the bourgeois of private means. As a highly practical person with a bourgeois education, Schopenhauer knew perfectly well that his intellectual existence depended on the stability and augmentation of his investments, for which he waged a tough and shrewd battle all his life with his family, the administrators of his fortune, and so on. In these 'practical' features of his character and conduct he shows a certain

affinity with, for instance, important figures of the Enlightenment (e.g., Voltaire). This we must briefly examine because – as we shall see – it also extended to intellectual matters and is characteristic of Schopenhauer's way of thinking. Voltaire too battled unceasingly to attain a complete independence, in his case from feudal and courtly patronage. He did so, however, not only on behalf of his individual productive work but so as to be able to make a stand as an independent intellectual force against feudal absolutism in respect of all the important topical issues (the Calas case, etc.). With Schopenhauer we find not the slightest sign of such a relation to public life. His 'independence' was that of the self-willed, sheerly egotistic eccentric who uses it to retire from public life completely and to free himself of all obligations existing towards it. Schopenhauer's striving for independence thus bears only a formal resemblance to Voltaire's and has nothing in common with it intrinsically, not to mention the heroic struggles which Diderot or Lessing, say, waged with contemporary reactionary powers for their intellectual independence and freedom to serve social progress.

We needed to sketch in these biographical features because they rapidly lead us to the heart of Schopenhauer's specific type of bourgeois existence. Schopenhauer expressed very lucidly what he understood by independence: 'For "I thank God every morning that I do not need to concern myself with the Roman Empire" has always been my motto,' he said, scornfully referring to Hegel's adulation of the State as the worst philistinism, whereby men are consumed in State service. 'According to this outlook the official and the human being were one and the same. It was a downright apotheosis of philistinism.'[114]

Undoubtedly Schopenhauer's scornful criticism caught the really weak aspects of Hegelian philosophy of right and ethics. Hegel's progressive ideal of the *citoyen* was to be embodied in the wretched German reality, and because of the way his system was constructed, this incorporation was bound to mean a marked adjustment to the wretched

condition of contemporary Prussian society. So such an equating of State citizenship and State officialdom did indeed give expression to that philistinism from which, to quote Engels, not even the greatest Germans, including Goethe and Hegel, succeeded in escaping.

So far, therefore, this Schopenhauerian critique of Hegel finds its target. But what of its author's independence – supposedly a state rising above philistinism? Let us mention only in passing that the *Faust* quotation which Schopenhauer includes in his political credo appears in Goethe's original context as a statement characteristic of precisely the petty bourgeoisie. More important is the consideration that Schopenhauer's high-minded withdrawal from all politics was only how he behaved in normal times, when State machinery automatically safeguarded the fortunes and incomes of private investors against any possible attack. But there were times – and Schopenhauer experienced them in 1848 – when this automatic protection of fortunes was thrown in question or at least – as then, in Germany – appeared to be. At such moments Schopenhauer's aloof 'independence' vanished, and our philosopher made haste to hand his opera-glasses to a Prussian officer for a better view of the rioters at whom he was shooting. And it was assuredly with memories of this major scare in his life that he wrote a will making his universal heir 'the fund set up in Berlin to support Prussian soldiers invalided in the riots and insurrections of the years 1848 and 1849 in the name of maintaining and establishing law and order in Germany, as also the surviving relatives of those who fell in those struggles'.[115] Thomas Mann, a great admirer of Schopenhauer from his youth onwards, calls the motto we have quoted 'a true philistinism and sluggishness, a slogan whose adoption by an intellectual wrestler like Schopenhauer is hardly comprehensible'.[116]

Here Thomas Mann was mistaken. With Schopenhauer, certainly, this attitude manifests itself in a grotesque and scurrilous form, but in its social essence it was typical of

the bourgeois intelligentsia; indeed we may say that it becomes increasingly typical as capitalism develops. Thomas Mann himself – speaking of the older Richard Wagner, who was decisively influenced by Schopenhauer ideologically – calls this attitude *machtgeschützte Innerlichkeit* ('a passive inner state protected by power').[117] This accurately characterized the new decadent form of bourgeois individualism as opposed to the economic, political and cultural individualism of the period of bourgeois ascendancy. The latter form, in line with the structure of bourgeois society at that time, was the philosophy of a personal activity ultimately calculated, just by dint of its personal nature, to promote the social aims and ends of the bourgeois class. From Machiavelli and Rabelais via the economic theories of Adam Smith and Ricardo to Hegel's *List der Vernunft*, bourgeois intellectual edifices express such an individualism in a historically conditioned variety of forms. Not before Schopenhauer is the individuum inflated into an absolute end in itself. The individual's activity now becomes detached from its social basis, turning purely inwards and cultivating one's own, private peculiarities and wishes as absolute values. To be sure, as was evident in Schopenhauer in a most drastic form, this self-sufficiency exists only in the decadently bourgeois individual's imagination. The puffing up into an end in itself of purportedly self-sufficient individuality cannot alter, let alone annul a single social commitment. And in a critical case, such as Schopenhauer's in 1848, we find that this aloof self-sufficiency of the private person is only a decadently heightened version of normal capitalist egotism. Any capitalist, any man of private means would have behaved like Schopenhauer – only without adding to this axiomatic defence of one's own capital a subtly constructed philosophical system.

That is by no means to say that such a system – seen also from the social angle – is immaterial; on the contrary. The farther the bourgeoisie's decadent tendencies go, the less it puts up a struggle against the relics of feudalism, and the stronger its alliance with the reactionary powers becomes, the

greater will be the importance of thinkers of Schopenhauer's ilk to the cultivation of bourgeois decadence, even when or rather precisely when the bourgeoisie itself has only this aforementioned basis of Being in common with such thinkers; precisely when bourgeois intellectuals – within the ideological scope this life-basis affords – view the status quo in an extremely critical light. For decadent tendencies necessarily entail the incipient shaking of the faith shown by the bourgeoisie's retainers in their own social system, and even the faith of many actual members of the class. Philosophy (along with literature, etc.) will now have the objectively social class-task of plugging the resulting gaps or indeed of bridging the newly apparent gulfs ideologically. This is the task of that body of writing which Marx liked to term the apologetics of capitalism.[118] In general these tendencies became dominant after the quelling of the 1848 revolution in Germany, although of course they first set in earlier. Their fundamental character finds expression in their attempts to eliminate intellectually the capitalist system's increasingly salient contradictions by 'proving' all that is contradictory, bad and horrible about capitalism to be mere illusion or a temporary, removable surface blemish.

Schopenhauer's originality lies in the fact that at a time when this ordinary form of apologetics had not yet even developed fully, let alone become the leading trend in bourgeois thinking, he had already found the later, higher form of capitalist apologetics: *indirect apologetics*.

How do we formulate its essence in a nutshell? Whereas direct apologetics was at paints to fudge the contradictions in the capitalist system, to refute them with sophistry and to be rid of them, indirect apologetics proceeded from these very contradictions, acknowledging their existence and their irrefutability as facts, while nonetheless putting an interpretation on them which helped to confirm capitalism. Whereas direct apologetics was at pains to depict capitalism as the best of all orders, as the last, outstanding peak in mankind's evolution, indirect apologetics crudely elaborated the bad

sides, the atrocities of capitalism, but explained them as attributes not of capitalism but of all human existence and existence in general. From this it necessarily follows that a struggle against these atrocities not only appears doomed from the start but signifies an absurdity, viz., a self-dissolution of the essentially human.

This brings us to the centre of Schopenhauer's philosophy, his pessimism. It was directly through his pessimism that Schopenhauer became the leading thinker of the second half of the nineteenth century. Through it he founded the new type of apologetics. To be sure, he did no more than lay the foundations. Later, and particularly when dealing with Nietzsche, we shall see that the Schopenhauerian form of indirect apologetics represents only the initial stage of this philosophical genre. The chief reason for this was that its conclusion – the abstention from all social activity (seen as senseless) and certainly from any effort to change society – sufficed only to answer the needs of the pre-imperialist bourgeoisie; it sufficed only during a period when, because of the universal economic boom, this rejection of political activity matched the position of the class struggles and the needs of the ruling class. The social task which reactionary philosophy was set in the imperialist period went further, although this trend was far from dying out altogether: now the task was to mobilize active support for imperialism. In this direction Nietzsche surpassed Schopenhauer, although, as an indirect apologist at a riper stage, he remained his pupil and continuation in the methodological sense.

So pessimism means primarily a philosophical rationale of the absurdity of all political activity. That was the social function of this stage in indirect apologetics. In order to reach this conclusion, the chief necessity is to devalue society and history philosophically. If there is an evolution in nature, and if this evolution climaxes in man and his culture (and therefore, in society), it will necessarily follow that the meaning of even the most individual action and the most individual conduct must be somehow connected with this

evolution of the human race. However idealistically distorted this link may be, and however much it may concentrate upon purely ideological activities (thinking, art), meaningful action will still be inseparably linked with man's social and historical life (and, through the medium of the latter, with some kind of concept of progress). These connections can be found, for example, in Schiller's philosophy of art, and we shall see how Schopenhauer's high estimation of the aesthetic and philosophic attitude is diametrically opposed to Schiller's and Goethe's.

So if action is devalued, a world-outlook is bound to arise in which all historicity (and with it, all progress and evolution) is diminished to an illusion and deception; in which society is depicted as a superficiality interfering with the essence and obscuring knowledge of it instead of giving expression to it – an illusion in the sense of delusion. Only when the new irrationalism is able to carry out this destruction will its pessimism be able to have the effect, and achieve the social task on the bourgeoisie's behalf, which Schopenhauer's philosophy did in fact accomplish in the second half of the nineteenth century.

But we have not yet fully circumscribed the function of Schopenhauerian pessimism. Optimism and pessimism in general are among the vaguest expressions in traditional philosophical terminology, and one cannot analyse them concretely at all without discovering the class background behind the affirmation or denial of a *particular* development (however strong the cosmic mystification that may accompany it – as in the case of Schopenhauer). Without some such concretization, optimism will be equated with embellishing the facts and pessimism with a stop-at-nothing disclosure of the dark sides of reality, as so often occurs in bourgeois historical accounts after Schopenhauer. The French economic historian Charles Gide, for instance, calls the classic author of bourgeois political economy, Ricardo, a pessimist merely because he freely investigates capitalism in its negative aspects as well, although there is not a trace of pessimism in

Ricardo's perspective. Or again, Schopenhauer himself regarded Voltaire as an ally because he ridiculed Leibniz's rose-tinted conception of the 'best of all possible worlds' with devastating irony, although in respect of his perspective of social evolution Voltaire was anything but a pessimist.

It is evident that Schopenhauerian pessimism was an ideological reflection of the restoration age. The French Revolution, the Napoleonic era and the wars of liberation were past, and for decades the whole Western world had been in the throes of constant upheaval, but in the end everything remained as before, at least on the directly visible face of things. During and after these major events the German bourgeoisie lived in the same lack of class consciousness as before. Anyone lacking a perspective of human evolution — apart from that wrested from this social misery — was easily convinced that all historical endeavours were fruitless, especially if one approached the question from the bourgeois individual's standpoint and made the crux of it the question: how does all this affect my personal life? And whereas at the time of the French Revolution the international outlook could offer a perspective pointing far beyond the German *Misere*, the futility of a historical transformation of human life was now presented as a universal destiny. So whereas Herder and Forster, Hölderlin and Hegel managed to obtain a guideline for appraising Germany — possibly condemnatory but offering perspectives — from the international outlook, Schopenhauer's cosmopolitan purview engendered a philosophical generalizing of the German plight: its projection into the cosmic realm was an important basic part of his pessimism. (It is no anachronism to see in Schopenhauer, in contrast to German classicism's world citizens, a first forerunner of decadent cosmopolitanism.)

The other component part of pessimism, whose personal class roots we have already located, is bourgeois-individualistic egotism. It is self-evident and common knowledge that there can be no bourgeois ideology in which this egotism does not play an important role. However, as long as the bourgeoisie

was fighting feudalism and absolute monarchy as a revolutionary class, this egotism always appeared in close albeit problematic association with the progressive aims which the class entertained of reforming society. All bourgeois ideologists faced the problem of how to reconcile this egotism, which – in their inability to fathom the historically transitory character of bourgeois society – they viewed as a general anthropological attribute, with social life and the progress of society as a whole. Here we cannot undertake to give even a rough sketch of the various views emerging, from Mandeville's ironic critique of society to the dualism of Adam Smith's economics and ethics, the Enlightenment's 'rational egotism', Kant's *ungesellige Geselligkeit* ('Unsocial Sociality') and Hegel's *List der Vernunft*. Here it suffices to establish this general connection between them.

To be sure, a certain change began to occur in England after the so-styled Glorious Revolution of 1688: this era's theoreticians were already starting to work out a code of ethics for the victorious bourgeois, the master of bourgeois society, and to glorify bourgeois forms of life from the standpoint of their stabilization. And since, by virtue of the character of the 'Glorious Revolution', this was a compromise with the remnants of feudalism, there now came about a weakening of the former revolutionary impulse and ruthless criticism of society inasmuch as the accent began to shift from the social nature of action towards the bourgeois individual's contented self-sufficiency as a private person.

No wonder this provided Schopenhauer with certain pegs for his views. It is notable in the context of the history of philosophy in general, and proof of the purely bourgeois nature of his philosophy that he, in contrast to the restoration period's Romantic thinkers – who to a man were sharply opposed to the whole Enlightenment, was generally in sympathy with the Enlightenment minds. In appearance this line runs parallel with that of German classicism, which provided in Goethe and Hegel a continuation, a dialectical extension of Enlightenment tendencies. But this is only

apparently so. For Schopenhauer did not want to cultivate the Enlightenment's forward-looking tendencies, i.e., to continue the Enlightenment struggle to abolish the relics of feudalism under the post-revolutionary period's new conditions. Instead he sought support from the Enlightenment thinkers for the ultra-radical philosophical formulation of the bourgeois individual's self-sufficiency. Thus when he seemingly coincides with certain Enlightenment tendencies and singles out its representatives for praise in contrast to Romantic thinkers, this constitutes a reactionary distortion of Enlightenment tendencies, including the aforesaid tendencies found in eighteenth-century England. Later we shall also find the same distortion with Nietzsche, in the form of his sympathy with such French moralists as La Rochefoucauld and even Voltaire, a distortion equally expressing a falsification of those Enlightenment thinkers' true tendencies, albeit at a more highly advanced stage of reaction.

To be sure – and this is another expression of Schopenhauer's indirect apologetics – he represents ordinary bourgeois egotism as morally negative, but not as socially negative and therefore not as an attribute and tendency to be changed in socio-ethical terms. With Schopenhauer, ordinary bourgeois egotism is an unalterable, cosmic attribute of 'man' in general; it is, moreover, the unalterable cosmic attribute of each existence. From his epistemology and world-view, with whose foundations we shall concern ourselves later from the theoretical angle, Schopenhauer derived the cosmic necessity of the capitalist type of ruthless egotism as follows:

> Hence each person wants everything for himself, wants to possess or at least to control everything, and would like to stamp out everything which offers resistance. In addition, where percipient beings are concerned, the individual is the transmitter of the percipient subject and the latter the world's transmitter; i.e., the whole of nature outside of him, and hence all other individuals as well, exists only in his idea, and he is always only conscious of it as his idea,

> hence only immediately and as something which is independent of his own essence and existence; since the world necessarily escapes him along with his consciousness, i.e., its being and non-being become synonymous and indistinguishable . . . nature which is everywhere veracious at all times herself provides him with this knowledge with simple and immediate certainty, in the raw and independently of all reflection. The two necessary conditions we have stated will now explain why each individual, although disappearing completely in the unbounded world and reduced to nought, still makes himself the centre of the world and considers his own existence and welfare before all else; indeed is willing, from the natural standpoint, to sacrifice everything else to these and to destroy the world just so as to preserve his own self, that drop in the ocean, a little longer. This frame of mind is the *egotism* essential to every thing that is found in nature.[119]

It now appears as if Schopenhauerian morality transcends this egotism and negates it. But with Schopenhauer, the dismissal of conventional, cosmically inflated bourgeois egotism is similarly enacted in the individual spiritually isolated from society, and it even marks a heightening of this isolation. From aesthetic enjoyment to saintly asceticism, the individual's pure self-sufficiency is celebrated more and more in Schopenhauer's professed surmounting of egotism as the only exemplary moral attitude. To be sure, this 'elevated' egotism was meant to appear, in sharp contrast to ordinary egotism, as a turning away from illusion and the 'veil of *maya*' (i.e., the life of society) in which conventional egotism is bogged down. It is presented as a sympathy with all created things resulting from the insight that individuation is only an illusion, and one that conceals the unity of all existence.

This contrast which Schopenhauer draws between two types of egotism is one of the subtlest features of his indirect apologetics. Firstly, he bestows on this attitude the sanction

of aristocratic perspicacity as opposed to the plebeian's blind attachment to the world of phenomena. Secondly, this elevation above ordinary egotism entails no obligations on account of its 'sublime', mystico-cosmic generality: it discredits social obligations and replaces them with empty emotional promptings, sentimentalities which may on occasion be reconciled with the greatest crimes against society. In the excellent Soviet film *Tchapayev*, the bestially cruel counter-revolutionary General keeps a canary, feels cosmically united with it – in the true spirit of Schopenhauer – and plays Beethoven sonatas in his leisure time, thus fulfilling all the 'sublime' commandments of Schopenhauerian morality. Schopenhauer's own behaviour, which we have discussed already, also belongs in this category.

To be sure, the philosopher clears himself in advance of any accusation that might be levelled against him in this respect. Once again he is a very modern moral reformer in that he avows that the morality which he himself has propounded and argued philosophically places no obligation on himself. 'In general it is a strange thing to ask of a moralist that he should commend no virtue unless he possesses it himself.'[120] This guarantees the decadent bourgeois intelligentsia the maximum of spiritual and moral ease: it has at its disposal a morality liberating it from all social duties and elevating it to a sublime height above the blind, uncomprehending riff-raff, but a morality whose very founder exempts the intelligentsia from obeying it (where it becomes difficult or even just inconvenient). Schopenhauer – and in this he was acting quite consistently – arranged his whole way of life with this convenience in mind.

We now have in outline an important example, a long-effective model, of bourgeois ethics in the period of decline. Admittedly, what Schopenhauer initiated in this dualistic and undemanding form his successors, and chiefly Nietzsche, carried on with a view to liberating through ethics all men's bad, anti-social and anti-human instincts, giving them a moral sanction and proclaiming them to be, if not always

commandments, then at least the prescribed 'fate' of 'man', i.e., of the bourgeois citizen and bourgeois intellectual of the imperialist age.

Here we see quite plainly the resemblance and the difference between Schopenhauer and the irrationalist philosophy of the restoration era. Both sought to educate their followers in a social passivity. The latter, however, stigmatized all revolutionary upheavals as inorganic, merely 'fabricated' and diabolical by glorifying as the will of God the 'organic growth' of society, i.e., the exclusive justification of the feudal-absolutist order. Schopenhauer, on the other hand, presents the irrationalism of society and history as a pure, naked absurdity, and the endeavour to participate in the life of society or even to change it as so lacking in insight with regard to the essence of the world as to verge on a criminal act. Schopenhauer, therefore, defends the established order as firmly as feudal or semi-feudal irrationalism defended the restoration, but with a totally contrary, bourgeois method of indirect apologetics. Whereas the restoration ideologists defended the concrete feudal-absolutist social order of their day, Schopenhauer's philosophy was an ideological safeguard for *any* existing social order capable of effectively defending bourgeois private property.

Thus Schopenhauer's bourgeois nature is expressed in just the fact that for him – given adequate protection of private property – the political character of the ruling system is totally irrelevant. In the commentaries he wrote to his main work in *Parerga and Paralipomena*, Schopenhauer voices this standpoint even more clearly than in the main work.

> Everywhere and always there has been much dissatisfaction with governments, laws and public institutions; but this is largely so only because we are always ready to tax these with misery inseparably attached to human existence itself since the latter is, to speak in mythical terms, the curse laid on Adam and his entire race with him. Never, though, has that false impression been promoted with

> more hypocrisy and audacity than by the demagogues of *Jetztzeit* (the 'now-time' movement). For these, being enemies of Christianity, are optimists: the world is their 'end in itself', and hence in itself, i.e., according to its natural disposition, it is quite excellently arranged, a proper haven of happiness. The colossal evils of the world that cry out against this view these demagogues ascribe entirely to governments: if, they argue, our governments were to do as they are supposed to, we would have a Heaven on Earth. That is to say, everyone would be able to eat his fill, to drink, to propagate himself and to expire without sweat and tears: for this is a paraphrase of their 'end in itself' and the goal of the 'unending progress of mankind' which they tirelessly proclaim in pompous catchphrases.[121]

It is clear from these statements wherein the social significance and function of Schopenhauer's pessimism lies, and why he stigmatized optimism in his main work as intellectually and morally wicked. There he writes: 'Here, by the way, I cannot refrain from stating that *optimism*, if not the thoughtless babble of men who have nothing but words in their thick skulls, seems to me not only an absurd but also a downright *ruthless* way of thinking, a bitter mockery of mankind's untold sufferings.'[122]

The resemblance and (class-based) difference we have described between Schopenhauer and irrationalist restoration philosophy is most clearly expressed in the stance which each adopted to the religious question. We have already examined this problem in dealing with Schelling. As we have seen, the general philosophical struggle in Germany was not between materialist atheism and religion; the extremely shaky and irresolute tendency towards eliminating religious elements from the philosophical world-picture concentrated upon the problem of pantheism. On the one hand this could never really overcome the religious outlook on account of its idealist foundation. On the other hand, its tendency to

explain the world from its own premises evoked – as we have also noted – the resistance of philosophical reaction, and it was repeatedly denounced as atheism. Not until the dissolution of Hegelianism did Feuerbach, as has been likewise noted, come forward with a Left critique of pantheism by taking apart the religio-theistic restrictedness of classical German philosophy from the standpoint of an atheistic materialism.

Schopenhauer perceived very clearly the inadequacy and inconsistency of all pantheism: 'In the main my only objection to pantheism is that it does not tell us anything. To call the world God is not to explain it but only to enrich the language with a superfluous synonym for the word "world". It is all the same whether you say "the world is God" or "the world is the world".' But he also saw the other side of the coin, pantheism's connection with theistic religion. In this context he had this to add to the remarks just quoted: 'For only insofar as we proceed from a God, thus taking God for granted and enjoying familiarity with God, can we finally reach the point of identifying him with the world, which we do really in order to oust God in a respectable manner.'[123]

Here Schopenhauer apparently approaches Feuerbach's critique of Spinoza and classical German philosophy; only apparently, though. For in the latter, Spinoza especially, pantheism was in its principal tendency really only a 'polite atheism'. Granted, Schopenhauer likewise avowed allegiance to atheism, but again he gave it a distinctive accent. It does not mean the destruction of religion and the religious life, as for the great materialists of the seventeenth and eighteenth centuries, and it does not even show an unconscious striving in this direction, as with the progressive idealist pantheists. It was meant, on the contrary, to serve as a substitute for religion, to create a new – atheistic – religion for those who had lost their old religious faith as a result of social evolution and progress in the knowledge of nature.

Accordingly, Schopenhauer's atheism not only failed to bear any relation to materialism. The substance of it, on the

contrary, was a most bitter struggle against materialism, a diversion of the incipient anti-religious trends away from materialist atheism and their redirecting towards a religious life without God, a religious atheism. Schopenhauer wrote on this subject:

> But do the gentlemen know what times we are living in? – An epoch has commenced that has long been foretold: the Church is rocking, rocking so heavily that it is doubtful whether it can regain its balance: for faith has gone missing . . . The number of those whom a certain degree and breadth of knowledge has rendered incapable of faith has swelled considerably. This attests to the universal dissemination of coarse rationalism, whose bulldog features are growing more and more widespread. It is quite calmly preparing to measure with its tailor's yardstick the profound mysteries of Christianity over which the centuries have brooded and quarrelled, and imagines itself to be marvellously clever. Above all the central Christian dogma, the doctrine of original sin, has become a risible plaything for the level-headed rationalists; that is because they think that nothing is clearer and surer than that each man's existence begins at his birth, hence he cannot possibly have entered the world in a state of guilt. How acute of them! – And just as wolves will start to prowl when poverty and neglect take hold of a village, so an ever-lurking materialism will raise its head in these conditions and assume control along with its companion, bestiality (which certain people call humanism).[124]

A notable thing about these statements in the negative sense is that they accept the religious crisis as a fact, yet contain a sharp polemic exclusively attacking 'coarse rationalism' and materialism. And in a positive respect we should note that here, as in many other key passages in his philosophy, Schopenhauer sides with the Christian dogma of original sin. Thus it is only logical of him repeatedly to stress the novelty

and timely nature, in principle, of his religious atheism. He characterized the pre-Kantian situation thus: 'Up to *Kant* there existed a real dilemma between materialism and theism, i.e., between the supposition that blind chance brought the world into being or an intelligence ordering it from outside, according to ends and concepts, *neque debatur tertium*. Hence atheism and materialism were the same!' Now Kant, he argues, prompted the following change: 'But the validity of that disjunctive major term in the proposition, that dilemma between materialism and theism, rests on the hypothesis that the world presented to us is that of things-in-themselves, and that consequently there is no other order of things than the empirical order . . . Thus Kant, in removing the basis of theism through his important distinction between phenomenon and thing, opened up an avenue to quite different and more profound accounts of existence.'[125] So Kant was the means of opening up the way out of this dilemma, the path to Schopenhauer's religious atheism, which had materialism as its principal target and adopted a great deal from Christian ethics, remodelling its arguments.

From this it is already clearly discernible where the essence of Schopenhauer's religious atheism is located: it is a kind of religious substitute for those no longer able to believe in the dogmatic religions. It offers them a world-view matching scientific requirements on the one hand and 'metaphysical' needs on the other, a world-view broadly accommodating the lingering emotional attachment to religious or semi-religious prejudices. Whereas pantheism, albeit idealistically entangled, with its world-immanence and – in classical German philosophy – its theory of evolution, led objectively away from the religious world-views, Schopenhauer's overtly atheistic philosophy pointed a way back to a religion imposing no obligations. Hence Schopenhauer repeatedly invokes the atheistic character of Buddhism;[126] hence he stresses that in the decisive question of original sin, the morality deriving from his atheistic philosophy is, 'if new and unfamiliar in expression, anything but that in essence, being in full

agreement with the authentic Christian dogmas';[127] hence he denounces Hegel as 'actually a bad Christian'[128] and so on. Again serving as a model for decadent developments later, there came into being that religious atheism which assumed, for a large section of the bourgeois intelligentsia, the function of the religion which had become intellectually untenable among this class.

Here again, of course, Schopenhauer did not round something off but only paved the way. His social starting-point in the restoration period dictated the fact that his atheism – like the religion of this era – inculcated a social passivity, a mere turning aside from social action, whereas his later successors, above all Nietzsche and the subsequent fascists, expanded these points of departure morally in the direction of an active, militant underpinning of imperialist reaction, which again ran parallel to the course taken by the Churches in the imperialist world wars and civil wars. (The complex stratification of capitalist society and the harsh changes in the course of the imperialist period's class struggles necessarily meant that religious atheism during this age could – without needing to hark back directly to Schopenhauer – have quietist variations as well, e.g., Heidegger's existentialism.)

The strength of these parallels in social function between Schopenhauerian atheism, political reaction and the positive religions and their Churches is most clearly manifest in his discourse on religion. Schopenhauer begins with a sharp critique of the historical role of religions, levelled primarily at the intolerance of the monotheistic ones. But he concludes his dialogue thus:

> *Philalethes*: Certainly the matter appears in a different light if we take into account the usefulness of religions in supporting the Crown: for as long as heads are crowned by the grace of God, altar and throne have a clearly defined relationship. And accordingly, every wise prince who loves his throne and family will always set his people an example

> of true religiosity; just as even Machiavelli urgently commends religiosity to princes in his Chapter 18. Moreover one could state that the revealed religions bore the same relation to philosophy as divinely appointed sovereigns bore to the sovereignty of the people; and for that reason the two primary terms of this equation were natural allies.
> *Demopheles*: Oh, don't you adopt that tone! Consider rather that you would then be sounding a fanfare for ochlocracy and anarchy, the arch-enemy of all law and order, all civilization and humanity.
> *Philalethes*: You are right. It was just sophistry . . . I therefore take it back.[129]

All this provides a clear outline of the social function fulfilled by Schopenhauerian philosophy. This function also determined its philosophical problems in the narrower sense. Its methodological and systematic significance can only be understood when we see how its social *terminus ad quem* was constituted in reality. For only by ascertaining this can we define Schopenhauer's stance towards the history of classical German philosophy and his place within it, the authentic philosophical character of the irrationalism he founded.

It is a well-established fact that on all crucial philosophical questions, Kant occupies a shifting, equivocal position. With matchless lucidity Lenin characterized Kant's position between materialism and idealism as follows: 'The basic feature of Kantian philosophy is the reconciling of materialism and idealism, a compromise between the two, a systematic binding together of heterogeneous, mutually contradictory philosophical orientations. When Kant assumes that something outside of us, some thing-in-itself corresponds to our ideas, he is a materialist. When he states that this thing-in-itself is unknowable, transcendent and from the Beyond, he is making an idealist stand. By acknowledging experiences and sensations as our sole source of knowledge he gives his philosophy a bent towards sensualism and beyond sensualism, under specific conditions, to materialism as well. By

acknowledging the a-priority of space, time, causality, etc., Kant gives his philosophy an idealist bent.'[130] In this crucial respect the whole of German classical philosophy marks a major step backwards in relation to Kant. Fichte already 'purifies', to use Lenin's term, Kantian philosophy of its materialist fluctuations and creates a purely subjective idealism. Schopenhauer's epistemology was always moving in this direction. It too, as we are about to see, reduced Kant's fluctuations to Berkeley's consistently subjective idealism.

But Kant's position was variable and provisional not only as regards this question, a crucial one for philosophy in general, but also on the question of dialectics. The contradictions which became manifest in mechanical-metaphysical thinking at the end of the eighteenth century (Diderot, Rousseau, Herder, etc.) come to a head with Kant. His comprehension of contradiction as a point of departure, as a logical and epistemological basis, is a tendency to be found throughout his *oeuvre* – although never taken to its conclusion or consistently worked out. Granted, with Kant all these preliminary moves still end in the reinstatement of metaphysical thinking and in a philosophical agnosticism. But we know from our discussion of the young Schelling how important even these inconsequential moves became as starting-points for the development of dialectics in Germany.

With Schopenhauer's position regarding materialism we are already familiar. Here it is just a matter of showing that Schopenhauer's 'purifying' of Kant's materialist inconstancies, his reduction of Kantian to Berkeleyan epistemology not only marks the establishing of a consistent subjective idealism, but also implies a striving to eradicate all dialectical elements from Kantian philosophy and to replace them with an irrationalism based on intuition, with an irrationalist mysticism. Thus while Schopenhauer's and Fichte's tendencies are in total conformity from the standpoint of the crucial epistemological question, the division of

idealism and materialism, they are equally contrasted in the question of dialectics. In this respect, Fichte's subjective-idealist view of the relation between Ego and non-Ego was an attempt to extend Kant's dialectical tendencies more logically. Hence the important role played by Fichte in the origin of the young Schelling's objective-idealist dialectics; hence Schopenhauer's sharply dismissive attitude to classical German philosophy's dialectical efforts in their entirety, even though his system shows many a point of contact with the irrationalist tendencies ever-present in Schelling, and even though he borrowed a thing or two from Schelling in this field – without, of course, admitting it.

In his critique of Kantian philosophy, Schopenhauer investigates the central problem of consistent subjective idealism in a very determined manner. He charges Kant above all with not having 'deduced the merely relative existence of the phenomenon from the simple, so apparent and undeniable truth *No object without subject*, so as to portray the object as dependent on the subject from its very root, as determined by the latter and hence a mere phenomenon which does not exist in itself, unconditionally, because it will always exist only in relation to a subject'.[131]

He formulated the same idea even more firmly, if anything, in his first book, *On the Fourfold Root of the Principle of Sufficient Reason*: 'Just as the object is posited with the subject (since the very word is otherwise meaningless), and likewise the subject with the object, and to be a subject is therefore tantamount to having an object, and to be an object tantamount to being known by the subject: in exactly the same way, the subject is posited along with an object *determined in any way* as *knowing it in just that way*. To that extent it does not matter whether I say that objects have such and such determinants pertinent and peculiar to them, or that the subject perceives in such and such ways; it does not matter whether I say that objects are to be divided into such classes, or that such differing powers of recognition are peculiar to the subject.'[132]

In this respect, then, Schopenhauer goes back firmly to Berkeley and defends him against Kant: 'That important thesis to whose merit Kant did not do justice Berkeley had already made the keystone of his philosophy, thereby creating a lasting memorial to himself, although he did not himself draw the appropriate inferences from the thesis and was consequently partly not understood, and partly not sufficiently heeded.'[133] Hence he rejected the second, revised edition of the *Critique of Pure Reason* as a falsification of Kant's true tendencies and always adhered to the first edition when interpreting Kant. This sharp contrast which Schopenhauer drew between the first and second edition of Kant's *magnum opus* has played a major part in Kant philology.[134] But the crucial question has to do not with philological history but with philosophy. We have noted how Schopenhauer viewed Kant's relationship to Berkeley. Now Kant wrote in the preface to the second edition of the *Critique of Pure Reason* that he had added a 'refutation of idealism' (aimed against Berkeley) which he justified thus: 'However innocuous idealism may be considered with regard to the basic purposes of metaphysics (though in fact it is not innocuous), it is still scandalous for philosophy and universal human reason to have to accept merely *on trust* the existence of things outside of ourselves (since, after all, we obtain all the actual material for knowledge from our inner mind), and – should anyone happen to cast doubt on this – not to be able to answer with any satisfactory proof.'[135] Thus what Schopenhauer regarded as Kant's great, though inconsistently sustained philosophical feat, Kant himself termed 'scandalous for philosophy'.

This firm adoption of the course of Berkeleyan subjective idealism would in itself ensure Schopenhauer the place of an important forerunner in reactionary bourgeois philosophy. For when Mach and Avenarius adopted Berkeley's epistemology afresh, just as fully in essence but using a much more veiled form of expression, they continued along lines which started with Schopenhauer. Lenin too ascertained the affinity

in his Mach critique: 'One is above not only materialism but also the idealism of "any old" Hegel, yet not averse to flirting with an idealism in the spirit of Schopenhauer!'[136]

But in two respects Schopenhauer outstripped his successors. On the one hand he supported unreservedly Berkeley's solipsistic subjectivism and idealism; it was still wholly alien to him to mask his idealism as a 'third road' between idealism and materialism, as an 'elevation' above this antithesis. On the other hand, he did not content himself, like Mach and Avenarius, with a mere agnosticism, but developed that mysticism and irrationalism inherent (consciously or not) in all consistent idealism overtly from it with thorough-going logic. In this, likewise, he came nearer to Berkeley than to his own successors. There is, admittedly, the important historical difference that his development of subjective idealism merges it not with Christian religion, as Berkeley's did, but with the religious atheism we have previously noted.

Now, in order to find an epistemological rationale for this, Schopenhauer does not repudiate the existence of things-in-themselves in general but simply puts an irrationalist-mystical interpretation on them by equating the thing-in-itself with the will, exaggerated and mysticized irrationalistically. He wrote: 'Phenomenon means idea and nothing further: all idea, of whatever kind, all *object* is *phenomenon*. But the *thing-in-itself* is *will* alone: as such it (Translator's note: i.e., the will) is never idea but different from idea *toto genere*: it is that of which all idea, all object constitutes the manifestation, the visible nature, the *objectivity*. It is the most intrinsic element, the core of each separate entity and equally of the whole: it appears in every blindly operating force of nature; it appears also in man's deliberate actions; the great difference between the two concerns only the degree of manifestation, not the essence of what is manifesting itself.'[137]

Thus Schopenhauer, like Schelling previously, presents us with two diametrically opposite modes of comprehending reality: an inessential reality (objective reality as really given) and a genuine, essential one (that of mystical irrationalism).

But as we have seen, the young Schelling rejected with this conjunction only conceptual (discursive) knowledge of reality. With his intellectual intuition he was striving to comprehend, albeit in a confusedly mystical manner, the essence of the same reality, the motive forces of evolution as a universal principle behind all reality. Schopenhauer, on the contrary, automatically discredited all scientific knowledge and created a far deeper rift between knowledge of the phenomenal world and that of the thing-in-itself than Schelling did, even in his later period when he opposed positive to negative philosophy. For here we are dealing with two different kinds of reality, or rather with reality and non-reality, and the difference between these is exactly reflected in the two kinds of cognition.

In part this is connected with their different epistemologies. Schelling was an objective, Schopenhauer a subjective idealist. For Schelling, in consequence, the objectivity of reality is still somehow present, although in a form that was growing more and more distorted through mystical irrationalism. His early conception of the identical subject-object especially is a mystificatory form of expressing the notion that human consciousness is, on the one hand, the product of natural evolution, and that, on the other hand, the achieving of this identity in intellectual intuition implies a knowledge, an elevation of this objective natural process into self-consciousness. With Schopenhauer, however, the association between subject and object is constituted quite differently from the outset. We have already quoted Schopenhauer's statements in this regard: they culminate in the thesis that there can be no object without subject, and that what we call reality (the world of appearance) is identical with our ideas. He therefore identifies himself with the Berkeleyan *Esse est percipi*.

From this it follows that for Schopenhauer — as later for Mach, Avenarius, Poincaré, etc. — the external world cannot have any real objectivity that is independent of human consciousness; that cognition — this too agrees with Machism

– possesses only a purely practical significance in the 'struggle for existence', the preservation of the individual and the species. 'Therefore knowledge in general,' Schopenhauer wrote, 'rational as well as merely intuitive, proceeds in the first place from the will itself and belongs to the essence of the higher stages of its objectivation as a mere *mekhane*, a means of preserving the individual and the species as much as every bodily organ. Originally determined, then, to serve the will and to accomplish its purposes, it remains entirely the servant of the will almost continuously: this is the case in all animals and in nearly all human beings.'[138]

Without futher ado Schopenhauer was able to deduce from this epistemological viewpoint that, in the case of phenomena, the mode of comprehension thus determined is incapable in principle of telling us anything about their essence. He divided knowledge of the external world into morphology and aetiology. Of the former he said: 'This presents us with innumerable shapes for our ideas, infinitely manifold and yet related through an unmistakable family resemblance, shapes which on this plane remain strange to us and, if regarded simply from this angle, look like baffling hieroglyphs.' Aetiology 'teaches us that, according to the law of cause and effect, one particular state of matter gives rise to the other, and has thereby accounted for it and done its task'. But this will not have affected our knowledge of objective reality. Schopenhauer sums up his epistemology as follows:

> But this does not enlighten us in the least about the inner essence of any of those phenomena. This is called *natural force* and lies outside the realm of aetiological explanation which gives the name of *natural law* to the immutable constancy of the occurrence of such a force's externalization, as long as the conditions it knows are present. But this natural law, these conditions and this occurrence, in respect of a particular place at a particular time, are all that it knows and ever can know. The actual force externalized, the inner essence of the phenomenon occurring

> according to those laws will remain for ever a mystery, quite strange and unknown, in the case of both the simplest and most complex phenomenon . . . In consequence, even the most thorough aetiological explanation of the whole of nature would actually never be anything beyond a catalogue of inexplicable forces and a reliable list of the rules whereby manifestations of those forces occur in time and place, succeed and give way to one another. It would however have to leave the inner essence of the forces manifested for ever unexplained, because the law it obeys does not go that far, but stops with the phenomenon and its classifying.[139]

Here we can distinctly see both the purely bourgeois character of Schopenhauer's epistemology and the energy with which it anticipates irrationalist philosophy's later development. Schopenhauer's close contact with eighteenth-century English philosophers, with Berkeley and Hume, stems chiefly from the fact that they were trying to meet the ideological needs of a bourgeoisie which had already gained control economically, by means of a compromise with the landowning class and the religious views of the old régime. For that reason, they tried to create an epistemology which did not, on the one hand, obstruct the free development of natural science indispensable to capitalist production (unlike, for instance, the religious ideas of feudal or semi-feudal philosophy which affected science itself). On the other hand, the epistemology they were seeking repudiated all philosophical consequences of scientific developments liable to hamper the compromise made with the ruling powers of the *ancien régime* by a bourgeoisie mostly inclining to reaction. This attitude's purely bourgeois character is manifest in the fact that the decisive argument for banishing such consequences is once again an indirect one. They are not dismissed (as in feudal or semi-feudal philosophy) because they fail to agree with Christian dogmas, but on account of their 'unscientific nature' and because they cross frontiers defined by

epistemology as impassable for the intellectual apprehension of the phenomenal world. Schopenhauer's anticipatory character, his 'genius' is indicated by the fact that he recognized this trend of bourgeois development in backward Germany at the start of the nineteenth century; that in the political unawareness – socially, matters still stood quite differently – of the German bourgeoisie of his age, he clearly surmised and raised to a high stage of generalization tendencies which only gained the upper hand in Germany and right across the Continent after the defeat of the 1848-9 revolution.

As we have seen, this knowledge of the phenomenal world could only possess, in Schopenhauer's opinion, a practical, pragmatist significance. He now countered it with apprehension of the essence of things-in-themselves, apprehension of will. At this point the irrationalist mysticism in his philosophy becomes fully evident. Even for the mode of perceiving the phenomenal world, Schopenhauer stresses the outstanding role played by intuition. Schelling's intellectual intuition which, as we know, was for him solely the mode of knowing things-in-themselves – in sharp contrast to that of perceiving phenomena – he made a universal principle governing every kind of knowledge. 'Accordingly our everyday, *empirical intuition* is an *intellectual* one, and to *this* is due the predicate which Germany's philosophical windbags have attached to a purported intuition of imagined worlds in which their favoured *absolutum* performs its evolutions.'[140]

Naturally this irrationalist principle of intuition makes an even bolder appearance in knowledge of the thing-in-itself, the will. Apprehension of this will occurs, as regards each man as an individual, purely intuitively and directly 'as something, namely, which is directly known to that Everyone which the word "will" denotes'.[141] That this entails a complete solipsism, a denial of the reality of our fellow-men and the external world in general, Schopenhauer can contest only with sophistry and the tools of Schelling's philosophy, the philosophy he otherwise challenges so strongly. We judge the existence of our fellow-beings, Schopenhauer says, 'according

to the analogy of that life',[142] that is, according to our own, and in both instances we distinguish between idea (phenomenon) and will (thing-in-itself). The same method is then used to apply the will by analogy to the entire phenomenal world as to its underlying Being-in-itself. Schopenhauer expounds this analogizing, this extension of human will to the whole cosmos as follows:

> It must however be observed that here, all we need is a *denominatio a potiori* through which, for that very reason, the concept of will is expanded further than before. Perception of the identical in different manifestations and of the incongruous in similar ones is, as Plato so often comments, the very precondition of philosophy. Until now, however, we have not recognized the identity, with the will, of the essence of every single force straining and operating in nature. Hence we have not regarded the manifold phenomena as the different species of the same genus which they are but have taken them for heterogeneous: that is also why there could not be a word to denote the concept of this genus. Hence I give the genus the name of its most admirable species, a nearer, immediate knowledge of which leads us to indirect knowledge of all other species.[143]

This analogizing, needless to say, again occurs in an intuitive way, on the basis of direct knowing: 'But the word *will*, which is supposed to reveal the innermost essence of each thing in nature like an open sesame, by no means signifies an unknown quantity, something that is reached by drawing conclusions; it signifies rather something which is directly perceived and so well known that we know and understand what will is far better than anything else, anything whatever. Hitherto the concept *will* was subsumed under the concept *force*; but I do the exact opposite and ask for every force in nature to be conceived as will.'[144] So here Schopenhauer anthropologizes the whole of nature with the help of plain

analogy, which he loftily declares to be myth, and hence truth.

Here we are neither able nor disposed to analyse in all its details the philosophical system which arose in this way. We shall only indicate those crucial elements in which the new Schopenhauerian irrationalism – which had a tremendously strong bearing on nineteenth-century philosophy – found expression. From Schopenhauer's return to Berkeley as we have traced it so far, it necessarily follows that for Schopenhauer, space, time and causality are purely subjective forms of the phenomenal world and can never be applied to things-in-themselves, to will as Schopenhauer grasped it. Kant's fluctuating position derived from the fact that here, he was similarly striving for a sharp dichotomy, but was forever trying to escape from the prison of this metaphysical dualism in the course of his concrete accounts. These steps taken by Kant towards a dialectical view of phenomenon and essence (objective reality, thing-in-itself) were mostly hesitant and equivocal. Schopenhauer radically abolished them and used the dualism, carried through in a more consistently metaphysical, anti-dialectical argumentation, to bring about a total irrationalisation of the world of things-in-themselves.

Let us take an important case in natural philosophy. 'Force itself', Schopenhauer said, 'lies right outside the chain of causes and effects, which presupposes time by having meaning only in relation to it: but the former also lies outside time. The particular mutation is always an equally particular variation, but not so the force, on the cause whose externalization it is. For just that which always gives a cause its efficacy, however many times it occurs, is a natural force and as such groundless, i.e., it lies right outside the causal nexus and the domain of the principle of reason, and is perceived philosophically as immediate objectivity of the will, which is entire nature's In-itself.'[145]

Thereupon, the whole of nature is turned into a mystery, although all the particular mutations needed for capitalist praxis may be comprehended in terms of causal laws and

used in production. But philosophically speaking, everything is inexplicable and irrational: 'It is as inexplicable to us that a stone should fall to the earth as that an animal should move.'[146] And by pursuing this idea to its logical conclusion, Schopenhauer arrived at findings very close to the reactionary mysticism of imperialist natural philosophy, which they anticipate in methodology. Let us remember from Spinoza's deterministic statements that a stone flying through the air, if it had consciousness, would imagine that it was flying of its free will – a graphic image to illustrate the illusion of free will; as has been shown, we find analogies of it in Bayle and Leibniz as well. Schopenhauer similarly refers to Spinoza's image but completely reverses its philosophical meaning by adding 'that the stone would be right. The push is the same for the stone as the motive for me, and what is manifested in the stone's case as cohesion, gravity, persistence in the assumed state is, in esoteric essence, the same as that which I recognize in myself as will and which the stone too would recognize as will, were it to acquire perception.'[147] Schopenhauer, of course, was not familiar with today's bourgeois atomic physics, but he would surely have assented enthusiastically, at least from the methodological angle, to the a-causal movements of electrons and 'free will' in the movement of particles.

The results of this metaphysical-irrationalist splitting asunder of phenomenon and essence emerge even more clearly in the human world. Since Schopenhauerian will lies beyond the operational field of space, time and causality, and since he regards the individuation principle as thereby dissolved, every will is identical with will itself. This has very important human (ethical) consequences: 'Only the *inner* processes, as far as they concern the *will*, have true reality and are real events; because will alone is the thing-in-itself. In each microcosm there lies the whole macrocosm, and the latter contains no more than the former. Multiplicity is phenomenon, and the external processes are mere configurations of the phenomenal world, hence possessing no direct

reality or meaning, which they only have indirectly through their relation to the will of individuals.'[148]

This, therefore, is not merely to say that it is exclusively the inner factor which counts in every deed. That is also implied in Kant's 'categorical imperative', albeit with the important difference that Kant was always striving to give his pure abstract ethics a social content as well, and in order to achieve this he did not flinch from sophistic methods, from an unconscious abandonment of his own methodological starting-point. With Schopenhauer, on the contrary, we are dealing with inwardness pure and simple, with the philosophical and ethical devaluation of every action, every real deed. But over and beyond this, the identity of macrocosm and microcosm, of the essential world and the pure inwardness of the *individuum* is also implied in the passage just quoted. Certainly, the path to this is an *askesis*, a dismissal of the cruelties of existence, a vision of the inner identity of all beings, and therefore a surmounting of ordinary egotism. On all these issues Schopenhauer speaks in a wide-ranging, picturesque and often witty manner. But we must never forget that – again in abrupt contrast to Kant and indeed to all the genuine moralists of the past – he regards his own ethics as optional for the philosopher expounding and justifying them. Why, then, should they be obligatory for his readers and followers? But if they are not so, all that these 'sublime' ethics leave us with is the inflation of the individual to a cosmic potency, plus a philosophical *carte blanche* to look down on all social activity in a superior way.

This side of Schopenhauer's philosophy is further reinforced by the most popular part of his system, his aesthetics. Here again, bourgeois historians blur the picture by discerning in Schopenhauer's aesthetics a continuation of German classicism. In fact they are the exact opposite. The aesthetics of Goethe and Schiller, those of the young Schelling and the mature Hegel, held art and knowledge to be two significant, mutually co-ordinating forms of comprehending the world. Goethe wrote: 'The Beautiful is a manifestation of secret

natural laws which, without the appearance of the Beautiful, would be forever hidden from us.'[149] On the face of it, Schopenhauer's aesthetics with their connection between Platonic ideas and aesthetic contemplation, and their view of music as a 'reflection of the will itself',[150] come very close to this view. But let us not forget that in German classicism, knowledge and art were oriented to the same reality and that they both sought in it different but converging solutions for the same dialectic of phenomenon and essence, whereas Schopenhauer defined art precisely '*as the mode of considering things independently of the principle of reason*'.[151] Thus with Schopenhauer, in contrast to German classicism, knowledge and aesthetic contemplation form diametrically opposite poles.

Despite an equally superficial and deceptive resemblance, an antithesis just as sharp obtains in the relation of the aesthetic sphere to praxis. We do not need to expatiate on the fact that in classical aesthetics, from Kant's 'without interest' to Schiller's 'aesthetic education', there exists a strong element of artistic isolation, an element of escape from social reality and praxis. But this was still only one element. Even 'aesthetic education' was originally designed as a preparatory stage, as one phase in the education of mankind in social action. Only with Schopenhauer (and in reactionary Romanticism before him) does this escape become the central problem of aesthetics. Here too Schopenhauer was an important forerunner of Europe's later decadence. For such a total flight from social action is inextricably linked with the distortion of man which this aesthetic attitude occasions. Whereas German classicism's aesthetic ideal was the normal human being, Schopenhauer posits an essential, intimate link between pathology and artistic excellence. For him the genius is no longer 'Nature's darling', as for Kant,[152] but a *monstrum per excessum*.[153]

Here we find the reactionary irrationalism of the late-bourgeois development anticipated in embryonic form. This anticipation takes on grotesque overtones if we briefly touch

on the stance which the 'atheistic' Schopenhauer adopted to those problems which later gained popularity among the decadent bourgeoisie in such diverse forms as 'depth psychology', occultism and so on. Thomas Mann has rightly pointed to the connection between Schopenhauer and Freud.[154] But more important is Schopenhauer's standpoint regarding the problem-complex of clairvoyance, spiritualism, etc. To these questions – which were also very important for the reactionary Romantics – he devoted a detailed separate study which, needless to say, we cannot now examine at length. The important thing is to establish that Schopenhauer's subjective-idealist epistemology (as we have noted, it sought, on the one hand, to inculcate a general scepticism regarding the philosophical value of natural scientific findings) offered a philosophical 'foundation' for all such superstition. Thus Schopenhauer wrote of clairvoyance that it would lose 'at least its absolute incomprehensibility if we carefully consider what a mere cerebral phenomenon the objective world is, as I have so often said: for it is this phenomenon's laws and principles, resting as they do on space, time and causality (as cerebral functions), which are eliminated to some extent in somnambulistic clairvoyance'.[155]

After briefly recapitulating his doctrine of the subjectivity of time, Schopenhauer continues: 'For if time is not a condition of the authentic essence of things, then in respect of this essence, Before and After are without significance: accordingly, then, it must be just as possible to perceive an event before it has happened as afterwards. All divination, whether in dreaming somnambulistic foresight, second sight, or whatever, consists only in locating the way to liberate knowledge from the condition imposed by time.' That means that we must concede 'a real influence by the dead on the world of the living to be also possible', seldom though it may occur, and so on.[156] This dual tendency: an agnosticism (or sometimes plain empiricism flinching from any real generalization) towards real natural phenomena and natural principles on the one hand, and a blind credulity in assessing

'occult phenomena' on the other, only becomes a widespread ideology in the second half of the nineteenth century. At the turn of the 1870s-1880s, Engels criticized strictly empiricist English natural scientists for such tendencies and summed up his characterization thus: 'Here it is palpably evident which is the surest road from natural science to mystification. Not the rank theory of natural philosophy, but the very plainest empiricism that despises all theory and distrusts all thought.'[157] But since Schopenhauer went much further than the English empiricists in dethroning reason, his true direct succession in this respect did not evolve until the imperialist age. The dual epistemological tendency is clearly visible in Simmel, for instance, and methodologically it later played an important part in the projection of myths up to fascist racial theory.

Hence the breeding of an irrationalist megalomania among the bourgeois intellectuals. It was aggravated by the fact that Schopenhauer not only took over the aristocratic character of Schelling's epistemology, but also extended it in a radical way. He too found that ordinary, conceptually discursive knowledge was 'available and comprehensible to anyone who only has reason'. The comprehension of the world as it really is, as it objectifies itself in art, is a different matter; this is 'attainable only for the genius and also someone in an inspired state by virtue of a raising of his pure apperception, a process which is mostly induced by the works of the genius'. The art-works in which this Being-in-itself appears are so constituted that they 'must remain books forever closed and inaccessible to the dull majority of men, with a wide gulf separating them, just as the society of princes is closed to the rabble'.[158]

We have briefly outlined how Schopenhauer's rigorous irrationalism grew out of his reduction of Kant's inconstancies to Berkeley's solipsism. It just remain for us to demonstrate with regard to several philosophically crucial problems how this irrationalism, as a backlash, meshes with the development of dialectics; how, in this respect,

Schopenhauer's philosophy is pervaded by a wholly conscious struggle against dialectics; and how it substituted a mystico-metaphysical irrationalism for the advance of dialectical knowledge.

Schopenhauer's conscious and bitter hostility to Fichte, Schelling and, above all, Hegel is known to us from the history of philosophy. But the sharp theoretical antithesis of dialectical and metaphysical thinking which in fact separates the two parties has scarcely ever received concrete elaboration. And precisely this side of the subject has great significance for the development of irrationalism. Not only because, as we have repeatedly explained, every important phase of irrationalism originates in the antithesis to a stage in the development of dialectics. It is important also because (and this finds especially vivid expression in Schopenhauer) every irrationalism requires, as a logico-epistemological complement to and underpinning of metaphysical thought, the appeal to a logical formalism.

Without having referred expressly to the problems of dialectics before, we were nonetheless obliged in substance to mention some of the most important dialectical problems. Let us recall the relation of phenomenon and essence, the inward and the external, theory and praxis. The sharp contrast will at once be evident from even a cursory glance at the development of dialectics from Kant to Hegel. With Hegel, the dialectical relativizing of phenomenon and essence leads to a correct solution of the thing-in-itself problem, a knowledge of the thing through knowledge of its attributes, and the logical transformation of things-in-themselves into things-for-us in the course of a dialectical unending approximation to objects. With Schopenhauer, on the contrary, there is no mediation at all between appearance and essence, between phenomenon and thing-in-itself; they are two worlds radically divided from each other. Whereas, for Hegel, the inward and the external continually interact, a metaphysical abyss separates them for Schopenhauer. (We shall discuss in detail this question's anti-dialectical and irrationalist

significance when we deal with Kierkegaard.) With Hegel, theory and praxis are portrayed – as far as is possible in an idealist philosophy – in intimate dialectical interaction, so that theoretical category problems, such as that of teleology, are at once explained as deriving from human labour and the use of the tool.[159] But, with Schopenhauer, theory and praxis are so inimical to each other that its relation to praxis is presented as a downright dishonouring of theory, an important symptom of the inferior and superficial character of praxis; real theory and real philosophy must be pure contemplation strictly isolated from all praxis.

This contrast becomes even clearer, if anything, when we consider the category of causality. We have already touched on this issue in the context of Schopenhauer's Berkeleyan solipsism and pointed out his extreme subjectivism, even in comparison to Kant. This aspect of the question is important for later developments because Schopenhauer's radical stress on causality as – along with space and time – a unique category of the phenomenal world is in seeming contrast to tendencies emerging in the imperialist age, from the repudiation of causality by Mach and Avenarius via its relativizing and enfeeblement in later thinkers (e.g., Simmel) down to the substitution of probability calculation by present-day natural philosophers, viz., the advocates of physical idealism. In fact, however, this line marks a uniform trend to destroy the objectivity and objective principles of the external world existing independently of our consciousness. The common aim was to reduce to the subject the outer world's own coherent relations and to deprive them of any objective character. In this respect Schopenhauer was, as we have already shown, an important forerunner and pioneer of the imperialist age's agnosticism and irrationalism. This is especially so because his concept of causality, precisely on account of the mechanical-metaphysical exclusiveness of his fatalist determinism in the phenomenal world, served only as a springboard for reaching a totally irrational indeterminism, a total denial of any objectivity and laws in the area of things-

in-themselves. It is no accident but a necessary consequence of Schopenhauer's interpretation of causality that one of the few older philosophers he revered was Malebranche, the founder of occasionalism.

From the angle of the dialectical or metaphysical development of logic at the start of the nineteenth century, Schopenhauer's attitude to Kant on the causality question is of exceptional importance. Kant, as we know, set up a table of categories in which causality, although acquiring a key role in his concrete exposition, nevertheless forms only one of twelve categories he listed of the coherence of objects. All Kant's dialectical successors raised critical objections to this table, chiefly to the effect that its contents and composition were simply adopted from formal logic and that a philosophical deduction of its coherence had not even been seriously attempted. True, Hegel praises the 'great flair of the concept' in Kant in his history of philosophy, because the latter sought to arrange it in triplicate (positive, negative, synthesis), but he censures Kant for 'not deducing' these categories and simply taking them from experience 'with the adjustments they undergo in logic' (i.e. formal logic — G.L.).[160] Thus Hegel was praising and censuring the extension of formal logic into dialectical logic, already discerning in Kant a precursor, albeit unclear and uncertain, of the dialectical method.

Schopenhauer too criticized Kant's derivation of the categories but in a totally opposite direction. His end was to destroy completely Kant's tentative steps towards dialectics. Whereas he saw in Kant's 'transcendental aesthetics' an enormous achievement, namely a purely subjectivist conception of space and time, he regarded the 'transcendental analytics', the deduction of the categories, as completely 'obscure, confused, undefined, shaky, unsure'. In his view they contained 'mere assertions that it is thus and must be thus'. Schopenhauer concluded his comments as follows: 'We may further remark that Kant, whenever he wants to illustrate a statement with an example, almost always resorts to the

category of causality, and what he has stated then turns out aright – and this is because the law of causality is the real and also sole form of understanding, while the other eleven categories are only blacked-out windows.'[161] About the causal nexus he adds, entirely in the spirit of this argument: '. . . of this real and sole function of understanding'.[162] Schopenhauer took this sovereignty of causality so far as radically to reject any extension of it beyond the single, mechanical chain of cause and effect. Thus he wrote, for instance, 'that the concept of *reciprocity* is, strictly speaking, empty';[163] that 'the effect can never be the cause of its cause, and hence the concept of reciprocity in its true sense is not admissible'.[164]

It is very interesting to compare this denial of reciprocity with Hegel's statements, which show in detail, on the one hand, the objective reality and effectiveness of reciprocity, but also see in it merely a relatively humble form of the universal dialectical bonds between all objects – a form, therefore, at which dialectical logic must not halt. 'Reciprocity', Hegel wrote, 'is, and this we admit, the closest truth of the relationship of cause and effect, standing so to speak at the threshold of the concept; but for that self-same reason we must not content ourselves with applying that relationship, insofar as knowing with comprehension (*das begreifende Erkennen*) is concerned. If we stop to consider a given content merely from the angle of reciprocity, the concept is in fact entirely missing from our act of considering.'[165] Since here we are only concerned with elaborating the antithesis between dialectical and metaphysical-irrationalist logic, we cannot now examine the very interesting details of this question-complex. It will suffice as a summing up to quote some comments which Lenin made on dialectics and causality in Hegel and to state that what he said about causality in neo-Kantian thinking also applies to Schopenhauer in its entirety. Lenin wrote: 'If we read what Hegel says about causality, it will at first appear strange that he occupies himself so relatively little with this theme when it was so

popular with the Kantians. What is the reason? The reason is that for him, causality is only *one* of the determinants of the universal coherence which he was already grasping earlier, *throughout* his account, in a considerably profounder and more universal sense, underlining this coherence, the reciprocal crossings, and so on, *constantly*, and from the very outset. It would be most instructive to compare the "birth pangs" of neo-empiricism (or "physical idealism") with Hegel's solutions or rather his dialectical method.'[166]

With regard to the question of space and time the contrast is equally clear-cut. Here, to be sure, there is far greater agreement between Kant and Schopenhauer than over the issue of the categories of understanding. For here Kant was much less of a dialectician, at least in his endeavours. Not only did Kant, like Schopenhauer, regard space and time as universal *a priori* preconditions of all objectivity, and therefore as principles to be comprehended philosophically in independence of and prior to all objectivity; he also stressed their mutual total independence of each other. Schopenhauer throws this metaphysical dualism of space and time into even sharper relief: 'Thus we see that both forms of empirical ideas, although known to have infinite divisibility and infinite expansion in common, are still fundamentally different in that what is essential to the *one* has no significance at all in the *other*; juxtaposition has none in time, and succession none in space.'[167] If space and time appear united in practical understanding's knowledge, the principle of unification does not, in Schopenhauer's view, lie in space and time themselves but exclusively in the understanding, in subjectivity.

The young Hegel already took issue with Kant's metaphysical dualism on the matter of space and time, as in his *Jena Logic* (1801-2). The most striking aspect of this is that Hegel deals with space and time not in the section concerned with epistemological logic, but in his book's natural-philosophical section, in the chapter on the concept of movement; and even here the theme is not discussed in epistemological isolation but in connection with the question of ether.

As regards the treatment itself, it should be stressed that space and time are presented, on the one hand, as elements of a concrete natural unity, and on the other – this automatically follows dialectically – as interacting elements. 'The single like-unto-itself, space, is an element when isolated; but as self-realizing, as being what it is in itself, it is its own opposite, it is time – and vice versa, the infinite as the element of time: it realizes itself or is as an element, i.e., annulling itself as that which it is, it constitutes its opposite, space . . .'[168]

With the mature Hegel this question undergoes many vicissitudes, but the dialectical principles remain the same. In his *Encyclopaedia*, too, space and time are developed under natural philosophy, not logic; this time, to be sure, by way of an introduction to mechanics. Now although Hegel as an idealist was still unable to find the real dialectic of space and time (it requires a dialectical theory of the reflection of objective reality), he nevertheless regarded the inner compatibility, the ceaseless interaction of space and time as axiomatic. Here we cannot possibly give a detailed analysis of his views, but must limit ourselves to several examples which particularly characterize the method. In one passage he writes, for instance: 'The truth of space is time, thus space turns into time; we do not pass into time subjectively, but space itself makes the transition. In imagination space and time are far apart, we have first space and then time *as well*; philosophy contests this "as well".'[169] For Hegel the dialectical thinker, then, Kant's dualism of space and time (and also the dualism found in Schopenhauer, whom Hegel never read) meant remaining stationary on the level of idea, a non-attainment of the philosophical standpoint. Hegel too constantly emphasizes the conceptual indivisibility of space and time from the real agitation of the world of objects. For him, space and time are never empty – and merely subjective – vessels within whose frame objectiveness and movement occur but are, on the contrary, themselves elements of the world of agitated objectiveness, the objective dialectic of reality. Thus Hegel says of time: 'Everything does not originate

and expire *in* time, but time *itself* is this *becoming*, originating and expiring.'[170]

Only on the face of it do these questions have an abstractly epistemological character. In reality the mode of comprehending space and time crucially affects the construction of any philosophy. Let us remark just in passing that the sharp metaphysical division of space and time which, with Schopenhauer himself, was still a mechanical juxtaposing constitutes the epistemological hypothesis for the opposition of space and time in the irrationalist philosophy of the imperialist age (Bergson, Spengler, Klages, Heidegger, etc.). Here again Schopenhauer appears an important initiator of irrationalism's later development, but he was only a forerunner once again. That slant so characteristic of the movement later, whereby mechanistic-fatalistic 'dead', rational and 'objective' space was placed in antithesis to vital irrationalist, truly subjective time, lay outside the scope of his thinking.

And this was so for socio-historical reasons. It was only the fiercer class struggles of the imperialist age that forced this time-conception upon reactionary bourgeois philosophy, as the philosophical basis for a mythicizing pseudo-history intended to counter the increasingly victorious advance of historical materialism. Nietzsche, on the eve of the imperialist age, was likewise a transitional figure in this respect, although certainly on the basis of acuter class struggles. His *mythos* was already a pseudo-history but lacked a time-theory of its own in the aforementioned sense, whereas Schopenhauer's *mythos* still consisted in a radical repudiation of all historicity.

We again find the explanation for this in the class struggles of Schopenhauer's day and the ideological antithesis they promoted. We have already remarked in other contexts that during the period of Schopenhauer's activity, the ideological fronts were drawn up in opposition as historism and pseudo-historism. On the one side, there was the progressive-bourgeois historical defence of progress founded on the lessons of the French Revolution, and on the other, the semi-feudal legitimist doctrine of an 'organic' development – which in fact

implied an endeavour to revert to pre-revolutionary conditions behind the mask of historicity and was thus the ideological defence of feudal-legitimist reaction. On the surface, Schopenhauer's standpoint in this dilemma was a peculiar *tertium datur*: namely a dismissal of the significance of all historicity for the essence of reality. But we have seen that this was antithetical to Romantic-reactionary philosophy only in its argumentation and in specific concrete contents. In truth, Schopenhauer was likewise bitterly hostile to all social progress, with the sole difference that since he lacked inner ties with absolute monarchy and the nobility supporting it, he did not mind which 'strong' régime defended bourgeois property against the exploited masses as long as it did so efficiently. (This is another reason for Schopenhauer's popularity in the period of Bonapartism.)

Only when regarded from this angle does the real philosophical meaning of the category problems we are discussing become clear. The change which classical German philosophy signifies in man's thinking rests not least on the fact that in objective idealism, Hegel's above all, dialectics became – after major preparatory steps in the seventeenth and eighteenth centuries – the historical method for knowledge of nature and history. (With, of course, all the limitations of philosophical idealism which the bourgeois dialecticians were incapable of surmounting.) The subjectivist view of space, time and causality, the restricting of their validity to the phenomenal world, the sovereignty of causality as the linking category of objects, the strictly metaphysical division of space and time: all this served primarily to repudiate in a radical fashion any historicity of nature and the world of men.

Schopenhauer designed a world-picture in which neither the phenomenal cosmos nor that of things-in-themselves knew change, development or history. The former, to be sure, consisted of a ceaseless changing, an apparent becoming and expiring, a changing moreover that was subject to a fatalistic necessity. But this becoming and expiring was still

static in essence: a kaleidoscope in which alternating combinations of the same components give the direct, uninitiated beholder the illusion of constant change. And anyone possessing real philosophical insight, Schopenhauer claimed, must be aware that behind this brightly coloured veil of surface phenomena continually succeeding one another, there is hidden another world without space, time and causality, a world regarding which it would be pointless to speak of history, development or even progress. This initiated mind, wrote Schopenhauer, 'will not share people's belief that time produces something really new and momentous, that through it or in it something sheerly real will come into existence . . .'[171]

It is here that Schopenhauer's animosity towards Hegel has its objective roots. Having converted Kantian philosophy into a radical anti-historicism, he then had to see Hegel's equally resolute dialectical historicism triumph over his system. Hence his doctrine largely took the form of bitter polemical imprecations directed against Hegel: 'As far, finally, as the striving to comprehend world-history as an orderly whole is concerned – a striving encouraged by Hegelian quack philosophy with its universally corrupting and stupefying influence; its actual basis is a coarse, humdrum realism which takes the *phenomenon* for the world's *essence in itself* and thinks that everything hinges on the former, its shapes and its processes . . .'[172]

It necessarily follows from this conception that Schopenhauer should deny any evolution in nature. In contrast to Goethe, with whom he purportedly agrees on every question, he was with regard to the natural sciences an admirer of Linnaeus and Cuvier, ignoring the attempts that his great contemporaries were making to discover a historical evolution in nature. Of course not even he could fail to observe the gradations in nature (inorganic and organic nature, living beings, species, etc.). But he regarded them as perennial objectivation forms of the will, '*stages in the objectivation of the will*' that were 'nothing else than *Plato's*

Ideas'.[173] For him these perennial prototypes of every individual phenomenal form were 'permanent, not subject to change, always being, never become'. Here again it is clear how vapid the conceptions were of those bourgeois historians who saw in Schopenhauer a continuation of Goethean traditions, and how they distorted any real connection. In all that crucially mattered about Goethe in terms of (natural) philosophy, in respect of his opposition to the unhistorical mechanicalism of Linnaeus and Cuvier, Schopenhauer was Goethe's adversary and not his heir.

For Schopenhauer, therefore, history does not exist. 'For we are of the opinion', he wrote, 'that everyone is still infinitely far from a philosophical knowledge of the world who presumes it possible to grasp its essence in some *historical* way, however finely clothed; but that is the case as soon as any *Becoming* or Having-Become or In-the-Process-of-Becoming (*Werdenwerden*) occurs in one's view of the world's essence in itself and any Earlier or Later has the slightest significance . . . For all such historical philosophy, however superior its manner, takes *time* for a condition of things-in-themselves as though Kant had never existed, and hence stops at what Kant terms phenomenon as opposed to thing-in-itself . . . it is just knowledge which is accommodated by the principle of sufficient reason that never takes us to the inner essence of things but only pursues phenomena into infinity, moving without purpose or goal . . .'[174] In principle, said Schopenhauer, history can never become the object of a science; it is 'false not only in the exposition but in its essence'.[175] Hence for Schopenhauer there exists no difference in history between important and trivial, major and minor; only the individual is real, whereas the human race is an empty abstraction.

Thus only the individual, isolated in a world without meaning, is left over as the fateful product of the individuation principle (space, time, causality). An individual, certainly, that is identical with the world-essence by virtue of the aforestated identity between microcosm and macrocosm

in the world of things-in-themselves. This essence, however, located as it is beyond the validity of space, time and causality, is consequently – nothingness. Hence Schopenhauer's *magnum opus* logically ends with the words: 'Rather we freely acknowledge that what is left after the complete annulment of the will is, for all those who are still full of will, assuredly nothingness. But conversely also, for those in whom will has turned round and denied itself, this very real world of ours with all its suns and Milky Ways is – nothingness.'[176]

And at this point, with our survey of the most important problems in Schopenhauer's philosophy completed, we ask once again: what is the social task it fulfils? Or, to put this question from another angle: what is behind its widespread and lasting influence? Here pessimism is not by itself an adequate answer, for first pessimism requires a further concretization in addition to that we provided earlier. Schopenhauer's philosophy rejects life in every form and confronts it with nothingness as a philosophical perspective. But is it possible to live such a life? (Let us mention only in passing that Schopenhauer – in line with Christianity, here as on the question of original sin – rejected suicide as a solution to the meaninglessness of existence.) If we consider Schopenhauer's philosophy *as a whole*, the answer is undoubtedly yes. For the futility of life means above all the individual's release from all social obligations and all responsibility towards men's forward development, which does not even exist in Schopenhauer's eyes. And nothingness as the pessimist outlook, as life's horizon is quite unable, according to Schopenhauer's ethics as already expounded, to prevent or even merely to discourage the individual from leading an enjoyable contemplative life. On the contrary: the abyss of nothingness, the gloomy background of the futility of existence only lends this enjoyment an extra piquancy. Further heightening it is the fact that the strongly accented aristocratism of Schopenhauer's philosophy lifts its adherents (in imagination) way above the wretched mob that is short-

sighted enough to fight and to suffer for a betterment of social conditions. So Schopenhauer's system, well laid out and architecturally ingenious in form, rises up like a modern luxury hotel on the brink of the abyss, nothingness and futility. And the daily sight of the abyss, between the leisurely enjoyment of meals or works of art, can only enhance one's pleasure in this elegant comfort.

This, then, fulfils the task of Schopenhauer's irrationalism: the task of preventing an otherwise dissatisfied sector of the intelligentsia from concretely turning its discontent with the 'established order', i.e., the existing social order, against the capitalist system in force at any given time. This irrationalism thereby reaches its central objective – no matter how far Schopenhauer himself was aware of it: that of providing an indirect apologetic of the capitalist social order.

5. Kierkegaard

Kierkegaard's philosophy, like that of Schopenhauer and Nietzsche, was slow to attain world influence. It only came into vogue in the imperialist period or, to be more precise, between the First and Second World War. Certainly, during his active life as a writer Kierkegaard was by no means so neglected a figure in his homeland as Schopenhauer was in Germany before 1848. His first major writings, and the only crucial ones philosophically, the works appearing under pseudonyms, immediately caused a certain stir, nor did his later overt stand against the official Protestant Church lack sensational elements. In the later decades his spiritual influence even became decisive for a time in Scandinavia. Not only Ibsen's dramatic poem *Brand* bears witness to this; the influence is also tangible in later Scandinavian literature (I will only mention Pontoppidan's novel *The Promised Land*). However, although translations of his works and individual essays on him had already appeared abroad much earlier,

Kierkegaard did not emerge as a leading intellectual force decisively influencing European (and American) philosophical reaction until between the two world wars, on the eve of Hitler's seizure of power. This position he has held up to the present day.

Speaking in general terms, Kierkegaard's intellectual anticipation of the later development poses no more of a mystery than Schopenhauer's and Nietzsche's. But in order to give a real concretization of it, we would need a knowledge of class relations and class struggles in Denmark during the second quarter of the nineteenth century far more intimate than the author of this book possesses. Hence he would prefer to leave the concrete analysis of this question to others, rather than cast a false light on it through inadequately founded generalizations. We are therefore obliged to treat Kierkegaard from the outset merely as a figure within the European philosophical development, omitting to discuss the concrete social foundations of his mental foreshadowing of much later irrationalist-reactionary tendencies, which were rooted in the Danish society of this age.

To be sure, such a mode of treatment does find certain points of connection in Denmark's intellectual development too. Georg Brandes has shown in detail how profound an effect German philosophy and imaginative literature had in Denmark in the first half of the nineteenth century.[177] That goes for Kierkegaard himself as well. His chief philosophical campaign was directed against Hegel, who represented the philosophically dominant trend in Denmark too at that time, and closely connected with this was Kierkegaard's constant attack on Goethe. His thinking has close points of contact with German Romanticism, Schleiermacher and Baader; he travelled to Berlin especially to hear the old Schelling's lectures, and although they were a severe disappointment to him after the violent first flush of enthusiasm, Schelling's new philosophical standpoint and the manner in which he criticized Hegel were not without a far-reaching influence on Kierkegaard's ideas. He also studied in depth the Left

opposition to Hegel, especially Feuerbach; Trendelenburg, as we shall see, had a crucial influence on his arguments against Hegel; after having elaborated his own standpoint he read Schopenhauer and held him in high esteem, and so on and so forth. Of course all this does not sufficiently compensate for the aforestated gap in our account. It merely gives us enough pointers to prevent it from being – even on this score – entirely speculative.

Kierkegaard's philosophy, for all the points of contact with Schopenhauer's that we shall demonstrate shortly, is distinct from the latter historically in being closely bound up with the process of Hegelianism's dissolution. During the restoration period, it was possible for Schopenhauer to combat Hegelian dialectics as pure nonsense and to counter them with a Kant 'purified' à la Berkeley, a metaphysical and overtly anti-dialectical subjective idealism. At the time of the greatest crisis in idealist-dialectical thought, in which there originated the highest form of dialectics completely surmounting its idealist limitations – namely the materialist dialectics of Marx and Engels, Kierkegaard, so as to be able to challenge Hegel in the name of a new, more advanced irrationalism, had to clothe the latter in the guise of an allegedly superior dialectic, the 'qualitative' dialectic. As we shall see, this had to do with the attempt, typical in the history of irrationalism, to thwart the further development of dialectics by inverting the true forward-looking problem of the period, to lead dialectics astray and to present the inverted proposition in a mythico-mystificatory form as the answer to the concrete question. Kierkegaard, who was an acute, ingenious and subjectively honest thinker, had an occasional inkling of this complex of ideas. He wrote in his *Journals* in 1836: 'Mythology is a hypothetical claim which is transposed into the indicative.'[178] The inability of bourgeois historians to define Kierkegaard's position in this development also manifests itself in their inability and refusal to comprehend the real meaning of materialist dialectics, and their consequent failure to understand the whole process of

the dissolution of Hegelianism in the 1840s.[179]

Hegel's significance in the history of dialectics lies chiefly in his finding a concept for the most important dialectical conditions and connections of reality. Marx outlined both the greatness and the limitations of Hegelian dialectics precisely when describing his own dialectical method as the 'direct opposite' of Hegel's. 'The mystification which dialectics undergo in Hegel's hands in no way lessens the fact that he was the first to represent their universal forms of motion in a comprehensive and conscious way. With him they are turned upside down. We need to right them in order to discover the rational core within the mystical shell.'[180] This statement also sheds light on the influence which Hegelian dialectics had. Their method, resulting as it did from the major revolutionary crisis in society and the natural sciences at the turn of the eighteenth to nineteenth century, became an important organ of the ideological preliminaries to democratic revolution, above all in Germany. Hegel's system, on the other hand, the systematizing of his findings, implied a recognition of the Prussian State of the restoration period and therefore exerted a conservative, indeed reactionary influence. The non-organic joining of these diverging tendencies could appear tenable only so long as the class conflicts in Germany were undeveloped or at least remained latent. With the July Revolution it became inevitable for the dissolution of Hegelianism, the working out of the antithesis between system and method and thereupon the refashioning of the method itself to begin. This struggle produced an increasingly clear differentiation between the camps or parties in the philosophical domain. After the statements which we have just quoted, Marx characterized this situation as follows: 'In its rational shape it is annoying and abhorrent to the bourgeoisie and its doctrinaire spokesmen because it includes in the positive understanding of the existing order an understanding of its negation, its inevitable collapse as well; it comprehends every realized (*gewordne*) form in the flux of movement and hence also from its transitory side; it

does not let anything impress it and is essentially critical and revolutionary.'[181]

It is anything but an accident that, in the dissolution of Hegelianism, one of the chief points of contention was the question of the relation of dialectics to reality. In Hegel's mysticizing of true dialectics it was his objective idealism, the theory of the identical subject-object that played the decisive role. As long as the antithesis had not yet collided in life and hence in philosophy, it was possible for such an artificial twilight to continue: an objective reality posited as independent of individual consciousness but still that of a mysticized mind (the world-spirit, God). The exacerbation of the social conflicts forced philosophy to come down more firmly on one side or the other: what each thinker understood by reality was something that had to be clearly worked out.

Is the dialectic, then, the objective motive form of reality itself? And if so, how does consciousness relate to it? As we know, the materialist dialectic answers the latter question to the effect that the subjective dialectic in human knowledge is precisely the reflection of the objective dialectic of reality, and that as a result of the structure of objective reality, this process of reflection likewise proceeds dialectically, not mechanically as the old materialism would have it. That answers the basic question in a clear, unambiguous and scientific manner.

But what was the stance that the bourgeois thinkers adopted to this question? Their class situation made it impossible for them to go on to materialist dialectics and the materialist theory of reflection. When, therefore, the problems of the objectivity of the dialectical categories and their mode of perception receive prominence, they can – at best – critically dissect Hegel's false synthesis, but are forced either to repudiate dialectics virtually altogether (Feuerbach) or to reduce them to a purely subjective one (Bruno Bauer). We shall concern ourselves with just one example taken from the copious literature of this period,

Adolf Trendelenburg's Hegel critique. Not only because this work shows the central problem-situation at its clearest, relatively speaking, but also because Trendelenburg, on Kierkegaard's own admission, exerted a strong influence on the Dane.[182]

Trendelenburg's critique starts out from an important and well-justified question. Hegelian logic rests – in accordance with the theory of the identical subject-object – on the principle of the logical categories' autonomous motion. If we view these as accurately abstracting reflections of the movement of objective reality, as materialist dialectics do, then autonomous motion is given a foothold. But if we approach the examination of this problem from an idealist viewpoint, there then arises the question – one which is fully justified with regard to Hegel – with what right does he introduce motion into logic as a fundamental principle? Trendelenburg challenged this right; he promptly examined the first fundamental transition in Hegel's logic, that from Being and Non-Being to Becoming, and arrived at the result that the dialectic which has been apparently deduced logically is 'presupposed without explanation by dialectics that claim to make no hypotheses'. He elucidates his idea as follows: 'Pure Being, like-unto-itself, is repose; Nothingness – the Like-unto-itself – is similarly repose. Now does agitated Becoming result from the union of two ideas in repose? Nowhere in the preliminary stages is there prefigured the motion without which Becoming would be only a Being . . . But if thinking engenders something else from that union, it is evidently adding this other factor to it and tacitly introducing motion in order to bring Being and Non-Being into the flux of Becoming. Otherwise the intrinsically mobile, ever-alive intuition (*Anschauung*) of Becoming would never result from Being and Non-Being, these immobile concepts. Becoming could never *come about* at all from Being and Non-Being were it not preceded by the idea of Becoming. Pure Being, an admitted abstraction, and Nothingness, again an admitted abstraction, cannot all of a sudden give rise to Becoming, this

concrete intuition governing life and death.'[183] Trendelenburg adds that Hegel investigates motion only in natural philosophy.

This, it is plainly evident, reaches to the crucial epistemological question of the Hegelian system and clearly reveals its central idealist weakness. Trendelenburg however never managed to get beyond the variation and restatement of this – intrinsically justified – critique. Certainly he draws attention to motion in objective reality; but because he again views it idealistically, he cannot discover in the real movement of nature and society the objective prototype of the categories' movement in logic, a logically generalized prototype reflected in accordance with consciousness.

So while he was able to indicate the central idealist flaw in Hegelian dialectics, it was unrectifiable from Trendelenburg's standpoint. For a solution to the difficulties which Hegel failed to overcome is possible only by obtaining a methodological, theoretical-scientific inversion along with the epistemological inversion of dialectics achieved by Marxism, and by locating concretely in the real categories of objective reality those prototypes which appear in abstract reflection in logic.

In his discussion of Marx's book *On the Critique of Political Economy*, Engels raises the question of whether the correct methodological treatment of these problems is historical or logical. Like Marx, he decides in favour of the latter and now defines its essence in an account which casts much light on our present problem. 'The logical mode of treatment was therefore the only apposite one. But this is none other in fact than the historical mode, only devoid of the historical form and disruptive contingencies. The train of thought must start where this history starts, and its further progress will be nothing but the mirror-image, in an abstract and theoretically consistent form, of the historical course of events; a corrected mirror-image, but corrected according to laws which the real course of history itself provides, in that every element can be considered in its classical stage, the stage of full maturity.'[184]

That is the only way to surmount the real flaws in Hegelian logic: through a scientific comprehension of that real motion which is reflected in the motion of logic. Hence in Hegel's logic, motion may rightly be criticized as mysticized, but this criticism will only take evolution beyond the Hegelian stage if the correct relation is established between what is reflected and the reflection. This cannot be done on an idealist basis. Trendelenburg, in company with others, discovered individual idealist flaws in Hegelian dialectics with occasional perspicacity, although frequently lapsing into triviality.[185] But the result of their critiques can only be either a universal rejection of dialectics or the construction of a subjectivist pseudo-dialectic.

Kierkegaard's role in the history of irrationalism is based on the fact that he took the latter tendency to a radical conclusion, so that at the time of his revival in the imperialist age, very little that was new could be added to what he had already expounded. He put paid to Hegelian dialectics and dissolved them just as completely, in substance, as Schopenhauer, with the one difference that whereas the latter wrote off dialectics *en bloc* as 'hot air', Kierkegaard seemingly countered them with a different dialectic laying claim to a higher value, a so-called qualitative dialectic. However, all the key conditions constituting the dialectical method are radically eliminated from this dialectic.

Thus 'qualitative' dialectics signify above all a denial of the conversion from quantity into quality. Kierkegaard did not even think it worth the trouble to develop a detailed polemic on the theme, contenting himself with an ironic reference to the absurdity of this Hegelian theory. 'It is therefore heresy to think in logic that a new quality may originate through a continued quantative determining; and it is an unacceptable fudging of the issue if, without concealing that all is not quite right, one hides the consequence of this proposition for the whole of logical immanence by including it in logical motion, as Hegel does. The new quality comes with the freshness, the jump and the suddenness of the enigmatic.'[186]

These thoughts do not have very much substance, since they are merely declarative without proving anything. But they are very characteristic of Kierkegaard's attitude to the problems of dialectics. Here he chiefly echoes Trendelenburg's criticism that Hegel's mistake was to deal with such a question under the heading of logic and especially as a problem of motion, and in a note appended to this criticism he sought to clarify the history of this problem. Like Trendelenburg before him, Kierkegaard strove here as elsewhere to lay down spontaneous Greek dialectics as the only model and one that also applied to his times, i.e., he was striving to annul all the advances made by dialectics in classical German philosophy, Hegel's especially, on the historical plane as well. After mentioning Schelling's tendency to explain distinctions quantatively, he said of Hegel in closing: 'Hegel's misfortune is precisely that he wants to validate the new quality and yet does not want to, since he wants to validate it in logic. But the latter must acquire a quite different awareness of itself and its meaning as soon as this is recognized.'[187]

Here Kierkegaard does not offer a clear statement, and it cannot even be verified if he ever became conscious of not only contesting a crucially original principle that carried the development of dialectics far beyond the stage of antiquity, but also of rejecting the very principle which, for Hegel, was the intellectual means (stemming from his coming to terms with the French Revolution) of his tentative comprehension of revolution as a necessary historical element. It is no accident that the idea of the conversion of quantity into quality already cropped up during Hegel's Berne period in this very context. 'The great, conspicuous revolutions must have been preceded by a quiet, secret revolution in the spirit of the age, one not apparent to everybody. An unfamiliarity with these revolutions in the spiritual world will then cause surprise at the outcome.'[188] This connection of the quantity-quality problem with the intellectual grasp of revolution manifests itself in Hegel's further development and receives in logic the universal definition of the leap as a necessary

element of change, growth and decay in nature and history.

Closer acquaintance with Kierkegaard's mental world will show two things. Firstly, that the denial of this element of evolution, the most important one, was as much of a central philosophical problem for him as its rationale was for Hegel. And secondly, that the fight against revolution occupied the centre of his world-view as much as the deduction of the contemporary situation from revolution occupied the centre of Hegel's. The passage from Kierkegaard we have quoted shows only the extreme consequences of this position, and not its whole scope. His chief concern here was to make a sharp division between the religio-moral sphere and the leap in it (the origin of the new quality) on the one hand and the process of gradual, quantifiable origination on the other. Hence with regard to the qualitative leap he stresses 'the suddenness of the enigmatic', i.e., the character of the irrational. In that the leap is divided from the transition of quantity, its irrational character comes about as a matter of necessity.

So while it seems that we are only dealing with a tiny fragment, a single question in Kierkegaard's world-view, it is already clear with what strict inevitability the denial of dialectical principles (motion and its laws, the conversion of quantity into quality) leads to irrationalism if this denial is thought out to a logical conclusion and if there is no eclectic blunting of its edge, as happens in Trendelenburg. And therefore – as we shall see more and more distinctly in the course of our discussion – Kierkegaard's qualitative dialectics are not a new and different dialectic set in antithesis to Hegelian dialectics, but a repudiation of dialectics. And since with Kierkegaard, who was disputing the most advanced dialectical form of his time, this occurs not fortuitously in the forms, categories and terminology of dialectics themselves, there arises a pseudo-dialectic, and irrationalism is clad in pseudo-dialectical forms.

This is the most essential step, the one with the greatest repercussions on irrationalism's later history, that Kierkegaard

takes beyond Schelling and Schopenhauer. The latter represents dialectics as pure nonsense; hence Schopenhauer's universal success during the period of Positivism. Schelling countered the most advanced dialectical form of his time with a more primitive one – and even this was distorted. Hence the collapse of Hegelianism was bound to plunge this answer to it into the same abyss. Naturally the dominance of Positivism also obstructed Kierkegaard's general international influence for decades. Only when Hegel's dialectics were converted into an irrationalist pseudo-dialectic at the time of his imperialist 'revival', only when the campaign against the real highest form of dialectics, the suppression and discrediting of Marxism-Leninism became bourgeois philosophy's central task, did Kierkegaard reappear internationally as a dialectician 'in tune with the age'. In this regard it is significant that Kierkegaard's own central philosophical problem, the campaign against Hegel, came to matter less and less. They now stood shoulder to shoulder in an increasingly fraternal and amiable fashion; indeed 'modern' Hegel interpretation contained a growing amount of existentialist-irrationalist Kierkegaardian motives.[189]

If we now use the term pseudo-dialectic, we do so because every irrationalism, as far as it is concerned with logical problems (as any irrationalism must be to a certain minimal level), always resorts to formal as opposed to dialectical logic. With Schopenhauer this happened quite overtly. The portentous change occurring with Kierkegaard consisted precisely in the masking of this recourse to formal logic and metaphysical thought as a qualitative dialectic, a pseudo-dialectic.

This retrograde movement to formal logic plus irrationalism in the guise of a pseudo-dialectic, in order to thwart an advance beyond Hegelian dialectics, had to be aimed first and foremost against those elements in Hegel constituting his idealist, inconsequential progressiveness at that time: against the historical and social nature of the dialectical method. Hence it is typical of Kierkegaard (and here again

he continued along the path taken by Trendelenburg) that he did not criticize the abstract forms of dialectics, those of the ancient Greeks and above all Heraclitus and Aristotle; on the contrary, in affirming them he strove to find a weapon against Hegel. Whereas Marx and Lenin discovered in Aristotle the seeds of dialectics and developed them further, Trendelenburg and Kierkegaard took care to reduce Aristotle to formal logic once more so as to do away with the Hegelian achievements in dialectics. Whereas Hegel already emphasizes strongly the patently dialectical tendencies in Heraclitus in order to work out the abstract framework of a dialectical method, and Marx and Lenin too vigorously stressed the materialist tendencies in him, Kierkegaard sought to read that 'genuine' form into the historically determined abstract generality of Heraclitan dialectics so as to turn them into a refutation of Hegel's 'spurious' dialectics.

This 'spurious' element in Hegel was precisely the historical and social nature of his dialectics. As we have already noted, it was just this which constituted the step forward taken by Hegel: he made conscious and raised to a method the historicity and sociality of dialectics. In fact he had a number of forerunners in this respect – it will suffice to refer to Vico, Rousseau or Herder. Before Hegel, however, with the Greeks, Nicholas of Cusa and in the Renaissance, the dialectical method was not yet associated, *qua* method, with the objective structure and the objective laws of movement of history and society. A considerable part of Hegel's progressiveness lies in this association; his limitation lies in the fact that, as an idealist, he was unable to carry these principles through consistently.

The dissolution of Hegelianism, before Marx took the decisive step to the materialist overthrow of Hegelian dialectics, has the peculiarity that the attempts to break through the Hegelian barriers engendered a retrograde movement in these questions objectively. Bruno Bauer, in the effort to develop Hegelian dialectics further in a revolutionary way, lapsed into the extreme subjective idealism of a 'philosophy

of self-consciousness'. By thus caricaturing – as the young Marx was already demonstrating at that time – the subjectivist aspects of the *Phenomenology*, and by reducing Hegel to Fichte, he too eliminated the social and historical motives from dialectics and made them far more abstract than they were in Hegel himself; he thus de-historicized and de-socialized dialectics. This tendency reaches a climax which tilts over into the absurdly paradoxical with Stirner. On the other hand the materialist turn we find in Feuerbach, since it was not a turn to *dialectical* materialism but the opposite, a demolishing of dialectics, was generally speaking a similar switch to the de-socializing and de-historicizing of subject and object in philosophy. Hence Marx rightly said of Feuerbach: 'As far as Feuerbach is a materialist, history does not occur for him, and as far as he takes history into account, he is not a materialist.'[190] And several decades later Engels demonstrated that man, the subject of Feuerbach's philosophy, 'therefore does not live in a real world originating in and determined by history'.[191]

Kierkegaard linked himself with the aforestated tendencies of the dissolution of Hegelianism, although Hegel's philosophy itself formed the main object of his polemics. It was these trends in ideas which determined his polemics' tendency and method to a large extent, and we may state by way of an advance summary: Kierkegaard took to a radical conclusion all the philosophical arguments which de-historicized and de-socialized Hegelian dialectics. What, in those arguments, was a mere product of the analytical process, became ossified in Kierkegaard into a radical irrationalism. This connection also shows how far we are justified[192] in regarding Kierkegaard and Marx in the same historical context: as long as we clearly see how Marx achieved the decisive step of raising dialectics to a really scientific method, while at the same time perceiving how the analytical method of idealist dialectics, which Marx could simply lay aside in surmounting Hegel, became with Kierkegaard the cornerstone of the most highly advanced irrationalist philosophy

which had hitherto existed.

This sharp contrast may also be portrayed as follows: Marx wrote in his Feuerbach critique '. . . that the individual's real spiritual wealth depends entirely on the wealth of his real connections . . .'[193] In the new, scientific dialectic, man is comprehended as essentially historical and social, so as to make us clearly recognize that to overlook his essential nature at any time is to turn our concept of him into a distorted abstraction. In contrast, Kierkegaard's irrationalism and his qualitative dialectic rest on the fact that in this dialectic, the distorted abstraction is presented as the sole true reality, the sole genuine human existence. Hence history and society need to be abolished in Kierkegaard's philosophy in order to create space for the existence of the artificially isolated individual, the only existence which is relevant here.

Let us start by considering Kierkegaard's struggle against the historicism of Hegelian dialectics. Above all Kierkegaard recognized that the Hegelian view of history, whatever Hegel himself may have thought about it, is atheistic in its objective core. Bruno Bauer before him already gave clear expression to this in the *Trumpet of the Last Judgement* (although in the context of his subjectifying of Hegel): 'The World Spirit only finds its reality in the human mind, or it is nothing but the "concept of mind" developing and perfecting itself in the historical spirit and its self-consciousness. It has no domain to itself, no world or heaven to itself . . . Self-consciousness is the only power in the world and history, and history has no other meaning than that of the Becoming and development of self-consciousness.'[194] It may be said without exaggeration that Kierkegaard's great polemic against Hegel is a *Trumpet* with the value sign reversed. Kierkegaard rejected Hegel's philosophy of history because of its atheism: 'Hence God does not play the master in the world-historical process as men see it . . . In the world-historical process, God is laced metaphysically into a corset half metaphysical, half aesthetico-dramatic, a corset that is immanence. May the devil be God in this way.'[195]

Kierkegaard sees quite correctly that there is no more scope for God in a world-history which is conceived as a uniform process with its own laws, and that Hegel's philosophy of history, despite all the references to the World Spirit, God and so on, can therefore be only a polite form of atheism. Evidently he quite failed to grasp in all its implications the most important progressive idea in Hegel's view of history, namely the idea that man has become human through his own labour and that men themselves make their history, even if they bring about something completely different from what they intended. Kierkegaard saw only the objective necessity, independent of individual will and consciousness, of the course of history as portrayed by Hegel, and protested against it in the name of God. 'As a result of involvement with the idea of the State and sociality and community and society, God can no longer take hold of the single individual. However great God's wrath, the punishment designed for the guilty person must propagate itself through all the authorities; in this way God has been excluded in practice, in the most binding and appreciative philosophical termini.'[196] And the disappearance of all dialectics from the world-picture, the conversion of dialectical into a formal logic (as a complementary basis for irrationalism) are expressed in the disappearance of all human activity from Kierkegaard's account of history and the conversion into a pure fatalism of the objectivity of history. Naturally Kierkegaard took this Hegelian view of history – in his own distorted interpretation of it – as an insult to God: 'The world-historical drama advances infinitely slowly: why does God not make haste if this is all that he wants? What undramatic forbearance, or rather, what a prosaic and tedious dawdling! And if this is all that he wants: how horrible of him to expend myriads of human lives like some tyrant.'[197]

At bottom this gives rise to a total repudiation of historicity; here Kierkegaard came very close to Schopenhauer. But as a result of the circumstances under which he developed his theory of the denial of historicity in combating Hegel's

historicism, the overall conception nonetheless acquires a different accent. There is a history – but not for man as a participant, but exclusively for God as the only spectator capable of surveying the entire course of history in its totality. The unique and complex problem of the knowledge of history, viz., that we are active producers of history and can still perceive it in its objective principles, hence that, here again, action and contemplation are closely linked with each other dialectically, was one whose unravelling Hegel strove for and surmised methodologically, rather than actually solved. Kierkegaard unravelled it with the proposition that action and contemplation are strictly separate; that man, who acts in a concrete and hence necessarily more or less small sector of history, is quite unable in theory to survey the whole. Knowledge of history in its totality remains the prerogative of God alone. Kierkegaard wrote: 'Let me now use a metaphor to remind us of the difference between the ethical and world-historical, the individual's ethical relationship to God and world history's relationship to God . . . The individual's ethical development, then, is the small private theatre where the spectator is God, but also the individual man himself occasionally, although he is meant in essence to be an actor . . . World history, on the other hand, is the royal arena reserved for God where he is essentially, and not by chance, the one spectator, because he is the only one who *can* be. The entrance to this theatre is closed to any spirit in existence. If this spirit imagines itself to be a spectator, it is merely forgetting that it is itself meant to be an actor in the little theatre, leaving it to that royal spectator and dramatist how the latter wishes to . . . employ it in the royal drama.'[198]

The difference between Schopenhauer and Kierkegaard is thus reduced to the fact that Kierkegaard did not proclaim the plain senselessness of the course of history – which, after all, would similarly be bound to lead to atheistic consequences. Instead he attempted to save religion and God by means of a consistent historical agnosticism. It looks as if

Kierkegaard was thereby turning back to the theodicies of the seventeenth and eighteenth centuries, which tried to pin down intellectually the contradictory and refractory elements in manifested history by invoking its totality, seen from the vantage point of God's omniscience. But the distinction that these also ascribed to human perception an approximative knowledge or at least a notion of history's true, complete interconnections is only apparently a difference of degree compared to Kierkegaard's radical agnosticism. It expresses the qualitative difference between two evolutionary periods: the gradual (but by the nineteenth century particularly rapid) withdrawal of the claim to a religious interpretation of concrete phenomena in history in the face of the scientific explanation of the world, which was gaining ground with increasing vigour. Religion had to leave bigger and bigger parts of the phenomenal world to objectively scientific research and withdraw increasingly to the pure inner man. In Kierkegaard too this retreat is clearly visible: 'An objectively religious person in the objective human mass does not fear God; he does not hear God in the thunder, for that is a law of nature, and perhaps he is right, nor does he see God in outward events, for that is the necessity of the immanence of cause and effect, and perhaps he is right . . .'[199] Kierkegaard's historical agnosticism is therefore an attempt, like Schleiermacher's previously, to abandon to science all the outposts of world-elucidation that could no longer be defended, in order to find in pure inwardness a terrain where it seemed to him that religion could be rescued and reinstated philosophically.

Obviously this retreat had to move in the direction of irrationalism, for with regard to the problems of pure inwardness, the surrender of the external world's (history's) rationality inevitably turns into irrationalism. Therefore the affinity between the positions of Schopenhauer and Kierkegaard also manifests itself in the fact that with both of them, the repudiation of history, or its knowability, implies a profound pessimism: if all events remain thrown back on the individual

mentally isolated from history and all human community, this will make his life not only irrational in general (which, considered in the abstract, could also occur in a form of mythical optimism), but also irrational in the sense of complete futility and absurdity. Hence in both cases – with, to be sure, a very different accentuation – despair is the basic category of all human behaviour.

There is a difference between them which is important to the development of irrationalism. It is that, with Kierkegaard, there arose a mythicized pseudo-history with a qualitative dialectic in place of Schopenhauer's overtly anti-dialectical anti-historicism. Certainly the historical element, with Kierkegaard, is only an irrationalist abyss dividing the whole of history into two: the appearance of Christ in history. Accordingly his historicity is a contradictory paradox: on the one hand, it means a change in the purpose, content, form, etc., of every mode of human conduct (consider the comparison between Socrates and Christ as teachers in the *Philosophical Fragments*). Here, therefore, the different and indeed opposed character of historical periods is to be deduced from the structural transformation of the cardinal intellectual types, ethical behaviour and so on, as later with Dilthey and other proponents of *Geisteswissenschaft* (human science). On the other hand, this did not give rise to a real periodizing of a real historical course of events. It is a unique, sudden leap in the middle of a 'history' which is otherwise motionless. For the philosophical point of the *Fragments* lies just in the fact that with regard to the relationship of the inner man to Christ – the sole essential relation in Kierkegaard's view – the two millennia that have passed in the meantime have no significance and cannot mediate in any way for those who have lived later. Kierkegaard wrote: 'There are no pupils at one remove. In essence the first and last are the same; it is just that the later generation finds an inducement in the report of contemporary witnesses, whereas Christ's contemporaries have this inducement in its immediate simultaneity and owe nothing to another generation in

this respect. But this immediate simultaneity is the inducement only . . .'[200] Thus history, again, does not exist in respect of the one matter which appeared essential about history to Kierkegaard, namely the salvation of the individual man through the appearance of Christ.

Certainly this qualitative-dialectical negation of historicity has the greatest importance for the philosophical essence of Kierkegaard's thinking. Whereas with Schopenhauer the intuitive experience of true reality is directly Nothingness, located beyond space, time and causality, beyond the individuation principle, with Kierkegaard it is only the individual's subjectivity developed to extremes which can attain to the highest and only genuine stage of reality, paradox. And this qualitative-dialectical pseudo-historicity is not to be separated from just the essence of paradox. 'Eternal truth has originated in time, that is the paradox,' wrote Kierkegaard.[201]

Here Kierkegaard distinguished – and this becomes very important to irrationalism's later development – the 'simple historical fact' both from the 'absolute fact', which is similarly held to be historical, but in a quite different sense, and from the 'eternal fact' situated right outside the historical course of events. This marks the creation of the methodological model for all later irrationalist distinctions, from that of Bergson between abstract time and real duration to Heidegger's contrast between 'authentic' and 'vulgar' historicity; and with all the irrationalists who came after Kierkegaard, 'authentic' time or history is always subjective and merely experienced as opposed to objective. According to Kierkegaard, only someone who 'receives the condition from God himself'[202] has access to the absolute fact and can become a pupil of Christ. For the simple historical fact, on the contrary, an 'approximative' knowledge is both possible and necessary.

This distinction has a major bearing on the character of Kierkegaard's qualitative dialectic. In order, however, to appraise it fully, we must first consider the historical milieu in which it originated. It was the decade of the writings of

D.F. Strauss, Bruno Bauer and Feuerbach; and therefore – especially where the first two are concerned – the age of the scientific-historical analysis of Gospel tradition. Kierkegaard saw clearly that the factual historicity of Christ contained in the Gospel traditions could not be defended any longer on the basis of a study of history that was at all scientific. Therefore he did not polemicize directly against the theories of Strauss or Bauer in order to rescue this historicity itself in the sense of a scientific objectivity, but extended his philosophical methodology so as to disparage and discredit, with regard to its philosophical cognitive value, the whole kind of historical knowledge that had led to such findings. He saw clearly that the historical reality of the Christ figure outlined in the Gospels was completely dissipated on a basis of scientific debate. His polemic was therefore levelled exclusively against the competence of the historical mode of examination in these questions concerning 'true' reality and 'existence'.

With the general dismissal of the knowability of the historical process in its totality we are already acquainted. Now we must recall the fact that Kierkegaard's qualitative dialectic rejected in theory the passage from quantity into quality, and thus a leap deduced through rational dialectics and therefore explained scientifically. The 'epistemological rationale' of Kierkegaard's attitude to history – whittled down to the problem of the knowability of Christ's historical appearance – was now accomplished in an extended polemic against the worth of any knowing based on approximation. This too shows us how radically this qualitative dialectic demolishes all the essential elements of real dialectics.

It was one of the major achievements of Hegelian dialectics that they tried to argue scientifically the concrete reciprocity between absolute and relative elements of knowledge. The doctrine of the approximative character of our knowledge is the necessary result of these endeavours: approximation, in this context, means that the relative element's irremovable presence does not annul the objective, absolute

character of a correct knowledge, but merely denotes the stage our knowledge has reached in the process of advancing approximation in the given phase. Approximation's objective basis is that the concrete, phenomenal object is always richer and more substantial than are those laws with whose aid we seek to know it. No kind of relativism, therefore, is contained in the consequent Hegelian conception of approximation, especially in the materialist further development it underwent with Marx, Engels and Lenin, where the reflection of objective reality guarantees the absolute element.

Here Hegel himself, because of his idealistically mysticizing starting-point of the identical subject-object, was unable to achieve any final clarity. But if we compare his version of dialectical approximation with the infinite progress of our knowledge as taught by Kant, we see the extraordinary advance. According to Kant the realm of true reality (independent of our consciousness) is eternally closed to us because of the unknowability of the thing-in-itself; with Kant infinite progress moves exclusively in the medium of the phenomenal world separated from this true objectivity. Despite all Kant's efforts to introduce into this sphere the element of objective knowledge, the immanent tendency to a subjectivism and relativism remains ineradicable, since the (*a priori*) disposition of the subject of knowledge can offer only an extremely problematic guarantee of its objectivity.

Here, Kierkegaard also contested Hegel by splitting the vital dialectical unity of the contradictory elements and puffing them up in their rigid isolation to autonomous metaphysical principles. Thus the element of approximation became the principle of pure relativism. Kierkegaard wrote: 'Historical knowing is an illusion, since it is an approximative knowing.'[203] And his demonstrations show how much he was focusing exclusively on the 'bad infinitude' of a philological historical discipline, and excluding any element of objectivity from this approximation from the very outset. 'The world-historical material is infinite, and a delimiting must therefore rest on some kind of arbitrariness. Although the world-

historical is something past, it is not finished as material for percipient contemplation but arises through ever new observation and investigation, which is always making discoveries or amending them. Just as in the natural sciences one augments the number of discoveries by sharpening the instruments, one can also do so with the world-historical by intensifying the critical observation.'[204]

So, as we see, Kierkegaard converted approximation to objective reality into a pure relativism by giving it the slant that the scientific progress which every further approximation signifies in this respect is, in truth, a march into nothingness. For a really objective knowledge is not attainable at all in this way, and the principle of selection and limitation is pure arbitrariness.

This nihilistic attitude to knowledge of objective reality rests on the fact that, for Kierkegaard, there is no question whatever of a real influencing of our perceiving relation by reality existing independently of our consciousness. Subjectivity decides everything. The only question is whether this subjectivity is genuine or false, passionately interested and intimately linked with the thinker's existence, or shallow and indifferent. And the objection which Kierkegaard made to Hegel's scientific knowledge of history (and objective reality as a whole) is that this knowledge lacked 'infinite interestedness', passion and pathos, and therefore degenerated into idle curiosity, a magpie learning, knowledge for its own sake. Thus he directed his attack against the purely contemplative character of knowledge in classical German philosophy, whose (to Kierkegaard's mind, specious) objectivity arises from just this absence of the subjective attitude.

This is not the only time we find that a critique of real central flaws in idealist dialectics has become the starting-point of the retrograde movement to irrationalism. The criticism of the old contemplative nature of Hegel's philosophy of history is not wholly unfounded here, although all along Kierkegaard presented a distorted caricature of Hegel and completely eliminated the vague pointers which his

philosophy of history provides in the direction of praxis. However, this – relatively – justified critique of a mere contemplation of history, of a history that has nothing to do with cardinal human problems in life, Kierkegaard used as a rationale for his specifically irrationalist denial of all real historicity.

In the first place, an absoluteness of 'existence', 'praxis' and 'interestedness' is posited to counter the worthless relativist contemplative attitude; an absoluteness which purports to contain no element of relativity or approximation. Thereupon the absolute and the relative, contemplation and action are transformed into neatly divided, sharply antithetical metaphysical potencies: 'A Christian is a person who accepts the teaching of Christianity. But if, in the last analysis, the What of this teaching decides whether a person is a Christian, then our attention is instantly turned outwards in order to find out what the Christian teaching is down to the smallest detail, because this What is supposed to decide not what Christianity is, but whether I am a Christian. In the same instant there begins the learned, concerned and anxious contradiction of approximating. Approximation may be continued as long as we wish, and by way of it the decision whereby the individual becomes a Christian is ultimately forgotten altogether.'[205]

But, in the second place, we must not only look at the methodology in the passage just quoted. Certainly this has a significance crucial to irrationalism's development, for it shows how, with each step in the concretization of the qualitative dialectic, all real dialectical categories and interconnections are removed and the dialectic is converted back into a metaphysic (irrationalism plus formal logic). This was the methodological model for many movements in the imperialist age, especially existentialism which was consciously affiliated to Kierkegaard. Albeit without express theology, and indeed in an atheist guise, the opposition we have demonstrated between absolute and relative became the core of Heidegger's philosophy. But exceeding this abstract

methodology, although very closely related to it, is the concrete Kierkegaardian antithesis: the antithesis between solely 'existing', solely absolute individual subjectivity on the one hand and, on the other, the abstract generality of socio-historical life, which inevitably vanishes into the nothingness of relativism.

An absolutely clear-cut gulf has now opened up between the quantative dialectic of mere approximation in the knowledge of history and the qualitative dialectic of the essential, 'existential', infinitely interested human relation. It is the Kierkegaardian gulf between theory and praxis, an antagonism which in this instance implies an antagonism between history and ethics. In the paradoxical definition of this antitheticality Kierkegaard goes so far as to declare: 'Constant association with the world-historical causes unfitness for action.'[206]

Action, for Kierkegaard, means an ethical enthusiasm whereby one must never think of 'whether one is thereby accomplishing something or not'. This antagonism implies the absolute incompatibility of the ethical with any human tendency to orient one's action to historical reality or to historical progress, which does not even exist in Kierkegaard's view. The ethical takes place in a purely individual, purely inwardly looking medium; all relating of action to – quantitative-dialectical – historical reality must therefore have a distracting effect, removing man from the ethical realm and destroying the ethical element within him. The relation to history neutralizes 'the absolute ethical distinction between Good and Evil in the aesthetico-metaphysical definition "the great", "the significant" on the world-historical and aesthetic plane'.[207] It is a downright temptation 'to associate too much with world history, a temptation which can lead to the desire to be world-historical as well whenever one should act for oneself. In being continually occupied with that contingent, adventitious factor through which world-historical figures become what they are, one can be easily misled into confusing these with the ethical element and into contemplating

one's own navel and showing a craven concern for the adventitious, instead of being ceaselessly concerned with the ethical factor in one's own existence.' Hence Kierkegaard could sum up his thinking as follows: 'World-historical immanence is always confusing for the ethical realm, and yet world-historical contemplation lies in immanence. If an individual sees an ethical element, it is the ethical within himself . . . For it would not be right to conclude: the more ethically advanced a person is, the more that person will see the ethical in world history. No, the very opposite applies: the more he develops ethically, the less concerned he will be about the world-historical realm.'[208]

We have now reached the central problem of Kierkegaard's philosophy, the real reason why he contested Hegelian dialectics. One of the most important motives in the dissolution of Hegelianism was its inadequate historicity, which did not point into the future. For all the mental confusion and woolliness of the Left Hegelians, they were spiritually united in challenging this. It was this crisis which engendered that view of history which is not only qualitatively superior but also exclusively scientific, and for the first time illuminates past, present and future in a really clear way: namely historical materialism. Without suspecting this momentous outcome to the philosophical crisis of his times, but consciously polemicizing against the radical Young Hegelians, Kierkegaard originated this new form of irrationalism, the most advanced so far: the pseudo-dialectical repudiation of history and the attempt to extrude – in the very name of his action – the man of action from all historical interconnections.

This is the meaning of the sharp antagonism of ethics and history, the antithesis between a praxis conceived in a purely subjective, individual light and an illusory immanence, an illusory historical objectivity.

Now the next step in making Kierkegaard's philosophy more concrete must be to elucidate what these ethics mean. It will be already clear from our studies that they signify not

only man's de-historicizing but, at the same time and going inseparably hand-in-hand with it, his de-socialization.

Kierkegaard did not draw this inference at once, and never drew it in a completely radical manner. Indeed his position is even more contradictory here than on the historical question. For we saw that he was obliged to counter the Hegelian view of history with an ethic, and he constantly accused Hegelian philosophy in general terms of lacking an ethic. Thus ethics appear to be Kierkegaard's effective answer to the claim laid in Hegel to history's objective immanence, a methodological tool for arguing subjectivity as the basis of truth.

But is an ethic possible if man is not viewed as a social being? Here let us avoid all discussion of Aristotle and Hegel, for whom this was axiomatic. Kant's *Gesinnungsethik* (ethic of conviction), the Ego-based Fichtean ethic and even Schleiermacher's were similarly unable and unwilling to renounce altogether the sociality which even conceptually is inseparable from the essence of man. Naturally the resultant inner contradictions lie outside the scope of our present studies. Here we must confine ourselves to showing briefly that these contradictions were not individual limitations in the thinking of single philosophers, but efforts to come to terms intellectually with the objective contradictions in bourgeois society that had emerged with the 'declaration of human rights' in the American and French Revolutions. Marx, polemicizing against Bruno Bauer, formulated their social basis as follows in the *German-French Yearbooks*:

> *Political revolution* dissolves bourgeois life into its component elements without *revolutionizing* these elements themselves and submitting them to criticism. It treats bourgeois society, the world of needs, labour, private interests and personal right as the *foundation of its existence*, a *hypothesis* argued no further, and hence as its *natural basis*. Ultimately man as a member of bourgeois society is taken for *authentic* man, for the *homme* as distinct from the *citoyen*, because he is man in his sensual

> individual *nearest* existence, whereas *political* man is only an abstracted, artificial man, man as an *allegorical*, *moral* person. Real man is only acknowledged in the shape of the *egotistic* individual, *true* man only in the shape of the *abstract citoyen*.[209]

Bourgeois philosophy expresses in very conflicting forms these contradictions between 'real' and 'true' man pervading the entire life of society. Either thinkers will attempt – without having discerned the true interrelations – a conceptual systematization of human activity from the angle of bourgeois society, like Hegel, in which case the antithesis of the 'world-historical' and the 'supporting' individual crops up as an uncomprehended contradiction (Balzac also formulated this question in very similar terms). Or they will endeavour to advance from individual ethics to the problems of social praxis, as was the case with, above all, Kant and Fichte, and with the Smith-Bentham school in England. Here we cannot examine in more detail the very graduated variations in these often extremely distorted reflections of a fundamental conflict in bourgeois society. But it can be stated that the duality and unity of *citoyen* and *bourgeois* growing out of life determines the structure, superstructure, propositions, etc., of the entire bourgeois ethic. And the shift to reactionary irrationalism finds expression, as early as the German Romantic period, in the attempt to weaken, diminish and indeed do away with the *citoyen* in man.

Kierkegaard too, especially at the beginning, could not wholly escape these universally bourgeois propositions. In his first major work *Either – Or*, ethics not only occupy a very important place; here, in contrast to the desperate solipsism of the aesthetic phase, the function of the ethical relation consists precisely in realizing the universal (i.e., the State citizen). Regarded in abstractly formal terms, somewhat from the standpoint of Kierkegaard's system-building, this position and function of ethics as the link between aesthetics and religion remained unchanged. In reality,

however, with the concrete development of Kierkegaard's world-view and philosophical method, this sociality of ethics and their realization of the universal became more and more problematic and contradictory, so that, considered objectively, they increasingly dissolved into nothing.

To be sure, we must not overestimate the sociality of even the early Kierkegaard's ethics. We would seek in vain for that wealth of human social relations which characterizes ethics with Hegel (and which also disappears with Feuerbach, but for opposite reasons than with Kierkegaard). They are, in essence, ethics of the private person, except that, as yet, Kierkegaard could not possibly blind himself to the fact that the private person – even as such – lives in society. In this early phase the advocate of the ethical vision of life declares: 'I am wont to appear in public as a husband . . . because that is really my . . . most important position in life.'[210] And precisely in polemical dispute with conscious immediacy and the solipsistic subjectivity of the aesthetic stage, the ethical categories are inevitably presented as those of the generality, of man's (private) life as it is consciously lived in society. 'Marriage', Kierkegaard makes his ethical advocate say in the later *Stages on the Road of Life*,[211] 'is the foundation of bourgeois life: through it a man and woman in love are bound to the State and the fatherland and the common public interest.' But in accordance with Kierkegaard's whole conception, the ethical sphere is 'only a transitional sphere',[212] a bridge to the authentic reality of the subjectivity which alone has existence: a bridge to the religious relation. Hence we must briefly investigate how it is that these bridging ethics (with their very reduced sociality) are not sublimed in the Hegelian sense, and thus both surpassed and preserved, but completely dissipated and destroyed instead.

Here, naturally, we cannot take it upon ourselves to give a full account of Kierkegaard's ethics systematically or even in their historical genesis. Our one concern is to indicate the decisive philosophical motives which of necessity entailed this inner collapse of those ethics. A principal motive was the

polemic against the Hegelian dialectical identification of the internal and external, a polemic of the greatest importance to Kierkegaard's philosophy. With Hegel, this identification has the epistemological purpose of refuting the subjective-idealist division of phenomenon and essence and showing them to be inseparably connected dialectically in contradictoriness: 'The external is thus *primarily the same content* as the internal. What is internal is also present externally and vice versa; the phenomenon exhibits nothing that is not in the essence, and there is nothing in the essence that is not manifested.'[213] This signifies for ethics – here we must pass over all the intermediate conditions – 'that it must be said: a man *is* what he *does* . . .' Kierkegaard saw in this position Hegel's endeavour to apply the category of the aesthetico-metaphysical to ethics and religion. But he expounds this as follows: 'Already the ethical poses a kind of antithetical relation between the external and internal inasmuch as it sets the external in indifference; as the material of the deed, the external is indifferent, for the ethical emphasis is placed on intention, the outcome being indifferent as the external side of the deed . . . The religious posits the antithesis between the external and internal definitely, definitely as antithesis, and therein lies precisely suffering as an existential category for the religious, but therein also lies the internal, inwardly directed infinitude of inwardness.'[214]

It will be clear without going into details that the view that the entire 'external' life is wholly indifferent for ethics also demolishes the private-ethical construction of Kierkegaard's stages. For how is marriage – to dwell on Kierkegaard's own very restricted interpretation of the realization of the universal – conceivable as a sphere of ethics, as a higher and no longer merely immediate stage of love, if the purely inward conditions, those remaining purely subjective, have sole ethical relevance for every marriage partner, and if the consequences of the one partner's aforestated convictions, deeds, etc., have to be regarded as wholly indifferent for the other partner's life? For in that case marriage is no longer

distinguishable (epistemologically) from the aesthetically immediate solipsism of eroticism, where the lovers belong to two completely separate worlds and cannot communicate with each other on the human plane at all.

Certainly Kierkegaard was at pains to sublime ethically the sensual-aesthetic immediacy of love. But this endeavour could only result in something if marriage, in his account, were to create a real, human communion between husband and wife. And Kierkegaard indeed attempted to follow this course in his writings, especially *Either – Or*. But as soon as he begins to develop his thinking's epistemological and philosophical foundations, it turns out that even that extremely limited circle of human relations which his ethics allow is irreconcilable with these foundations. Kierkegaard offers the clearest evidence that an 'ethic of conviction' taken to a rigorous conclusion can only produce a moral solipsism.

But this objective tendency in Kierkegaard to the self-dissolution of ethics is not – as seen from the angle of the logic of his system – the sole decisive reason why ethics and the extremely modest sociality permitted in them recede increasingly into the background. The crucial factor is his basic view of the religious element. We have already noted how important a motive the accusation was, in his polemic against the 'immanence' of Hegel's dialectical view of history, that this necessarily ousts God from history, thereby providing a historical rationale for atheism. In the first work in which Kierkegaard's theory of religion appears overtly and concretely (in *Fear and Trembling*), the same question crops up with regard to ethics. Not, to be sure, in so violently polemical a form as with regard to history, but no less decidedly in essence. Here Kierkegaard defined ethics as 'the universal, that which is valid for all'.[215] They are immanent, have their objective within themselves and do not point beyond themselves: 'The ethical is as such the universal, that which is valid for all; expressed from another angle, that which is valid at every moment. It rests immanently in itself;

it has nothing outside itself that constitutes its *telos*, but is itself *telos* for everything it has outside of itself; when it has assumed this within itself it goes no farther.' He closes this observation with the significant words: 'If this is the utmost that may be said of man and his existence, then the ethical has the same meaning as man's eternal bliss, which is man's *telos* in all eternity and at every instant. For it would be a contradiction for the possibility to exist that eternal bliss could be surrendered, i.e., suspended teleologically: since as soon as it is surrendered it will be frittered away . . .'

Thus, to Kierkegaard's mind, an ethic which does not exceed the generality (and clearly, the general or universal is now merely an idealistically distorted synonym for sociality) would be atheistic. Thus in his extremely individualist-irrationalist way he answers the old question – often debated in bourgeois ethics since Bayle's day – of whether a society of atheists would be possible with a yes as regards the ethical possibility, although with a sharp no as regards his value judgement. And he added (again, this is typical of him) that if such a state of affairs obtained, Hegel's definition of the relation between the particular and universal, between the individual and society would be correct.

For Kierkegaard, therefore, the only saving factor of the religious element, of faith, is that 'the individual as the individual ranks higher than the universal'.[216] Granted, he repeatedly added that his individual did not proceed from immediacy, that before reaching these heights he had to pass through the fulfilment of the universal in ethics. This, however, is an empty assertion, without any methodological significance for ethics whatever. For this sublimation of the ethical into the religious realm leaves no traces whatever behind it: from the standpoint of the individual, the 'paladin of faith' who lives in paradox – a paradox forever inaccessible to thought – it is completely irrelevant whether he has really passed the stage of the predominance of the universal over the particular. As far as a connection can be established here, it rests on the fact that the Kierkegaardian stage of

ethics was already far less rational and social than he represented it in this marked contrast with aesthetics on the one hand, and religion on the other.

As we have pointed out, the Kierkegaardian ethic too acknowledges no common medium, no real community between men; and with regard to the ethically essential, the inner realm sharply divided from the exterior, those practising this ethic likewise live in an insuperable incognito. The quantative heightening occurring between ethics and religion, one that is converted into quality (what a grotesque sequel for qualitative dialectics!), seems to be based only on the fact that ethical solipsism, the incognito contradicted the traditional categories with whose aid Kierkegaard formulated his ethics. Thus whereas this incognito displayed a vacillating, relative character, his temperament found its appropriate medium in faith, in paradox and in the absolute incognito. So the religious stage is, on the one hand, an aristocratic heightening of ethics where, because of the predominance of the universal, the aristocratic principle of the chosen individual cannot be practised so adequately as in the religious relation to life. On the other hand, the realization of the universal serves Kierkegaard's religious man as an ironical mask, as a deceptive and extremely petty-bourgeois attitude permanently concealing the latent pathos of the religious 'paladin of faith'.

Kierkegaard's entanglement in this web of contradictions certainly does not derive from the architectonic tripartite system-construction of his 'stages'.[217] There were social and philosophical reasons for it. Kierkegaard was always wanting to challenge the Romantic-ethical type of his age with which, he sensed, his own intellectual persona was most profoundly related. In his case, however, this defensive stance was far more than psychological. Here we are dealing with something objective and more important: namely the socially determined deep-seated affinity between his conception of aesthetics and of religion.

This applies above all to the methodology. Where religion

is not to be regarded as something objective, as doctrine – and we have yet to see how passionately Kierkegaard rejected any such method – an attempt will arise to rescue it from the angle of the individual person's subjectivity and of religious experience, whereupon the close proximity to aesthetics is already irrefutable. For in both instances we are dealing, on the one hand, with a world-picture steeped in fantasy whose truth and reality can only be argued from pure subjectivity. And, on the other hand, we are dealing with an extremely subjectivist mode of behaviour whose collisions with the universal (i.e., the ethical, social) again appear soluble only in the purely subjective evidence.

Feuerbach, who studied Kierkegaard in great detail and esteemed him highly, already saw perfectly clearly – naturally from a diametrically opposed viewpoint, with diametrically opposite intentions and inferences – this affinity between aesthetics and religion with regard to the objectivity of that which is reflected in them. He resisted the idea that his dissolution of religion, because of the demonstration of its purely subjective character, was bound to entail a dissolution of poetry. 'So little', he wrote, 'do I annul art, poetry and imagination that I rather annul religion only *insofar* as it is *not* poetry but ordinary prose.'[218] He did not dispute that religion may also be poetry; poetry, however, does not profess that its creations are any different to what they are, whereas 'religion, however, makes its imagined beings out to be *real* beings'.

It is, needless to say, not only the basic philosophical tendency which is at opposite poles in Feuerbach and Kierkegaard, but accordingly the relation of aesthetics and religion as well. With the former, the discovery of the subjective character of religion signifies its dissolution, and aesthetics survive as an important part of man's terrestrial life. Thus the aforestated affinity applies only within the terms of this hypothesis. With Kierkegaard, on the contrary, precisely the extremely rigorous subjectifying of the religious is deemed to provide a philosophical basis for religion itself and to

establish its autonomy, its absolute validity through qualitative dialectics. It is patent that under these conditions, the separation of religion from the aesthetic sphere was bound to become, for Kierkegaard, a vital philosophical issue. With Feuerbach the non-existence of its objects – where religion claimed their existence – in objective reality could easily elicit a clear delimiting. But for Kierkegaard this problem was much more involved, and it jeopardized the whole survival of his system.

This was not only because, in order to vindicate religion philosophically, he needed and wanted to prove that the existence of the religious sphere contested by Feuerbach was even the sole absolute reality. It was also because, in Kierkegaard, the aesthetic sphere denotes something different and far more comprehensive than in Feuerbach: not only products of art, their production and aesthetic contemplation but also, primarily even, an aesthetic attitude to life. Not for nothing does the erotic play so crucial a role in Kierkegaard's aesthetics.

In this we can see, despite all Kierkegaard's polemical digressions, an enduring and living legacy of Romanticism. With regard to this, the basic problem in his philosophy, he came very close in methodology to the moral philosopher of early Romanticism, the Schleiermacher of the *Talks on Religion* and *Intimate Letters on Friedrich Schlegel's Lucinde*. Certainly the resemblance of the propositions is limited to the fact that, as a result of the passing of Romantic aesthetics into an aesthetically determined 'art of living' on the one hand, and of a religion founded purely on subjective experience on the other, the two areas were bound to mesh all the time. But just that was the young Schleiermacher's intention: it was just by that route that he sought to lead his romantic-aesthetically oriented generation back to religion and to encourage the Romantic aesthetic and art of living to sprout into religiosity. If, then, the resemblance and the structural closeness of the two spheres were of advantage to Schleiermacher's arguments, the self-same factors gave rise

to the greatest intellectual difficulties for Kierkegaard.

This proximity, affinity and unbridled overflowing of the one into the other obtained both in early Romanticism and in Kierkegaard's works, as could be readily demonstrated at every point. Here, to indicate the affinity, let us pick out from Kierkegaard's *Journals* just one passage that also clearly expresses the joint aristocratic opposition of both orientations to the mediocre majority of men. In 1854, and thus not in the romanticizing period of his youth but at the time of his overt struggles to reinstate religion, Kierkegaard wrote: 'Talent ranks in proportion to its arousing of sensation; genius in proportion to its arousing of resistance (religious character in proportion to its arousing of annoyance).'[219] Clearly it is none too difficult here to draw a dividing-line between talent and genius (for this entirely matches Kierkegaard's aristocratic outlook on the world within the aesthetic sphere as well). But equally clearly, a high degree of theological-irrationalist sophistry is needed to draw even a specious line between resistance and annoyance (genius and the religious character). That applies all the more in that this contrast again vividly expresses the aristocratic outlook shared by the Romantics and Kierkegaard. In this respect Kierkegaard was a logical heir of Romantic thinkers (and Schopenhauer); to him it was axiomatic that entry to every sphere he deemed essential was available only to the 'chosen'. The reason why he defined the ethical stage in such a contradictory and self-defeating way was, the motives previously stated aside, the necessarily non-aristocratic character of an ethic which was intended to realize the universal. As soon as his ethics were translated into the paradoxically religious, Kierkegaard again found himself – in contradiction, it must be said, to his initial hypotheses – on the familiar basis of aristocratism. So the borderline between aesthetics and religion is just as blurred in his writings as in the Jena period of Friedrich Schlegel or Tieck and in Novalis and Schleiermacher.

But whereas for the Romantic thinkers of Jena, these fluid

dividing-lines were an attainable end, they implied for Kierkegaard's philosophy a danger which threatened to undo the whole system, a danger to be surmounted – and it never really was. It was more the changing times, the change in class relations and the class struggle than the thinkers' personalities which determined this contrast in philosophical propositions, in spite of a deep-seated affinity in cardinal philosophical hypotheses. The untroubled merging of Romantic aesthetics and religion was very closely connected with the thermidorian moods of the post-revolutionary intelligentsia in Germany; with the hope of managing to establish a harmonious 'art of living' subliming the crisis contradictions upon the basis of the new possibilities to be enjoyed in post-revolutionary society. Kierkegaard shared with the Romantics the life-basis of a reactionary-parasitical intelligentsia whose behaviour in the capitalist society taking shape was strongly oriented to a subjectivist 'art of living'. But since he was living in a deeply disturbed time of crisis, he had to try and rescue religion from its close relationship with aesthetics and above all with the parasitic-aesthetic art of living. In this respect, therefore, he represents the Ash Wednesday of the Romantic carnival as much as Heidegger represents that of the imperialist parasites in the universal capitalist crisis after the First World War, as opposed to the pre-war revels of Simmel or Bergson.

So in appearance – and from the subjective emotional angle – Kierkegaard was far removed from early Romanticism in his conception of both aesthetics and religion. Certainly, we have just established the affinity of the structure of both spheres (aesthetics, closely linked with the 'art of living', and religion as purely subjective experience). And the difference in, indeed, antitheticality of, the emotional emphasis predominant in both spheres only reinforces this merging of them – which Kierkegaard did not intend and indeed fought against. For the atmosphere of the Kierkegaardian aesthetic stage is determined by despair. The aphoristic confessions of the 'aesthetician' in *Either – Or* begin:

> What is a poet? An unhappy man who in his heart harbours a deep anguish, but whose lips are so fashioned that the moans and cries which issue forth from then sound to the stranger like ravishing music. His fate is like that of the unfortunate victims whom the tyrant Phalaris slowly tortured in a brazen bull over a low-burning fire; their cries could not reach the tyrant's ears so as to strike terror into him; to him they sounded like merry music.[220]

And in Kierkegaard's reply to Plato's *Symposium*, in which representatives of the aesthetic stage gather and discuss their views of eroticism (the central question in the 'art of living'), Johannes the Seducer, after hearing all the speeches, bursts out with the following reproaches to his companions: 'My noble friends, has the Devil got into you? For you are talking like mourners, your eyes are red not with wine but with tears.'[221] All Kierkegaard's aesthetic studies are pervaded by different shades of this despair.

Now as opposed to this, the religious relation shows a qualitative heightening and indeed a still profounder despair, an even stronger emphasis on the solipsism and irrationality in the subject left to its own devices. For in Abraham's sacrifice of Isaac, to take Kierkegaard's paradigmatic example, that which distinguishes Abraham from the tragic (and therefore the aesthetic or ethical) hero consists just in the absolute incommensurability of the motives for his deed, the impossibility in principle of communicating his authentic, decisive experiences. But this is to proclaim a complete extinction (and not a sublimation) of the ethically universal where the religious sphere is concerned. Here, comparing the sacrificing Abraham with the outwardly similar, but inwardly merely tragic conflict of Agamemnon when called upon to sacrifice Iphigenia, Kierkegaard wrote: 'The tragic hero too concentrates in a moment the ethical, which he exceeds teleologically; but in so doing he has a prop in the universal. The paladin of faith depends solely and uniquely on his own resources, and that is the terrible thing.'[222] Kierkegaard's

Abraham has nothing in common with a tragic hero but is 'something quite different; either a murderer or a believer. What lies between and saves the tragic hero is not applicable to Abraham.'[223]

So we have: despair as a spiritual basis, irrationality as a content and, connected with it, the theoretical impossibility of spiritual communication between men, the absolute incognito. These, with Kierkegaard, characterize both the aesthetic and the religious. In order to give rise, at least in appearance, to a polarity of interrelated tendencies at least, but not a complete identity, Kierkegaard had to stress (for the sake of a dividing factor) the anti-ethical aspect in aesthetics and the necessary passage through the ethical sphere in religion. And this although the ethical leaves no traces behind it, thus being wholly irrelevant to a concrete treatment of the problems, and although the tragic, precisely in Kierkegaard's account of it, creates a more intimate bond between aesthetics and ethics than he ever established between ethics and religion. For as we have noted, the tragic hero seeks and finds his justification in the universal (and therefore, according to Kierkegaard, in ethics); Kierkegaard never succeeded in locating so strong a concrete link between ethics and religion. All the more intimate was his link between aesthetics and religion. Kierkegaard himself admits as much in his *Journals*. Under the heading 'On My Production, Seen as a Whole' he wrote: 'In a certain sense the contemporary age is faced with a choice: one must choose between making either the aesthetic sphere the total idea and explaining everything in these terms, or the religious.'[224]

In our opinion, this desperate situation of his philosophy of despair forced Kierkegaard into the empty declaration of a relation between ethics and religion which never exists in his work. He was forced to make it to avoid admitting (the objective truth) that his religion was nothing more than a refuge for stranded decadent aesthetes. And since Kierkegaard, in view of the period in which he lived, was not a Huysmans and still less a Camus, who both found in despair itself a vain

and trifling self-satisfaction, he had to resort to such hollow constructions, unconsciously and reluctantly recognizing that a mental de-socializing of man implies at the same time the annihilation of any ethics.

To be sure we find in Kierkegaard's *oeuvre* another, even more important motive, one that is outwardly constituted quite differently but closely linked with the above motive objectively: the social function he wished to assign to religion and to Christianity. Kierkegaard perceived the mounting crisis of his age – he was a romantic anti-capitalist –, and the events of 1848 'promoted' his development (like the development of Carlyle, who was of course originally far more socially oriented) in the sense that they brought all the seeds of the reactionary in him to fruition. As early as 1849 he wrote in his *Journals*: 'Should Providence go on sending prophets and judges, it must happen solely in order to assist the government.'[225] Several years later he said very firmly: 'My whole work is a defence of the established order.'[226] And finally in 1854, when he thought that revolution 'could break out at any moment', he saw it as a dire misfortune that 'Christianity has been abolished as the regulating weight'.[227] Kierkegaardian Christianity, by imprisoning the individual as such in his incognito, by rendering the whole world of society about him of no value to him and concentrating his energies solely on the salvation of his own soul, was intended to become this 'weight'. 'And this weight was calculated to regulate temporalness.'

This social function of the solitary subject, the incognito as a prop of the established order and of retrogression, represents nothing that is radically new in the history of irrationalism; very analogous connections can be verified in Schopenhauer. Kierkegaard's only original contribution was the nuance of individual despair, despair as the elevation and mark of distinction of true individuality (in contrast to Schopenhauer's abstractly general pessimism, which was related to the species). And he raised the pathos of its subjectivity and the nothingness confronting it as its adequate

object to a pitch in the face of whose sublimity all 'petty' differences of social life were meant to fade away. Here too it is not hard to ascertain where Kierkegaard resembles Schopenhauer and where he differs from him. In both cases nothingness appears in a mythicizing, mysticized form. But with Schopenhauer, nothingness is the real substance of his Buddhist *mythos*, whereas its inevitable coming into force refutes and dissolves Kierkegaard's Christian *mythos*. Kierkegaard thereupon became the pioneer of a reactionary attitude whose repercussions are palpable even today in the philosophies of Heidegger, Camus and so on.

We have referred to nothingness as the adequate object of Kierkegaardian subjectivity – but does not this make us at odds with the facts? Have we not projected into his world-view, unjustifiably, the findings of his later, imperialist successors? Was not Kierkegaard a Christian believer, an orthodox Protestant? If we are to trust Kierkegaard's protestations – and there is no need to discuss the psychological question of how far they were genuine to the last, and how far products of self-deception, etc. – he was not only an orthodox Christian believer but even at pains to restore the lost purity of Christianity. Our task, however, is to decipher the real, factual substance of these protestations.

First and foremost: Christianity was not a doctrine for Kierkegaard. As his own position, to be sure, he countered this negation with the realization in practice, the imitation of Christ. That this imitation was placed emphatically at the centre of his thinking does not, it must be admitted, constitute anything startlingly new in the history of religion. But here we must bear in mind the difference that in the earlier forms of emphasizing the *imitatio*, nothing was set in antithesis to an objective theory – no kind of revealed doctrine whatever. The *imitatio* was presented as the individual's avenue to bliss, but only if his convictions and deeds agreed exactly with the revealed doctrine. With Kierkegaard, however, this opposition was rendered absolute. For Kierkegaard, Christianity was not a doctrine at all; for that would mean

its objective down-grading to a system or part of a system. He wrote: 'Objective faith makes it sound as though Christianity were also being proclaimed like a minor system, although not as good as the Hegelian system.'[228] Subjectively, the appropriation of such a doctrine – like any relation to objectivity – would be only an approximation, something relative, not the Absolute and not God. Thus once again, theory and praxis, objectivity and subjectivity are presented as mutually exclusive antinomies. '*Objectively*', Kierkegaard wrote, '*the stress is on what is stated; subjectively on how it is stated*,' and it is again highly characteristic of the closeness of aesthetics and religion in his system that he added: 'This distinction already applies in the aesthetic realm.'[229]

But the stark antithesis had decisive consequences for Kierkegaard's whole view of religion. He took the idea expressed in the above aphorism to a detailed conclusion: 'If there is an objective inquiry after truth, then there is objective reflection upon truth as an object to which the perceptive mind stands in relation. The reflection is not upon the relation but upon the fact that it is truth, the true, to which it stands in relation. If that to which the perceiving mind stands related is only the truth, the true, then the subject is in truth. If there is a subjective inquiry after truth, there is a subjective reflection upon the relation of the individual . . .'[230] And not omitting to draw all the conclusions that stem from this, he states immediately after the above passage: 'As long as the How of this relation is in truth, the individual is in truth, even if related thus to untruth.' Here it is plain to what degree Kierkegaard was more honest than his imperialist successors. Both reflected upon the subjective act, not upon the object. But whereas Kierkegaard drew from this the only possible inference, namely that no knowledge whatever can be reached by this route, the later Existentialists simply removed the 'parentheses' in which, following the method of Husserlian phenomenology, they set the – real or imagined – objective world while reflecting upon the subjectivity of the act, asseverating that they had

then attained to an 'ontology', a true objectivity. Kierkegaard, on the contrary, stated what was implied in his previous, general philosophical studies with great lucidity and in concretely theological terms: 'One man prays in truth to God, although he is worshipping an idol, the other prays in untruth to the true God and hence in truth is worshipping an idol.'[231]

Kierkegaard was therefore in earnest with the theory he directed against Hegel and all objective knowledge: 'Subjectivity is truth.' But what becomes of religion itself and of God in this – purported – rationale of the existence of religious subjectivity? In his studies pertaining to this, Kierkegaard again took up the approximative character of the apprehension of any objectivity by a subject, and therefore of any knowledge, and demonstrates the untenable position which results from it for the person existing religiously: 'Because he is deemed to need God at the same moment, because every moment in which he does not have God is wasted.'[232] And in a footnote to these lines he added: 'In this way *God certainly* becomes *a postulate* (my italics, G.L.) but not in the casual ordinary sense of the word. Rather it becomes plain that the only way in which an existing person enters into a relation to God is that the dialectical contradiction casts passion into despair and helps to apprehend God with the "category of despair" (faith). So the postulate is by no means arbitrary but a downright *self-defence*, so that God is not a postulate but the postulation of God by the existing being is – a necessity.'[233] We see how hard Kierkegaard was endeavouring here nonetheless to soften his rigorous deductions and to reduce his God's postulate character to a mere, albeit necessary, distinguishing feature of the subjective relation.

Such endeavours, however, do not in any way alter the state of affairs inexorably resulting from his premises. And Kierkegaard was far too much a child of his time, far too 'modern' seriously to set about changing anything essential to these deductions in the concrete realm or to attempt, for

instance, to demonstrate a real fulfilment of his God-postulate. He bore contemporary witness to the dissolution of Hegelianism, was clearly informed of the significance of Feuerbach's critique of religion, and indeed was downright fascinated by his reduction of religion to human subjectivity, although it was Feuerbach's purpose to dissolve religion. Thus he wrote of Feuerbach: 'On the other hand, a derisive man attacks Christianity and at the same time expounds it so brilliantly that it is a joy to read him, and anyone who has difficulty in finding a clear-cut account of it is almost obliged to resort to him.'[234]

This sympathy with the contemporary atheists is no accident. Not only because Kierkegaard grasped as clearly as they did the untenability of an objective, scientific defence of religion, but also because particular conditions in the ideological reflection of the socio-political crisis of the 1840s brought them very close to each other. We have already stressed more than once how much the disruption of objective idealism formed the centre of this crisis, and how much – barring the realization of a dialectical-materialist surmounting of Hegel – every bourgeois attempt at the revolutionary surpassing of Hegel was bound to turn into a philosophical subjectivism. This was manifested quite openly in Bruno Bauer or Stirner. But such elements of subjectification are also inherent in the flaws in Feuerbach's anthropologism. Here too – because a dialectical theory of reflection was lacking – the rigorously materialist theory, the object's theoretical independence of the subject often had to be watered down. Granted, Feuerbach himself was constantly at pains to pursue this materialist line strictly, but he only succeeded in the area of epistemology in the narrower sense. Everywhere else, as Marx, Engels and Lenin have pointed out, the illogicalities of anthropologism emerge more or less distinctly in Feuerbach's work too. It must therefore be emphasized that the philosophical materialism of Marx and Engels is not identical with Feuerbach's materialism, any more than Marxian dialectics are identical with Hegel's.

Through the subjectifying elements, the atheistic consequences of a materialist critique of religion of this type are likewise thrown into vivid relief: atheism is represented as a new form of religion. This may be observed very clearly with Heine. But even with Feuerbach, such illogicalities arising from the perpetuation of religion in atheistic forms are still present. And Engels, in criticizing these flaws, drew attention to their universal dissemination in this period. He gives as an example the maxim of Louis Blanc's followers, who used to say: 'Atheism, therefore, is your religion.'[235]

With Kierkegaard, of course, there is never any question of an overt allegiance to religious atheism; that was an unconscious, undesired product of his conception. Since Kierkegaard wished to release the defence of religion from Hegel's false idealist objectivism, he was caught up in the subjectivist movement that sought to retract every kind of objectivity into the subject and to have it proceed from the latter exclusively. For that very reason, every object (and with it, every trace of God as well) had to vanish in the – as it were – epistemological contemplation of the religious subject. But this methodology was at the same time an exact expression of his spontaneous world-sense, thereby determining the typically given surroundings and milieu of his religiously existential relation: it was nothingness. Kierkegaard asked of his religiously existing man that he should retain 'objective uncertainty', 'that I am in objective uncertainty "upon the seventy thousand fathoms of water", and believe nonetheless'.[236]

But belief – in what? Doctrine has disappeared, because every doctrine is 'either a hypothesis or an approximation, because every permanent resolution lies precisely in subjectivity'.[237] The community has disappeared because every religious person lives in an absolute incognito: 'But in absolute passion, which is the ultimate in subjectivity, and in the internal How of this passion the individual is farthest removed of all from this indirectness.'[238] Kierkegaard goes on to state that if two religious persons conversed, 'the one would have

a comic effect on the other . . . , because neither of them would be permitted to express the latent inwardness directly'.[239] And what of the imitation of Christ? Since there was no doctrine, since to Kierkegaard's mind Christ's earthly life itself logically formed the acme of the incognito: how could religious subjectivity know whom to imitate and in what deeds or convictions? Thus it had as a guideline that which it found in its own subjectivity, and with Kierkegaard that was despair and nihilism.

And Kierkegaard, obeying his innermost feelings, affirmed this tenuous perfect solitude, this atmosphere of nothingness precisely from the standpoint of the subjective element's highest development. Not for nothing did he write (1848) in his *Journals*: 'In a sense a disciple leads a crippled existence as long as his master is also alive. In a certain sense the disciple cannot achieve the stage of being himself.'[240] And the God of Kierkegaard's *Journals* has the same physiognomy of the desperately eccentric bourgeois intellectual (in such passages Kierkegaard was an unconscious and inconsistent follower of Feuerbach, an unwitting caricaturist). We read in the *Journals* for 1854: '. . . God is assuredly a person, but whether he wishes to be so towards the single individual depends on whether that is to God's liking. It is by the grace of God that he wants to be a person in relation to you; if you fritter it away he will punish you by adopting an objective relation to you. And in that sense we may say that (in spite of all proofs) the world does not have a personal God.'[241]

And it is wholly in line with this, Kierkegaard's profoundest inner attitude, his solipsistic aristocratism, that he stated just in his last period, when fighting overtly and publicly to restore the purity of Christianity, that there was no Christianity at all in the modern age. 'Now I have yet to see a single person whose life, according to the impression I gained of it (ignoring the *Protestations*, which I cross out), expressed even remotely that he had expired and had become spirit (any more than I believe myself to be such). So how on earth has it come to pass that entire states and countries are

Christian, that we are Christians in our millions?'[242] And the protestations of the Christianity of the past would likewise hardly stand up to his criticism, were he to choose to apply it.

Although the two movements exhibit directly opposing trends, they derive from the same causes socially speaking. To begin with, the religious conversion which overtook atheism in otherwise progressively minded thinkers only reflects a vacillation and floundering in the face of their own standpoint's ultimate consequences. But with the growing decadence of the bourgeois classes and their ideology, it developed more and more into an abdication of any critical viewpoint in respect of philosophical questions. It is the same process as that of the agnosticism of philosophicizing natural scientists, which was an 'abashed materialism' (Engels) for a time before it turned increasingly into reactionary idealism and myth-fabrication in the imperialist age. On the other hand, the conversion to atheism of the religiously disposed attitude was, regarded directly, a spontaneous process of disintegration in the religious outlook. However, the reactionary bourgeoisie's elastic defensive tactics were able to turn it into a new means of defence, in that with the help of this disintegration, that crisis within the bourgeois intelligentsia, which would have otherwise induced a falling away from all religion, could be arrested and redirected into a religious safeguarding of the established order. So gradually, in the imperialist period, the two trends intertwined and were already often hard to tell apart.

We have mentioned the reactionary bourgeoisie's tactics. The accuracy of our statement would suffer however were we, for instance, to charge Kierkegaard with such tactics. Subjectively, Kierkegaard was a sincerely convinced thinker whose contradictions originated in the fact that he was borne along on social currents whose nature he understood in part not at all, and in part very inadequately. (That he did not lack all awareness of his socio-political position is shown by his aforestated view of religion as a conservative power.)

In Kierkegaard we encounter the mode of feeling, spontaneously expressed, of an intellectual bourgeois stratum which had become deracinated and parasitical. How little this was to do with a personal problem, or with a narrowly Danish one, is evident not only from Kierkegaard's later international influence but also from the fact that, wholly independently of him, similar versions of religious atheism were starting to spring up and to take effect all around him.

Here it is impossible to discuss this question even in outline. I will just refer briefly to Dostoievsky who, under totally different concrete social conditions and with totally different objectives and means, often adopted a thoroughly similar position with regard to the intertwining of religion and atheism. An investigation of the parallels and divergences would be interesting and instructive, certainly. But we must be content with pointing out that with Dostoievsky's 'holy man', atheism is represented as nothing less than the 'penultimate step to perfect faith'. Admittedly Dostoievsky, in marked contrast to Kierkegaard, attempted to portray even this 'most perfect faith' in its humanly practical fulfilment. But typically, he always represented it such that, while it was destined to signify an overcoming of the Kierkegaardian incognito of human beings in their mutual relations, it always expressed the close affinity of this 'clairvoyant goodness' with the deepest scepticism towards men and a nihilistic contempt for them.[243]

Here in Kierkegaard's case, then, we are dealing with a more advanced form of religious atheism than Schopenhauer's. The contradictions we have just indicated in him may be amplified by comparing them with a fresh aspect: that of their relation to praxis. Schopenhauer's pessimistic irrationalism culminated in a complete ascetic withdrawal from all praxis. Kierkegaard, on the contrary, firmly stressed the role of deeds and action for existing subjectivity; indeed he polemicized, and not without reason, against the fanciful element in German idealism's pure contemplation. Quite correctly, he called the identical subject-object propounded

by Schelling and Hegel a phantom.

This antithesis between Schopenhauer and Kierkegaard was again a result of historical developments, of the mounting crisis in the social being of the bourgeois class. What, in the quagmire of the restoration period, was the typical form of reactionary withdrawal from participation in social praxis, and thus the typical form for the intelligentsia's reactionary 'neutralization', and what again became the universally typical form after the defeat of the 1848 revolution, could no longer suffice in the crisis-stricken 1840s. Regarded objectively, Kierkegaard accomplished a reactionary 'neutralization', a reactionary diversion from social praxis just as Schopenhauer did. But he countered social praxis not with the pure form of contemplative dissociation from life, but with an 'authentic', 'existential' action, albeit an action which, as we have noted, was just as carefully purged of all social determinants and was thus in reality only a quasi-acting. To be sure, this was endowed with the 'inner' attributes of action, and its conceptual description implied the most diverse active spiritual deeds. It therefore gave the illusion of being a copy of action itself, although everything whereby action really becomes action, namely the objectivity of social life, was extinct in it.

It did dawn on Kierkegaard himself in certain moments of self-criticism that this central portion of his thinking presents basically a caricature of action. He wrote in his *Journals* (1854): 'Can you imagine anything more ridiculous than wanting to use a crane to pick up a pin?'[244] It must be said, however, that just this illusory essence, distorted as it was – because of pure inwardness – lent to Kierkegaard's philosophy in the crisis of the 1840s a certain influence which became widespread in the major crisis between the two world wars and still exists today. For, on the one hand, the extinction of the social determinants of praxis made it easier to decide in favour of the established order. And, on the other hand, the semblance of praxis bestowed on the intelligentsia's irrationalist neutralization a firmer and more active reactionary

accent than we find in Schopenhauerian contemplation. At the time of Kierkegaard's later imperialist influence, this accent underwent a heightening in that modern Existentialism – through the help afforded by Husserl's phenomenological method – had at its disposal more subtle means of eradicating the concrete social determinants than Kierkegaard himself possessed. His modern successors eliminated all that was concrete in praxis, concretely historical and social, but retained nonetheless a distorted framework of both in the form of an allegedly ontological objectivity. (Heidegger's *das Man*, 'the one', is an example of this.) Thus unlike Kierkegaard, existentialist praxis no longer placed empty, purposeless, anti-ethical, 'world-historical' doings in antithesis to the purely inward concern for one's own salvation, but sought to give the impression that we make a free choice and realize our 'project' (Sartre) in 'true' reality purified ontologically, in the 'situation'. Existentialism's erasing of the contents, evolutionary direction, etc., of the social determinants enabled Heidegger to exercise his 'free choice' by opting for Hitler.

This conception of quasi-activity was the crucial step which Kierkegaard took beyond Schopenhauer in the history of irrationalism. In this respect, Nietzsche subsequently took a further step towards a still firmer, more militant reaction. But for all the contrasts manifest here, we must not neglect the close affinity of Kierkegaard and Schopenhauer, particularly in questions of ethics. When he read Schopenhauer in the 1850s, Kierkegaard showed a warm appreciation of his philosophy. With his intellectual acumen, to be sure, he at once pointed out the weakest aspect of Schopenhauer's ethics, 'that it is always hazardous to propound an ethic when the teacher is not in its power . . .'[245] In another passage he brusquely dismissed as 'academic claptrap' Schopenhauer's claim 'to be the first to have allocated asceticism a place in the system'.[246] And from this angle he investigated Schopenhauer's stance towards the academic philosophy which they both affected to despise: 'But what is the difference between Schopenhauer and a professor? In the last

resort it is only that Schopenhauer has private means.' His conclusion was that in the Socratic sense – which to Kierkegaard meant a great deal, as denoting the non-Christian form of 'existence' – Schopenhauer was not wholly innocent of mere sophistry.

But how does Kierkegaard himself pass the test in which Schopenhauer was found wanting? First of all he had to admit that the 'existential' significance of a material independence through private means was as crucial in his own case as in Schopenhauer's. He was honest enough to admit this openly, at least in his *Journals*: 'My becoming a writer is basically due to my melancholy, to that and my money.'[247] And in another passage: 'But even if I considered my life as a writer in total detachment from the rest of my life – there is still a danger, the danger that I have been privileged in respect of my ability to lead an independent life. This I fully recognize, and to that extent I feel very small in comparison to those who have managed to develop a genuine life of the mind in real poverty.'[248] So here Kierkegaard had nothing with which to tax Schopenhauer: both their philosophies culminate in an 'independent', purely inward attitude away from the bustle of the everyday world of society. From this vantage point they both looked down with great contempt on the wage-earning philosophers (the professors, and chiefly Hegel). And it turns out that the basis for this aloofness is not to be sought in their ethic itself but in the financial independence of its authors. This point is not without historical significance because in its heyday bourgeois philosophy produced thinkers who effectively adopted the same attitude to the 'trade' – although without the irrationalistically reactionary premises and deductions – while making many personal sacrifices. It will suffice to mention Spinoza, Diderot or Lessing.

Even more important is the fact that with regard to the 'existential' realization of his ethics, Kierkegaard too came very close to the Schopenhauerian answer, albeit in a more veiled and less cynical form. Let us reconsider the passage

where Kierkegaard denies his contemporaries the right to call themselves Christians. Here we find in parentheses the phrase: 'any more than I believe myself to be one'. And in the book's concluding reflections we read: 'If, on the other hand, nobody in our age will dare to adopt the task and character of the Reformer, then let the established order stand and retain validity – just as long as it is ready to subscribe to the truthful admission that, considered in Christian terms, it is only a modified approximation to Christianity.'[249]

Now what else does this express other than Schopenhauer's attitude to asceticism in theory and in his own praxis? If we substitute 'Christianity' for 'asceticism' in Kierkegaard's commentary on Schopenhauer's position, from which we are about to quote, we not only have from Kierkegaard a self-criticism which is unconscious but all the more devastating on that account. We also find a further agreement for the thesis that the gist of his philosophy was less a regeneration of Christianity than a new variety of irrationalist religious atheism. Kierkegaard wrote: 'The fact that asceticism now has a place in the system – does that not signify indirectly that its time is over? There was a time when men were ascetic in character. Then there came a time when the whole business of asceticism was consigned to oblivion. Now somebody is boasting of being the first to allocate to it a place in the system. But precisely this kind of preoccupation with asceticism shows that it does not exist for him in the true sense of the word . . . Schopenhauer, far from actually being a pessimist, represents at most – something interesting; in a way he renders asceticism interesting, which could not be more dangerous for an age bent on pleasure, for this age will suffer the most harm of all by distilling pleasure even out of asceticism; that is to say, contemplating asceticism without having the character for it, and allotting to it a place in the system.'[250]

This unconscious self-criticism is all the more telling because in the first place, Kierkegaard is confessing – involuntarily again – that Christianity belongs to the past, and that

it is precisely his qualitative-dialectic treatment, the place of religion in the *Stages* (the place in the system), which provides proof of this. Especially considering that, as we have just demonstrated, the purely ethical, practical-subjective character of religion is a self-deception on Kierkegaard's part, because he – like Hegel or Schopenhauer – only created a system. In the second place, and most importantly, Kierkegaard pointed out with heavy emphasis here how frivolous and inappropriate to crucial ethical questions it was of Schopenhauer to render asceticism 'interesting', and how far he was pandering to the pleasure-seeking tendencies of a hedonistically decadent world. But exactly the same criticism applies to Kierkegaard. And that is no coincidence, for such demands as Buddhist asceticism or 'paradoxical' Christianity would – if taken literally – be anachronistic absurdities in the capitalist, not to say imperialist, period. Their exponents would be pure eccentrics of no interest to anybody.

The reason why Schopenhauer and Kierkegaard achieved a world-wide influence lies in the essential nature of their systems as analysed above. It is of the essence of capitalism that every bourgeois ethic is bound to be contradictory in character. Marx rightly said of the ordinary bourgeois: 'The bourgeois has the same attitude to the institutions of his régime as the Jew to his law; he dodges round them as often as is feasible in every single case, but expects everybody else to abide by them.'[251] The bourgeois intelligentsia reflected the same state of affairs, but in greater complexity. When the class was in the ascendant and entertained illusions about its own being that were world-historically justified, there arose endeavours to solve the contradictions intellectually on the basis of the bourgeoisie's socio-historical mission in life. The relation between *bourgeois* and *citoyen* is one of the key questions in this complex, an honest attempt to comprehend intellectually the objective contradictions of bourgeois life.

With the marked emergence of the contradictions in capitalism, with a cessation of the struggle to dissolve the

feudal leftovers completely, and the origin of the bourgeoisie's defensive front against the proletariat as its one serious battleground, the period of apologetics naturally commenced in ethics as well. Their vulgar form was a direct sanction of all the hypocrisies that this social evolutionary trend prompted in the average bourgeois. Their indirect forms succeeded in affirming bourgeois society from the moral viewpoint by means of complicated detours. For in very general terms, indirect apologetics were based on repudiating reality as a whole (society as a whole) in such a way that this repudiation's ultimate consequences led to the affirmation of capitalism or at least to a benevolent tolerance of it. In the ethical realm, indirect apologetics chiefly discredited social action in general, and in particular any tendency to want to change society. They achieved this goal by isolating the individual and by setting up ethical ideals so lofty and sublime that in the face of them, seemingly petty and fleeting social objectives would fade and disintegrate. But if such ethics are to gain an influence which is real, broad and profound, they must not only set up this lofty ideal but also waive the pursuit of it (again with the assistance of ethically lofty arguments). For to realize such an ideal could confront the decadent bourgeois individual with a task posing as much personal difficulty as social action does. And that would render problematic the efficacy of the diversionary function of indirect apologetics. The decadent bourgeois, and in particular the decadent intellectual, requires a morally aristocratic boost that imposes no obligations. To heighten his enjoyment still further, he will want – while posssessing *de facto* all the privileges of bourgeois life – to feel that he is the exception, and even the rebellious, 'non-conformist' exception. This granted, he will reproduce the totally self-absorbed egotism of the ordinary bourgeois in the sphere of 'pure spirituality' and have at the same time the pleasurable sense of being infinitely superior to the latter and radically opposed to ordinary bourgeois morality.

Only through such twofold suppositions and suspensions

can indirect apologetics entirely fulfil their social function in the realm of morality: the function of creating a complicated system of modes of conduct remote from practical everyday life and meeting the intelligentsia's spiritual needs and demands. And yet the innermost core of these modes remains – in an etherealized, inflated and distorted way – that basic form of bourgeois social being and the ethic expressing it as defined above by Marx. Indirect apologetics in ethics have the task of steering intellectuals, sometimes rebellious ones, back to the path of the bourgeoisie's reactionary development, while preserving all their intellectual and moral pretentions to a superior ease in this respect. In devising such methods, Schopenhauer and Kierkegaard played pioneering roles. Their epigones (Nietzsche was not, of course, one of them, since he carried on the trend towards militant reaction) did not invent anything fundamentally new. They merely adapted these methods to the imperialist bourgeoisie's increasingly reactionary needs. Casting off more and more that residue of consistency, of good faith, which Schopenhauer and Kierkegaard still evinced in part, they increasingly became pure apologists of bourgeois decadence, and nothing else.

NOTES

1 Cf. especially F. Kuntze: *Die Philosophie Salamon Maimons*, Heidelberg 1912, pp. 510ff.
2 Schelling: *Collected Works*, Stuttgart 1856ff., Section I, Vol. VI, p. 22.
3 Fichte: *Works*, edition by F. Medicus, Vol. IV, p. 288.
4 Hegel: *Encyclopaedia*, para. 231. *Collected Works*, Berlin 183ff., Vol. VI, p. 404.
5 Ibid., Vol. IV, p. 145f.
6 Lenin: From the *Posthumous Works*, Berlin 1949, p. 70.
7 Hegel: op. cit., Vol. IV, pp. 150 and 145.
8 Quoted from F. Toennies: *Hobbes*, 2nd impr., Stuttgart, n.d., p. 147.
9 Marx-Engels: *Collected Works* (MEGA), Section I, Vol. III, p.164.
10 Marx: *Theories on Surplus Value*, Vol. II.

11 Marx-Engels: *The German Ideology*.
12 Engels: *The Dialectics of Nature*.
13 Engels: *Anti-Dühring*.
14 Hegel: *Encyclopaedia*, para. 73, Vol. VI, p. 141.
15 Jacobi's *Über die Lehre des Spinoza*, Munich 1912, p. 66.
16 Ibid., p. 78.
17 Published in: *Die Schriften zu Fichtes Atheismusstreit*, Munich 1912, p. 179.
18 Hegel: *Encyclopaedia*, para. 66, Vol. VI, p. 134.
19 Jacobi's *Über die Lehre des Spinoza*, pp. 74f.
20 Ibid., p. 77.
21 Friedrich Schlegel: *Early Prose Works*, Vienna 1906, Vol. II, p.85.
22 Ibid., p. 88.
23 L. Feuerbach: *Collected Works*, Leipzig 1846ff., Vol. II, p. 289.
24 Ibid., p. 245.
25 Ibid., p. 285.
26 Vico: *The New Science*.
27 Ibid.
28 Ibid.
29 Engels: *Anti-Dühring*.
30 Ibid.
31 Schelling: Op. cit., Part I, Vol. III, p. 628.
32 Marx: MEGA, Part I, Vol. 1, 2, p. 316.
33 This ambiguous dual tendency is already to be found in Boehme himself. Cp. Marx-Engels: *Early Philosophical Works*, Berlin 1953, p. 258.
34 Translator's note. *Heinz Widerporst's Epicurean Confession*, written in 1799 in opposition to Novalis.
35 Kant: *Critique of Judgement*, para. 77, translated by J.C. Meredith, O.U.P.
36 Ibid.
37 Ibid., para. 75.
38 Goethe's essay: *Anschauende Urteilskraft* (Intuitive Judgement).
39 Schelling: Op. cit., Part I, Vol. III, pp. 89f.
40 Spinoza: *Ethics*, Part II, 7th statement.
41 G. Lukács: *The Young Hegel*, translated by Rodney Livingstone, London 1975.
42 Schelling: Op. cit., Part I, Vol. IV, p. 361.
43 Ibid.
44 Ibid., p. 362.
45 Ibid., Part I, Vol. III, p. 369.
46 Ibid., Part I, Book V, p. 269.
47 Ibid.

48 Ibid., p. 267.
49 Ibid.
50 Quoted from: J.E. Erdmann: *Versuch einer wissenschaftlichen Darstellung der Geschichte der neueren Philosophie*, Stuttgart 1831-2, Part III, Vol. III, pp. 298f. and 304.
51 Schelling: Op. cit., Part I, Vol. V, p. 259.
52 Ibid., p. 261.
53 Fichte: Op. cit., Vol. II, p. 747.
54 Schelling: Op. cit., Part I, Vol. III, p. 625.
55 Ibid.
56 Ibid., pp. 627f.
57 Ibid., Part I, Vol. V, pp. 386f.
58 C.A. Eschenmayer: *Die Philosophie in ihrem Übergang zur Nichtphilosophie*, Erlangen 1803, p. 25.
59 Ibid., p. 54.
60 Hegel: Op. cit., Vol. XV, p. 647.
61 Schelling: Op. cit., Part I, Vol. VI, pp. 26f.
62 Ibid., p. 26.
63 Ibid., p. 35.
64 Ibid., pp. 38f.
65 Ibid., p. 58.
66 Hegel: Op. cit., Vol. II, pp. 13f.
67 Ibid., pp. 11f.
68 Cp. G. Lukács: *The Young Hegel*, London 1975, pp. 457ff.
69 Rosenkranz: *Hegel and his Contemporaries*; and Hegel: Op. cit., Vol. VIII, p. 21.
70 F. von Baader: *Writings and Essays*, Münster 1831, Vol. II, pp. 70f. Friedrich Schlegel described Hegelian philosophy as downright Satanism: *Lectures*, Bonn 1837, Vol. II, p. 497.
71 F. von Baader: Op. cit., Vol. I, p. 160.
72 Ibid., Vol. II, p. 86.
73 Ibid., Vol. II, p. 119.
74 Translator's note. Taken, with slight modifications, from the prose translation by Peter Branscombe (*Heine*, Penguin Books, 1967).
75 Marx: MEGA, Part I, Vol. I, 2, p. 316.
76 Engels: MEGA, Part I, Vol. II, p. 188.
77 Ibid., p. 225.
78 Ibid., pp. 204f.
79 It is characteristic of this trend that Baader polemicizes not only against the atheism of Fichte and Hegel, but also against the Pietists' religiosity, irrational and harnessed purely to feeling, and against Jacobi's abstract intuition philosophy. Op. cit., Vol. II,

pp. 71, 116, 126, etc.

80 Schelling: Op. cit., Part II, Vol. III, p. 81.

81 Ibid., p. 80.

82 Ibid., p. 6.

83 Ibid., p. 7. Here Schelling directly anticipates a favourite idea in the modern existentialism of Heidegger and Jaspers, the idea that man is unknowable in principle.

84 Ibid., Part II, Vol. I, p. 230.

85 Ibid., p. 238.

86 Ibid., p. 239.

87 Ibid., p. 498.

88 Ibid., p. 500.

89 Ibid., p. 513.

90 Ibid., pp. 537 and 540.

91 Ibid., p. 547.

92 Ibid., p. 374.

93 Ibid., Part II, Vol. III, p. 80.

94 Ibid., Part I, Vol. X, p. 161.

95 Ibid., Part II, Vol. I, p. 587.

96 Ibid., Part II, Vol. III, p. 161n.

97 Ibid., Part I, Vol. X, p. 239.

98 Ibid., p. 240.

99 Ibid., Part II, Vol. III, pp. 247f.

100 Ibid., p. 171.

101 Ibid., pp. 57f.

102 Ibid., p. 59.

103 Ibid., Part II, Vol. I, p. 569.

104 Ibid., Part II, Vol. III, p. 185.

105 Ibid., p. 155.

106 Ibid., Part II, Vol. I, p. 497.

107 Ibid., p. 499. This relation of present immediate awareness to pre-human reality returns in Machism. Cf. Lenin: *Empirio-Criticism*.

108 Ibid.

109 Ibid.

110 This becomes especially evident in Baeumler. Cf. his introduction to Bachofen: *Der Mythus von Orient und Okzident*, Munich, pp. CLXXIf.

111 Engels: *Peasant War in Germany*. The reference contained in the text relates to Engels's work: *Zur Wohnungsfrage*, Berlin 1948, p. 45. Franz Mehring has accurately characterized the social reasons for Schopenhauer's influence. Mehring: *Werke*, Berlin 1929, Vol. VI, pp. 163f.

112 Cf. G. Lukács: *Skizze einer Geschichte der neueren deutschen Literatur*, Berlin 1953.
113 Engels: *Peasant War in Germany*.
114 Schopenhauer: *Collected Works*, Reclam, Leipzig, Vol. IV, pp. 173f.
115 Ibid., Vol. VI, p. 213.
116 Thomas Mann: *Schopenhauer*.
117 Ibid.
118 Marx: *Capital*, Vol. I.
119 Schopenhauer: Op. cit., Vol. I, p. 429.
120 Ibid., p. 492.
121 Ibid., Vol. V, pp. 266f. Cf. also the passage on 'Corrupt Factory Workers' and Young Hegelians, Vol. II, p. 544, etc.
122 Ibid., Vol. I, p. 422.
123 Ibid., Vol. V, p. 112.
124 Ibid., Vol. III, p. 139.
125 Ibid., Vol. I, pp. 650f.
126 Ibid., Vol. III, p. 143. Mehring is therefore mistaken in regarding Schopenhauer as a 'freethinker'. Op. cit., Vol. VI, p. 166.
127 Ibid., p. 522.
128 Ibid., Vol. II, p. 521.
129 Ibid., Vol. V, pp. 376f.
130 Lenin: *Empirio-Criticism*.
131 Schopenhauer: Op. cit., Vol. I, pp. 554f.
132 Ibid., Vol. III, pp. 159f.
133 Ibid., Vol. I, p. 555.
134 Let us briefly point out here that this interpretation of the revision of the *Critique of Pure Reason* impressed even a Marxian like Mehring. He concludes – wrongly – from Schopenhauer's analysis that Kant's actual idealist tendencies would emerge from precisely the second edition. Cf. *Works*: Op. cit., Vol. II, pp. 232f. This is to turn the Kant problem elucidated by Lenin on its head again.
135 Kant: *Critique of Pure Reason*.
136 Lenin: *Collected Works*, Vienna/Berlin 1927ff., Vol. XIII, p. 186.
137 Schopenhauer: Op. cit., Vol. I, p. 163.
138 Ibid., p. 214.
139 Ibid., pp. 147f.
140 Ibid., Vol. III, p. 67.
141 Ibid., Vol. I, p. 151.
142 Ibid., p. 157.
143 Ibid., p. 164.
144 Ibid., p. 165.

145 Ibid., p. 188.
146 Ibid., p. 181.
147 Ibid., pp. 182f.
148 Ibid., Vol. II, p. 520.
149 Goethe: *Sayings in Prose*, Section II.
150 Schopenhauer: Op. cit., Vol. I, p. 340.
151 Ibid., p. 252.
152 Kant: *Critique of Judgement*, para. 41.
153 Schopenhauer: Op. cit., Vol. II, p. 443. Also Vol. I, p. 258.
154 Thomas Mann: Op. cit., p. 394. According to Mann this line runs via Nietzsche.
155 Schopenhauer: Op. cit., Vol. IV, pp. 299f.
156 Ibid., p. 348.
157 Engels: *Dialectics of Nature*.
158 Schopenhauer: Op. cit., Vol. I, p. 311.
159 Cf. Marx's Feuerbach theses, Marx-Engels: *The German Ideology*, as well as Lenin's *Posthumous Philosophical Writings*, especially op. cit., p. 133. This question receives a chapter to itself in my book on the young Hegel.
160 Hegel: Op. cit., Vol. XV, pp. 567f.
161 Schopenhauer: Op. cit., Vol. I, pp. 569f.
162 Ibid., p. 571.
163 Ibid., Vol. III, p. 55.
164 Ibid., p. 170.
165 Hegel: *Encyclopaedia*, para. 156, Supplement, op. cit., Vol. VI, p. 308.
166 Lenin: *Posthumous Philosophical Writings*, op. cit., pp. 82f.
167 Schopenhauer: Op. cit., Vol. III, p. 42.
168 Hegel: *Jenenser Logik*, Leipzig 1923, p. 202.
169 Hegel: *Encyclopaedia*, para. 257, Supplement, op. cit., Vol. VII, I.T., p. 53.
170 Ibid., para. 258, p. 54.
171 Schopenhauer: Op. cit., Vol. I, p. 249.
172 Ibid., Vol. II, p. 519.
173 Ibid., Vol. I, p. 186.
174 Ibid., pp. 357f.
175 Ibid., Vol. II, p. 521.
176 Ibid., Vol. I, p. 527.
177 Cf. especially Brandes's essay: 'Goethe and Denmark' in *Menschen und Werke*, Frankfurt 1894.
178 Quoted by J. Wahl: *Etudes Kierkegaardiennes*, Paris, n.d., p. 623.
179 Löwith, who in respect of his content occupies himself at length with radical Hegelianism and also with Marx, and thus does not

fall into the usual error (at least in this respect) committed by bourgeois historians of philosophy, that of openly or covertly ignoring Marx, sees nothing of the significance of the central problem, the materialist change-over to objective reality independent of our consciousness and to its objective dialectic. He therefore makes a kind of equation between objective reality and irrationalist-mythologized pseudo-reality, between Kierkegaard, Feuerbach and Marx or even Ruge and sees in all of them merely an 'attack on the existing order', etc. He thereby confuses and muddles together completely all the crucial philosophical problems – which, to be sure, is not surprising when the intention is to trace a line of development from Hegel to Nietzsche. K. Löwith: *From Hegel to Nietzsche*, Zurich/New York 1941, pp. 201, 217f., etc.

180 Marx: *Capital*.

181 Ibid.

182 Cf. Kierkegaard: *Collected Works*, Jena 1910ff., Vol. VI, pp. 194f.; also Höffding: *Kierkegaard als Philosoph*, Stuttgart 1912, p. 63, etc.

183 A. Trendelenburg: *Hegel's System*.

184 Marx-Engels: *Selected Writings*, Berlin 1951, Vol. I, p. 348.

185 Trendelenburg quotes, for instance, the phrase used by Chalybaeus, who called the dialectical transitions in Hegel 'the diseases of the joints in the system', op. cit., Vol. I, p. 56n. Engels calls such a kind of criticism 'pure beginners' stuff'; he states that 'the transitions from one category or antithesis to the next' are 'almost always deliberate' but adds, 'to speculate a lot about it is a waste of time'. Letter to C. Schmidt, 1.11.1891, Marx-Engels: *Selected Letters*, Berlin 1953, p. 525.

186 Kierkegaard: *Works*, op. cit., Vol. V, pp. 24f.

187 On the problem of quantative conditions in Schelling and Hegel cf. my book: *The Ycung Hegel*, London 1975, pp. 433-4.

188 Hegel, *Theologische Jugendschriften*. Edited by H. Nohl, Tübingen 1907, p. 220.

189 It is not by chance that Kierkegaard and Hegel are now brought into the closest possible association, since the irrationalizing of Hegel is a principal task of this movement. An important advocate of this association is J. Wahl, who regards the chapter in the *Phenomenology* on 'unfortunate consciousness' – torn out of any context – as the key to Hegel's intellectual world, but interprets this as though phenomenology were to reach its conclusion and climax here. The reader may soon begin to suspect that Wahl only read as far as this chapter. J. Wahl: *Le malheur de la con-*

science dans la philosophie de Hegel, Paris 1929.

190 Marx-Engels: *The German Ideology.*

191 Marx-Engels: *Selected Writings*, op. cit., Vol. II, p. 355.

192 In radical contrast to Löwith's interpretation.

193 Marx-Engels: *The German Ideology.*

194 B. Bauer: *Die Posaune des jüngsten Gerichtes über Hegel, den Atheisten und Antichristen*, Leipzig 1841, pp. 69f.

195 Kierkegaard: Op. cit., Vol. VI, p. 234.

196 Ibid., Vol. VII, p. 227.

197 Ibid., Vol. VI, p. 236.

198 Ibid., p. 235.

199 Ibid., Vol. VII, p. 227.

200 Ibid., Vol. VI, p. 95.

201 Ibid., p. 283.

202 Ibid., pp. 90f. Here the affinity with Baader is plainly visible.

203 Ibid., p. 168.

204 Ibid., p. 228.

205 Ibid., Vol. VII, p. 285.

206 Ibid., Vol. VI, p. 215.

207 Ibid., p. 214.

208 Ibid., p. 235.

209 Marx-Engels: *Early Philosophical Works*, Berlin 1953, p. 56.

210 Kierkegaard: Op. cit., Vol. II, p. 142.

211 Ibid., Vol. IV, p. 101.

212 Ibid., p. 442.

213 Hegel: *Encyclopaedia*, paras. 139 and 140, Supplement op. cit., Vol. VI, pp. 275, 279.

214 Kierkegaard: Op. cit., Vol. VI, p. 367n.

215 Ibid., Vol. III, p. 51.

216 Ibid., p. 53.

217 Translator's note. 'Stage' in the special Kierkegaardian sense of 'viewpoint' – the aesthetic, the ethical and the religious.

218 Feuerbach: *Collected Works*, Vol. VIII, p. 233.

219 Kierkegaard: *Journals*. Edited by Th. Häcker, Innsbruck 1923, Vol. II, p. 341.

220 Kierkegaard: *Either – Or*, New Jersey 1971, Vol. I, p. 19. (Translation modified.)

221 Kierkegaard: *Works*, op. cit., Vol. IV, p. 61.

222 Ibid., Vol. III, p. 75.

223 Ibid., p. 54.

224 Kierkegaard: *Journals*, op. cit., Vol. II, p. 108.

225 Ibid., p. 22.

226 Ibid., p. 242.

227 Ibid., pp. 357f.
228 Kierkegaard: *Works*, op. cit., Vol. VI, p. 289.
229 Ibid., p. 277.
230 Ibid., p. 274.
231 Ibid., p. 276.
232 Ibid., p. 275.
233 Ibid., p. 275n.
234 Ibid., Vol. VII, p. 291. Similarly he wrote of Börne, Heine and Feuerbach in the *Stages*: 'Often they are very well informed about the religious realm.' Vol. IV, pp. 418ff.
235 Marx-Engels: *Selected Writings*, op. cit., Vol. II, pp. 352ff.
236 Kierkegaard: *Works*, op. cit., Vol. VI, p. 279.
237 Ibid., p. 269.
238 Ibid., Vol. VII, p. 194.
239 Ibid., p. 196.
240 Kierkegaard: *Journals*, op. cit., Vol. II, p. 80.
241 Ibid., p. 392.
242 Kierkegaard: *Works*, op. cit., Vol. XI, p. 121. From Kierkegaard's standpoint, to be sure, one would have to ask: How does he know that none of his contemporaries is a Christian? According to the absolute incognito which he himself laid down, each of them could just as easily be a Christian. Certainly Kierkegaard has no criterion for deciding this question in his own epistemology.
243 From the copious literature on religious atheism let us give just one significant quotation to suggest the trend's universality. Berdyaev wrote: 'Atheism is only one of the experiences of which man's life is composed, a dialectical element in his knowledge of God. The passage through the stage of atheism can signify the purifying of the idea of God, the deliverance of man from bad sociomorphism.' The last term shows that Berdyaev too saw the main 'achievement' of religious atheism in de-socialization. Berdyaev: *The Divine and the Human* (Geoffrey Bles Ltd., 1949, out of print).
244 Kierkegaard: *Journals*, op. cit., Vol. II, p. 383.
245 Ibid., pp. 345f.
246 Ibid., pp. 368f.
247 Ibid., Vol. I, p. 373.
248 Ibid., p. 384. There are any number of such passages. We refer readers interested in this biographical side of Kierkegaard primarily to the conversation with Emil Boesen shortly before Kierkegaard's death, ibid., Vol. II, p. 407, and to the memoirs of his niece Henriette Lund, ibid., p. 413. Here we are not concerned with the biographical details but only with demonstrating

the connection between a 'sublime', meta-social ethic and its vulgarly bourgeois financial basis.

249 Kierkegaard: *Works*, op. cit., Vol. XI, p. 188.

250 Kierkegaard: *Journals*, op. cit., Vol. II, pp. 368f.

251 Marx-Engels: *The German Ideology*.

CHAPTER III

NIETZSCHE AS FOUNDER OF IRRATIONALISM IN THE IMPERIALIST PERIOD

1

It may be postulated as a general statement that the decline of bourgeois ideology set in with the end of the 1848 revolution. Of course we can find many latecomers – especially in literature and art – for whose work this thesis by no means holds good (we need only to mention Dickens and Keller, Courbet and Daumier). These latter names apart, the period between 1848 and 1870 was rife with significant transitional figures who, while their work does reflect features of the decline, were in no wise party to it with regard to the central substance of their output (e.g., Flaubert, Baudelaire). Certainly the decline started much earlier in the sphere of theoretical learning, particularly economics and philosophy; bourgeois economics had produced nothing original and forward-looking since the demise of the Ricardo school in the 1820s, while bourgeois philosophy had yielded nothing new since the demise of Hegelianism (1830s and 1840s). Both these fields were completely dominated by capitalist apologetics. A similar situation obtained in the historical sciences. The fact that the natural sciences continued to make enormous strides during this period – Darwin's great work appeared between 1848 and 1870 – does not affect the picture one bit; there have been new discoveries in this area right up to the present. This in itself did not forestall a certain degeneration of general methodology, an increasingly reactionary slant in the bourgeois philosophy of natural sciences, and an ever-growing zeal in the use of their findings

for the propagation of reactionary views. (We are not now speaking of ideological evolution in Russia. Here the year 1905 corresponded to 1848 in the West – and only twelve years afterwards came the socialist revolution.)

Only in the light of all these facts are we entitled to claim – without losing a just sense of proportion – that the years 1870-1 marked another turning-point in the development of ideology. In the first place, it was then that the rise of the great nation-states in Central Europe reached completion, and many of the most important demands of the bourgeois revolutions their fulfilment; at all events such revolutions had had their day in Western and Central Europe. Some very essential features of a real bourgeois-revolutionary transformation were lacking in Germany and Italy (to say nothing of Austria and Hungary), and there still existed very many relics of feudal absolutism, but from now on it was only thinkable that these could be liquidated through a revolution led by the proletariat. And in those years, the proletarian revolution was already clearly delineated in the Paris Commune. Not only in a French but also in a European context, the battle of June in the 1848 revolution had already signified the turning-point. Its occurrence strengthened the bond between the bourgeoisie and the reactionary classes, and its outcome sealed the fate of every democratic revolution of the period. The illusion that these bourgeois victories had secured 'law and order' once and for all was to crumble forthwith. After what was only a short pause, historically considered, the movements of the working-class masses acquired fresh life; in 1864 the First International was founded, and in 1871 the proletariat succeeded in gaining power, albeit only for a relatively short time and on a metropolitan scale: there came into being the Paris Commune, the first dictatorship of the proletariat.

The ideological consequences of these events were very widespread. The polemics of bourgeois science and philosophy were increasingly directed against the new enemy, socialism. While on the upsurge, bourgeois philosophy had

challenged the feudal absolutist system, and the interpretation of this challenge had occasioned its controversies over objectives, whereas the chief enemy now was the proletarian world-view. This, however, changed at once the subject and mode of expression of each and every reactionary philosophy. When bourgeois society was a rising force, reactionary philosophy had defended feudal absolutism and subsequently the feudal remnants, the restoration. As we have noted, Schopenhauer's special position stemmed from the fact that he was the first to proclaim a markedly *bourgeois*-reactionary world-view. But at the same time he remained on a par with the feudal reactionary, Schelling, inasmuch as what they both considered the chief enemy were the progressive tendencies of bourgeois philosophy: materialism and the dialectical method.

With the battle of June and with the Paris Commune in particular, reactionary polemics underwent a radical change of direction. On the one hand, there was no longer a progressive bourgeois philosophy to combat. Insofar as ideological disputes arose – and they figured prominently on the surface – they related primarily to differences of opinion as to how socialism could be disarmed most effectively, and to class differences within the reactionary bourgeoisie. On the other hand, the principal foe had already appeared in theoretical as well as palpable form. In spite of all the efforts of bourgeois learning it was becoming increasingly impossible to hush up Marxism; the bourgeoisie's leading ideologues sensed with ever-growing clarity that this constituted their decisive line of defence, upon which they had to concentrate their strongest forces. True, the accordingly defensive character of bourgeois philosophy only had a slow and paradoxical influence. The hushing-up tactics continued to prevail for a long while; from time to time it was attempted to incorporate 'what was usable' from historical materialism – correspondingly distorted – in bourgeois ideology. But this tendency assumed a wholly distinctive form only after the first imperialist world war, and after the victory of the great

socialist October Revolution in Russia. Right from the start, however, the defensive character was manifested in the fact that bourgeois philosophy was driven to the formulating of questions and into methodological controversies which did not arise out of any intrinsic need, but were forced upon it by virtue of the opponent's existence. It goes without saying that the solutions corresponded in every instance to the bourgeoisie's class interests.

In Nietzsche, of course, we perceive solely the initial stage of this development. But we can already confirm some important changes at this stage. The most telling fact is that in the battle against Hegel's idealist dialectics, the older irrationalists such as Schelling and Kierkegaard were occasionally in a position to indicate its real flaws. Although backward-looking inferences inevitably resulted from their critique, which was only partially accurate, their correct critical observations are of significance in the history of philosophy nonetheless. The situation was completely altered as soon as the enemy had become dialectical and historical materialism. Here bourgeois philosophy was no longer in a position to exercise a real critique, or even to understand correctly the target of its polemics. All that it could do was either to polemicize – at first openly, later increasingly surreptitiously – against dialectics and materialism altogether, or else to play the demagogue in trying to establish a system of pseudo-dialectics by which to counteract genuine dialectics.

Another point to consider is that the bourgeois philosophers ceased to possess any first-hand knowledge when the great arguments over objectives within the bourgeoisie abated. Schelling, Kierkegaard or Trendelenburg had still had an exact knowledge of Hegelian philosophy. In criticizing Hegel without knowing him even superficially, Schopenhauer was once again a forerunner of bourgeois decadence. It seemed that when it came to opposing the class enemy, no holds were barred and all intellectual morality vanished. Scholars who were conscientious in other areas, only venturing

to express themselves after accurately digesting their material, now permitted themselves the most facile assertions, which they had gleaned from other, similarly unfounded expressions of opinion. Even when presenting facts they never thought of resorting to the actual sources. This further helps to explain why the ideological struggle against Marxism took place on an incomparably lower level than did, in its own day, the reactionary irrationalist critique of Hegelian dialectics.

In view of this, how can we maintain of Nietzsche that his whole life's work was a continuous polemic against Marxism and socialism, when it is perfectly clear that he never read a single line of Marx and Engels? We believe that the claim is still feasible, for the reason that every philosophy's content and method are determined by the class struggles of its age. Although philosophers – like scholars, artists and other ideologists – may more or less fail to recognize it and sometimes remain totally unaware of it, this conditioning of their attitude to so-called 'ultimate questions' takes effect notwithstanding. What Engels said of the lawyers is valid in an even acuter sense for philosophy: 'The reflecting of economic conditions in legal principles operates without impinging on the awareness of the agents, and the lawyer imagines that he is operating with *a priori* theses, whereas they are simply economic reflexes . . .' Hence each ideology is consciously attached to 'a specific intellectual fabric which has been transmitted by its predecessors'.[1] But this does not alter the fact that the selection of these traditional strands, one's attitude towards them and method of treating them, the results obtained from a critique of them, etc., are, in the final reckoning, determined by economic conditions and the class struggles to which they give rise. Philosophers know instinctively what is theirs to defend, and where the enemy lurks. Instinctively sensing the 'dangerous' tendencies of their age, they try to combat them philosophically.

We exposed in our preceding chapter this kind of modern reactionary defence against philosophical progress and the dialectical method, and we traced the essence and

methodology of modern irrationalism back to precisely this type of reaction. In the observations we have just made, we have likewise attempted to outline the social reasons for the radical change in the representation of the enemy, and how this change was registered philosophically. Now when we consider the period of Nietzsche's activity, it can be clearly discerned that the Paris Commune, the evolution of the socialist parties of the masses, especially in Germany, as also the manner and success of the bourgeois struggle against them, impressed him most profoundly. We shall postpone until later a thorough examination of the relevant details and their manifestations in Nietzsche's life and work. First we intend to moot the general possibility that for Nietzsche, as for the other philosophers of the age, socialism as a movement and world-view had become the chief opponent, and that only this change on the social front and its philosophical consequences enable us to portray his outlook in its true context.

What determined Nietzsche's particular position in the development of modern irrationalism was partly the historical situation at the time of his appearance, and partly his unusual personal gifts. With regard to the former, we have already touched on the most important social happenings of this period. Another circumstantial factor – one favourable to his development – was that Nietzsche concluded his activity on the eve of the imperialist age. This is to say that, on the one hand, he envisaged the impending conflicts of Bismarck's age from every perspective. He witnessed the founding of the German Reich, the hopes that were pinned to it and their disappointment, the fall of Bismarck, and the inauguration by Wilhelm II of an overtly aggressive imperialism. And at the same time he witnessed the Paris Commune, the origins of the great party of the proletarian masses, the outlawing of socialists, and the workers' heroic struggle against it. On the other hand, however, Nietzsche did not personally live to see the imperialist period. He was thus offered a favourable opportunity to conjecture and to solve in mythical form –

on the reactionary bourgeoisie's terms – the main problems of the subsequent period. This mythical form furthered his influence not only because it was to become the increasingly dominant mode of philosophical expression in the imperialist age. It also enabled him to pose imperialism's cultural, ethical and other problems in such a general way that he could always remain the reactionary bourgeoisie's leading philosopher, whatever the variations in the situation and the reactionary tactics adopted to match them. Nietzsche had already acquired this status before the first imperialist world war, and he retained it even after the second.

But the lasting influence whose objective possibility we have just outlined could never have become a reality, were it not for the peculiar features of Nietzsche's not inconsiderable talent. He had a special sixth sense, an anticipatory sensitivity to what the parasitical intelligentsia would need in the imperialist age, what would inwardly move and disturb it, and what kind of answer would most appease it. Thus he was able to encompass very wide areas of culture, to illuminate the pressing questions with clever aphorisms, and to satisfy the frustrated, indeed sometimes rebellious instincts of this parasitical class of intellectuals with gestures that appeared fascinating and hyper-revolutionary. And at the same time he could answer all these questions, or at least indicate the answers, in such a way that out of all his subtleties and fine nuances, it was possible for the robust and reactionary class insignia of the imperialist bourgeoisie to emerge.

This Jekyll-and-Hyde character corresponds to the social existence, and hence to the emotional and intellectual world, of this class in a triple sense. Firstly, an oscillation between the most acute feeling for nuance, the keenest over-sensitivity, and a suddenly erupting, often hysterical brutality is always an intrinsic sign of decadence. Secondly, it is very closely linked with a deep dissatisfaction concerning contemporary culture: an 'unease about culture' in Freud's phrase, a revolt against it. Under no circumstances, however, would the 'rebel' stomach any interference with his own parasitical

privileges and their basis in society. He therefore waxes enthusiastic if the revolutionary character of his discontent receives a philosophical sanction, but is at the same time deflected – with regard to its social substance – into a rebuttal of democracy and socialism. And thirdly, it was just at the time of Nietzsche's activity that the class decline, the decadent tendencies reached such a pitch that their subjective evaluation within the bourgeois class also underwent a significant change. For a long while, only the progressive opposition critics had been exposing and condemning the symptoms of decadence, whereas the vast majority of the bourgeois intelligentsia clung to the illusion of living in the 'best of all worlds', defending what they supposed to be the 'healthy condition' and the progressive nature of their ideology. Now, however, an insight into their own decadence was becoming more and more the hub of these intellectuals' self-knowledge. This change manifested itself above all in a complacent, narcissistic, playful relativism, pessimism, nihilism, etc. But in the case of honest intellectuals, these often turned into sincere despair and a consequent mood of revolt (Messianism, etc.).

Now as a diviner of the cultural psyche, as aesthetician and moralist, Nietzsche was perhaps the cleverest and most versatile exponent of this decadent self-knowledge. But his significance went further: in acknowledging decadence as the basic phenomenon of bourgeois development in his time, he undertook to chart the course of its self-conquest. For in the most spirited and vigilant intellectuals who succumbed to the influence of the decadent outlook, there ineluctably arose a desire to conquer it. Such a desire rendered the struggles of the burgeoning new class, the proletariat, extremely attractive for most of these intellectuals. Here, and particularly with regard to personal conduct and morality, they perceived auguries of a possible social recovery and, in connection with it – naturally this thought was uppermost – of their own recovery. At the same time, the majority of the intellectuals had no inkling of the economic and social

implications of a real socialist transformation. Since they contemplated it in purely ideological terms, they had no clear notion how far and how profoundly such a realignment would mean a radical break with their own class; or how such a break, once accomplished, would affect the lives of the persons concerned. Confused though this movement may have been, it did embrace wide sections of the move advanced bourgeois intelligentsia. Naturally enough, it revealed itself with particular vehemence in times of crisis (for instance, the ban on socialists, the fate of Naturalism, the First World War and the Expressionist movement in Germany, *boulangisme* and the Dreyfus Affair in France, etc.).

Nietzsche's philosophy performed the 'social task' of 'rescuing' and 'redeeming' this type of bourgeois mind. It offered a road which avoided the need for any break, or indeed any serious conflict, with the bourgeoisie. It was a road whereby the pleasant moral feeling of being a rebel could be sustained and even intensified, whilst a 'more thorough', 'cosmic biological' revolution was enticingly projected in contrast to the 'superficial', 'external' social revolution. A 'revolution', that is, which would fully preserve the bourgeoisie's privileges, and would passionately defend the privileged existence of the parasitical and imperialist intelligentsia first and foremost. A 'revolution' directed against the masses and lending an expression compounded of pathos and aggressiveness to the veiled egotistic fears of the economically and culturally privileged. The road indicated by Nietzsche never departed from the decadence proliferating in the intellectual and emotional life of this class. But the new-found self-knowledge placed it in a new light: it was precisely in decadence that the true progressive seeds of a genuine, thorough-going renewal of mankind were deemed to lie. This 'social task' found itself in pre-established harmony, as it were, with Nietzsche's talents, his deepest intellectual inclinations and his learning. Like those sections of society at whom his work was aimed, Nietzsche himself was principally concerned with cultural problems, notably

art and individual morality. Politics always appeared as though on an abstract, mythicized horizon, and Nietzsche's ignorance of economics was as great as that of the average contemporary intellectual. Mehring was quite right to point out that his arguments against socialism never surpassed the level of Leo, Treitschke, etc.[2] But the very association of a coarsely humdrum anti-socialism with a refined, ingenious, sometimes even accurate critique of culture and art (for example the critiques of Wagner and Naturalism) was what made Nietzsche's subject-matter and modes of exposition so seductive for the imperialist intelligentsia. We can see how great the temptation was right through the imperialist period. Beginning with Georg Brandes, Strindberg and Gerhart Hauptmann's generation, its influence extended to Gide and Malraux. And it was by no means limited to the reactionary part of the intelligentsia. In the essence of their overall work, decidedly progressive writers like Heinrich and Thomas Mann or Bernard Shaw were equally prey to this influence. Indeed it was even capable of making a strong impression on some Marxist intellectuals. Even Mehring – for the time being – assessed it as follows: 'The Nietzsche cult is still more useful to socialism in another respect. No doubt Nietzsche's writings have their pitfalls for the few young people of literary talent who may still be growing up within the bourgeois classes, and are initially labouring under bourgeois class-prejudices. But for such people, Nietzsche is only a transitional stage on the way to socialism.'[3]

We have, however, explained only the class basis and the intensity of Nietzsche's influence, and not its long duration. This rests on his undoubted philosophical abilities. From Julius Langbehn (author of *Rembrandt als Erzieher*) to Koestler and Burnham in our own day, the standard pamphleteers of the reactionary wing have never done more than satisfy, with more or less skilful demagogics, whatever happened to be the bourgeoisie's tactical needs. But Nietzsche, as we shall see in more detail later, was able to enshrine and formulate in his works some of the most important *lasting*

features of reactionary attitudes to the imperialist period, and to the age of world wars and revolutions. To perceive his standing in this field, one has only to compare him with his contemporary, Eduard von Hartmann. The latter epitomized as a philosopher the ordinary, reactionary-bourgeois prejudices of the age after 1870, the prejudices of the 'healthy' (i.e., sated) bourgeois. This is why he at first enjoyed a much greater success than Nietzsche, and also why he fell into complete oblivion in the imperialist period.

Certainly Nietzsche, as we have already noted, achieved everything in a mythicizing form. This alone enabled him to comprehend and define prevailing tendencies because, lacking any understanding of capitalist economics, he was solely capable of observing, describing and expressing the symptoms of the superstructure. But the myth-form also results from the fact that Nietzsche, the leading philosopher of the imperialist reaction, did not live to see imperialism. Exactly like Schopenhauer as the philosopher of the bourgeois reactionaries after 1848, he wrote in an age that was nurturing only the first shoots and buds of what was to come. For a thinker incapable of recognizing the real generative forces, these could only be portrayed in a utopian, mythical manner. True, his task was facilitated both by the expressive mode of myth and by its aphoristic form, whose characteristics we are about to discuss. This is because such myths and aphorisms, depending on the bourgeoisie's immediate interests and their ideologues' endeavours, could be arranged and interpreted in the most diverse, often diametrically opposed ways. But the constant harking back to Nietzsche – in each instance a 'new' Nietzsche – shows that there was a definite continuity beneath it all. It was the continuity of the basic problems of imperialism in its *entirety* from the standpoint of the reactionary bourgeoisie's *lasting* interests, viewed and interpreted in the light of the *permanent* needs of the parasitical bourgeois intelligentsia.

There can be no doubt that such an intellectual anticipation betokens a not inconsiderable gift of observation, sense

of the problematic, and capacity for abstraction. In this respect Nietzsche's historical position is analogous to that of Schopenhauer. The two are also closely associated in the fundamental tenor of their philosophy. We shall refrain here from raising the historio-philological questions of influence, etc. The current attempts to dissociate Nietzsche from Schopenhauer's irrationalism, and to connect him with the Enlightenment and Hegel, I regard as childish, or rather, as an expression of history-fudging in the service of American imperialism on the lowest level yet seen. Of course there exist differences between Schopenhauer and Nietzsche, growing ever deeper as Nietzsche clarified his efforts in the course of his development. But they are more in the nature of differences of period: differences in the methods of combating social progress.

From Schopenhauer, however, Nietzsche took over the principle of the methodological coherence in his intellectual structure, merely modifying and extending it to suit the age and the opponent. It amounted to what we identified in our second chapter as the indirect apologetics of capitalism. Naturally this basic principle partly assumed new concrete forms in consequence of the conditions of a more acutely developed class struggle. Schopenhauer's struggle against the progressive thinking of his times could be summed up by saying that he condemned all action as intellectually and morally inferior. Nietzsche, on the contrary, called for active participation on behalf of reaction, of imperialism. This in itself obliged him to cast aside the whole Schopenhauerian duality of *Vorstellung* and *Wille*, and to replace the Buddhist myth of will-power with the myth of the will-to-power. Similarly, a further consequence of the heightened class struggle was his inability to make anything of Schopenhauer's abstract rejection of history in general. A real history, of course, did not exist for Nietzsche any more than for Schopenhauer, yet his apologetics of aggressive imperialism take the form of a mythicizing of history. Lastly – here we can only enumerate the most essential points – while

Schopenhauer's apologetics were indirect with regard to form, he voiced his socio-politically reactionary sympathies in an open, even provocatively cynical manner. With Nietzsche, on the contrary, the principle of indirect apologetics also permeates the mode of exposition, his aggressively reactionary siding with imperialism being expressed in the form of a hyper-revolutionary gesture. The fight against democracy and socialism, the imperialist myth and the summons to barbarous action are intended to appear as an unprecedented reversal, a 'transvaluation of all values', a 'twilight of the false gods'; and the indirect apologetics of imperialism as a demagogically effective pseudo-revolution.

This content and method of Nietzschean philosophy were most intimately connected with his literary manner of expression, namely the aphorism. Such a literary form made the element of change possible within the context of his lasting influence. When a shift in interpretation has become a social necessity – as, for example, in the age immediately preparatory to Hitlerism, and as again today, after Hitler's downfall – there are no obstacles to the revision of the enduring content such as we find with thinkers who have expressed the coherence of their intellectual world in a systematic form. (Granted, the fate of Descartes, Kant and Hegel in the imperialist period shows that the reactionary is capable of surmounting even these obstacles.) With Nietzsche, however, the task was far simpler: at each stage different aphorisms would be singled out and brought together, in accordance with the needs of the moment. There is one further point to consider as well. Much as the basic objectives accorded with the ideological outlook of the parasitical intelligentsia, to voice them in a systematic, brutal and open fashion would have repelled a wide and not insignificant circle. Thus it is far from an accident that, with but few exceptions (notably the immediate pioneers of Hitlerian fascism), Nietzsche-exegesis has stuck to his cultural critique, moral psychology and so forth, and has seen in Nietzsche an 'innocent' thinker concerned only with the spiritual problems

of an intellectual and moral 'élite'. Brandes and Simmel saw him thus, as did Bertram and Jaspers later, and as does Kaufmann today. And correctly so from the class standpoint, since the overwhelming majority thereby won for Nietzsche has later been ready to take practical steps matching this outlook. Writers like Heinrich and Thomas Mann have been exceptions.

This, however, is merely the result of the aphoristic mode of expression. Let us now consider the mode itself. Academic schools of thought have often reproached Nietzsche with having no system, something they held to be necessary to a real philosopher. Nietzsche himself roundly condemned all systems: 'I mistrust all systematic thinkers and give them a wide berth. A deliberate systematization means a lack of honesty.'[4] This tendency we have already observed in Kierkegaard, and it is not fortuitous. The bourgeoisie's philosophical crisis, as evidenced in the demise of Hegelianism, amounted to far more than the recognition of a given system's inadequacy; it signified the breakdown of a concept that had swayed men for thousands of years. When the Hegelian system collapsed, so did the whole endeavour to co-ordinate, and so to comprehend, the world's totality and its principle of growth from idealist sources, i.e., from elements of the human consciousness. This is not the place to give even a rough outline of the fundamental changes resulting from this final breakdown of the idealist system-concept. Granted, we know that even after Hegel academic systems were created (Wundt, Cohen, Rickert, etc.), but we know also that they were totally insignificant for the evolution of philosophy. We know too that the demise of the system in bourgeois thought prompted the outbreak of a bottomless relativism and agnosticism, as though the now obligatory renunciation of idealist systematizing were at the same time to mean renouncing the objectivity of knowledge, a real coherence of the actual world, and the possibility of knowing this. But equally we know that the burial once and for all of the idealist system coincided with the discovery of the real framework of

objective reality, namely dialectical materialism. Engels, polemicizing against Nietzsche's contemporary Eugen Dühring, formulated the new philosophical position thus: 'The real unity of the world lies in its materiality . . .'[5] This unity the individual branches of learning seek (with ever greater accuracy) both to reflect and to embrace conceptually; the principles and laws of this cognitive process are summed up by philosophy. So the systematic framework has not disappeared. It no longer appears, however, in the form of idealist 'essences', but always as an approximating reflection of that unity, that coherence, that set of laws which is objectively – or independently of our consciousness – present and operative in reality itself.

Nietzsche's rejection of systems arose out of the relativistic, agnosticizing tendencies of his age. The point that he was the first and most influential thinker with whom this agnosticism turned into the sphere of myth we shall investigate later. To this outlook his aphoristic mode of expression is no doubt intimately related. But he also had another motive beyond this. It is a general phenomenon in ideological history that thinkers who can observe a social development only in embryo, but who can already perceive the new element in it and who – especially in the moral area – are striving for an intellectual grasp of it prefer the essayistic, aphoristic forms. The reason is that these forms guarantee the expression most fitted to a mixture of a mere scenting of future developments on the one hand, and an acute observation and evaluation of their symptoms on the other. We see this in Montaigne and Mandeville, and in the French moralists from La Rochefoucauld to Vauvenargues and Chamfort. Stylistically, Nietzsche had a great liking for most of these authors. But a contrast in the basic tenor of the content accompanied this formal preference. The important moralists had already criticized – the majority in a progressive way – the morality of capitalism from within an absolutist, feudal society. Nietzsche's anticipation of the future was, on the contrary, approvingly oriented to an impending

reactionary movement, qualitatively heightened, that is to say imperialist reaction. It was solely the abstract fact of the anticipation which determined the formal affinity.

We must now ask whether, in Nietzsche's case, we are justified in speaking of a system. Are we entitled to interpret his individual aphorisms in a systematic context? We believe that the systematic coherence of a philosopher's thoughts is an older phenomenon than the idealist systems and can still survive when they have collapsed. No matter whether this systematic framework is an approximately correct reflection of the real world or one distorted by class considerations, idealist notions and so forth, such a systematic framework is to be found in every philosopher worth his salt. Admittedly, it does not tally with the structure which the individual philosopher himself intends to give his work. While indicating the need thus to reconstruct the real consistency in the fragments of Heraclitus and Epicurus, Marx added: 'Even with philosophers who give their works a systematic form, Spinoza for instance, the actual inner structure of the system is quite different from the form in which they consciously present it.'[6] We shall now venture to show that such a systematic coherence may be detected behind Nietzsche's aphorisms.

2

In our view, it was only little by little that the nodal point in the framework of Nietzsche's ideas took definite shape: the resistance to socialism, the effort to create an imperial Germany. There is ample evidence that in his youth, Nietzsche was an ardent Prussian patriot. This enthusiasm is one of the most significant factors in his early philosophy. It cannot possibly be regarded as a matter of chance or youthful whim that he wanted to be involved in the war of 1870-1; nor that, since a Basle professor could not enlist as a soldier, he at least took part as a volunteer nurse. It is at any rate characteristic

that his sister (although we must view her statements in a highly critical light) recorded the following memory of the war. At that time, she wrote, he first sensed 'that the strongest and highest will-to-live is expressed not in a wretched struggle for survival, but as the will to fight, the will to power and super-power'.[7] At all events this bellicose philosophical state of mind, which was an extremely Prussian one, in no way contradicts the young Nietzsche's other views. In his papers of autumn 1873, for example, we find the following: 'My starting-point is the Prussian soldier: here we have a true convention, we have coercion, earnestness and discipline, and that also goes for the form.'[8]

Just as distinct as the source of the young Nietzsche's enthusiasm are the features of his principal enemy. Directly after the fall of the Paris Commune he wrote to his friend, Baron von Gersdorff:

> Hope is possible again! Our *German* mission isn't over yet! I'm in better spirit than ever, for not yet everything has capitulated to Franco-Jewish levelling and 'elegance', and to the greedy instincts of *Jetztzeit* ('now-time'). There is still bravery, and it's a German bravery that has something else to it than the *élan* of our lamentable neighbours. Over and above the war between nations, that international hydra which suddenly raised its fearsome heads has alarmed us by heralding quite different battles to come.[9]

And the content of this battle, which initially was waged directly against the movement obstructing the full fruition of his ideology, Nietsche moreover defined in the draft, several months earlier, of his letter dedicating *The Birth of Tragedy* to Richard Wagner. Once more the Prussian victory was his point of departure. From it he drew such conclusions as these: '. . . because that power will destroy something which we loathe as the real enemy of all profounder philosophy and aesthetics. This something is a disease from which German life has had to suffer since the great French Revolution in

particular; ever-recurring in spasmodic fits, it has afflicted even the best type of German, to say nothing of the great mass of people among whom that affliction, in vile desecration of an honourable word, goes under the name of liberalism.'[10]

The connection between the battle against liberalism and that against socialism very soon became apparent. The Strauss pamphlet attacked the liberal 'cultural philistine', and did so with such energy and brilliance that it succeeded in deceiving even such a Marxist as Mehring about its true nature, for Mehring thought that 'indisputably' Nietzsche had here defended 'the most glorious traditions of German civilization'.[11] But Nietzsche himself wrote in his notes for the lectures 'On the Future of our Cultural Institutions' (1871-3): 'The most widespread culture, i.e., barbarity is just what Communism presumes . . . universal culture turns into a hate of genuine culture . . . To have no wants, Lassalle once said, is a people's greatest misfortune. Hence the workers' cultural associations, whose aim has been often described to me as that of creating wants . . . The drive, therefore, to disseminate culture as widely as possible has its origins in a total secularization, by which culture is reduced to a means of gain and of earthly happiness in the vulgar sense.'[12] As we see, Nietzsche's philosophical thinking was opposed to democracy and socialism from the beginning.

This attitude and these perspectives form the basis of Nietzsche's understanding of Ancient Greece. Here his opposition to the revolutionary traditions of bourgeois development is quite plainly perceptible. We are not thinking mainly of the Dionysian principle which made Nietzsche's first writings famous, for there the idea was still, in his own words, part of his 'artist metaphysics'. It took on actual significance only after the conquest of decadence had become a central problem for the mature Nietzsche. We want to put the chief emphasis on the principles upon which his new image of Ancient Greece was founded in the first place. And prominent among these is the idea that slavery is necessary to

any real civilization.

If Nietzsche had stressed the role of slavery in Greek culture merely from the historical standpoint, this perfectly correct observation would be of no great importance; he himself referred to Friedrich Wolf, who had made it before him.[13] It was bound to gain an even wider currency, and not only because of progress in historical studies. It followed also from a review of the 'heroic illusions' of the French Revolution, whose ideologists had ignored the slavery issue in order to create out of the democratic city-state the model of a modern revolutionary democracy. (These same views influenced the German image of Ancient Greece in the period from Winckelmann to Hegel.) What is new in Nietzsche is that he used slavery as a vehicle for his critique of *contemporary* civilization: 'And while it may be true that the Greeks perished because of their slave-holding, it is far more certain that we shall perish because of the *absence* of slavery.'[14]

So if Nietzsche – showing certain methodological affinities with Romantic anti-capitalism – contrasts a great bygone period with the capitalist present which he was criticizing, it is not the same thing as Sismondi's contrast between the peaceful, simple trade in goods and an age of crisis and mass unemployment. Not is it the same as ordered and purposeful artisan labour in the Middle Ages, as contrasted by the young Carlyle with the division of labour and an age of anarchy. What Nietzsche contrasts with present times is the Greek dictatorship of an élite which clearly recognizes 'that work is an ignominy', and which creates immortal art-works at its leisure. 'In more recent times', he wrote, 'it is not the person who needs art but the slave who has determined the general outlook. Such phantoms as the dignity of man, the dignity of labour are the shabby products of a slave mentality hiding from its own nature. Unhappy the age in which the slave needs such ideas and is spurred to reflect upon himself and the world around him. Wretched the seducers who have deprived the slave of his innocence by means of the fruit from the Tree of Knowledge!'[15]

Now what are the qualities of this 'élite' whose revival, assisted by a return of slavery, aroused in the young Nietzsche the hope of a cultural renaissance on a utopian and mythical plane? That it springs up from a barbarian condition is something we might accept as confirming historical facts. Indeed Nietzsche depicted it in the most lurid colours in 'Homer's Contest' (1871-2). But if we are to understand Greek civilization, stated Nietzsche in a polemic against the Orphic thinkers – who held that 'a life rooted in such an urge is not worth living' – then 'we must start out from the idea that the Greek genius accepted this so fearfully active urge and regarded it as *justified*'.[16] Thus it is a matter not of conquering, civilizing and humanizing the barbarian instincts, but of constructing the great civilization on their bedrock and diverting them into suitable channels. Only in this context, not from the standpoint of some vague 'artist metaphysics', can the Dionysian principle be properly grasped and appreciated. Moreover, Nietzsche rightly said in a later draft of the preface to his début work on the Dionysian principle: 'What a disadvantage my timidity is when I speak as a scholar of a subject of which I might have spoken from "experience".'[17]

For the young Nietzsche, the organ for the social utilization of the barbarian instincts is the contest (*agon*). This, as we are about to note from Nietzsche's own statements, was a mythicizing of capitalist competition. He quotes from Pausanias the Hesiod passage about the two goddesses Eris: 'She (the good Eris, G.L.) spurs even the inept to work; and if a man without property sees a wealthy man, he will make haste to sow and plant likewise and to put his house in good order; neighbour competes with neighbour in striving for prosperity. This Eris is beneficial for mankind. One potter will resent another, one carpenter the other, beggar envies beggar and singer envies singer.'[18] And this state of affairs he contrasted with modern depravity: 'Nowadays self-seeking is feared as "the devil incarnate" ', whereas for the ancients the goal of the agonal training was 'the welfare of the whole, the commonwealth'.[19]

If we now return to slavery as the alleged bedrock of any genuine civilization, we can see how much of the later Nietzsche this early work – albeit in an immature manner – anticipated. In this context the Schopenhauer and Wagner portraits which he produced with such fervent eloquence resemble mythicized pretexts for expressing something not yet fully developed, half in poetic and half in philosophical form. His own later criticism of his first writings – especially in *Ecce homo* – all tended in this direction: '. . . that what I learnt from Wagner about music in those years has nothing at all to do with Wagner; that when I described Dionysian music I was describing *the* music that *I* had heard, – that I had instinctively to transpose and transfigure into the new spirit all that was latent within me. The proof of this, *the strongest possible proof*, is my piece *Wagner in Bayreuth*: I am the sole subject in all the psychologically crucial passages – one may automatically read my own name or the word "Zarathustra" wherever the text reads "Wagner" . . . the latter himself sensed this; he was unable to recognize himself in the piece.'[20] Modified somewhat, this also applies to the Schopenhauer portrait in the work of Nietzsche's youth. The third, similarly mythologized, Socrates portrait is a totally different matter. In the début work the great antithesis was already 'The Dionysian and the Socratic'.[21] And Nietzsche – at first in predominantly aesthetic terms – enlarged this antithesis to encompass that of instinct and reason. In *Ecce homo* he reached his conclusion: the discovery that Socrates was a 'décadent' and that one must rate 'morality itself as a symptom of decadence' the mature Nietzsche regarded as 'an innovation, a discovery of the first order in the history of knowledge'.[22]

When investigating in general the determining causes of Nietzsche's further development, one usually lays the chief stress on the Wagner disappointment. But the points just raised concerning Nietzsche's attitude to Wagner already show us that it was a symptom of his shift rather than its actual cause. In Wagner, and with increasing acuteness,

Nietzsche challenged the art of his own German period in the name of the imperialist future. When, especially after the First World War, it became the fashion to challenge the nineteenth century's ideology (the age of 'security') in the name of the twentieth, Nietzsche's split with Wagner and late polemics against him furnished the methodological 'model' for this conflict. The fact that the ideological spokesmen of the Hitler period continued this tradition, though linking it with Wagner idolatry, does not prove anything. Their rejection of 'security' was combined also with the glorification of Bismarck, whom Nietzsche in his final period nearly always attacked in conjunction with Wagner. For the older Nietzsche, Wagner was the greatest artistic expression of that decadence whose most important political representative he saw in Bismarck. And in going beyond the philosophy of Schopenhauer he followed the same direction. We must not forget that even the young Nietzsche was never a really orthodox disciple of Schopenhauer with regard to radical a-historicism. From the start he had toyed with a mythicizing of history, whereas his master had totally avoided history. This tendency, already present in *The Birth of Tragedy*, grew more pronounced in the second *Untimely Consideration*. Activism – of the counter-revolutionary variety – was moreover gaining in significance for Nietzsche. And thus, along with Wagner and Bismarck, Schopenhauer too came more and more within the area of that decadence he wanted to conquer. This, naturally enough, did not prevent Nietzsche from adhering all his life to Berkeley-Schopenhauer epistemology, as we are likewise soon to see. He adapted it, however, to suit his own particular purpose.

Now where do we look for the real causes behind Nietzsche's development, and for the basic features of his so-called second period? It is our belief that they can be found in the aggravation of those socio-political conflicts which governed the second half of the seventies (cultural conflict, but above all the anti-socialist laws). We have observed how strongly Nietzsche's first works were affected by the war of 1870-1

and hopes of a general cultural regeneration in the aftermath of victory. We have further observed how tenuous the young Nietzsche's hopes were and how apolitical his perspectives, despite his general social and historico-philosophical stand in favour of slavery. Now this changed quite decisively in the second half of the seventies. Not that Nietzsche by now had acquired clear ideas on politics and more particularly on their underlying economics; we shall soon see his naive ignorance when it came to the latter. But in spite of all the facts speaking against him and the confusion in his views, Nietzsche's cultural and historico-philosophical studies were moving in a direction oriented towards the concrete present and future.

Let us anticipate for a moment what we are going to amplify on this subject. Nietzsche's new political position was centred upon the idea of rebutting and disarming the socialist threat, his chief adversary now as before, with the aid of democracy. Here we must note that Nietzsche regarded Bismarck's Germany as a democracy. And so – no matter how far Nietzsche was aware of it – his hope that here lay the cure for socialism was very closely connected with Bismarckian politics. We cannot take it as pure coincidence that his first work of this period, *Human, All-Too-Human*, appeared roughly half a year before the promulgation of the socialist ban. To be sure, this was also the date of the centenary of Voltaire's death. And very far-reaching conclusions have been drawn from the dedication with which Nietzsche prefaced his first edition on this occasion. Their validity, however, is extremely limited. For if we read Nietzsche's Voltaire treatise we perceive that it was still dealing with the same conflict we have defined as the most important in his life. But with the difference, characteristic of this period, that Nietzsche now thought the evolution which he praised Voltaire for representing was the surest antidote to revolution (i.e., socialism). In this light he drew his parallel between Voltaire and Rousseau (the aphorism's title, 'A Falsity in the Doctrine of Revolution', is typical of Nietzsche at the time). 'Not *Voltaire's* moderate nature with

its bias towards ordering, purifying and reconstructing, but *Rousseau's* passionate follies and half-truths have awakened the optimistic revolutionary spirit, and against it I cry, "*Écrasez l'infâme*!" It has long been responsible for banishing *the spirit of enlightenment and progressive development*.'[23] Nietzsche was to persist in this view of Voltaire long after he had overcome the illusions of *Human, All-Too-Human*. Indeed, in line with his later radicalism, he now saw Voltaire's universal historical significance solely in this opposition to Rousseau and revolution. Thus he wrote in *The Will to Power*: 'Only at this point does Voltaire (hitherto a mere *bel esprit*) become the man of his century, the philosopher and representative of tolerance and unbelief.'[24]

Thus in the second half of the seventies, Nietzsche became a 'democrat', 'liberal' and evolutionist precisely because he found in this the most effective counterpoise to socialism. His enthusiasm for this – as he then believed – inevitable transitional step was very temperate; one must, he wrote, 'adapt oneself to the new circumstances as one adapts when an earthquake dislocates the earth's old borders and contours'.[25] But in the second part of the same work he thought it possible 'that the democratization of Europe is one link in the chain of those enormous *prophylactic measures* constituting the idea of the new times and dividing us from the Middle Ages. Only now has the era of Cyclopean structures arrived! At last we have stable foundations on which the whole future can safely build! Impossible, henceforth, for wild and senseless mountain waters once more to ruin the fertile fields of civilization overnight! Stone dams and bulwarks against barbarians, pestilence, physical and mental thraldom!'[26] In this vein Nietzsche went so far as even to condemn exploitation as stupid and futile: '*The exploitation* of the worker was, as we now recognize, a piece of stupidity, a maverick enterprise at the future's expense which imperilled society. Now we are already on the verge of war: from now on, at all events, there will be a very high price to pay for maintaining peace, sealing contracts and winning confidence, because the

exploiters' foolishness was very great and long-lasting.'[27] The new form of government – and here he expressly sided with Bismarck – was to be an admittedly unhistorical but shrewd and useful compromise with the people, whereby all human relations would undergo a gradual transformation.

In Nietzsche's opinion – one which fully harmonized with the views just quoted – the positive value of such 'democratic evolution' rested in its ability to rear a new 'élite'. Thus in completing the turn to 'democracy' à la Bismarck, Nietzsche gave up none of his youthful aristocratic convictions. For now he still saw the salvation of culture solely in a more resolute bestowal of privileges on a minority, one whose leisure was based on the hard physical labour of the majority, the masses. He wrote: 'A higher civilization can only come about when there are two distinct social castes: that of the working people and that of the leisured, those capable of true leisure; or, to put it more strongly, the caste of forced labour and the caste of free labour.'[28] So close to liberalism was he coming that temporarily he even appropriated its concept of the State. He wrote the oft-quoted sentence: 'Modern democracy is the historical form of the *decay of the State*.' But just how Nietzsche amplified this idea is seldom quoted: 'The prospect opened up by this assured decay is not, however, a gloomy one in every respect: of all human attributes, shrewdness and self-seeking are the most highly developed; when the State is no longer a match for these forces' demands, chaos will be the least likely result. It is more likely that the State will be defeated by an even more practical invention than itself.'[29]

Here it becomes palpably clear why Nietzsche arrived at the views he did. No longer did he consider socialism to be an ally of liberalism and democracy, their consummation carried to radical extremes – in which guise he had previously opposed it along with the other two. Socialism was now 'the imaginative younger brother of the near-defunct despotism'.[30] And Nietzsche ended the aphorism in such a way that his current attitude to the State is quite plain to behold: 'Socialism

can serve to teach men most brutally and forcefully the danger of all accumulations of State authority, and so inspire a distrust of the State itself. When its hoarse voice mingles with the battle-cries of "*as much State power as possible*", these will at first become louder than ever: but soon the opposite cry will ring out all the more strongly – "*as little State power as possible*".'[31]

It is not worth examining more closely how Nietzsche envisaged this democracy in concrete terms. To do so would merely reveal his political naivety and economic ignorance. If, in conclusion, we quote one more statement by him, this will clearly illustrate not only both the aforesaid points but also the constant leitmotif of all stages in Nietzsche's development: the campaign against socialism, the chief adversary. In the second part of *Human, All-Too-Human*, Nietzsche maintained that democracy would of all parties profit most from the general dread of socialism, and he concluded: 'The people are the farthest away from socialism as a doctrine of reform in the acquisition of property: and should they ever have access to the taxation screw through their parliaments' large majorities, they will assault the principality of capitalists, businessmen and stock exchanges with progressive taxation, thus in fact slowly creating a middle class which may forget about socialism as it would a disease it has recovered from.'[32] That was the focal point of Nietzsche's utopian dream of this period: to achieve a society where socialism could be forgotten as easily as 'a past illness'. For this dream's sake he regarded Bismarck's 'democracy' with – qualified – benevolence: the 'democracy' of the anti-socialist laws and the professed social policies, the 'democracy' of the carrot and the stick.

How far these views were associated with reactionary illusions about the socialist ban is indicated by the new and final turn they took. Again this occurred side by side with the bourgeoisie's disillusionment as a result of the growing, and increasingly successful, courageous resistance of the German working class. Assuming more and more passionate

forms, Nietzsche's new line of thought reached its peak in his final works. We shall not retrace it step by step; our concern here is the essential social content, above all the fact that, despite the chopping and changing, the actual pivot and real centre never shifted, but was still hostility to socialism.

The estrangement from the 'democratic' illusions of the transitional period already takes a very distinct form in the *Joyful Science* (1882). In a passage that the fascists have often quoted, and with understandable enthusiasm, Nietzsche sided with military command and subordination, officers and soldiers, playing off this hierarchy against the capitalist exploiters' want of refinement and aristocratic character. Indeed he saw in the lack of aristocratic form the very reason for the rise of the socialists: 'Were they (namely the capitalists – G.L.) to share the hereditary nobility's distinction in glance and gesture, then perhaps there would be no socialism of the masses.'[33] What determined the sharper tone and mounting passion was that Nietzsche, becoming more and more sceptical about the chances of putting down the workers by time-honoured methods, strongly feared – at least for the time being – a workers' victory. Thus he wrote in *The Genealogy of Morals* (1887): 'Let us face facts: the people have triumphed – or the slaves, the mob, the herd or whatever you like to call them . . . Masters have been abolished; the morals of the common man have triumphed . . . Mankind's 'redemption' (namely from its masters) is well under way; everything is becoming visibly Judified or Christified or mobified (what do words matter!). To arrest this poison's progress throughout the body of mankind seems impossible . . .'[34]

At this point it might be quite interesting to glance at the differences and similarities in the careers of Nietzsche and Franz Mehring. We may then see what the socialist ban and the German proletariat's resistance meant to the crisis in bourgeois ideology. Both authors – although always proceeding from totally different starting-points and on equally different lines – had a period of illusionary perspectives:

Mehring wrote a pamphlet attacking social democracy, while Nietzsche entered upon his 'democratic' phase. Both underwent a crisis during the workers' ever-mounting and increasingly successful resistance. But whereas this crisis led Mehring into the socialist camp, it exacerbated Nietzsche's hostility to socialism to the point of fury and brought about the final formulation of his mythical foreshadowing of imperialist barbarity. 'Whom do I hate most', said Nietzsche in his *Anti-Christ*, 'among the rabble of today? The socialist rabble, the Shandala disciples undermining the worker's sound instinct, good spirits and sense of contentment – making him envious and instructing him in vengeance . . . Injustice never lies in unequal rights; it lies in the claim to *equal* rights . . .'[35] And it is typical of Nietzsche's shift that in his last period, in the *Twilight of the Idols*, he expressly returned to the statement we quoted earlier, concerning democracy as the decaying form of the State; but this time he made it in a decidedly condemnatory sense.[36]

In summing up, it only remains for us to show how Nietzsche described his attitude to the worker question in *The Twilight of the Idols*:

> The stupidity, at bottom the degenerate instinct, which today is the cause of *all stupidities*, rests in the fact that there is a worker problem at all. There are certain questions that *one does not ask*: number one imperative of the instinct. I quite fail to see what we wish to do with the European worker once he has become a problem. The worker is faring far too well not gradually to start asking more questions and to ask them less modestly. In the last resort he has the strength of numbers in his favour. We have said good-bye to the hope that here a humble and contented kind of man, a Chinese type might form an emergent class: and that would have made sense, and would have been a downright necessity. But what have we done? Everything to nip in the bud even the first requirement – through the most irresponsible thought-

> lessness, we have killed outright the instincts enabling the worker to exist as a class, enabling the *worker himself* to exist. We have taught him military efficiency and given him the coalition right and the political vote: so why be surprised if now the worker is already regarding his condition as a deprived one (in moral terms, an *injustice*)? But I ask once more: what is it we *want*? If we have some end in view we must also wish for the means. If it is slaves we want, we are fools to raise them as masters.[37]

Two points in Nietzsche's thought warrant particular emphasis. Firstly, the fact that he considered the whole 'worker problem' to be a purely ideological issue: the ruling-class ideologues were to decide the course of conduct that the workers should follow. Nietzsche quite overlooked the fact that the question had objective economic foundations. The sole deciding factor, for him, was how the 'masters' stood on the question; they could achieve anything if they were determined enough. (Here Nietzsche was a direct forerunner of the Hitlerian view.) Secondly, this passage unwittingly provides a historical summary of the constant and inconstant elements in Nietzsche's thoughts on this central problem. It is evident both that the 'breeding' of a slave type adapted to modern circumstances was his permanent social ideal, and that his hostility was directed against those – the socialists – who were frustrating this development. But the inconstant element is equally clear: if Nietzsche was levelling sharp criticisms against others of his class, he was at the same time practising self-criticism and overcoming the illusions of his *Human, All-Too-Human* period.

At all events, since the crumbling of his 'democratic' illusions Nietzsche had been predicting an era of great wars, revolutions and counter-revolutions. Only out of the resulting chaos could his ideal arise: absolute rule by the 'lords of the earth' over a henceforth compliant herd, the suitably cowed slaves. In Nietzsche's jottings from the time of *The Genealogy of Morals* we already find: 'The problem – whither now? The

need is for a new reign of terror.'[38] And in the prolegomenon to *The Will to Power* he said of the new barbarians and future overlords: 'Obviously they will come into view and consolidate themselves only after immense socialistic crises.'[39] The older Nietzsche's optimistic perspectives derived from this vision of the future (of imperialism): 'The sight of the present European affords me much hope: a daring master race is being formed upon the broad basis of an extremely intelligent herd of the masses.'[40] And whilst dreaming up these goals and the path that would lead to them, he occasionally conceived of the future in images whose content directly anticipates the Hitlerian saga: 'The putrid ruling classes have corrupted the image of the ruler. For the State to exercise jurisdiction is cowardice, because it lacks the *great man* who can serve as a criterion. There is so much uncertainty in the end that men will kow-tow to *any old* willpower that issues the orders.'[41]

In order to be completely clear about Nietzsche's sociopolitical line, it only remains for us to cast some light on his attitude to Bismarck. This is not an irrelevant question; indeed it is central both to his influence on basically Left-oriented circles and to his role in fascist ideology.

The Left saw the problem thus: Nietzsche criticized Bismarck very sharply – hence he could not possibly be a reactionary. Since this was a case of mistaking criticism from the Right for criticism from the Left, our concrete treatment of the Nietzsche-Bismarck relationship will tacitly answer this question to the effect that he always criticized Bismarck from a Right-wing standpoint, and considered Bismarck to be not decidedly enough the imperialist reactionary.

The fascist ideologists too started out from the contrasts between Nietzsche and Bismarck. But since the Third Reich needed a synthesis of all the reactionary currents in German history, it had to regard itself as a fusion of Nietzsche and Bismarck on a higher (i.e., reactionary) level. Franz Schauwecker, for example, said of the need to reconcile Nietzsche and Bismarck in the Third Reich: 'It will be an

empire guaranteeing the ultimate world-order. It will be the empire in which Frederick the Prussian and Goethe the German are at one. Then the meeting which was prevented from taking place between Bismarck and Nietzsche will be a *fait accompli* strong enough to withstand all attacks by hostile powers.'[42] Hitler's official philosophical ideologue, Alfred Baeumler, for his part used Nietzsche's Bismarck critique – entirely in the spirit of *Mein Kampf* – to prove the Third Reich's superiority to the Bismarck-Hohenzollern empire. Accordingly he passed over all Nietzsche's chopping and changing, and summed up his views thus: 'The history of the Empire became the story of Bismarck's intellectual defeat. This process took place before the horrified eyes of the other great realist (namely Nietzsche, G.L.) . . . The empire prospered, but it was a sham prosperity, and the concomitant philosophy ("ethical idealism") was a sham philosophy. In the world war the ostentatious romantic-liberal structure collapsed, and in the same instant the two great contestants from the past became visible.'[43]

Now let us look at Nietzsche's Bismarck critique itself. Both men were so-called 'up-to-date' reactionaries who, along with the usual weapons of popular subjugation and brutal terror – although this remained the favourite weapon of both – attempted above all to employ individual 'democratic' measures or institutions against the chief adversary, the proletariat. (Universal suffrage, etc., in Bismarck's case.) Bismarck, however, being essentially a diplomat of the Bonapartist period, was only briefly carried beyond the narrow aims of a Prussian reactionary policy by the movement for German unity. He failed to grasp the German bourgeoisie's imperialistic aspirations, based on the reactionary foundation of the Empire and now gradually gaining in momentum. Nietzsche, on the contrary, was the ideologist and prophet of this very tendency. Hence his often bitterly ironical, scornful criticism of Bismarck, and hence – precisely in the last years of his active life – his opposition to him. What Nietzsche found wanting in Bismarck was a grasp of the prin-

ciple of the will to power, which was why he said that he knew as little about philosophy as 'a farmer or an army recruit'.[44]

But that was simply a polemical invective. The essence of Nietzsche's quarrel with Bismarck comprised two complexes of ideas. Firstly, in the domain of home affairs Nietzsche called for a determined break with the semblance of a democracy and with that form of demagogic flirting with democracy, that is to say parliamentarianism, which Bismarck represented. For Nietzsche the crucial question was this: 'The increasing emergence of democratic man, and the consequent stultification of Europe and *belittling* of European man.' Hence his precept: 'A break with the English principle of popular representation: it is the big interests which need to be represented.'[45] Here Nietzsche anticipated the fascist 'class State'. The second complex of ideas covered world affairs. In *Beyond Good and Evil* – significantly, and in contrast to Bismarck's policy at the time, in the form of a demand that Europe unite against Russia – Nietzsche declared: 'The time for small politics is over: the very next century will bring a struggle for dominion over the earth, the *obligation* for great politics.'[46] This era which Nietzsche accused Bismarck of failing to understand was to be the era of great wars. In *Ecce homo* Nietzsche expressed himself thus on the subject: 'There will be wars the like of which have never been seen on earth before. *Great* politics on earth are only beginning with me.'[47] That is why Bismarck was not militaristic enough for Nietzsche. Exactly like Hitler, he believed that Germany's salvation depended on renewing in up-to-date form the traditions of the Prussian military State: '*The upholding of the military State* is the ultimate means of adopting or sustaining the *great tradition* with regard to the *highest type* of person, *the type that is strong*.'[48] As these few passages show us perfectly plainly, Nietzsche's Bismarck critique rested solely on the contention that Bismarck did not grasp the problems of the impending imperialist period, and was incapable of solving them by way of reactionary aggression. He was, therefore, criticizing Bismarck from the Right.

3

Only on the basis of the aforesaid can we apprehend both the unity behind Nietzsche's philosophy and its various changes. It implied an active rejection of the chief enemy, namely the working class and socialism. And as the class struggle intensified and one illusion crumbled after another, it expanded into an intellectual anticipation of the imperialist phase in capitalist evolution. Only in an imperialist bourgeois state of a decidedly aggressive reactionary hue could Nietzsche find a sufficiently strong defence against the socialist danger; only the emergence of such a power inspired in him the hope of succeeding in neutralizing the working class once and for all. His bitterness about the Germany of his time stemmed from its failure to adopt this measure and its continued hesitancy in doing so.

These tendencies are best seen in Nietzsche's ethics. That is because Nietzsche, in view of his class situation, his ignorance of economics and the fact that his activity pre-dated imperialism, was naturally in no position to foreshadow imperialism in economic and social terms. In his works he portrayed the bourgeoisie's consistent imperialist morality all the more clearly for that. Indeed he here anticipated in theory the true course of developments. Most of his statements on ethics became a dreadful reality under the Hitler régime, and they also retain a validity as an account of ethics in the present 'American age'.

Nietzsche was frequently associated with the Romantic movement. The assumption is correct inasmuch as many motives of Romantic anti-capitalism – e.g., the struggle against the capitalist division of labour and its consequences for bourgeois culture and morals – played a considerable part in his thinking. The setting up of a past age as an ideal for the present age to realize also belonged to the intellectual armoury of Romantic anti-capitalism. Nietzsche's activity, however, fell within the period after the proletariat's first seizure of power, after the Paris Commune. Crisis and

dissolution, Romantic anti-capitalism's development into capitalist apologetics, the fate of Carlyle during and after the 1848 revolution – these already lay far behind Nietzsche in the dusty past. Thus the young Carlyle had contrasted capitalism's cruelty and inhumanity with the Middle Ages as an epoch of popular prosperity, a happy age for those who laboured; whereas Nietzsche began, as we have noted, by extolling as a model the ancient slave economy. And so the reactionary utopia which Carlyle envisioned after 1848 he also found naive and long outdated. Admittedly the aristocratic bias of both had similar social foundations: in the attempt to ensure the leading social position of the bourgeoisie and to account for that position philosophically. But the different conditions surrounding Nietzsche's work lent to his aristocratic leanings a fundamentally different content and totally different colouring from that of Romantic anti-capitalism. True, remnants of Romanticism (from Schopenhauer, Richard Wagner) are still palpable in the young Nietzsche. But these he proceeded to overcome as he developed, even if – with regard to the crucially important method of indirect apologetics – he still remained a pupil of Schopenhauer and preserved as his basic concept the irrational one of the Dionysian principle (against reason, for instinct); but not without significant modifications, as we shall see. Hence an increasingly energetic dissociation from Romanticism is perceptible in the course of Nietzsche's development. While the Romantic he identified more and more passionately with decadence (of the bad kind), the Dionysian became a concept increasingly antithetical to Romanticism, a parallel for the surmounting of decadence and a symbol of the 'good' kind of decadence, the kind he approved.

With regard therefore to the philosophy of human behaviour (ethics, psychology and social philosophy always coalesce in Nietzsche), he harked back to the epoch paving the way for bourgeois ascendancy, to the Renaissance, French classicism and the Enlightenment. These interests are important because

they offered connecting links both for Nietzsche's admirers from the bourgeois Left, and for his updating in the service of ideological preparations for a third imperialist world war. Kaufmann, for instance, treated Nietzsche as the consummator of great philosophy after Descartes (indeed after Aristotle), intending to depict him as carrying on the Enlightenment traditions.[49] Having been apparently compromised by the Hitlerists' enthusiasm, he was – in company with Hjalmar Schacht and General Guderian – to be 'denazified' to suit the purposes of American imperialism.

The reader will have already observed the scientific worth of such essays from our previous quotation concerning Voltaire and Rousseau. Voltaire, whose work formed a great focal point for the mobilization of all the progressive forces of his age, was – according to Nietzsche – to become the spiritual head of the anti-revolutionary brigade. And it is extremely characteristic of this so-called link with the Enlightenment that Nietzsche, seeking an analogy with Voltaire's conduct, found one in the life of Schopenhauer – who was, he stated, 'unsullied as no German philosopher before him, living and dying a Voltairean'.[50] We are asked to believe that Voltaire, who used his world-wide fame effectively to combat the antediluvian feudal absolutism of his times, and who risked his neck to save the innocent victims of the clerical-absolutist reactionary party (or at least to preserve their memory), led a life comparable to that of Schopenhauer, whose only personal conflict involved a family squabble over his inheritance; who in 1848 offered the counter-revolutionary officers his opera-glasses to help them shoot at those fighting on the barricades; who bequeathed part of his wealth to the counter-revolution's disabled, etc. It is not, I think, worth adducing similar proof with respect to all Nietzsche's supposed ties with earlier progressive traditions; to do so would be only too easy. It will suffice if we quote, in conclusion, Nietzsche's own comment about the relationship of his 'new Enlightenment' to the 'old' for Nietzsche, in contrast to his hypocritical imperialist

interpreters, expressed his views with a candour leaving nothing to be desired. He said: '. . . the old movement was in the spirit of the democratic herd: a universal levelling. The new Enlightenment aims at showing dominant natures the way; inasmuch as to these (as to the State), *everything is permitted* that is barred to the herd mentality.'[51]

Quite contrary to those commentators who sought to bring Nietzsche into close alignment with the Enlightenment, he actually stood – after the brief episode of relative propinquity in the 'Democratic Phase' we have examined – at extreme loggerheads with such Enlightenment epigones as Mill, Guyau and others. The inconsistent development in the period of bourgeois ideology's decline found expression in this conflict. The Enlightenment itself, under the illusion that it was establishing the empire of reason, had opposed the theology and the irrationalism of feudal traditions. The bourgeoisie's victory in the great French Revolution meant a realization of these ideals, but the necessary consequence was, as Engels says,[52] that the empire of reason proved to be the bourgeois empire idealized, with all its insoluble contradictions. Marx says tellingly of the difference between Helvétius and Bentham: 'Bentham only reproduces dully what Helvétius and other eighteenth-century Frenchmen had expressed with wit.'[53] The contrast of wit and dullness was not just a matter of their respective talents, however. It illustrates two different stages in the development of capitalism and, accordingly, in that of bourgeois ideology. Helvétius was capable of wit because a clairvoyant loathing of the decayed feudal-absolutist society, the obscurantism of church and religion, and the ruling classes' hypocrisy lent wings to his thinking. Bentham was bound to grow dull because he was doggedly defending a capitalism that had already triumphed, and to do this he had to overlook the most significant social phenomena or distort reality with the aid of rose-tinted spectacles. With the epigonal Bentham's own epigones, the positivists Mill and Spencer, Comte and Guyau, the bourgeoisie's further decline could only hasten

this tendency to superficiality and dullness. Nietzsche, in turn, could become witty once more because, as a result of his method of indirect apologetics, he commanded a wide field for ruthless criticism, especially in the cultural sphere. From the artistic character of such criticism derived his aesthetic preference for individual Enlightenment authors, and the French moralists in particular. But this professional, formal allegiance must not be allowed to conceal the ideological antithesis in their basic lines of thought. Occasionally Nietzsche voiced these contrasts quite openly, as for instance when – as early as the time of *Human, All-Too-Human* – he discovered an ally of Christianity in La Rochefoucauld's moral critique.[54]

The connecting link between Nietzsche's ethics and those of the Enlightenment, the French moralists and so on is the fact that they all perceived in the egotism of the 'capitalist' individual the central phenomenon of social life. Since, however, they were writing in different periods, the historical development of the class struggle produced qualitative differences in content and indeed incompatible elements in orientation and evaluation. As progressive ideologists of the era leading up to the bourgeois-democratic revolution, the rationalists were bound to idealize bourgeois society and, first and foremost, the social functions of egotism. Without any knowledge, for the most part, of classical British economics and often before they appeared, these ideologists expressed in their ethics Adam Smith's basic economic tenet that the individual's economically self-seeking actions are the mainspring of the productive forces' development, leading necessarily, in the last resort, to a harmonizing of the collective interests of society. (Here we lack space even to outline the complicated paradoxes occasioned by 'theory of utility', the ethics of 'rational egotism' which flourished in this soil among the Enlightenment's great representatives.) It is clear, however, that after the Adam Smith doctrine had itself foundered on the real facts of capitalism, it could only be preserved in economics in the shape of popular economics

(starting with Say), and in ethics and sociology in the form of direct apologetics for capitalism (starting with Bentham). The Positivists' dull-wittedness and eclecticism are indicated by, among other factors, their inability to adopt an unequivocal line on the question of egotism. Their position amounted to a generally obfuscating 'on the one hand . . . on the other hand'. Now if Nietzsche, standing for indirect apologetics, took up once more the question of whether to commend egotism – and we see that in his youth, this policy played an important role in the mythicizing modernization of the *agon* and the 'good Eris' – it was no longer, in his case, an idealization of a rising, still progressive, and indeed revolutionary, bourgeois society. He was, on the contrary, idealizing those egotistic tendencies in the declining bourgeoisie that were burgeoning in his own lifetime and became truly, universally prevalent in the imperialist period. That is to say, it was the egotism of a class which, having been condemned by history to its doom, was mobilizing all mankind's barbaric instincts in its desperate struggles with its grave-diggers, the proletariat, and was founding its 'ethics' on these instincts.

We know that in his so-called Voltaire phase, Nietzsche was for a short while closely associated with Paul Rée, a Positivist epigone of Enlightenment ethics, and even fell temporarily under his influence. Hence the motives behind his rift and critical controversy with Rée are most instructive with regard to our problem. He voiced them with unambiguous clarity: 'I challenge the idea that egotism is harmful and reprehensible: I want to give egotism a clear conscience.'[55]

The chief task of Nietzsche's mature period, then, was to extend the ethics (the psychology and, so Nietzsche thought, the physiology as well) of this new egotism. In drafts for a sequel to *Zarathustra* he set out perhaps the most revealing programme for the task. And significantly, he began with his aforementioned definition of the 'new Enlightenment': ' "Nothing is true, everything is permitted." Zarathustra: "I deprived you of everything, a god, a duty – now you must

provide the *greatest proof* of a *noble* action. For *here* is the open road for the impious – behold!" – A contest for dominance, with the herd still more of a herd in the end, and the tyrant still more of a tyrant. – No secret society! The *consequences* of your doctrine must wreak fearful havoc: but *countless are destined to perish from them*. – *We are submitting truth to an experiment*! Maybe mankind will perish in the process! So be it!'[56]

To accomplish this upheaval, this 'transvaluation of all values' new men were needed. Nietzsche intended his ethics to effect their selection, education, breeding. But this called for a liberation of the instincts before all else. In Nietzsche's opinion, each previous religion, philosophy, morality, and so forth, had the function of opposing a liberation of the instincts, of suppressing, neglecting and perverting them. Only with his own ethics did the liberating process commence: 'Every *sound* morality is governed by a life instinct . . . *Unnatural* morality, i.e., nearly every morality that has been hitherto inculcated, venerated and preached, is aimed, conversely, directly *against* the vital instincts – it is a *condemnation*, sometimes clandestine and sometimes loud and bold, of these instincts.'[57] Here Nietzsche emerges as a vigorous critic of ethics past and present, philosophical and above all Kantian as well as Christian-theological. Taking a purely formal view, one might at first glance assume that he had in mind a link with the great ethical ideas of earlier men, such as Spinoza's doctrine of the emotions. But as soon as we consider content and programmatic bias in concrete terms, we see how appearances can deceive. With Spinoza, the dialectics of the conquest of one's own emotions were an endeavour to project the ideal of a harmonious, humanistic, self-controlled social being through mastery over (not just the suppression of, as in Kant) mere instinct and the anti-social passions. With Nietzsche, on the contrary, as we have seen already and will see again in more detail, we have a veritable conception of an unleashing of the instincts: the declining bourgeoisie, he maintained, had to let loose all that was bad and bestial in

man so as to obtain militant activists who could save its dominion.

That is why the acknowledgement of the criminal type was so important to Nietzsche. Here too there is a surface affinity with certain tendencies in the earlier literature of the period of the bourgeois rise (the young Schiller's *Robbers*, Kleist's Michael Kohlhaas, Pushkin's Dubrovsky, Balzac's Vautrin, etc.), but once again with a radically different content. At that time, the injustices of feudal-absolutist society were driving high-principled men into crime, and the study of such criminals constituted an attack on that society. Granted, Nietzsche too was bent on attacking. But where he put the emphasis was on deforming a specific human type, on transforming it into the criminal type. And his chief concern was to give even the criminal a clear conscience and thus to cancel out his degeneration and make him a member of the new élite. In *The Twilight of the Idols* he stated: 'The criminal type is the strong type under unfavourable conditions, a strong man rendered sickly. What he lacks is the jungle, a certain freer and more dangerous form of nature and existence where all that serves as arms and armour – in the strong man's instinctive view – is his *by right*. His *virtues* society has prohibited; the liveliest impulses he has borne within him are quickly entangled with the crushing emotions of suspicion, fear and ignominy.'[58] And then in *The Will to Power*, the necessary, organic connection between greatness, in Nietzsche's sense, and criminality (which means belonging to the criminal type) was distinctly stated: 'In our civilized world we are almost solely acquainted with the stunted criminal, weighed down by society's curse and contempt, mistrusting himself, often belittling and calumniating his own deed, a *failed criminal type*; and we find it repugnant to think that *all great men were criminals* (but in the grand manner, not miserably) and that crime belongs to greatness . . .'[59]

Here already Nietzsche has very plainly raised and answered the question of 'sickness' and 'health', so central to his

mature philosophy. If we complement these statements with a further one from his drafts for his final works, it will not be for the sake of comprehensiveness, for we could devote many more pages to such quotations. We shall do so because many of Nietzsche's interpreters, especially in recent times, have been eager to water down all his tendencies towards the revival of barbarity, glorification of the white terror and moral sanction of cruelty and bestiality – eager indeed to eliminate them from his works. Often they give one the impression that the 'blond beast' is only a harmless metaphor within a delicate cultural critique. To counter such distortions we must always refer back to Nietzsche himself who, in all such matters, – and in this he was a sincere thinker, no hypocrite or sneak – wrote with a downright cynical candour. Thus he stated in the aforesaid passage: 'Beasts of prey and the primeval forest show that *depravity* can be very healthy and works wonders for the body. Were the predatory species beset by inner torments, they would have become stunted and degenerate long ago. The dog (which moans and whines so much) is a degenerate predator, and so is the cat. Innumerable good-natured, depressed people are the living proof that *kindliness* is *connected* with a lessening of vital powers: their feelings of anxiety *predominate* and govern their organisms.'[60] As we shall see, the biological language too is in complete accord with the mature Nietzsche's basic philosophical bias. But this terminology only serves a mythicizing purpose, for the beast of prey's 'depravity' is of course a myth attendant on the imperialist glorification of the bad instincts.

All this contains an explicit avowal of belief in a revival of barbarity as the means of saving mankind. (It is irrelevant that in his early writings, and occasionally later, Nietzsche also used the word 'barbarity' in a pejorative sense; in such instances he meant cultural philistinism, narrow-mindedness in general.) Nietzsche stated in the same drafts that 'today we are tired of civilization'.[61] In even Nietzsche's eyes, to be sure, this would simply be chaos, a state of decadence. But it is interesting to observe the constant growth of his optimism

concerning the future as he foresaw it. Where was the way out of the chaos? Here again Nietzsche gave an unequivocally clear reply: the era of 'great politics', wars and revolutions would compel men (i.e., the ruling class) to reverse their course. The crucial signs of this saving transformation would appear in no other guise than that of the revival of barbarity. We have already quoted several important comments by Nietzsche on this subject in the previous paragraph.

Admirers of the 'purified' Nietzsche have been hard put to unite his sanctioning of barbarity with an often subtle and rarefied cultural critique. But we can easily dispose of this dichotomy. In the first place, the union of ultra-refinement and brutality was by no means a personal quirk requiring psychological elucidation, but a universal, psychical-moral distinguishing mark of imperialist decadence. I have demonstrated the kinship of these contrasting qualities in other contexts in the *oeuvre* of Rilke, who practised a far greater refinement still.[62] Secondly, in the *Genealogy of Morals* Nietzsche gave an excellent description of the type he favoured. Unlike the passages previously quoted, it not only reveals its psychology and ethics, but also sheds much light on the subterranean class basis of this contrasting duality and unity. Here Nietzsche examined pairs of moral opposites: the aristocratic concept of good and bad, and the concept of good and evil dictated by plebeian disapproval. And to the question of how the concept of evil arose he replied as follows:

> To answer with all severity: it is *precisely* the other code's 'good man', noble, powerful and dominant, only given a different hue, meaning and perspective by malicious, resentful eyes. Here we are glad to admit that anyone getting to know those 'good men' only as enemies would find them evil enemies indeed. The very men whom etiquette, respectful feelings, custom and gratitude keep strictly within the pale, as do mutual surveillance and jealousy to an even greater extent, who, on the other hand,

> prove so resourceful in consideration, self-control, tact, loyalty, pride and friendship – once estranged from these confines, they will behave little better than predatory beasts at large. For then they will enjoy a freedom from all social constraints; out in the jungle they are immune from the tensions caused by long incarceration and domesticating in the calm of the community. They step *back* into the wild animal's state of innocence, the kind of exuberant monsters that might quit a horrible scene of murder, arson, rape and torture with the high humour and equanimity appropriate to a student prank. They would do so in the conviction that the poets would have plenty to celebrate again. Behind all these noble breeds there is no mistaking the beast of prey, the magnificent *blond beast* in greedy search of spoils and conquest . . . It is the noble races that have left the word 'barbarian' in their tracks wherever they prowled; even their highest culture betrays this awareness and their pride in the fact.[63]

To sum up: we find aesthetic, moral and cultural refinement within the ruling class, brutality, cruelty, barbarity towards 'the alien element', i.e., the oppressed and those it means to oppress. As we see, the young Nietzsche's enthusiasm about slavery in ancient times remained a constant – indeed constantly heightened – motive of his philosophical work. To be sure, a romantic element thus entered into his 'prophetic' anticipation of the imperialist future. For Nietzsche's prototype, for instance the slave-holding and culturally refined Pericles, adapts itself most awkwardly to such persons as Hitler and Göring, McCarthy and Ridgway. Apologetic aims aside, his ignorance of the socio-economic differences between two ages necessarily led to this romantic idealism. Certainly it is no coincidence that Nietzsche lapsed into romantic fatuity in this particular area; after all, it is the main problem in his philosophizing. Nietzsche's cultural concern was definitely not just the bait for the decadent intelligentsia, but always occupied a central place in his life, emotions and

thoughts. In challenging cultural decline and in trying to pioneer a future revival he was no doubt sincere in his own mind, albeit personally sincere from an extremely reactionary class standpoint. In this light the romantic dream of a culturally highly-developed ruling stratum, representing at the same time an indispensable barbarity, takes on a special colouring. And the subjective sincerity of this false prophetship was itself an important source of Nietzsche's fascination for the parasitic intelligentsia of the imperialist period. With his assistance it was able to conceal its cowardice, compliance with imperialism's most repugnant forms and mortal fear of the proletarian revolution behind the mask of a 'concern about culture'.

But we can leave this subject and still find ourselves at the heart of Nietzsche's philosophy. Superficial commentaries have interpreted his 'Superman' as a biologically more highly developed form of man, a view which certain remarks in *Zarathustra* tend to support. But in the *Anti-Christ* Nietzsche very firmly disavowed such a reading: 'Not what is to supersede man in the biological series is the problem which I am now posing (man is an *end*), but what type of man we should be *breeding*, *willing* into existence, a superior being more worthy of life and more assured of a future. This superior type has already dwelt among us frequently enough, but as a stroke of good fortune, an exception, and never something willed.'[64] But in this case the 'Superman' is identical with the 'lords of the earth' and the 'blond beast' whose barbaric morality we have just examined. Nietzsche plainly indicates that this type has repeatedly existed in isolation, seeking deliberately to make the rearing of it the focal point of the social will of the ruling class.

With this construction, Nietzsche foreshadowed in the most concrete fashion possible both Hitler's fascism and the moral ideology of the 'American age'. And likewise, the fact that barbarity and bestiality are the very essence of such 'Supermen' was plainly stated in *The Will to Power*: 'Man is a *brute* and *super-brute*; the higher man is the monster and

Superman: thus the two go together. Whenever man adds to his greatness and stature he also increases in lowness and fearsomeness. The one is not to be desired without the other – or rather, the more thoroughly you want the one, the more thoroughly you will achieve the other.'[65]

What Nietzsche provided here was a morality for the socially militant bourgeoisie and middle-class intelligentsia of imperialism. In this he again occupied a unique historical position. From the objective, social angle, there had of course been a morality of the class struggle in bourgeois ideology from the beginning. But during the campaign against feudal absolutism it had a universal human, universally humanitarian character. Because of this bias it was progressive in its main orientation. The abstract generalizing – which, as regards facts, often distorted the problems – had its own social justification too, since it was a reflection of actual class conditions, albeit one that never attained to proper consciousness. For, on the one hand, the bourgeoisie at this time was truly the spearhead of all those classes challenging the feudal remnants of absolutism, and thus had a certain right to identify its own interests with those of social evolution considered as a whole. Admittedly this was only so up to a point. Conflicts of policy, for example within the Enlightenment, clearly show that a differentiation within the 'third estate' had already set in, at least on the ideological plane, before the French Revolution; typically for this social situation, each faction claimed to represent the common interests of society (Holbach, Helvétius, Diderot, Rousseau). And, on the other hand, those who were acting as the spokesmen for collective capitalist interests were equally able to declare themselves for this commonalty with a certain subjectively sincere, and relatively justified, pathos. For they also identified it with society, as opposed to the isolated endeavours of individual capitalists or capitalist sectors (among such spokesmen were Ricardo and moralists like Mandeville or Ferguson).

In the nineteenth century this relative justification, and

the subjectively sincere pathos in which it found expression, both ceased to exist. True, capitalist ideologists spoke ever more volubly of society's collective interests and the universal principles of progress and humanism. But such talk was growing increasingly apologetic and dissembling, becoming more and more obliged to hush up, gloss over and misrepresent the actual facts of social life and their immanent contradictions. The clash of class interests between bourgeoisie and proletariat in particular was disappearing from these treatises, and doing so to precisely the degree that it was moving towards the centre of social events in objective reality.

The ethics of Nietzsche which we have briefly outlined have the historical significance that they are exclusively a morality of the ruling, oppressing and exploiting class, a morality whose content and method were determined by this explicitly militant position. Here Nietzsche's extension of indirect apologetics in the ethical domain took concrete shape, and two elements need stressing in particular. The first point is that even here Nietzsche defended capitalism through apologetics on behalf of its 'bad sides'. Whereas the popular fellow-apologists, concentrating on an idealization of capitalist man, strove to dismiss all capitalism's darker aspects and contradictions, Nietzsche's writings centred exactly on what was problematic about capitalist society, on everything that was bad in it. Of course he too went in for idealizing; but what he emphasized with his ironic criticism and poeticizing pathos were the capitalist's egotistic, barbaric and bestial features, seen as attributes of a type desirable for the good of mankind (i.e., capitalism). Thus Nietzsche likewise spoke of mankind's interests and identified them with capitalism.

However, and this is the second point to be stressed, unlike the neo-Kantians or Positivists, etc., Nietzsche had absolutely no wish to establish a morality valid for all. On the contrary, his ethics were expressly and consciously an exclusive code of the ruling class: beside it and below it there was

a qualitatively differing morality – that of the oppressed – which Nietzsche passionately rejected and opposed. The conflict between two moral codes which, although changing according to historical conditions, in essence stood for two permanent types of morality, determined all the crucial historical questions to Nietzsche's way of thinking. His ethics thereby acknowledged the fact of the class struggle to a certain extent, again in violent contrast to direct apologetics, which sought to banish the whole idea or at least to lower its moral tone with the very weapon of a code eternally valid for all. Nor would Nietzsche tolerate such a toning down; once again he levelled against his age the criticism that democracy was blunting the struggle between masters and mob, and that the master-race morality was making too many concessions to slave morality. In his campaign against socialism, therefore, Nietzsche did come to recognize up to a point the fact of the class struggle as underlying the nature and transformation of all morality.

Far be it from us to suggest that he had even partially enlightened views about classes and the class struggle. Without a doubt, the class struggle appeared to Nietzsche to be a conflict between higher and lower races. This formulation, of course, already points towards the fascist takeover of bourgeois ideology. All those seeking to absolve Nietzsche from any connection with Hitler now cling to the assertion that his racial concept was utterly different from the Gobineau-Chamberlain-Rosenberg view. And unquestionably there is indeed a considerable difference. This holds good in spite of the fact that Nietzsche too gave his social categories a 'biological' basis, that his ethics take as their premise and seek to prove a supposedly radical and permanent inequality between men, and that the racial theories of Nietzsche and Gobineau fundamentally agree, therefore, in their moral and social conclusions. They differ in that the supremacy of the 'Aryan' race carried no weight with Nietzsche. Understanding master races and slave races only in a very general and mythicized sense, he took into account only ethico-social considerations.

Hence in this respect he was a direct forerunner of Spengler rather than Rosenberg.[66] Today, however, the stressing of this difference is only a means of 'denazifying' Nietzsche. Since, as we have noted, Nietzsche drew the same barbaric imperialist conclusions from a racial theory as did Rosenberg from Chamberlain's, the difference is – to borrow Lenin's phrase – merely that between a yellow devil and a blue one. We must also remember that the obfuscating and disordering of the social sciences in the imperialist age proceeded largely along the lines of racial theory (race replacing class). And in this area, too, Nietzsche gave rise to the same obscurantist irrationalism as Gobineau or H.S. Chamberlain.

Nietzsche's ethics further differ from those of the idealist and Positivist epigones in that he treated problems of the individual as inseparable from social problems. Questions which play a decisive part in, for instance, neo-Kantian thought, such as those of legality and morality, never even occur in his work. To be sure, he was undertaking not a practical deduction of individual morals from concrete social conditions, but an intuitive, irrational association of highly personal psychological and moral problems with a society and a history transferred to mythical realms. But just this philosophical approach – deliberately witty in form, in content serving the permanent interests of the most reactionary monopoly capitalism – is one of the most important reasons for Nietzsche's lasting influence in the imperialist period. Neo-Kantians (and also neo-Hegelians) too often derived their propositions from the age of 'security' and too openly aimed at consolidating capitalism for them to be of any real use to the bourgeoisie in the great new ages of global crisis and revolution. On the other hand, those decadent-intellectual movements which had many affinities with Nietzsche, and which often were in some measure influenced by him (Gide's *acte gratuit*, existentialism, etc.), proceeded all too exclusively and narrowly from the ideological needs of the individualistic, parasitic intelligentsia. While expressing a nihilism similar to Nietzsche's, though at a still higher pitch of inner

disintegration, they were however much more limited and specific in their propositions and conclusions. They lent themselves more readily to a philosophy of the 'third way' than to a philosophy of the reactionary avant-garde. Just this union of an ingeniously decadent individualism with an imperialist commonalty of reactionary hue – a union full of tensions and paradoxes – decided the duration of Nietzsche's influence in the imperialist age and caused it to survive particularities.

For similar reasons Nietzsche's influence outstripped those equally resolute reactionaries who resorted to more direct methods (e.g., the Pan-Germans, reactionaries in the mould of Treitschke). Whereas the latter found their starting-point in the type of the 'normal' petty bourgeois, Nietzsche took his from the type of the decadent intellectual. The moral disintegration of bourgeois and petty bourgeois, which became increasingly marked as imperialist economics and politics gained ground, confirmed the 'prophetic' foresight of Nietzsche's ethics. And his lasting influence had not a little to do with the fact that he went a long way towards catering for the needs of the decadent wing. He brought up questions from within its sphere of interests, answered them in its own spirit. Above all he commended and encouraged its decadent instincts, professing that this was just the way to conquer decadence. Hence Nietzsche's 'dialectics' in this respect lay in a simultaneous acceptance and rejection of the decadent movement, whereby he could enable the militant reactionaries to reap the benefits. For his own part, Nietzsche gave his blessing to these dialectics; in his *Ecce homo* he said: 'For granted that I am a *décadent*, I am also the antithesis.'[67]

This antithesis is represented in the ethics of barbarism which we have portrayed above. And Nietzsche turned the whole problem of decadence firmly on its head when he defined as its most important sign the view that 'we are fed up with egotism'.[68] For patently the predominance of individualist-egotistic propensities over social ones was among the movement's most significant features. But it was possible for

Nietzsche to 'salve' the decadents, i.e., to induce in them absolute self-confidence and give them a clear conscience without fundamentally altering their psychological-moral structure. And he did so precisely by suggesting that they were not over-egotistic but rather lacking in egotism, and that they must – with a good conscience – become more egotistic still.

Now we can also clearly discern the 'social task' which we mentioned initially, namely that of diverting discontented intellectuals from socialism and driving them towards reactionary extremes. Whereas socialism called for both an outward and an inward change of position (a break with one's own class plus a reform of personal attitudes), no radical reform was needed to conquer decadence in the manner Nietzsche proclaimed. One could go on as before (with fewer inhibitions and a clearer conscience) and feel oneself to be much more revolutionary than the socialists. And an additional point is the socio-historical nature of Nietzsche's answers in his ethics. The chief manifestations of decadence he perceived quite correctly: 'What does nihilism signify? – *That the highest values are depreciated.* A goal is absent; an answer is absent to the question "Why?" '[69] It is on this very point that the 'Superman', the 'lords of the earth' and company provided the decadent intellectual of the imperialist age with the perspective he needed and hitherto lacked. This handful of examples may suffice to illuminate the methodology behind Nietzsche's relationship to the intelligentsia, one of the most important sources of his lasting influence. We could give umpteen examples, but they would add nothing basically new. By actively serving the most extreme imperialist forces of reaction (Hitler's), decadence 'overcame' itself and became 'healthy' without having undergone any inner change beyond releasing its worst instincts, instincts that were previously half or wholly suppressed.

4

Only if we proceed from Nietzsche's ethics can we comprehend his attitude to what are called the 'ultimate questions' of philosophy, to religious belief or unbelief. As is widely know, Nietzsche declared a fervent allegiance to atheism; and with the same fervour he denounced all religions, but especially Christianity. That was of great importance for his influence on the intelligentsia, large sections of which were increasingly breaking away from the old religions. Nonetheless, as we have shown in the case of Schopenhauer, the resultant movement split up into quite different directions. On the one hand, we have an atheism truly materialist in character and based primarily on the development of natural sciences. This, although Darwinian theory gave it a strong temporary impetus (E. Haeckel), always exhibited major weaknesses on account of its inability to provide a materialist explanation for social (and hence moral, political, etc.) phenomena. Bounded by a narrowly bourgeois horizon, it usually remained in perpetual oscillation between pessimism and apologetics with regard to such questions. There can be no question of a widespread influence of dialectical and historical materialism upon the bourgeois classes; even within the workers' parties its significance – except in Russia – was continually played down through philosophical revisionism in the imperialist age. 'Religious atheism', on the other hand, was constantly gaining in strength. It had the function of satisfying the religious need of those classes that had broken with positive religions, and it did so in the form of polemics against them which became very forceful at times. This accounts for the semblance of an 'independent', 'non-conformist', indeed 'revolutionary' attitude in its adherents. But at the same time, it had to preserve the vague religiosity that mattered to the survival of capitalist society. Thus 'religious atheism' is another manifestation of indirect apologetics.

Occupying a special position in this development, Nietzsche

carried religious atheism far beyond the Schopenhauerian stage. We see this from a negative angle above all in the fact that Nietzsche transformed the argument of his atheism into myth to an even greater extent than was the case with Schopenhauer's Buddhism. He dissociated himself more strongly still from the connection with the natural sciences, and his views ran increasingly and more deliberately counter to 'vulgar' (scientifically based equals materialistically based) atheism. A famous passage in the *Joyful Science* states that God is dead, indeed that men have murdered him.[70] That is to say that there used to be a God, only he no longer exists today. Thus Nietzsche was expressly arguing that atheism is not a result of the incompatibility of our scientifically acquired world-view with the idea of God (in which event the new knowledge would have retrospective validity for the past). On the contrary, he asserted, it is the moral conduct of men in our time that rules out the existence of God, which hitherto accorded with it and found a veritable support in it – to be sure, Nietzsche was here referring to the long dominance of slave morals (Christianity). Nietzsche's atheism had therefore a pronounced tendency to base itself exclusively upon ethics. And these, as we have noted, meant to him both the philosophy of history and social philosophy. On occasion he voiced this thought quite clearly: 'The *refutation* of God: to tell the truth, we are only refuting the *moral* God.'[71]

No doubt traces of Feuerbach are visible in this conception. The contrasts, however, appear of far greater moment than the similarities. For with the materialist Feuerbach, the idea of God (and God for him is never more than a human concept) was causally derived from man's real being. Nietzsche, on the other hand, laid down only an ineluctable reciprocal relationship between specific moral forms of human behaviour and mankind's gods. Whether such gods existed independently of man's imagining or were only projected figments of this imagining remained – true to the essence of Nietzsche's method, the creating of myths – deliberately obscure. Granted, the connecting threads are not limited to a mere

concrete co-existence – unexplained as far as Nietzsche is concerned. Nietzsche took over from Feuerbach the weakest, most ideological side of his philosophizing: that which assumed that the change in men's religious ideas constituted the most important and decisive part of history. Even here, though, there is the significant difference that for Feuerbach the man-God relationship, while stemming from life, was in character a product of thought and contemplation, whereas for Nietzsche the essential determining factor of the relationship was to be found in men's social actions, in their morality.

As our detailed study of Nietzsche's ethics has demonstrated, he linked atheism – saying that Zarathustra had deprived men of God – with the new ethics of 'All is permitted'. The killing of God was only one means of liberating men from the restraints acquired in the course of millennia and turning them into those immoralists which the tyrannically ruling class of the future was to become in opposition to the herd. When Nietzsche happened to touch on the theme of 'Back to nature' he at once stressed the contrast with Rousseau. For Nietzsche, there is only one way that something purposeful can come of this: 'nature, i.e., daring to be as immoral as nature'.[72] And it would be equally false to draw a parallel between such passages and Hobbes's natural state, for the latter was concerned with the starting-point of man's development, with a 'Whence?', whereas Nietzsche's concern was the goal to be realized, the 'Whither?'. So here again we may clearly observe the contrast with the Enlightenment, with which individual commentators have tried to associate Nietzsche because of his atheism. In the Enlightenment, the idea was to prove that belief in God might not signify any kind of moral imperative for mankind, that the moral laws would operate in a society of atheists just as much as in one where religious patronage held sway (Bayle). Nietzsche, on the contrary, wanted to show that the demise of the idea of God (or the death of God) would entail a moral renaissance in the sense we have noted above. Apart, therefore, from the other ethical contradictions in the 'old'

and 'new' Enlightenment, about which we again already know Nietzsche's opinion, we find another contrast here in respect of the socio-ethical role of religion. The 'old' Enlightenment regarded the religious concept as irrelevant to men's morality, actions, views etc., which in reality were adequately determined by a combination of society and men's reason. On the other hand, Nietzsche – and here he far exceeded all Feuerbach's weaknesses in the realm of historico-philosophical idealism – regarded the switch to atheism as a turning-point for morality. (At this point let us just briefly remark that here Nietzsche's world-view is very close to certain tendencies in Dostoievsky. Since he had only read the *Notes from the Underground*, the *Memoirs from a House of the Dead* and *The Insulted and Injured*, and none of Dostoievsky's major novels,[73] the parallels in the relationship of religious atheism and morality appear all the more striking.)

The extremely subjective and idealistic character of Nietzsche's atheism needs stressing immediately because on the most important philosophical questions, he continually and effectively stood against idealism. Later, when we discuss the close affinity of his epistemology with that of Mach and Avenarius, we shall see how Nietzsche, like these, attacked idealism passionately but mendaciously in order to mask his principal campaign against materialism. He was always striving to give the impression that his philosophy represented something new, a 'third solution' contrasting with idealism as well as materialism. In the circumstances we deem it necessary to point out the striking parallels which also exist between Nietzsche and Mach on the question of God. Just as, for example, the Russian Machists (Lunacharsky, etc.) gave currency to an interpretation of religious atheism as the search for a 'new god', as the creation of a god, thus drawing from the Nietzschean death of God the inference of his possible resurrection in a new form, so too did Nietzsche himself. Here too his position is contradictory, opalescent. On the one hand, we read in his Zarathustra notes: 'You call

it God's self-dissolution: but it is only his fleecing – he is peeling off his moral skin! And you shall soon see him again, beyond good and evil.'[74] And later, in *The Will to Power*: 'Again we say: how many new gods are still possible!' Here, to be sure, Nietzsche is expressing his own doubts under Zarathustra's hat, and Zarathustra is 'merely an ancient atheist believing in neither old nor new gods'. But he ended the train of thought with the words: 'A God-type corresponding to the type of the "great men's" creative minds.'[75] These comments suffice to give a clear indication of the whole nature and historical position of Nietzsche's atheism. But in his last writings, on the other hand, the antagonist he conceived to Christianity and the Crucified is not a world liberated from all gods, not atheism or at least not *only* that, but also – as we shall later observe in detail – the new god, Dionysos.

So, then, this kind of 'radical' atheism blurs all religion's dividing lines and – within specific limits which we are coming to – offers an open house to the most diverse religious tendencies. Here again the uniqueness of Nietzsche's influence stands out: what he created was a blanket ideology for all the imperialist age's firmly reactionary tendencies. Socially and hence ethically, his *mythos* was quite unequivocal. In every other respect, however, it was wrapped in a mental haze which admitted of any interpretation one chose; and this lack of intellectual definition did not take away the immediate suggestive power of Nietzsche's symbols. That is why it was equally possible to find in Nietzsche a prop for the (fascist) myth of 'one's own kind' as opposed to the 'foreign' (Christian) myth, as Baeumler[76] does, and to bring his 'radical' atheism into an amicable rapport with Christianity itself. This Nietzsche's sister tried from the start to achieve by heavy-handed Pan-Germanic methods; later minds found for the same bent a stylistically more refined expression. Thus Jaspers, for instance, writes of Nietzsche's relationship to Christianity: 'Although we may reproach Nietzsche with atheism and point to his "Anti-

Christ", Nietzsche's atheism is not a flat straightforward denial of God, nor is it the indifference of a man so far from God, and so far from seeking him out, that God does not exist. The very manner in which Nietzsche decrees for his age that "God is dead" conveys his emotion . . . And even when he . . . is straightforward to the point of a radical No to all faith in God whatsoever, Nietzsche is still remarkably close to Christianity: "It is after all the best piece of idealism with which I have really become familiar: since childhood I have pursued it into many nooks and crannies, and I believe I have never dealt it an unfair blow at heart" ' (to Peter Gast, 21 July 1881).[77] And for a contemporary American such as Kaufmann, Nietzsche's conformity with Christianity outweighs his departures from it.

All these seemingly very marked contradictions are resolved if we consider more closely the socio-ethical content of Nietzsche's anti-Christian polemics. Here too we must refrain from taking tone and style as our criterion, or else we could easily say with Baeumler: 'He felt with acute clarity that his own position was infinitely bolder, infinitely more perilous than that of the eighteenth-century Church's most daring rationalist opponents.'[78] This paradox is not hard to account for. Even in the case of Voltaire, no atheist, the Enlightenment's attack on the Church was chiefly directed against the real central pillar of feudal absolutism. And hence its content embraced every area of human life and thought; it extended from the most general questions of philosophy and epistemology to the fields of ethics and aesthetics. Nietzsche's polemics, on the other hand, railed exclusively against the putative ideological forerunners of democracy and socialism, against the spokesmen for slave morality. The whole struggle against Christianity thereby took on a very narrow and firmly reactionary character, but apart from that, it also lost its social reality. The Enlightenment was challenging the real ideological pillar of absolute monarchy; but was Nietzsche not berating ideologies and institutions that were actually his best allies in his central campaign against socialism and

democracy? Of course there are elements in Christian teaching, and occasional proclivities in the development of Christian religion, where the idea of the equality of all human beings – which Nietzsche hated – finds powerful expression. But the churches' development, and also that of the dominant religious mood, tends towards completely disarming that idea in the social sphere by so interpreting it that it lends itself perfectly to the system of exploitation and oppression currently obtaining, and to supporting the resultant inequality. That is the social basis of the reason why Elisabeth Förster-Nietzsche was just as assiduous as Jaspers or Kaufmann in detecting links between Nietzsche and Christianity or the Christian Church. And in this they are absolutely right from the social angle, for the political praxis of the Pope, Cardinal Spellman, etc., has been in total agreement with the Nietzschean ethics we have outlined. The fact that the theoretical-ethical declarations accompanying this praxis hardly bear Nietzsche's frankly cynical tone is a secondary point compared with the essential unanimity. Hitlerian propaganda, on the other hand, could directly exploit just this side of Nietzsche's critique of Christianity.

We may now confine ourselves to the brief citing of several crucial passages from Nietzsche's works. They distinctly show that the theme we have emphasized was not one picked at random from others of equal value, but the very core of Nietzsche's anti-Christianity. We shall begin by quoting some concluding sentences of *Ecce homo*. Significantly, all that comes afterwards is the antithesis which was decisive for Nietzsche at the close of his career: '*Dionysos versus the Crucified*'. It is equally characteristic that the passage about to be quoted ends with Voltaire's phrase '*Écrasez l'infâme*!' Precisely this passage illustrates in the grossest way the extreme contrast between that which Voltaire wanted to abolish in Christianity, and that which Nietzsche thought should be abolished. Nietzsche wrote as follows:

> The *discovery* of Christian morals is an event without parallel, a veritable catastrophe . . . The concept of God, devised as a rival concept to life – it makes a horrible union of everything harmful, poisonous and deceitful, the whole deathly conspiracy against life! The concept of the Beyond and the true world, invented to devalue the *only* world that there is – leaving no purpose, reason or task for our earth-reality! The concept of soul, spirit and, to cap it all, immortal soul, invented to pour scorn on the body and to make it sick – 'holy' . . . The concept of sin, invented along with the instrument of torture attaching to it, the concept of free will, so as to bemuse the instincts and make one's distrust of them second nature! In the concept of selflessness, self-denial: the real mark of *décadence*, the process of being *enticed* by what is harmful, the *inability* to see one's purpose any more, self-destruction being made the very sign of one's worth, a duty, a thing that is 'sacred' and 'divine' in man! Finally – the most dreadful thing of all – in the concept of the *good* person, supporting all that is feeble, sick, botched, the own cause of its suffering, all that *is intended to perish* – the law of *selection* confounded, an ideal born of gainsaying the proud and well-fashioned man, yea-saying, confident, guardian of the future – this man is now called the *evil* one . . . And all this passed *for morality*! – '*Écrasez l'infâme*!'[79]

This hate-inspired lyrical effusion finds the requisite factual, ethico-social and historical rounding-out in Nietzsche's *Anti-Christ*, which also appeared in his last period. We do not need direct quotatiun to show that here Nietzsche, from first to last, was trying to made the idea of human equality intellectually contemptible and to wipe it out: that was his basic aim throughout his career. Let us just point out once more that Nietzsche never, of course, rejected equality out of general ethical considerations; his attitude was the direct result of his stance with regard to democracy, revolution and socialism, which to his mind were necessary fruits of the

dominion of Christianity. Nietzsche wrote: 'And let us not underestimate the destiny that has crept all the way from Christianity into politics! Today, nobody has any longer the courage of special rights, or rights of command, or a sense of respect towards oneself and one's peers – a *pathos of distance* . . . Our politics are *sick* through this absence of courage! The fib of the equality of souls undermined the aristocratic outlook in the most insidious way; and while faith in the "prerogative of the most" is making and *will make* revolutions – it is Christianity, let there be no mistake about it, and it is *Christian* judgements that turn every revolution into mere crime and bloodshed! Christianity is the revolt of all grovelling creatures against that which has *stature*: the gospel of the "lowly" *makes for* lowliness . . .'[80] And as a kind of historico-typological rider to this statement he added somewhat later: 'The pathological limitation of his perception turns a man of conviction into a fanatic – Savonarola, Luther, Rousseau, Robespierre, Saint-Simon – the opposite type to the strong mind, the mind become *free*. But the grand attitude struck by these *sick* minds, these intellectual epileptics, acts upon the broad masses – fanatics are picturesque, and mankind would rather see gestures than hear *arguments* . . .'[81] The basic thinking is patent: out of Christianity came the French Revolution, out of this came democracy, and out of this came socialism. When, therefore, Nietzsche takes his stand as an atheist, the truth is that he is out to destroy socialism.

5

In Nietzsche's polemics against Christianity, as indeed in all his social and ethical writings, the naive reader will gain the impression that all these phenomena are being examined as they are manifested in real, material existence, from the angle of biological needs and laws. But this is an illusion, and it is

highly likely that Nietzsche was labouring under it himself. Specific branches of classical philology apart, Nietzsche's knowledge was certainly very extensive, and his grasp of it lively and vivid, but this knowledge was always superficial and acquired at second or third hand. Jaspers concedes as much even for the philosophical classics with which Nietzsche was in vigorous dispute throughout his life.[82] But much more than just superficiality is involved. For Nietzsche, biology was one of the means of arguing and making concrete on quasi-scientific lines an essential element in his methodology. The method itself, of course, came into being long before him. In all reactionary biologist social theories (it may be no accident that the two make a regular habit of appearing together), the 'biological law' – the 'organic' in *Restauration* philosophy, the 'struggle for survival' in Social Darwinism – constantly appears as the basis from which the most diverse regressive conclusions are drawn in the fields of society, morals, etc. In reality the situation is the reverse of this. Out of the 'restoration' need to create a concept of society which – logically and ontologically – precluded any revolution *a priori*, there arose that notion of the 'organic' which this philosophy thereupon took as its basis without worrying about whether the analogy was possible and arguable in scientific terms. Any analogy will fit the bill if, as has happened from Adam Müller to Othmar Spann, the corresponding reactionary conclusions can be drawn with some semblance of plausibility. Scientifically speaking, this methodology has not advanced since the famous fable of Menenius Agrippa.

In Nietzsche's time, Social Darwinism emerged as one such ideology supporting the reactionary presentation of social processes. The term 'reactionary' still holds good where the thinkers concerned, e.g., F.A. Lange in Germany, subjectively placed themselves on the side of progress. These thinkers chose a method which did not lead to a concrete examination of social phenomena; on the contrary it diverted them from concrete perception because, in every period, the 'universal law' of the 'struggle for survival' explains every event in the

same way, i.e., it explains nothing at all. And with this methodology they supported the bias of declining liberalism: they substituted for class warfare various freely invented forms of the 'laws of motion' of society.[83]

In books on Nietzsche there was at one time a violent controversy as to whether and how far Nietzsche should be considered a Darwinist. We regard this discussion as idle for two reasons. In the first place, Nietzsche was never more than a *social* Darwinist in the aforesaid sense of the term. And secondly, his relationship to Darwinism is the clearest illustration of the fact that it was not scientific discoveries and knowledge that guided his thinking into specific channels and forced specific roles upon him. On the contrary, it illustrates that the development of his struggle against socialism determined every single one of his pseudo-scientific attitudes. He only differed from his like-minded contemporaries in that the programmatic arbitrariness of the 'scientific' argumentation emerged, in his case, with cynical frankness and did not put on a mask of objectivity with the aid of a pseudo-scientific apparatus.

If we recall our study of Nietzsche's interpretation of ancient society, we will realize that Social Darwinism strongly influenced his view of the *agon*, Eris, and so on. Darwinism accordingly receives a positive emphasis in this phase. For example, Nietzsche reproached D.F. Strauss with praising Darwinism in general terms without having the courage to apply it rigorously to moral problems, and so taking refuge in a form of idealism.[84] Occasionally, moreover, and quite as a matter of course, he used images borrowed from Darwinism in order to elucidate individual phenomena: 'Darwinism is also right with regard to thinking in images: the stronger image devours the weaker ones.'[85] Darwinism played a far slighter role for Nietzsche in the period of *Human, All-Too-Human*. Although he did not polemicize against it, he drew on it in his explanations far less often. This consigning of it to the background is understandable if we consider at the same time the evolutionist tendencies of this transitional

phase that we stressed earlier. Only when Nietzsche had overcome this illusion did he adopt a dismissive attitude of increasing sharpness towards Darwin and Darwinism. As early as the *Joyful Science* he treated Darwinism with irony on account of its plebeianness: 'The whole of English Darwinism smacks of England's stuffy air of over-population, of a provincial whiff of misery and close confinement.' This ironic argument *ad hominem* is, however, only a prelude to the theoretical rejection: 'The struggle for survival is only an *exception*, a temporary restriction of the life-will; big or small, the struggle revolves everywhere around ascendancy, around growth and expansion, around might in accordance with the will to power, which is nothing other than the life-will.'[86]

But we can study the actual content of this shift only in the more detailed statements of the last works and sketches, where its real motives are voiced with Nietzschean candour. In *The Twilight of the Idols* and *The Will to Power* the decisive motive of his – new – anti-Darwinism is now clearly expressed. Here again it becomes patent how Nietzsche resembled and how he differed from the general run of 'Social Darwinists'. Instead of considering the facts of natural evolution itself, both sides used 'the phrase of the struggle for survival' (Marx) from the standpoint of their assessment of the perspective on the present and future resulting, they thought, from the class struggle between bourgeoisie and proletariat. Capitalism's ordinary 'Darwinist' apologists started with the experiences of the age after 1860, which they superficially generalized. If, they thought, the 'struggle for survival' operated in society unchecked, it would end ineluctably in the victory of the 'strong' (the capitalists). This is where Nietzsche's sceptical, pessimistic critique begins. 'Normal' conditions for the social struggle for survival will inevitably lead the 'weak' (the workers, the masses, socialism) to a position of command. Very special measures must be taken to prevent this. Here Nietzsche was not only, as in his ethics, a 'prophet' of imperialist barbarity, but was moreover

looking for those *new* types of forms of dominion which could thwart the rise of the proletariat. The accent is on the word 'new' because Nietzsche, as we have seen, was highly sceptical about those methods of oppression practised in his own times (he had witnessed the failure of the anti-socialist laws). He did not believe that the contemporary capitalists, politically conservative as they were, were capable of carrying out such a policy. That calling awaited none else than the 'lords of the earth' whose deliberate training was the principal idea behind Nietzsche's ethics. (Here we see that he anticipated in his thinking not only imperialism, but also fascism to boot. Of course it was impossible for this to happen in an even relatively concrete form; it was only possible on a mythical, universal level.) Now that we have presented the sharp contrast between Nietzsche and the ordinary direct apologists of capitalism, we must briefly remark on the methods they shared in connection with Darwinism. Each side started out not by examining the objective correctness and applicability of Darwinism in respect of social phenomena, but from its own political aims and the perspectives which these provided. Thus in the last resort, it boils down to the same method whether the ordinary apologists, out of a narrow optimism about capitalist evolution, are commending Darwin, or whether Nietzsche, as a result of the scepticism we have just indicated, is rejecting and attacking him. In both cases, Darwinism was only a mythologized pretext for the ideological war against the proletariat.

It was in the light of such considerations that Nietzsche taxed Darwin as follows in *The Twilight of the Idols*: 'Darwin has forgotten men's wits (how English of him!), *the weak have their wits more about them* . . . One must need wit in order to acquire it – one loses one's wits when they are no longer needed. He who has strength on his side forgoes his wits ("Never mind all that!" is current thinking in Germany, "we shall still have the *Empire*" . . .). As you see, by wit I mean caution, patience, cunning, dissimulation, great self-

control and everything under the heading of mimicry[87] (which covers a large part of so-called virtue).' In the above statements Nietzsche was, as we have already noted, contesting the struggle for survival as a universal phenomenon; the latter, for him, was the will to power, and the former only an exceptional instance. From this there now follows his programmatic rejection of the Social Darwinism of his contemporaries, which of course appears in his book as Darwinism itself: 'But assuming that there is this struggle – and it does in fact occur – it unfortunately amounts to the reverse of that which the Darwin school desires, that which one might perhaps be *entitled* to wish for: namely to the detriment of the strong, the privileged, the happy exceptions. The species do *not* grow perfectly: the weak will always become master of the strong – that is because they are the great number and they are also *shrewder* . . .'[88]

This problem receives more detailed treatment in *The Will to Power*. So as to avoid repetition, we shall pick out only the motives which complement these statements, and which, indeed, became very significant for the development of the militantly reactionary world-view in the imperialist age. Nietzsche summed up his opposition to Darwin in three points: '*First thesis*: man is *not* progressing as a species. Higher types may well be reached, but they are not enduring. The level of the species is *not* being raised.'[89] It is clear how this thesis derives from the social reflections we have just cited: since the class struggle (the struggle for survival) does not automatically bring about the higher type of human being Nietzsche desired, it cannot possibly be the law of evolution in nature and society. But over and beyond this, Nietzsche's thesis points to the reactionary future: mankind's peak achievements are of equivalent merit, and the spontaneous dynamics of society can only corrupt them and condemn them to perish. Everything depends on creating devices whereby these peak achievements of nature can be not only preserved but also systematically produced. Here we have the methodological 'model' for fascist racial theory

and in particular for its practical application. The significance of Nietzschean ideology for Hitlerian philosophy is in no way diminished by the fact that the latter derives from Chamberlain's racial theory, and not Nietzsche's; we have already remarked on the difference between them.

The subsequent thesis contains, on the basis of the same reflections upon the fragility and vulnerability of the higher type, a bland denial of any development in nature and history. Nietzsche states that 'man as a species represents no advance in comparison to any other animal. The entire animal and plant world does not develop from the lower to the higher . . . but everything at once, one thing over and through and against another.'[90] This thesis too, although objectively it does not go beyond the commonest anti-Darwinist argumentation, likewise assumed no little importance in the development of the imperialist age's reactionary views. As we have noted, when Nietzsche advanced beyond Schopenhauer in indirect apologetics he made their historicizing the main point of his advance. And we have also indicated the cause of this change of method, which lay in the fact that it was now no longer the bourgeois idea of progress which constituted the chief adversary (Schopenhauer's denial of all historicity could serve as a weapon against this). The new adversary was the socialist idea of progress pointing beyond a capitalist society. To this dialectical view of history, irrationalism had to reply with another, though again historical-seeming explanation of reality if it wanted to remain up-to-date and effective within the reactionary sphere. But at the same time, the reactionary content, the apologetic defence of capitalist society as the unsurpassable peak and final end of human evolution had to bring about the repeal of history, evolution and progress. This simulated keeping in step with needs of the times (which diverted attention from objective reality), along with a mythicizing of history in nature and society leading not only to the emergence of other reactionary evolutionist contents and aims, but also to the self-annulment of evolution in the mythical presentation – this

was the most fundamental intellectual attainment of Nietzsche the irrationalist.

The third thesis includes nothing that is especially new for us. In it Nietzsche is chiefly opposed to the liberal interpreters of Social Darwinism, such as Spencer, who perceived in the – as Nietzsche put it – 'domestication' of man, in the taming of barbaric instincts, an important area over which Darwinian doctrine could be applied to social evolution. Nietzsche wrote: 'Man's domestication (his "culture") has no depth to it . . . Where it does go deep, it immediately means degeneracy (the type: Christ). The "savage" man (or, in moral terms: the *evil* man) means a return to nature – and, in a certain sense, his recuperation or *convalescence* from "culture" . . .'[91] Nietzsche was scoring a valid point against the liberal apologists inasmuch as the humanizing of the instincts cannot possibly go truly deep in capitalism. But it is perfectly evident from this very point how exclusively both Spencer and Nietzsche projected their own ideals on to Darwinism, from which they gained no fresh insights. This apart, it merely shows us once more the great extent to which – notwithstanding the aphoristic form – Nietzsche's work has a systematic intellectual coherence, although it is only from the real social core that we may discern its ramifications.

The method we have described can be precisely traced in all Nietzsche's statements in scientific vein. These have considerable significance for imperialist philosophy in that here again his boldness, coupled with a rigour touching on cynicism, made him the forerunner of methods and theories which did not come into the open until much later. As we have mentioned (we shall go into details shortly), Nietzsche's epistemology was closely related to that of Machism. Initially, however, Machism emerged in the guise of an agnostic 'neutrality' regarding concrete solutions to concrete questions; behind it, of course, lay an allegiance to subjective idealism. To be sure, this 'neutrality' was already manifesting itself in the period before the imperialist world war: for

Duhem, the Ptolemaic and Copernican theories were equally true, while Simmel, from his 'perspective of the future', placed the great nineteenth-century discoveries in the natural sciences on the same level as the belief in witchcraft. But an open mythicizing of the natural sciences on this basis – as in the theory of the free will of atomic particles – is, after all, a product of a far more advanced irrationalist subversion of scientific thinking. Thus, here again, Nietzsche's special position is characterized by the fact that as early as the eighties he was resolutely starting to mythicize all scientific categories. Having resolutely projected the main principles of his social philosophy on to natural phenomena, he then read these principles in them in order to bestow a mighty 'cosmic' background on his constructions and to present them as manifestations of a general world-principle. As paradigms of this method let me quote the well-known passage from *Beyond Good and Evil* where Nietzsche claims to prove the indestructability, harmlessness and positive merits of exploitation by demonstrating – through the method outlined above – that exploitation contains an irrefutably basic and universal principle of every form of life, which naturally includes every form of social life. 'Here', he stated, 'one must think things through thoroughly and beware of all weak sensitivity: life itself is *in essence* appropriation, doing injury, overpowering the alien and the weaker, oppression, hardness, the imposing of one's own forms upon others, physical adoption and at the least, at the mildest, exploitation . . . "Exploitation" does not belong to a corrupt or undeveloped and primitive society: it lies in the *essence* of living things as a basic organic function, it is a consequence of the actual will-to-power, which is precisely the life-will.'[92]

Once this method has been devised, it is child's play to arrive at that world-view whereby everything animate and inanimate is just as much a manifestation of the will-to-power as it was a manifestation of the will for Schopenhauer. The basic principle's mythical concretization, applied with an equal degree of arbitrariness, brings about the matching acts

of concretization that we have already discussed. It naturally follows that the body itself is a 'power structure';[93] that 'the supposed "natural laws" are formulae for power relationships';[94] that the will-to-power governs the whole of physics: 'It is my idea that every specific body is striving for mastery over the whole of space, to expand its strength (its will-to-power) and to repel everything which resists its expansion. But it continually meets with other bodies that are likewise engaged and finishes by adjusting ("uniting") itself to those which have enough affinity with it: thus *they then conspire to achieve power*. And the process goes on . . .',[95] etc. And in *Beyond Good and Evil* Nietzsche – with some reservations in respect of verifiability that are wholly absent from his later statements – formulated his programme for natural philosophy: 'The world seen from within, the world determined and designated with regard to its "intelligible character" – this would be sheer "will-to-power" and nothing else.'[96]

All these tendencies revolve round the pith of Nietzschean philosophy, the doctrine of 'eternal recurrence'. In its farrago of pseudo-science and wild fantasy, this doctrine has caused many Nietzsche interpreters a lot of embarrassment. Baeumler even tries to take it right out of Nietzsche's 'authentic' fascist system.[97] And he was quite correct from that particular standpoint. For 'national socialist philosophy' had a fully adequate substitute for the crucial social function of eternal recurrence in Nietzsche's thought, the function of denying that history could produce anything that was new in principle (such as socialism after the class society). This substitute was the dogma of racial immutability, which taught that the 'Third Reich' was only a consciously induced renewal of primal racial energies that had never changed. Other bourgeois commentators were hard put to treat eternal recurrence as a harmless intellectual affair. Kaufmann, for example, regards it as a glorification of the passing moment (even drawing a parallel with Faust) or as a training method; of course he always keeps silent about Nietzsche's purpose behind this training.[98]

For Nietzsche himself, eternal recurrence is the decisive counter-idea to the concept of becoming. This counter-balance was needed because Becoming cannot give rise to something new (in the context of capitalist society) without betraying its function in Nietzsche's system. We have already encountered the tendency to transform Becoming into a simulated movement, to assign to it the mere role of providing variations within the 'eternally cosmic' laws of the will-to-power. Eternal recurrence narrows the scope even more: the emergence of something new is a 'cosmic' impossibility. 'The rotating cycle', wrote Nietzsche no later than the time of his *Joyful Science*, 'is not something that has *become* but a first principle, just as *mass* is a first principle, without exception or transgression. All Becoming is within the cycle and mass.'[99] One of the most detailed passages in the late sketches gives a clear picture of this. There is small interest for us in Nietzsche's allegedly scientific argumentation,[100] which counts for as little as his other sorties in this field. Far more important are his conclusions; Nietzsche regards as theologians all who acknowledge the origination of something new in the world. 'This notion – that the world is deliberately *evading* a goal and can even prevent artificially the entry into a cyclical process – is one to which all those must succumb who would like to decree upon the world the power of *eternal innovation*, i.e., to invest such a finite, specific, constant and immutable force as "the world" with a miraculous capacity for the *infinite* shaping anew of its forms and conditions. They insist that the world, even though bereft of a God, must be capable of divine creativity, the infinite power of transformation. It must deliberately *restrain* itself from reverting to one of its old forms, and must have not only the intention but also the *means* of *preserving* itself from all repetition . . .'[101]

We have laid stress on the 'becoming' in Nietzsche's ethics. This, we believe, is right because it contains the immediate reasoning behind these ethics and particularly their revolutionary gestures such as the transvaluation of all

values. In order to break the old moral 'tablets' on which 'eternal laws' of morality were inscribed, Nietzsche used the concept of becoming – which he often traced back to Heraclitus – as a philosophical battering-ram. The 'innocence of becoming' was the immediate prerequisite for Nietzsche's activism, his reactionary militancy, his conquest of Schopenhauerian passivity. Hence the Nietzschean concept of becoming had to surpass Schopenhauer's wholly senseless, patently merely apparent agitation of 'the world as appearance'. But it is of the very essence of Nietzschean philosophy that all this can be only a prelude. Let us recall the structure of *Zarathustra*, where the idea of becoming reigns supreme in the first part, e.g., in the call to create the Superman, but where the same type's recurrence forms the crowning conclusion in the 'Drunken Song'. (That the idea of recurrence figures in several earlier episodes does not affect the underlying construction.) Baeumler is thinking in a very shallow and anti-Nietzschean manner when he scents in this a contradiction of the will-to-power. For here Nietzsche is quite lucid about the true hierarchy of his system. In *The Will to Power* we read: 'To *impress* on Becoming the character of Being – that is the *highest will-to-power* . . . The fact that *everything recurs* is the very *nearest approach of a world of Becoming to the world of Being – a contemplative peak*.'[102] For Nietzsche, moreover, the will-to-power, though admittedly the moving principle of all Becoming, is in itself – like Schopenhauer's will – something that has not come into being: 'One cannot locate the cause of the fact that there *is* any development at all by following the same road in one's investigation; one must not attempt to grasp it as "becoming", and even less as that which has become . . . The *Will to Power* cannot have come into being.'[103] Here we plainly see how superficially Nietzsche treated all Becoming, all historical events: as merely a manifestation of 'eternal' principles.

In itself, of course, this hierarchy is – if regarded logically – a crass contradiction. At the same time, it is also the

philosophical expression of the fact that, after subjective idealism and irrationalism had triumphed over Hegel, bourgeois philosophy became incapable of any dialectical linking of becoming and being, freedom and necessity; it could express their mutual relationship only as an insoluble antagonism or an eclectic amalgam. Neither in purely logical nor in general philosophical terms did Nietzsche surmount this irrationalist barrier either. His myth of eternal recurrence as the highest fulfilment of the will-to-power combines, we might say, hard antagonism and picturesquely blurred eclecticism. The two extremes, however, perform a single function from the viewpoint of his central polemical stance, his fight against socialism and for imperialist barbarity. They have the function of removing all moral restraints with a view to the ruthless termination of this social conflict. As we have noted, Nietzsche's boundless freedom created for the 'lords of the earth' the principle that everything is permitted; fatalistic necessity led, in his view, to the same result. In *The Twilight of the Idols* he quite unequivocally posed this question: 'What can *our* only doctrine be? That nobody *gives* man his attributes, neither God nor society nor his parents and forefathers, nor *he himself* . . . Nobody is responsible for his being here at all, his disposition to this and that, his existing in these surroundings under these conditions. The fatality of his essential being is not to be puzzled out of the fatality of all that was and will be . . . We are necessary, a portion of destiny, we belong to the whole, we *are* in the whole – and there is nothing which could judge, measure, compare and condemn our being, for that would mean judging, measuring, comparing and condemning the whole . . . *But there is nothing outside the whole*! . . . Only then is the *innocence* of Becoming restored . . .'[104] And the indirectly apologetic, moral function of eternal recurrence is exactly the same. In *Zarathustra*, in fact, by way of introducing the crucial proclamation of eternal recurrence, the 'ugliest person' suddenly voices as an inspiration the Nietzschean wisdom: ' "Was *that* – life?" is what I would say to death. "Well and

good! One more time!" '[105]

Thus from the standpoint of this central motive of Nietzsche's philosophy, the – logically disjointed – series of thoughts combine in a unified content. From the 'innocence of Becoming' stems Nietzsche's pseudo-revolution, the bourgeois transition from the liberal age of 'security' to that of 'great politics' and the struggle for control of the earth. Despite all the exaggerated pathos over the change in values, this upheaval is just a sham revolution, a mere heightening of the reactionary contents of capitalism tricked out with revolutionary gestures. And eternal recurrence has the function of expressing the ultimate meaning of this myth: the barbaric and tyrannical social order thus created is to be a definitive order, the conscious realization of that which was always sought in past history, that which usually came to grief and enjoyed a partial success only now and again. Now if we consider the methodological structure of this system of thought, we see that it fully tallies with Hitler's, except that instead of eternal recurrence, Hitler incorporates the Chamberlain racial theory as the new, complementary element. Therefore one cannot dismiss the closeness of Nietzsche's thinking to Hitler's by disproving false assertions, misrepresentations, etc., by Baeumler or Rosenberg. Taken objectively, the two were even closer than these men imagined.

6

The reader may have been struck by the fact that we have left Nietzsche's epistemology until the end of our study. In this way, however, we think we can adequately represent the real coherence of his system of ideas. During the rise of irrationalism, epistemological questions played a decisive role in philosophy. It was in this very area that, for instance, crucial collisions between idealist dialectics and irrationalism occurred in the conflict over the 'intellectual intuition', the

'positive philosophy' of Schelling. And their outcome determined – philosophically – the concrete questions of the interpretation of history, etc. With Nietzsche this question is completely reversed. His philosophy takes issue with an adversary wholly unknown to it – even in the realm of philosophical theory – that adversary being the world-view and scientific method of socialism. Nietzsche had not an inkling of the philosophical problems of dialectical and historical materialism. He contested socialism wherever he thought he could confront it in the flesh: socially, historically, morally. The concrete contents of these philosophical areas are therefore primary to his system. For him epistemology was only a tool whose character and disposition were dictated by the purposes it served.

This new situation too is typical not only of Nietzsche but of all bourgeois philosophy in the age of its decline. The period of its rise, whose import was determined by the struggle against feudal ideology and by conflicts of direction within bourgeois ideology, accordingly evinces a great variety of epistemological trends; idealism and materialism, subjective and objective idealism, metaphysics and dialectics vied with one another for predominance. Objective idealism, whose bourgeois perversion was considerably fostered by the 'heroic illusions' of the democratic revolution, died out with increasing speed as this period came to an end. After the French Revolution, mechanical materialism lost its earlier universality; Feuerbach's purview was already much narrower than that of his seventeenth- and eighteenth-century predecessors. (While developments in Russia form an exception to this, they were not known to contemporary thinkers outside Russia.) After a brief period of supremacy in natural philosophy, mechanical materialism forfeited its leading position in this sphere also. Although, as Lenin demonstrates, every genuine scientist's praxis remained spontaneously materialistic, philosophical idealism falsified and deformed the great scientific discoveries. So epistemology sank very low precisely as a result of the near-total hegemony which subjective

idealism exercised in the bourgeois philosophy of this period. On the surface, admittedly, epistemology governed the content and method of philosophizing much more firmly than ever before; it is as though philosophy consisted of almost nothing else. But in actual fact an academic scholasticism was growing up, and trivial professorial squabbles over insignificant nuances were replacing the great philosophical conflicts.

The pre-imperialist period energetically paved the way for this decline. Here the social grounds for subjective idealism's total control over bourgeois philosophy are also clearly visible. This idealism, along with the agnosticism to which it was inseparably linked, enabled the bourgeois ideologist to take from the progress of science, and first and foremost the natural sciences, all that served capitalist interests, while at the same time avoiding taking a stand with regard to the altered world-picture. Hence Engels very rightly calls this period's agnosticism a 'shame-faced materialism'.[106]

In not only the imperialist period but also in the years immediately preceding it, the ideological needs of the bourgeoisie underwent a change. A mere 'abstention' from questions of viewpoint no longer sufficed, and philosophy was obliged to make a stand, above all a stand against materialism: more and more clearly the positivist agnostics' 'shame-faced materialism' was acquiring an anti-materialist accent. Neo-Kantianism and Machism were their chief orientations as they completed this shift, which was concurrent with Nietzsche's activities.[107] The bourgeois ideological position, however, permitted less and less of a clear and public platform on the decisive questions of outlook. Lenin has clearly demonstrated the contrast between Berkeley's open war on materialism and that which the Machists waged behind their anti-idealist camouflage. The very fact that bourgeois thinking was forced – in order to defend idealism against materialism – to take a 'third road', i.e., to act as if it were criticizing and rejecting both idealism and materialism from a 'higher vantage point', indicates that – on the world-historical scale – it had been already forced into a defensive posture. Its propositions,

methods and so forth were more in the nature of protective measures than means of analysing and interpreting objective reality in a way of its own. It goes without saying that this defensive character did not exclude the most violent attacks on the declining bourgeoisie's opponents or a passionate advocacy of its class interests, etc. These actions even gained in intensity with the onset of the imperialist age, where it is precisely the ever-growing 'need of a world-view' that characterizes the contrast with the age which Engels described. The 'world-views' which now came about were, however, qualitatively different from those of the ideological heyday. Then, the bourgeois view of the world – albeit emerging in a more or less idealistically distorted form – had been designed to reflect the essence of objective reality. But now every such 'world-view' had its basis in an agnostic epistemology, in a denial that what was objectively real was perceptible. For that reason it could only be a myth, something subjectively contrived with pretentions to (an epistemologically unarguable) objectivity, an objectivity resting solely on an extremely subjectivist foundation, on intuition and the like, and so never more than a feigned objectivity. The bourgeoisie's age of decline finds a clear expression in this mounting and increasingly uncritical need of myth. In the pseudo-objective form of myth, the bourgeoisie countered real evolution with wishful thinking. In its heyday, on the contrary, its philosophical systems had sought to oppose the feudal legends precisely by appealing to real evolutionary trends in nature and history.

Now Nietzsche's special position is determined by the fact that he, at the same time as Machism, introduced the new agnosticist method into epistemology. But in doing so he went much further than his contemporaries. Anticipating the spread of agnosticism into the sphere of myth, he showed in his myth-making a careless daring that general bourgeois developments only came close to matching at the end of the first imperialist world war, as in the work of Spengler. Thus Nietzsche was by no means original in his epistemology

either; his treatment of individual problems is entirely on the general level of Machism. To be sure, he did strike a special note in his determination to think reactionary bourgeois tendencies through to the most extreme consequences and openly to state their conclusions in a crude and paradoxical form. This is connected with an attitude in which we see the binding centre of Nietzsche's philosophical system: with his unceasing and passionate open warfare against the peril of socialism. He subordinated all the principal contents of his thought to the needs of this battle; he always allowed these needs to dictate the content.

Hence his epistemology too, though very close to the Machist in general, far exceeded that of his contemporaries and allies in its cynically frank conclusions. A salient example will clearly illustrate the similarity and difference. Nietzsche was in complete agreement with the Machists in respect of the 'immanence' of philosophy, of the programmatic denial of all 'transcendence'. But what did both parties mean by the terms? 'Immanence' signifies the world of our intuitions and ideas, 'transcendence' all that in reality goes beyond these, i.e., objective reality itself, existing independently of our consciousness. There is a further agreement in that both parties – so it appears – polemicize against idealism's purported claims to be able to perceive objective reality; here, therefore, anti-idealist polemics mask the denial of materialism. But Nietzsche went still further along this road by linking the campaign against 'transcendence' and the Beyond with his anti-Christian views. Hence he was capable on occasion of misleading those who failed to see that the Christian Heaven and the materialist view of objective reality are mythically synthesized in his concept of the Beyond. (Incidentally, even the Machists criticized materialism as 'metaphysical' theory.) But whereas the Machists were largely content to present the 'immanence' of the realm of ideas as the sole scientific basis for comprehending the world, Nietzsche, with nihilistic openness, formulated this theory in bold paradoxes. In *The Twilight of the Idols* his mocking

polemics inveigh against the conception of a 'true world' (of objective reality), and his deductions climax in the sentences proclaiming the 'end of the longest error' and the 'peak of mankind': 'The true world we have abolished: what was left? the apparent world, perhaps? . . . But no! *Along with the true world we have also abolished the apparent one*!'[108]

But Nietzsche was not content with mere epistemological statements. His whole epistemology was for him just one weapon in the main battle against socialism. Hence it follows that in the same work he should give a socially concrete definition of that which he understood by 'immanence', namely not only – epistemologically – the world of ideas but also, inseparable from it on the general philosophical level, the actual condition of society at any given time: in concrete terms, capitalism. And anybody who stepped beyond this 'immanence' was in his eyes a bad reactionary from the philosophical angle. Here again, of course – as we have noted in earlier sections – Christians and socialists alike are made to look philosophically and morally reprehensible because they represent 'transcendence' and are therefore reactionaries. 'But', Nietzsche wrote, 'even if the Christian condemns, slanders and vilifies the "world", he does so from the same instinct as the socialist worker who condemns, slanders and vilifies *society*: the "Last Judgement" itself continues to offer sweet revenge – the same revolution that the socialist worker awaits, only carried somewhat further . . . The "Beyond" itself – what good might a Beyond have except as a means of vilifying this world? . . .'[109] In the last analysis all 'immanence' in imperialist bourgeois philosophy is aiming at this target: to deduce from epistemology the 'everlastingness' of capitalist society. Nietzsche was particularly important because he publicly voiced in suggestive paradoxes this common idea in imperialist philosophy. Hence in the epistemological field, too, he became the leading ideologist of the militant reactionaries.

Nietzsche's individual epistemological statements are of little interest. Where they do not jump across to the overtly

social sphere, as in the above passage, they proceed along well-known Machist lines. They challenge the perceptibility of objective reality, indeed all objectivity of knowledge (hence Nietzsche also opposed the materialist side of the Kantian *Ding an sich* or 'thing-in-itself'). They regard causality, laws, etc., as categories of an idealism that has been conquered once and for all. Here we wish only to dwell briefly on those elements in which Nietzsche's special historical individuality finds expression. One such element is that Nietzsche's subjective idealism and agnosticism – which, while certainly derived via Berkeley and Schopenhauer, belong to modern imperialism – are avowedly based on Heraclitus. This lends his agnosticism a 'philosophical' character that exceeds the drily scientific and helps him to transpose agnosticism into myth-making. (Small wonder that it is precisely his fascist followers, such as Baeumler, who lay so much stress on his derivation from Heraclitus. For this makes it easier to extract him from mainstream bourgeois philosophy, where he belongs, and to make him a 'solitary' forerunner of Hitler.)

But even more instructive, on the other hand, is the point that the Heraclitus-based interpretations offer a perfect example of our general view that in reactionary hands, dialectical problems turn into irrationalist myths. In his notes for *Philosophy in the Tragic Age of the Greeks* (1872-3), Nietzsche touches on a central thesis of Heraclitus's dialectics, 'Everything always contains its opposite', and Aristotle's polemics against this thesis. His commentary is highly significant: 'Heraclitus possesses the regal gift of the highest power of intuitive thinking, while showing himself cool, insensitive and indeed hostile towards that other type of thinking which is accomplished in concepts and logical combinations, i.e., towards reason and he seems to take pleasure in any chance to contradict it with a truth intuitively arrived at.'[110] So we see that, for Nietzsche, the critique of understanding (*Verstand*) through its own contrariety – Heraclitus's great dialectical discovery – is simply identical with the sovereign supremacy

of intuition over reason.[111]

Nietzsche then goes on, quite logically, to establish a close link between Heraclitus's dialectics and Schopenhauer's consciously anti-dialectical irrationalism, whereby he likewise establishes the link with Berkeley and Mach. The Heraclitean concept of becoming he interprets in exactly the same context. In his studies from the time of *The Birth of Tragedy* (1870-1) he wrote of it: 'In Becoming is manifested the ideational nature of things: there *is* nothing, nothing *exists*, everything becomes, i.e., is idea.'[112] Let us not suppose that this view belongs only to Nietzsche's youth, when he stood under Schopenhauer's influence. This view of Being and Becoming dominates the whole epistemology of Nietzsche's *oeuvre*. When, at the end of his career, in *The Twilight of the Idols*, he again touched on Heraclitus, he stressed the very same idea: 'But Heraclitus will be forever right in that Being is an empty fiction. The "apparent" world is the one and only: the "true world" is only *a mendacious gloss* . . .'[113] Indeed Nietzsche's intrepid lack of concern for the facts of philosophical history was continually on the increase. In the preparatory writings for *The Will to Power* even the materialist Democritus has to testify to Nietzschean irrationalism. And the development reaches its acme – characteristically once more – in the Machists' patron saint, Protagoras, who 'united in himself both Heraclitus and Democritus'.[114]

We can properly appreciate Nietzsche's doctrine of eternal recurrence as a victory of Being over Becoming only if we review it in the light of these epistemological findings. We now see that the concept of Being employed therein has nothing to do with real Being (existing independently of consciousness); on the contrary, it is invoked purely in order to lend myth – which can be apprehended only intuitively, through 'illumination' – a semblance of objectivity. Nietzsche's concept of Becoming, as we could see in his Heraclitus interpretations, serves principally to destroy all objectivity, all perceptibility of reality. In *The Will to Power* he wrote: 'The character of the becoming world as defying

formulation, as "false", as "self-contradictory". *Knowledge and Becoming* are mutually exclusive.'[115] Quite logically for Nietzsche, the same consideration determines the purely fictive character of Being: 'The *assumption of that which is in being* is necessary in order to be able to think and summarize: logic only deals in formulae for unchanging things. Hence this act of assuming could still furnish no proof of reality: "That which is in being" (*Das Seiende*) belongs to our optics.'[116] But if Being is a mere fiction, then how can a Being arise in eternal recurrence which is higher than a real Becoming – real at least in our idea of it?

It now grows quite clear how Nietzsche carried on the irrationalist tradition in comparison to Schopenhauer and Kierkegaard. These authors, in contesting idealist dialectics as the highest form of the bourgeois conception of progress, had likewise to oppose the dialectical self-agitation of Being and to fall back on a contrastingly mythical, only intuitively apprehensible Being. But since their polemics against Hegelian dialectics were only a conflict of orientation within bourgeois philosophy, they could content themselves with narrowing and distorting dialectics in a reactionary irrationalist spirit. (Schelling's distinction between 'negative' and 'positive' philosophy, Kierkegaard's 'stages'.) True, the resultant distinctions between 'lower' and 'higher' types of Being have an anti-scientific character and structure, but formally they remain – at least until Kierkegaard's 'leap' – within the sphere of a certain logical order. One might say that the tattered pieces of dialectics taken over in garbled form from Hegel restore, for Schelling and Kierkegaard, the appearance of a modicum of rational coherence. Nietzsche, however, did away with the connecting links from the outset in his epistemology, which followed the line of Berkeley, Schopenhauer and Mach. And to the extent to which we can speak of a logico-philosophical order in his work here at all, it can have but one meaning. The more fictive a concept is and the more purely subjectivist its origins, the higher it stands and the 'truer' it is in the mythical scale of values.

Being, so long as its concept contains even the slightest vestiges of a relationship to a reality independent of our consciousness, must be displaced by Becoming (equals idea). Being, however, when freed from these shackles and viewed purely as fiction, as a product of the will-to-power, may then, for Nietzsche, be a still higher category than Becoming: an expression of the intuitive pseudo-objectivity of myth. With Nietzsche, the special function of such a definition of Becoming and Being lies in supporting the pseudo-historicity vital to his indirect apologetics and in simultaneously dismissing it, confirming philosophically that historical Becoming can produce nothing that is new and outruns capitalism.

But the significance of Nietzschean epistemology as a structural tool for the systematic articulation of his thoughts exceeds this single instance, central though it is. It encompasses the full totality of his universe. To help complete the picture, let us take another important example. In contrast to contemporary neo-Kantianism and Positivism, whose basic approach was a specific objectivism, an avowedly solely scientific abstention from any explicit attitude and relationship to praxis, Nietzsche vigorously shifted the connection between theory and praxis to the centre of his whole epistemology. Here, too, he drew all the inferences of agnosticism and of the relativism succeeding it earlier and more radically than his contemporaries. By rejecting any criterion of truth other than usefulness for the biological survival of the individual (and the species), he became an important precursor of imperialist pragmatism. 'We have always', he stated, '*forgotten* the main thing: *why* does a philosopher want to *know*? Why does he value "truth" more highly than appearance? *This valuation* is older than any *cogito ergo sum*: even presupposing the logical process, there is something inside us which *affirms* it and *denies* its opposite. Whence the preference? Every philosopher has neglected to explain *why* he *values* the true and the good, and none has sought to attempt the same for the opposite. Answer: the True is more *useful* (for preserving the organism) – but not *in itself*

more acceptable. Enough; from the very beginning we find the organism speaking as a whole, with "purposes" – therefore making value judgements.'[117] It goes without saying that this applies to an even greater degree to the truths of morality: 'All moralists join in drawing lines regarding good and evil, depending on their sympathetic and egotistic impulses. I regard as good that which serves some end: but the "good end" is nonsense. For the question is always "good for what?" Good is always merely a term for a *means*. The "good end" is a good means to an end.'[118] And in *The Will to Power*, Nietzsche summed up this doctrine in the suggestive words: '*Truth is the type of error* without which a particular type of living being could not exist. In the last resort the decisive valuc is the value for *living*.'[119]

Nietzsche, however, was not satisfied with tracing the good and true back to biological vital interests, thereby depriving them of all absolute, objective worth. The object of his endeavours went even beyond his referring in general to biological usefulness for the species, rather than merely for the individual. For the life of the species – this returns us to the sphere of Becoming – is, firstly, a historical process and, secondly, as historical content, the uninterrupted conflict between two human types, two races, namely masters and slaves. In *The Genealogy of Morals*, Nietzsche expressly emphasized that his starting-point was an etymological one: the insight that the morally positive element is identical with the socially eminent man, and the negative with the socially subordinate.[120] But this 'natural' condition is dissipated in the course of history: there arises that embittered struggle between masters and herd whose philosophical, moral and other consequences, as well as its perspectives for Nietzsche, we have portrayed in detail in other contexts. And the function which all categories acquire in this struggle determines the degree of truth they possess. More precisely, the determining factor is their potential usefulness to the master race in obtaining and establishing ultimate control. To refer back just briefly to what we have already expounded,

let us quote the statement, likewise from the *Genealogy*: 'Egotism and a kind of *second innocence* go hand in hand.'[121]

Once this condition, a 'clear conscience' for the master race's most extreme egotism and every sort of cruelty and barbarity, has been fulfilled ('the innocence of Becoming'), then – and only then – this concept is finally established and set free in the mythical realm through eternal recurrence. Only for the 'lords of the earth', of course, but then it was only for them that Nietzsche wanted to provide a militant philosophy. Hence he wrote of eternal recurrence: 'It is the great *disciplinary* idea: those races which cannot endure it are condemned, those that find it of the greatest benefit are destined for mastery.'[122] And it totally accords with this conception that, in Nietzsche's view, eternal recurrence must be a deadly poison for the herd. We have already noted that in defining epistemological 'immanence' he launched a violent attack on all 'transcendence', and identified the Christian belief in a Beyond with socialism's revolutionary perspectives on the future. But eternal recurrence revokes, in his opinion, all transcendence and hence the basis of all Christian (or socialist) morality. Thus we read in *The Will to Power*: 'Morality protects the *defeated type* from nihilism by attributing to *each* person of this type an infinite, metaphysical worth and by assigning each to an order which differs from worldly power and hierarchy: it taught submissiveness, humility, etc. *Supposing that faith in this morality perishes*, the defeated would no longer have their consolation – and would *perish*.'[123]

The 'lords of the earth' are, of course, the decadent parasites of imperialism. This definition of the decadent man as a central figure in future developments, and of decadence as a springboard for the desired future condition, again distinguishes Nietzsche from the other reactionary philosophers. The latter, who wanted to save capitalist society as typified by the 'normal' man (bourgeois and petty-bourgeois), found themselves increasingly at loggerheads in the course of time with the capitalist reality, with its mounting and

increasingly total distortion of man. Nietzsche proceeded resolutely from this distortion, which manifested itself in his age as world-weariness, pessimism, nihilism, dissipation, lack of self-belief, lack of perspectives and so on. Recognizing himself in these decadent types, he regarded them as brothers. But in his opinion, it was precisely these decadent attributes which would provide the right material for the new lords of the earth. As we have noted, he considered himself to be decadent and to be its antithesis at one and the same time. This avowal is just an epigrammatic summary of the concluding section of *Zarathustra*: here the 'higher men' gather round Zarathustra – a gallery of the most diverse decadent types that Nietzsche characterizes with shrewd psychology – and to them is addressed the prophetic announcement of the Superman and eternal recurrence. The conquest of decadence, or its own self-conquest, is not Nietzsche's aim. When he praises the philosophical merits of his eternal recurrence, he is chiefly praising its nihilistic, relativistic and perspectiveless character. 'Let us think this idea in its most fearful form: existence just as it is, without meaning or goal, but inevitably returning into nothingness without a finale: *eternal recurrence*. That is the most extreme form of nihilism. Nothingness (the "meaningless") for ever more!'[124] Hence this new perception was intended to reinforce decadent nihilism rather than to supersede it. What Nietzsche wanted was to obtain on this basis a change of direction, a turn-round, without affecting the status quo. All decadent attributes were to be converted into tools for a militant advocacy of capitalism, and the decadents themselves into activists supporting the – both outwardly and inwardly – aggressive and barbaric imperialist cause.

Dionysos is the mythical symbol for this turn among the ruling class. Although the connection between the crowning figure of Nietzschean myth – '*Dionysos versus the Crucified* . . .', reads the closing line of *Ecce homo*[125] – and its first, youthful version is fairly tenuous, a very important motive does link the two: the domination of understanding and

reason by the instincts (hence Socrates was the contrasting figure to Dionysos in the début work). But with the later Nietzsche, the liberation of the instincts poses much wider questions – moral and social – than did his youthful, largely artistically oriented Dionysos sketch. At the end of his career, the complex of ideas is summed up again in this much transformed mythical figure. Decadence is now, to Nietzsche's mind, a universal problem, and Dionysos appears as a symbol of the forward-thrusting, commendable type of decadence, decadence in strength, as opposed to paralysing, debilitating pessimism (Schopenhauer) or a liberation of the instincts with plebeian overtones (Wagner). Nietzsche said of this pessimism of strength: 'Man now needs a "justification of the bad" *no longer*, it is precisely "justifying" that he abhors: he enjoys the bad in its raw purity and finds the *meaningless* bad the most interesting . . . Under such conditions it is precisely *the good* which needs "justifying", i.e., it must have an evil and dangerous undercurrent or incorporate a great stupidity: *then it will still find favour*. Animality now no longer shocks; a lively and cheerful bravado in favour of the beast in man is, in such times, the most victorious form of mental activity.'[126] 'It is part and parcel of this', he stated somewhat later, 'to grasp the hitherto *rejected sides* of existence not only as *necessary* but also as desirable: and not only as desirable with regard to the hitherto approved sides (as, say, their complements or preconditions), but for their own sake as the mightier, more fruitful and *truer* sides of existence through which its will is distinctively voiced.'[127] The god of this decadence 'redeemed' for activity is Dionysos; his distinguishing marks are 'sensuality and cruelty'.[128] He is the new God: 'God, conceived as a state of liberation from morality, cramming into himself the whole abundance of life's antitheses and *redeeming*, *justifying* them in divine torment: – God as the Beyond, superior to the pitiful workaday morality of "good and evil".'[129]

There is no need, we think, to go into any further details of Nietzschean epistemology and its application. As we can

already see, Nietzsche hereby created for the whole imperialist period a methodological 'model' of the indirect apologetics of capitalism, showing just how a fascinating and colourful symbol-realm of imperialist myth could be evolved from an extremely agnosticist epistemology, a theory of the most extreme nihilism. We have avoided dwelling – deliberately so – on the blatant contradictions in his myth structures. Were we to study Nietzsche's statements in this area from a logico-philosophical angle, we would be confronted by a dizzy chaos of the most lurid assertions, arbitrary and violently incompatible. Nevertheless we do not believe that this observation contradicts the view we developed at the outset, the view that Nietzsche had a consistent system. The binding or systematic factor lies in the social content of his thinking, in the struggle against socialism. Regarded from this viewpoint, Nietzsche's brightly variegated, mutually irreconcilable myths will yield up their ideational unity, their objective coherence: they are imperialist bourgeois myths serving to mobilize all imperialist forces against the chief adversary. The fact that the struggle of masters and herd, of nobles and slaves amounts to a mythical counterpart, in caricature form, to the class struggle is not too hard to discern. We have demonstrated that Nietzsche's challenge to Darwin was a myth arising from the justified fear that the normal course of history must lead to socialism. We have also shown that behind eternal recurrence there hides a self-consoling, mythical decree that evolution can produce nothing fundamentally new (and therefore no socialism). Another point we can see quite easily is that the Superman came about in order to steer back on to capitalist lines, etc., etc., the yearning spontaneously springing from the problems of capitalist life, its distortion and stunting of human beings. And the 'positive' part of the Nietzschean myths is no more than a mobilization of all the decadent and barbaric instincts in men corrupted by capitalism in order to save by force this parasitical paradise; here again, Nietzsche's philosophy is the imperialist myth designed to counter socialist humanism.

Perhaps a point which we have expounded earlier, viz., that the ideology of the declining bourgeoisie was forced on the defensive, is now becoming even clearer. It is of the essence of bourgeois thinking that it cannot manage without illusions. Now if, from the Renaissance to the French Revolution, men were projecting as a model an image of the Greek polis that was full of such illusions, its nucleus was nonetheless made up of real evolutionary currents, the real evolutionary trends of a rising bourgeois society; hence of elements of its own social life and perspectives of its own concrete future. But with Nietzsche, all his contents stem from the fear – which sought refuge in myth – of the fall of his own class, and from an inability genuinely to measure up to the adversary in intellectual terms. It is material from 'enemy territory', problems and questions imposed by the class enemy which ultimately determine the content of his philosophy. And the aggressive tone, the offensive approach in each individual instance barely disguises this underlying structure. The epistemological appeal to adopt the most extreme irrationalism, to deny completely all knowability of the world and all reason, coupled with a moral appeal to all the bestial and barbaric instincts, is an – unconscious – admission of this position. Nietzsche's uncommon gift is manifest in his ability to project, on the threshold of the imperialist period, a counter-myth that could exert such influence for decades. Viewed in this light, his aphoristic mode of expression appears the form adequate to the socio-historical situation. The inner rottenness, hollowness and mendacity of the whole system wrapped itself in this motley and formally disconnected ragbag of ideas.

NOTES

1 Engels to Conrad Schmidt, 27.10.1890. Marx-Engels: *Ausgewählte Briefe*, Berlin 1953, p. 508ff.

2 Mehring: *Works*, Berlin 1929, Vol. VI, p. 191.

3 Mehring: Review of Kurt Eisner's 'Psychopathia spiritualis', *Neue Zeit*, Yr. X, Vol. II, pp. 668f.
4 Nietzsche: *Works*, Vol. VIII, p. 64. All quotations of Nietzsche come from the 16-volume *Complete Works* published by Kröner, Leipzig.
5 Engels: *Anti-Dühring*.
6 Marx to Lassalle, 31.5.1858, Ferdinand Lassalle's posthumous *Letters and Writings*, edited by G. Mayer, Berlin 1922, Vol. III, p. 123.
7 Elisabeth Förster-Nietzsche: *Der einsame Nietzsche*, Leipzig 1914, pp. 433f.
8 Vol. X, p. 279.
9 Nietzsche to Baron von Gersdorff, 21.6.1871. *Works* ed. Schlechta, III, pp. 1092f.
10 Vol. IX, p. 142.
11 Mehring: op. cit., Vol. VI, p. 182.
12 Vol. IX., p. 425.
13 Ibid., p. 268.
14 Ibid., p. 153.
15 Ibid., p. 149.
16 Ibid., p. 276.
17 Vol. XIV, p. 368.
18 Vol. IX, p. 277.
19 Ibid., p. 280.
20 Vol. XV, p. 66.
21 Vol. I, p. 86.
22 Vol. XV, p. 63.
23 Vol. II, p. 341.
24 Vol. XV, p. 215.
25 Vol. II, p. 325.
26 Vol. III, p. 338.
27 Ibid., pp. 349f.
28 Vol. II, p. 327.
29 Ibid., p. 349.
30 Ibid., p. 350.
31 Ibid., p. 351.
32 Vol. III, p. 352.
33 Vol. V, p. 77.
34 Vol. VII, pp. 315f.
35 Vol. VIII, pp. 303f.
36 Ibid., p. 151.
37 Ibid., p. 153.
38 Vol. XIV, p. 334.

39 Vol. XVI, p. 288.
40 Ibid., p. 336.
41 Ibid., p. 194.
42 Franz Schauwecker: '*Ein Dichter und die Zukunft*', in *Des deutschen Dichters Sendung in der Gegenwart*, Leipzig 1933, p. 227.
43 A. Baeumler: *Nietzsche, der Philosoph und Politiker*, Leipzig, n.d., p. 135.
44 Vol. VII, p. 205.
45 Vol. XIII, p. 352.
46 Vol. VII, p. 156.
47 Vol. XV, p. 117.
48 Vol. XVI, p. 180.
49 W.A. Kaufmann: *Nietzsche*, Princeton 1950.
50 Vol. V, p. 130.
51 Vol. XIV, p. 321.
52 Engels: Op. cit., pp. 18ff.
53 Marx: *Capital*.
54 Vol. XI, p. 34.
55 Vol. XIII, p. 111. There follows a critique of Guyau, ibid., p.112.
56 Vol. XII, p. 410.
57 Vol. VIII, p. 88.
58 Ibid., p. 157.
59 Vol. XVI, pp. 184f.
60 Vol. XIV, p. 82.
61 Ibid., pp. 207f.
62 Cf.: '*Karl Marx und Friedrich Engels als Literaturhistoriker*,' Berlin 1952, p. 31f. and '*Skizze einer Geschichte der neueren deutschen Literatur*,' Berlin 1953, pp. 115ff.
63 Vol. VII, pp. 321f.
64 Vol. VIII, p. 218.
65 Vol. XVI, p. 377.
66 Ibid., pp. 305f.
67 Vol. XV, p. 11.
68 Ibid., p. 147.
69 Ibid., p. 145.
70 Vol. V, pp. 163ff.
71 Vol. XIII, p. 75.
72 Vol. XV, p. 228.
73 L. Zahn, *Friedrich Nietzsche*, Düsseldorf 1950, p. 282.
74 Vol. XII, p. 329.
75 Vol. XVI, p. 381.
76 Baeumler: Op. cit., p. 99.

77 Karl Jaspers: *Nietzsche*, Berlin 1947, pp. 431f.
78 Baeumler: Op. cit., p. 103.
79 Vol. XV, pp. 125f. Since such commentators as Kaufmann (e.g. Op. cit., p. 329) associate Nietzsche's anti-Christianity with Heine's, let us briefly point out that the purpose and content of Heine's polemics against Christianity are diametrically opposed to Nietzsche's. The similarity to which Kaufmann draws attention is of a purely external, stylistic nature. For Heine's world-outlook cf. my essay in *Deutsche Realisten des 19. Jahrhunderts*, Berlin 1951, pp. 39ff.
80 Vol. VIII, p. 273.
81 Ibid., p. 295.
82 Jaspers: Op. cit., p. 36.
83 Marx criticizes Social Darwinism with annihilating acuteness in the letter to Kugelmann, 27.6.1870, Engels at length in the letter to Lavrov, 12-17.11.1875. Engels emphasizes that the Social Darwinists should be criticized in the first place as bad economists, and only then as bad natural philosophers.
84 Vol. I, pp. 220f.
85 Vol. X, p. 137.
86 Vol. V, p. 285.
87 Translator's note. Nietzsche uses this English term.
88 Vol. VIII, p. 128.
89 Vol. XVI, p. 147.
90 Ibid.
91 Ibid., p. 148.
92 Vol. VII, pp. 237f.
93 Vol. XVI, p. 126.
94 Vol. XIII, p. 82.
95 Vol. XVI, p. 114.
96 Vol. VII, p. 58.
97 Baeumler: Op. cit., p. 79.
98 Kaufmann: Op. cit., pp. 282, 286ff.
99 Vol. XII, p. 61.
100 'We disallow the concept of an *infinite* force *as incompatible with the concept of "force"*. And thus – the world also lacks the power of eternal innovation.' Vol. XVI, p. 397.
101 Vol. XVI, pp. 396f.
102 Ibid., p. 101.
103 Ibid., p. 155.
104 Ibid., Vol. VIII, pp. 100f.
105 Vol. VI, p. 462.
106 Engels: On historical materialism in *Feuerbach*, Berlin 1927, p. 85.

107 As early as 1876 Avenarius published his 'Prolegomena', in 1888-90 his *Critique of Pure Experience*; although Mach's crucial philosophical works had not yet appeared, he likewise emerged as a theorist in the seventies and eighties, as too did Schuppe, the leader of 'philosophy of immanence'. Vaihinger, the Kantian closest to this trend, published his *Philosophy for the Common Man* only much later, but wrote the essence of it between 1876-8. If this whole movement subsequently claimed Nietzsche's support – Vaihinger taking the initiative – it was not a question of a direct influence (for obviously Nietzsche never even came across most of these works). It stemmed from an essential similarity in epistemological orientation brought about through the new ideological needs of the bourgeoisie.
108 Vol. VIII, p. 83.
109 Ibid., p. 142.
110 Vol. X, p. 32.
111 Nietzsche had no notion of the difference between understanding (*Verstand*) and reason (*Vernunft*), which he employed as synonyms. This indicates not only his ignorance of the most important philosophers, which even Jaspers concedes, but at the same time – and far more importantly – the coarser, intellectually inferior nature of irrationalism in imperialist times. Kierkegaard, for instance, contested Hegel with a far finer intellectual apparatus.
112 Vol. IX, p. 197.
113 Vol. VIII, p. 77.
114 Vol. XV, p. 456.
115 Vol. XVI, p. 31.
116 Ibid., pp. 30f.
117 Vol. XIV, pp. 12f.
118 Vol. XI, p. 251.
119 Vol. XVI, p. 19.
120 Vol. VII, pp. 306f.
121 Ibid., p. 388.
122 Vol. XVI, p. 393.
123 Vol. XV, p. 184.
124 Ibid., p. 182.
125 Ibid., p. 127.
126 Vol. XVI, p. 371.
127 Ibid., p. 383.
128 Ibid., p. 386.
129 Ibid., p. 379.

CHAPTER IV

VITALISM (*LEBENSPHILOSOPHIE*) IN IMPERIALIST GERMANY

1. Essence and Function of Vitalism

Vitalism or *Lebensphilosophie* was the dominant ideology of the whole imperialist period in Germany. But in order to appreciate properly the breadth and depth of its influence, we must bear clearly in mind that this philosophy, as such, was not so much a school or even a plainly defined subject, as was, for instance, neo-Kantianism or phenomenology, but rather a general trend pervading nearly all schools or at least influencing them. And its influence was constantly increasing. In the pre-war period, for example, only Simmel of the neo-Kantians was a declared adherent of vitalism, whereas in the post-war period both neo-Hegelianism and the Husserl school in its advanced stage became entirely guided by vitalism.

In order to delineate in full the vitalists' sphere of influence, we must step beyond the field of philosophy in the narrower sense of the term. On the one hand, they had an influence on all the social sciences from psychology to sociology, most especially historical studies, the history of literature and art. On the other hand, their influence extended far beyond the university campus; precisely the more widely influential writings of freelance philosophers were decidedly vitalist very early on. This is not only to do with Nietzsche's constantly growing influence on wide literary circles; relatively early, we also find similar echoes of Dilthey in Weininger, of Simmel in Rathenau, and of both in the Stefan George school. In the post-war period, virtually the whole of

bourgeois philosophical literature that was being read by wider circles was vitalist.

The cause of vitalism's universal effect can only be sought in the social and ideological situation of imperialist Germany. Naturally vitalism was a general product of the imperialist period and had important representatives in different countries (Bergson in France, pragmatism in the Anglo-Saxon lands, etc.). But here as elsewhere in this book, we shall confine ourselves to the specific features of German developments.

Vitalism, as it emerged and evolved as a philosophical subject in the imperialist period, was a specific product of this age: an attempt philosophically to solve from the standpoint of the imperialist bourgeoisie and its parasitic intelligentsia the questions raised by social evolution, by the class struggle's new forms. Obviously, the philosophers concerned supported their arguments with the findings and methods of those thinkers of the immediate and more distant past who had voiced ideas which tended in the same direction and appeared of importance to them. This was all the more so since the social circumstances under which philosophical propositions and methods arise will show, despite all the – often qualitative – changes, a certain continuity which must naturally be also reflected ideologically. In the present case, it was the ruling classes' reactionary hostility to progress since the French Revolution which determined this continuity. In our earlier chapters, we attempted to show in detail how irrationalism's specific problems of methodology and content arose from an endeavour to lend philosophical support to the increasingly decayed rule of these classes. As far as these aims and means have some continuity, it is also present philosophically. Every period harks back to the past, to specific phases of past development whenever and insofar as it seeks and finds in them analogies to its present needs.

This all indicates that this continuity can only have a relative character. The ruling classes' tendency towards conservation and opposition to the new forces hammering on the door is subject to perpetual social transformation. As we

saw earlier, the first manifestations of irrationalist philosophy at the start of the nineteenth century arose out of a resistance by the exploiters of feudal absolutism to the general bourgeois progressive movement sparked off by the French Revolution. Only with Schopenhauer did the expressly bourgeois bias of this reactionary movement emerge, and it was, as we showed in the relevant chapter, a matter of historical necessity that his philosophy gained universal currency only after the defeat of the 1848 revolution. For the age between 1789 and 1848 was, in Germany, the age marking the mobilization and assembling of forces of the bourgeois-democratic revolution. The leading reactionary class forces were still directed against the aspiring tendencies of bourgeois democracy. Only with the defeat of the 1848 revolution was the transformation completed: the result was the development of a bourgeois irrationalism, of an extreme philosophical reaction from the bourgeoisie's class standpoint which served its own particular class interests. Hence the popularity of Schopenhauerian philosophy after 1848.

The battle of June had already revealed the bourgeoisie's new and true adversary, the proletariat, in armed combat, thereby causing the bourgeoisie to betray its own revolution. The appearance of the *Communist Manifesto* showed this adversary clad in all its ideological armour: from now on, bourgeois philosophy was no longer fighting against the remnants of feudal thinking and for the establishment of a bourgeois society purged of such remnants. Instead it allied itself to all reactionary forces in order to suppress the revolutionary working class. In the ideological field, of course, this process was a gradual one and had its contradictions. Only after the second great historic battle between bourgeoisie and proletariat, the Paris Commune, which already adumbrated the social transformation that would come about in the event of a proletarian victory, did Nietzsche conceive fully fledged the form of new bourgeois irrationalism in which all the trends in this change are clearly expressed. While demonstrating this in our Nietzsche analysis, we elucidated at the

same time his relationship to Schopenhauer in philosophical-historical terms: the shared class origin in the specifically bourgeois character of their irrationalism and, this notwithstanding, Nietzsche's need to advance beyond Schopenhauer's conceptions philosophically. (This explains why Schelling's irrationalism, even in its later form, became more and more neglected after 1848. Why, later on, imperialist philosophy returned to Schelling and still more to Kierkegaard we shall explain in due course.)

But the philosophy of the imperialist age entailed no instantaneous direct association with the founders and 'classics' of irrationalism. This again has socio-historical reasons. A chief reason lies in the fact that the great social crisis expressed, at the outset of the age, in Bismarck's fall and the repeal of the anti-socialist laws quickly abated, and that the development of German imperialism up to the First World War presented – outwardly and superficially – a picture of prosperity without any deep-seated social crises. Of course this was merely a surface impression. But it was in the imperialist bourgeoisie's interests to have this impression portrayed and propagated as a reality. And the imperialist parasitical intelligentsia from which the creators and readers of vitalism were recruited could carry this out all the more readily because their social situation generally endowed them with a 'beneficial' blindness in respect of impending social changes and incipient crises. Thus very often they could play their social role spontaneously and in good faith.

Somehow, of course, this crisis-torn character of the collective condition did show itself in various ways. But as a result of the leading thinkers' social situation, it did so in the form of a cultural crisis, a crisis of culture pure and simple (although its actual concrete elements, distortedly reflected, were necessarily derived without exception from the cultural crisis of imperialist capitalism). Hence the bourgeoisie was able to exploit this largely spontaneously engendered intellectual movement for its own class ends. It used it partly to divert attention from the economic-social character of the

objective crisis itself, and partly as an element of the general hostility to progress, of the tendency – already discussed and due to be discussed again later – to glorify Germany's social and political backwardness as a 'higher' form of the State and culture. All this is also related to the fact that while the stimuli provided by Nietzsche played a major part in vitalism's development before the First World War, here his influence was primarily that of the 'cultural philosopher'. Only when the crisis of the imperialist system had become publicly apparent to all after the First World War did his extremely reactionary questions and solutions begin to exert an effect.

This latency of the crisis supplies the link between pre-war vitalism and its immediate forerunners, the philosophers after the 1848 revolution. At the same time it accounts for the important differences that existed between them. The post-1848 period saw the burial of almost the whole of post-Hegelian philosophy; most of the survivors covered – at a varying pace, some resolutely and some hesitantly – the road leading from Hegel to Kant (Vischer, Rosenkranz, etc.). To the bourgeoisie, it seemed as though they had landed in a period of unlimited capitalist prosperity and of true social security where nothing could weaken the confidence of bourgeois society. To be sure, this was also the time of the German bourgeoisie's unconditional surrender to Bismarck's 'Bonapartist monarchy'. These motives determine the fact that, along with Schopenhauer's growing fame and the diffusion of a scientifically mechanistic, socially liberal-opportunistic materialism (Büchner, Moleschott, etc.), a Positivist-agnosticist neo-Kantianism was becoming the dominant philosophy. Bourgeois social self-confidence and an imperturbable trust in the 'everlastingness' of capitalist growth led to the rejection of universal questions and to the confining of philosophy to logic, epistemology and, at the most, psychology. This reflects, on the one hand, a belief that the development of economics and technology would solve all life's problems 'just like that' (at most the Prussian State would still be needed for its 'ethical' value). And on

the other hand, the predominance of epistemology was intended to be a defence against such fantastic, excessive, 'unscientific' aberrations as the German bourgeoisie had been forced to experience in the 'year of madness' (1848). This instrument of defence was chiefly levelled against the consequences of Hegelian philosophy (and thus the pre-1848 democratic movement). But gradually, as the German working class gained in strength and awareness and became better organized, this instrument was increasingly used to challenge its world-view. Here we find to a growing degree the social roots of the furious struggle – in the name of neo-Kantian agnosticism – against the 'unscientific' nature of materialist 'metaphysics'. But it was deemed sufficient to outlaw questions of *Weltanschauung* (world-view) from philosophy. The need for a world-view only became explicit with the latent crisis in the imperialist period, and it was the central task of the vitalist philosophy which arose at this point to satisfy that need.

It was that need which gave rise to the difference between vitalism and its immediate antecedents. We have already indicated the important external difference: pre-imperialist German philosophy was largely a scholastic discipline, far removed from seeking a wide influence (the outsider position of Eduard von Hartmann, Nietzsche or Lagarde merely underlines this basic feature). Vitalism's sphere of influence – on the intelligentsia – on the other hand, far exceeded these bounds; and a change in the mode of presentation was both its precondition and its consequence. The growing acknowledgement of Nietzsche as a fully qualified philosopher, and not as a 'poet', is a symptom of this change. But at the same time, as we shall discuss in detail later, the agnosticist epistemological basis of philosophy remained intact.

Now how is this superstructural change reflected in vitalism's stand on such decisive problem complexes as dialectics and materialism?

As we know, pre-imperialist German scholastic philosophy

took a resolutely dismissive view of dialectics. On this the now influential Schopenhauer and the positivist neo-Kantians agree: dialectics are nonsense and unscientific in principle; the course of German philosophy from Kant to Hegel is a major aberration, a cul-de-sac of learning; back to Kant! must be philosophy's catchphrase. (Liebmann: *Kant und die Epigonen*, 1865.) Admittedly, other tendencies emerge in the philosophical outsiders: Eduard von Hartmann, for instance, sought to create an eclectic synthesis of the late Schelling, Schopenhauer and Hegel, while even the later Nietzsche occasionally referred to Schopenhauer's unreasonable animosity to Hegel and so forth. But these tendencies remained episodic, all the more so because many vestiges of the pre-1848 period were concealed in Hartmann's eclectic views. In part, to be sure, they were also in a specific sense an intellectual anticipation of the imperialist-vitalist position. They express – in Nietzsche's case, to particularly marked effect – the decisively altered social situation and its intellectual reflection: the neo-Kantians believed, in the age of 'security', that they could remove the new enemy, socialism (dialectical and historical materialism), through hushing it up. They thought that Kantian agnosticism, as the sole 'scientific' philosophical method, when combined with the categorical moral imperative to submit unconditionally to the Hohenzollern system, would wholly suffice to remove all ideological dangers. If therefore the idea of progress cropped up at all on the neo-Kantian liberal wing, it was purely positivist-evolutionary, i.e., the idea was of progress within a capitalist system unaltered in either structure or content. Already, capitalist triumphs and their consolidation had long ago made this positivist evolutionism the dominant direction in the countries of the West; Prussian-tinged 'security' produced its own particular German nuances. At any rate, from this standpoint any movement of history by way of contradictions and antitheses appeared a pure unscientific absurdity. This theory of evolution could – especially since it was presenting itself as the theory of the revolutionary worker

movement – be simply dismissed as a ridiculous utopia.

How the experience of the disruption of such 'security' affected bourgeois philosophical thinking, and how it radically altered all methodological attitudes in this respect, we have been able to trace in Nietzsche. Because Nietzsche clearly perceived the new enemy, the working class, for him dialectics were no longer a theoretical problem which had long been settled on the academic plane. And that is what they meant to those of his contemporaries for whom this adversary was not so dangerous as to make its intellectual destruction their primary task. Hence they thought that they could wave aside with a superior gesture those forms of dialectics (the Hegelian) that had in fact been overtaken by historical events – whereby, to be sure, they totally misread the historical and objective meaning of even Hegelian dialectics. Similarly, we have shown that Nietzsche merely perceived (or rather, sensed and felt) the danger, merely apprehended the enemy and did not really study its theory and praxis. With Nietzsche, therefore, there ensued no conscious wrangling with dialectics such as we find in Schelling or Kierkegaard. All he did was to oppose materialist dialectics, historical materialism with an irrationalist myth as his counter-concept. Granted, the fundamental structure of this conception corresponds to that of the earlier irrationalist opposition to dialectics. But as we have seen, even in its method it was, in principle, anti-scientific, emotional and irrationalist.

As the philosopher whose thought anticipated the crisis of capitalist society in imperial times, Nietzsche only acquired real readers and a real following after this crisis became generally evident in society, i.e., after the First World War and the setting up in Russia of the first dictatorship of the proletariat. The history of vitalism in its relations with dialectics constitutes the ideological development which led from latent crisis to acute crisis. Hence this process advanced slowly, but with occasional jerks, before the First World War; hence its development ran parallel with various sociological wrangles with Marxism. These, while aiming primarily at

destroying Marxism 'scientifically', also attempted in part to incorporate its 'serviceable' and suitably 'purified' elements in the bourgeois view of history (in a reciprocal relationship to the revisionist movement in social democracy). And hence bourgeois philosophy harked back to the Romantic era, to Kant's successors, as well as to Hegel and so on. All these tendencies are – very distorted – reflections in thinking of the same fact, namely that even during the time of what we have called their latency, the contradictions in social developments were already emerging so publicly that it became impossible to ignore them, as previously, with a show of academic *hauteur*. But the ensuing controversy was most half-hearted. Nobody wanted a rupture with the immediate forerunners; there was simply a desire to develop philosophy in accordance with the philosophical needs that now existed for the aforesaid reasons. To a constantly increasing extent, it was becoming recognized that valuable allies could be found in the expressly reactionary, irrationalist philosophy of the age before 1848, in the reactionary foibles of idealist dialectics. Thus whilst preserving its epistemology, philosophy struck out beyond positivist neo-Kantianism in a reactionary direction. Here again we find an irrationalist reversal of objective progress as reflected in dialectics and their extension. And already it was – in essence, though not couched in the outward form of most controversies – a case of philosophically demolishing dialectical and historical materialism in this way. In this and the following chapter, we shall analyse in detail the growth of this development and those important stages in it that depended on the adversary's growth and activities.

In the second place, the struggle against materialism also governed the philosophical development of imperialism. Thus it was unable to detach itself from the epistemology of subjective idealism. It made no difference whether it was chiefly oriented towards Kant, as in Germany, or towards Hume and Berkeley: the unknowability, indeed the non-existence, the unthinkable nature of an objective reality

independent of consciousness was the implicit axiom of every philosophy of this age.

It is clear that here the age's 'need for a *Weltanschauung*' came into conflict with the epistemological precondition of its own thinking. And at this point vitalism appeared in an attempt to resolve the dilemma. It was very easy for it to adopt the dominant forms of modern agnosticism, for since the classic basic question of epistemology – the relationship between consciousness and being – was gradually shrivelling and dwindling into the formula: understanding (reason equated with understanding and reduced to reasonableness) versus comprehended being, it was possible to initiate a critique of understanding, an attempt to surpass its limits, without disturbing the foundations of subjective idealism. The key to all these difficulties, it was thought, could be located in the concept of 'life', especially if this was identified, as always in vitalism, with 'experience'. Experience, with intuition as its organon and the irrational as its 'natural' object, could conjure up all the necessary elements of *Weltanschauung* without renouncing, *de facto* and publicly, the agnosticism of subjective idealist philosophy and without revoking that denial of a reality independent of consciousness which had become crucial to anti-materialism. Outwardly, to be sure, this struggle now acquired other forms. On the one hand, the appeal to the richness of life and experience, as opposed to the barren poverty of the understanding, permitted philosophy to counter the materialist inferences from social and scientific developments in the name of a natural science, biology. (But as we shall see, vitalism's relationship to biology was very loose, metaphysical rather than concrete, and never a philosophical assessment of concrete problems of biological science.) On the other hand, the appeal to experience gave rise to a pseudo-objectivism, an apparent self-elevation above the antithesis of idealism and materialism.

The tendency to be raised above the allegedly false dilemma of idealism and materialism was a universal endeavour of philosophy in the imperialist age. To the bourgeois conscience,

both 'isms' seemed compromised in various ways: idealism because of the sterile academicism of its advocates (with, as its background, the collapse of the great idealist systems); and materialism chiefly because of its association with the worker movement. And it is worth mentioning that the new, dialectical materialism seldom cropped up in these debates. Materialism as preached by Marx was simply identified with the old materialism (Moleschott, Büchner, etc.), and the latter philosophy's failure to grasp conceptually the new achievements of physics was interpreted as a failure of materialism in general. Thus on the eve of the imperialist period, a philosophical 'third road' came into being with Mach, Avenarius and Nietzsche almost simultaneously. In fact, however, this amounted only to a revival of idealism. For whenever the mutual inseparability of being and consciousness is posited, there necessarily arises an epistemological dependence of the first on the second – which is idealism. As long, therefore, as the philosophical 'third road' remained purely epistemological, it differed not at all or barely from the old subjective idealism (Mach-Avenarius in relation to Berkeley). The actual problem of pseudo-objectivity arose only when this philosophy went beyond the purely epistemological sphere. For the age's need for a *Weltanschauung* demanded a concrete world-picture, an image of nature, history and man. Granted the proposed objects can only be created by the subject in accordance with the prevailing epistemology. But in order to satisfy the need for a *Weltanschauung*, they must at the same time stand before us as objects of objective being. The central position that 'life' occupied in the method of this philosophy, particularly in that specific form wherein life is always subjectified into 'experience' and experience 'objectified' as life, allowed of such a swing between subjectivity and objectivity – one, to be sure, that never stands up to a proper critique of knowledge. The tendency – its first marked occurrence was in Nietzsche – was reinforced when the idea of myth entered into philosophical conceptions. There can be no

doubt that mythical objects are creations by the subject. On the other hand, the long historical survival of myths, their universal and unchallenged validity for wide cultural circles gave rise to the uncritical illusion that, despite their subjective origin and the subject-bound nature of their validity, they might represent a special type of objectivity. And precisely as the result of the aforesaid swing between subjectivity and objectivity (experience and life), the new central concept of philosophy further reinforced these illusions and gave them a fashionable accent. It seemed as though it was the destiny of precisely this age, out of its 'experience' of 'life' and with new figures of a new myth, to restore coherence to a world become godless and ravaged through understanding, to make it meaningful and to make new perspectives discernible.

In fine: the essence of vitalism lies in a conversion of agnosticism into mysticism, of subjective idealism into the pseudo-objectivity of myth.

This mythical 'objectivism', behind which there always stood a subjectivist-agnosticist epistemology, exactly matched the philosophical needs of the imperialist reaction. The general feeling prevailed that a period of great inner and external historical decisions was imminent (Nietzsche first voiced the feeling openly). Hence the need to say something substantial and positive, something philosophical about social developments, history and society, i.e., to surpass neo-Kantian formalism.

In the intelligentsia, one can sense a constant growth of anti-capitalist attitudes. During the final Bismarck crisis, the time of the repeal of the anti-socialist laws, when the Naturalist ferment was taking place in German literature, the vast majority of the young and gifted intellectuals, for instance, was to be found in the social democrat camp. Therefore these tendencies had to be assimilated in the philosophical world-outlook so as to combat the intelligentsia's socialist tendencies more effectively than was possible for ordinary reactionary ideology. With its contrast between the living and the

dead, petrified and mechanical, vitalist philosophy took over the task of 'deepening' all concrete problems to such an extent that they created a major diversion from these imminent social consequences.

But the atmosphere that was threatening the reactionary forces in Germany by no means confined itself to a sympathy with socialism. By the eve of the imperialistic period, the Bismarckian compromise was already cracking in every joint of the structure of the German Reich. A need for reconstruction was universally felt, by the Right as much as the Left. Reactionary historians and sociologists were making strenuous efforts to portray the second Reich's backward political structure as historically outstanding, new and superior to Western democratic forms, and these efforts met with great success among broad sections of the intelligentsia.

Vitalism came to their assistance philosophically. Its relativism effectively undermined the belief in historical progress, and hence in the possibility and value of Germany's radical democratization. The polar 'primal phenomenon' of vitalism, the antithesis of the living and the petrified, could be readily applied to this problem complex and could, on the philosophical plane, compromise democracy as something mechanical and petrified. Here we cannot do more than outline this important connection. We shall discuss later the historical role of German sociology, philosophy of law, history and so on insofar as they affect the problems under consideration.

There is the additional point that the central position of experienced life in vitalistic epistemology necessarily nurtured an aristocratic feeling. An experiential philosophy can only be intuitive – and purportedly it is only an elect, the members of an aristocracy, who possess a capacity for intuition. In later times, when the social contrasts emerged more strongly still, it was overtly stated that the categories of understanding and reason belonged to the democratic crowd, whereas the truly eminent appropriated the world only on the basis of intuition. Vitalism had in principle

an aristocratic epistemology.

All these motives, of which we have set down only the most important, contributed to the dominance of vitalism and to the inflation of its agnostic relativism into a new philosophy. At first, official scholastic philosophy and the State authorities adopted a sceptical attitude towards these tendencies. Only gradually did vitalism infiltrate the entire thinking of imperialistic Germany. Imperialistic vitalism's founder and most important forerunner, Dilthey, occasionally voiced sharply programmatic statements about this situation. He portrayed the major role that a philosophical *Weltanschauung* had played in bygone politico-social struggles. He went on to write: 'A lesson for the politician! In turning away from ideas and their philosophical expression, today's State officials and our bourgeoisie may assume as lofty an air as they please: it signifies not a sense of reality but their intellectual poverty: not only naturally powerful feelings but also a closed system of ideas give social democracy and ultramontanism an advantage over the other political forces of our times.'[1]

We intend, in these studies, to trace in its main phases the development beginning at this point and ultimately leading, in its consequences, to 'National-Socialist philosophy'. Of course the line we are tracing does not mean that German fascism drew its ideas from this source exclusively; quite the contrary. The so-called philosophy of fascism based itself primarily on racial theory, above all in the form developed by Houston Chamberlain, although in so doing, to be sure, it made some use of vitalism's findings. But for a 'philosophy' with so little foundation or coherence, so profoundly unscientific and coarsely dilettantish to become prevalent, what were needed were a specific philosophical mood, a disintegration of confidence in understanding and reason, the destruction of human faith in progress, and credulity towards irrationalism, myth and mysticism. And vitalism created just this philosophical mood.

Of course it did not achieve this consciously, and the

less so the farther we move away in time from Hitler. It would be absurd to regard Dilthey or Simmel as witting forerunners of fascism; not even in the sense in which Nietzsche or Lagarde were its ancestors do they merit this description. Here, however, we are concerned not with a psychological analysis of intentions, but with the objective dialectics of the development itself. And in the objective sense, every thinker whom we have discussed contributed to the creation of the aforesaid mood in philosophy.

2. Dilthey as Founder of Imperialistic Vitalism

Wilhelm Dilthey is next to and after Nietzsche the most important and influential forerunner of imperialistic vitalism. But whereas Nietzsche achieved the decisive turn to vitalism by focusing his attack on the new agent of historical progress, the proletariat, thereby initiating the open attack on every scientific method very early on, Dilthey was a forerunner, a transitional figure in a much truer sense. His starting-point was the positivistic neo-Kantianism of the sixties and seventies. This he wanted gradually to reconstruct into a new philosophy. Subjectively he always adhered to a scientific standpoint, without overtly breaking with Kantianism and in particular with the individual sciences. Objectively, to be sure, he proceeded to undermine the scientific method of philosophy in a way that had many repercussions, and in the long run this proved quite as effective as Nietzsche's direct attacks.

Dilthey's starting-point was psychological and historical. His life-work was actually intended to be a 'Critique of Historical Reason'; Kant was to be adapted to contemporary needs and his philosophy developed in such a way that it would lend itself to laying the foundations of the human sciences, and chiefly history. (History, needless to say, in the sense of Ranke or Jakob Burckhardt, not that of the

progressive period of bourgeois society.) The underlying character traits of the positivistically comprehended Kant – agnosticism, phenomenalism – were to be preserved unchanged; in Dilthey, as in all modern Kantians, the master's uncertainties regarding materialism were completely eliminated in the doctrine of the *Ding an sich*. But despite Dilthey's Kantian 'orthodoxy', his philosophy took an important step beyond neo-Kantianism in the direction of vitalistic irrationalism. It promoted not only the upsurge of vitalism proper but also, in close connection with it, the rebirth of post-Kantian philosophies (neo-Romanticism, neo-Hegelianism). At the same time it ran parallel to the phenomenological school, whose vitalistic advances Dilthey anticipated and influenced more than anybody, and to Bergson and pragmatism in countries outside Germany. Naturally these tendencies only emerged with absolute clarity in Dilthey little by little. He stood very close to positivistic neo-Kantianism in his beginnings, even if the seeds of innovation are visible right from the outset. Here we can only provide a brief résumé of his most important views.

Dilthey's epistemological rationale of vitalism proceeds from the thesis that experiencing the world is the ultimate basis of knowledge. 'Life itself, liveliness, behind which I cannot penetrate, contains structural connections from which all experiencing and thinking is explained. *And this is the decisive factor for the whole possibility of knowing*. There is a knowledge of reality only because the full structural coherence which emerges in the forms, principles and categories of thinking is contained in life and experience, and because this coherence can be shown analytically in life and experience.'[2] At first this sounds like an attempt to argue an objective idealism epistemologically. If all categories are contained in objective reality and our perception descries them there alone, the subjectivistic narrowness of neo-Kantian idealism with its inability to provide a proper world-image is overcome.

This impression becomes even stronger if one acquaints

oneself more closely with Dilthey's position. Correctly, Dilthey sensed that an epistemological solution to man's relationship with the objective external world could only be elucidated by way of praxis. 'Supposing we had a man who was all observation and intelligence, then this intellectual apparatus might contain every possible means of projecting images: yet all of it would never succeed in differentiating a subject from concrete objects. The core of the distinction is far rather the relation of impulse and thwarted intention, of will and resistance . . .' (*Realität der Aussenwelt*). If, however, we pursue Dilthey's statements further, we will see that at every point he was by no means speaking of objective reality itself. For Dilthey, impulses, etc., are not organs or agencies through which to comprehend and progressively to master intellectually a reality existing independently of consciousness. They merely form 'the inner side, as it were, of the coherent framework of our observations, ideas and thought processes. Now impulse, pressure and resistance are, as it were, the fixed components imparting their solidity to all external objects. Will, struggle, labour, need and satisfaction are the ever-recurring nuclear elements comprising the framework of intellectual activity' (*Realität der Aussenwelt*). The world portrayed in Dilthey's epistemology is as purely determined by the consciousness as that of the neo-Kantians, for all the 'practical' categories he cites are just as much elements of a subjective world as the 'purely intellectual' ones against which he polemicized, and which he strove to surmount. At this period the attempt to comprehend the objectivity of the real world was seldom conscious and seldom decided, and it proceeded from the vague sensing of a connection between praxis and comprehension of objective reality. The very fate of the attempt shows the correctness of our view that vitalistic epistemology never surpassed, in principle, the subjective idealism of the preceding age.

But precisely here it is necessary to show the new and distinguishing aspect of the vitalistic terms of inquiry. Dilthey concluded his train of thought with the words: 'Here we have

life itself. It is perpetually its own proof.'[3] And, he added in another passage, all the problems of transcendence contained in the Kantian 'thing-in-itself' were thereby automatically solved: 'From the standpoint of life no proof can be obtained by proceeding beyond what is contained in consciousness to something transcendent. We are only analysing that which belief in the external world rests upon in life itself. *Life gives the fundamental preconditions of knowledge, and thinking cannot reach behind them*. It may test and investigate them from the angle of the extent of their realization in science. But they are hence not hypotheses but principles or preconditions arising out of life which enter science as the means to which they are tied. Let us suppose the existence of a reason without will or feelings. This intellectual world, which would be a consciousness, might well develop differing degrees of dependence when it appeared, and a regularity therein, which would match the causal idea and the distinction between Ego and objects. But in the last resort, even the difference of subject and object still attaches to the functions, and so to the activities and image. And the knowledge value of the antithesis of subject and object is not that of a transcendent fact: the subject and otherness or externality are nothing else than that which is contained and given in the experiences of life itself. *This is all reality*.'[4] Here we have the complete epistemological basis of vitalism in undiluted form. As a result of the (unconscious) identification of life and experience, we obtain that equivocation between (apparent) objectivity and (real) subjectivity which is the essence of vitalistic pseudo-objectivity. For had Dilthey carried to a rigorous conclusion his original aim at objectivity, he would soon have been obliged to recognize that the 'resistance' met by his impulses, etc., is something broader and more comprehensive, something quite other than merely the 'objective' side of life. Here experience encounters objective reality, and life forms only part of it unless – and this was alien to Dilthey – one hylozoistically views the whole of objective reality as life. But Dilthey's inquiry

remained bogged down in a unity of experience and life which he never thought through to a conclusion or really analysed. He did not acknowledge at all an objective reality independent of consciousness.

There is present in this a distant analogy with the problems of classical German philosophy. Here a similar subject-object was sought and professedly located (subject and substance in Hegel's *Phenomenology of Mind*). But in this very instance the differences are far more revealing than the analogies. Firstly, Hegel wittingly and resolutely surpassed the subjectivism of Kantian epistemology, whereas Dilthey arrived at its neo-Kantian, even more decidedly subjectivist sequels. Secondly, the object side of the thinking subject-object embraced the whole of reality in classical German philosophy, whereas Dilthey's subject-object is merely an equating of experience and life, with a marked preponderance of the former. In classical philosophy, therefore, there did arise a type of objectivity, albeit beset with all the problems pertaining to objective idealism, whereas Dilthey's inevitably remains a pseudo-objectivity. And thirdly, the classical philosophical solution permitted of, and indeed demanded, a rational-dialectical perception of the world; the transformation of substance into subject was also, with Hegel, a discovery of reason's governance in reality – all-embracing, encompassing all depths. Dilthey's obscure union of life and experience, on the other hand, necessarily posits the essence of reality thus apprehended as something fundamentally irrational.

Dilthey's great discovery is, therefore, that our belief in the reality of the external world springs from the experience of resistance and obstruction forced upon us by our will-controlled relations to persons and things in the external world. This is a vitalistic revival of the Kantian *Affektion* of the subject through the 'thing-in-itself' (the stumbling block for all his disciples from Maimon to the Marburg and South-West German school). But vitalism robbed it of its original materialist flavour. Dilthey set forth his views as follows: 'The thing and its conceptual formula, the substance, is . . .

not a creation of the understanding, but one of the totality of our spiritual powers.'[5] Thus the external world is not independent of human consciousness, but its 'producer' is not understanding or reason but the totality of the human mind, vitalistically grasped. This apparent extension of the basic epistemological questions would, in Dilthey's view, bring about an insolubly paradoxical concept of that which transcends consciousness if intellectually treated. But, he continued, the basis of these categories 'lies in the experiences of our will and of the associated emotions. All sensations and thought processes clothe, as it were, this naked experience.' In proportion to the accumulation of experiences 'that character of reality will grow which images have for us. It will become a power completely encircling us . . . Here is life itself, it is perpetually its own proof.'

We have quoted Dilthey in rather more detail so as to make it clear how little, despite his 'discovery' and his new terminology, he advanced beyond the agnosticist-solipsistic character of neo-Kantianism on the central epistemological question. But like all modern idealists, he protested against the conclusions rightly drawn from his epistemology, against the interpretation of his position as a subjective idealism and agnosticism. The further he moved in concrete statements from the original problem, the more vigorously he acted as though he acknowledged an external world independent of the consciousness. Thus he once stated that the laws of the natural sciences and their presuppositions of facts confounded all scepticism. 'They do clearly show us that there is an objective order behind appearances, independent of us and with its own laws. This is the expression of a great reality existing independently of us.' To be sure, he at once added: 'It is certain that we never perceive reality itself',[6] only symbols, signs and so forth.

This vitalistic twist to the basic Kantian epistemological question necessarily brought psychology to the centre of philosophical interest. This again is a general trait of the Positivist renewal of Kant and of Dilthey's initial tendencies.

But here, as Dilthey developed his own particular views, there arose something qualitatively new: a programme for a special type of psychology. It amounted to an antithesis between the previous 'explanatory' psychology (which was causal and sought out laws) and a 'descriptive' or 'understanding' psychology. This new science was intended to lay the basis for all 'human sciences' (*Geisteswissenschaften* – Dilthey's term for the social sciences), principally history.

The history of the rise of vitalism in general takes concrete shape around this problem. A certain relative justification for the proposition itself existed in the critique of Positivism's prejudices and limits, for the positivists thought it possible to reveal the course of history and, even more, its coherence, with the aid of some abstract psychological categories. But the vitalists' dissatisfaction was not applied to studying the true causes of the historical framework and of society's economic structure and its vicissitudes. Hence the false answer: the need for a new, qualitatively total and vital psychology.

The answer was false because in respect of the course of history, the new psychology was just as abstract, just as secondary as the old had been. Since the objective basis of history is broader, wider and deeper than any individual consciousness – a fact which Dilthey himself, as we shall see, was obliged to recognize in other contexts – all psychology is perforce abstract as a fundamental method of history and bypasses the cardinal problems. There can be no psychology that lays the foundations for the study of history, since the psychology of human beings acting in history can only be grasped from the material basis of their lives and deeds, and above all from their work and its objective conditions. Here too, naturally, there are complicated reciprocal influences, but the material basis remains the primary factor, that which is decisive 'in the last resort' (Engels). Thus Dilthey's attempt so to reconstruct psychology as to make it a basis for the 'human' (social) sciences turned its relationship to objective, socio-historical reality on its head just as much as it reversed

that of the positivism he was challenging. All that Dilthey did was to replace the false abstraction of that which is governed by mere understanding with an irrational, putative totality of experienced life. The only difference – and this 'only' exactly expresses the transition to the new age of vitalism – was that the positivists' psychology represented a shallow, mechanical rationalism, whereas Dilthey, while divining a real dialectic question, posed and answered it irrationalistically from the outset, thus causing its dialectic character to disappear.

The chief lack that Dilthey found in the old 'explanatory' psychology was an ability to solve the problem of the spiritual world's relationship to the physical; it contained a tangle of equally unprovable hypotheses blocking the path to reality. Here again, he was relatively justified in his dissatisfaction with a psychology which would not concede that spiritual phenomena depended in a materialistic sense on material-physical ones, but shied away from an openly idealistic answer. The vitalistic solution, however, consisted merely in an irrational sweeping aside of the real problem. Life was to have the unity of body and soul as its content. But since, as we already know, life actually meant experience to Dilthey, he clothed a radically subjectively-rooted answer in quasi-objective terminology and 'eliminated' the dualism of body and soul with the result that all the objects of psychological study appeared projected on the level of experienced life. A simple description of the psychic facts was to succeed the old hypotheses. This meant the relegation to a subsidiary role of all causal and ordered knowledge in this field and the creation of more scope for irrationalism.

Dilthey's proposition had as its purpose a new methodological foundation for the historical sciences. Now in positivism, these were degenerating to the extent that the actual reality of history was receding more and more in the face of academic controversies with scholars concerning the phenomena of history, literature and art, philosophy and so on. Dilthey's opposition to this Alexandrinism, the 'turning to

the matter itself' which he had already demonstrated in his praxis, and which he now formulated in theoretical-methodological terms, is understandable, and it subsequently became of great influence. (The fructifying effect of the phenomenological method had similar sources.) Hence Dilthey became the founder of the 'humanistic method'. But whilst fully recognizing the relative rights of its critique of academic positivism, we must also stress at this point that the 'matter itself' to which Dilthey and the phenomenologists gave central importance is simply not the matter itself in its totality and objectivity. It is not total, for actual social connections and conditions disappear behind the 'uniqueness' of isolated objects, and where these are linked together, this happens with the aid of mythicized abstractions and analogies. It is not objective, for experience as the organon of knowledge creates an atmosphere of subjective arbitrariness in selection, emphasis, designation, etc. With Dilthey there was still a certain tendency towards objectivity; but in Gundolf subjective arbitrariness as a consciously applied method clearly comes to the forefront.

Granted, with Dilthey – as somewhat later with the neo-Kantians Windelband and Rickert – this struggle by 'descriptive psychology' against law and causality relates only to the social sciences. In these, objects appear 'from within, as reality and as a living structure *originaliter*', whereas the natural sciences have as their object 'facts which enter the consciousness from without, as phenomena and separate data'. Therefore: 'Nature is something we explain, the spiritual life something we understand.'[7]

Here we should note an inconsistency in this recognition of the ordered (if also phenomenalistic) objectivity of nature from the angle of Dilthey's epistemology. If mythicized life replaces the Kantian 'thing-in-itself', there is no reason why nature should form an exception. This very point shows us how instinctively Dilthey identified life and experience. For, considered from the angle of experience, the bi-partition is a logical one, albeit also a purely subjectivist one. Thus it is no

coincidence that later developments corrected Dilthey's illogicality to the extent of including nature too in the subjective-irrationalistic equation of life and experience.

And so irrationalism came to occupy the centre of Dilthey's philosophy, at least as far as it dealt with the social sciences, and these virtually encompass his entire *oeuvre*. He defined the essence of the 'understanding' process as follows: 'Hence there is an irrational element in all understanding, just as life itself is irrational; it cannot be represented by formulae arrived at by logical processes. And an ultimate, though completely subjective certainty that lies in this re-experiencing (*Nacherleben*) can find no substitute in an examination of the knowledge value of the chains of reasoning by which the process of understanding may be represented. The very nature of understanding imposes these limits on its logical treatment.'[8] And Dilthey summed it up more astringently still in the course of his later statements: 'Life cannot be brought before the judgement-seat of reason.'

The inevitable result of this is an aristocratic epistemology. Here again Dilthey proceeded consistently to the last. He said of the hermeneutics, the systematic application of 'understanding', that they 'are, however, conjectural and never produce demonstrative certainty'. And in other places he stressed that interpretation, 'as the *artistically governed* (*kunstmässig*) reproductive understanding',[9] must always involve a touch of genius. Thus in Dilthey's view, the new psychology is by definition the privilege, the secret doctrine of a specific aesthetic-historicist spiritual aristocracy.

Seen from the angle of Dilthey's propositions, which, as we have noted, express a deep-seated ideological need among the bourgeois intelligentsia of the imperialist age, this methodologically central position of intuition is an inevitable consequence. Hopeless situations call for desperate remedies. And as always in the history of philosophy when a remedy is sought and, it is believed, found in a *salto mortale*, the real epistemological and methodological preconditions of the 'solution' escaped examination. Its adherents overlooked

the crassest methodological *quid pro quo* because the need for a 'solution' was so strong that it obscured all possible doubts.

The new 'objectivity' presupposed a new organ of knowledge. It was a central issue of imperialist philosophy to place this new mode of knowledge, this new organ, intuition, in opposition to conceptual, rational thought. In reality the fact is that intuition constitutes a psychological element of every scientific working method. Superficial study can evoke the immediate impression that intuition is more concrete and synthetic than abstract, discursive thinking in concepts. Certainly this is only an impression; for psychologically, intuition signifies nothing else than the sudden conscious realization of a thought process that has hitherto gone on partly unconsciously. Objectively, therefore, it is never separable from the largely conscious working process. And for conscientious scientific thinking, it is a serious task firstly, to check whether these 'intuitively' obtained results stand up scientifically, and secondly, organically to build them into the rational conceptual system so that it will afterwards be quite impossible to tell what was discovered by the power of deduction (consciously), and what was discovered with the aid of intuition (below the threshold of consciousness, and only later become conscious). Thus considered in its proper place, as a psychological element of the working process, intuition is a supplement to conceptual thought and not its antithesis. And the intuitive discovery of a correlation can never become a criterion of truth.

A superficial psychological study of scientific investigation will foster the illusion that intuition is an organ independent of abstract thought for the comprehension of higher correlations. This illusion, a confusing of subjective investigation with the objective scientific method, became, with the support of the general subjectivism of imperialistic philosophy, the bedrock of the modern theory of intuition. The relationship between the resulting process and dialectic knowledge further heightened the illusion. From a

subjectivist perspective, it was tempting to assume that the dialectic contradiction came about through a conceptual process, whereas its resolving synthesis, its assimilation into a higher unity was the product of intuition. This is naturally an illusion, for true dialectics express every synthesis conceptually once more, and do not recognize any synthesis as a definitive answer. Precisely because it is an accurate reflection of the objects of the real world, genuine scientific dialectic thinking always contains the conceptual association and analysis of ideas. For that reason intuition is not an organ of knowledge, not an element of the scientific method. As we have seen, Hegel clearly expounded all this in answer to Schelling in the introduction to his *Phenomenology*.

In the philosophy of the imperialist period, on the other hand, intuition occupied a central position in the objective theory of method. This need emerged directly because thinkers were turning away from the epistemological formalism of the preceding period. This they had to do, for the quest for a *Weltanschauung* already signifies in itself a substantial proposition. Subjective idealism's epistemology, however, was of necessity a purely formal and not a dialectic analysis, not an ideational formulating of the conceptual content. If thought aspires beyond such limits, if it seeks to perceive real contents philosophically, then it must have a twofold support. It must find support in, on the one hand, the reflection theory of materialism and, on the other, the dialectically grasped universal order, which is to say an order which is not to be taken as merely a static framework of objectivities and structures, but as the dynamic framework of evolution (the ascending movement) and of rational history as well. Intuition helped imperialist philosophy to turn away from the formalism of epistemology, and also from subjective idealism and agnosticism, without in the least disturbing their foundations.

So this philosophy will always put forward the claim that the content to which it aspires, the philosophical reality which it seeks to attain, is to be appreciated as a qualitatively

different, higher reality than the conceivable world. And in this context, the subjectively interpreted fact of intuition will give the impression of being the sign of a flash of inspiration in comprehending this higher world. It now became crucial for the new philosophy to refute at all costs the criticism coming from the side of conceptual analysis. This protective action by intuition appeared in similar old philosophies (it already did so in a part of ancient religious mysticism), where it already took the line of an aristocratic epistemology. It was based on the standpoint that it was not given to everybody to grasp the higher reality intuitively. Thus anybody who sought conceptual criteria for intuitive perception was merely proving that he lacked all capacity for the intuitive grasping of the higher reality. And thus his criticism merely revealed his own lower nature, just as those people who failed to see the fine new clothes on Hans Andersen's naked Emperor were 'unqualified or intolerably stupid'. Such an 'epistemology' of intuition was also needed for the reason that, by virtue of its very nature, all 'reality' thus comprehended is arbitrary and cannot be checked. As the organ of higher knowledge, intuition at the same time provided a justification for this arbitrariness.

This proclamation of the irrationalism of life's ordered framework – which, formally speaking, found a coolly sober expression in Dilthey himself – and of conjectural intuition as its organ of knowledge formed the basis of the great influence which Dilthey exercised even before the war. Let us refer only to the chiefly literary-historical and aesthetic activities of the George school. For its spiritual leader, Gundolf, the division of explaining and understanding was no longer sufficient. Even within the realm of experience, he drew a distinction between 'primal experience' and 'educated experience', whereby the anti-historical, anti-social character of the doctrine of intuition found a far firmer expression than in Dilthey or even in Simmel. For if we examine more closely the content and methodology of Gundolf's distinction, we see that the criterion of actual

unfalsified experience, of the 'primal experience', consists in the very fact of its being torn out of the context of its social surroundings, surroundings comprehensible through understanding and reason. Its direct content outleaps its defined limits, its philosophical substance has become purely irrationalistic (meta-rational). 'By primal experience', wrote Gundolf, 'I understand, for instance, the religious, titanic or erotic – by Goethe's educational experiences I understand his experience of the German heritage, of Shakespeare, classical antiquity, Italy, the Orient, even his experience of German society.'[10]

Dilthey, to be sure, was not an irrationalist of post-war proportions. This is already manifest in the fact that he confined his method to the social sciences. But here too irrationalism, although it was the logical conclusion of his method, was a consequence which he constantly endeavoured to surmount and to direct back on to the path of a quasi-scientific method. For Dilthey did not believe in an irreconcilable antithesis between reason and life, science and intuition. He thought, rather, that it was possible to evolve the full splendour of the subjective and objective world out of experience; to proceed from experience, via its understanding and the systematization of this understanding in the methodical interpretation of hermeneutics, to a higher and more comprehensive concept of the scientific method. Dilthey, who all in all was a man of exceptional knowledge and genuine learning, himself frequently noticed that his two basic tendencies were mutually contradictory, and he overtly stated the resulting antinomies. But again and again, he attempted – vainly – to overcome them.

Our exposition so far shows us already that these antinomies were irrevocable because of his starting-point and because of his method. Dilthey himself said of the circle inherent in the vitalistic argumentation of the science of history: 'History is intended to teach what life is. And it must find its resources in life.'[11] So a vicious circle existed at the very outset of the method. And the false circle was

none other than that of pseudo-objectivity. It had its basis in Dilthey's idea of the identical subject-object: life equals experience. With a truly objective method (even if it be that of an objective idealism), it is clear that the categories, at least in their Being-in-itself, are contained in objective reality and only 'read off' by the perceiving subject. Thus Dilthey's dilemma contains the ambiguous basic character, the epistemological dichotomy of his philosophical starting-point.

But still more important, because more concrete and substantial, was the impossibility of locating in experience a path to laying the foundations of the historical sciences. Dilthey, certainly, laboured under the illusion that all categories of objective reality are contained in experience, and that it only requires the correct method ('understanding' psychology, hermeneutics) in order to develop them. He overlooked the fact that experience, epistemologically, presupposes these categories as forms of objective reality; they determine experience, but experience does not determine them. And we are setting aside the fact that this starting-point dictates a basically uncritical attitude in the first place to the experiences on which the method is founded. The Diltheyan method does not, however, take into account the whole historically decisive complex that the consciousness (experiences) of man acting in history does not by any means necessarily provide the key to an adequate causation of the historical connections. This problem Hegel had already raised, and Marxism solved it with the theory of 'false consciousness'.

Dilthey's historical knowledge, his own theory of historical method confronted him – albeit inadequately and incompletely – with that which he failed to perceive epistemologically. Even with Dilthey the dissolving of all historical phenomena into experiences, i.e., into subjective facts of consciousness, was bounded by the 'objective spirit' which he himself regarded as the central category of history. For his own part he saw the difficulty, the antinomy, perfectly

clearly. Thus he said of the problem of the objective spirit: 'There now arises the question as to how a correlation which is not produced as such in somebody's mind, and which, therefore, is neither experienced directly or indirectly, nor traceable to a person's experience, from his expressions and statements about them, form itself as such in the historian? This presupposes the possibility of forming logical subjects which are not psychological . . . It is soul we are looking for . . . but by what route can we discover soul when no individual soul is involved?'[12] Thus Dilthey saw the difficulty very clearly, while failing to recognize its epistemological roots. And hence he failed to see that in order to solve it, he would have had to renounce his whole new science of psychology and foundation of history. There is the further point that Dilthey's two viewpoints of modern relativism, the psychological-anthropological and the historical, likewise formed an antinomy, an insoluble contradiction. By virtue of its very nature, Dilthey's psychological-anthropological argumentation of the social sciences tended to accept the basic facts that it had discovered as constant and supra-historical. For it appears to be quite clear that man, ever since he became man, was subject to changes no longer cardinal from a anthropological standpoint; those changes which we ascertain in men's thoughts, emotional life, etc., are of a socio-historical character. For an objective historical theory, such as historical materialism, the result is no kind of antinomy but simply the mutual dialectical complementing of both viewpoints; it may even render the most rewardingly anthropological viewpoints of service to historical knowledge, and vice versa. In Dilthey's theory of experience, however, the two points of view inevitably polarized in an antinomy: from the anthropological viewpoint, the result was the supra-historical character of man, while from the historical viewpoint it was a boundless relativism which admitted of nothing thorough-going.

And for Dilthey there was no way out of this antinomy; he could not plump for one viewpoint and discard the other. He needed them both – partly out of the historian's

understandable feeling that both principles are inextricably caught up in reality itself, and partly because of imperialism's philosophical needs, to which both anthropological supra-historicity and historical relativism were equally essential. So he perceived the antinomy and remained stuck with it .... (This standpoint was not only Dilthey's; it is found in nearly all the historians working during the imperialistic period. Thus racial theory, at this time, was always based on an – imagined – permanence of the life of the race, which might become degenerate but was fundamentally incapable of developing into something qualitatively different.) Dilthey, coming up against this problem time and again, gave the most diverse, contradictory answers to it. Thus he said, on the one hand: 'Human nature is always the same.'[13] In analysing, on the other hand, the 'natural system' of the seventeenth-eighteenth century, i.e., in polemics against the Enlightenment view of history, he said: 'The human type melts away in the process of history.'[14] And he knew also that he could not answer the question. He said 'that for us, the question as to whether men of different periods may be regarded as the same within certain limits in respect of strength of motives cannot be answered at all at present'.[15] This made the whole psychological-anthropological rationale of the social sciences of problematical value. But since the interpretation of all historical and social phenomena from the angle of experience formed the core of Dilthey's philosophy, his whole basic conception was thereby rendered illusory.

Dilthey succeeded only in compromising and pulling apart the causal psychology of positivism, for which he substituted an essentially non-causal, indeed anti-causal 'morphology' of spiritual phenomena which became of decisive moment for vitalistic relativism in all later developments. Although 'descriptive psychology' and its intuitive method were, as we have noted, uncommonly hazy and contradictory, these very qualities ensured their long-lasting effect. There arose a morphological bias whereby the original meaning of morphology increasingly faded away, and where morphology was

more of a colourful catchword than a clearly defined method.

Imperialism's general philosophical needs – products of an increasing intensity in both the external and inner conflicts – were driving philosophy further and further beyond the abstract and insubstantial formalism of the strict neo-Kantians and urging it towards a concrete, substantial treatment of the problems at issue. But since they did not, in the class and hence methodological context, allow philosophy to tackle the concrete problems of content with a concrete method, precisely such an equivocal 'method' as the one we have indicated above was the fittest expression for the regressive demands of the day. From the same historical source as Dilthey's 'descriptive' psychology there sprang, parallel to but independent of it, Husserl's phenomenology, with which it had many affinities. Dilthey immediately welcomed the latter as 'epoch-making'.[16] For his own part, Husserl at first confined himself to the descriptive treatment of purely formal-logical problems. But under Dilthey's influence, Husserl's most influential pupils (Scheler, Heidegger) went outside this group of problems, as we shall show in detail later. Like Dilthey, they were to strive for a universal philosophical method based on the 'descriptive' approach.

Dilthey's whole thinking was determined by the need for a concrete and substantial philosophy capable of exerting on current affairs an influence similar to that enjoyed by philosophy in its great bygone eras. (We have already quoted a programmatic statement by him to this effect.) On the other hand, Dilthey detected that the old philosophies in their original form could not possibly play this role in the present. Although his concerns with the history of philosophy, in association with a general cultural history, outwardly formed the greater part of his *oeuvre*, they were not for him an end in itself. Just as he intended the development of experience into understanding and hermeneutics to culminate in a world-view, so he intended his historical treatment of the problems of philosophy to be only a prelude to the

presentation of a modern world-view (*Weltanschauung*).

Dilthey's historical innovations were important and influential. Along with Nietzsche and Eduard von Hartmann, he was among the first to inaugurate the campaign against great rationalistic philosophy since Descartes, with its natural-scientific bias. With his Schleiermacher biography and works on Novalis, Hölderlin, etc., he was one of the initiators of the Romantic renaissance in the imperial period. His discovery and annotation of the young Hegel's manuscripts became crucial to the vitalistic interpretation of Hegelian philosophy in the post-war period; his Goethe study likewise ushered in the vitalistic interpretation of Goethe subsequently leading from Simmel and Gundolf to Klages, and so on.

Thus we see that the initiative was considerable and of historical significance. The philosophical results, however, remained exceedingly meagre. Here, we shall consider Dilthey's researches in the history of literature and philosophy only insofar as they served the argument of his vitalistic world-outlook. In this respect they had the function of proving that metaphysics (a philosophy of being in itself) were impossible in principle, and that the mediaeval theological system, the scientific 'natural system' of the seventeenth-eighteenth century and the attempt by Kant's major successors to revive metaphysics in a new way were all, therefore, necessarily doomed to failure.

Here, however, the profound contradictions in intuitionism appear once again. Dilthey wrote: 'Philosophies are not products of thinking. They do not arise out of the mere volition of knowing. The comprehension of reality is an important element in their shaping, but only one among others.'[17] This was a genuine question concerned with the broader, and not narrowly philosophical, basis of the origins of world-views in man's social being; and Dilthey, in facing it, endeavoured to exceed the limits of positivism. But, as always happens in the history of irrationalism, he at once twisted the question into a false subjectivism by transforming into the subjective, into an antithesis of intuition and reason,

the objective contradictions resulting from the dialectics of being and consciousness. Dilthey stated: 'Every genuine philosophy (*Weltanschauung*) is an intuition springing from the state of being-within-life (*Darinnensein im Leben*).'[18] Once again, he was turning rich, real, objective historical life into a mere subjective experience. At the same time, the scientificness of the world-view, the methodological value of its scientific argument ceased to exist. Thus in Diltheyan philosophy, the scientific method was limited to leading up to the threshold of the world-view, at which point it was revoked. Hence Dilthey – partly against his own intentions – became a founder of irrationalistic arbitrariness in questions of world-view or outlook.

Dilthey's own solution had its basis in his relativism – in which respect it was also most successful. It is clear from what we have expounded so far that Dilthey could not possibly come down on the side of an outlook with a clearly outlined content and method. His efforts led only to the achievement of a psychological and historical typology of philosophical outlooks. This marked the onset of a development which, as we shall see, was to govern the philosophy of the whole imperialistic period: typology as the expression of historical relativism. The impossibility of discovering real historical connections from these hypotheses, the increasing denial of a set of principles behind history and, in particular, of an ascertainable progress within it, inspired in Dilthey the idea of giving expression to historical (and generally social), spiritual connections by setting forth a typology of the standpoints which might be adopted. First of all, this was an assertion of pure relativism: typology afforded the possibility of a concealed abstention from judgement which posited different, and often opposing standpoints as being of equal value. Meanwhile, imperialism's needs for a philosophical outlook were fast advancing beyond this typological stage. On the one hand, the critical abstention formally expressed in typology became increasingly formal, i.e., a standpoint was adopted *de facto*, chiefly in opposition to materialism but

mostly, to be sure, without renouncing the relativistic advantages which typology provided. On the other hand, the anthropological foundation of the types very quickly condensed into a myth-like 'substantiality', into a 'figure' (*Gestalt*). The typological figures were seen as the leading actors in the drama of history. To a large extent this was already the case with Nietzsche, who occupied an advanced position in the rise of the irrationalistic myths and was, therefore, regarded for a long time as unscientific. Not before Spengler did the overtly myth-creating function of typology strongly resume operations, which reached their height in the types of fascist anthropology. It is easy to see that here the dilemma between anthropology and history which we have analysed, and which idealism could not resolve, was returning in a more concrete form. In the course of irrationalism's development it determined a *de facto* anti-historicity, the creation of a mythicized pseudo-history.

Now with regard to his philosophical typology, Dilthey discovered in history three major basic types: naturalism (by which Dilthey meant materialism with its – in his totally mistaken opinion – historically unavoidable transition to positivism); the idealistic freedom doctrine (subjective idealism); and objective idealism. Psychologically, he traced these three types back to understanding, volition and feeling respectively. In his methodological and historical discussions, he revealed the inevitable narrowness and one-sidedness of each type.[19] He believed, however, that these confines resulted from the hitherto dominant practising of philosophy along the lines of understanding: 'The contradictions come about, therefore, through the independent status that objective world-images acquire in the scientific consciousness. It is this acquisition of independence which turns a system into metaphysics.' And Dilthey was under the illusion that the contradictions could be removed if this tendency towards systematic extension, towards metaphysics were blocked. For he opined the following: 'In the sphere of objective interpreting, each of these outlooks contains a combination of

world-knowledge, life-appreciation and principles of action.'[20]

Here too Dilthey was starting out from a question which is in fact raised by life. That mental reflections of reality, intellectual syntheses of its elements were undertaken from different viewpoints in the course of history, is a fact of the history of philosophy. Another fact which merits examination is that – under specific historical conditions – different viewpoints may be of assistance in comprehending important sides of objective reality. But here Dilthey was guilty of distortion, just as he had already distorted, in a subjectivistic and intuitionistic way, that side of the origin of a world-outlook transcending philosophy in the narrower sense. For all the questions in this complex may only be posed and answered correctly if one proceeds from the objective structure of society, the lines along which it develops and the concrete class struggles within it. The neo-Kantian history of philosophy ignored all such lines of inquiry. Dilthey's need for a world-outlook impelled him in this direction. The importance which he attached to the question, as well as his immediate subjective-idealistic distortion of it, indicates how strongly the imperialist period's need for a world-outlook demanded that historical materialism be constantly polemicized against, instead of ignored, and that such polemics should claim to answer in a 'deeper' way the questions it raised. In Dilthey himself, this was still manifested in a more or less spontaneous, unconscious form; he wishes to oppose the general materialistic view of history with something philosophically 'higher'. In Simmel's case the polemics appear to be quite conscious, and they became increasingly strong up to Mannheim and Freyer.

And as they did so, that antinomy between an anthropological and a historical viewpoint which we have already stressed also came into its own. Dilthey, in this typology, wished to raise himself above the historical (which for him was synonymous with historical relativism) and to locate in the anthropological principle a basis for his typology, and in particular for his types' philosophical synthesis. This

attempt was doomed as soon as he set up the typology, because major historical phenomena can never be adduced from such threadbare psychological-anthropological principles, and certainly not from artificially isolated 'spiritual faculties' like understanding, volition or feeling. (According to the Diltheyan typology, the anthropological basis of Aristotle or Hegel would have to be sought in feeling.) A scientifically practicable typology could only be discerned from history itself by abstracting out of it, out of the historically conditioned standpoints which men may adopt to objective reality, the pervasive elements in this process. But then the deciding factors would no longer be anthropological-psychological attributes, but the essential types of philosophical positions (e.g., separation of materialism and idealism according to the basic philosophy, according to whether being was given priority over consciousness or vice versa). Dilthey had an occasional inkling of this. He wrote: 'The great homomorphic relations existing between individuation and circumstances must be developed theoretically.'[21] His methodology, however, had no organ through which to comprehend such interacting influences since it was devised precisely in order to circumvent such questions, to conceal them in irrationalistic obscurity.

An even more evident point is the failure of Dilthey's attempt to surpass anthropological relativism through a synthesis of types. In tracing back the psychologically rooted types to understanding, emotion and volition, Dilthey dreamt of a harmony of philosophical types similar to the harmony which these psychical forces may achieve in a human being. But all this remained a dream, objectively not least because the lack of harmony troubling Dilthey by no means stemmed primarily from psychological or anthropological causes. Since it was a consequence of the social division of labour within capitalism, it could never – within the frame of capitalism's continued existence – be superseded psychologically or philosophically. Here we are dealing with the subjective-idealistic distortion of a problem arising

out of life, and not for the first time in Dilthey. And here the mystification he accomplished did in fact weigh heavily on his conscience. For in rendering this question concrete, Dilthey did not in reality advance from his typology to a philosophical synthesis but destroyed the abstract anthropological foundations of his own typology. He himself conceded that every real philosophy must spring from the unity of understanding, volition and emotion. Now from this position, Dilthey had either to regard the earlier philosophers as monsters fossilized in partiality, or else to discard his whole typology. And not even the rejection of it, according to his hypotheses, could point the way to a world-outlook with philosophical-scientific foundations.

Of course he did not resort to either of these extremes. But that he often sensed the insoluble nature of the question, and hence the fragility and hollowness of the basis of his own philosophy, is distinctly visible.

The presentation of such a world-outlook is confined in Dilthey's *oeuvre* to obscure intimations. For once understanding, volition and emotion have been hypostasized into autonomous, historically operative entities matched by their own sharply contrasting, mutually exclusive philosophical types, they cannot be converted back into purely psychical factors without pulling down the whole structure. In particular, one cannot annul the autonomous existence of the philosophical tendencies in order to achieve the imagined harmony. Scientifically speaking, Dilthey as a historian of philosophy could substantiate only a complete relativism – an unceasing battle of rival philosophies in which a specific selection is made, but there is no single choice: 'Its (i.e., philosophy's, G.L.) major types stand beside one another, autonomous, unprovable and indestructible.'[22] Indeed, Dilthey now and then came to refute in principle the possibility of the imagined synthesis: 'It is denied to us to behold these facets together. The pure light of truth we can glimpse only via an irregularly broken ray.'[23]

So Dilthey's *oeuvre* sounded a final note of resignation

and despair. At the end of his life he said quite candidly that sometimes he deeply envied such personalities as Rousseau or Carlyle who dared to express their convictions publicly, deterred by no scientific scruples. And this dilemma of science and philosophy in the broader sense was again highly characteristic in respect of the bankruptcy of Dilthey's philosophical endeavours. Neo-Kantianism had, because of this dilemma, dismissed every question of world-outlook from its (purportedly scientific) philosophy. The later vitalism rejected science and scientific philosophy in the name of irrationalism. Dilthey was a transitional figure between these extremes of pre-imperialistic bourgeois philosophy. Not for nothing did he add, when recalling his friend Graf Yorck von Wartenburg: 'Is not my own historical viewpoint a barren scepticism, measured by such a life as his?' Nonetheless, even here he declared his allegiance to a scientifically based standpoint – one useless to his search for a *Weltanschauung*: 'Then I became determined not to seek even happiness through a belief which did not stand up to thought.'[24]

In this respect, therefore, Dilthey differed very sharply from the thinkers who later carried on and extended the drift of his argument. Even with Dilthey, to be sure, the resignation was not devoid of illusions: 'The knife of historical relativism which has dissected all metaphysics and religion must also provide the remedy. We must be thorough. We must make philosophy itself the object of philosophy.'[25] This was an illusion not only methodologically, but also in respect of historical reality: further advances along the lines he had pursued were to produce no outlook with a new, scientific basis such as he had envisaged. On the one hand, his great influence, as broad as it was profound, extended both psychological and historical relativism, bringing them closer to nihilistic scepticism. And on the other, by way of the increasingly extreme intuitionistic and irrationalistic movements, it set philosophy on the track of disordered fantasy and arbitrary myth-making. Later developments removed from

his work all his attempts at a scientific argumentation and cast them aside. His suggestions were only exploited in order to oppose the scientific spirit, in order to combat it. That this, even if it ran counter to Dilthey's subjective intentions, was objectively possible both accounts for his influence and stamps it a reactionary one. As regards his contents and the methodology to which he aspired, Dilthey had precious little to do with fascism. Yet objectively speaking, these by no means fortuitous repercussions of his work made him a pioneer, albeit unwittingly and only indirectly, of the subsequent open struggle against reason, the eclipse of philosophical awareness in Germany.

3. Vitalism in the Pre-War Period (Simmel)

In his whole mentality and education Dilthey was a man of the pre-imperialistic period, but he sensed the new problems very strongly in advance and subsequently passed into this problem-complex. In Simmel, his junior by twenty-five years, the intellectual tendencies of pre-war imperialism were concentrated in an incomparably more salient and immediate way: he was truly the child and representative of the new period.

As in Dilthey's case, to be sure, Kant and positivism formed his philosophical starting-point. But with Simmel we are dealing with the positivism of a more advanced age, and no longer with Comte, Taine or Buckle. Influenced very strongly by Nietzsche, Simmel attained eminence in the struggle against the philosophical and social consequences of historical materialism. From the outset, his thought spontaneously ran parallel to Anglo-American pragmatism and developed a close affinity with Bergsonian tendencies. His Kantianism too had a different, more imperialistic nuance: he was resolutely subjectivistic, and the objective reality of the external world was already, for him, no longer a problem at all.

On the contrary, the chief bias of his epistemology was an energetic battle against every kind of imitation, every kind of mental reproduction of reality as it really is. Thus he said of historical knowledge that it was 'no mere reproduction but an intellectual activity which fashions out of its material . . . something that, in itself, it does not yet constitute'.[26] With Simmel we see perfectly clearly how the Right-wing critique of the narrowly mechanical theory of imitation, given an idealistic basis and a dominance of formal logic, necessarily led to vitalistic subjectivism. Simmel, like many modern idealists, saw that the old materialism's mechanical theory of imitation was unable to solve complicated problems of concreteness in a satisfactory form. And as with many modern idealists, this observation caused him to reject the knowability, indeed the existence of objective reality. But Simmel was far more decided in this rejection than most of his predecessors or contemporaries. This followed from his vitalistic stance, which allowed him radically to deny any objective reality independent of the subject and yet to confront man with a pseudo-objective external world, because life here offered itself to him as a real intermediary: 'Life appears to be the most extreme objectivity to which we may penetrate directly as animated subjects, the farthest and most permanent objectifying of the subject. With life we occupy a position half-way between the ego and the idea, subject and object, person and cosmos.'[27] Accordingly he dismissed the epistemological question in its only correct and clear formulation, namely the priority of being or consciousness, in the name of a vitalistic 'third road'. The question was to be modified as follows: 'Does consciousness depend on life, or does life depend on consciousness? For after all, life is the being which stands between consciousness and being in general . . . Life is the higher concept and higher actuality beyond consciousness; this is life at all events.'[28] Epistemologically speaking, real life belongs to being and experience to consciousness. But with the explanation of 'life' as a third concept contrasted with being and consciousness, that

irrationalistic pseudo-objective intermediate realm is created which not only permits but demands an unlimited preponderance of subjectivity.

Thus the structure of Simmel's world-picture came into being. Simmel no longer acknowledged any actual object-world, but only various forms of the vitalistic attitude to reality (knowledge, art, religion, eroticism, etc.), each of which produced its own world of objects: 'The coming into effect of certain fundamental spiritual forces and impulses means that they create an object for themselves. The meaning of the object of this function of love, art or religious feeling is only the meaning of the functions themselves. Each of these enlists its object for its own world by thereby creating it as its own. Hence it does not make the slightest difference whether the contents assembled in this particular form already exist in other forms or not . . .'[29] This epistemological standpoint shows a striking congruence with that aesthetic reasoning employed to surmount Naturalism in pre-war imperialism; Simmel's epistemology generally was very strongly oriented towards the aesthetics of his time.

The consequence of this position was a relativism still more radical than Dilthey's had been. Accounts of Simmel's philosophy frequently state that his path led from positivism to metaphysics, i.e., to a surmounting of relativism. This view is mistaken: Simmel did develop in the sense that the vitalistic tendencies which had always been dormant in him shifted more and more consciously to the centre of his thinking. This, however, meant an increase and not a decrease in relativism. And it is characteristic of vitalism, as the chief philosophical bias in the imperialist era, that the central content of the relativistic thought process was always a depreciation of the scientific method, a creating of space for faith and a subjective religious feeling without a definite object, using just this relativistic scepticism as a weapon. Let us quote a longer passage from one of Simmel's last works. It illustrates how markedly the extremely relativistic bias was manifested precisely in his late phase:

Despite the stress on the ever-advancing and immeasurable progress of our knowledge, it should not be overlooked that at the other end, so to speak, much that we formerly possessed as 'sure' knowledge is sinking into doubt and recognized error. How much mediaeval man 'knew', and the enlightened thinker of the eighteenth century or the materialistic scientific researcher of the nineteenth, which for us is either completely obsolete or at least completely dubious. How much of that which is now undoubted 'knowledge' will suffer the same fate sooner or later! The effect of man's whole spiritual and practical disposition is that – *cum grano salis* and speaking of the broad basis – he apprehends only that which matches his convictions and simply overlooks the counter-examples however startling: a fact totally inexplicable to later eras. Proofs no less 'factual' and 'convincing' were adduced for astrology and miracle cures, for witchcraft and the direct efficacy of prayer as are now adduced for the validity of universal laws of nature. And I by no means exclude the possibility that later centuries or millennia, perceiving as the core and essence of each individual phenomenon its indissoluble, unified individuality, not ascribable to 'universal laws', will declare such generalities to be as much of a superstition as the aforesaid articles of faith. Once we have abandoned the idea of the 'absolutely true', which is likewise only a historical construction, we might arrive at the paradoxical idea that in the continuous process of perception, the standard of the truths newly adopted differs only in degree from the standard of the errors we have abolished; that, as in a never-halting procession, just as many 'true' perceptions mount the front steps as 'illusions' are cast down the back steps.[30]

We have quoted Simmel's statements at such length in order to show quite plainly the partisan nature of vitalistic relativism. What we are dealing with is not an extreme scepticism, which may, in given circumstances, in a reactionary

culture's drift towards dissolution, have progressive functions (as, for example, mediaeval nominalism or the scepticism of Montaigne, Bayle, etc.). Modern relativistic scepticism was directly undermining objective scientific knowledge and, no matter whether its begetters intended this or not, providing scope for the wildest reactionary obscurantism, for the nihilistic mysticism of imperialistic decadence. And this development made such rapid strides that for today's reader there is something comical about Simmel's view that the universal laws of nature would seem a superstition centuries or millennia later. For as we know, it was in the year of Simmel's death that Spengler published the book in which vitalism undertook to realize this viewpoint. This destructive relativism was imperialistic philosophy's self-defence against dialectical materialism. With Spengler this tendency emerged clearly and overtly, but it was already present in Simmel.

The problem of faith, religiosity and religion had already occupied much of Dilthey's attention. And even Dilthey saw in religion an eternal type of human attitude towards reality; but he also sensed that the historical religions, the ideas of God handed down through history, had lost their significance for contemporary man. (Hence his strong sympathy towards Schleiermacher who had given prominence to the priority of religious inwardness in his youth.) Simmel adhered more resolutely than Dilthey to the viewpoint that the historical religions and old types of metaphysics had fallen apart. But for him, Schleiermacher's turning inwards was not radical enough. He wanted to obtain for religion and metaphysics a self-governing autocracy of the kind for which the art-for-art's-sake movement was striving in art. Thus he wrote of metaphysics: 'They present a world-picture in accordance with categories which . . . have nothing to do with the categories of empirical cognition: the metaphysical interpretation of the world lies beyond truth and error, which are decisive to a realistically exact one.'[31]

So men's various kinds of attitude stand beside one another in self-sufficiency and create autonomous worlds which

contradict one another no more than – in the sense of an art-for-art's-sake aesthetic – the dramatic treatment of an event contradicts its epic treatment. 'The religious life', wrote Simmel, 'creates the world afresh, it signifies the whole of existence set in a particular key, so that in its pure idea it cannot clash with the world-picture constructed according to other categories or contradict it in the least . . .'[32] This view of religion was not only the most rigorous application of Simmel's epistemology in this field, but sprang at the same time from his view of the religious situation in his day. Simmel saw that contemporary man had set himself free from the established religions, but that needs hitherto satisfied through a religious fulfilment still survived and sought to assert themselves.

Of course Simmel failed to see that the basis of these religious needs was the social being of capitalism, whose essential determining factors appeared further heightened in the imperialist period: it was, as Lenin showed, the insecurity of this being. The special nuance which Simmel gave to the religious need similarly arose on this basis; the insecurity manifested to the worker in brute materiality appeared to the bourgeois intellectual in a 'sublimed', far less direct form. There was an increasingly obvious incongruity between the imperialist period's social being and all the ideological forms which capitalism had produced or – where it suited its needs – taken over from earlier formations. Now for the bourgeois intellectual, this incongruity meant the mixed blessing of a total freedom: it presented the intoxicating feeling of being left wholly to one's own devices on the one hand, and a disconsolate helplessness on the other. And along with the urge to seek within his own ego the standards of all action and behaviour, he was faced with a mounting nihilism in respect of all standards. This growing senselessness of individual life brought about the origin of modern religious atheism, of which the Protestant theologian Schleiermacher was a forerunner. For all traditional religious ideas paled in the face of these developments, and yet the world-feeling

which dismissed them preserved the uncritical religious anthropomorphism which Feuerbach did most to expose.

In pre-war imperialism the elements of insecurity, which appeared in purely intellectual forms, still occupied the forefront of the bourgeois intelligentsia's ideology; the elements of the ecstasy of freedom, of liberation from old bonds still formed the dominant pole in the dichotomy of this world-feeling, a dichotomy which was present even then. Only when the first imperialist war shook the foundations in a manner felt by everyone, only when the great economic crisis of 1929 destroyed hopes that the 'relative stabilization' would endure, did the pole of despairing nihilism become the central focal point of philosophy (Heidegger).

Simmel's new view of religion was based, therefore, on religious being, which was 'a form of the whole of vital life itself'. Through perceiving it, contemporary man glimpsed the possibility that 'out of its substantiality, its link with transcendent contents, religion becomes by back or upward formation an intrinsic form of life itself and of all its contents'.[33] Thus vitalistic nihilism was intended to provide the basis for a seasonable form of religiosity.

This attitude was – considered in purely epistemological terms – a logical continuation of neo-Kantian tendencies. Neo-Kantianism, besides rejecting the perceptibility of an objective reality independent of consciousness, had constantly ensured religion a place in the philosophical world-picture. Here Simmel was doing just that. But in the same way as he went beyond the revival, prompted by Dilthey, of Schleiermacher's religious subjectivism, so too he went beyond its neo-Kantian acknowledgement.

The particular note struck by Simmel lay, as we have seen, in the fact that while he radically separated the religious attitude from a connection with any kind of content, he viewed this attitude as creating an autonomous world independent of and equivalent to the other worlds likewise created by human subjectivity (the scientific, artistic, erotic, etc.). And so Simmel's philosophy merged with that stream

of 'religious atheism' which found its first major philosophical formulations in Schopenhauer and above all in Nietzsche ('God is dead'), whose ethico-philosophical consequences effectively emerged on a European scale in Dostoievsky's *oeuvre* (Kirilov, Ivan Karamazov, etc.), and which became a question central to the interpretation of the world in the later existentialism. The old atheism, by and large closely connected with mechanical materialism, had always been a pure negation of religiosity altogether. But in line with the evaporation of those hopes of social revolution which had animated the French materialists, and whose echo was still discernible in the pre-1848 Feuerbach, it either became totally empty and shallow (Büchner, etc.) or it acquired a note of desperation (Jacobsen's *Niels Lyhne*).

Naturally, all these views had been already long refuted at the time in Marxism. But this fact had no influence on bourgeois thinking, chiefly for the reason that all the problems of 'religious atheism' had stemmed from the bourgeoisie's social being in capitalism, which was why all solutions transcending bourgeois horizons were a closed book to the ideologists of the bourgeois class. (The assimilation into the bourgeoisie of the workers' aristocracy and bureaucracy even prevented such solutions from affecting the workers' movements of Central and Western Europe.) Despite the ignorance of Marxism's real views on the religious question, here again the vitalistic modification of 'religious atheism' included, objectively speaking, an attempt to repel the influence of dialectical and historical materialism on the bourgeois intelligentsia. In particular, it attempted to destroy all hopes of a purposeful life within the human community and of a social answer to the loneliness of the bourgeois individual. It was, let us remember, this loneliness in which vitalism – whilst elaborating on the 'tragedy' of it – perceived the highest value of civilized life.

Thus religious atheism was the product of a situation in which scientific findings had totally alienated large circles of the intelligentsia from the official churches and religions.

On the other hand, this intelligentsia's social situation (the uncertainty of existence, lack of a concrete perspective on public and private life, and so on) nonetheless awakened a religious need whose essential content may be summed up as follows. In itself, and considered immanently, my individual life is completely meaningless. The external world does not offer me a meaning, for scientific knowledge has 'desanctified' the world, while the standards of social intercourse do not provide a signpost – so where can I now discover the meaning of my life? Naturally, bourgeois philosophy could not provide the individual with an answer, for it summed up in theory, after all, the very questions which capitalism's social being had posed for the bourgeois individual in an unanswerable form. The purely agnosticistic 'answer' from positivism could have adequate validity only in times and for class-sectors in and for which the uncertainty, the meaninglessness of life in capitalism had not yet become obvious. But the imperialist period was increasingly bringing this uncertainty and meaninglessness to the forefront. Hence the withering of positivism among the élite of the bourgeois intelligentsia, and hence that need for *Weltanschauung* from which vitalism emanated and which vitalism promoted. Of course vitalism could no more provide a real answer than could positivism. As in other spheres, it only brought about a sprouting of agnosticism into mysticism, enveloping the agnostics' clear '*ignorabimus*' in the parti-coloured rags of an individualistic, subjective mythology. So all that it achieved in this sphere was that the socially determined psychological state we have described appeared to be dictated as universally philosophical in general (through 'man's' eternal situation in the cosmos) or historico-philosophical (through mankind's present world-historical situation). Thus the spiritual state acquired first and foremost a philosophical sanction, a justification of its perennial nature. Here originated, moreover, a philosophical linking of questions of conduct, and primarily that of morality, with the – largely negative – world-picture thus provided. In Nietzsche and the characters of Dostoievsky this gave rise

to the morality of 'Everything is permitted' on the one hand, and, on the other, the claim that in a world without a God or in one which God has abandoned, man can and must become God. Thus 'religious atheism' cultivated both sides of modern Nietzscheanism: both the repeal of all the old socio-ethical laws, which however were no longer replaced by fresh ones but autonomously appointed by sovereign individuality, and the apprehension of objective reality, especially the socio-historical world, as nihility. Both aspects, in continuing the Nietzschean proposition, had serious consequences for later developments: they led to the 'heroic pessimism', the 'heroic realism' of pre-fascist and fascist philosophy.

With Simmel himself, we can observe in this respect a moderating, if anything, of the shrillness of Nietzsche and the characters of Dostoievsky. Sovereign individualism expressing itself in its religiosity without a God, although an acknowledgement of nihility in objective reality, nevertheless led, as we shall see later, to a self-indulgent compliance with the 'tragedy' of human civilization. Here Simmel was voicing the basic mood of the imperialist period before the First World War: the insolubly problematical nature of life was already palpable – but life in the midst of these problems was quite agreeable and one could feel at one's ease; vitalism supplied the clear conscience, the philosophical cushion.

Here we clearly see Simmel's inclination to turn the period's extreme relativism into a philosophy, to give modern agnosticism in mythical dress a positive slant. That he belonged to a different generation from Dilthey is shown even more markedly in the concrete achievement. To Dilthey modern economics and sociology were still wholly alien; with Simmel they were central concerns during his first period, and they had repercussions lasting until the end of his work. The task now facing him consisted of interpreting the problems of the capitalist culture of imperialism in a philosophically positive sense. For that reason Simmel no longer ignored historical materialism. He contested – in a most vulgar and superficial way – the materialism in it as

well as its concrete historico-social inferences, but he ventured to reinterpret the facts ascertained by this method, facts which played a role in the psychology of the intelligentsia in the form of tendencies towards an anti-capitalist cultural critique. These facts he attempted to incorporate in the idealist outlook of vitalism and to reconcile with conventionally inperialist theories of history. Methodologically, this was essentially a 'deepening' process: social reality itself and its concrete socio-economic principles were portrayed as the mere manifestation of a universal 'cosmic' order, thereby losing their concrete substance as well as their revolutionary bite. In the introduction to his *Philosophie des Geldes* ('Philosophy of Money') Simmel formulated this task as a matter of 'constructing a basement underneath historical materialism such that the inclusion of economic life in the causes of spiritual culture retains its explanatory value, but such that those very economic forms are recognized as the product of profounder estimations and currents of psychological, indeed metaphysical hypotheses'.[34]

There thus originated with Simmel a broad, highly effective and influential philosophy of culture. It was designed to comprehend sociologically the specific features of the present and thereupon to incorporate them in 'deeper' philosophical thinking. Here again, Simmel proceeded in a radically subjectivist manner. What interested him in economics was only the subjective reflex of definite, economically conditioned situations. Since these were immediately evoked by categories pertaining to the surface of economic life, he gave all his attention to these without considering their true economic dependence and function (money). In so doing – and precisely as a result of his 'depth' – he came quite close to the vulgar economics of imperialism. The same applies to Simmel's sociology, where he was concerned only with the immediate and most abstract relational categories of social life, assiduously avoiding all serious problems of content.

In his concrete analysis of individual phenomena, Simmel was a pupil of Schopenhauer and Nietzsche. They – Nietzsche,

to be sure, to far greater effect than his teacher – had developed a new philosophical theory of method for the defence of the established order. Before their time, apologetics on behalf of capitalism had proceeded from its – supposed – ultimate harmony and had stamped the illogicalities and dissonances of existence as surface manifestations, as mere transitory foreground phenomena. But for the new apologetics of Schopenhauer and especially Nietzsche, the world's essentially contradictory and divided nature was at the same time its ultimate ground. With Schopenhauer, this gave rise to a pessimism whereby the meaninglessness of universal substance drowned every single disharmony of the present (in the socio-historical world in general). All attempts to improve our real world appeared meaningless. The established order was defended from the angle of the senselessness of the universe. On the one hand, Nietzsche extended this pessimism in the context of a great historical myth; he historicized Schopenhauer into myth. And on the other hand, he inferred from this pessimistic interpretation of the world's basis an active affirmation of capitalism *quand même*, rejecting all revolutionary positions as decadence and slave morality. Thus in Schopenhauer and Nietzsche, complicated indirect apologetics replaced ordinary, direct apologetics on behalf of the established order. Theirs amounted to a *credo quia absurdum* in relation to the prevailing social order.

As heir to Schopenhauer and Nietzsche, Simmel never tried simply to deny the illogical and problematical nature of contemporary culture, as was the wont of the vulgar apologists. He contested not even the most repugnant phenomena, and not even those current imperialist tendencies which were culturally unfavourable. Precisely here, on the contrary, he seemingly went the whole hog and endowed the problem with a 'deeper' perspective by representing the concrete, socio-economic problems of culture as the manifestation of a universal 'tragedy of culture in general'. This tragedy, according to Simmel, rested on the antithesis of 'soul' and

'mind' (*Geist*), on the antithesis of the soul and its own products and objectifications.

Dilthey too represented culture, the objective spirit, as something surpassing experience, therein revealing the illogicality and limitation of the psychological method. This situation appeared to be an objective antinomy of the philosophical methodology, an antinomy which Simmel showed great energy in making a central issue. Thereupon vitalism's central problem, the antithesis of 'rigid' and 'alive', appeared in a new concrete form. Simmel wrote: 'Everything which is a product of the mind, everything which the continuing life-process has ejected as its result has something rigid and prematurely finished about it in relation to this directly live, creative reality. With mind, life has run into a cul-de-sac . . . But the remarkable thing is that this really miserable portion, which has no room at all for the full richness of subjective life . . . is, on the other hand . . . nevertheless perfection.'[35]

The objective spirit therefore possessed its own logic. Although its formations sprang from individuals' most personal and inward spontaneity, once they had done so they went their own ways. The capitalist division of labour and above all money were, according to Simmel, formations of this kind. 'The "fetish character" which Marx assigns to economic objects in the era of mercantile production is only a specially modified case of this general fate of our cultural contents.'[36] Thus the 'deepening' of historical materialism consisted in the subsumption of its findings under the vitalistic programme, represented in this instance as an indissoluble opposition between subjectivity and cultural construction, between soul (*Seele*) and mind (*Geist*). According to Simmel, this opposition was the true tragedy of culture.

Here the basic tendency is plain: that of inflating elements of the imperialist epoch specific to the situation of the individual (notably the intellectual individual associated with this culture) into the 'eternal' tragic conditions of 'culture' in general. This 'deepening' process had very diverse but

converging consequences. Above all, it distracted attention from the concrete economic situation and concrete socio-historical causes. Although economics and sociology were dealt with in broad terms, they lost their independence and even their priority; they were presented, rather, as superficialities which men of a 'deep' disposition had at all costs to exceed. It is, for example, very characteristic that when discussing both Goethe and Nietzsche, whose features he falsified in each case, Simmel emphasized that they had always distanced themselves from all social problems.[37]

So by dint of this philosophical generalization, the intelligentsia's anti-capitalist discontent was perverted into self-satisfaction, complacency and narcissism. After Simmel had revealed all the problems related to a monetary culture that he could see, he found something to commend in these very problems. 'The factual substance of life', he stated, 'is growing more and more matter-of-fact and impersonal in order that the unobjectifiable remainder of life may become all the more personal, something all the more indisputably peculiar to the first person.'[38] Thus money was of benefit to 'pure inwardness'; money was presented as nothing less than the 'guardian of inwardness, which may now develop within its intrinsic limits'. This apophthegm exposes the 'tragic condition of culture' as the philosophy of parasitical imperialist capitalism. (This cultural critique by Simmel exerted a powerful influence and had all kinds of repercussions. Here we shall mention only Walter Rathenau.)

Simmel's vitalistically revised Kantianism served a parasitical aim. The remodelling of Kant had as its chief purpose the removal of all bourgeois-revolutionary elements from his philosophy, on the grounds that they were historically outmoded. Kantian ethics, the 'freedom of essentially homogeneous individuals', were for Simmel merely a correlate of the world-concept mechanistically based on understanding. And the two had grown obsolete together. After Goethe, Schleiermacher and Romanticism, ran the argument, one had the ethics of the 'uniqueness' of the individual, which

replaced all Kantian ideals of equality. The social and moral equality of human beings was thus presented as a purely time-conditioned and already outmoded element of Kantian ethics. Here it was Simmel's (highly sophistical) intention to prove that his conception of the uniqueness of the personality and its liberty as a new foundation for morality did not turn this freedom into a relativist-anarchistic chaos. For the unique individuals would, he asserted, be mutually complementary. Here, while avowedly only interpreting Kant in the spirit of the times, he achieved a total break with Kant's ethics, whose abstract demands were a theoretical reflection of the bourgeois-democratic revolution. Certainly Simmel was in the right when he referred to the historically conditioned character of these ethics. The real historical step beyond Kant, however, was the concrete, economic abolition of social classes to be realized by socialism after the overthrow of capitalist society. Now when Simmel pointed to the temporal limitation of Kantian ethics, he did so in the name of the parasitical, privileged intelligentsia of the imperialist period, on behalf of an aristocratic morality à la Nietzsche, who regarded the 'crowd' as unworthy of an ethical study. The only difference between them was that Nietzsche stated this aristocratic bias in an overt, reactionary-militant manner whereas Simmel, in accordance with the pre-war social situation, contented himself with a haughty aloofness from the 'crowd'. We have already touched on his further remodelling tendency, i.e., the total subjectification of Kantian a-priority. Simmel presents us with a juxtaposition of the various *a priori* 'worlds', and philosophy is to a certain extent a genre-theory of this juxtaposition. This constituted a further heightening of the relativism of Dilthey's doctrine of types.

For Simmel, life formed the ultimate unity as against this fragmentation into umpteen autonomous worlds. 'I place myself in the concept of life as the centre; from that point the way leads to the soul and the first person on the one hand, and to the idea, the cosmos, the absolute on the other . . . Life appears to be the most extreme objectivity to

which we, as subjects with souls, may penetrate directly – the farthest and most permanent objectification of the subject. With life we stand centrally situated between the first person and the idea, between subject and object, person and cosmos.'[39]

Here life has already become a purely mythical concept and has discarded all relation to scientific biology. Vitalism thereby advanced a step further along the road to anti-scientific thinking. To be sure, Simmel – like Dilthey, only in a heightened form – was still consciously concerned with a reconstruction of science; his struggle against law and causality still took the form of an attempt to work out an epistemological concept of individual causality. But the irrationalistic and anti-scientific bias was far more salient than in Dilthey: 'Everything that can be proved may also be challenged. Only the unprovable is beyond dispute.'[40]

The central position of life in this sense within Simmel's philosophy lent a new 'depth' perspective to the antinomy he saw in culture. It involved not only a general antithesis between the currents of life and the delimitations of the mind, for both principles were carried into the living 'ego'. 'It is not that we are divided into unlimited life and the limits of secured form, living partly in continuity and partly in individuality, with the two states "neutralizing" each other; these two principles are at odds in the ego itself.' Life's paradox: 'that it can only be accommodated in forms, and yet cannot be accommodated in forms' is every ego's fundamental problem. Hence the fundamental feature of life for Simmel was: 'The transcending of its own self'.[41] Life, each life is at the same time 'surplus life' (*Mehr-Leben*) and 'more than life'.

So the tragedy of culture was represented as only a manifestation of the ultimate illogicality of life itself. Simmel formulated for our epoch that antithesis previously conceived to be beyond time as follows: 'Perhaps our present life includes too much ego on the one hand, and too much that is mechanical on the other. It is not yet pure life.'[42]

But just as Simmel had, in presenting the tragic condition of society and culture, penetrated only as far as the tragic conflict and had then given it a pacific, parasitical slant, so he now slanted the question of life's ultimate philosophical illogicality. Let us quote his last piece of worldly wisdom from his posthumous private notes: 'For the deeper man there is one possibility only of enduring life: a certain degree of superficiality. For were he to ponder over all the contradictory, irreconcilable impulses, duties, endeavours and longings too deeply, and to register them as completely and absolutely as both their and his nature demands, he would be bound to explode, become crazy, run away from life. Beyond a certain limit of depth, the lines of being, volition and moral feeling collide so radically and violently that they would inevitably tear us apart. Only by not allowing them beyond that mark can one keep them sufficiently separated for life to be possible.'[43]

Schopenhauer and Nietzsche had founded those indirect apologetics which defended the capitalist system by acknowledging and stressing its bad aspects, but inflated them at the same time into cosmic paradoxes. In Simmel, they were publicly declared bankrupt. Though perspicacious enough to see the insoluble nature of the paradoxes, he was far too much an ideologist of imperialist parasitical capitalism to meet a tragic fate in consequence. On the contrary, his vitalism's esoteric morality was a deliberate evasion of ultimate consequences; exoterically, their teeth were drawn in a gesture of reconciliation. The superficiality for which vitalism asked established a crumb of comfort for man's soul in the nihilistic self-dissipation of relativism. Thus the Simmelian variety of relativism and scepticism introduced something new into the German philosophical consciousness; complacent cynicism. With Simmel himself, this was still a product of his philosophical methodology, a moral reflection of the situation of his philosophical endeavours under the conditions of Wilhelmine Germany. From a mixture of purely theoretical radicalism and absolute conformity, in practice,

to conditions which could never have stood up to criticism, there came about this sapping of the thinking personality even in such lively and gifted men as Simmel. This was a general symptom of the age, a situation of (imagined) social security accompanied by a thinking and feeling for which there was no longer anything absolute, any really objective object. It was the situation of 'inwardness supported by might', as Thomas Mann neatly characterized it. With Spengler, Simmel's involuntary cynicism grew into a frivolous dilettantism elevated to a methodology, and thereupon made devastating and destructive inroads on the scientific spirit of philosophy. And thence the development rapidly continued up to fascism. Simmel himself was, in the direct sense, no more than Dilthey a pioneer of this decline of scientific honesty in philosophy, or of its replacement through a cynical playing with delberately contrived myths. But he did allow his juggling with intellectual points to lead to conscious, sometimes openly cynical compromises. Hence the process of dissolution is already manifested at a far more advanced stage in Simmel than in Dilthey.

4. War and Post-War Period (Spengler)

This line of vitalism's development was rudely interrupted by the outbreak of the first imperialist war. On the day that war was declared, nearly the whole of intellectual Germany 'learnt differently'. The resignedly contemplative voices of vitalism (like those of all other philosophy, official and unofficial) fell silent, and a publicistic philosophy arose to argue the case for imperialistic aggression and the world-conquering aims of Wilhelmine Germany.

It goes without saying that vitalism too participated in this general change of tack. Despite the superficiality of these wartime products, despite their total worthlessness and insignificance from a philosophical viewpoint, they

were nevertheless of import as the beginnings of a new phase in German vitalism. The old basic antithesis of 'life' versus 'rigidity' and 'the moribund' was naturally preserved, but it acquired a new and seasonable content. The 'German character' (*das deutsche Wesen*) which was to 'restore the world's health' now constituted the 'life' conception, and the national character of other peoples (chiefly the Western democracies and especially England) was what was moribund and rigid. And in particular, there arose the new equations and antitheses of war as equalling life, and of peace as the rigid and moribund. The publicistic catchwords of this ephemeral writing soon faded, and the crisis of the lost war buried the whole of this Babel beneath its ruins. But we can discern in this philosophically worthless literature an important prelude to the second decisive change of course in vitalism, the turn to fascism.

Theoretically, this war-mongering, aggressively imperialistic philosophical writing offered little that was important. To give a single example, let us just mention the war pamphlet by Max Scheler, with whose philosophy we shall concern ourselves later. In that pamphlet the 'vital root' of war in human nature itself was emphasized as strongly as possible so as to discredit any economic interpretation of the war. Hence the affirmation of war was given a vitalistic reasoning à la Nietzsche: 'The true root of all war lies in the fact that a tendency towards ascent, growth and development is inherent in all life itself . . . Everything that is moribund and mechanical seeks only to "maintain" itself . . . whereas life is growing or decaying.'[44]

In an immediate sense, vitalistic wartime literature soon disappeared without trace. Nonetheless, it signified a decided change in the development of vitalism. The collapse of the war was not, however, the only cause of the change. The first imperialist war also meant the first major, lasting, world-historical victory of socialism, and this victory entailed a fundamental change in vitalism. We have noted with Nietzsche how socialism became the chief adversary in, and the target

of, irrationalist philosophy's crucial struggle. We have already observed how Simmel continued these polemics – in, to be sure, a form modified to suit the times – in the pre-war period (and in a later chapter on German sociology, we shall analyse similar tendencies in Toennies, Max Weber, *et al.*). With the triumph of the 1917 October Revolution this ideological struggle by Germany's imperialistic bourgeoisie, and with it vitalism, entered upon a new phase.

The extent of the change, as well as the nature of its most important consequences with regard to methodology and content, finds its clearest illustration in Oswald Spengler's famous two-volume work, *The Decline of the West* (1919 and 1922). It had such a powerful and lasting effect because Spengler gave this change its most radical expression. It was the representative work of this phase and at the same time a veritable, direct prelude to fascist philosophy.

Spengler's philosophical level is essentially inferior to that of the previous leaders of vitalism, and that was no accident. We have been able to observe more and more distinctly this lowering of philosophical standards in the course of our studies so far. The more that the new enemy, socialism, became the focal point of their polemics, the more the irrationalists were faced with a problem of whose true content they understood nothing and, for the most part, did not care to understand anything. And to the same degree, their arguments dispensed with a real, scientific knowledge of the object and also, in the majority of cases, with intellectual honesty, the *bona fides*. But it is highly likely that Spengler's influence in general was related to this dimunition of standards. Basically, vitalism's new phase was distinguished by the fact that the degrading of the scientific method, which was hitherto partly half-conscious, partly tactfully concealed and at first sought only to obtain room for vitalism's intuitive-irrationalist world-view alongside the established, materially unquestioned individual sciences, now went over to an open attack upon the scientific spirit in general, upon the competence of reason adequately to

treat of important human questions. This bias towards a firm separation from the scientific method inevitably introduced a dilettantish element into its exponents' mode of thinking and presentation. (We can see this already in Nietzsche.) With Spengler, this became a conscious methodology, and one which had serious consequences for later developments. For in that, as we shall see, he rejected causality and laws, recognizing them as only the historical phenomena of given epochs and denying them any competence for scientific and philosophical methodology, and in that he substituted analogy for causality, he made a sporting with (often very shallow) similarities the canon of investigation. Moreover, he made all fields of human knowledge subservient to his philosophy of history, no matter whether he personally had truly mastered them or whether they, in themselves, had already yielded unequivocal, philosophically applicable results. And this meant that all the time, he had to proclaim as a method a dilettantish playing with analogies, a readjustment of the facts. Measured by the standard of Dilthey or even Simmel, therefore, Spengler was nothing more than an amateur, often ingenious but mostly shallow and frivolous. At all events the amateurism did not damage Spengler's general and far-reaching influence, even on the international scale. On the contrary, it was just this which gave rise to his unscrupulously cynical candour, his cheerful boldness in making uncritical generalizations. Precisely in this respect he was infinitely superior to his like-minded contemporaries (I shall mention only Leopold Ziegler and Hermann Graf Keyserling).

Spengler aimed at creating a universal science from history. In Spengler, Dilthey's historical relativism was transformed from a bias that Dilthey himself constantly – though unsuccessfully – laboured to overcome into the avowed basis for the conception. The pre-war neo-Kantians (the principal ones besides Simmel were Windelband and Rickert) had evolved a special philosophical epistemology for the science of history in order to prove it of equal standing to the

natural sciences. This consisted of the rigorous elimination of any kind of laws from history. On account of their less exact laws, extreme positivism had pronounced the historical sciences to be sciences of an inferior rank, and many positivist sociologists were striving to prove the unaltered governance of natural laws in history. (Cf. my section on Gumplowicz, etc., in the chapter 'Social Darwinism, Racial Theory and Fascism'.) In this situation, Windelband and Rickert in their scientific doctrine had simply canonized the reactionary praxis of Ranke and his successors. In substance that meant, on the one hand, the removal of the idea of progress from history (Ranke versus Hegel: every epoch as being equally close to God), and on the other, the elevation of the uniqueness and unrepeatability of all historical events and constructions to the sole essence of historical science. Certainly this uniqueness and unrepeatability is a real *element* of the historical framework. If, however, it is inflated into the sole determining factor of what is historical, and if all elements of law are banished from history, there will come about a reactionary distortion and perversion, an irrationalizing of history, the destruction of its reasoned and orderly nature. Although Windelband and Rickert were not deliberate irrationalists in their general philosophy, they did irrationalism's development with regard to history a great service nonetheless. For the 'value relation' through which Rickert tried to secure a certain rationality for historical connections could only establish a pseudo-objectivity. This was especially so in view of the inevitable instability and subjectivity of that which the historical methodology of bourgeois philosophy understood in the concrete instance by valid worth, as also of the manner in which that methodology could realize the relatedness of the unique historical phenomenon to such values. With Simmel, this association with irrationalism already became consciously intended, although even he still sought to establish an 'individual causality' and had not yet wholly given up the standpoint of a modicum of rationality. And with Spengler, all this amounted to the

unquestioned dominance of the subjectivist-relativistically reasoned historical categories over even mathematics and natural science.

Spengler's epistemology was therefore only a means of rounding off the victory of extreme historical relativism. It was an extremely primitive theory resorting to catchwords and catchphrases. It simply applied to history the old vitalistic antithesis of life and death, intuition and reason, form and law: 'Form (*Gestalt*) and law, simile and concept, symbol and formula have a very different organ. What we have here is the relationship of *life and death*, of procreating and destroying. The understanding, the concept kills in the act of "perceiving" . . . The artist, the genuine historian *intuits* (*schaut*) how something comes about.'[45] Here we can readily see how industriously Spengler, through simplification, fashioned popular slogans for the absolute rule of the vitalistic standpoint out of the pre-war methodology of history. Here the Diltheyan method of 'perception through men of genius' was already burgeoning into a sharply anti-scientific, aristocratic epistemology.

With this epistemology Spengler intended to degrade all causal and law-controlled knowledge. 'The means of grasping dead forms is the mathematical law. The means of understanding live forms is the analogy.'[46] Spengler now extended analogy, as the central category of history, into the method of a universal morphology, into a 'symbol-system', a 'physiognomy' of history. He recognized as forerunners of this new method Goethe, whom he interpreted from a purely vitalistic angle and hence falsified, and Nietzsche, who had now attained to maximum influence. There was also a smattering of Bergson, whom Spengler simplified as vigorously as he simplified Dilthey and Simmel. Cause and effect, whose framework Spengler called the 'logic of space',[47] were to be replaced in history by the framework of destiny, the 'logic of time'. Thus he achieved the identification of irrationalist life and history: '*life* is the alpha and omega, and life has no system, no programme, no rationality; it exists for itself and

through itself, and the profound order in which it realizes itself can only be intuited and felt – and then perhaps described . . .'[48] Thus he declared history to be a universal science and, in the same breath, denied it any scientific character: 'The wish to treat of history scientifically is, in the last analysis, always a paradoxical thing . . .'[49]

This shallow and arbitrary epistemology in which everything boiled down to experience, to intuition, was Spengler's way of asserting the undisputed mastery of historical relativism. Everything is historical: with Spengler that meant that everything was historically relative, purely relative. Whereas the methodology of pre-war German imperialism had allotted to the natural sciences an isolated place in a kind of National Trust area of rationality, Spengler sought to 'historicize' the whole knowledge of nature, i.e., to subordinate it to historical relativism. Here again the issue itself, namely that of regarding nature historically, of conceptualizing the historicity objectively present in nature, was not invented by vitalism but had been raised by the evolution of society and the natural sciences. But Spengler also turned this question irrationalistically upside-down: for him, it was not to do with the historical character of the real process in nature but with a pseudo-historical dissolving of the objectivity of all natural-scientific categories. With vitalism's assistance, this question could not but succumb to an increasingly radical relativism and also to a mysticism which was becoming more and more audacious and uncontrolled. The question of a historical treatment of nature (in its objective laws, to be sure) had been in the air since Darwin, and indeed since the Kant-Laplace theory; the natural philosophies of the young Schelling and of Kant were bold attempts to answer it, albeit with totally inadequate tools. Here Spengler reversed the proposition in a subjectivist-vitalistic manner: while ignoring the objectively historical evolution of nature, he 'historicized' knowledge of nature by making it a mere function of the character-type of a given 'cultural cycle'. This 'historicizing' therefore removed all nature's

independence and autonomy, thus causing the complete disappearance of the genuine problem, the historical being of nature itself within objective natural laws. Certainly we must not forget that, again, a genuine problem lay hidden behind even this totally distorted proposition, namely how and to what extent the historical evolution of society affects the compass, character, etc., of our perception of nature. But Spengler dismissed from consideration the necessary basis for the correct proposition, the objectivity of nature and evolution of the productive forces of a given society, and the stage in the growth of science and technology which they determine. By making an absolute principle of the element of historical relativity in our perceptions of nature, he likewise eliminated the fact of their progressive approximation to nature's objective reality. Not acknowledging the interaction between the evolution of productive forces and perceptions of nature, he intuitively derived the separate forms or results of natural science directly from the 'morphological form' of a 'cultural cycle'. And in so doing, he engendered a myth based on the radical and permanent relativity of all knowledge.

Spengler did not, in the process, shrink from making the most daring assertions; in many respects he owed his sudden and widespread influence to this fondness for startling paradoxes. Number, for instance, was for him a purely historical category: '*A number in itself does not and cannot exist*. There are several worlds of numbers because there are several civilizations. We find an Indian, Arabic, ancient and occidental type of number each at bottom unique, each the expression of a different course of events . . . Accordingly there is more than one kind of mathematics.'[50] This ridiculously consistent denial of all objectivity Spengler took to the point where he was capable of saying of causality that it was 'an occidental and more precisely a Baroque phenomenon'.[51]

For Spengler, history took precedence over nature as a general rule: 'Thus history is the original world-form and

nature a late one which only men of a mature culture may fulfil, not the reverse as a prejudice in urban scientific understanding tends to assume.'[52] And so the whole science of physics along with its object was a myth of the late occidental 'Faustian' culture. The atom, speed of light and gravitation were just as much the mythical categories of 'Faustian man' as poltergeists and household demons were categories of the period that believed in magic.[53] (If we recall Simmel's statements on the historical relativity of knowledge we can see how Spengler was merely drawing all the conclusions of pre-war imperialist vitalism and popularizing them.) For those reasons, culture was for Spengler the 'primary phenomenon of all past and future world-histories'.[54]

We have noted already that in Spengler's view, culture provided the organon for a consistent relativizing of all phenomena. But in now proclaiming a world-history to be a universal science, he also abolished the unitary character of world-history. Spengler ardently polemicized against the division of history into antiquity, the mediaeval period and the modern age. These periods, to be sure, had become a pure convention in the study of history, which failed to recognize for the most part that its real objective foundation lay in the great economic formations of slavery, serfdom and hired labour.

It might seem as if Spengler's polemics were aimed against this convention, but that was only immediately and apparently so. For it is no accident that such attacks (on behalf of racial theory, H.S. Chamberlain similarly made a stand against this division *before* Spengler), such fundamental revisions to the whole construction of world-history ensued only at that stage of irrationalism at which the latter took up arms against socialism. To the bourgeois concept of progress as formulated in, say, Hegel's philosophy of history and later – suitably ironed out – in Anglo-French liberal sociology, Ranke's elevation to a principle of the absence of ideation and its philosophical transfiguration through neo-Kantianism offered

an adequate answer. But the bourgeois historical theorists found their situation thoroughly altered when historical materialism presented the major periods of history as an orderly succession of social formations and proved that the economic laws of their change led to the higher formations of socialism. Chamberlain and Spengler just drew the most rigorous conclusions from this position: the only effective challenge to the notion of socio-historical progress lay in denying the unitary and ordered character of the course of history and human evolution in general. (Although the immediate, surface polemics may have been aimed against the pedantic tripartite scheme, citing as an argument the discovery of oriental cultures which had indeed been overlooked, this was only shadow-boxing. For historical materialism was able to elucidate their development too in economic terms and to trace the – admittedly tortuous – orientation of content from primitive communism to socialism. Therein lay the true target of Spengler's polemics.)

From the concretely methodological angle, Spengler's view of culture as a 'primary phenomenon' was tantamount to saying that there were several qualitatively different cultures each of which evolved in its own way in every respect. Here we can clearly see how the Diltheyan concept of the type grew into a myth. The relativistic basic character of Dilthey's typological conception was, if anything, heightened further; Dilthey's dream of a philosophical synthesis that would remove the rigid relativism of typology was thoroughly discredited; for Spengler, the typology of cultures constituted their ultimate and sole fundamental perception. The radicalization which exaggerated the relativistic element in typology also marked the point at which it tipped over into myth. With Dilthey (and far more strongly still with, for example, Max Weber) typology was an auxiliary tool of historical knowledge whose value was only established in the elucidation of historical reality. In calling his types 'primary phenomena' Spengler was responsible for much more than a terminological innovation: he declared the

'form' (*Gestalt*) of each culture to be the real basis of all its separate manifestations, in content as in form, in structure as in dynamics. The scientific auxiliary construction had become a concrete ground, albeit irrationalist in principle and comprehensible only via intuition.

The automatic result was that these self-enclosed 'forms' were necessarily 'monads without windows': only within its unique essence could each be intuitively grasped and described. (Here the Windelband-Rickert theory of history, the individualizing method, tipped over into myth.) But Spengler, as we have seen, was unwilling to stop at a mere description of his unique 'forms'; after juxtaposing them in mutual exclusiveness, he wanted to reveal connections between them after all. It is however plain that these could not possibly be of a scientific character. In the worst, anti-scientific traditions of Romanticism, Spengler found for this another intuitive, irrationalist category: manifestations of different cultures were comparable only by analogy. For example, Euclidean geometry as a manifestation of antiquity compared to non-Euclidean geometry as a manifestation of occidental culture. Historical 'morphology' now ascertained definite and necessarily recurring stages in all cultural development: 'Every culture goes through the different ages of individual man. Each has its childhood, youth, adult life and old age.'[55]

Now since, according to Spengler, each culture proceeded to evolve on these lines towards an inevitable destiny, there arose a new and, for Spengler, crucial category: 'I am naming *simultaneously* two historical facts which, each in its own culture, appear in exactly the same – relative – situation and therefore have a precisely corresponding significance.'[56] Thus Archimedes and Gauss, Polignot and Rembrandt, etc., were 'contemporaries'. This was the ancient and hackneyed dictum of the successive ages of civilization. But as voiced in Vico, Herder and Hegel before the origin of historical materialism, it did show at least an inkling of the ordered rise and decline of social formations, whereas Spengler turned it into an

occasionally ingenious but mostly downright false juggling with unreasoned analogies.

This view had, however, become important for the later course of events. In the first place, it denied the unified evolution of the human race, and this denial later became a dogma in the fascist interpretation of history based on racial theory – which admittedly owed more to Chamberlain than to Spengler. Secondly, it made for a new and, from the propaganda angle, effective challenge to historical progress. As we have seen, pre-war vitalism already had a major share in contesting the idea of progress from a reactionary and sceptical standpoint. Here Spengler's paradoxy, original in form and trivial in content, did no more than draw all the conclusions. We have already seen that Spengler's struggle against socialism as the chief enemy formed the social basis of this more advanced stage of the irrationalist denial of all historical progress. And thirdly, the Spenglerian theory of 'forms' with regard to individual cultures gave rise at this point to a solipsism of cultural cycles. With Spengler, the vitalistic and irrationalistic anthropomorphizing of cycles of culture was not limited to ascribing to them a growth and an ageing; they also acquired the inner psychological structure of humans (intellectuals) of the imperialist period: they 'lived' in a solipsistic fashion. This solipsism, as the mode of feeling of the imperialist age's parasitical classes, had hitherto expressed itself openly only in the psychology of the decadent *belles-lettres* of the time. As we have noted, it governed the epistemology of most of vitalism's exponents, but largely tacitly and hidden behind a mythical pseudo-objectivity.

At this point Spengler, since these 'forms' had acquired an overt and fully developed mythical pseudo-objectivity, also allowed these features of the solipsistic relation to the world to emerge overtly and fully developed. In principle each cultural cycle can experience only itself; there exists no bridge of mutual understanding whatever between one cycle and another. The definition of this inner structure of Spengler's 'forms' is of importance chiefly for the light it

sheds on the imperialist myths' inner historical substance: they claimed to unearth at last primeval, scattered connections, but in reality they constituted nothing more than the insertion of the psychology of the imperialistic age's parasitical intelligentsia into a suitably adjusted, purportedly historical reality. (That the method behind this insertion derived on the one hand from Nietzsche, and on the other from Mach-Avenarius, needs no detailed commentary.)

But this definition also has a forward-looking significance: the solipsistic character of historical 'forms' was the methodological prototype for fascist racial theory. The 'philosophical' substantiation of the fascist precept of barbaric inhumanity towards those of other races was built on the conception of such a solipsistic racial structure: the various races were regarded as just as alien, hostile, hermetic and uncommunicative towards each other as Spengler's cultural cycles. Granted, we shall find that with Gobineau and to an even greater extent with Chamberlain, racial theory reached this stage under its own power, and we have remarked that Nietzsche was similarly far advanced in this respect. But that does not lessen the significance of the fact that vitalism led to this pass. In the first place, we notice in Spengler the fulfilment of Nietzsche's barbarizing tendencies; in the second, we see the deep-seated concurrent development of the various streams of reactionary imperialist philosophy, and their tendency to merge in theoretical preparation for the barbaric ideas and actions of Hitler and Rosenberg.

Similarly, it is patent that the construction of this irrationalist, solipsistic myth of history had as its ultimate, crucial purpose another attempt to resist the socialist perspective on social evolution. Nietzsche, the first to take up this philosophical challenge, was still obliged to present the whole of world-history, which was unitary in his eyes, as a contest for leadership between masters and rabble. Therefore he had to lay stress on awakening the masters' 'will-to-power' with all the available means in order that their struggle might end in the future defeat of socialism. Spengler entertained hopes

that were far weaker than Nietzsche's. His conception was a consoling melody rather than a battle-hymn, an opiate rather than a stimulus. The cyclical life of the cultural spheres, he thought, had repeatedly given rise to dangers similar to the contemporary one, namely the proletarian threat to capitalism. This danger, however, had been dismissed from every cycle, and each culture had died a 'natural' death of superannuation, of cultural paralysis. Why should a different fate befall the Faustian civilization of capitalism? There was, after all, intuitive-analogical morphology, the only sure knowledge of history, and this indicated that destiny was about to introduce the rule of the 'Caesars' (i.e., the monopoly capitalists). The fact that this rule signified the beginning of the end of the culture concerned did not interest any capitalist or parasitical intellectual. We shall manage to survive – *après nous le déluge*: that was Spengler's song of consolation, and very effective it was.

Another powerful effect of his *oeuvre* Spengler owed to the consequences of an overall conception which allotted a central place to the asserted antithesis of culture and civilization. This antithesis had long played a major part in the reactionary German philosophy of history. The ideological battle against Germany's democratization was waged under its flag. By 'civilization' it meant everything that was bad about capitalism and principally Western democracy, which was now confronted with an autochthonous, organic and genuinely German 'culture'. Here Spengler was uniting reactionary Prussian tendencies with an artificially paradoxical modern form. Again, the problem of civilization acquired a vitalistic slant: it was presented as the problem of decay contrasted with life in full bloom, with culture. The question of the decline of the Western world was this: 'Every culture has its own civilization . . . Civilization is a culture's inescapable destiny . . . Civilization constitutes the *most extreme and artificial* conditions of which a higher kind of man is capable. These conditions are a final terminus; as things that have come about they are the sequel to

becoming, as death they are the sequel to life, as paralysis they are the sequel to evolution . . . are an *end*, irrevocable, but they have always been reached as a matter of the innermost necessity.'[57]

In this statement Spengler answered the question in the spirit of the Prussian reactionary movement. Admittedly it sounds like a disconsolate answer at first, as the prospect of a fateful paralysis. But, like Nietzsche's pessimistic critique of culture in its day, this gave reassurance to the extreme reactionaries. For it stressed once again that the present was not a revolutionary period which threatened to overthrow German reaction; on the contrary, the prospect of the consolidation of reactionary forces was 'proved' to be irrefutable. For to Spengler's mind, the dominant form of civilization was Caesarism. It was the amorphous method of governance pertaining to every decaying culture, to every civilization. The people were transformed into a peasantry without a history over whom the Caesars erected their dominion, a dominion whereby 'history reverts to the absence of history, to the primitive beat of pre-history'.[58] This, then, was the Spenglerian prospect for the Western world, for the present day: the fateful, irresistibly growing dominion of the 'Caesars' of monopoly capitalism over a merely amorphous mass of 'peasant' proletarians, an undisputed dominion lasting until the end of the 'Faustian' culture.

This prospect originated in a pessimistic analysis of the contemporary fate, and it was highly agreeable to the reactionaries. Spengler gave it concrete expression in a specific book which is of importance to fascist ideology, *Prussianism and Socialism*. Here he expounded the 'morphological' basic idea in the following way. Every civilization, according to Spengler, has its socialism (Zeno, Buddhism, etc.; present-day socialism is the Faustian form of these manifestations). But this generalization did not satisfy Spengler's analogy hunt. He had, in addition, to discover the 'real' socialism, namely Prussianism; the types of the military officer, civil servant and worker. The adversary of this 'socialism' was not capi-

talism but England.[59] (Here Spengler was enlarging on the ideas in Scheler's war pamphlets and Sombart's *Dealers and Heroes*.) Prussians and Englishmen represent two major types in the development of civilization. There are 'two moral imperatives of a contrasting kind, slowly evolved from the Viking spirit and the code of the Knights of the Teutonic Order. The one group carried the Germanic idea within them, the others felt it *over* them: *personal independence and supra-personal commonalty*. Today they are called individualism and socialism.' Karl Marx and working-class socialism have only complicated this question and are being thrust aside by the fateful logic of world-history. The victor will be 'Prussian socialism', the 'socialism' founded by Friedrich Wilhelm I. The true Internationale will also be built on this basis: 'A *genuine* Internationale is possible only through the triumph of the idea of a *single* race above all others . . . *The genuine Internationale is* imperialism.'[60] The worker, in this 'socialism', becomes an economic officer, and the entrepreneur a responsible administrative official. The German working class will be bound to realize that only this 'socialism' has real possibilities. No ideology is needed, only 'a brave scepticism, a class of socialistic master-natures'.[61]

Here, what was new in Spengler as compared with Nietzsche is perfectly clear. The latter had made a direct, frontal assault on socialism – of which he knew little. Of course it cannot be claimed that Spengler was any better acquainted with socialist literature, but his mode of attack was different, a dodging of the issue and a demagogic ruse: socialism, he conceded, would triumph – but the 'genuine article' was Prussianism. That the historical prospect he outlined here is essentially different from that of *The Decline of the West* will interest only those wishing to see in Spengler a thinker with a coherent system. It seems to us that an important connection, a social one, exists between the two perspectives. If, in his *magnum opus*, he had rebuffed the prospect of socialism with arguments taken from his theory of cultural morphology, here he sought the intellectual redemption of

German imperialist capitalism, with its aristocratic-militaristic features, by dubbing it the 'real' socialism. This, however, was already to anticipate the basic idea of Hitlerian social demagogy.

Thus we see how close, in the time of the immediate post-war crisis, this reactionary prelude of vitalism turned militant came to fascist ideology. Naturally there were still many elements dividing Spengler from fascism. His racial conception was a Nietzschean one. So too was his concept of dominance: by rejecting all social demagogy, all appeals to the masses, he strongly differed from Rosenberg and Baeumler at the time of fascist dominion. (Compare his book *Years of Decision*.) But that makes no difference to Spengler's significance in the history of the preliminaries to fascism. By reconstructing vitalism as a philosophy of militant reaction, he completed the change of course which led in a roundabout way to fascism. And notwithstanding all their reservations and polemical comments, the fascist ideologists always acknowledged Spengler's services to them.

5. The Vitalistic Philosophy of 'Relative Stabilization' (Scheler)

The ebbing of the revolutionary tide after 1923 marked the start in Germany, as in the whole of Western and Central Europe, of the period of 'relative stabilization'. With its illusory hopes of a long period of economically and politically consolidated, gradual and peaceful development, it also brought different contents and tendencies to the fore in vitalism. Although large sectors, particularly among the petty bourgeoisie, hoped for a return of pre-war times, public opinion among the intelligentsia was increasingly recognizing that so simple a return was objectively impossible. The new conditions engendered by the war and collapse determined a militant politicizing of vitalism, which meant

its going beyond the pacifically parasitical, complacently sceptical and purely individualistic resignation of the pre-war period. Nevertheless there arose for the time being a prevalence of thinkers and tendencies that, although still rooted in their essential philosophy and method in pre-war times, sought henceforward to reconcile the dominant philosophical traditions of yesteryear with the new situation.

The most important figure in this transitional period was Max Scheler. He was a lively-minded, flexible, versatile writer without firm convictions, very strongly susceptible to whatever was most in vogue. But for all that, he did take a basic line which largely matched the requirements of 'relative stabilization'. It was his desire to found a philosophy rich in content and surpassing neo-Kantian formalism, a fixed hierarchy of values suited to playing an important part in the consolidation of German bourgeois society.

This meant a resumption, under radically altered circumstances, of the Diltheyan philosophical programme with which we are already familiar. And Scheler in fact spoke most appreciatively of Dilthey's 'pre-intuiting genius'.[62] His affinity with the latter's tendencies is also evident in the fact that Scheler was far removed from a vitalistic relativism as overtly expressed and radically paradoxical as Spengler's. Indeed it has sometimes been asked if Scheler can be fully credited with vitalism in the orthodox sense, since his hierarchy of values constantly went beyond life to culminate in higher values than life. Scheler shared with Dilthey the conviction – which he attempted to build up and argue with the intellectual methods of Husserlian phenomenology – that categories, i.e., norms, values, etc., were to be organically obtained and developed from a materiality of the philosophical objects intuitively grasped and experienced through 'intuition of the essence' (*Wesensschau*). The intuitive character of this method brought him very close to vitalism. Despite Dilthey's enthusiasm for Husserlian phenomenology, it had hitherto stood apart from vitalism's philosophical tendencies (Husserl himself actually rejected them and strove for a

philosophy that was a 'strict science'[63]). But we may go so far as to say that Scheler, with his intuitive mind, led phenomenology into the mainstream of vitalistic irrationalism.

To be sure, we should not overestimate the worth of Husserl's rejection of vitalism. Although he acted as though divorced from vitalism's agnosticistic excesses, he turns out to stand quite close to Machism when he himself takes up basic questions of epistemology. Thus Scheler was only extracting from Husserl the somewhat latent irrationalist-relativistic core. We have only to quote Husserl's exposition of the reality of the external world: 'The question of the existence and nature of the "external world" is a metaphysical one. Epistemology, as a general explanation of ideal essence and of the valid meaning of cognitive thinking, does encompass the general question of whether and how far a knowledge or reasoned surmising of concretely "real" objects is possible – objects transcending in principle the experiences perceiving them – as also the question of the norms to which the true meaning of such cognition would have to conform. But epistemology does not include the empirically slanted question of whether we human beings may truly gain such knowledge on the basis of the data in fact offered to us, or even the task of realizing this knowledge. In our view, epistemology in the proper sense of the word is not a theory at all. It is not a science in the meaningful sense of a unity derived from theoretical explanation.'[64] As we are about to show, the Husserlian method of 'leaving in parentheses' the question of the datum of reality implies the same proximity to Machism.

Scheler was a transitional figure, and the period in which he acquired a leading influence was also a transitional one. It marked a temporary breathing space between two major crises in German democracy and its ideologies. Scheler's versatility and impressionable nature made him well qualified to become a central figure of this period. Although originally a pupil of Eucken and subsequently an adherent of Husserl, he promptly tried to enlarge phenomenology in respect of

both content and world-outlook. His most important pre-war works have as their content the search for a morality of substance, against Kantian formalism and on behalf of an objective classification of values. For a long while catholicizing, hierarchical tendencies reminiscent of scholasticism were still present in this apparent objectivism – tendencies which had been already operative in the logical method of phenomenology since Bolzano and Brentano. The catholicizing Scheler provides a certain parallel to the social philosophy of Spann, and in that radical reactionary currents overtook them during the second post-war crisis, both authors met the same fate.

Another sign of Scheler's lability and his impressionable nature is the fact that in his war-time writings, he propounded a vitalistic attack on the 'English mind' first and foremost, more or less along Sombartian lines. During the age of relative stabilization, on the other hand, he developed a considerable open sympathy with contemporary Western culture. During this period, he also attempted to harmonize his objective hierarchy of values with the dominant historical relativism by helping to found a 'sociology of knowing' in which this compromise was central to the methodology. The impending crisis, which Scheler did not live to experience in its acuter phases, cast a pessimistic gloom over his philosophy and increased the weight it gave to anthropological relativism. And the latter increasingly weakened the dogmatics of a classification of values. Whereas at the outset, his ideas of God had almost echoed Aquinas, his philosophy of religion was now gradually shifting to an almost complete godlessness in that he proclaimed a God evolving together with man. In his late period, this doctrine already amounted almost to a semi-religious, semi-atheistic deification of man.

So Scheler's attempt to link vitalistic relativism with a fixed classification was only a rather fleeting episode in the development of vitalism up to fascism. But it was not without its significance, for it carried phenomenology along with it into the vitalistic stream. Or to put it more precisely:

phenomenology's vitalistic-irrationalistic tendencies first emerged openly with Scheler; he made public that which Husserl had concealed by confining his method to problems of formal logic. Here 'descriptive' psychology too, the 'understanding' of historical phenomena (as opposed to causal explanation) was married to Husserl's 'intuiting of the essence'. The 'timeless' proofs of phenomenology (the legacy of Bolzano and Brentano) were exposed as a mirage as soon as Scheler applied the method to concrete socio-historical phenomena: the profound affinity with the relativism of Dilthey and Simmel came to light.

Let us now examine Scheler's phenomenological method rather more closely. Scheler provided a clear picture of it in an essay dating from 1913. Phenomenology is the 'name for an attitude of intuitive contemplation in which one receives something to intuit or to experience which would otherwise remain hidden.'[65] Here Scheler openly admitted the total subjectivity of the method: 'What is experienced and intuited is "given" only in the experiencing and intuiting act itself, in its accomplishment: it appears herein and only herein.' Its basic character is 'the most lively, intensive and immediate *experiential commerce with the world* itself'. He was here polemicizing against the well-known Husserl critique by Wilhelm Wundt, who poked fun at the Husserlian mode of presentation by saying that Husserl produced a long series of definitions of what a concept was not, and then finished with a pure tautology – such as 'love is love'. Wundt's misunderstanding, according to Scheler, lay in a failure to recognize the phenomenological 'attitude' of mind, 'which must *bring* the reader . . . something *to intuit* which in essence may only be intuited'. The whole statement was, Scheler maintained, only a preliminary, and the final 'tautology' was tantamount to: 'Now look, and then you will see it!'

As these statements show, the phenomenological method had had its strongly vitalistic-irrationalistic features from the outset. And Scheler remained throughout his life a loyal and grateful pupil of the Husserlian method, always adhering to

the phenomenological working method. This method 'set in parentheses', as Husserl conceived it, every object whose 'intuitive contemplation' was intended. That is to say, it left the object's reality out of consideration in order to attain to a 'sight' of the objective 'pure essentials' unencumbered by the question of the data of reality, and to express this apodictically in a purportedly objective form.

This method shows very clearly both facets of the imperialist period's general philosophical development, viz., the close association of intuitivistic irrationalism and pseudo-objectivity. It was an acknowledged fact that the method rested upon intuition, nor did Scheler, as we have just noted, make any attempt to conceal it. Initially, the basically irrationalistic character was masked by the fact that Husserl and his first pupils concerned themselves largely with problems of formal logic, with analyses of meaning. Hence it was possible for Husserl himself to imagine that with phenomenology he had discovered a method of treating philosophy as a 'strict science'. But we must at once point out that formal logic's important position in the methodology by no means precluded irrationalism. On the contrary: although formal logic and irrationalism constitute an antinomy from the philosophical angle, they are nonetheless modes of relating to reality standing in polar co-ordination. The origin of irrationalism is always closely associated with the limits of the comprehension of the world through formal logic. Case facts which are here adduced as the starting-point, as proof and verification of the irrationalistic character of reality will be raised to categories of reason in every dialectical treatment of the contradictory nature of the forms of understanding, of the reflectional conditions. And it is characteristic of the thinkers marking the transition to extreme irrationalism that this conflict, which had made previous appearances in history as a conflict between opposing tendencies, played a decisive role in the internal structure of their philosophy. So, with Scheler too, the ethical hierarchy, although acquiring its real substantiation through intuition, was constructed with

the aid of extremely logical considerations and divided into distinct types. This function of formal logic as a kind of conceptual corset for intuitions and irrationalisms may be observed in all the philosophers coming from the Husserl school, even Heidegger. But for all of them, it was only an auxiliary tool. The essential content was irrationalistic to a growing degree, and the decisive, externally non-constructive structural principles were also irrationalistic.

The tendency towards pseudo-objectivity was present in phenomenology from the start. But with Husserl, phenomenology seemed at first to be only a renewal of the Bolzano-Brentano tradition. Only when phenomenologies had left the purely logical realm and taken phenomena of social life as the object of 'essential intuition' did the question of true objectivity emerge at its sharpest. And in its later stage of development, phenomenology claimed more and more insistently to be arguing a science of reality, an ontology. Here, however – even within the phenomenological context – it would have been obliged to ask when, and on what conditions, one could remove the 'parentheses' in which the phenomenologically intuited 'essentials' were placed, and where one could locate and register the criterion of whether 'essential intuition' included reality independent of consciousness. But the 'setting in parentheses' radically excluded this question; 'essential intuition' could be applied not only to a significant correlation, but to a purely imaginary formation as much as to a (correct or false) image of reality. The essence of the 'setting in parentheses' lay precisely in the fact that all these thought-formations, so radically different in respect of their relation to reality, were reduced to a common denominator in phenomenological investigation, which took them as being homogeneous. It is clear, therefore, that the whole question of reality, of whether the object remaining after the 'removal of the parentheses' is a mere formation by the consciousness or the image of something with a being independent of consciousness, had become inescapable. Now it is very interesting that this major shift from the investigation of consciousness

to the science of being, from phenomenology to ontology – the self-styled 'turning to the facts' – was accomplished almost unnoticed. One simply declared the phenomenological objects to be objects of ontology and surreptitiously transformed 'essential insight' into a revival of 'intellectual intuition'. This development characterized the often imperceptibly and gradually but irresistibly mounting strength in post-war imperialism of a thinking oriented to the mythical. Pre-war neo-Kantian epistemology was avowedly left behind (in reality, its subjectivism and agnosticism were preserved intact). And at the same time, a 'reality' that was irrational and comprehensible only by intuition was granted automatic evidence for its being on the basis of its purely intuitive comprehensibility.

In order to illustrate quite clearly the epistemological hollowness and untenability of the phenomenological method and the ontological method deriving from it, we have deliberately avoided starting with a critique of its hypotheses. A true critique would have to go right back to the 'setting in parentheses'. For it is obvious that this celebrated method tells us nothing more than that, for instance, the idea of man and the idea of the Devil are both just ideas. Without logical devices, however, no substantial conclusions can be drawn from so purely formal an identification. And 'essential insight' claimed to do just that. Were the phenomenologists to analyse in some measure this central point of their method, they would be forced to recognize that any investigation of an idea with regard to content is impossible without reference to objective reality, no matter whether the procedure is intuitive or discursive. The content can only be obtained by comparing its individual features, coherence and so forth with objective reality, by enriching, complementing, correcting, etc., the original idea through these comparisons. If Scheler, to return to his example, conducts an 'intuition of the essence' with regard to love, then those mental pictures of the objective reality constituting the phenomenon of love must be collected, summed up and collated, and that

which does not belong to it (mere sympathy, friendship, etc.) excluded; only then would he be in a position to accomplish his 'essential insight'. In fact, therefore, he will not have set reality 'in parentheses' but will have constantly referred to it. 'Setting in parentheses' is only a specific method of phenomenology inasmuch as the subjective-idealistic irrationalistic arbitrariness of it acquired from the outset a pseudonym giving an impression of objectivity. The relation of the ideas to objective reality is disrupted not only from the epistemological standpoint but also from that of concrete content, and a 'method' is created that blurs and indeed erases the distinction between true and false, necessary and arbitrary, real and merely imagined. If, say, man and the Devil are likewise 'placed in parentheses', then, by dint of the fact that we are dealing – in a psychologically immediate way – with ideas in both cases, we are overlooking the difference that in determining the content, we are resorting to reality in the first instance, but only to ideas again in the second. This is why phenomenological ontology also fails to investigate the questionable right to 'open the parentheses'. For it introduced them only in order to reduce truth and fiction, reality and myth to a common level and to create a haze of mythical quasi-objectivity. That method which Husserl declared to be 'strictly scientific' is therefore nothing more than the subjective-idealistic statement: it is my ideas which determine the essence of reality. Husserl's epistemological closeness to Mach was no accident. It was just that where the Machists and the Kantians attempted deductions, Husserl contented himself with proclaiming intuitive certainty.

Scheler, who admittedly stood at the beginning of this development, claimed along with the whole school to have overcome the Kantians' formalism and subjectivism. How much this method had to do with a subjectivistic arbitrariness surpassing even neo-Kantianism we have just shown, and we can now illustrate the point with a short example from Scheler's major early work of moral philosophy. There he stated: 'The *institution* of slavery was not, therefore, an

institution permitting the *subjugation of persons* . . . , but vice versa: because the slave depicted *himself* . . . *not as a person* but only, for instance, as man, ego, psychical subject and so on, i.e., still as a "fact", it was normally permissible for him to be killed, sold, etc.'[66] Slave consciousness, therefore, did not arise out of the socio-economic institution (it is, by the way, very dubious whether this consciousness was always – even, say, in Spartacus – identical with that which Scheler's 'essential intuition' 'saw' in it). On the contrary, it was slave consciousness which created slavery in a society. Here it becomes patent that one may 'see' whatever one chooses by means of the professedly objective 'intuiting of the essence'.[67]

We see, then, the extent to which the foundation upon which Scheler sought to build his pyramid of an objective and permanent classification was rotted and riddled with subjectivistic arbitrariness. All that supplemented mere experiencing was an extremely threadbare formal logic, such as in Scheler's statement that the existence of the positive values was something positive, their non-existence something negative and so forth. In this way such formal logic could produce at best an abstract context. The important factor dictating the content was the subjective arbitrariness of the 'intuiting', as we have characterized it above. The very definition of the individual types of ethical attitude (Scheler, like Dilthey, did not get beyond a typology) was therefore arbitrary, and their professedly objective classification thoroughly so. For this, according to Scheler, could 'never be *deduced* or *inferred* . . . There is for this (the adoption of preferences, G.L.) an *intuitive "preferential evidence"* which no kind of logical *deduction* can replace.'[68]

So Scheler's ethics gave rise to a purely arbitrary arrangement and hierarchy of types. Scheler included among them the saint, the genius, the hero, the intellectual leader and the hedonistic artists, in that 'order of precedence'. Occasionally, to be sure, he stated some quasi-scientific, quasi-objective characteristics, such as whether the one phenomenon was

'founded' on the other, etc. But since these quasi-logical arguments were similarly based on a purely subjective intuition, they could in every instance be reversed at will. Therefore Scheler's ethical doctrine of types was just as much a simple juxtaposition as Dilthey's typology of world-views, and like Dilthey he was forced to admit that in reality, these types were separated by insoluble contradictions which not even the new world-view could resolve and so establish a really valid order of precedence. Scheler designated this confession of extreme relativism the 'essential tragedy' of all finite personal being and its (essential) moral imperfection.[69] No finite person could be simultaneously a saint, hero, genius, etc. 'Hence every possible conflict of will, i.e., every possible "dispute" between representatives of personal types (as model examples), *eludes settlement* through a finite person . . . Tragic is therefore the word for a dispute whose just settlement is conceivable *only* through the judgement of the Godhead *exclusively*.' Thus Scheler himself was indicating that his ethics, were they not to dissolve into total relativism, needed supplementing with an 'ontology of God'. And we have already shown how the God whom Scheler grasped phenomenologically underwent a gradual dissolution in the course of the author's development.

It is clear that as soon as the social world experienced a real upheaval, the allegedly objective and permanent order of values would be bound to collapse. The subjectivistic, relativistically arbitrary tendency would break through in triumph. The tendency towards dissolution in his own philosophy is visible in Scheler's late works, where an allegedly permanent objectivity no longer ordered the human types and the philosopher had to try and argue everything on overtly anthropological grounds. 'All forms of being depend on the being of man. The whole objective world and its essential being do not constitute a "being-in-itself", but only a counter-projection and extract from this being in itself, tailored according to man's total mental and physical organization. Only from the image of man's essence . . . may we

draw a *conclusion* as to the true attributes of the highest ground of things.'[70] Here Scheler was already approaching Spengler's nihilistic scepticism. It is also significant that in the post-war period, he broke with all the Husserlian traditions of 'strict' scientific thought and openly allied himself to the most irrational anti-scientific thinking. 'Science', he said, 'has *absolutely no* significance ontologically for acquiring and establishing a world-outlook.'[71] So Scheler, like all vitalists, did not go beyond a relativistic doctrine of types; even Spengler's doctrine of cultural cycles was nothing better than a pompously inflated and, factually considered, superficially historical typology.

Scheler's personal character enabled him to give vitalism a slant matching the requirements of 'relative stabilization'. His new and opportune intermediate link was his 'sociology of knowledge'. We shall deal with its individual findings, its specific methodology in connection with an analysis of German sociology in the imperialist period. The one philosophically important element to be established is that Scheler believed, on the one hand, that he could dispose of his increasingly extreme relativism by finding a new term with which to describe it; the new magic word was 'perspectivism'. (Similarly, Mannheim 'overcame' relativism with the magic word 'relationism'.) Scheler revived, on the other hand, the ageing Dilthey's illusion, the fictive hope, as though extreme relativism pursued to the farthest limit could engineer its own resolution.

But in accordance with the more advanced development of imperialism, Scheler went much further than Dilthey. The latter saw an irremovable relativism only in the judging of historical phenomena. Scheler took the view that the relativism applied to the events themselves. He stated: 'Not only our *perception* (which has its own stages of relativity) of the "historical facts of the case", but also these *themselves* are relative to *being* and to *being-thus*, not just to the mere "consciousness of the beholder". There is only a metaphysical, not a historical "thing-in-itself".'[72] Here Scheler, like

Mannheim soon afterwards, was striving to have relativism resolve itself precisely by taking it to its extreme conclusion. On the basis of a superficial analogy – which was then in fashion – with a garbled version of Einstein's theory of relativity, Scheler intended to found a historical 'perspectivism' starting from these hypotheses. This meant the strict denial of all objective existence of the historical facts (denial of the historical 'thing-in-itself'), and at the same time the dependence 'of all "possible" historical images on the substance of the individual moment and the beholder's individual position in absolute time'. That is to say: the student of history actually creates it. The task of Scheler's 'sociology of knowledge' in this respect was to furnish historical proof of this relativism, especially through proving the different basic direction of European and Asiatic knowledge (in the former 'from matter to the soul', in the latter 'from the soul to matter'). Here again we can see that historical 'perspectivism' was serving to discredit Western materialist philosophy as 'provincial prejudice'. This epistemological relativism was given a basis quite superficial enough: 'A man who – to take a crude example – spends today in Rome, the next day in Paris, and will shortly be in Berlin or Madrid already feels the extended physical world to be less real and substantial on account of the changes of location. The physical world will take on for him an increasingly objective figurative character.'[73]

So Scheler was aiming at producing a compromise between vitalistic relativism and his objective, permanent hierarchy of values. Hence he met the needs of 'relative stabilization' and came correspondingly closer to specific tendencies of pre-war vitalism. We can almost think that Simmel is speaking when Scheler states: 'Everything that can be mechanized *ought* to be mechanized.'[74] But Simmel's vitalistic precept about money as the 'guardian of the inner life' was still quite a general tenet of faith. With Scheler, in the period of 'relative stabilization', this bias denoted a stand in favour of a democracy 'from above' (in contrast to the French Revolution's

plebeian democracy and even more to proletarian democracy), and in particular on behalf of the cultural expectations of capitalism entertained by broad sectors of German society during 'relative stabilization'. Scheler viewed the contemporary state of affairs as a battle for a new metaphysics, the origins of which were closely linked to the current politico-social crisis. 'The sociological form of democracy "from below" . . . is as a whole more foe than friend to *all* higher forms of knowledge. It is the democrats of *liberal* origin who have supported and developed positive scientific thinking first and foremost.' The 'proofs' were the revolutionary developments from the Peasants' Wars to Bolshevism, as also the 'class myths'; for Scheler, fascism was also included. They were 'beacons of a mighty metaphysical need we would do well to notice, and if we fail to meet this need through developing good, rational metaphysics afresh in a new, relatively metaphysical European epoch, they will be all the more likely to shatter the scientific edifice'. Scheler's new relativism was to take over this diversionary 'stabilizing' function. For there were signs all around of 'the *end* of positive scientism, as a type of thinking which is hostile to metaphysics in principle'. 'Thus the trend towards the self-conquest of parliamentary democracy strangely chimes together with the aforesaid self-conquest of materialist or semi-materialist sham and *ersatz* metaphysics, and with the self-conquest through historical perspectivism of a historical approach which is hostile to metaphysics.'[75]

With Scheler vitalism, which owed its popularity chiefly to the vague discontent with the contemporary state of civilization, to the hardly conscious uneasiness about the existing social situation, was 'consolidated' hierarchically or later through perspectivism. Vitalism itself underwent a 'relative stabilization' without, of course, blunting its attacking edge, which was aimed principally at socialism; only the mode of battle changed in accordance with bourgeois illusions about 'relative stabilization'. This inner elective affinity of the versatile, adaptable, rather spineless Scheler with the ideological

needs of this short transitional period raised him for a while to the authoritative thinker of bourgeois Germany. But Scheler could not strive for and achieve anything more than a compromise. It is a very telling fact that, profoundly steeped as he was in the relativism and irrationalism of the times, he had daydreams of a 'good and rational metaphysics'. These compromising tendencies brought him into close association with the dominant trends of a brief transitional phase. The same forces, however, were very soon to consign his whole philosophy to oblivion.

6. The Ash Wednesday of Parasitical Subjectivism (Heidegger, Jaspers)

Scheler's tempered feelings of uneasiness about the contemporary situation burst into the open in the philosophy of his younger fellow-pupil in phenomenology, Martin Heidegger. With the latter, phenomenology came to occupy the centre of the German intellectuals' philosophical interest for the time being. But it now turned into the ideology of the agony of individualism in the imperialist period. Already the 'consolidation' of Scheler's philosophy echoed only faintly that self-awareness which imperialistic subjectivism had voiced in the philosophy of Dilthey and above all Simmel. It was just extreme relativism which seemed to account for the sovereign assurance of this self-awareness: everything solid resolved into a matter of subjective viewpoint, and all objectivity into a purely relative function or relation conditioned by the subject. This meant that, for all the relativistic resignation, the subject appeared to itself as creator of the spiritual universe, or at any rate as the power creating – in line with its own model, own assessment and own inner needs – an ordered cosmos out of an otherwise senseless chaos, bestowing on it a meaning to its own greater glory, and appropriating it as the realm of its experiences. Vitalism, even Simmel's,

expressed this general feeling more cautiously than did imaginative literature in the imperialist period (we are thinking chiefly of the lyric poetry of Stefan George and Rilke).

The grim years of the First World War, which were full of abrupt changes of fortune, and the ensuing period brought a marked change of mood. The subjectivistic tendency remained, but its basic tenor, its atmosphere was completely altered. No longer was the world a great, multi-purpose stage upon which the I, in ever-changing costumes and continually transforming the scenery at will, could play out its own inner tragedies and comedies. It had now become a devastated area. Before the war, it had been possible to criticize that which was mechanical and rigid about capitalist culture from a lofty vitalistic angle. This was an innocuous and safe intellectual exercise, for the being of society appeared to stand undisturbed and to guarantee the safe existence of parasitical subjectivism. Since the downfall of the Wilhelmine régime the social world had started to constitute something alien to this subjectivism; the collapse of that world which subjectivism was continually criticizing, but which formed the indispensable basis of its existence, was lurking at every door. There was no longer any firm means of support. And in its abandoned condition, the solitary Ego stood in fear and anxiety.

As a rule, relatively similar social situations produce relatively similar tendencies in thought and feeling. Before the outbreak of the 1848 revolution, which was an international, European event, Romantic individualism went to pieces for good. The most important thinker during its crisis and fall, the Dane Søren Kierkegaard, formulated in the most original way the philosophy of the then current Romantic-individualistic agony. No wonder that now, when this depressed mood was already starting to make itself felt — years ahead of the actual crisis — as a foreboding of future gloomy events, a renascence of Kierkegaard's philosophy was proclaimed by the new phase's leading minds, Husserl's pupil Heidegger and the former psychiatrist Karl Jaspers. Of course they did so with up-to-date modifications. Orthodox

Protestant religiosity and Kierkegaard's strictly Lutheran faith in the Bible were of no use to present needs. But Kierkegaard's critique of Hegelian philosophy, as a critique of all striving for objectivity and universal validity by reasoned thought, and of all concepts of historical progress, acquired a very strong contemporary influence. So did Kierkegaard's argumentation of an 'existential philosophy' from the deepest despair of an extreme, self-mortifying subjectivism which sought to justify itself in the very pathos of this despair, in its professed exposure of all ideals of socio-historical life as mere vapid and vain ideas, in contrast to the subject, which alone existed. The altered historical situation did, of course, dictate far-reaching changes. Again, these lay chiefly in the fact that Kierkegaard's philosophy was aimed against the bourgeois idea of progress, against Hegel's idealist dialectics, whereas the renovators of existential philosophy were already principally at odds with Marxism, although this seldom found overt and direct expression in their writings; at times they attempted to exploit the reactionary aspects of Hegelian philosophy on behalf of this new campaign. That in Kierkegaard existential philosophy was already no more than the ideology of the saddest philistinism, of fear and trembling, of anxiety, did not stop it conquering wide intellectual circles in Germany on the eve of Hitler's seizure of power and the nihilistic period of so-called heroic realism. On the contrary: this pretentiously tragic philistinism was precisely the socio-psychological reason for the influence of Heidegger and Jaspers.

It was this mood of despair, and not deep-seated programmatic differences, which distinguished existential philosophy from the rest of vitalism. Admittedly it was more than a matter of chance or merely terminology that the emphatically used catchword of 'life' was succeeded by an emphasis on 'existence'. Although the difference was one of mood far more than philosophical method, it nevertheless expressed something new in content and not trivial: the intensity of the loneliness, disappointment and despair created a new

content. The emphatic stress on 'life' signified the conquest of the world through subjectivity; hence the fascist activists of vitalism, who were about to succeed Heidegger and Jaspers, revived this catchword, although they gave it a new content once more. 'Existence' as a philosophical leitmotif implied the rejection of a great deal that vitalism had elsewhere approved as 'alive', and this was now presented as inessential, non-existential.

Certainly this mood was not unknown in pre-war vitalism. It is obvious in Nietzsche, although in his case the selection from 'life', the rebuttal of a portion of 'life' suggests rather the militant vitalism of fascism and pre-fascism. But Dilthey and Simmel were no strangers to such moods either. Let us remember Simmel's 'tragedy of culture' and his cynically resigned attempts at solving it. And even Dilthey stated once: 'And the contemporary analysis of human existence fills us all with a feeling of fragility, of the might of the dark impulses, of being afflicted with obscure visions and illusions, of the finiteness in everything that constitutes life, even where these things give rise to the highest constructions of communal life.'[76]

But it would be wrong to see only a quantitative difference here, a difference of accent. Granted, in order to recognize that the social and psychical motives which existentialism engendered were operative from the start, it is important that we heed the communal foundation, the being of society in the imperialist period. It is equally important, on the other hand, not to overlook what was specifically new about it. We might say that the same motives now appeared in different proportions, thus bringing us closer to that which was new. For the basic philosophical mood of existentialism is expressed in just this qualitative change of proportion. Whereas the earlier vitalism had been mainly concerned with rejecting the 'moribund formations' of social being and confronting them with the vivacity of total subjectivity as organ of the conquest of 'life', the cleft now appeared within the subject. Whereas before – in the context of the aristocratic epistemo-

logy this necessarily entailed – human beings were divided to some extent into two classes, the one living out life and the other torn from it, now the life of each human being, life in general was considered at risk. And the peril was expressed in the very feeling of becoming inessential, of succumbing to the un-living. The emphatic stress on existence instead of life, even in contrast to life, expressed precisely this fear of life's becoming inessential in general; and it indicated a search for that core of genuineness in subjectivity which, it was hoped, man could still endeavour to rescue from the imminent general destruction. So the pathos of the new orientation expressed the yearning to rescue naked existence from a universal collapse, and therein lay this basic mood's affinity with Kierkegaard's.

Heidegger united Diltheyan tendencies and phenomenology more resolutely and consciously than Scheler. He even brought description and hermeneutics closer together than Dilthey himself had done, and this naturally meant a reinforcement of overt subjectivism. He stated: 'The methodical meaning of phenomenological description is *interpretation*.'[77] With him even contemplation and thought appear as 'distant derivatives of understanding. The phenomenological "intuition of the essence" too is based on existential understanding.'[78]

Despite this heightening of subjectivistic tendencies, Heidegger represented perhaps even more strongly than his predecessors the philosophical 'third way': the claim to be above the antithesis of idealism and materialism (which he terms realism). 'That which-is-in-being (*Seiendes*) *is* independent of experience, cognition and comprehension, through which it is inferred, discovered, defined. But Being (*Sein*) "is" only in the understanding of that which-is-in-being, to whose Being belongs something like an understanding of Being.'[79] This epistemological hocus-pocus, so typical of the whole imperialist period, was carried out by Heidegger such that he always says 'existence' (*Dasein*), thus giving the impression of an objectivity independent of human consciousness,

although by 'existence' he meant nothing more than human existence, indeed only, in the final analysis, its manifestation in the consciousness.

Heidegger solved this crucial question of the philosophical 'third way' on the basis of apodictic statement and 'essential intuition'. He himself was obliged to see that through his position, he was approaching that vicious circle which Dilthey had perceived with alarm in the earlier vitalism. 'But if interpretation must operate within the bounds of the understood and be sustained by it, how then is it to yield scientific results without travelling in a circle, especially if, moreover, the presupposed understanding moves within the general ken of mankind and the world?'[80] But whereas Dilthey paused to regard the circle with scientifically honest alarm, Heidegger resolutely cut the knot with the aid of 'essential intuition' (with which, because of its irrationalistic arbitrariness, anything at all can be sought out, especially by means of an ontological transition to Being). For understanding 'proves' (?) to be 'the expression of the existential pre-construction of existence itself . . . Because understanding, in its existential sense, is the potential Being of existence, the ontological hypotheses of historical perception surmount, in principle, the rigour of the exact sciences. Mathematics are not stricter than history, but only narrower with regard to the radius of the existential foundations pertaining to mathematics.'

The special significance of the historical in Heidegger we shall discuss later. Here it is only important to establish that Heidegger 'ontologically' smuggled 'understanding', i.e., a procedure governed purely by consciousness, into objective Being and thus tried to create, in his own way, just as ambiguous a contrast between subjectivity and objectivity as Mach, in his own period, had done with regard to the sphere of apprehension. Both, in reality, were carrying out the same transference – though in a different form, as befitted their different intentions – of purely subjective-idealistic positions into objective (i.e., pseudo-objective) ones. It is just that the Machists were far more open and straightforward in

translating direct observations into the only (pseudo-objective) reality accessible to us, whereas Heidegger was presenting the project of a – professedly – special science of pure objectivity, of ontology. To be sure he was no more successful than the earlier phenomenologists in showing how to find a way from objective reality 'set in parentheses' to genuine objectivity independent of consciousness. On the contrary: he posited a close and organic connection between phenomenology and ontology, allowing the latter to grow out of the former without further ado. 'Phenomenology is the mode of access to and the deciding mode of determining that which is to become the theme of ontology. *Ontology is only possible as phenomenology*.'[81] That this had to do with the intuitivistic (and hence irrationalistic) arbitrariness of 'essential intuition' is indicated by the definition of the object which directly precedes it as: 'Patently that which generally is *not* immediately manifest, which is *concealed* in relation to that which generally is immediately manifest, but which at the same time intrinsically belongs to that which generally is immediately manifest, and so as to constitute its meaning and ground.' This is the very '*Being* (*Sein*) of that which-is-in-being (*Seienden*)': the object of ontology.

The advance in Heidegger's proposition as against Machism lies in the fact that he zealously made the difference between essence and phenomenon his central concern, whereas Machism could only draw overtly subjectivistic ('thought-sparing') distinctions in the phenomenal world. But the advance, which contributed much to Heidegger's influence in a period hankering after objectivity, promptly defeated its own ends in the manner of his answers. For in this method, 'intuition of the essence' alone can decide what is to be comprehended as 'concealed essence' in immediate present reality perceived directly by the subject. Thus with Heidegger too, the objectivity of the ontological materiality remained purely declarative, and the proclamation of ontological objectivity could lead only to a heightening of the pseudo-objectivism and – owing to the intuitivistic selection principle

and criterion – irrationality of this sphere of objectiveness.

But the terminological camouflaging of subjective idealism was exposed each time that Heidegger came to speak of concrete questions. Let us quote just one example: ' "*There is*" *truth only insofar and as long as there is existence* ... Newton's laws, the thesis of contradiction, every truth in general, these are true only as long as existence *is*. Before there was any existence and after there is existence no longer, there was and will not be any truth because, as a thing inferred, a discovery and thing discovered, it *cannot* then be.'[82] That is not less subjective-idealistic than the view of any follower of Kant or Mach-Avenarius. This juggling with quasi-objective categories on an extremely subjectivistic basis pervades Heidegger's entire philosophy. He claimed to be arguing an objective doctrine of Being, an ontology, but he then defined the ontological essence of the category most central to his world on a purely subjectivistic basis, with pseudo-objectivistic expressions. He said of existence: 'Ontologically, existence is fundamentally different from all that is present and real. Its "permanency" is grounded not in the substantiality of a substance, but in the "*autonomy*" of the existing self whose Being was grasped as care.'[83] And in another place: 'That which-is-in-being ... is always we ourselves. The Being (*Sein*) of this which-is-in-being (*das Seiende*) is *always mine*.'[84] The arbitrariness examined above in the transition to (professed) objectivity is voiced quite plainly in some foregoing methodological remarks: 'Higher than reality stands *possibility*. Phenomenological understanding lies solely in seizing it as possibility.' For clearly, in any serious attempt to conquer subjectivist-irrationalistic arbitrariness scientifically (and also philosophically), only objective reality can produce a standard for genuine or merely imagined possibility. Hegel, therefore, was very right to distinguish sharply between abstract and concrete possibility. Kierkegaard's conscious subjectivism first reversed the philosophical-hierarchical positions and placed possibility higher than reality in order to create room – a vacuum – for the free

decision of the individual concerned with absolutely nothing beyond saving his soul. Heidegger followed Kierkegaard in this, albeit with a difference which very much impaired the logic and honesty of his philosophizing. For in contrast to his master on this point, he still avowed the objectivity of the categories thus arising (the so-called existentials).

The claim to objectivity is even more marked with Heidegger than with Scheler, and yet he made the subjectivistic character of phenomenology far more salient. And the Husserlian tendency towards a strictly scientific approach had now already faded completely. In striving to argue an objective doctrine of Being, an ontology, Heidegger needed to draw a sharp dividing-line between it and anthropology. But it turns out that when he came to his central problems and was not engaged in pure, detached methodology, his ontology is in actual fact merely a vitalistic anthropology with an objectivistic mask. (So here again Heidegger was faced with an insoluble dilemma of the kind we have noted with Dilthey. And here again the same contrast between the two holds good: Dilthey shrank from the dilemma and tried to evade it, whereas Heidegger cut the knot in a loftily declarative, overtly irrationalistic manner.) Characteristic, for example, are his efforts to prove the underlying anthropological bias in Kant's 'transcendental logic', efforts intended to make Kant just as much a forerunner of existential philosophy as Simmel had made him out to be a forerunner of vitalism.

Over and above his reading of Kant, however, Heidegger expressed this tendency at every point. Anthropology today, in hiw view, is not a special discipline, 'but the word signifies a *basic tendency* of man's present attitude to himself and to the whole of that which-is-in-being (*das Seiende*). In accordance with this basic attitude, something is only perceived and understood if it has found an *anthropological explanation*. Anthropology not only seeks the truth *about* man, but now lays claim to decide *what truth can signify in general*.'[85] And he clarified this attitude, which implied a factual identity between his ontology and anthropology, by saying that

while no age had known as much about man as the present one, it was also true that 'no age knew less what man is than the present age. To no age has man become so questionable as to ours.'

This plainly expresses the negativity of Heidegger's philosophical tendencies. For him philosophy was no longer the detached 'strict' science of Husserl, but also no longer the path to a concrete world-outlook, as vitalism from Dilthey to Spengler and Scheler had been. Its task was rather: 'to keep the investigation open by means of questions'.[86] With a pathos reminiscent of Kierkegaard, Heidegger expounded his position as follows: 'Does it make sense and are we entitled to comprehend man as "creative" and hence as "infinite" on the basis of his intrinsic finiteness – the fact that he needs "ontology", i.e., understanding of Being –, when it is just the idea of infinite essence that rebuffs nothing so radically as an ontology? . . . Or have we already become all too much the dupes of organization, industry and speed for it to be possible for us to be familiar with the essential, simple and permanent . . .?'[87]

Thus what Heidegger termed phenomenology and ontology was in reality no more than an abstractly mythicizing, anthropological description of human existence; in his concrete phenomenological descriptions, however, it unexpectedly turned into an – often grippingly interesting – description of intellectual philistinism during the crisis of the imperialist period. Heidegger himself admitted this to a certain degree. His programme was to show that which-is-in-being 'as it *immediately and mostly* is, in its average *everyday state*'.[88] Now what is really interesting about Heidegger's philosophizing is the extremely detailed account of how 'the human being', the supporting subject of existence, 'immediately and for the most part' dissipates and loses himself in this everyday state.

Here reasons of space, apart from anything else, prevent us from retailing this account. Let us stress just one element, namely that the unauthenticity of the Heideggerian everyday

existence, that which he calls the 'fallen state' (*Verfallensein*), is caused by social being. According to Heidegger, man's social character is an 'existential' of existence, which he regards as a term in the sphere of existence equivalent to categories in thinking. Now, social existence signifies the anonymous dominance of 'the one' (*das Man*). We need to quote at some length from this account in order that the reader can receive a concrete picture of Heidegger's ontology of the everyday state:

> The Who is not this person or that person, not oneself and not several and not the sum of all. The 'Who' is the neutral, the one (*das Man*) . . . It is by being inconspicuous and incapable of being pinned down that 'the one' evolves his actual dictatorship. We enjoy and amuse ourselves in the way *one* enjoys himself; we read, view and judge literature and art in the way *one* looks and judges; but we also withdraw from the 'great mass' of people in the way *one* withdraws; we find 'outrageous' whatever *one* finds outrageous. The one, which is no specific person and all persons, although not as the sum of them, dictates the type of being of the everyday state . . . Each is the other and nobody is he himself. The *one*, the answer to the question as to the *Who* of everyday existence, is the *nobody* to which all existence in the being-among-one-another (*im Untereinandersein*) has already delivered itself up. In the ontological characteristics of everyday being-among-one-another on display: staleness, mediocrity, levelling, public life, shedding of being and acquiescence lies the nearest 'permanence' of existence . . . One is in the mode of non-independence and unauthenticity. This mode of being does not signify any reduction in the facticity of existence, any more than 'the one' as nobody is a cipher. On the contrary, existence is, in this ontological type, an *ens realissimum*, provided that 'reality' is understood as being governed by existence. To be sure, 'the one' is as little present as is existence in general. The more obviously

> 'the one' behaves, the more incomprehensible and latent it is, but it is also all the less of a nought. To unprejudiced ontic-ontological 'vision' it will reveal itself as the 'most real subject' of the everyday state.[89]

Such descriptions constitute the strongest and most suggestive part of *Being and Time*, and in all likelihood they formed the basis of the book's broad and profound effect. Here, with the tools of phenomenology. Heidegger was giving a series of interesting images taken from the inner life, from the world-view of the dissolute bourgeois mind of the post-war years. These images are suggestive because they provide – on the descriptive level – a genuine and true-to-life picture of those conscious reflexes which the reality of post-war imperialist capitalism triggered off in those unable or unwilling to surpass what they experienced in their individual existence and to go further towards objectivity, i.e., towards exploring the socio-historical causes of their experiences. With these tendencies, Heidegger was not alone in his time; similar tendencies were expressed not only in Jaspers's philosophy, but also in a large part of the imaginative literature of the period (it will suffice, perhaps, to mention Céline's novel, *Journey to the End of the Night*, and Joyce, Gide, Malraux, etc.). However, even if we acknowledge the partial accuracy of these accounts of spiritual states, we must ask how far they square with objective reality, how far their descriptions go beyond the immediacy of the reacting subjects. Of course this question is chiefly of philosophical moment; imaginative literature operates within far more elastic limits, although its stature is still determined by the comprehensive concreteness and depth of the representation of reality. But to treat the problems arising from this is not within the scope of these studies.

Heidegger's descriptions are related to the spiritual conditions prompted by the crisis of post-war imperialistic capitalism. There is evidence for this not only in the influence exercised by *Being and Time*, far beyond the sphere of the

really philosophically-minded – it was repeatedly singled out for praise and censure by philosophical critics. What Heidegger was describing was the subjective-bourgeois, intellectual reverse side of the economic categories of capitalism – in the form, of course, of a radically idealistic subjectifying and hence a distortion. In this respect Heidegger was carrying on Simmel's tendency 'to construct a basement underneath historical materialism', professedly in order to render visible the philosophical, indeed metaphysical hypotheses of this doctrine. The difference, however, tells us more than the affinity. It is a difference expressed in both the methodology and the mood of Heidegger's work. Methodologically, in the fact that, in contrast to Simmel, who was expressly criticizing historical materialism and trying to 'deepen' it through personal reinterpretation, Heidegger did not give the least indication of doing anything similar. Not only is the name of Marx absent from *Being and Time*, even from allusions where it is patently relevant. The content also dispenses with all objective categories of economic reality.

Heidegger's method was more radically subjectivistic: without exception his descriptions pertain to spiritual reflexes to socio-economic reality. Here we have manifested in practice the inner identity of phenomenology and ontology, the purely subjective character of even the latter in spite of all declared objectivity. Indeed it is even manifest that this shift to ontology – an allegedly objective ontology – rendered the philosophical view of the world still more subjectivistic than it was at the time of the overtly radical subjectivism of a thinker like Simmel. For in the latter, there are at least glimmers of objective social reality with its contours distorted, whereas in Heidegger this reality is reduced to purely a series of spiritual states described phenomenologically. This shift of method is intimately connected with the change in the basic mood. Simmel was philosophizing in the very hopeful early days of vitalism. Despite establishing a 'tragedy of culture', and for all his critique of capitalist civilization, he still considered money, as we may recall, the

'guardian of inwardness'. In Heidegger, these illusions had crumbled long ago. The individual's inner life had long since renounced all world-conquering plans; no longer was its social environment regarded as something problematical in itself, but in whose domain pure inwardness could nonetheless lead a free life. The surrounding world was now an uncanny, mysterious permanent threat to everything that would constitute the essence of subjectivity. This again, to be sure, was not a new experience for bourgeois man under capitalism; Ibsen, for example, had portrayed it many decades earlier in the famous scene where his Peer Gynt – symbolizing the problem of the essentiality, or lack of it, in his own life – peels an onion and finds no core, only peel. In Heidegger this expression of the ageing and despairing Peer Gynt became the determining maxim of his descriptions. This is the meaning of the dominance of 'the one' (translated back into the language of social life: of bourgeois-democratic public life in the imperialist period, and thus, say, the Weimar Republic): 'But the understanding of existence in "the one" perpetually *overlooks* itself, in its projects, in respect of the genuine ontological possibilities.'[90] For Heidegger, this was something akin to an ontological proof for anti-democratism. And he amplified this idea in a graphic concept: 'Existence hurtles out of the him-self into the it-self, into the bottomlessness and nothingness of the unauthentic everyday state.' It is just this which is concealed through public life and is manifested as 'concrete life'. But this is a deceptive whirlpool. 'This continual breaking loose from authenticity while always simulating it, at one with the process of tearing into "the one" . . . Accordingly *the average everyday state of existence* may be defined as the falsifying-disclosed, dejected-projecting (*geworfen-entwerfend*) state of being-in-the-world, concerned with its intrinsic ontological potential in its being with the "world" and in its co-being with others.'[91]

This makes it clear that with Heidegger, the transition from phenomenology to ontology was, at root, as much directed against the socialist perspective on social develop-

ment as the irrationalistic method of all leading bourgeois thinkers since Nietzsche. Germany's post-war crisis and the class struggles exacerbated as a result of it – with, in the background, the existence and growing strength of the socialist Soviet Union and, among both the working class and intelligentsia, the spread of a Marxism taken a stage higher by Lenin – impelled all men into making a personal choice far more strongly than was the case in quieter times. Heidegger, as we have noted, did not explicitly contest the economic doctrines of Marxism-Leninism or the political consequences they entailed – neither he nor the caste he represented was capable of it. He attempted rather to avoid the necessity of drawing social conclusions by 'ontologically' branding all man's public activity as 'unauthentic'.

Bourgeois man's sense of becoming inessential, indeed a nonentity, was a universal experience among the intelligentsia of this period. Hence Heidegger's complicated trains of thought, his laborious phenomenological introspections struck upon the material of experiences widespread among this class and found an answering chord. Heidegger was here preaching a retreat from all social dealings just as much as Schopenhauer, in his time, had proclaimed a withdrawal from the bourgeois idea of progress, from the democratic revolution. Heidegger's retreat, however, implies a reactionary stand far stronger than that to be found in Schopenhauer's quietism. At the height of the revolution, to be sure, even this quietism could, within the thinker advocating it, all too easily tilt over into counter-revolutionary activity, and Nietzsche demonstrated how easily a counter-revolutionary activism could be evolved from Schopenhauer's hypotheses on the philosophical level as well. One may say without undue exaggeration that in the period of the imperialistic bourgeoisie's struggle against socialism, Heidegger was related to Hitler and Rosenberg as Schopenhauer, in his own day, was related to Nietzsche.

All the same, events never repeat themselves mechanically – not even in the history of philosophy. The human emotional

emphasis in the withdrawing process was totally different, indeed opposed, in Schopenhauer and Heidegger. With the latter, the feeling of despair no longer left the individual free scope for a 'beatific' aesthetic and religious contemplation as in Schopenhauer. His sense of peril already encompassed the whole realm of individual existence. And although the solipsism of the phenomenological method may have distorted the depiction of it, it was still a social fact: the inner state of the bourgeois individual (especially the intellectual) within a crumbling monopoly capitalism, facing the prospect of his downfall. Thus Heidegger's despair had two facets: on the one hand, the remorseless baring of the individual's inner nothingness in the imperialistic crisis; on the other – and because the social grounds for this nothingness were being fetishistically transformed into something timeless and anti-social – the feeling to which it gave rise could very easily turn into a desperate revolutionary activity. It is certainly no accident that Hitler's propaganda continually appealed to despair. Among the working masses, admittedly, the despair was occasioned by their socio-economic situation. Among the intelligentsia, however, that mood of nihilism and despair from whose subjective truth Heidegger proceeded, which he conceptualized, clarified philosophically and canonized as 'authentic', created a basis favourable to the efficacy of Hitlerian agitation.

This everyday state of being, dominated by 'the one', was therefore actually a non-being. And in fact Heidegger defined Being not as immediately given, but as extremely remote: 'The state of being (*das Seiende*) in which each of us rests is ontologically the remotest state.'[92] This most intrinsic part of man, he maintained, was forgotten and buried in everyday life; and it was precisely the task of ontology to rescue it from oblivion.

This programmatic attitude to life (the social life of his period) determined Heidegger's whole method. We have already indicated, more than once, the unsurmountable subjectivism of the phenomenology, the pseudo-objectivity

of the ontology. But only now that Heidegger's world-picture stands before us in a certain concreteness with regard to both content and structure is it plain that this method, for all its objective fragility, was the only possible one for his purposes. For in Heidegger's conception, man's life in society was a matter not of a relation between subjectivity and objectivity, not of a reciprocal relationship between subject and object, but of 'authenticity' and 'unauthenticity' within the same subject. Only in appearance, in the methodological expressions, did the ontological surpassing of objective reality 'set in parentheses' tend towards objectivity; in actual fact it was turning to another, purportedly deeper, layer of subjectivity. Indeed it may be said that with Heidegger, a category (an existential) expressed Being all the more genuinely and came all the closer to Being the less it was encumbered by the conditions of objective reality. For that reason his defining terms (mood, care, fear, summons, etc.) were without exception of a decidedly subjective character.

But for that very reason, Heidegger's ontology was bound to grow more irrationalistic the more it developed its true nature. Admittedly, Heidegger was constantly trying to shut himself off from irrationalism. Here too it was his aim to elevate himself above the antithesis of rationalism and irrationalism, to find a philosophical 'third road', just as in the question of idealism and materialism. But for him it was impossible. He repeatedly criticized the limits of rationalism, but would then add to his critique: 'No slighter matter, therefore, is that falsification of phenomena which banishes them to the refuge of the irrational. Irrationalism – as the counterpart of rationalism – speaks only squintingly of that to which the latter is blind.'[93] But since, in Heidegger's eyes, this blindness lies in the fact that rationalism takes into account the observable facts and laws of objective reality, a loss of all real possibility results from his exclusion of irrationalism. For if one removes from a concrete state every condition relevant to observable reality, if this concrete state arises solely in the inner life, it is inevitable that the consequent

findings will take on an irrationalistic character.

This was already so with Kierkegaard. The latter, however, although able to work with theological categories and hence to attain a quasi-rationality or quasi-dialectic, did not shrink from the most extreme conclusions and spoke, with regard to precisely the decisive questions of 'existence', of the paradox, i.e., of irrationality. Heidegger lacked, on the one hand, the possibility of resorting to overtly theological categories, and, on the other, the courage openly to declare his allegiance to irrationalism. Yet every one of his ontological statements shows that the de-reification of all conditions of objectivity in reality – however we may phrase this – leads to irrationalism. Let us give a single example. Heidegger writes of 'mood' (*Stimmung*). This is realized in principle in its Why, Whence and Whither. 'This ontological character of existence which is shrouded in its Whence and Whither, but which is all the more openly revealed to existence itself, this "That it is" we call the thrownness (*Geworfenheit*) of this state of being in its There, and this means that it constitutes the There *qua* being-in-the-world.' But the resulting '*facticity is not the matter-of-factness of the factum brutum of something which is present, but an ontological character of existence which, although at first forced away, has been taken up into existence*'.[94] As long as Being – in Heidegger's 'project' – intervenes or intends to intervene, the findings (and the road to obtaining them) can only be irrationalistic. The road to Being means a casting aside of all objective conditions of reality. At all times, Heidegger's ontology imperiously demanded this in order that man (subject, existence) might escape the power of 'the one' that rendered him unauthentic and took away his essence.

We thus see that, inadvertently, Heidegger's ontology was turning into a moral doctrine, indeed almost a religious sermon; this ethico-religious epistemological shift also shows the determining influence of Kierkegaard on Heidegger's propositions and method. The gist of the sermon is that man should become 'essential' and make ready to hear and

understand 'the call of conscience' in order to mature to 'resolution'. Heidegger gave a very detailed account of this process too; again, we can give only a brief outline of it here. The disclosure of the nothingness concealed in the 'fallen state' (*Verfallensein*) is achieved through ontology: 'The essence of the originally nullifying nothing lies herein: it begins by putting being-there (*Da-sein*) before the state of being (*das Seiende*) as such . . . Being-there means: bound immanency (*Hineingehaltenheit*) in nothingness.'[95]

That is the essence of Heidegger's 'existence', and men were deemed to differ merely in respect of whether or not they were conscious of it. The attainment of awareness took place through the conscience: 'Conscience is the call of anxiety from the uncanniness of being-in-the-world, summoning existence to its most intimate potential state of guiltiness . . . Understanding of the summons initiates personal existence into the uncanniness of its isolation.'[96]

The understanding of this summons brought man to a state of resolution. Heidegger stressed the significance of this 'existential' with great pathos. After what has gone before, it comes as no surprise when he strongly denies that 'resolution' (*Entschlossenheit*) in respect of man's surroundings might bring about even the slightest change; not even the dominance of 'the one' is disturbed. 'The "world" close at hand does not become another "in substance", and the circle of the "other ones" remains unchanged . . . The irresolution of "the one" still holds sway, only it is incapable of combating resolute existence.'[97] Here, the methodology and content of Heidegger's philosophy are expressing in an extremely complicated (but above all, mannered) terminology the intellectual philistine's feelings in a time of severe crisis: the threat to personal 'existence' is so deflected as to prevent its giving rise to any obligation to alter one's external living conditions or indeed to collaborate in transforming objective social reality. Difficult though Heidegger may be to grasp, this much was correctly read out of his philosophy.

So the only result arrived at here was the insight that

existence as such is to blame. And the authentic life of the resolute man now constituted a preparation for death; 'a foreshadowing of the possibility', in Heidegger's terminology. Here again there are traces of Kierkegaard, though without his pronounced Protestant theology.

Like every vitalistic philosophy, this Heideggerian theology without positive religion or a personal God was, of course, bound to contain a new doctrine of time of its own. This too was a methodological necessity. For the rigid opposition of space and time was one of the weakest points of undialectical rationalism. But whereas a true way of surmounting that opposition must lie in the dialectical interaction of space and time founded in objective reality, irrational vitalism had always directed its sharpest attacks against the rationalistic time-concept, taking time and space – like culture and civilization in the realm of social philosophy – as diametrically opposed, indeed warring principles. To conquer time was very important to vitalism in a positive respect – this is the reverse side of the aforesaid polemical intention – because the identification of experience and life (existence) crucial to its pseudo-objectivism was only possible if there was a subjectified, irrationalistic conception of time to meet this demand.

Heidegger laid much weight on this. He sharply divorced himself from Bergson whom he condemned – along with Aristoteles and Hegel – as representing the 'vulgar' view of time. This 'vulgar' time was the accepted one that knows past, present and future; the time of the 'fallen' world of the 'one', the time of measurement, clock-time, etc. Genuine time, on the contrary, knew no sequentiality: 'The future is *not later* than that which has come to pass, and the latter *not earlier* than the present. Temporaneity proceeds as futurity which has come to pass and is bringing to pass (*gewesende-gegenwärtigende Zukunft*).'[98]

Epistemologically, the contrast to Bergson (but not to Aristotle and Hegel) was merely a difference of nuance. For each of them – Bergson *and* Heidegger – posited a subjectively

experienced time as authentic time in opposition to real objective time. Only, in the case of Bergson, who in the essence of his epistemology was a pre-war figure whose thought shows many affinities with Simmel and with pragmatism, experienced time was an organon of the subjective-individualistic conquest of the world. In Heidegger's diseased philosophy, however, 'real' time is de-secularized and becomes devoid of content, theological, concentrated purely on the element of personal decision. Hence Bergson aimed his sallies chiefly against 'spatial' time, against concepts formed in the exact sciences, and his 'real' time was oriented to aesthetic experience, whereas with Heidegger, vulgar time corresponds to an existence that has fallen foul of the 'one', and real time points towards death. (Here again it can be easily spotted that the difference between Heidegger's and Bergson's view of time was of a social character and determined by their respective adversaries. In essence Bergson was polemicizing against the scientific-materialistic world-view obtaining during the rise of the bourgeoisie. Heidegger, even with regard to the theory of time and the reading of historicity closely associated with it, was chiefly attacking the new adversary, the historical materialism whose influence was being felt in all areas of life.) In both cases, however, this antithesis within the concept of time was a means to setting up an irrationalistic philosophy. Granted, Heidegger did 'discover' that time played a hitherto unobserved role in Kant's *Critique of Pure Reason*, above all in the chapter on schemata or essential forms. The central position of time, Heidegger stated, 'thus disrupts the dominion of reason and understanding. "Logic" has lost its long-standing primacy in metaphysics. Its idea is becoming questionable.'[99] Thus Kant becomes, for Heidegger, one of the fathers of modern irrationalism.

In view of this interpretation of time Heidegger's second chief programmatic point, proof of the elementary historicality of 'existence' as the basis for comprehending history, turns out to be pure shadow-boxing. Heidegger was right in

making a stand against the neo-Kantians who were trying to argue historicality from a subjective 'setting', and in indicating that Being must be historical in order for there to be any historical science. As on many points, vitalism was here preempting the collapse of undialectic idealism. But Heidegger still lagged far behind the neo-Kantians in the concrete definition of his 'existential' historicality. As a consequence the primary phenomenon of history was, for him, existence, i.e., the life of the individual, the 'universal coherence of life between birth and death'. And this too – quite in accordance with the Diltheyan vitalistic method – was defined from experience: 'It (this coherence, G.L.) *consists of* a sequence of experiences "within time".'[100] The result was a double distortion. Firstly, Heidegger did not take the historical data in Nature as the 'originals' (Kant-Laplace theory, Darwinism, etc.), but presented the coherence of human experiences far removed from the 'original state' as the starting-point, the 'primal phenomenon'. Secondly, he failed to observe that his 'primal phenomenon' was derivative: a consequence of that social Being and praxis of men in which alone such a 'coherence' of experiences could come about at all. As far as he did notice a link, he rejected it as belonging to the domain of the 'one'. In so doing, he not only isolated a distorted derivate of human social praxis – as a historical 'primal phenomenon', as 'original' – from real history, but also set them up as antinomies. The tendency to falsify in this way the structure of reality graphically expresses the prefascist character of Heidegger's thinking. Now since the primary historicality was 'ontologically founded' on this basis, the automatic product of it was Heidegger's crucial distinction between 'authentic' and 'unauthentic' history. 'In keeping with the rooting of historicality in anxiety, existence exists as authentically historical or unauthentically historical, all depending.'[101]

But according to Heidegger's reading of history, it was precisely real history which is unauthentic, just as real time is the 'vulgar' kind. In giving history an apparently

ontologically reasoned basis, Heidegger actually took away any kind of historicality, whilst acknowledging as historical only a philistine's moral 'resolution'. In his analysis of everyday existence, Heidegger had already rejected all human orientation towards objective facts or trends in socio-historical life. There he stated:

> One would completely mistake phenomenally *what* mood (*Stimmung*) reveals and *how* it does so, were one aiming at collating with the revealed material that which existence, in the given 'mood', knows, knows about and believes 'simultaneously'. Even if existence is 'secure' in the belief of its 'Whither', or thinks it is rationally enlightened about the Whence, none of this affects the established phenomenal fact that the 'mood' confronts existence with the That of its There, a remorselessly sphinx-like sight. Existentially-ontologically, one has not the least right to suppress the 'evidence' of the existing state through judging by the apodictic certainty of a theoretical perception of that which is purely present.[102]

The illumination of existence can come only from within, for every (to Heidegger's mind: purported) objectively directed perception brings about a casting down (*das Verfallen*), a state of surrender to the 'one' and unauthenticity. Thus it was only logical for Heidegger, in positing the historicality of existence, to refute equally firmly everything objectively historical; Heidegger's historicality, then, has nothing to do with the point 'that existence occurs in a "world-history" '.[103] Here he was polemicizing – quite rightly to some extent – against the old idealistic argumentation of the theory of history. The 'location of the historical problem', he said, 'must not be sought in history as a science of history . . . How history may become a possible *object* of history (in the abstract) can only be inferred from the ontological character of the historical, from historicality and its rootedness in temporaneity.'[104] Here again Heidegger was

pre-empting the collapse of idealism, not unskilfully, by giving the impression that he planned to make the historical nature of existence itself the starting-point of history. But in one breath he was giving this existence itself, as we have observed, a thoroughly subjectivistic definition, while in the next he radically 'purged' the original historicality of existence of all relation to real, objective history. For: 'In accordance with the rooting of history in anxiety, existence exists as either authentically or unauthentically historical.'[105] From this we may logically conclude that 'the authentic being-unto-death, i.e., the finiteness of temporaneity is the latent ground of the historicality of existence'.[106]

This, of course, implies the positing of an 'unauthentic' historicality as well. And here, in accordance with the main substance of his conception, Heidegger almost compromised himself. For if the sole historical issue at stake is that of what one might – in theological language – term 'saving the soul', then there is no clear reason why everything else, whose role cannot be more than, at most, a distraction from Being in history, should likewise have a historical character. But sometimes Heidegger acknowledged a primary and secondary, and sometimes an authentic and unauthentic historicality. 'Implement and work (*Zeug und Werk*) . . . Institutions have their history. But nature too is historical. Granted, that is *not* the case precisely as long as we are speaking of "natural history"; it may be so, on the contrary, as landscape, scene of human settlement and exploitation, as battlefield and shrine.'[107] So not much more emerges from Heidegger's 'unauthentic' history than a Spenglerian 'historicality' (*Geschichtlichkeit*). But whereas, with Spengler, this was an organic part of his conception, with Heidegger it damaged the basic idea and was, in the last analysis, unnecessary ballast. In part it arose from Heidegger's reluctance openly to conform to radical irrationalism, to the radical rejection of any scientific approach; and in part it was a legacy – no longer organic – of the basic theological conception of Heidegger's path to saving the soul, a path which in Heidegger

– godless and soulless – had lost its earlier guiding principles.

This brings to light an important factor in Heidegger's relationship to Kierkegaard. For Heidegger arrived at this twofold view of history as authentic and unauthentic under the influence of Kierkegaard's polemics against Hegel. But as always in history, the reactionary thinker at the less advanced stage was more candid, forthright and rigorous than his imperialistic epigone. (This too, as we have shown more than once, is connected with the fact that Kierkegaard was contesting the bourgeois concept of historical progress, whereas Heidegger was striving to combat the appeal of the socialist view of future developments.) Kierkegaard acknowledged no world-history save in the eyes of God. For man, who in his view – significantly enough – could be only a spectator in history, there is no history but only an individual moral-cum-religious development. Kierkegaard stated: 'For the ethical sphere, world-historical immanence is always confusing, and yet world-historical contemplation lies precisely in immanence. When an individual beholds something ethical, it is the ethical element within him that he sees . . . For it would not be correct to conclude: the more ethically advanced a man is, the more he will see the ethical element in world-history – no, the very opposite is true: the more a man progresses ethically, the less concerned he will be with the world-historical sphere.

> Let me use a metaphor to convey more graphically the difference between the ethical and world-historical spheres, the individual's ethical relation to God and the relation of the world-historical to God. There may be a time when a king has a royal theatre all to himself, but this exclusion of his subjects is fortuitous. It is a different matter when we speak of God and the royal theatre which he has to himself. So the individual's ethical development is the small private theatre where God is the spectator, but occasionally also individual man himself, although he should be essentially the actor, viz., an actor who does not dissemble

> but bares himself, just as all ethical development is a process of exposure to the sight of God. World history, on the contrary, is the royal theatre for God where he is the sole spectator not by accident but essentially so, because he alone *can* be. An existing spirit has no access to this theatre. If he then supposes himself a spectator he is simply forgetting that he himself is meant to be an actor in the little theatre, leaving it to his royal spectator and dramatist to decide how to employ him in the royal drama, the *drama dramatum*.[108]

This forcefully expresses the backlash against Germany's classical literature and philosophy. Whereas for Goethe, the fulfilment of and solution to his Faust's truest ethical problems was possible only in the 'wide world' of Part Two of his play, Kierkegaard restricted ethics to the 'little world' of the first part. And whereas Hegelian ethics coursed into world history, Kierkegaard excluded just this in principle from men's 'existential' activity.

Admittedly with Kierkegaard, as often occurred in this period, vitalism was linked with unresolved questions of bourgeois idealistic dialectics. It was only the weakness of the Hegelian philosophy of history, which ended by contemplating the total course of events to date, that made the Kierkegaardian proposition possible, in that Kierkegaard could pour scorn on this contemplation as being an abstract, professorial, inadequate and indeed humiliating attitude to take towards the important questions of human life, and could counter it with at least the semblance of a praxis. This Kierkegaardian praxis was an ironic revenge on Hegel because the latter, unable to think historical praxis through to its logical end, stopped at the present and let it turn into contemplation ('Minerva's owl'). But in its real essence, Kierkegaard's praxis had nothing to do with the sole really historical praxis. Indeed the fact that Kierkegaard, as we have noted, vehemently disavowed it implied the possibility of reviving, with a certain limited consistency, the old duality of

theological thinking about history. In this, too, the individual soul's path to salvation was the authentic content of history. But the old theology, especially Catholic theology, was capable of incorporating the individual paths to salvation in a theological history of the cosmos and mankind and thus of still arriving, within its own terms of reference, as with Bossuet, at a unified view of history. As we have seen, the soul's path to salvation as the content of history was also the basis of Kierkegaard's view of history. But for Kierkegaard, each man seeking his existence and the saving of his soul had to enter into a direct relationship to Christ, as source of salvation, a relationship that he could realize only from within. And here, in the sphere of authentic existence, all historicality is abolished (and every man as much related to Christ as his first disciples), so that history itself becomes wholly transcendent; only in the recognition that before Christ's appearance, men had a fundamentally different attitude to their own existence are there still traces of a theological historicality. But even here, in the last analysis, two 'types' of existential behaviour confront one another, whereby each type in and for itself lacks history, and the historicality is defined simply by Christ's appearance – which separates periods and types.

It was only possible for Kierkegaard to take his aforesaid ironic revenge on Hegel because, despite the latter's energetic efforts – successful in part – to interpret history purely as the product of human praxis, the salient points of his philosophy of history disappeared in the mists of an idealistic theology. And this gave rise to a contemplation of history at once 'god-like' and *ex cathedra* instead of a theoretical study, which was merely a summing up of the experiences of praxis so far on behalf of a better, more conscious praxis to come. With regard to this contemplation, Kierkegaard's critique had a certain qualified justification. But only, to be sure, *qua* criticism, for as soon as his critique becomes concrete it turns – in contrast to rational Hegelian theology, which rises to the conceptual heights – into an irrational

theology. And it loses its relative justification when Hegel's historicism gives way to the irrationalist's open denial of history.

In Heidegger we find a problem-complex similar to that found in Kierkegaard, but lacking a God, Christ or a soul. Heidegger wanted to create a theological philosophy of history on behalf of 'religious atheism'. Hence the disappearance of all the substantial elements of theology, even Kierkegaard's, with only the now totally empty theological framework remaining. For Kierkegaard too, such categories of the forlorn life of (the Philistine's) isolated individuality as anxiety, care, guilt-feelings, resolution, etc., were the 'existentials' of 'authentic' reality. But Kierkegaard, because of the residue of a theological philosophy of history positing, to his mind, a real history for God, was capable of radically denying historicality for the individual man working out his own salvation. Heidegger, on the other hand, had to disguise this unhistorical existence as 'authentic' history in order to achieve a contrast to the denial of real history (the 'unauthentic'). Again the socio-historical content was the deciding factor in this antithesis. Kierkegaard, whose thinking rejected bourgeois-democratic progress, could still envisage a way back into the feudal religious world; even if, as we have shown, this conception was already susceptible in his work to a decadent, bourgeois dissolution. Heidegger, who wrote during the crisis of monopoly capitalism and in the vicinity of a socialist State ever gaining in strength and appeal, could evade the consequences of the crisis period only by disparaging real history as 'unauthentic'. This also meant acknowledging as 'authentic' history only such a spiritual development as would, through care, despair and so forth, lead men away from social actions and decisions, at the same time confirming them inwardly in such a state of disorientation and perplexity as would encourage to the utmost a switch to reactionary activism of the Hitlerian variety.

So the whole pretentious point of Heidegger's philosophy of time and history does not go beyond his ontology of

everyday life. For its content is still merely the inner life of the modern philistine frightened to death by nothingness, a nonentity in himself, and gradually becoming aware of his nothingness.

After this analysis of Heidegger's existential philosophy we can discuss that of Jaspers far more briefly. For in both cases, both the point of departure and the conclusions are remarkably similar. That Jaspers was openly writing as a psychologist is instructive inasmuch as this, in connection with the development of phenomenology in Scheler and Heidegger, and with the growing influence of Dilthey's descriptive psychology, completes the exposure of their original pseudo-objectivity.

Jaspers's first influential philosophical work, *Psychology of World-Outlooks* (1919), was an attempt to fulfil the Diltheyan programme for a typology of philosophies. In this book, to be sure, Jaspers had already completely renounced Dilthey's dream that typology might point the way to an objective philosophical world-view. He sought precisely the opposite. Under the influence of Kierkegaard and Nietzsche, whom Jaspers regarded as *the* philosophers of the day, and also under the influence of Max Weber's sociological relativism, this typology was meant to proclaim the total rejection of the very possibility and value of an objectively philosophical knowledge.

In this respect, Jaspers took radical vitalistic relativism farther than any of his predecessors. For everything objective about knowledge he used the scornfully ironic term 'shell' (*Gehäuse*), thereby restating the old vitalistic antithesis of the alive and the moribund, though with the special nuance that here, it is avowedly all objectivity which appears as moribund and extinct. Jaspers wrote of this question: 'Every doctrine formulated of the whole becomes a shell devoid of the original experiencing of the ultimate situations, and it thwarts those energies which are actively seeking the meaning of future existence in self-willed experience. For this it substitutes the calm of a fully perceived and perfected,

soul-appeasing world of eternally present meaning.'[109]

If we just recall Simmel's statements – extensively quoted earlier – on the relation of the soul to the objective spirit, and on the fairly relativistically conceived 'tragedy of culture', we can see how far vitalism has proceeded towards relativistic nihilism in the meantime. Jaspers regarded every 'shell' not only as fateful for life in general or for individual man's development – the only development that mattered to him – but also as a social threat: '. . . with the assertion of the one truth as universally valid for all men . . . *falsehood* immediately sets in.'[110] That is taking a Kierkegaardian line. The statement proceeds from the supposition that all universal, commonly binding objective truth is necessarily opposed to the inner subjective veracity and sincerity of the individual, that the two are hostile and mutually exclusive. (We find Nietzsche already pursuing similar arguments.) Anti-scientific thinking thereby acquires an ethico-metaphysical slant. And with Jaspers, as with his exemplars, this slant has an anti-democratic character. Jaspers saw the powers of objectivity that threatened subjective truth as residing almost exclusively where a democratic rule by the masses was springing up. Hence fanaticism and brute force were, for him, the salient necessary consequences of such a 'falsehood', born of the world's belief in the truths of the 'shells'. Already in Heidegger, we find a plainly anti-democratic tendency: the mythical, 'phenomenological' figure of the 'one' is a distilled caricature of that 'anonymity' and 'lack of responsibility' which reactionary propaganda has always taken as the chief characteristic of any democracy. In Jaspers, this tendency amounted to the most extreme philistinism. Only with the 'inwardly' turned, purely self-reliant individuum (in the intellectual philistine rejecting all public life) could, Jaspers believed, truth, integrity and humanity be found; and – in true German petty-bourgeois style – he represented all mass influence as falseness and barbarity.

This radical subjectivism manifested in the doctrine of the 'shell' is what is specific to Jaspers's philosophy. Any

knowledge of the objective world had, accordingly, only a technical use; and only the 'illumination of existence' (*Existenzerhellung*) had a real significance that touched on Being. Jaspers expressed himself as follows on this central point of his thinking:

> Existential philosophy would be *lost* at once if it *believed it knew again what man is*. It would again provide the basic outlines for an investigation of human and animal life in its types, and would revert to being anthropology, psychology, sociology. It can have meaning only if it remains without a base in its concreteness. It awakens that which it does not know; it illuminates and activates, but it does not pin down . . . Because it remains without a concrete object, illumination of existence does not yield any results. The clarity of awareness contains the demand without fulfilling it. As observers we must be content with that. For I am not that which I perceive, and I do not perceive what I am. Instead of observing my existence I can only set in motion the process of clarified awareness.[111]

This position gave rise, in Jaspers, to a Kierkegaardian bias which is in many ways linked with Heidegger's: seeing something real only in inwardness, in one's own soul, in the 'existence'-preserving stance of the totally isolated individual. Heidegger, however, elaborated this standpoint with a certain abstract rigour, and only where he planned to reveal the historicality of existence on this basis did his sorry philistinism become fully apparent. Jaspers planned to set out a broad, substantial and finished concrete philosophy, cultural critique, etc., on the basis of his Kierkegaardian solipsism. Hence his petty-bourgeois, intellectual cant – a vain and philistine self-indulgence – became much more quickly apparent.

Jaspers even demanded something that seems absurd in the light of his hypotheses, political action; he condemned both 'apolitical conduct and blind political volition'. Now this gave

rise to the following petty-bourgeois ideal: 'Only patience in the long term coupled with secret resolution as regards a sudden intervention, comprehensive knowledge which stays open to the infinite realm of possibility beyond urgently real matters, can perform something here which is more than mere tumult, destruction, driving things away.'[112] This demand looks all the more comical in that Jaspers logically rejected any forecast or foresight: 'That knowledge of the run of things which considers them with foresight remains a knowledge of possibilities among which that which will really come true does not even have to occur.'[113] So, after all these fruitless excursions into the world of reality, it is only the Kierkegaardian perspective that retains its validity: 'Since the course of the world is unfathomable, since up to now the best has failed and may fall short again, and since, therefore, *the course of the world in the long run is not at all the one and only issue*, all plans and actions with an eye to the distant future are curtailed so as to create and animate existence here and now . . . To do genuine deeds in the present is, in the last resort, the only thing which assuredly remains for me.'[114]

This final dictum, which is closely related to Heidegger's teaching, gives rise to a somewhat amusing contradiction in Jaspers. He saw in the contemporary, wholly self-reliant human being a step forward (a discarding of the 'shell', a conquest of the fallaciously objective philosophies of the past achieved with the aid of Kierkegaard and Nietzsche). Really, therefore, he should have been obliged to affirm the present age that had produced this human being and this one genuine philosophical proposition, as did the more logical Simmel with regard to his subjectivism. But since Jaspers harboured a deadly hate of the masses and a quivering fear of them, democracy and socialism, a romantic glorification of earlier ages emerged hand in glove with his polemics against the 'shell'. Thus, for example, he occasionally defended the Church as the 'existential precondition for the freedom evolving at any given time',[115] completely forgetting that

according to his theory, every church would necessarily constitute a 'shell'. Here again we see the superiority of the 'class authors' of philosophical reaction over their epigones: from the standpoint of his existential Protestantism, Kierkegaard had constantly raised the most passionate objections to the Church. This contradiction renders Jaspers's would-be sublime gesture comical, compromising and trivial. Time and again nihilism was converted into a petty-bourgeois Calvinistic, modernized 'inner-worldly *askesis*', giving rise to a vitalistic caricature of Max Weber's relativistic sociology.

Heidegger went only so far as to elaborate the 'existential'. Jaspers, on the other hand, published a massive three-volume philosophical system under the title, at once proud and modest, of *Philosophy*. In the introductory studies (on world-orientation and existential illumination), the matter indicated here is expounded on a broad scale. Only in the third part (on metaphysics) does there occur a 'cryptology' whereby the impossibility of perceiving reality objectively was to be read afresh as a positive form of world-comprehension. Jaspers wanted, on the one hand – after the model of Kierkegaard and Nietzsche – to maintain the pose of an undaunted hammer of objectivity, while, on the other, he had neither Kierkegaard's faith in pristine Christianity nor Nietzsche's vision of an imperialistic epoch to come. And yet, instead of logically drawing the nihilistic conclusions, he aimed at conjuring something loosely positive out of Heidegger's murderous nothingness. Herein lies his half-heartedness compared to Heidegger's radical nihilism.

Thus Jaspers's philosophy, like Heidegger's, bore no philosophical fruit whatever, but still had uncommonly far-reaching consequences for society. Heidegger and Jaspers carried the most extreme individualistic, petty-bourgeois-cum-aristocratic relativism and irrationalism to their farthest logical limits. They ended up with an ice age, a North Pole, a world become empty, a senseless chaos, a nought as man's environment, and a despair about oneself and one's inescapable loneliness was the inner content of their philosophy.

They thus provided an accurate picture of what was widely going on within the German intelligentsia at the end of the twenties and the start of the thirties. But they did not stop at description. Their account was at the same time interpretation: an exposition of the meaninglessness of any action in this world. Their partisan attitude is manifest in the fact that they related the negative features of what they called the 'world' exclusively to democratic society. And that, on the eve of the crisis and during it, was tantamount to a decisive *parti pris*. For it deepened the general mood of despondency among broad sections of the German bourgeoisie, above all, its intellectuals, side-tracked potential rebellious tendencies and thus afforded significant assistance, in a negative way, to aggressive reaction. If fascism could inculcate a more than benevolent neutrality in broad sections of Germany's intelligentsia, this was due in no small measure to the philosophy of Heidegger and Jaspers.

In this context it matters hardly at all how both of them personally responded to the Hitler movement, particularly as neither was to become so disloyal to the hypotheses and conclusions of his own thinking as really to make a stand against Hitler. The fact, therefore, that Heidegger emerged as an overt fascist, whereas Jaspers could not go so far for purely private reasons – and for a while, as long as a Leftist climate seemed to prevail, used his *otium cum dignitate* under Hitler to strike an anti-fascist pose after his downfall – does not affect the basic facts of the matter. In the substance of their philosophy, both still paved the way for fascist irrationalism.

7. Pre-Fascist and Fascist Vitalism (Klages, Jünger, Baeumler, Boehm, Krieck, Rosenberg)

Vitalism itself rapidly passed beyond the 'existentialist' episode we have just portrayed and applied itself to a more

overt, belligerent preparation for the impending barbaric reaction. Herein lies the significance of the philosophy of Ludwig Klages. As a writer he had already appeared in the pre-war period. Originally a leading member of the Stefan George circle, he then separated from it and went his own way. It was he who actually transformed vitalism into an open combat against reason and culture. (How much this had to do with current trends rather than with single individuals is indicated by the striking similarity of the philosophical line taken by the politically Left-oriented Theodor Lessing.) With Klages, vitalism's anthropological side emerges still more distinctly than it did with his predecessors. A major part of his literary activity was based on this subject, on the argumentation of the new science of 'characterology'. Here all objective knowledge in the theory of types has already dissolved completely.

With Dilthey, anthropological typology had still been subservient to objective scientific thinking, while with Jaspers it already took precedence over the latter. With Klages, it signified a frontal attack upon the scientific spirit, upon the role which reason, knowledge and the mind played and continue to play in the collective development of mankind.

Klages's basic conception was extremely simple: there is a universal cosmic life in which men, at the start of their evolution, participated as by a law of nature: 'Wherever there is a living body there is also soul; wherever there is soul, there is also a living body. The soul is the meaning of the body, and the image of the body the manifestation of the soul. Whatever is manifest has a meaning, and every meaning reveals itself as it becomes manifest. The meaning is experienced inwardly, the manifestation outwardly. The first must become image if it is to communicate itself, and the image must be internalized again in order to take effect. Those are literally the two poles of reality.'[116]

This cosmic and nature-ruled, organic and alive state is suppressed and disrupted by the 'intellect'. 'The law of

intellect secedes from the rhythm of cosmic life.'[117] The substance of human history is 'that *intellect* may elevate itself above the soul, comprehending *wakefulness* may be raised above the dream, and an activity aimed at staying put above life coming into being and expiring'.[118] How this mighty reversal has taken place, nobody knows: but it is a fact '*that an extra-mundane power burst into the sphere of life*'.[119] (Here Klages was offering a mystical and reactionary distortion of Bachofen's account of primitive communism.) But if how the intellect has gained dominance is unknown, its effect is fully evident to Klages: 'the killing of life'.[120]

Klages's whole philosophy is only a variation on this one primitive idea. His significance lies in the fact that never before had reason been challenged so openly and radically. He called its activity a 'scandal'[121] and an 'outrage'.[122] The thirst for knowledge was equated with vulgar curiosity. On one occasion Klages described the youth who, as legend has it, wanted to remove the veil from the image of Sais: 'Why does the youth really wish to lift the veil? From scientific interest or, to put it plainly, from *curiosity*? There is no essential difference between scientific and ordinary curiosity. The first, like the second, stems from a disquieting of the understanding, which is disquieted by everything that it does not yet possess. The urge to perceive is an urge to appropriate . . . and whatever the intellect takes possession of is invariably stripped of magic and destroyed in the process – if it was, in essence, a mystery.'[123] And precisely therein, to Klages's mind, lay the scandalous nature of all scientific thinking, for what was philosophically essential was by no means a perception, but only a 'knowing about secrets'.[124]

Only through maintaining this respect towards the secret was an alive relationship to life possible. Clearly the category of 'life' thus loses, with Klages, any relation to biology; he openly stated that biology was ignorant of 'wherein the aliveness (*Lebendigsein*) of living things consists'.[125] It is characteristic that Klages, like all his fellow-vitalists, claimed to be setting himself above the antithesis of idealism and

materialism. For the apparent antithesis of Being and consciousness obscured, in Klages's opinion, 'what is neither *cogitare* nor *esse*, neither spirit nor matter, but more important than either for temporal entities: namely life . . . The mind perceives that Being is, but only life lives.'[126]

This view of life was the acme of vitalistic irrationalism so far. Here, however, it no longer constituted a simple nihilistic negation, but an about-turn into direct myth. Klages put forward an epistemology of his new doctrine of myths, playing off image against thing. A thing is a dead product of the mind, the image an animated manifestation. It was to this contrast that Klages linked his epistemology – which, in turn, became characteristic of and important to vitalism in its myth-creating phase, although it was, in itself, pure sophistry. That is, Klages accepted for the world of the intellect the epistemology of the neo-Kantians and Positivists in order to confront it, in the world of the soul, with a demagogic, pseudo-materialist view of subject and object. He stated: 'The image has a reality independent of consciousness (for it remains totally unaffected by whether or not I recall it hereafter); the thing is thought into the world of consciousness and exists only *for* an inwardness of *personal* entities.'[127] As we know, the independence of the material world forms the basis of the epistemology of philosophical materialism. It is typical that Klages professed to be advocating it precisely when dealing with the most subjective issues, with products of fantasy. But this very sophistry is characteristic of the pseudo-objectivism of the vitalistic doctrine of myths.

This epistemology of vitalism with a mythical slant naturally had its own time-theory, a discovery of 'real' time which differed from that of the world of understanding as radically as in Bergson or Heidegger. But here Klages's polemics were directed against the future, which was 'not a property of real time'. Only 'Promethean mankind raised what was to come to the *same* stage of reality as the past . . . the Heraclitean man of "world-history" toppled and is toppling the reality of what has been with the mirage of the "future" . . . is shattering

the fruitful connection of the near and the far so as to substitute for it the present's Ahasverus-like *fascination* with that distant phantom called the future.'[128] Real time, on the other hand, was a 'stream coursing *from* the future *into* the past'.[129] Thus in Klages too we behold a struggle against the reality of a world-history which is presented as an outrage perpetrated by intellect and reason, and whose most disreputable feature is that it ventures to set objectives for the future, thereby disturbing a soul snugly embedded in myth, in the pre-eminence of what has gone before. It is perhaps superfluous to stress that Klages's time-theory and the view of history closely linked to it stemmed from the same social need of the imperialistic bourgeoisie – the need to challenge socialism – as the corresponding doctrines of Spengler or Heidegger. Objectively the degree of divergence is unimportant, since in each case the real connections of objective reality were turned resolutely upside-down; all of them simply mark various stages of German irrationalism on the road to Hitler.

Thus there came into being an empty, barren, soulless, discredited world. Although incapable of defending itself against the incursions of the intellect, the world of myth was deemed to reign over the world of ruling reason in a darkly fateful way. In everything from the fall of Rome to the prophesied collapse of the present-day States Klages saw this act of revenge by the downtrodden powers of myth. The only task his philosophy could set mankind was self-liberation from the infamous world of the intellect: 'to save the soul!'[130]

In Klages we already discern in a very marked form the new vitalistic phase. On the one hand, vitalism has now become the overtly militant enemy to reason in a manner quite different from that of the thinkers discussed earlier. On the other hand, Klages was – if we disregard the Spengler episode – the first thinker since Nietzsche in whose works vitalism was overtly creating concrete myths. Hence he became a direct forerunner of the 'National Socialist world-

view', a fact which that movement's official philosophy always gratefully acknowledged. Granted, it did so with certain reservations. For, in the first place, although Klages was a militant vitalist, he still took old apolitical individualism as his basis; his only territory could be the coffee-house or drawing-room; he could not possibly carry the battle on to the streets. In the second place, and above all, Klages regarded war as another of the pernicious, culture-sapping consequences of the intellect. That was, of course, a point at which all National Socialist piety towards a meritorious forerunner had to cease. His fascist admirers criticized this pacifism and individualism in Klages's thought.

In its transition to fascism, vitalism also produced several militant thinkers who interpreted the antithesis of life and death in social and political terms, and in whose writings the effort to destroy reason acquired a social accent. This phase of vitalism arose largely on the basis of those small groups and alliances which had proliferated in the second half of the twenties. Their socio-political aims oscillated between a sometimes sincerely felt sympathy with socialism and an outlook very close indeed to National Socialism – mostly, to be sure, with a marked preponderance of the latter trend. Of the authors producing fairly copious works in this vein, let us quote here just one particularly salient, sharply Right-oriented representative: Ernst Jünger. As a young man Jünger took part in the First World War, and he subsequently depicted the horrors of the war machinery in effective, by no means worthless stories. He always treated this subject in connection with the edifying 'experience of the front' which, in the opinion of the militant younger generation of vitalists, formed the inner basis of the future renewal of Germany. The association of mechanized warfare and battle-front experience made Jünger one of the first propagandists for 'total mobilization'.

This proposition modified the content of the antithesis between the alive and the rigid. Because they approved of modern warfare, writers of Jünger's kind had to refrain from

rejecting all manifestations of modern capitalism as moribund, as dead 'shell' after the manner of Heidegger, Jaspers and Klages, who all took the same line on this issue. With Jünger, the dividing-line between death and life ran between the pacifistically bourgeois capitalism of the Weimar Republic and the envisaged revival of an aggressive, Prusso-Germanic imperialism. It was here that the introduction of social demagogy and the incorporation of the working class into these imperialist projects began. War literature of the sort published by Scheler and Sombart, and above all Spengler's *Prussianism and Socialism*, had anticipated this new synthesis. But Jünger was the first to interpret the antithesis of proletariat and bourgeoisie vitalistically, so as to obtain the requisite broad social basis for the longed-for new imperialistic war, seen as liberating life from the dead bourgeois world. Thereupon vitalistic irrationalism quite openly took up its reactionary historical mission, the direct combating of Marxism-Leninism and the world-outlook of the proletariat. We now find things openly stated which, in the case of the earlier proponents of vitalism, had to be shown by first deciphering convoluted, obscure and seemingly irrelevant theories. At the same time – this, to be sure, we already find in Spengler – it turns out that for all its openness and frontality, this struggle was an indirect and demagogic one. Spengler and Jünger do not even attempt, as did the early or pre-imperialistic apologists, to prove the superiority of capitalism over socialism. Instead they play off against real socialism a monopoly capitalism which they dub 'socialism' and present as the social system of the future. But in so doing Spengler still ignored the proletariat, whereas Jünger, like Hitler, was already making demagogic statements in the proletariat's name.

Jünger summarized this philosophy in a programmatic book entitled *The Worker – Government and Form* (*Der Arbeiter. Herrschaft und Gestalt*). 'Form' had already been one of the central categories of vitalism for a long time – remember Spengler's 'morphology'. Here it emerged as a

central concept of the myth-creating tendency. According to Jünger the very methodology proceeding from the forms was revolutionary: 'The beholding of forms is a revolutionary act inasmuch as it perceives a being in the whole and unitary fullness of its life. It is the great advantage of this process that it takes place beyond the moral and aesthetic as well as the scientific law.'[131] Here, needless to say, 'revolution' is to be understood in the fascist sense: as a destroying of democratic parliamentary forms of government, in a manner demagogically professing to overcome bourgeois society along with those forms and in them. Jünger's militant vitalism repudiated mind and reason just as radically as did Klages's, but the mood and tone had changed completely; morality and the philosophy of history now turned into politics. Jünger wrote not of outrage and scandal, but of the 'high treason of the intellect'.[132] With Jünger, vitalism's radical subjectivism too was further heightened and given a politico-historical slant. Of the origin of myth he wrote: 'The victor creates the historical myth.'[133] This cynically open statement marked the climax of the repudiation of all historical objectivity.

The basic philosophico-historical idea behind this new, militant phase of vitalism was fairly simple and primitive. The 'form' of the worker, from which every trace of economics and social class has been carefully removed, represents the elemental force in contemporary culture, the life-force – as opposed to the bourgeoisie, which has never had any notion of its presence. This new conception, as we have indicated, carried on specific tendencies from Spengler's 'Prussian socialism', but we must point out the difference as well. Spengler undertook a straightforward identification. Jünger saw in Prussianism a 'restraining of the elemental' and went on to state: 'working life does not exclude the elemental, it includes it'.[134]

This was a vitalistic rationale of irrationalistic social demagogy. The dead bourgeois world is a world of 'security'. This vitalistic-demagogic critique of bourgeois culture was

of the greatest importance to the philosophical argumentation of fascism. In contrast to other reactionary movements which preached a return to earlier, secure, 'restrained' eras, fascist agitation proceeded from the crisis itself and the dissolution of all secure conditions. And since it planned to set up a totally arbitrary government internally, its chief object being to organize the imperialistic war of aggression, it was striving towards this militant nihilism and a deliberate undermining of all secure conditions in the existence of the individual. Hence the ideology of 'security', as a moribund bourgeois concept, was to be rendered contemptible at all costs: fascism planned to rear the type of a brutal bully-boy, deterred by nothing and stopping at nothing. Now since 'security' was a category of German classical humanism (Wilhelm von Humboldt first formulated it with great clarity and force), we begin to understand the leading fascist ideologists' hostility to this entire period. (Let us mention in passing that the existential thinking of Heidegger and Jaspers contributed much, in its own ways, to the undermining of 'security'.)

The two forms, that of the worker and the bourgeois, confronted each other in total mutual exclusiveness. The worker stood for an absolute otherness from the bourgeois citizen. This is where Jünger's radically anti-historical, mythicizing view of history – a complete tearing asunder of history – commences. 'A form *is*, and no development can add to or detract from it. Hence evolutionary history is not a history of form . . . Evolution knows beginning and end, birth and death, from which the form is removed. History does not produce any forms, but changes along with the form. History is that tradition which a victorious power bestows on itself.'[135] And that is tantamount to abolishing history. Originally, with Dilthey and Simmel, vitalism had proceeded to safeguard the independence of history in the face of the laws of nature. Even then, to be sure, and especially with Dilthey, it showed a secondary tendency to obtain a foothold against historical relativism by means of an

anthropological reasoning; with Dilthey, as we have noted, this led to an antinomy of the anthropological and historical viewpoints. The need for a world-outlook, the necessity of the outlook expressible through vitalism meant expending more and more energy on turning history into a myth, the more so the greater the pretention to concreteness. Only the 'forms' of vitalistic anthropology and typology, inflated into entities, could inhabit the resultant myths. The more evolution advanced, the more real history lost any significance for the proponents of vitalism. With Spengler, real history was supplanted by the myths; with Heidegger it sank into unauthenticity; with Klages it was presented as a set of parables on the Fall of man resulting from the dominance of reason and the infamous intellect. Much as all these conceptions may have differed, they had in common the feature that the historical process appeared the spurious movement of a number of types. And the more militantly reactionary these myths became, and the more directly they anticipated the fascist myth, the more strongly they polarized into adversaries; and the more the whole mysticized history of life served to illustrate the sole right to life of the one 'form' and the total reprehensibility of the other. With Jünger this line was taken to the farthest stage possible in pre-fascist times. From here to Rosenberg it was only the shortest of steps.

Thus the 'form' of the worker (which, as with Spengler and Hitler, included not only the soldier but also the entrepreneur) determined the myth of the contemporary world. This world was a 'workshop landscape' and, as far as the bourgeois world was concerned, a 'museum'. It would fully become a workshop landscape only with the victory of the worker-form, and at that point it would be converted into a 'battleground landscape', into 'imperial space or territory'.[136] In Jünger, the myth of the worker was the belligerently aggressive imperialist myth.

As we see, vitalism in militant dress was now already only a few steps away from 'National-Socialist philosophy'. What

kept them apart was, basically, only the sectarian streak in the philosophy of Jünger and thinkers like him. Inwardly they had already made up their minds to carry vitalism out of the scholar's study and intellectual coteries on to the streets, for their ideas were already tending to have a distinctly political character. But their methodology and terminology were still steeped in the esoteric wisdom of tiny closed, interlocking groups.

The 'philosophical' representatives of National Socialism took over the legacy of this whole irrationalistic development of vitalism in the imperialistic period, above all in its final phase. They used it to build ideological bridges between Hitlerian propaganda, which could never stoop too low, and the German intelligentsia raised on vitalism. By speaking the intellectuals' language – this was both externally and intrinsically the case – they enticed them into the camp of National Socialism or at least rendered them benevolently neutral in their attitude to it. Thus National-Socialist propaganda had a circulation of varying range. Rosenberg stood more or less mid-way between Hitler and the official Nazi thinkers in the narrower sense, ideologists such as Baeumler and Krieck.

These two, whom we may regard as representative of official National-Socialist thinking, incorporated Jünger's idea of 'total mobilization' in their fascistic completion of vitalism. Both of them continued its demagogic polemics against bourgeois life, the bourgeois age and culture. It is significant that – since these writings were not addressed to workers – Baeumler and Krieck, in line with the traditions of bourgeois philosophy and sociology, largely confined themselves to cultural criticism. They had little to say of socialism, even in terms of the demagogic agitation of Hitler and Rosenberg.

Baeumler posed the task of a general 'de-bourgeoisifying' only in a very general way. While he depreciated bourgeois culture and poured contempt on it, he did so chiefly in his pursuit of a general militarization. Intellectuals were to be educated for the 'life of political soldiers'. Baeumler painted

the misfortune of nineteenth-century German history as follows: 'The really fateful aspect of the nineteenth century was the discrepancy between humanistic thinking and the tacit thinking of the soldiers of the Prussian militia.'[137] In another passage, he saw in the fact that Nietzsche and Bismarck could not agree a symptom of incorrect development when the bourgeois class was predominant.[138] In this, Baeumler was very close to Spengler's idea of 'Prussian socialism', as amended by Jünger. He now wanted to emphasize what was specific to and new about National Socialism and divorce himself from the older reactionary trends. Hence he criticized the old militarism in the sense that this was 'heroism with a bad conscience'. 'Germany was "militaristic" before the war because it was not heroic enough.' All in all a military man was a 'soldier degraded to a civilian', and militarism held sway only where the civilian 'determines the spirit of the army'. However – and here vitalism came in, 'with a virile people the *soldier's life* represents a *life-form*'.[139] The ideal of the 'political soldier', the S.A. and S.S. man, was therefore life incarnate, in contrast to the fossilized bourgeois world.

Thus we encounter once more the antithesis of alive and dead. Dead was the bourgeois world of 'urbanity' and 'security' with all its social and cultural categories like economy and society, secure living, pleasure and the 'inner life'. Dead was its thinking, both that of classical humanism and that of Positivism, since it lacked intuitions and daring and was therefore – soulless, despite all the inwardness.[140]

With its sharp attacks on everything that it called bourgeois culture, militant fascist vitalism proudly declared an allegiance to irrationalistic nihilism and agnosticism, albeit in a language which appeared to give them a mythical, positive element. This mythical element now became the core of the epistemology of the new vitalistic stage. The fascist thinker Boehm stated: 'For German though, the uninvestigable is not a limiting condition but an eminently positive one . . . It permeates our entire reality and governs all things

great and small . . . An insoluble part of the fabric of our reality, the uninvestigable is essentially inaccessible but not at all – unfamiliar. We are acquainted with it even though it cannot be voiced, it operates in our life, determines our decisions, has control over us . . . It cannot be said what profundity is, but it can be demonstrated through men in whom it exists.'[141] (Here it is patent that the vitalistic argumentation of that which is alive and German represents nothing other than a base for Hitler's boundless arbitrariness as *Führer*.)

The relation of myth to history Baeumler defined in the same spirit as Boehm: 'The problem of myth will remain hopeless as long as one clings to the question of how myth has *come into being*. For then one is presupposing a fixed basis to human evolution and proceeds to ask how myth must have arisen *within history*. A satisfying answer can never be offered to this question because the formulation is wrong. Myth is downright unhistorical . . . Myth reaches down not only into pre-history but also into the *primal grounds* of the human soul.'[142]

Causality, from the lofty angle of this mystical insight into the uninvestigable and primal grounds, was contemptuously dismissed as a category of 'absolute security'. We already know from Jünger the social basis of this disparagement of 'security'. For the National-Socialist philosophers in the narrower sense, the struggle against law and causality as expressions of 'security' also tended to portray the complete internal arbitrariness of the Hitler régime as 'philosophically' higher, closer to life and the Germanic soul than the defeated bourgeois world-order.

So the antithesis of life and death cropped up in every domain, and it now signified the contrast of war and peace, of German and un-German, of National-Socialist and 'bourgeois' ('plutocratic'). And thus the basic categories of vitalism were so reshaped as to lay a foundation for the slogans and deeds of the National-Socialist 'revolution'. The nihilism of late vitalism became the basis for fascist 'heroic realism'.

For, precisely in the spirit of Kierkegaard's modern followers, Baeumler too regarded life as signifying: decision. Action on the basis of the National-Socialist outlook had to be irrational and unarguable in principle. Action, Baeumler stated, 'is not however a realizing of recognized values. A truly active man always finds himself in uncertainty, he is "devoid of knowledge", as Nietzsche puts it. It is precisely the hallmark of action that no value covers it. The man of action lays himself open, his share is never *securitas* but *certitudo*.'[143] (That is to say: belief in the *Führer*, G.L.) But whereas a nihilism was the consequence of the Kierkegaardian position, logically so with Heidegger and somewhat reconditely with Jaspers, Baeumler cut the Gordian knot very simply by confronting the biological life-concept with life as a 'cosmic fact'. While the former would certainly lead to relativism, the latter 'would resist all relativizing'.[144]

Here again we notice how fascist vitalism took previous tendencies to their conclusion and exacerbated them. We have been able to observe the gradual, ever-stronger separation of the vitalistic life-concept from that of biology; here there is already a strict antithesis which is energetically expressed not only by Baeumler, but also by Krieck and others. In Krieck's view the theses of biology, like those of other sciences, were only parts of the myth.[145] Even the chief categories of orthodox fascism, race and blood, he interpreted as symbols only.[146] Hence it was only logical to present the new science of life as follows: 'Universal biology is perfected in man's image of himself. The image is described through a racial-cum-popular-cum-political anthropology . . . This anthropology replaces the exhausted philosophy.'[147] Here we can clearly see whither the final consequences of that anthropological principle timidly, hesitatingly introduced by Dilthey were bound to lead, and how fascist vitalism 'solved' what it found to be the insoluble dilemma of anthropologism in philosophy.

This brings us to the concrete explanation of what 'cosmic

life' signifies. Baeumler spoke with scorn of the 'imageless idealism' of German classicism. And he added by way of a contrast, an expression of the philosophically positive: 'Hitler is not *less* than the idea – he is more than the idea, for he is real.'[148] Krieck gave an extremely clear picture of how this reality of life is manifested: 'Destiny demands the heroic man of honour who is receptive to every order.'[149] The order was, of course, to come from the *Führer*: 'The personality of the pre-ordained *Führer* is the arena in which the fate of the whole is decided.'[150] What the *Führer* and what the National-Socialist movement wanted was nothing else than a religious revelation. Krieck vigorously defended the notion that such a revelation was possible even today: 'But God speaks within us directly as the people setting out to battle.'[151]

Thus all the antinomies of vitalism's nihilistic relativism were resolved in the National-Socialist myth. Every question was solved through obedience to Hitler's orders; following these orders meant eliminating the antithesis of the mere theorist (fictive, unalive, bourgeois) and the alive man, interested and active in Kierkegaard's sense. Baeumler clearly stated what leadership meant in practice for the new period of 'political soldiering': 'a college of education which . . . does not speak of leadership through Adolf Hitler and Horst Wessel is unpolitical',[152] which is to say unalive, bourgeois, reprehensible. And Krieck supplemented this proclamation of 'leadership through mind and idea' with the lucid comment: 'He who wishes to devise his own answer is assuredly good for nothing; the predestined course of events will sweep him aside as a useless hindrance and cast him on the dung-heap.'[153]

In this way vitalism merged with fascist demagogy. It does not matter how far Baeumler, Krieck and company were really drawing logical conclusions, and how far cynically complying with that power of brutal exploitation and suppression whose coming they foresaw. From the objective philosophical viewpoint, they drew the ultimate conclusions

of vitalism and completed that journey which began with Nietzsche and Dilthey on the eve of the imperialistic era, a journey whose fitful progress we have traced in its most important stages. That thinkers such as Dilthey and Simmel would have recoiled in horror from the fascist reality and would have deeply despised its so-called philosophy is certain, but this does not diminish the objective historical connection. In the substance of his writing, Spengler was far closer to fascism than they were but still found himself in continual dispute with its official representatives. And Stefan George, whose school played a major part in the dissemination of vitalism (Gundolf, Klages and the fascist Kurt Hildebrandt were among its products), while individual poems of his contain and herald a prophetic foreboding of the *Führer*, so that his influence certainly carried in this direction, even died in voluntary exile. That, however, does not at all affect the fact that the Baeumler-Krieck-Rosenberg philosophy would not have been possible without Spengler, and that Spengler's would not have been possible without Dilthey and Simmel.

Hitler himself was far too uneducated and cynically lacking in convictions to see in any philosophy something more than an instantly effective means of agitation. But it is patent that even his views were formed under the influence of the same destructive and parasitical imperialistic trends which gave rise to vitalism among the intellectual 'élite'. A nihilistic lack of convictions and a faith in miracles as related polarities also determined the particular nature of Hitlerian propaganda. In Hitler himself, to be sure, cynical nihilism had the upper hand. Indeed, as we know from the conversations with Rauschning, Hitler regarded even racial theory as a hoax but ruthlessly exploited it for his predatory imperialistic ends.[154] The general atmosphere surrounding his agitation was a popular, vulgar version of the basic tendencies of vitalism. In his propaganda he rejected any conviction governed by the understanding and was only concerned to produce and maintain a frenzy;[155] agitation, to him, was merely a 'working on men's freedom of will'.[156] For all that

the technique derived from the American advertising world, Hitler's agitation stemmed just as much, in content, from the same soil as vitalism.

The influence of vitalism can be seen more directly in Rosenberg. Admittedly even with him, a cynical lack of convictions was quite blatantly the overriding factor, with the slight difference that as a pupil of the Russian White Guard and a student of Mereshkovsky and other decadent reactionaries, Rosenberg was already predisposed by training to a receptiveness to German vitalism. Thus his book *The Myth of the Twentieth Century* was a crudely propagandistic vulgarization of the final period of vitalism. (Irrespective of all critical reservations, he even expressly admitted his borrowings from Spengler and Klages.) With Rosenberg too we find a mythical history without historical substance, a repudiation of world-history that was intended to 'prove' the absolute pre-eminence of the Germans in the world (and of the Nazis in Germany). With him too we find that the antithesis of life and death, of intuition and reason has acquired a brutally militant slant; with him too, a vehemently demagogic attack upon the intellect and science was one of the central points of the new myth's rationale. Here the antithesis of life and death was presented as one of Germans and Jews, of productive and grasping capitalists, etc. That aristocratic epistemology which Dilthey had reinforced became the mythical infallibility of the *Führer*. Spengler's theory of cultural cycles, that sociological solipsism, was presented as a doctrine of the perennial nature of sharply divided races which could associate with one another only in the form of mutual destruction. The vitalistic doctrine of types was presented as a call for the creation of types: as the rule of the ruffians of the S.A. and S.S.

Philosophically, there was no longer anything new in all this, even if measured by the philosophical level of vitalism's final phases. The vitalism of a Rosenberg was just a powerful tool for the crimes of the fresh imperialistic world war and of its preliminaries. But it is not without significance that

vitalism was concluded in exactly this fashion, or that the 'National-Socialist philosophy' sprang from these roots. For this barbaric cul-de-sac thereupon appears a necessary climax to the self-dissolution of German imperialistic ideology in vitalism, whose earliest philosophical forerunners we traced to the irrational reaction of German feudal absolutism to the French Revolution. And this climax was by no means fortuitous, but the merited fate of the immanent tendencies of vitalism itself. Hegel, who came to vitalism when it was not yet far advanced, when it was a doctrine of 'direct knowing', prophetically wrote of it: 'From the thesis that *direct knowing* must be the criterion of truth it follows . . . that all superstition and idolatry are declared to be true, and that the most wrongful and indecent content of the will is justified . . . Natural desires and inclinations automatically deposit their interests in the consciousness, and the immoral purposes are directly located in the same.'[157]

NOTES

1 Dilthey: *Collected Works*, Leipzig-Berlin 1914, Vol. II, p. 91.
2 Ibid., Vol. V, p. 83.
3 Ibid., pp. 130f.
4 Ibid., pp. 136f.
5 Ibid., p. 125.
6 Ibid., Vol. VIII, p. 225.
7 Ibid., Vol. V, pp. 143f.
8 Ibid., Vol. VII, pp. 213, 261.
9 Ibid., Vol. V, p. 278.
10 Gundolf: *Goethe*, Berlin 1920, p. 27.
11 Ibid., Vol. VII, p. 262.
12 Ibid., p. 282.
13 Ibid., Vol. V, p. 425.
14 Ibid., p. XCI.
15 Ibid., p. 62.
16 Ibid., Vol. VII, p. 14.
17 Ibid., Vol. VIII, p. 36.
18 Ibid., p. 99.

19 Ibid., p. 7.
20 Ibid., Vol. V, p. 404.
21 Ibid., p. 272.
22 Ibid., Vol. VII, pp. 86f.
23 Ibid., p. 222.
24 Ibid., p. 231.
25 Ibid., p. 232.
26 Simmel: *Probleme der Geschichtsphilosophie*, 3rd ed., Munich-Leipzig 1922, p. 55.
27 Simmel: *Fragmente und Aufsätze*, Munich 1923, p. 7.
28 Ibid., p. 263.
29 Simmel: *Die Religion*, Frankfurt-am-Main 1906, p. 32.
30 Simmel: *Lebensanschauung*, Munich-Leipzig 1918, pp. 104ff.
31 Simmel: *Probleme der Geschichtsphilosophie*, p. 153.
32 Simmel: *Die Religion*, p. 11.
33 Simmel: *Philosophische Kultur*, Leipzig 1911, pp. 235, 237.
34 Simmel: *Philosophy of Money*.
35 Simmel: *Fragmente und Aufsätze*, p. 264.
36 Simmel: *Philosophische Kultur*, p. 270.
37 Simmel: *Kant und Goethe*, Berlin 1906, pp. 52, 54.
38 Simmel: *Philosophy of Money*.
39 Simmel: *Fragmente und Aufsätze*, p. 6.
40 Ibid., p. 4.
41 Simmel: *Lebensanschauung*, pp. 19f.
42 Simmel: *Fragmente und Aufsätze*, p. 6.
43 Ibid., pp. 15f.
44 Scheler: *Der Genius des Krieges und der deutsche Krieg*, Leipzig 1915, p. 42.
45 Spengler: *The Decline of the West*.
46 Ibid.
47 Ibid.
48 Spengler: *Prussianism and Socialism*.
49 Spengler: *The Decline of the West*.
50 Ibid.
51 Ibid.
52 Ibid.
53 Ibid.
54 Ibid.
55 Ibid.
56 Ibid.
57 Ibid., p. 43.
58 Ibid., Vol. II, pp. 418 and 541ff.
59 Spengler: *Prussianism and Socialism*.

60 Ibid.
61 Ibid.
62 Scheler: *Posthumous Works*, Berlin 1933, p. 290.
63 Husserl: *Philosophy as a Rigorous Science*.
64 Husserl: *Logical Investigations*.
65 Scheler: *Schriften aus dem Nachlass*, pp. 266ff.
66 Scheler: *Der Formalismus in der Ethik und die materiale Wertethik*, *Jahrbuch für Philosophie und phänomenologische Forschung*, Vols. I and II, Halle 1913 and 1916, Vol. II, p. 353.
67 Ibid., Vol. I, p. 483.
68 Ibid., p. 491.
69 Ibid., Vol. II, pp. 472ff.
70 Scheler: *Philosophical Perspectives*.
71 Scheler: *Moralia*, Leipzig 1923, p. 8.
72 Scheler: *Versuch einer Soziologie des Wissens*, Munich-Leipzig 1924, p. 117.
73 Ibid., pp. 114f.
74 Scheler: *Der Formalismus in der Ethik*, etc., Vol. II, p. 384.
75 Scheler: *Versuch einer Soziologie des Wissens*, pp. 133ff.
76 Dilthey: *Collected Works*, Vol. VII, p. 150.
77 Heidegger: *Being and Time*.
78 Ibid.
79 Ibid.
80 Ibid.
81 Ibid.
82 Ibid.
83 Ibid.
84 Ibid.
85 Heidegger: *Kant and the Problem of Metaphysics*.
86 Ibid.
87 Ibid.
88 Heidegger: *Being and Time*.
89 Ibid.
90 Ibid.
91 Ibid.
92 Ibid.
93 Ibid.
94 Ibid.
95 Heidegger: *Was ist Metaphysik?*, Bonn 1926, pp. 19f.
96 Heidegger: *Being and Time*.
97 Ibid.
98 Ibid.
99 Heidegger: *Kant*, p. 233.

100 Heidegger: *Being and Time*.
101 Ibid.
102 Ibid.
103 Ibid.
104 Ibid.
105 Ibid.
106 Ibid.
107 Ibid.
108 Kierkegaard: *Collected Works*, Jena, from 1910, Vol. VI, p. 235.
109 Jaspers: *Psychologie der Weltanschauungen*, 2nd ed., Berlin 1922, pp. 254f.
110 Jaspers: *Reason and Existence*.
111 Jaspers: *Man in the Modern Age*.
112 Ibid.
113 Ibid.
114 Ibid.
115 Ibid.
116 Klages: *Vom kosmogonischen Eros*, 2nd ed., Munich 1926, p. 63.
117 Ibid., p. 65.
118 Klages: *Der Mensch und das Leben*, Jena 1937, p. 32.
119 Ibid., p. 33.
120 Ibid., p. 51.
121 Ibid., p. 33.
122 Ibid., p. 214.
123 Ibid., pp. 215f.
124 Ibid., p. 79.
125 Klages: *Vom Wesen des Bewusstseins*, Leipzig 1921, p. 4.
126 Ibid., pp. 137ff.
127 Klages: *Kosmogonischer Eros*, p. 79.
128 Ibid., pp. 137ff.
129 Ibid., p. 140.
130 Klages: *Vom Wesen des Bewusstseins*, p. 52.
131 Jünger: *The Worker – Government and Form*.
132 Ibid.
133 Ibid.
134 Ibid.
135 Ibid.
136 Ibid.
137 Baeumler: *Männerbund und Wissenschaft*, Berlin 1934, p. 127.
138 Baeumler: *Nietzsche, der Philosoph und Politiker*, Leipzig 1931, p. 125.
139 Baeumler: *Männerbund und Wissenschaft*, p. 63.
140 Ibid., p. 62.

141 Boehm: *Anticartesianismus. Deutsche Philosophie im Widerstand*, Leipzig 1938, pp. 34f.
142 Baeumler: *Der Mythos vom Orient und Occident*, Introduction to Bachofen's Works, Munich 1926, pp. XCf.
143 Baeumler: *Männerbund und Wissenschaft*, p. 91.
144 Ibid., pp. 95f.
145 Krieck: *Völkisch politische Anthropologie*, Vol. I: *Die Wirklichkeit*. Leipzig 1936, p. 27.
146 Ibid., p. 74.
147 Ibid., p. 43.
148 Baeumler: *Männerbund und Wissenschaft*, p. 127.
149 Krieck: *Anthropologie*, p. 59.
150 Ibid., pp. 90f.
151 Ibid., p. 60.
152 Baeumler: *Männerbund und Wissenschaft*, p. 35.
153 Krieck: *Anthropologie*, p. 35.
154 Rauschning: *The Voice of Destruction*, New York 1940, p. 232.
155 Hitler: *Mein Kampf*.
156 Ibid.
157 Hegel: *Encyclopaedia*, para. 72.

CHAPTER V

NEO-HEGELIANISM

The relatively short 'Hegel renaissance' in the imperialist era was preceded by a much longer period during which Hegel was accorded no recognition at all. But the fact that Hegel fell into oblivion is, historically considered, only one side – by far the less important one – of the history of his influence. Germany's post-1848 bourgeoisie took the view that in order to reach its goals, it no longer needed even the reactionary elements in Hegel's philosophy, and that neo-Kantian positivism and agnosticism rendered Hegel completely superfluous as far as it was concerned. But whereas at the one extreme, Hegel's reactionary systematizing tendencies vanished from the philosophical scene, that which was alive, forward-looking and progressive in his thought, namely the dialectical method, entered into the higher world-outlook, into dialectical materialism. This is not the place to discuss how fundamental a reconstruction of Hegel's dialectics, as well, had to be carried out in the process. It would be to simplify and falsify history to assume that a certain changing of the terms would suffice to get from Hegel's idealist to Marx's materialist dialectics. Between Hegel and Marx there was a qualitative leap of world-historical significance; with Marx there came about – as compared to all that had gone before – a qualitatively new philosophy, a new dialectic. The result of this relationship of Hegel to Marx was that even those progressive elements in Hegel's dialectic with which Marx could associate himself had to be thoroughly transformed, as regards both form and content, and critically re-worked in the materialistic dialectic. Little though this procedure was understood by bourgeois philosophy, its

presence must have likewise become a co-determining reason for bourgeois thought's turning away from Hegel. Bernstein, a blind adherent of bourgeois philosophical tendencies and the founder of revisionism, expressed this state of things the most clearly when he simultaneously sought to make Kant the philosopher of 'seasonable' Marxism and attacked Marx on account of his 'Hegelianism', because of the dialectical (revolutionary, not evolutionary) character of his doctrine. Meanwhile Bernstein had, like all revisionists, taken in tow many bourgeois tendencies that were already obsolete. Hardly had he accomplished his 'purge' of Marxism from its Hegelian traces than more perspicacious bourgeois thinkers began to realize that the reactionary elements in Hegel – under imperialistic conditions – could, suitably recast, be rendered useful to the bourgeoisie's needs for a world-outlook. (One can often discern echoes of this change in bourgeois thinking about Hegel in the Social Democrats of the Weimar period.)

The defeat of the 1848 revolution finished off the collapse of the Hegelian system on the German philosophical scene. Rudolf Haym's book on Hegel (1857), which was crucial to the assessment of Hegel for a long period and carries weight even now as regards numerous points, summed up most effectively this coming to terms with the dialectical method. Naturally it cannot be said that all Hegelians had now disappeared from the face of the Earth. Many continued their activities; indeed for a long time there existed in Berlin a society of Hegelians which even published its own periodical (*Der Gedanke*, 1860-84). But only a handful, as for example Adolf Lasson, remained loyal to orthodox Hegelianism. To be sure, this orthodoxy must be properly understood from the historical angle. Those contradictions openly emerging between Hegel's dialectical method and the Hegelian system in the period spanning the July Revolution and 1848 found in dialectical materialism a solution on a qualitatively higher plane. The bourgeois Hegelians distanced themselves more and more from this 'algebra of revolution', as Alexander

Herzen called it. Orthodoxy of the type which Lasson was practising signified adherence to the Hegelian system, with all its often retrograde results. And precisely this adherence – amid a German development which, around 1870-1 and beyond, was leading into Wilhelmine imperialism – inevitably exacerbated the conflict between system and method from the reactionary side and forced the dialectical method into the background. Even Lassalle, who considered himself an orthodox Hegelian and wanted to be a revolutionary at the same time, was obliged to subjectify the dialectical method in many ways and to bring it nearer to Fichte. Under the pressure of current events and trends, there arose with the majority of Hegelians a – conscious or unconscious – movement away from Hegel's doctrine and method to an increasing degree. Many of them were now drawing closer to the Kantianism increasingly in evidence, without always registering the fact that they were thereby breaking with the Hegelian method. (Cf. Lassalle's review of Rosenkranz.) Others, drawing closer and closer to the positivism also emerging at that time, were already starting to bring irrationalist tendencies into philosophy (cf. the development of Franz Theodor Vischer). A sharply dismissive criticism of dialectics, represented chiefly by Trendelenburg, Schopenhauer, etc., dominated philosophical opinion to a growing extent; Hegelian philosophy was treated as an outdated metaphysic. Hence Marx was quite right to say that in Germany, Hegel was being treated as 'old hat' just as much as Spinoza had been in his own period.[1] The neo-Kantianism which had notably gained in strength after the defeat of the 1848 revolution officially voiced the philosophical burial of Hegel. It interpreted the development of German philosophy from Fichte to Hegel as a major aberration for which amends could only be made by a resolute divorce from it and an unqualified return to what was purportedly the sole scientific philosophy, that of Kant (Liebmann: *Kant und die Epigonen*, 1865). This view held sway in German philosophy until the imperialistic period.

Only in this period did it become more widely and strongly

palpable that purely positivistic neo-Kantianism was incapable of mastering the problems which the age was setting philosophers. In the so-styled South-West German school (Windelband-Rickert), there very soon sprang up a movement back to Fichte. Nietzsche's influence was growing all the time. And parallel to it in all spheres of the historical sciences, there was now originating a markedly positive revaluation of Romanticism which related not only to the Romantic school in the narrower sense, but also led to a revival of Schelling and Schleiermacher (Dilthey, Ricarda Huch, etc.). All such tendencies were connected with that general 'need of a world-view' by the imperialistic German bourgeoisie which we have already encountered. They were connected with the insight that it was impossible to prepare ideologically for the great internal, and, above all, outward struggles of the time on the basis of formalistic neo-Kantian thinking. It was in this intellectual milieu that the revival of Hegelian philosophy began in the pre-war period.

Earlier on, the origin of a new Hegelian bias had already been ascertained by the accredited philosophers, above all Windelband in his Academy speech.[2] He too saw that the general 'hunger for a world-view' formed the basis of this movement. But whilst recognizing its existence and its relative justification, his speech aimed chiefly at defining in advance the limits of the neo-Hegelian movement and warning the philosophical world of the dangers which such a movement could induce. Here Windelband formulated – albeit in the form of an advance staking of boundaries – an important element of the neo-Hegelian movement in the imperialistic era: the preservation of the link with Kant. The neo-Kantian concept of 'value' (*Geltung*) – i.e., subjective idealism – was, to his mind, 'the farthest point to which critical philosophical analysis can penetrate'.[3] The rejection of the dialectical method was very closely bound up with this standpoint. Our later studies will show that here, too, Windelband anticipated an important element in the later development of neo-Hegelianism: the rejection of the dialectical

method, whether explicit or tacit, was to become a constant feature of the whole Hegelian revival. Granted, as a Kantian Windelband formulated this in a negative spirit, in that he did not allow that 'such a dialectic as a whole' might form 'the method of philosophy again'.[4]

This eloquent warning from Windelband was superfluous. For the German neo-Hegelians had not the least thought of repeating Hegel's break with Kantian philosophy. As we know, Hegel always strongly repudiated Kant's subjective idealism, and in particular its denial of the perceptibility of the 'thing-in-itself'. The knowableness of it was a salient point in his dialectical epistemology, for this implied the dialectical relativity of phenomenon and essence, of the phenomenon and the thing-in-itself. If the properties of things (their phenomenal modes) have been perceived, then so have the things themselves, and the in-themselves become for-us, and under certain conditions for-themselves. Leaving aside this process of concrete perception leading from phenomenon to essence, the thing in itself, according to Hegel, was an empty and meaningless abstraction. The imperialist revivers of Hegel were far from even considering this criticism of Kant, let alone adopting it. They continued to abide by a modified neo-Kantian standpoint suited to the conditions of the imperialistic era, i.e., they went on mechanically dividing phenomenon from essence and did not admit of the existence and perceptibility of objective reality.

If they were renewing Hegel, they presented him – in contrast to his true historical character – as the consummation of Kant's philosophy, not as a thinker surmounting it. This epistemological foundation was very vividly expressed in a small book by Julius Ebbinghaus (*Relativer und absoluter Idealismus*, 1910), a book which, although it did not become widely known, had a decisive influence on the method and views of the later, more influential neo-Hegelians. We may briefly summarize Ebbinghaus's basic idea by saying that Hegel simply thought through to their logical conclusion all the consequences of Kant's transcendental method, whereas

Kant himself only half thought them out. Thus Hegelianism was nothing beyond a really rigorous, consistent Kantianism. Hence Ebbinghaus formulated the task facing neo-Hegelianism as follows: 'to develop the form of the philosophical *principle* out of the determinants of the Kantian "I", liberated from its faint-heartedness'.[5]

This leads to the second important thesis in the neo-Hegelian conception of the history of philosophy: the unity of classical German philosophy, which amounts to the blurring of any basic difference between Fichte, Schelling and Hegel. Ebbinghaus stated 'that no difference can be found as regards the *principle* in the constructions of that speculative philosophy preached from Fichte to Hegel, if they are grasped at once in their full scope'.[6] That was a considerable step backwards in comparison to the findings reached in Hegel's *History of Philosophy* and subsequently by Erdmann or Kuno Fischer. Although they too presented the development from Kant to Hegel in an all too straightforward way, one does however see very well – especially in Hegel's own account – that, precisely with regard to philosophical principles, notable cracks, clefts, gaps, etc., occur along this line (e.g., in the transition from subjective to objective idealism). But a searching and open-minded historical investigation would be bound to show that the road from Kant to Hegel was by no means so straight and direct as Hegel himself portrays it. To be sure, the development did have a certain unity to it. This was already so by dint of the fact that, without exception, the important German classical thinkers sought answers to the concrete questions of their time, the time of the French Revolution. But here the unity lay in the common social Being and in its intellectual reflections; the roads to realization, on the other hand, were far more complicated, circuitous and uneven than Hegel himself portrayed them. (For Hegel's own development, see my book, *The Young Hegel*, London, 1975.) Now Ebbinghaus, by laying down a unity of principle behind the development from Kant to Hegel, lowered the whole of German classical

philosophy to the plane of Kantian subjective idealism. He was thereby discounting its cardinal achievements, in particular the elaboration of the dialectical method, which Ebbinghaus and his successors presented as just an organic continuation of Kantian transcendental philosophy which never surpassed the latter in theory. So Hegelian philosophy was seen as the peak of an unbroken continuation of Kantianism. Thus Hegel was traced back to Fichte, objective to subjective idealism. In absolute idealism, Ebbinghaus wrote, 'the not-I is completely dissolved in the process of the I . . . The object is wholly and fully a knowing'.[7] That was, at best, a modernized Fichte, but it passed over the new element in the young Schelling's natural philosophy regardless and ignored all that Hegel had done to enrich philosophical knowledge. These theses of Ebbinghaus became exemplary for and fundamental to the development of German neo-Hegelianism in the imperialist period.

This was not, however, the only contribution to the renewal of Hegel, indeed not even the chief contribution. The book most important to the 'Hegel renaissance' in Germany was the old Dilthey's *Die Jugendgeschichte Hegels* ('The Story of Hegel's Youth', 1905). On the crucial epistemological questions, however, this most influential pioneer of the Hegel revival stood, as we have noted, extraordinarily close to neo-Kantianism. With regard to the speculative method Dilthey stated very firmly: 'Here, too, Kant's limiting definitions remain victorious.'[8] Similarly, and despite all their other differences, he agreed with Windelband in rejecting the dialectic method. Analysing the speculative method, he wrote: 'Equally the means of solving this falsely set task, namely the dialectic method, is completely useless, as Trendelenburg has convincingly proved.'[9] The otherwise greatly diverging tendencies of the neo-Hegelians were therefore at one concerning the central question – in their rejection of the dialectic method.

But the importance of Dilthey's book lay elsewhere. In that he discovered, as it were, the young Hegel, he wrought a

change that was of great moment for Hegel interpretation: he brought him into direct proximity to the irrationalistic 'vitalism' of the imperialist period, whose most important proponent was Dilthey himself. To be sure, his carrying over of vitalism into Hegel's thought was confined to the young Hegel, in whose work he ascertained a period of 'mystical pantheism'. During this period, Dilthey thought, Hegel represented vitalism: 'Hegel defines the character of all reality through the concept of life.'[10] This was a misrepresentation that stood on its head the whole of the young Hegel's development. Dilthey, by introducing an imperialist-vitalistic slant, was distorting both the crisis in which Hegel renounced the republican enthusiasm for the French Revolution and his investigation into the economic foundations of bourgeois society (Steuart, Smith), as also the dialectic method originating in this context. But this distortion enabled the new view of Hegel to fit in with the great vogue of irrationalism. (On this question, too, see my aforementioned book on the young Hegel.) And that Dilthey confined this interpretation to the young Hegel was, as we shall see, rich in consequences inasmuch as later, there arose in neo-Hegelianism a strong tendency to play off the young Hegel, as the authentic and genuine one, against the old.

There are two further considerations. Firstly Dilthey, himself one of the most important renewers of Romantic thought in the imperialist era, complemented Ebbinghaus's uniting of Kant, Fichte, Schelling and Hegel by laying down also a unifying link between Hegel and the whole Romantic movement (Friedrich Schlegel, Schleiermacher, Schelling). And in order to prove it, he did not shrink from the grossest distortion of history. For Hegel was a decided adversary to every form of German Romanticism from the very outset. His early polemic against F.H. Jacobi was aimed at the Romantics, even where the latter are not expressly mentioned; in the conclusion of *Belief and Knowledge*, he openly and sharply opposed a chief theoretical work of Romanticism, Schleiermacher's *Talks on Religion*. (He maintained an

intensely hostile attitude towards this author all his life.) The Romantic theory of art Hegel dismissed in the introduction to his *Philosophy of Art*, his *Philosophy of Right* teemed with the sharpest polemics against the representatives of the historical school of law and Romantic political and social theory (Hugo, Haller, Savigny), while the introduction to his *Phenomenology of the Mind* was directed against Schelling's Romantic and intuitionistic epistemology, against 'intellectual intuition' and so forth. Let us mention in passing that for their part, the Romantics judged Hegel in an equally hostile and dismissive fashion. Friedrich Schlegel, for instance, saw in the Hegelian dialectic a kind of satanism. Only between Hegel and the most important of Romantic aestheticians, Solger – whose dialectic surpassed the Romantic age in various ways – do we find mutual respect despite the numerous critical reservations on both sides. If a historian of Dilthey's knowledge and standing could ignore such obvious facts, if he could leave out of his Hegel portrait precisely the original's essential features, there is only one explanation. It is that Dilthey unhistorically and uncritically ascribed to Hegel his own attitude, which was vitalistic in the modern sense; in Romantic thinking he correctly located tendencies which had affinities with his own.

Secondly, Dilthey was seeking a historical basis for linking Hegel with the modern age. This bent had a real foundation inasmuch as the effects of Hegelian philosophy on German historical studies, religious studies, law, aesthetics, etc., were indeed uncommonly wide-ranging and profound, and they long survived the collapse of the philosophical influence in the narrower sense. In other words, specific tendencies, elements and fragments of Hegelian thinking continued to affect the German social sciences for a very long while, although here again the dialectic method was completely shunned. Since, as we have seen, Dilthey himself rejected it, the Hegelian influence on social studies was almost all that mattered to him. The two endeavours of Dilthey that we have touched on go hand in hand. At the same time that he

was blurring the distinctions between Hegel and Romantic thought with the 'historical school' belonging to it, he was giving exaggerated weight to Hegel's repercussions on the old Strauss, Zeller and so on. Thus Dilthey, in his renewal of Hegel, was inclined towards proving the hitherto lasting continuity of his influence in the aforestated sense.

The historians too helped to reinforce this latter Diltheyan tendency. Those who were carrying on the Ranke tradition in the imperialist period aimed at portraying Bismarck's foundation of the Reich and the Prussianizing of Germany as though no break with classical culture had occurred, as though the Second Reich and, above all, Bismarck had evolved from specific tendencies of around 1900 in the course of a wholly uninterrupted process. They now fitted Hegel into this context. The most influential work in this vein, Meinecke's *World Citizenship and the National State* (1907), deliberately drew a line running from Hegel through Ranke to Bismarck. Meinecke stated: 'Thus we now venture to name as the three great liberators of the State: Hegel, Ranke and Bismarck.'[11] Here similar tendencies prevailed as in Dilthey; but the blurring of the antithesis between Hegel on the one hand, and Romantic thought as well as the 'historical school' and, above all, Ranke on the other, now had a marked historico-political character. The existing Bismarck-Hohenzollern Reich was to be presented as the peak and the legacy of the whole German development in the nineteenth century; Hegel as a supporting figure on a large statue of Bismarck.

But all these attempts to make of Hegel a live and efficacious contemporary power, a power-house of Prusso-Wilhelmine conservatism, proceeded independently before the first imperialist war and did not yet constitute a clearly defined movement, far less a school. Beside the aforestated tendencies, another aspect of the incipient Hegel vogue was that his philosophy suggested an intellectual force which might be successfully played off against Marxism. In itself, as we have noted, the combating of Marxism – though seldom openly avowed, very often hardly consciously registered – had been

the main bias of irrationalism since Nietzsche. So it is understandable that before the war, there were already attempts to exploit the reactionary facets of Hegelian philosophy against Marx and socialism, on behalf of the ends of the imperialist bourgeoisie. Hammacher and, above all, Plenge came forward with such views. But the influential revisionist wing of German social democracy openly dissociated itself from Marxism's Hegelian legacy, and likewise, the 'orthodox' Marxists who were polemicizing against revisionism had no live contact with it (this applies not only to Kautsky, a man of the Centre, but also to the bright ideological leader of the Left, Franz Mehring). For the chief line of imperialist philosophy's ideological struggle at that time, it thus seemed sufficient to distort Hegelian doctrine in the style of Ebbinghaus or Dilthey. Hence the endeavours of Hammacher and Plenge remained episodes without major consequences.

Neo-Hegelianism only became a real movement after the German defeat in the First World War. The German bourgeoisie – threatened by revolution and constantly trapped in increasingly critical situations in respect of its attempts at consolidation, its striving to prepare Germany ideologically for fresh imperialist aggression – now sensed the 'need for a world-view' more strongly and was developing it more vigorously than ever. Now neo-Hegelianism also went towards meeting this ideological need; it too was carried along on this general reactionary current, which moved slowly at first but then with torrential force.

But it would be wrong to suppose that neo-Hegelianism was ever the really dominant ideology of the German bourgeoisie between the two world wars. During that period its ruling ideology was always, as we have seen, the ever-increasingly radical irrationalism of 'vitalism', the philosophy which did so much to pave the reactionary German bourgeoisie's way to fascism. Naturally neo-Hegelianism too was quite reactionary enough, but it expressed bourgeois tendencies that were more moderate, more eclectic in a reactionary way, more 'consolidated'. It was – philosophically speaking – an

attempt to incorporate irrationalism in a system without giving up rational principles or scientific thinking completely or to a decided extent. We are dealing with a philosophical bias matching those German bourgeois tendencies which were ever-present and sometimes came to the forefront, but always remained episodic in the final analysis. And these consisted in absorbing the 'constructive' elements of fascism into a reactionary, unified bourgeois front as a partial and not a principal element. (This bias emerged most clearly during the short period that General Schleicher was Chancellor of the Reich.)

There arose on this basis a synthesis of the neo-Hegelian orientations which had proceeded separately in the pre-war period. Synthesis must here be understood in a very broad and manifold sense. It implied not only the summing up and unification of the pre-war tendencies of which we have spoken, but also a new idea of synthesis which was foisted on Hegel. Interpreting Hegelian philosophy as a synthesis of all orientations of past ages and the age of Hegel himself, the neo-Hegelians now wanted to produce a similar synthesis of all the current philosophical tendencies on a neo-Hegelian basis. They could not or would not see that Hegel took a clearly defined line of his own for the sake of which he fiercely contested all the orientations of his time (Kantians, Jacobi, the Romantics, the historical school of right, Fries, etc.). Nor could they see that he did not seek in past ages an uncritically eclectic unity, but aimed at demonstrating how dialectics had evolved from the first beginnings of human thought up to what he considered their most advanced form – that inherent in his own system. Thus Hegel synthesized different philosophical trends only to the following extent. On the one hand, he showed that the entire history of philosophy was man's intellectual quest for the genuine philosophical method, the dialectical method. He further showed that while, in the course of this development, the most diverse thinkers – according to their times, culture and personality – had raised the most diverse problems from the angle of both content and form, there was, nonetheless, a

unity behind this variety: the objective unity of philosophy, the unity of its cardinal substance, namely the reproduction of reality, as it exists in itself. That is to say, dialectically – the unity of the determining form: of the dialectical method. On the other hand, Hegel saw his own philosophy as an intellectual crowning of sorts of the entire development, for it endeavoured to encompass everything which, in the way of progressive tendencies and especially the extending of the dialectical method, past philosophy had first produced and then superseded, thus eliminating its shortcomings while at the same time preserving it and raising it to a higher plane. Not for one second, however, did Hegel contemplate a synthesis of the philosophical orientations of his time, a synthesis, say, with Kant or Schleiermacher.

The neo-Hegelians, on the contrary, were seeking a peaceable union of all the reactionary tendencies of their day, a kind of philosophical 'consolidation', and they now imposed this idea upon Hegel. The methodological basis of this tendency was the complete elimination of dialectics from their picture of Hegel. So the contradictory movement of history that we find in his work was transformed into an Alexandrian eclecticism, a peaceful and static juxtaposition of events. It was such a portrait of Hegel that Kroner tried to sketch in his speech on the hundredth anniversary of his death. He compared Hegel with Aristotle and Aquinas as though the former had sought to achieve with Plato, and the latter with Jewish religious thinkers and Mohammedanism, a synthesis akin to that which Kroner was imputing to Hegel. The simple formulation of the question shows his intentions in all clarity: the reason for the influence of Hegel's world-view, he opined, lay in the fact that 'it brilliantly does justice to the eternal basic motives of thought by arranging the fullness of reality in a hierarchy in which every single thing has its appointed place. Through these architectonics it is capable of uniting even opposites, of achieving a balance between conflicting facts.'[12] Here, let us note, Hegel is alleged to have created an architectonic edifice and to have converted the dialectical resolution

of opposites (in a given system or orientation) into an agreement between conflicting facts, as though it had ever occurred to him to obtain agreement between, say, Bacon and Descartes!

This, however, was only the methodological basis; more important is the concrete content. Kroner stated it programmatically in his inaugural speech at the first Hegel Congress. He dealt with Hegel's adversaries, *Kritizismus* and phenomenology, 'dialectical theology' (Kierkegaard), Heidegger, and so forth, before stating: '. . . they are *disunited* among themselves only because they do not grasp their mutual need for integration, do not mutually penetrate one another and band together. And they are *united* in opposing Hegel only because in their one-sidedness they exclude not only each other, but by the same token the whole in which they are reduced to elements as well.'[13] Glockner supplemented this programme very clearly with the following statements, which in part went farther still – in an irrationalistic direction. 'Everywhere there exists a desire to escape from the rationalism which was generally prevalent in the last third of the century, and which we may label as the "new Enlightenment". But it will not do simply to side with the "new romanticism" which that rationalism summoned up as its antithesis. Here the task is to "mediate" . . . Hegel performed that act of "mediation" which is required in Germany at present. In the name of Hegel the factions can conclude peace and make common cause.'[14]

Neo-Hegelianism's social content emerges clearly from these remarks. Firstly, Kroner saw in the various lines of thought of the time (including fascism) only partisan views which had not grasped the mutual need for integration, and were combating one another for that reason alone. Their struggles, he believed, had no authentic factual substance to them, and these trends – we must stress this – were not moving in a reactionary direction. So all that was needed for everlasting peace in philosophy (as in social life) was a generally acceptable compromise proposal. Glockner further

supplemented this content by adding that there was justification for a struggle against the 'new Enlightenment' (i.e., the remnants of rationalism). Only, one had to stop short of radical or militant irrationalism. Naturally the world-outlook of the working class, Marxism, was excluded from the synthesis; it was rather the case that it opposed Marxism, if not always to a decided extent. The purpose of a philosophical synthesis under Hegel's aegis was a coalition of all bourgeois orientations against the proletariat. The neo-Hegelians' petty-bourgeois narrow-mindedness, which had not a few parallels in politics at that time, consisted chiefly in their reluctance to acknowledge that an effective defensive action on the part of the bourgeoisie would involve violent policy conflicts ending with the victory of the most reactionary wing of monopoly capitalism. And this at a time when the class struggle between bourgeoisie and proletariat was become more and more embittered. Here, neo-Hegelianism, seemingly doing the obvious practical thing but really in a wholly utopian way, was putting itself forward as a suitable umbrella organization for all current reactionary (and hence philosophically reactionary) trends of thought.

By thus undertaking a synthesis of the various philosophical orientations, neo-Hegelianism was setting itself the task of guiding the imperialistic post-war crisis of world-outlook into 'normal' and 'ordered' channels. In this we can read an essential difference to pre-war times. In its attempt to find a reactionary compromise solution, neo-Hegelianism acknowledged the fact of such a crisis; this motive could not, in the context of Being, have arisen in pre-war philosophy. Siegfried Marck interpreted neo-Hegelianism as such a 'crisis theory' in contrast to orthodox Kantianism. Hence he wrote of Rickert: 'He therefore affirms the "bourgeois" world-epoch, regards its solutions as sound and the epoch itself as in no danger of collapsing . . . But are not Hegel and Kierkegaard, those mighty and affiliated antipodes of the nineteenth century, are not the *dialecticians of the real* and *ideal* (here Marx is mentioned along with Hegel and Kierkegaard, G.L.) . . . harb-

ingers of a *post-Kantian, post-bourgeois* and also *post-Christian* world-epoch?'[15] Kroner too stated: 'Modern Kantianism has entered a crisis.'[16]

All this obviously implies a certain distance from neo-Kantianism. But the repudiation of it was far less radical than that which we have discerned in Glockner with regard to the 'new Enlightenment', i.e., all Left-oriented thinking. For nearly all the leading neo-Hegelians came from neo-Kantianism, and chiefly from the south-west German school (Kroner, Glockner, Siegfried Marck, etc.), where Kantianism had always gone farthest in the direction of irrationalism. We must not fail to mention that in 1920, Rickert published a book attacking vitalism. But this book's (respectful) critique of vitalistic irrationalism cannot hide the fact that it was none other than Rickert (together with Windelband) who argued in philosophical terms the irrationalism of a large area of knowledge, namely that of historical studies. It matters precious little that the word 'irrationalism' did not actually occur in this epistemological argument; for in essence this theory of history certainly tended in that direction. It is true that by 1920, Rickert was already concerned about the consequences of an extreme irrationalism. This very fact demonstrates, from a different angle, his affinity with the neo-Hegelians; they too heeded irrationalism and simply wanted to evade its most extreme consequences. Both types of 'challenge' to irrationalism show the same weakness, the total vulnerability of a German intelligentsia which was wholly under its spell, fascinated by it in every respect, but which nonetheless wished to dodge its ultimate consequence – Hitlerian fascism. Without seeking to repel in any way or even to moderate reactionary tendencies to any appreciable extent, these intellectuals wished to steer the troubled post-war developments into 'ordered channels'. That this was politically impossible the outcome of the Weimar period showed clearly enough. The nature and destiny of neo-Hegelianism reflect the same plight.

With the neo-Hegelians, then, we note a specific dividing-

line from the neo-Kantians, but at the same time a far more marked emphasis on the continuity with Kant and neo-Kantianism. Glockner even stated: 'It may sound paradoxical, but in Germany today the *Hegel* question is primarily a *Kant* question.'[17] And in this respect, the great book by Kroner that had a central influence on neo-Hegelianism (*From Kant to Hegel*, 1921-4) was not much more than a concrete realization of the programme constructed by Ebbinghaus in his day: the attempt to prove that Hegel's philosophy had grown out of Kant's as a matter of inner necessity, without departing from the basic principle. Kroner stated: 'German idealism from Kant to Hegel should be grasped in its development as a single whole: as a line soaring in a splendid curve according to a law inherent in it, and impressing itself nowhere else . . . one must depict how the Hegelian philosophy of mind has grown out of the Kantian critique of reason.'[18] And he added 'that the major successors to Kant have surpassed him *because* they understood him'.[19] So for Kroner, as for Ebbinghaus, the unity of classical German philosophy (Fichte, Schelling, Hegel) was only an unfolding of what was implicitly present in the Kantian conception. And Kroner developed this schema in a consistent way. The Hegelian system, for example, he showed as deriving straight from Schelling's philosophy. Where, however, he could no longer conceal the open break between Hegel and Schelling in the *Phenomenology of the Mind*, he misconstrued Hegel's advance as – a harking back to Kant and Fichte. Thus Kroner commented on the *Phenomenology*: 'Hegel renews the subjectivism of Kant and Fichte by raising it to the stage of absolute idealism attained by Schelling . . . The book counters the idea behind Kant's critique of reason and Fichte's theory of scientific thought with the old identity-system of Schelling, thus countering the idea of "epistemology".'[20] In no sense does that square with the historical facts of the matter. Hegel did not have an epistemology at all in the Kantian sense. He rejected in principle the investigation of the cognitive faculty *prior to* knowledge. In order to learn to swim, he said, we

must get into the water, by which he meant that the correctness or otherwise of perception, the degree of our ability to know, etc., can be demonstrated only *within* the concrete cognitive process. Secondly, the *Phenomenology of the Mind* contains no sign of a return to the subjectivism of Kant and Fichte. This, for Kant and Fichte, was the corner-stone of their whole philosophy. The function of the *Phenomenology* in Hegel's system at the time was, on the other hand, a representation of the subject's development leading it to the point from which objective philosophy (logic, natural and humanistic philosophy) could be adequately mapped out and comprehended. And in line with this methodological task, the *Phenomenology* did not provide an analysis of the structure, capabilities, etc., of the subject, as did the Kant-Fichte epistemology, but the *history* of the subject in the course of the objective history of man's development. The work's 'mixture' of historical, psychological and epistemological considerations, faulted by Haym and others, was no failing but a methodologically rigorous carrying out of an intention radically different from that of Kant or Fichte. And Kroner, with his neo-Kantian blinkers, was unwilling even to see this intention, let alone understand it.

So the epistemological basis of neo-Hegelianism remains in essence Kantian. To be sure, this statement does full justice to neither the philosophical nor the historical endeavours of the neo-Hegelians. In the historical sphere, they carried on the Meinecke line. Rosenzweig, an avowed supporter of Meinecke, traced back to Hegel the ideological foundations of German national liberalism, that is to say the coupling of former German liberalism with Bismarck. In Hegel, he wrote, the national liberals had found 'the philosophical rationale for the hard, outwardly oriented power-character of the State'. Granted – and Rosenzweig himself had to admit this – they were no Hegelians in the stricter sense; but 'they believed it possible to utilize the "substance" of the system without needing to cling to the "formal letter" of the method. And this they were historically entitled to do.'[21]

With this glorification of the Hegelian system, i.e., its reactionary contents, and this radical rejection of the dialectical method, Rosenzweig believed he had established the ideological continuity in the development of the nineteenth-century German bourgeoisie. Like Meinecke, he was presenting Hegel as a forefather of the contemporary reactionary bourgeoisie, as a predecessor and accomplice to Bismarck. Of the neo-Hegelians Glockner, in particular, most vigorously adopted this line. He wrote monographs on Vischer and Erdmann in order to prove this continuity in the philosophical field as well. Naturally Glockner knew perfectly well that Vischer, for example, had expressly departed from Hegel. But it was just that which rendered him valuable in the eyes of such 'Hegelians' as Glockner; for he seemed to them an ally in the liquidation of the dialectical method. Vischer, according to Glockner, had preserved what was really lasting in Hegel precisely by turning away from his dialectics.

This historical bias now leads us back to Dilthey. In neo-Hegelianism, Dilthey's 'discovery' of the young Hegel as a 'vitalist' entailed the interpretation and presentation of the young thinker as the 'authentic' Hegel. Hegel's later development, his cultivation of the dialectical method was seen as a gradual ossifying, as a more or less life-negating logical ordering, etc., of the great achievements of his youth. Within neo-Hegelianism there were, of course, major distinctions with regard to this question. Kroner, for instance, generally confined himself to representing the historically significant later Hegel, while Herbert Marcuse, Hugo Fischer, Glockner, and so on, put the crucial emphasis on Hegel's departure from his youthful 'vitalism', though they had differing estimations of it. They shared, however, the basic line that the contemporary and forward-looking elements in his work had originated in his youth, whereas the mature Hegel was important only insofar as he had retained those tendencies. Here again neo-Hegelianism was proceeding in a wholly unhistorical manner. Not only did it completely neglect the essential unity in the young and old Hegel, namely his dialectical method. It also

overlooked the real historical changes in Hegel's life and thinking: his support for the French Revolution and the Frankfurt crisis, the hopes he staked on Napoleon and his corresponding philosophy of history during the Jena period, and finally the (resigned) turn of his thought after Napoleon's final defeat, and the building of his definitive system. It would be impossible to answer the primary question correctly without insight into this concrete development. For it shows that even through these vicissitudes, Hegel was able to sustain his *Logic* with continual improvements to it, but without any decisive reconstruction. But for the neo-Hegelians, as we have seen, Hegel's dialectic did not exist.

It was from such a standpoint that Glockner challenged the general view of the dissolution of Hegelianism. This, he claimed, was relevant only to the '*old* Hegel, the skilful systematizer, the Berlin headmaster, the conservative State philosopher'.[22] Dilthey, on the other hand, had supposedly discovered the young Hegel who had lighted on 'the mobile fullness of life impelling the youthful thinker to resolve the eternal problems of the irrational . . .' This doctrine was not affected by the dissolution of Hegelianism. 'So it was the *old* Hegel who was alive at the time. So it was *only* the old Hegel who died at the time.' Thus the present task was 'a "surmounting" of the old Hegel in the spirit of the young one'. Marcuse, deriving his ideas from Heidegger, drew the following conclusion from the aforestated historical interpretation: 'At the deepest level Dilthey took up "vitalism" again where Hegel left off.'[23]

Considered from the angle of philosophical history, this conception meant bringing Hegel another stage closer to Romantic thought. Just as the neo-Kantian line had blurred the distinctions between Hegel's objective idealism and the subjective idealism of Kant and Fichte, so we have here a blurring of all the sharp contrasts dividing Hegel from Schelling and particularly from Schleiermacher, from Friedrich Schlegel, Novalis, Savigny and Adam Müller. This line was taken by Metzger, Troeltsch, Hugo Fischer, etc. And here

again Glockner was the most radical, in that – entirely in Dilthey's spirit – he laid down a close connection between Hegel and Schleiermacher, who in reality passionately opposed each other all their lives. Glockner declared 'that a history of Hegelianism cannot be written without a history of Schleiermachism'.[24] As we have seen, Kroner himself toed the Kantian line. But when, at the very time of his *chef d'oeuvre*, Nicolai Hartmann wrote a history of German idealism which strongly emphasized Hegel's affinity with the Romantic thinkers, Kroner hailed the achievement as a first-class complement to his own.

This historical falsification of the origin and effect of Hegelian philosophy, its hypotheses and its growth, served a double purpose. One purpose was radically to banish the dialectic from the Hegelian method, 'correctly understood' and 'seasonably renewed'. The second was to make vitalistic irrationalism the constitutive basis of that new synthesis of the whole of German reactionary philosophy for which neo-Hegelianism was striving.

In the introduction to his Hegel analyses, Kroner made the following programmatic declaration: 'It was a matter of making good the damage caused through the catchword "Pan-logism" coined by J. E. Erdmann; this could only be achieved if, for once, we sharply stressed the *irrationalistic* instead of the rationalistic character of the dialectic . . .'[25] Thus he corrected Erdmann not through a dialectical interpretation of the, intrinsically, likewise misleading term 'Pan-logism', but by taking refuge in the dominant trend of imperialistic reactionary thinking, namely irrationalism. In the course of demolishing Hegelian philosophy, the programme he had set up was now assiduously developed. Kroner stated: '*Hegel is without doubt the greatest irrationalist* that the history of thought has known. No thinker before him succeeded in illuminating a concept as he did . . . Hegel is an irrationalist because he brought out the irrational aspect of thought, because he irrationalized thought itself . . . He is an irrationalist because he is a *dialectician*, because the dialectic

itself is *irrationalism converted into method, made rational* – because, finally, dialectical thought is rational-cum-irrational thought.'[26] And continuing this train of thought: 'Thinking in its dialectical, speculative form is in itself irrational, that is to say supra-rational, because it is *living*: it is life thinking itself.'[27] And of the *Phenomenology of the Mind* Kroner wrote – entirely in the spirit of imperialistic vitalism of the Diltheyan variety: 'Here the problem of perceiving is deepened, extended downwards to the problem of *experiencing*.'[28]

This expresses quite plainly the turn to irrationalistic vitalism. Kroner differed from Dilthey in only one respect. Dilthey, on the basis of Trendelenburg's critique, had rejected dialectics and achieved the transition from neo-Kantianism to vitalism the long way round, via an enlargement of Kant's epistemological propositions. Kroner, on the other hand, simply called dialectics irrationalism treated as a method. (Once again we see that the earlier upholders of a reactionary orientation are, as a rule, more consistent and honest than the later ones.)

We need not dwell for long on the fact that this neo-Hegelian stance had nothing in common with Hegel. As far as any forerunners of vitalism were about in his time (and only advocates of 'direct knowledge', i.e., intuition, like F.H. Jacobi qualify as such), Hegel always repudiated them with the utmost energy. He would only have laughed in scorn at a 'downward extension' of the problem of perceiving into the problem of experiencing. After all, the fundamental point in his theory of knowledge – this applies to his *Phenomenology* and thus to his earlier thinking also – was that each direct sensation, each experience is *just as* abstract as the categories of the understanding and reflective determinants; and the precise task of the reason, of the self-perfecting dialectic is to rise above *both* and to locate the real, concrete defining terms. Granted, Hegel could not have come across irrationalism yet as a central philosophical question. The very term he used only in its exact mathematical sense. But in his generalized analysis of those questions pertaining to know-

ledge arising here, it is clear that he saw in both objective and subjective sets of facts simply problems and tasks for rational, dialectical thought; whereas modern irrationalism has been wont to interpret the case-facts to suit its own ends, by treating them as basic structures of Being, as 'primary phenomena' and 'eternal' confines of thinking. Hegel, therefore, saw in the 'irrational' aspect of mathematics and geometry 'a beginning and trace of *rationality*',[29] i.e., a set question for dialectical thinking, whose 'irrationality' (Hegel ascertained a perversion of the term's meaning in common parlance) was resolved dialectically as a matter of course. So nothing was further from Hegel's mind than the neo-Hegelian celebration of the irrational. For that reason Kroner's position was, as a Hegel interpretation, untenable, unscientific, a travesty of the scientific positions of Hegelian philosophy. But it characterized all the more strongly the fundamental bias of neo-Hegelianism: a capitulation in the face of the chief irrationalistic trend of the imperialistic period, of the philosophical preliminaries to fascism. The one original element in Kroner's thinking is that he no longer presented irrationalism as a counter-movement to dialectics, as Dilthey had done; he simply identified dialectics with irrationalism.

That was unquestionably a symptom of the deepening crisis. We have frequently observed how irrationalism arises as a specious answer to a concrete question of life, and how it converts elements of the real question into the totality of an untrue, reactionary answer. Philosophically, however, this operation largely took the form of a repudiation of dialectics, the most effective means of diverting into a reactionary channel the genuine forward movement latent in the concrete question (in reality). Not until the years of crisis around 1848 did there originate with Kierkegaard a pseudo-dialectic irrationalistically aimed against the dialectical method. Kroner, of course, went to less trouble than Kierkegaard, contenting himself with passing off his own mediocre vitalistic irrationalism as dialectics. Nowhere do Kroner's contents exceed those of his vitalistic predecessors. All that was new –

and this is the crisis symptom – was the labelling of the dialectic.

Kroner's pronounced allegiance to irrationalism is notable in itself because otherwise, in this respect, he belonged to the moderate wing of neo-Hegelianism. In Glockner the bias was expressed far more radically; Glockner was not wholly satisfied with Kroner's account. For him it did not go far enough. 'Kroner did not fail to recognize Hegel's "irrationalism" but emphatically underlined it. But it was presented only by implication, so to speak: as an element of the dialectical method.'[30] Glockner, on the contrary, put forward the following programme: 'I would like to bring to awareness the irrational elements contained in all concrete thought in a subtler way than is found in Hegel himself. I would like to show that these elements may be linked with a scientific-philosophical method in a non-dialectical way.'[31] Accordingly, Glockner sought to transcend Hegel's putative 'pan-logism' with a 'pan-tragism'. This term is familiar to us from the writings of Hebbel. Its essential content had already cropped up, among none other than the Hegelians, during the 1848 revolution. (Wilhclm Jordan and Ruge in Frankfurt, Vischer in his memoirs of Stuttgart.) At bottom it meant two things. On the one hand, each 'tragedy' in history had to be acknowledged as an 'eternal' decree of fate (so that the decline of feudal Poland, for instance, was final and no longer remediable through the birth of a democratic-peasant revolution in Poland). And on the other hand, the reactionary party to every historical controversy had, objectively, the same justification as the progressive side. It was, therefore, the beginning of the liquidation of Hegel's concept of historical progress.

In reality this concept was by no means a simple optimistic 'pan-logism'; on the contrary. Admittedly Hegel adhered to the idea of progress in man's development, but he clearly perceived that the road was paved with a continuous series of personal and national tragedies. Thus he by no means contested the phenomenon of the tragic, but only moved it

to the appropriate place in the overall context of history. (That this point is also very closely connected with the basic idea of *Faust*, that here Hegel and Goethe were going in the same direction, I have attempted to show in my book *Goethe and his Age*, London, 1968.)

With the aforesaid Hegelians or sometime Hegelians, on the other hand, we have an approximation to Schopenhauer's anti-historical irrationalism whereby the 'cosmically' tragic factor casts an 'infamous' light on every idea of historical or social progress. Now when Glockner revived this idea, it was more than a philosophical working out of that historical line already familiar to us. It signified a conjunction of neo-Hegelianism with the vitalistic tendencies expressed initially in the Nietzschean '*amor fati*', then in Simmel's 'tragedy of culture', and subsequently leading via Spengler to Heidegger's existential nihilism, which was also, in its own way, a 'pan-tragism'. The tendency manifested therein will be obvious to anyone acquainted with the German philosophy of post-war imperialism: it is an approximation of neo-Hegelianism to that nihilistic world-view of Heidegger or Jaspers which we have already encountered.

Along with the transposition of irrationalism, disguised as dialectics, to the centre of neo-Hegelian methodology, all dialectics had to be carefully removed from the purportedly 'renewed' Hegel. Some neo-Hegelians carried this out by twisting Hegel's dialectics back, where possible, to Kant's doctrine of antinomies. Principal among them was Kroner who announced, entirely in the Kantian spirit: 'Philosophy cannot proceed beyond itself, it *ends* in contradiction.'[32] Among the rest of the neo-Hegelians this anti-dialectical trend had a greater prominence still. Siegfried Marck formulated his position with regard to 'critical' dialectics in the following terms: '*Kritizismus* affirms the dialectical element while rejecting the dialectic.'[33] Accordingly Marck accepted 'in the Hegelian term "supersession" (*Aufhebung*) only the "preservation and elevation", the *tollere* element', and rejected that which implied 'a negation of the negation'. Let us

remark in passing, so as to illustrate the neo-Hegelians' ignorance of Hegel with a crass example, that the *tollere* in the Hegelian definition of 'supersession' is by no means identical with the 'negation of the negation'. In Hegel the first negation was the – decisive – element in every supersession, which would be meaningless without it, whereas the negation of the negation signifies the specific concluding stage of a triadic-dialectical ordered framework. The confusion is typical inasmuch as here, Marck was rejecting exactly the conditions of the dialectic most deeply rooted in concrete history. His confusion between simple negation and the negation of the negation was a twofold repudiation of everything that is forward-looking and indeed revolutionary about the dialectical method. On the one hand, behind the *tollere* there lies the intellectual mirroring of an – often violent – historical change (dialectics in nature did not interest Marck at all). And on the other, the negation of the negation, if set up from the materialist angle, similarly points to the – again, often violent – revolutionary transformation of the social structure, to the antagonistic path of progress as Engels analysed it in Rousseau's social doctrine when rebutting Dühring.[34] The ignorance of Hegel apparent in his 'renewer', Marck, is therefore, a clear indication that Marck was far less concerned here with him than with Marx. The revolutionary consequences of Marxism were to be 'refuted' pseudo-dialectically, in a neo-Hegelian form, just as Bernstein had 'refuted' them in an overtly anti-dialectical way from a neo-Kantian standpoint. While the social tendency had remained the same – Siegfried Marck too was a social democrat – the philosophical form, in view of the exacerbation of the crisis, the existence of the Soviet Union and of Communist parties throughout the world, had changed accordingly in Germany as well. It is only too understandable that a philosophical orientation whose declared intention was conciliation with the reactionary thinking of its time was bound to choose such a policy. But this – like the other points we have stressed – goes to show that Hegel's renewers were treating him as 'old hat' just

as much as his detractors had formerly done. And it was only consistent of Marck to take issue with the 'Bacchanalian whirl' of dialectical concepts in the *Phenomenology*, of which he wrote: 'In this culmination the dialectic outstrips itself, at this point it really keels over into its own opposite, into meaninglessness.'

With Glockner, this tendency then turned into a decided irrationalism. Although he defended Hegel against the charge of 'pan-logism', he found it understandable and justified because of Hegel's doctrine of contradiction. 'I do not count the doctrine of contradiction among the on-going elements of Hegelian philosophy.'[35] One must acknowledge its historical existence but he personally, Glockner added, could not take it over as a systematizer . . . Contradiction was, he wrote, a central logical phenomenon; it would find its place within the system, but it did not determine the method. Here too the sharply anti-dialectical character of neo-Hegelianism in all important questions is clearly visible. With a vague, non-committal bow to the dialectic, incarcerated in the 'nature reserve' of a – needless to say – purely subjective, neo-Kantian logic, Glockner contested the possibility of applying it to reality. (This 'nature reserve' was carefully kept well apart from social reality; in similar fashion, the neo-Kantian social democrat Max Adler had already 'purged' the theory of contradiction of its revolutionary content.) Hence Glockner summed up the positive and negative sides of Hegel's philosophy as follows: 'Hegel attempted to think concretely, to philosophize objectively, to exist substantially as a philosopher . . .' (here he was kierkegaardizing Hegel, and characterizing as genuinely Hegelian just what, according to Kierkegaard, was from his existentialist viewpoint necessarily lacking in the Hegelian dialectic. Hegel was again being 'rescued' through an unwarrantable smuggling in of contents essentially alien to him, G.L.) . . . 'Hegel tried to let matters run their own course, to stand aside from realism and idealism (thus to choose the imperialist 'third road' in philosophy and to be, *de facto*, a Machist subjective idealist, G.L.) – and we

want all this today as well.'[36] To be sure, Hegel solved this task in a dialectical way and therefore, in Glockner's eyes, incorrectly from the methodological standpoint.

So neo-Hegelianism 'erased' the dialectic of Hegel with the greatest of respect, but just as firmly as Haym or Trendelenburg had done in a sharply polemical form. The one modern thinker to take a positive view of the dialectic, Nicolai Hartmann, treated it entirely as a mystery, as an enigmatic godsend bestowed upon genius: 'The dialectic cannot be arbitrarily divorced from the Hegelian store of ideas . . . It devolves on individuals like manna from heaven, and they then use it to produce works which others follow but barely understand, intellectual structures which other men think out only laboriously and circuitously. The talent for dialectical thinking is in that sense eminently comparable with the talent of the artist or genius. Like any gift of the mind it is rare and not something which can be acquired . . .'[37] This defence too turned Hegel into 'old hat'. For anybody who has really read the *Phenomenology of the Mind* and studied a little of its background history must know that the unlearnable quality which Hartmann ascribed to the Hegelian dialectic, and his comparison with the artist's mind, characterizes precisely Schelling's view of the dialectic. But the methodology of the *Phenomenology* was directed with great polemical force against that view and proclaimed the universal accessibility, in principle, of dialectics. Indeed, without doing violence to Hegel one may say that it was one of the book's chief aims to illustrate the learnable nature of the dialectic, and that one of its purposes as a whole was to guide conventional thinking to dialectics step by step. Here again the serious error in interpretation was not so important, except as a symptom; more so was the inherent capitulation to the aristocratic epistemology of irrationalism. And this tendency appears in the constructions put on Hegel, in respect of every question, by the otherwise very different thinkers of the time. It indicates the utter defencelessness of the German intelligentsia in the face of the irrationalist fascist takeover of philosophy.

Thus we observe that the Hegel, whose 'renaissance' German imperialism had brought about, had nothing to do with Hegel's progressive tendencies, either historically or systematically. Everything conservative or reactionary about his system, on the other hand, was carefully retained and fondly cultivated. We have been able to note exactly from many individual accounts that it was just the dialectical method which became the main victim of this Hegel 'renewal'. And that was far from an accident. For Hegelian dialectics are not one method among many others in modern philosophy. In origin and essence they marked a continuation, on a higher plane, of the efforts of the finest minds since the Renaissance to try and argue philosophically the rationality and progressiveness of man's development. The higher plane achieved by Hegel derived from the new historical situation in which he had to comprehend rationality and progressiveness: the socio-historical situation created through the French Revolution. That entailed two things. Firstly, Hegel comprehended reason in its contradictory nature, i.e., in contrast to the general Enlightenment tradition which often – though by no means always – presented the connection between reason and life in an all too direct, straightforward way. He perceived in contradiction itself the objective process whereby reason takes distinct shape in life. In simplifying and vulgarizing this inseparable unity of contradiction and reason, in calling it 'pan-logism', Hegel's successors were already deviating from his dialectical method. In neo-Hegelianism, as we have seen, the polemics against this deviation turned into an equation of dialectics and irrationalism – a total falsification of the Hegelian method, in that rationality, hitherto merely vulgarized, now vanished from the method completely. Secondly, the dialectical method signified a historical defence of progress. The philosophical reaction which followed upon the French Revolution had established a view of the historical process from which the idea of progress had disappeared, and which declared every social revolution in particular to be anti-historical. The gist of the Hegelian dialectical method was, on

the other hand – and this is inseparably united with the central place of contradictoriness – the proof that the convoluted, irregular paths of history themselves reveal its profound rationality, which is often not immediately visible. Hence the founders of dialectical and historical materialism were able to ally themselves with Hegel. They did so, of course, on the basis of a relentless critique of his idealism (with all its consequences in respect of content and methodology), his reactionary system, and so forth. The depth and universal range of this critique, the qualitatively new character of Marxism by comparison with Hegel, and the antithetical cast of the new materialist-dialectical method as compared to Hegel's idealist dialectic do not, however, remove the fact of the critical alliance. After all, dialectical and historical materialism is the philosophy in which progress and rationally cognizable principles of history are expressed in their highest form, the only philosophy which can argue the case for progressiveness and rationality in a fully consistent way. That neo-Hegelianism was – without always publicly admitting it – in all a polemical sally against the Marxist reshaping of the Hegelian dialectic we have already seen. We have seen also that the 'scientific' form of this polemic was a downright distortion of Hegelian thought: it took away its dialectic, progressiveness and rationality. Thus neo-Hegelianism, which in its subjective aims often resembled an effort to resist the despotism of irrationalist vitalism, led into the main tidal waters of the imperialist destruction of reason. The renewing of Hegel signifies nothing more, here, than an attempt by moderate reactionary sectors of the German bourgeoisie to reach a compromise with the reactionary extremists.

The attempt was a failure. Philosophically, the victory of the reactionary groups in the imperialist bourgeoisie led to the victory of the most extreme irrationalist 'vitalism' – and this in its most debased form, that of 'National-Socialist philosophy'. The neo-Hegelians naturally tried to carry out a compromise policy with regard to overt fascism as well. This effort had a specific external basis: Hitler (with an eye to

foreign relations) had somehow to keep the universities ticking over, and the neo-Hegelians were known to be sufficiently reactionary for a triumphant national socialism to tolerate them. (Only 'non-Aryan' neo-Hegelians like Kroner were obliged to emigrate.) So neo-Hegelianism continued to vegetate; in Göttingen there even sprang up a special neo-Hegelian school of law philosophy (Binder, Busse, Larenz, etc.); the publication of collected source-material, monographs, etc., went on.

The neo-Hegelians made various attempts at a rapport with the Hitler régime, all commending Hegel as a trustworthy reactionary ideologist. Of these very numerous attempts let us give just one example. Herbert Franz rested his case on the claim that in Italy Hegel was the political philosopher of fascism, 'whereas in Germany he has to suffer some hostility at present. Were we to concern ourselves with Hegel as *much* as this great mind truly deserves, we would soon recognize that the Hegelian concept of government largely takes into account just those conditions of vitality, the physicality of the organic cycle and popular feeling manifested as spirit which are intended to raise the rich and vital concept of "national government" (*Volksordnung*) above the mediocre, humdrum concept of a schematic State machine.'[38] Thus Hitler received a bouquet of all the reactionary contents of the Hegelian system, presented in order to make him more benevolently disposed towards Hegelianism.

These attempts misfired. In an official statement in which he sharply divided the 'National-Socialist world-view' from the fellow travellers' attempts at conciliation, Rosenberg declared that National Socialism regarded only Wagner, Nietzsche, Lagarde and Chamberlain as intellectual forerunners, as its own classical authorities.[39] Now it is widely known that both Lagarde and Chamberlain were sharply opposed to Hegel. Lagarde declined to recognize Hegel – along with the majority of thinkers and imaginative authors of the classical epoch – as a German: 'Our classical literature of the previous century . . . is German in the persons of

individual bearers of the tradition, but not as writers: it is, on the one hand, cosmopolitan, and, on the other, it strives after Greek and Roman ideals. In scholasticizing the content of this body of literature, Hegel typically passed over precisely its best parts.'[40] As for Chamberlain, he saw in Hegel a 'Protestant Thomas Aquinas',[41] a phrase which for him 'says it all' because Chamberlain, as we shall note in due course, saw in Rome the champion of the ruinous 'chaos of nations'. And since he saw the founder of his own racial philosophy in a Kant interpreted in a vitalistic, racialistic and mystical light, he scornfully dismissed the thesis of the uniformity of philosophical developments from Kant to Hegel. 'Kant is the outstanding representative of the purely scientific answer, but ignorant or malicious hacks are still misleading the public with the assertion that the thinking of Fichte and Hegel is organically connected with Kant's, thereby preventing any true understanding or serious deepening of our world-view . . .'

Rosenberg followed these lines in his fierce challenge to Hegel.[42] He expressed in clear terms the cardinal element in the reactionary extremists' rejection of Hegel: his relation to Marxism. This repulsed at one stroke all the compromise attempts of the social democrats from Bernstein to Siegfried Marck, as well as the post-war neo-Hegelians: on this question, the national-socialist 'theoretician' would not stand for any compromise. As we shall see, Rosenberg furthermore firmly rejected both rationality in the study of world-history and the Hegelian theory of the State. This shows us how fruitless all the neo-Hegelians' attempts at good relations were with pre-fascist and fascist reaction. The reactionaries were moving towards the total destruction of reason; compromise, concessions counted for little in their eyes: they demanded all or nothing. Through its concessions to vitalistic irrationalism, neo-Hegelianism managed only to disarm mentally a part of the intelligentsia that would have perhaps resisted the fascist takeover of thought more strongly had it not had such an 'ideological prop'.

The official thinking of German fascism now assiduously

carried out the anti-Hegelian line traced in advance by Rosenberg. Alfred Baeumler, who was appointed professor of political studies at the University of Berlin immediately after Hitler's seizure of power, spelled out this programme in his inaugural address: 'The systematic critique of the idealist tradition is a part of our future work.'[43] And drawing on the preparatory studies of Meinecke, Rosenzweig and Glockner – with, to be sure, the value sign reversed – he attacked Hegel as a philosopher of despicable national liberalism. 'National liberalism, whose ideological basis was laid by Hegel, was the most recent form of that synthesis of Enlightenment and Romantic thought which Nietzsche was summoned to abolish.'[44] Now when Nietzsche was, according to Baeumler, rightly challenging the State of his time, he was 'instinctively right in taking the Hegelian total State as a *culture-State* . . . Nietzsche is contesting the spirit of Goethe's Weimar made concrete in the State.'[45] Obviously all German fascists were behind Baeumler in disputing any possible association of their State with culture.

Official Hitlerian thinking was now challenging in actual philosophical terms the image of Hegel as the completion of that great and universally European movement which began with Descartes. Thus Hegel too belonged to those dangerous Western imports which National Socialism would have to eliminate. This is most clearly stated in the book written by Franz Boehm: 'With Descartes, the man tied to Western civilization in his unity and national roots was replaced by . . . *European man* – the creation of an unreal and non-historical rationality.'[46]

This development reached its climax in Hegel. '*Hegel perfected Western awareness as regards the history of thought in a way that has not been surpassed* . . . For it is Hegel's picture of history which gave Cartesianism its standing justification, after the best minds in German philosophy had led the *battle* against it down the centuries. Just as, conversely, Hegel's universalist conception steam-rollered the motives of German history of philosophy into Western thought and

partly buried them for a century.'[47] This was a logical extension of the fascist attack on Hegel to the whole of European rational philosophy. Hegel was under fire for having completed the separation from medieval philosophy that began with Descartes; it was a formulation, in terms of the history of thought, of the war of extermination vowed by Hitler's supporters against progressive European civilization and culture in their entirety. Here again, of course, the fascist ideologists were not showing any originality. We are already acquainted with the anti-Hegelian tradition from Schopenhauer to Chamberlain. But the thesis that the attack on Hegel had to commence historically with Descartes also has old roots in reactionary thought; the old Schelling initiated it, and he had successors in Eduard von Hartmann and his school. And the fact that we are, objectively speaking, dealing once more with those questions which we underlined earlier as being the central ones is indicated by Boehm's attacks on the concept of progress. 'Progress is a gradual heightening of present conditions. This denies the historical process all *creative* character and *disables* the future by a monstrous act of anticipation.'[48] As always in such polemics, Boehm was ignoring Hegel's dialectical and historical concept of progress (not to mention Marxism) and putting forward the vulgar concept as the only possible one.

So neo-Hegelianism with its imperialist-reactionary adjustments to Hegel was unable to establish itself as the 'synthesis' of all orientations (except progressive ones) after which it hankered. It eked out a tolerated existence in a few small corners of the German universities. Its results for the development of philosophy were precisely nil. The only historical interest that this trend evokes is a negative one: it plainly shows us how ineffective philosophical compromises are; how resistance, unless decided, is swept helplessly along by the main reactionary currents; and the unimportance of nuances and reservations in world-historical upheavals. The development of neo-Hegelianism is instructive inasmuch as it provides a philosophical reflection of the role that an increas-

ingly decaying liberalism (and its various splinter groups) not only played in the history of the reactionary upsurge, the fascist takeover, but will also play in the future.

NOTES

1 Marx: *Capital*, Vol. I, Afterword to the 2nd Edition.
2 Windelband: *Die Erneuerung des Hegelianismus*, Report of the Heidelberg Academy of Sciences, Heidelberg 1910, p. 7.
3 Ibid., p. 13.
4 Ibid., p. 15.
5 J. Ebbinghaus: *Relativer und absoluter Idealismus*, Leipzig 1910, p. 31.
6 Ibid., p. 4.
7 Ibid., p. 69.
8 Dilthey: *Collected Works*, Leipzig-Berlin 1921, Vol. IV, pp. 219f.
9 Ibid., pp. 229f.
10 Ibid., p. 138.
11 Meinecke: *World Citizenship and the National State*.
12 *Logos*, Hegel issue, 1931, p. 9.
13 Minutes of the 1st Hegel Congress, Tubingen 1931, p. 25.
14 Ibid., p. 78.
15 S. Marck: *Die Dialektik in der Philosophie der Gegenwart*, Tubingen 1929-31, Vol. 1, p. 33.
16 R. Kroner: *Von Kant zu Hegel*, Tubingen 1921-4, Vol. I, p. 25.
17 Minutes of the 1st Hegel Congress, p. 79.
18 R. Kroner: *Von Kant zu Hegel*, Vol. I, p. 21.
19 Ibid., p. 27.
20 Ibid., Vol. II, p. 364.
21 F. Rosenzweig: *Hegel und der Staat*, Munich-Berlin 1920, Vol. II, pp. 198f.
22 H. Glockner: *F. Th. Vischer und das 19. Jahrhundert*, Berlin 1931, pp. 155ff.
23 H. Marcuse: *Hegels Ontologie und die Grundlegung einer Theorie der Geschichtlichkeit*, Frankfurt a. M. 1932, p. 278.
24 H. Glockner: *Krisen und Wandlungen in der Geschichte des Hegelianismus*, Logos, XIII No. 3, pp. 355f.
25 R. Kroner: *Von Kant zu Hegel*, Vol. II, pp. VIIf.
26 Ibid., pp. 271f.
27 Ibid., p. 282.
28 Ibid., p. 364.

29 Hegel: *Encyclopaedia*, para. 231.
30 H. Glockner: *Hegel*, Vol. I, Stuttgart 1929, pp. XIf.
31 Ibid., p. XXI.
32 R. Kroner: *Die Selbstverwirklichung des Geistes*, Tubingen 1928, p. 221.
33 S. Marck: op. cit., Vol. II, p. 93.
34 Engels: *Anti-Dühring*.
35 H. Glockner: *Hegel*, p. XII.
36 Ibid., p. XIV.
37 N. Hartmann: *Hegel*, Berlin 1929, pp. 17f.
38 H. Franz: *Von Herder bis Hegel*, Frankfurt a. M. 1938, p. 149.
39 Rosenberg: *Gestalten der Idee*, Munich 1936, pp. 11f.
40 Lagarde: *Drei deutsche Schriften*, Leipzig, pp. 204f.
41 Chamberlain: *The Foundations of the Nineteenth Century*.
42 Rosenberg: *The Myth of the Twentieth Century*.
43 Baeumler: *Männerbund und Wissenschaft*, Berlin 1934, p. 125.
44 Baeumler: *Nietzsche, der Philosoph und Politiker*, Leipzig 1931, p. 134.
45 Ibid., p. 133.
46 Boehm: *Anticartesianismus*, Leipzig 1938, p. 55.
47 Ibid., pp. 24f.
48 Ibid., p. 99.

CHAPTER VI

GERMAN SOCIOLOGY OF THE IMPERIALIST PERIOD

1. The Origins of Sociology

Sociology as an independent discipline arose in England and France after the dissolution of classical political economy and utopian socialism. Both these, each in its own way, were comprehensive doctrines of social life and therefore treated all important problems of society in connection with the economic questions dictating them. Sociology as an independent discipline came about in such a way that its treatment of a social problem did not consider the economic basis; the supposed independence of social questions from economic ones formed the methodological starting-point of sociology. This separation is linked with profound crises in bourgeois economics that clearly express the social basis of sociology. One crisis was the dissolution of the Ricardo school in Britain, which prompted the drawing of socialist consequences from the classic authors' theory of labour value, and another was the disintegration of utopian socialism in France, which began with a tentative quest for that social path to socialism which Saint-Simon and Fourier had left unexplored. These twin crises, and more especially the solving of both through the appearance of historical materialism and Marxist political economy, terminated bourgeois economics in the classical sense, as a discipline fundamental to the knowledge of society. There arose at the one pole bourgeois 'vulgar economics', later so-called subjective economics, a specialist discipline confined to a narrow range of objects. This refrained from the start from explaining social manifestations and

regarded it as its chief task to banish the question of surplus value from economics. And at the other pole there sprang up sociology, a humanistic discipline divorced from economics.

Certainly it is true to say that initially, sociology also claimed to be a universal science of society (Comte, Herbert Spencer). For that reason it was trying to find a basis in natural science that would replace an economic basis. This again was closely linked with the – socially dictated – development of economics. Hegel, though he was scarcely understood at the time, had already discovered the principle of contradiction in the economic categories; with Fourier, the internal contradictoriness of capitalist economics was already openly manifest; with the dissolution of the Ricardo school, as with Proudhon, it appeared as nothing less than the central problem of economics, whatever the falsity of the individual answers to it. It was the Marxist doctrine which first discovered the correct dialectical framework in economics. The natural-scientific underpinning of sociology as a universal science was meant to exclude from its doctrine not only economics but the very contradictoriness of social Being, i.e., a thorough critique of the capitalist system. Admittedly to start with, in the case of its founders particularly, sociology adhered to the standpoint of social progress; indeed it was one of its main aims to demonstrate this scientifically. But it was a version of progress tailored to a bourgeoisie about to enter an ideological decline, a progress leading to an idealized capitalist society as the culmination of man's development. Already in Comte's time, not to say that of Spencer, the proof of this progress could no longer be furnished with the tools of economics. Hence a natural science – applied by analogy to society and in this way more or less mythologized – was sought as the sole foundation.

But just because of this bond with the idea of progress, sociology could not last as a universal science for long. Soon the natural-scientific, primarily biological argumentation was to lapse – in accordance with the bourgeoisie's general politico-economic development – into anti-progressive, often

reactionary ideology and methodology. Most sociologists turned to specialist investigations. Sociology became a pure, detached branch of learning which barely touched on the major questions of the structure and development of society. No longer, therefore, could it fulfil its original task of portraying the – economically no longer arguable – progressive character of bourgeois society and defend it, ideologically, against feudal reaction and socialism alike. As sociology, exactly like economics, etc., grew into this strictly specialized branch of learning, there sprang from it, as from the other divided social sciences, tasks dictated by the capitalist division of labour. Prominent among these was one that arose of its own accord and never became a conscious part of bourgeois methodology: namely, the task of transferring the cardinal problems of social life from a specialist discipline incompetent as such to solve them to the authority of another discipline. Then this second specialist discipline would, with equal logic, declare its own incompetency. Naturally it always involved cardinal social questions, for the declining bourgeoisie was increasingly interested in preventing them from being clearly raised and indeed answered. Social agnosticism, as a form of defending ideologically hopeless positions, thereby acquired an – unconsciously functioning – methodological organ. The process much resembles the behaviour of the capitalist or self-capitalizing, semi-feudal absolutist bureaucracy, which 'solved' awkward questions by perpetually passing the relevant documents from one office to another, with none of them pronouncing itself competent to make an objective decision.

2. The Beginnings of German Sociology (Schmoller, Wagner and Others)

But there was a stark difference between Germany's situation and that of the Western, capitalistically more advanced

countries with a long bourgeois-democratic development behind them. Germany lacked above all any original scientific study of economics. In 1875 Marx characterized the situation as follows:

> In Germany, political economy has remained a foreign science up to this day . . . It was imported ready-made from England and France; its German professors stayed pupils. In their hands, the theoretical expression of an alien reality changed into a collection of dogmas which they interpreted in the spirit of the petty-bourgeois world about them, and therefore misinterpreted . . . Capitalist production has developed rapidly in Germany since 1848, and nowadays it is already bearing its spurious fruit. But fate remained unkind to our experts. All the while that they were pursuing political economy in peace and quiet, modern economic conditions were absent from the German reality. As soon as those conditions became operative in real life, they did so in circumstances which no longer permitted of their unrestricted study within the realm of bourgeois thinking.

It was German minds, moreover, which gave birth to scientific socialism, and inevitably it was precisely on German soil that this first began to exert a wide literary influence. And finally, the situation of German sociology at its birth was complicated by the fact that in Germany, the bourgeoisie did not seize power as a political class in a democratic revolution, as had happened in France. Instead, the bourgeoisie reached a compromise with feudal absolutism and the *Junker* class under Bismarck. Thus the birth of German sociology took place within the context of the apologetics of this compromise; and these apologetics determined the tasks of German economics and social science.

Such a situation obstructed the origin of a sociology in the Anglo-French sense. The 'social doctrine' put forward by the epigones of the Hegelian distinction between State and Society

(L. von Stein, R. von Mohl), along with the reactionary 'idyllist' (Riehl), represents the first tentative attempts at a German bourgeois theory of society. At first this met with great resistance. The National-Liberal Treitschke, the later notorious historian of Prussianism, published a pamphlet attacking these attempts under the title of *Social Doctrine* (*Gesellschaftslehre*, 1859). In this he advanced the view that all social problems were merely political and juridicial ones; thus if all was well with political science, then no particular social science was needed at all. Social science, he maintained, had no object of its own; in reality everything which appeared to be an object of sociology could be settled by constitutional or civil law. Economics Treitschke considered from the viewpoint of popular liberal harmonism; the worker question was, for him, purely a police question.

After 1870-1 this rough and summary dismissal of all sociology had become untenable. The great upsurge of capitalism, the exacerbation of the class conflicts and Bismarck's battle against social democracy in connection with his 'social policy' changed the German bourgeoisie's attitude to these problems. Another factor was the divergence of Bismarck, taking large sections of the German bourgeoisie with him, from the popular dogma of free trade. In this new situation, a group of German economists attempted to expand popular economic doctrine into a social science (Brentano, Schmoller, Wagner, etc.). They planned to create a purely a-theoretical, empirical, historical and at the same time 'ethical' political economy which rejected classical economics and would additionally be capable of comprehending the problems of society. This eclectic pseudo-science grew out of the reactionary historical school of jurisprudence (Savigny) and older German economics (Roscher, Knies, etc.). Methodologically totally without principles, it was the ideology of those bourgeois circles which thought that Bismarck's 'social policy' could offer a solution to the class conflicts. In common with the older generation of German economists they did battle against classical economics, in

close association with the struggle against Marxism. In accomplishing a radical subjectification of economics, these circles wholly failed to see the objective economic problems of the classical thinkers, and merely polemicized against an allegedly narrow psychology that perceived in economic self-seeking the sole driving motive of economic behaviour. The intention was now to 'deepen' this psychology and also to give it an ethical character. According to Schmoller, the various theories of economics 'mainly furnished various ideals for the morality of economics'.[2] Or, to take a specific example, the whole problem of demand was 'nothing else than a slice of concrete ethical history related to a definite time and a definite nation'.[3] Hence these economists opposed all 'abstraction' and 'deduction', i.e., theory of any kind; they were pure historical empiricists and relativists. For that reason it was no accident that the positivistic neo-Kantianism then in the ascendant encouraged their views to drift in the direction of an empirical agnosticism.

The social systems of an 'organic' kind which were simultaneously springing up also set out to refute socialism. They sought to justify intellectually the connection between Bismarck's empire and the old semi-feudal, semi-absolutist Germany and so to find a seasonable theory for what the German bourgeoisie of the time called progress. This first German sociology also stemmed from reactionary Romantic philosophy and the 'historical school of law' (Schäffle, Lilienthal, etc.).

But even such a sociology-substitute evoked a sharp rejection of sociology as a scientific discipline on the part of the philosophical doctrine of science that was currently dominant. Most typical of the attitude of German philosophy to the nascent sociology is the critique we find in Dilthey's *Introduction to the Humanistic Sciences* (*Einleitung in die Geisteswissenschaften*, 1883). Dilthey, to be sure, was primarily combating the Anglo-French sociology of Comte, Spencer, and so on. He dismissed *a limine* its claim to comprehend historical processes in a unified way with the aid of

sociological categories.[4] His standpoint was radically empirical, specialist and relativist. He saw in the new sociology, not mistakenly, a successor to the old philosophy of history, but contested them both as being a kind of pseudo-scientific alchemy. Reality, he thought, could only be grasped through strictly specialized branches of science. Both the philosophy of history and sociology, on the other hand, were dealing with metaphysical principles.

Dilthey observed fairly clearly the consequences of Western sociology's methodology, namely the emergence of claims to a universal philosophy of history which had no foundation in the basic historical facts. But, since he understood even less (if that were possible) of this remoteness from reality and abstractness of sociology than its founders did, his critique remained completely fruitless. A large proportion of Western European sociologists set out on the road to establishing a strictly specialized single branch of science. But, in so doing, they renounced the very purpose of sociology; this course adopted by sociology was not a science, but its abdication. Dilthey's critique was therefore nothing beyond a phenomenon – one whose methodology was defined by German conditions – running parallel to the decline of sociology generally. Sociology was renouncing more and more a bourgeois argumentation of progress, and to an equal degree a unified theory of progress was, from Dilthey's standpoint, scientifically impossible.

3. Ferdinand Toennies and the Founding of the New School of German Sociology

The rapid capitalization of Germany rendered such a theoretical rejection of sociology as we have just described untenable in the long run. (Dilthey's later attitude to Simmel and other sociologists of the imperialist period also changed totally; indeed his own view of history, as it developed in

the course of time, became a co-determining factor in later German sociology.) A certain degree, a specific form of theoretical comprehension of social phenomena had become a matter of growing urgency, although it naturally remained, in essence, within the aforementioned politico-ideological compromise which the German bourgeoisie made with the Hohenzollern régime. But as the *Junker* class too turned increasingly capitalist, and as the country grew into the imperialist stage of its development (not by chance did Bismarck's downfall occur on the eve of it), all these questions had to be formulated anew. The irresistible growth of the social democrat labour movement also made new propositions obligatory: neither the police measures demanded by Treitschke and administered by Bismarck nor the unctuous sermons of Schmoller and Wagner were sufficient. A new form of anti-Marxist polemics was needed.

The chief upshot of these needs was a new economic doctrine which claimed to answer 'theoretically' the bourgeoisie's current economic problems and thereby to 'surmount' even Marxism in the economic field. It was at the same time so abstract and subjectivist that from the outset – if only for methodological reasons – it had to suppress any claim to lay the basis for a sociology. Thus from now on, the Western European separation of economics from sociology and prevalent coexistence of the two held good for Germany as well. We are referring now to the 'Austrian school' of Menger, Böhm-Bawerk, etc., which was just as radically subjectivist as the 'historical school'. Only, the blurred, unctuous moralizing was replaced by a purely psychological approach: the dissolution of all objective economic categories in the casuistry of the abstract antithesis of inclination and disinclination. So pseudo-theories arose which sought their sole object in the surface manifestations of economic life (offer, demand, production costs, distribution) and set up pseudo-laws of subjective reactions to these phenomena (*marginal utility*). The 'Austrian school' thought of itself as having overcome the 'teething

troubles' of the classic thinkers (Böhm-Bawerk), and hence of Marxism, on the one hand, and those of the 'historical school' on the other. Thereby the new popular economics arising from this cleared the way – as in Western Europe – for a separate science of sociology which was divorced from economics and 'complemented' it. In their economic views, the most important representatives of sociology in imperialist Germany belonged to this school either explicitly or tacitly. The methodological discussion between the two economic orientations associated with the works of Karl Menger is no longer of any interest. For us its only historical significance is that it opened up an avenue for the new sociology.

Seemingly linked only loosely with these struggles is what was for a long time the most influential publication of the new German sociology: *Community and Association* by Ferdinand Toennies (1887). This book occupies a special place in the development of German sociology. Above all, its author's ideological link with the classic German traditions was stronger than that of the later sociologists. Accordingly he had a closer relationship with the progressive scientific learning of Western Europe. (Later he wrote a biography of Hobbes which gained international renown, etc.) Moreover he was the first German thinker to appropriate research results concerning primitive society, primarily Lewis Henry Morgan's, and at the same time the first German sociologist who did not dismiss Marx out of hand but tried to rework him and render him of use to his bourgeois purposes. Thus Toennies expressly stood for the theory of labour value, and he rejected the claim of bourgeois criticism to have exposed insoluble contradictions between the first and third volumes of *Capital*. That, to be sure, was by no means tantamount to understanding Marxism and recognizing it. 'I have never', Toennies said, 'acknowledged as correct the Ricardo-Rodbertus-Marxian theory of value in the form propounded, but recognize all the more its core and basic idea.'[5] This statement, with its identification of Marx and Ricardo and Rodbertus, shows just how little Toennies understood

Marxism.

Nevertheless, the influence of Marx and Morgan on Toennies went deeper than is apparent from his explicit references to them in his book. It was the antithesis between the old classless primitive society and the capitalism that had come about in the course of socio-economic developments that formed the basis of his sociology. To be sure, Toennies radically reworked the basic ideas of his sources. Firstly, he banished all concrete economics, albeit less radically than later German sociologists. Secondly, he volatilized concretely historical social formations into supra-historical 'essences'. Thirdly, here again the objective economic basis of the social structure was replaced by a subjective principle – the will. And fourthly, socio-economic objectivity gave way to a Romantic anti-capitalism. Hence the findings of Morgan and Marx gave rise in Toennies's work to that contrast between 'community' and 'society' which continued to influence the whole of later German sociology. The process of subjectification was achieved through mysticized will-concepts. 'For it emerges from all this how the essential community will carries the preconditions within itself, whereas arbitrary will brings about society.'[6] Toennies presented these two mysticized concepts of will as the creators of the two formations.

'Society' is capitalism – as seen through the eyes of Romantic anti-capitalism. Admittedly, if we compare Toennies with the older Romantic anti-capitalists, we will notice the particular and subsequently important nuance that he was not voicing a desire to revert to social conditions now surmounted, and certainly not to feudalism. Toennies was a liberal. His position provided the basis for a cultural critique which strongly emphasized the problematic, negative features of capitalist culture, but which also underlined that capitalism was ineluctable and a product of fate.

The antithetical type of the 'community' now determined the character of this critique. It was the antithesis between what was dead, mechanical and machine-like about 'society'

and the organic nature of the 'community'. 'As an artificial implement or a machine designed for specific *purposes* is related to the organ-systems and individual organs of an animal body, so a will-aggregate of this kind – a form of arbitrary will – is related to the other kind – a form of essential will.'[7] This contrast was by no means original, but it became of methodological significance because Toennies proceeded from it to that contrast between 'civilization' and 'culture' which later became of crucial importance to German sociology.

This antithesis arose spontaneously out of the bourgeois intelligentsia's feeling of discontent with capitalist, and especially imperialist, cultural development. The theoretical problem which objectively existed behind this feeling was Marx's well-known discovery that capitalism in general has an unfavourable effect on the evolution of art (and culture as a whole). Now a real understanding of this problem – if really grasped and thought all the way through – would have turned any intellectual sincerely concerned about culture into an adversary of capitalism. But materially, a great many threads tied the majority of the intellectuals to the capitalist basis of their existence (or at least they thought that to sever those threads would mortally endanger their livelihood). They were, moreover, influenced by the bourgeois ideology of their time, which means that they had no inkling of the socio-economic foundations of their own livelihood.

It was possible for the false antithesis of culture and civilization to spring from this soil of its own accord. Conceptually formulated, the antithesis acquired the following – factually wrong and misleading – form: promoted by capitalism, civilization, i.e., techno-economic development, was constantly ascending, but its evolution put culture (art, philosophy, man's inner life) at an increasing disadvantage; the conflict of the two would be intensified to the point of a tragic, unbearable tension. Here we see how the case-facts of capitalist development ascertained by Marx were being distorted in a Romantically anti-capitalist, subjectively

irrational way. That we are dealing with the irrationalist distortion of a set of historio-social facts is indicated by the simple consideration that culture and civilization – properly understood – cannot be antithetical concepts at all. Culture, after all, encompasses all the activities through which man overcomes in nature, in society and in himself the original personal characteristics bestowed by nature. (For instance, we rightly speak of the cultivation of work, of human behaviour, and so on.) Civilization, on the other hand, is a comprehensive, periodicizing expression of man's history after his emergence from barbarity; it embraces culture, but along with it the whole of man's life in society. To pose such a conceptual antithesis, and to invent the myth of these counter-active forces, entities, etc., was thus simply an abstracting and also irrationalist distortion of culture's real contradictory nature in capitalist life. (This real contradictoriness applies also to the material productive forces; think of their destruction in a time of crisis, the contradictions of the machine in capitalist life in relation to human labour as portrayed by Marx, and so forth.)

The irrationalist distortion of the original facts of the matter derived spontaneously from the intellectuals' social situation in capitalism. This distortion, which on account of its spontaneity was continually self-reproducing, was extended in breadth and depth by the ideologists of capitalism. They did so partly in order to channel into an innocuous cultural critique the potentially rebellious tendencies of Romantic anti-capitalism, and partly because, to many intellectuals, to absolutize the false antithesis of culture and civilization seemed to be an effective weapon against socialism. For since socialism was developing further the material forces of production (mechanization, etc.), it too was unable to solve the conflict between culture and civilization. It was rather perpetuating the conflict – consequently, the argument ran, the intelligentsia afflicted by this dichotomy would be wasting its time by contesting capitalism for the sake of socialism.

Depicting society in the colours of Hobbes's philosophy of

law, Toennies described it as a condition in which all men were enemies and only the law preserved an external order. And he went on: 'This is . . . the condition of social *civilization*, in which convention and the mutual fear expressed in it maintain peace and social intercourse, and which the State protects and extends through legislation and politics; scientific learning and public opinion partly seek to comprehend it as necessary and permanent, partly glorify it as advancing towards perfection. But it is far rather the communal life-styles and rules in which *popular life* (*Volkstum*) and its *culture* find sustenance . . .'[8] Here Toennies's Romantic anti-capitalism is patent.

Morgan and Engels too contrasted primitive communism with the later class societies and indicated – for all the socio-economic necessity and progressiveness of its abolition – the moral decay, the ethical degradation ineluctably linked with this step forward. And in Marxism the contrast was by no means confined to the antithesis of primitive communism and the class-divided society. The idea of irregular development inevitably meant that the heights attained in specific cultural fields, in specific branches of art and philosophy for instance, and indeed the general cultural level in class societies very often failed to tally with the level of development reached by the material forces of production. Marx pointed out with regard to epic poetry, and Engels with regard to the golden ages of modern philosophy in the various leading nations, that under specific circumstances, the less advanced conditions more greatly favoured a partial cultural flowering of this nature than did more advanced conditions.[9] The confirmation of such connections as consequences of an irregular development was, however, always of a concretely historical character. To reveal the social principles which found expression herein did not permit of any simple and immediate application to the whole of culture.

With capitalist culture the position was different. Marx repeatedly pointed out that the development of capitalist economics usually had unfavourable consequences for specific

branches of culture (he was speaking of art and poetry).[10] And here we have the concrete starting-point of such Romantic anti-capitalist accounts as we have just found in Toennies. As we have seen, the striking contrast between the rapid development of material productive forces and, simultaneously, decadent tendencies in the fields of art, literature, philosophy, morality, etc., caused many thinkers to split in two the inherently unified and organically coherent domain of human culture. Those parts of it which capitalism had brought to a high level they contrasted as civilization with those of culture (in a narrower, special sense) in jeopardy; indeed they saw in this opposition the essential hallmark of the epoch, and even of the whole of mankind's development. Here again we can see that the point of departure behind this false proposition was a real set of social facts. But because of false, unhistorical generalizing, the directly and subjectively justified question was bound to give rise to a false proposition and a thoroughly erroneous answer. The falsity of these – and also their connection with the general reactionary-oriented philosophical trends of the time – is primarily manifested in the fact that such an opposition of culture and civilization was necessarily backward-looking, that it had to proceed in an anti-progressive direction. We can already observe this with Toennies, although he was very chary of drawing inferences. The more strongly that vitalistic tendencies, especially Nietzsche's, took hold of sociology and social studies in general, the stronger the emphasis became on the contrast between culture and civilization, the more energetic the turning to the past, and the more unhistorical, anti-historical the propositions. And the internal dialectic of ideological developments after the war inevitably meant that the dismissive attitude was extended more and more to culture as well. Culture and civilization alike were rejected in the name of the 'soul' (Klages), of 'authentic existence' (Heidegger), and so on.

It is only the start of this development that we find in Toennies. But from the results of Morgan's investigations he

was already making a – permanent – structure of supra-historical duration and forming in substance a permanent contrast to the structure of society. So Toennies not only placed in opposition to one another family and contract (abstract right); with him the antitheses of man and woman, youth and old age, the common people and educated people also mirrored the contrast between community and society. There thus arose a whole system of abstractly inflated, contrasting subject-concepts which we do not need to set out in detail.

This anti-historical exaggeration of concepts originally obtained from concrete analyses of concrete social formations not only diluted these concepts (and rendered them, for that very reason, highly influential in German bourgeois sociology). It also reinforced their Romantic anti-capitalist character. Community thus became a category covering everything pre-capitalist and a glorification of primitive, 'organic' conditions as well as a slogan to combat the mechanizing, anti-cultural effects of capitalism. This cultural critique of capitalism – characteristically for the next phase in German sociology – henceforth occupied the centre of interest and succeeded the vague ethical utopianism of the preceding phase. The change matched the growth of capitalism in Germany. It came a good way towards meeting widespread intellectual discontent with the increasingly palpable contradictions of the present, and it also diverted attention from the real and decisive economic and social problems of imperialist capitalism. The diversionary trend did not necessarily have to be a conscious trend. On the one hand, however, concrete social data deriving from the economic character of a particular social formation were being detached from their social roots as a result of the philosophical 'profundity' according to which an autonomous entity found expression in them. And, on the other hand, they were being totally de-historicized by this same abstracting process. This necessarily entailed the disappearance of the object of that protest and struggle which the concrete phenomenon, historically

viewed, could and would indeed have to evoke. (We already found advanced forms of this diversion through 'deepening' in Simmel.)

With Toennies himself, admittedly, all these tendencies were only latent. He emphasized the progressive factor more strongly than his successors did. The later, purely apologetic form taken by criticisms of capitalist culture, namely the 'proof' that Germany – because of its unique political development – ranked higher than the Western democracies socially and ideologically, is lacking in Toennies. Also, as yet the vitalist-irrationalist element was barely present in his work, at least in his conscious methodology; latently, to be sure, it was there already. The primitive 'organism' concept used by the 'historical school' and early German sociology was no longer adequate to the needs of this phase. It was only to make a comeback in the fascists' racial theory. But as we have noted, the new antithesis of the 'living' and 'mechanized' ('constructed') already constituted the centre of Toennies's sociological conception, although he did not imitate Nietzsche, his contemporary, in linking it with vitalistic lines of thought.

Granted, in Toennies too we find not a few hints and signs of this. As when, for instance, he sees in the development of Roman law a process whose reverse side is the 'decay of *life*'.[11] And where he discusses the life-destroying effects of the metropolis it is even more marked. We shall quote this passage because it clearly expresses Toennies's attitude to socialism. He wrote: 'So the metropolis and the condition of society in general spell the ruin and death of the common people vainly striving to attain power by virtue of their numbers and able, to their own way of thinking, to use their power only in the cause of rebellion if they want to cast off their misfortune . . . The ascent is from class consciousness to the class struggle. The class struggle destroys that society and State which it plans to reshape. And since the whole of culture has changed into a civilized society and State, culture itself in this altered form will come to an end . . .'[12]

We likewise find in Toennies the beginnings of the 'internalization' and 'deepening' of economic categories by the historian of culture – a line of development that was to culminate in Simmel. With the concept of money, Toennies was already pursuing analogies whose effects were to extend as far as the post-war vogue for a 'sociology of knowledge'. Thus he wrote on occasion of science and money: 'And consequently, scientific concepts which, in their usual origin and real disposition, are judgements which bestow *names* on affective complexes behave within science like goods within society. They combine in the system like goods on the market. The uppermost scientific concept, which no longer contains the name of anything concrete, resembles money, e.g., the concept of the atom or energy.'[13] Equally, Toennies anticipated the later sociology in exploiting his cultural critique as an ideological prop for reformism in the labour movement – as when, for example, he perceived in the building societies a victory of the community principle within capitalist society.

4. German Sociology in the Wilhelmine Age (Max Weber)

Toennies's book took a long time to attain influence. Similarly, the new sociology as a whole had to fight unceasingly for scientific recognition in the decades before the First World War. But the conditions and character of this struggle were altered. Above all, sociology in the imperial age increasingly desisted – on an international scale – from taking over the legacy of the philosophy of history or philosophy in general as a universal science. It changed, in connection with the general victory of philosophical agnosticism, more and more consciously into one limited specialist discipline among others.

In Germany, this development had the particular nuance that sociology showed a great rapprochement with Romantic-

irrationalist history conceptions in the Ranke tradition. Accordingly, the scientific doctrine of the prevalent Kantianism was increasingly willing to allow it a modest niche in the classification of the sciences. It is instructive to compare Rickert's critique of sociology with that of Dilthey. Rickert thought that from a logico-methodological angle, there was nothing contradictory in pursuing natural-scientific 'generalizing' studies of social phenomena, and that such a sociology was therefore eminently possible. We had just to contest the idea 'that this science might tell us how the life of mankind has really shaped itself in its unique individual course'.[14] Therefore a sociology was possible, but it could never take history's place.

This saved the methodological 'honour' of sociology. And the sociologists themselves (especially Max Weber) underlined the fact that they were not claiming to reveal the universal meaning of historical development, that sociology was rather merely a kind of ancillary study to that of history in the Dilthey-Rickert sense. Simmel's standpoint was typical in this respect. On the one hand, he stood with the most extreme vehemence for the possibility of an independent, strictly formalistic sociology, while on the other, he went just as far in his works dealing with the theory of history in abiding by the standpoint of the irrationalist 'singularity' and 'uniqueness' of historical objects.

This friendly, neighbourly relationship between sociology and history was also encouraged by the development of the latter. Even under pre-war imperialism, historical accounts went beyond the coarse forms of apologetics we find in Treitschke. With Lamprecht there were even definite tendencies, if also very inadequate ones, towards a 'sociologization' of historical studies. Although the majority of German historians rejected this project, it is still indubitable that many of them began ascribing greater importance than before to social categories (seen most distinctly in Delbrück's history of the war). This again was closely bound up with the development of capitalism in Germany: from now on it was

absolutely imperative to come to intellectual terms with the origin, character and perspective of capitalism (imperialist capitalism). The attitude to Marxism now changed as well: a straightforward total ignorance or a coarsely apodictic rejection of it appeared behind the times, not least because of the constantly growing might of the labour movement. A 'subtler' way of 'refuting' Marxism was called for. This went hand in hand with the equally necessary receptiveness to those of its elements which – in a distorted form, to be sure – seemed acceptable to bourgeois ideology in this period.

That such an attitude could emerge at all was caused by the growing strength of the reformist movement in social democracy, by theoretical and practical revisionism. As we know, the leading revisionist theoretician, Bernstein, wanted to eliminate everything revolutionary from the labour movement (materialism and dialectics from philosophy, dictatorship of the proletariat from political theory, and so on). Capitalism was to 'grow into' socialism in a peaceable way. Where the strategy and tactics of the labour movement were concerned, this meant that the labour organizations should – for the purpose of reforms viewed as stages in this 'growing-in' process – collaborate with the liberal bourgeoisie and form coalitions with it. Here we are dealing with an international trend caused by the influence on the labour élite and bureaucracy of the imperial economy's parasitical nature. In France it led to the admission of social democrat ministers into bourgeois cabinets (Millerand), etc.

This liquidation in both theory and practice of the class struggle, the proclamation of class co-operation between bourgeoisie and proletariat exerted a great influence on the bourgeois sociologists. For them too, revisionism offered a platform of collaboration; it seemed to them that Marxism – which they had so far tried to hush up or to refute as a universal system – might be fragmented on the revisionist model so as to incorporate into sociology those parts of it which were serviceable for the bourgeoisie.

We shall pick out only several principal elements of the

change now occurring. Above all the struggle against materialism was waged just as resolutely as earlier – and that meant, in the sociological sphere, a struggle against the priority of social being and the determining role played by the development of the forces of production. But the relativistic methodologism arising on the basis of neo-Kantianism and Machism made it possible to absorb into bourgeois sociology definite, abstract forms of the interaction between basis and superstructure. This we have seen very clearly in Simmel's *Philosophy of Money*. The same applies to Max Weber. In investigating the interaction between economic formations and religions, he sharply rejected the priority of economics: 'An ethic of economics is no simple "function" of economic forms of organization, no more than these ethics, conversely, unequivocally stamp their intrinsic character on these forms . . . However far-reaching the economically and politically conditioned social influences on religious ethics in individual cases – these ethics still acquired their hallmark primarily from religious sources.'[15]

Here Max Weber started out from the interaction of material motives and ideology. He challenged historical materialism because this, in a way he alleged to be scientifically inadmissible, established the priority of the economic factor. (He left unsaid that historical materialism too ascertains complicated reciprocal influences in the concrete reality of society; the economic grounds have, in Engels's words, a determining effect only in the last instance.) But this structure of reciprocal influences, which highly suited modern relativism, was not retained; it was only a polemical prolegomenon attacking historical materialism. Weber's line of thought continually led him into ascribing to ideological (religious) phenomena, more and more strongly, an 'immanent' development arising out of the phenomena themselves. Then this tendency was always so reversed that the phenomena received causal priority in respect of the entire process. This was already patent in the aforestated remarks of Weber. In the same context he stated further: 'Interests (material

and ideal), and not ideas, directly govern the actions of men. But the "pictures of the world" created through ideas have, by changing the points as it were, very often determined the lines along which the dynamic of interests drove those actions.'[16] Thus with Weber also, sociology switched to the lines of humanistic studies in general and a humanistic, idealistic interpretation of history. Nor was the irrationalist nuance absent, although Max Weber was opposed to irrationalism in his conscious aims. Precisely this sociology was intended to demonstrate that an irrationalism would necessarily arise on the basis of capitalist rationalism, indeed that it actually lay at the bottom of the whole movement. If we examine closely Weber's aforestated genesis of capitalism (the capitalist mentality), we find a particular significance in his wedding of modern rationalism to the idea that with it, religion was 'shifted into the domain of the irrational'. Troeltsch and others occupied a similar position, except that they stood nearer still to the irrationalist humanistic sciences.

This new, 'refined' form of criticism of historical materialism was, as we have noted, connected also with a change of attitude towards the labour movement. The elementary illusions that Bismarck's 'carrot and stick' could put an end to the proletarian class organizations had collapsed with the downfall of Bismarck and his anti-socialist laws. To be sure, experiments were repeatedly made to divert the labour movement from the road of class struggle (Stöcker, later Göhre and Naumann; in many cases the German sociologists supported these efforts). Later, however, it became of mounting importance for German sociology to lend ideological support to the reformist trends in social democracy. They included the aim of proving scientifically the necessity and usefulness of the trade union movement's independence of social democracy. Here Werner Sombart played the leading part.

For German sociology, the central problem in pre-war imperialism was to find a theory for the origin and nature of capitalism and to 'overcome' historical materialism in this

sphere through a theoretical interpretation of its own. What constituted the real bone of contention was the original accumulation, the forcible separation of the employed from the means of production. (As adherents to the *marginal utility* theory, the majority of German sociologists regarded the doctrine of surplus value as settled scientifically.) New hypotheses and theories were set up by the dozen as a sociological substitute for original accumulation. Sombart in particular developed a feverish activity in this field. He furnished a whole series of explanations for the origin of capitalism: the Jews, the war, luxury, city ground-rents, etc. With regard to later developments, however, Max Weber's conception became the most influential. Weber, as we have seen, started out from the interaction between the economic ethics of religions and economic formations, whereby he asserted the effective priority of the religious motive. His problem was to explain why capitalism had come about only in Europe. In contrast to the earlier view of capitalism as any accumulation of wealth, Weber was at pains to grasp the specific character of modern capitalism and to relate its European origin to the difference between ethico-religious development in the East and West. To achieve this his principal step was to de-economize and 'spiritualize' the nature of capitalism. This he presented as a rationalizing of socio-economic life, the rational calculability of all phenomena. Weber now devised a universal history of religion in order to show that all oriental and ancient religions produced economic codes constituting inhibiting factors in the rationalization of everyday life. Only Protestantism (and within Protestantism, chiefly the dissident sects) possessed an ideology agreeable to this rationalization and encouraging it. Time and again Weber declined to see in the economic codes a consequence of the economic structures. Of China, for example, he wrote: 'But here this lack of an ethically rational religiosity is the primary factor and seems, for its own part, to have influenced the constantly striking limitation in the rationalism of her technology.'[17] And in consequence of his identification of

technology and economics – a vulgarizing simplication that acknowledged only mechanized capitalism as the authentic variety – Weber then arrived at the 'decisive' historical 'argument' that the Protestant economic ethos which speeded up and fostered capitalist development was already there '*before* the "capitalist development" '.[18] In this he saw a refutation of historical materialism.

These few examples suffice to illuminate the German sociologists' methodology: an apparent comprehension of the essence of capitalism without having to go into its real economic problems (above all the question of surplus value and exploitation). Certainly they recognized the fact of the workers' separation from the means of production and free labour, and it played an important part in the sociology of Max Weber especially. But the cardinal distinguishing feature of capitalism remained rationality, calculability. There we see the sequel to Toennies's concept of society, albeit with many divergences in points of detail. This concept necessarily entailed standing the capitalist economy on its head, in that the popularized surface phenomena took priority over the problems of the productive forces' development. This abstracting distortion also enabled the German sociologists to ascribe to ideological forms, particularly justice and religion, a causal role equivalent and indeed superior to economics. That, in turn, now entailed an ever-increasing methodological substitution of analogies for causal connections. For instance, Max Weber saw a strong resemblance between the modern State and a capitalist industrial works. But since he dismissed on agnostic-relativist grounds the problem of primary causation, he stuck to description with the aid of analogies. These came to form the broad basis of a cultural critique which never got down to the fundamental questions of capitalism. Although giving free play to expressions of discontent with capitalist culture, it viewed the capitalist rationalizing process as the workings of 'destiny' (Rathenau) and thus, for all its criticisms, showed capitalism to be necessary and inevitable.

This thinking always culminated in proof of the economic

and social impossibility of socialism. The seeming historicity of sociological studies was aimed – but never explicitly – at arguing the case for capitalism as a necessary, no longer essentially changeable system and at exposing the purported internal economic and social contradictions which, it was claimed, made the realization of socialism impossible in theory as in practice. Here it is not worth examining the argument put forward in more detail. Since the German sociologists adhered, economically, to the standpoint of the new and subjectivist popular economics, they could neither know nor understand Marxian economics, let alone polemicize against them objectively. As bourgeois ideologists of the imperialist age, they merely drew all the conclusions of revisionism more rigorously than its spokesmen were capable of doing – out of tactical considerations in respect of their position in the labour movement.

The resulting cultural critique took on, in Germany, a particular nuance. Here pre-war sociology was the successor to earlier trends, in an altered form to be sure. It attempted to prove the superiority of the German political form and social structure over the Western democracies. Here again the change signified only an up-dating of methods. As we know, the contradictions in bourgeois democracy were becoming sharply apparent in the West at this time, and they found a strong literary echo not only in reactionary, anti-democratic sociological writings, but also in the theory of a part of the Western labour movement (syndicalism). The German sociology of the age now absorbed all the findings of this critique of democracy and lent to them a philosophically and sociologically 'deepened' form. Henceforth democracy was presented as the inevitable form of the mechanical violation of 'life', of liberty, of individuality, chiefly because of its *mass* character. The special development and the condition of Germany were then played off against it as an organic order compared with mechanical anarchy, as a rule of responsibly-minded and competent leaders compared with the irresponsibility of leadership through democratic 'demagogy'. Such

influential sociological works as Hasbach's *Modern Democracy* were nothing more than scientifically puffed-up pamphlets attacking democracy. Just as earlier, the 'historical school' of German economics had glorified the Bismarck régime as a superior political and social form, so now German sociology was writing apologetics for Wilhelmine imperialism.

Max Weber occupied a special position in this development. Admittedly, his methodological foundations were very similar to those of his contemporaries; he too adopted the Western sociological criticisms of modern democracy. But his attitude to it was totally reversed: despite all the criticism, he regarded democracy as the form most suited to the imperialist expansion of a major modern power. He saw the weakness of German imperialism as lying in its lack of internal democratic development. '*Only a politically mature* people is a "master race" . . . *Only master races are called upon to intervene in the course of global developments*. If nations attempt it without possessing this quality, then not only will the safe instinct of the other nations protest, but they will also come to grief in the attempt internally . . . *The will to powerlessness* in home affairs that the writers preach is irreconcilable with the "will to power" abroad which has been so noisily trumpeted.'[19]

Here the social derivation of Max Weber's democratism can be readily grasped. He shared with the other German imperialists the view of the world-political (colonizing) mission of the 'master races'. But he differened from them in that he not only failed to idealize German conditions under specious parliamentary government, but criticized them violently and passionately. Like the English or French, he thought, the Germans could become a 'master race' only in a democracy. Hence for the sake of attaining Germany's imperialist aims, a democratization had to take place internally and go as far as was indispensable to the realization of these aims. This Weberian standpoint implied a sharp rejection of the 'personal régime' of the Hohenzollern dynasty and the bureaucratic power closely connected with it. Not

only on the political plane did Weber continually challenge this régime; in his sociology, too, he constantly portrayed it as a gloomy prospect. Here he was turning the tables: he showed that a régime like the German one by no means meant 'organic freedom' but the opposite – a bureaucratic, mechanized cramping of all freedom and individuality. (We may note in passing that he also used the same prospect as a warning against socialism, which he interpreted as a total bureaucratization of life.) Weber criticized the inferiority of German foreign policy, which he believed to lie in the system and not the mistakes of individuals, and he stoutly affirmed the view that a proper choice of leader could only come about through a powerful parliament, and through democratization. Because of its imperialist basis this Weberian democratism had, to be sure, very curious nuances. Weber, according to his wife's notes, expressed himself as follows in a conversation with Ludendorff after the war: 'In a democracy the people elects as its leader a man it trusts. Then the man elected says, "Now hold your tongues and obey!" Neither the people nor the parties may contradict him . . . Afterwards it is for the people to judge – if the leader has erred, then away to the gallows with him!' It is not surprising that Ludendorff said to this: 'I like the sound of such a democracy!'[20] Thus Weber's idea of democracy lapsed into a Bonapartist Caesarism.

This concrete political basis of sociological critiques of culture shows even in their most opposed manifestations the deep affinity with the contemporary philosophy of the imperialist age, with the particular forms of neo-Kantianism and the burgeoning vitalism. In sociology too we find an extreme formalism in methodology, and an extreme relativism and agnosticism in its epistemology which now degenerated into an irrationalist mysticism. Sociology, as we have noted, went through the motions of being a specialist discipline, and indeed nothing other than an ancillary discipline to history. Its very formalism, however, removed all possibility of concrete historical elucidation. In this respect

the lines along which the different disciplines developed again ran parallel, becoming more and more formalistic, each creating for itself an immanent formal casuistry, and thereby passing from one to another the essential problems of content and origin. Thus Jellinek – to take jurisprudence as an example – regarded the substantive problems of justice as 'meta-legal' questions; thus Kelsen wrote of the origin of justice: 'It is the great mystery play of Justice and State which is performed in the legislative act . . .'[21]; thus Preuss stated: 'The content of legal institutions is, however, never of a juristic but always of a political, economic nature.'[22]

In appearance, sociology thereby acquired the important function of explaining, for its own part, these contents and processes of derivation in concrete terms. But that was only apparently the case. What did it really achieve? Instead of causal explanations, its equally formalistic sublimations yielded purely formal analogies. With Simmel this formalism sometimes amounted to a journalistic *jeu d'esprit*, as when he was discussing the possibility of identical social forms with completely different contents and discovered analogies between religious associations and bands of outlaws. This is concrete evidence of what we stressed in our introductory remarks, namely that the practice of the specialist branches of social theory meant postponing a resolution of the problems. In that they passed them round among themselves, their method bore a striking resemblance to the document transfers of bureaucratic authorities.

Although Max Weber occasionally polemicized against Simmel's exaggerated formalism, his own sociology was likewise full of such formalistic analogies. Thus he formally equated, for instance, ancient Egyptian bureaucracy with socialism, councillors (*Räte*) and estates (*Stände*); thus in speaking of the irrational vocation of leader (charisma), he drew an analogy between a Siberian shaman and the social democrat leader Kurt Eisner, etc. As a result of its formalism, subjectivism and agnosticism, sociology, like contemporary philosophy, did no more than to construct specified types,

set up typologies and arrange historical phenomena in this typology. (Here Dilthey's later philosophy had acquired a decisive influence on German sociology. Its real blossoming – after Spengler – we can witness in the post-war period.)

With Max Weber this problem of types became the central methodological question. The setting up of purely constructed 'ideal types' Weber regarded as a question central to the tasks of sociology. According to him a sociological analysis was only possible if it proceeded from these types. But this analysis did not produce a line of development, but only a juxtaposition of ideal types selected and arranged casuistically. The course of society itself, comprehended in its uniqueness on Rickertian lines and not following a regular pattern, had an irremediably irrationalistic character, although for the rational casuistry of the ideal type the irrational was the 'disruptive' element, the 'deviation'.

The ultimately subjective nature of Weber's sociology is best expressed in its concept of law. With regard to the categories of an 'understanding sociology' Weber specifically stressed that: 'the manner in which sociological concepts are formed is always largely a question of practicality. We are by no means *obliged* to form all . . . the categories set forth below.'[23] In accordance with this pragmatically oriented epistemology he wrote: 'The "laws" – our customary designation for a number of precepts in the "understanding sociology" – . . . are typical *chances*, hardened by observation, of a course of social action to be *actualized* in the presence of certain data, chances which are *understandable* from typical motives and the typically viewed mentality of the agents.'[24] This not only suspended subjectivistically the whole of objective social reality; the social data thereby took on a seemingly exact but in reality extremely blurred complexity. For instance Weber described the 'labour contract' in such a way that after enumerating the workers' obligations he wrote: '. . . that if he does all this, he (i.e., the worker, G.L.) moreover has the chance to receive at intervals certain specifically shaped metal discs or pieces of paper which,

when placed in the hands of others, enable him to acquire bread, coal, trousers, etc. And the upshot of it is that if somebody then wanted to take these articles away from him again, men in helmets would, with a certain degree of likelihood, appear at his bidding and help to restore them to him etc., etc.'[25]

It is evident from this that Weber's sociological categories – he defined as 'chance' the most diverse social formations such as might, justice, the State and so on – will yield simply the abstractly formulated psychology of the calculating individual agent of capitalism. Even here, with the German scholar who, in his subjective aims, made the most honest and rigorous effort to pursue his discipline purely objectively, to found and to translate into praxis a methodology of pure objectivity, the imperialist tendencies of pseudo-objectivity proved stronger. For Weber's conception of 'chance' was, on the one hand, modelled on the Machist interpretation of natural phenomena. And on the other, it was conditioned by the psychological subjectivism of the 'marginal utility theory'; it converted the objective forms, transmutations, happenings, etc., of social life into a tangled web of – fulfilled or unfulfilled – 'expectations', and its regular principles into more or less probable 'chances' of the fulfilment of such expectations. It is likewise evident that a sociology operating in this direction could go no further than abstract analogies in its generalizations.

Imperialist sociology, however, not only set itself the tasks we have outlined above. It also attempted to satisfy those 'needs for a world-view' evoked at this time by 'vitalism', the Hegel revival, the Romantic revival, etc., which were all bound in the direction of a mystical irrationalism. These tendencies took various forms in German sociology. Sometimes they expressed themselves quite directly, as when Rathenau was speaking of the irrational revolt of the 'soul' against the mechanical apparatus of capitalism (similarly in the Stefan George school, etc.). Simmel presented the dualism of formalistic sociology and irrationalistic 'vitalism'

in a more complex fashion in the problem of the 'tragedy of culture'.

Here too we must emphasize the special position of Max Weber, principally because in struggling against this irrationalism, it provided a bridge to a higher stage of it. Whilst Weber repeatedly defended himself against the charge of relativism, he considered his agnostic-formalistic method to be the only scientific one, since it prohibited the introduction into sociology of anything that was not exactly verifiable. In his opinion, sociology was able only to offer a technical critique, i.e., to investigate '*which* means are apt to lead to an envisaged end', and, on the other hand, 'to ascertain the *consequences* which the application of the required means would have . . . *besides* the achieving of the purpose intended'.[26] Everything else, according to Weber, lay outside the domain of science; it was an object of faith and therefore irrational.

Thus Max Weber's 'value-freedom' for sociology, its apparent purging of all irrational elements, finally amounted to a still greater irrationalizing of socio-historical events. Weber himself, although he certainly failed to see that this was to take away the whole rationality of his scientific methodology, had to accept that the irrational basis of 'value judgements' was deeply anchored in social reality itself. He wrote: 'The impossibility of a "scientific" presentation of practical standpoints adopted . . . follows for much profounder reasons. There is in principle no sense in it because the world's various orders of value are inseparably locked in mutual conflict.'[27] Here Weber ran up against the problem of the *Communist Manifesto*, the problem that history is a history of class struggles. But because of his world-outlook, he could and would not acknowledge these facts. Since, as a result, he was neither able nor willing to draw in his mind dialectical conclusions from this dialectical structure of social reality, he was forced to seek refuge in irrationalism. Here it is very evident how imperialist irrationalism arose out of false answers to questions that were justified, because

posed by reality itself. The situation was that reality itself was, with great and increasing force, confronting the ideologists with dialectical questions which – for social and hence methodological reasons – they could not possibly answer dialectically. Irrationalism was the form taken by the resulting flight from a dialectical answer to the dialectical question. So in truth this apparently scientific character and strict 'value-freedom' of sociology marked the highest stage of irrationalism hitherto reached. As a result of Max Weber's intellectual rigour, these irrationalist consequences emerged from his writings more clearly than from imperialist neo-Kantianism.

At the same time, Weber energetically opposed the conventional German irrationalism which held sway earlier and was continuing to do so. He observed perfectly clearly that something can be irrational only in relation to something else, and therefore only relatively irrational. He was contemptuous of the experiential irrationalism of his contemporaries: 'Anyone who wants "vision" (*Schau*) can go to the cinema.'[28] Certainly it is worth noting that he expressly exonerated from this charge the later leading lights of existential philosophy, Jaspers and also Klages. Thus his critical dismissal was only aimed against the outmoded and popular forms of irrationalism. Weber's own methodology was shot through with irrationalist tendencies which had arisen out of specifically imperialist motives and become insuperable for him, and which stemmed from the inner contradictoriness of his own position regarding German imperialism and the democratizing of Germany. Hence he was obliged to recognize the new, refined forms of irrationalism – forms determined in part by his own equivocal methodology. That he would certainly have repudiated them in their advanced pre-fascist or actual fascist form does not disprove in the least this historio-methodological connection. With regard to fascism Weber would – *mutatis mutandis* – have landed himself in a situation similar to that later occupied by Stefan George or Spengler.

Max Weber contested the outmoded irrationalism of German sociology as represented by Roscher, Knies and Treitschke. He challenged the more modern, but epistemologically still naive irrationalism of Meinecke and jeeringly wrote: 'So human actions would find their specific meaning in the fact that they are *inexplicable* and hence *beyond understanding*.'[29] He spoke just as ironically of the personality concept of Romantic irrationality 'which, after all, altogether shares the "person" with the animal'.[30] But this lively and just polemic against the vulgar irrationalism prevalent at that time does not cancel out the irrational core of Max Weber's method and outlook. Although Weber sought to rescue the scientific character of sociology through its 'value-freedom', he was only shifting all irrationality to the value judgements, the standpoints adopted. (Let us recall his historio-sociological statement about the rationality of economics and irrationality of religion.) Weber summed up his viewpoint thus: a scientific presentation of practical attitudes adopted is impossible.

> It is meaningless in principle because the world's various orders of value are inseparably locked in mutual conflict . . . if anything, we know again today that something can be holy not only although it is not beautiful, but *because* and *insofar* as it is not beautiful . . . and that something can be beautiful not only although, but in that it is not good. We have know this again since Nietzsche, and we find it previously in the *Fleurs du Mal*, as Baudelaire called his cycle of poems, – and it is a platitude to say that something can be true although and whilst it is not beautiful, not holy and not good . . . It is precisely here that even various gods are at loggerheads, and always will be . . . Depending on the latest view adopted, one thing is the Devil and the other God as far as the individual is concerned, and the individual must decide which, *for him*, is God and which the Devil. And this is so throughout the orders of life . . . The gods of ancient polytheism, bereft

> of their magic and hence appearing as impersonal powers, are climbing out of their tombs, striving for command over our lives and renewing their eternal battles with each other.[31]

According to Weber, this irrationality in the views which men will adopt – and precisely in respect of their cardinal praxis – is a supra-historical fundamental fact of social life. But his account bestowed on it some specific features of the present. Above all he put the stress on withdrawing from public life and thus raised the consciousness of the solitary individual to the status of an inappellable arbitrator; and by thus denying even the possibility of an objective authority, he further underlined the irrational character of the judgement. With Max Weber this universal condition was also connected with the world's 'disenchantment' and the origin of modern prose, in which the mythical figures of the warring gods have lost their mythical-religious-sensuous forms and are present only in their abstract antinomies (and the irrationality of their existence as well as of subjective reactions to them).

At this point Max Weber's outlook merged with the 'religious atheism' of the imperialist period. The disenchanting godlessness and god-forsakenness of life was presented as the historical face of the times. And whilst it had to be accepted as historical fact, it was bound to evoke a profound mourning, a profound yearning for the old, not yet 'disenchanted' ages. With Weber this attitude was less overtly romantic than with most of the 'religious atheists' among his contemporaries. In his work, the lack of socio-historical perspectives emerges all the more graphically as the real basis of 'religious atheism'. As always, he tackled this matter more cautiously than the later critics of culture who represented this standpoint, and was far more concerned not to lose touch with scientific thinking. So for him, the lack of perspectives did not rule out *a limine* and *a priori* the possibility of a perspective. It merely denied the present age this

possibility and made this denial a hallmark of intellectual integrity. Considering those views of Weber that we have expounded so far, this attitude may be readily understood. For even were everything that he wished for Germany to be realized, the realization could not decisively alter in any respect his basic assessment of the social reality. In his eyes, after all, the democratizing of Germany was only a technical step towards a better functioning imperialism, only an alignment of Germany's social structure with that of the Western European democracies. And these, he perceived clearly, were equally subject to the problems of 'disenchantment', etc., in respect of their essential social life. Hence when he began looking at the essence of the life of society, he saw nothing but general gloom all around. This universal condition he described most impressively: the scholars' highest virtue was, Weber wrote,

> simple intellectual honesty . . . But it commands us to state that for all the many people today who are awaiting new prophets and saviours, the situation is the same as that voiced in the beautiful song of the Edomite guards in exile, as recorded in the prophecies of Isaiah: 'The summons comes from Seir in Edom: dawn is breaking, but night lingers on. If you would ask, return another time.' The race to whom that was spoken had asked and waited for more than two thousand years, and we know its grievous fate. Let us draw a moral from it – that longing and waiting are not sufficient. Let us act differently, let us go to our work and satisfy the 'demand of the day' – on the human as much as the professional level. That demand, however, is plain and simple if each of us finds and obeys the daimon holding the threads of *his* life.[32]

Here Max Weber quite evidently carried 'religious atheism's' lack of perspectives resolutely beyond Dilthey and even Simmel. The existentialists' nihilism could now be directly linked to it, as indeed happened in the case of Jaspers.

So Max Weber banished irrationalism from his methodology and analysis of isolated facts only in order to introduce it as the philosophical basis of his world-picture with a firmness hitherto unknown in Germany. Granted, even this elimination of irrationalism from the methodology was not total. Just as Weber relativized everything in sociology into rational types, so likewise his type of the non-hereditary leader who attains office as a result of his 'charisma' was purely irrationalistic. That aside, however, imperialist neo-Kantianism really crossed the bridge into irrationalist existentialism for the first time in the lines quoted above. For that reason it was no coincidence that Jaspers saw in Weber a new type of philosopher. How strongly Weber was here expressing the general tendency of the most cultivated (and politically Left-oriented) German intellectuals of the imperialist period, how much his strictly scientific approach was only a path to the definitive establishing of irrationalism in men's outlook, and thus how helpless the best German minds were in the face of the irrationalist onslaught, is indicated – to quote just one example – in the following comment by Walther Rathenau: 'Let us press on with the language and images of the intellect as far as the gates of eternity; not in order to break them down, but in order to put paid to the intellect by securing its fulfilment.'[33] From here it was only a single step to the absolute predominance of irrationalism; only a firm renunciation of this 'detour' via the intellect and scientific thinking was needed. This step was not long coming. At bottom Spengler constructed in a merely amateurish and overtly mythologizing fashion the same bridge from extreme relativism to irrationalist mysticism which Weber expounded in the form of a credo as he crossed from scientific exactitude into the realm of world-outlook.

5. The Defencelessness of Liberal Sociology (Alfred Weber, Mannheim)

Max Weber's conception of society was permeated, as we have seen, by a profound dichotomy. Against Prussian *Junker* reaction, on the one hand, he affirmed the need for democratic development in Germany, albeit in the service of a more alert German imperialism. He took, on the other hand, a critical view of modern democracy and capitalist culture in general, and entertained a deep-seated pessimism about them. Hence his prognoses and perspectives were bound to be equivocal. We have observed his reactionary utopia of a democratic Caesarism. At the same time, after Germany's defeat in the First World War he was of the pronounced opinion that the possibilities of a German imperialism had been exhausted for a long time to come, and that the German people would have to reckon with this situation. Democracy he presented in this context as the political form of such an accommodation and also as the most effective safeguard against the revolutionary labour movement. We have just noted the same dichotomy in methodology and world-outlook in the matter of irrationalism.

Post-war German sociology took over this dichotomy as a legacy from him, as far as it was supported by the least vestige of a democratic idea. The most outstanding representative of this transitional form was Weber's younger brother, Alfred. With the latter, however, the dualism of rationalism and irrationalism assumed different proportions from the start (and already before the war). Alfred Weber was strongly influenced by Bergson and other vitalistic irrationalists. That is to say, he was more radical than Max Weber in grasping everything rational and scientific in a purely technical, pragmatic-agnosticist light, as merely external technical aids, since there could be only *one* entrance to the dead 'shell' of the external aspects of Being. For him, this entrance to 'life' was formed by the element of direct 'experience' in its irrationality. But Alfred Weber did not

therefore make a radical break with all science in the name of experience, as Stefan George's pupils had done before the war. Nor did he follow his brother in shifting the problem of irrationality to an extra-scientific philosophical plane. He attempted a 'synthesis', an intellectual 'illumination' of the irrational but without rationalizing it, a scientific approach which was intrinsically anti-scientific. So here Max Weber's dichotomy was reproduced at a higher stage.

This was not simply a difference of personal mentality. Before the war Alfred Weber's position was that of a lone wolf. The class struggles were gaining in intensity, the bourgeoisie was in a critical state, consciously revolutionary tendencies in the labour movement throughout the world were becoming stronger, while in the Soviet Union there existed a growing socialist society which was becoming increasingly established. And as we have noted in analysing Spengler's philosophy of history, the reaction of the bourgeois ideologies to all these events opened up the way to a new, full-blown irrationalist study of sociological problems. On the one hand, there arose an irrationalist 'method' in the social and historical sciences, with the typology of Dilthey and Max Weber branching out into a socio-philosophical 'morphology' and 'doctrine of forms'. In the vigorous class struggles over the new republic starting at the end of the war, on the other hand, irrationalism became to a mounting extent the ideological banner of entrenched reaction. Now since Alfred Weber's methodology sided with the tendencies of post-war reaction on the irrationalism question, but aimed at turning them into a sociological argumentation for a new democratic movement, his vague and vacillating eclecticism temporarily took on a wider importance.

Alfred Weber shared his brother's estimation of Germany in comparison with the Western democracies, thereby sharply dissociating himself from entrenched reaction, which idealized the German conditions. On this question he kept his distance from mythologies of history. He saw the difference as lying not in the national character but in the historical destinies of

the nations. He saw how the Western cultures had profited by the fact that their attainment to national status was linked with major revolutionary movements, whereas 'establishment as a political nation was handed to us on a plate'.[34] This implies a more or less firm rejection of the reactionary theories of history. But this rejection, which stemmed from Alfred Weber's liberal views, he promptly retracted and twisted into a reactionary direction. For he was also influenced very strongly by the Western criticism of modern bourgeois democracy, a criticism always connected with irrationalism. (Note Sorel's relationship to Bergson.) This criticism shows very clearly the reactionary decay of liberalism. Out of a fear of the socialist possibilities of a democracy carried all the way through, the oft-heralded democratic spirit was despicably betrayed. Here Alfred Weber allied himself with those critics of democracy who, following the general imperialist vogue, traced its problems back to its mass form. Thus instead of criticizing firmly the bourgeois, capitalist fetters of contemporary democracy – the real problem which life was posing – he flinched from the socialist consequences of such a critique and began to attack democracy's mass character, whereupon his criticism – for all its reservations – was bound to join the general trend of reaction. This steered him back to positions which, as we have seen, he was endeavouring to reject: to the world mission associated with Germany's social backwardness. And he now thought that Germany had the chance of finding a new road for which all mankind was looking.

Here we see the persistence of that reactionary German tradition which, taking its cue from Bismarck's solution for unifying the German nation, reached a temporary climax at the time of the First World War in the slogan, *Am deutschen Wesen soll die Welt genesen* (The essence of Germany will set the world to rights). It was, this tradition asserted, precisely the backward sides of the German people in comparison with Western democratic developments that constituted the source of its international superiority, its vocation for

international leadership. Max Weber's specific position was anchored not least in the fact that he was free from this chauvinistic prejudice. Alfred Weber (who, as we have remarked, was essentially in agreement with his brother in his assessment of German history) strayed from the road of sober judgement just where he was required to draw decisive consequences. He capitulated to the reactionary chauvinist view, to which he made major concessions. This surrender clearly illustrates his inconsistent, wavering position, which was connected socially with the weakness of democracy in the Weimar Republic and methodologically with his eclectic, undirected irrationalism.

That defines for us the task of Alfred Weber's sociology. It proceeded from the thesis that we find ourselves in a completely new world-situation. There were, Alfred Weber contended, three periods in the history of thought, and the present age marked the beginning of the third. Hence he deemed it necessary to make a clean break with the classical traditions. Philosophically, he allied himself with that campaign against Descartes and the rationalism derived from him which we have already analysed, a tradition which began with the older Schelling and ended in fascism. He saw the culture of the future in the emergence of a 'post-Cartesian period'. Here his reasoning is not without interest. He said of the legacy of German idealism: 'But this, paradoxical though it is, leads to the shaping of materialist propositions and to continued compromises with historical materialism.'[35] He vigorously reproached Troeltsch for making such compromises.

Here again Alfred Weber's conception of history came very close to that of extreme reaction. We noted in the Hegel dispute that such a rejection of the classical period ran from Lagarde to Baeumler. Now the nearer this line came to Hitlerism, the more important the discovery became that, intellectually, historical materialism had a profound link with the ideology of Germany's classical period; Rosenberg made this plain with regard to the link between Hegel and Marx.

This question is of such significance for the development of German culture that we must dwell on it for a moment. From the outset all anti-democratic reaction had tended to exclude Marx and Marxism from German culture, although it must have been clear to any student the least bit open-minded how profound the connection was between Marxism and the ideology of the golden age of German culture, the period from Lessing to Heine and from Kant to Hegel and Feuerbach. For a long time it was possible to employ the cliché that Marxism was 'un-German'. The aggravation of the class struggles, and in particular the inevitable first encounter in theory and praxis with the problems of democracy and socialism imposed by the loss of the First World War, now created a new situation, of which Alfred Weber's aforestated standpoint may be termed the ideological expression. The objective development of society wrested from him an insight into this link between the classical age and Marxism; for social democrat literature dealt with this question not at all or very feebly – with the sole exception of Franz Mehring. From both the methodological and the social angle, it is highly remarkable that Alfred Weber countered this correct definition of the concrete connection by dismissing the whole classical period. Methodologically, he drew his conclusions from the basic irrationalistic position; if the future of culture depended on the emergence of a 'post-Cartesian period', then it was only logical to discard the Lessing-Heine period and to see in Marx the – equally dispensable – final realization of this 'Cartesian' development. The struggle against Marxism made obligatory this very break with the greatest traditions of German culture. (That fascist demagogy laid down some exceptions – chiefly Hölderlin, and portions of Goethe – did not materially affect the principal line.)

In this methodology we can also observe once more how, in the imperialist age, points of departure that were correct in themselves – here, the connection between classical times and Marx – could lead to the most false and portentous conclusions – here, a rejection of the classical period. The

class struggles in the Weimar Republic formed the objective basis for this. It became more and more evident in the course of these struggles that a concrete maintenance and expansion of democracy, which would necessarily lead in the direction of socialism, was only possible with the support of the revolutionary working class. That so-called democracy which was being defended from this onslaught could, in turn, only be preserved with the aid of the extreme reactionaries. Under these conditions the social scope afforded to a purely Western democracy (of the British type) was growing narrower and narrower. So for these liberal middle-of-the road ideologists, of whom Alfred Weber was one, the task became that of saving their liberal conception of democracy. And this, for them, was only possible if they were in the most intimate touch with reaction, and through a resolute battle against the Left, allied to an – inevitably more than lame – resistance to the radical demands of the extreme reactionaries. The latter principle finds clear expression in Alfred Weber's irrationalist sociology. The energetic struggle against the Left and the true forces of democracy led him to associate Lagarde's rejection and Nietzsche's critique of the classical period with the attempt to destroy Marxism. That just this step cleared the way for fascist ideology, and for the theories of history and culture advanced by Baeumler and Rosenberg, is among the not uncommon facts of the development whereby convinced liberals, precisely because of their liberal ideology, have become pioneers of the ideology of extreme reaction in times of crisis.

Thus Alfred Weber's dismissal of historical materialism was more vehement and impassioned than that of Max Weber and Troeltsch. Like his brother, but more radically, more strongly detached still from all economic considerations, indeed, repudiating economics in radical fashion, he saw the basic character of contemporary society as lying in the general rationalizing process. But that it was precisely capitalism which had achieved this rationalization was, in his eyes, a 'historical coincidence – it could equally well have been . . .

the *State* which carried out the general rationalization'.[36] (This radical belittlement of economic life and economic motives again expresses the point that, to him, the real adversary was socialism and Marxism. And here too Alfred Weber was doing preliminary work on behalf of fascist ideology.)

For these reasons he called for entirely new forms of sociology: a new method of intuitive sociology of culture. This rested on the thesis that the world was split into three areas with 'different trends of movement': the social process, the process of civilization, and the cultural movement. We can see the significance now acquired by the false antithesis, which first became central with Toennies, between culture and civilization. But we see also how much farther this antithesis had been developed in a reactionary irrationalist direction since Toennies's day. The Romantic anti-capitalist critique of contemporary culture had petrified into a starkly mechanical opposition of culture and socio-economic life. It had become an assertion of the total other-ness of culture to all the rest of mankind's tendencies and forces of development: a mysticized fetish for decadent intellectuals who were timidly and artificially cutting themselves off from the public life of society.

When analysed the process of civilization showed, according to Alfred Weber, only a continuation of the biological stages of man's evolution 'through which, however, we preserve and extend *only* our *natural* existence'.[37] On the one hand, this evolution had, in principle, nothing to do with culture; culture no longer stemmed from human evolution as its finest flower, but was deemed radically independent of man's physical and social existence. On the other hand, the character of culture, as representing the peak of the human condition, was polemically contrasted to all other expressions of life. It was quite logical for Alfred Weber to recognize only works of art and ideas as forms of culture, and artists and prophets as its only transmitters. In its actual content, this sociology of culture was bound to proclaim a complete

abstention from social action, which in any case can never touch on essential matters. But since this sociology was, as we shall see, still turning its attention to the social sphere, there arose an important intellectual link between Alfred Weber, the Stefan George school and Hitlerism. Hitler and Rosenberg had only to invest the 'prophet' with a plainly reactionary content in order to complete this development of the irrationalist social doctrine in the fascist spirit. (There is a similarity here to the connection between Max Weber's 'charismatic leader' and the blind worship of the *Führer* demanded by Hitler.)

With Alfred Weber this antithesis of culture and civilization coincided with that of emotion and intellect, irrationalistic intuition and rationalism. All evolution was rationalistic and had a methodological import only outside the cultural sphere; in culture there was no development, no progress, but only a 'live stream' – a true Bergsonian expression. Here Alfred Weber repudiated all perspectives, all 'cultural prognoses' of the future; the future was – so irrationalist logic would have it – of necessity a secret. What he wished to achieve was a 'mere orientation in the present'.[38] It is striking from a logical viewpoint, but not surprising from that of Alfred Weber's hypotheses, that he did not so much as notice the contradiction occurring here. For if, as he himself repeatedly stressed, culture is – as Bergson would have it – a 'stream', then how can we orient ourselves in it without having investigated the direction of the stream (a question involving the matter of perspective)? According to Weber it was sociology's task precisely to attain to a vision of this 'stream' and to express it in 'affective symbols'. On such a basis it could provide an answer to the question of where we stand. Thus while consciously renouncing the scientific 'dignity' of sociology, Alfred Weber believed that a definite synthesis and analysis resting on intuition would still be possible on this basis, though they would have nothing to do with a causal explanation. It is perhaps superfluous to remark how close this new sociology comes to the

existentialism of Heidegger and Jaspers.

So let us now take the concrete central question of Alfred Weber's sociology – the respective positions of present things, our present position in history. To a large extent his diagnosis of this tallied with that of Max Weber: the mechanization, technical trappings and mass quality of existence, accompanied by a prognosis of the ineluctability of these social manifestations. Democracy too was, in Alfred Weber's eyes, part of this process of civilization. Already going beyond his brother at this point, he characterized democracy as the 'subjugation of the State's political will to mindless economic forces'.[39] Naturally this was closely connected with his rejection of the 'mass quality of existence' in democracy. It was however this diagnosis that gave rise to the particular perspective of Alfred Weber's sociology. Weber stated, with regard to the fate of democracy and of our tasks in its formation, that one had to penetrate to a deeper level; it was there that the authentic problem first originated. 'We must separate those parts of the democratic idea which follow simply from the development of man's self-consciousness from those which have sprung from the rational mediating apparatus of civilized thinking and contemplation.'[40] One must therefore begin to contemplate the 'primal facts of life'. In concrete terms that means: the manifestation is civilization, but the primal facts are the processes of 'leading' and of 'being led'. Thus the central problem of democracy is the creation of a new leader caste.

Here there is still a glimmer of a proper democratic instinct in Alfred Weber, inasmuch as he criticized the fact about the German development that the lower classes could not attain to leadership. But all that he could do positively was to set up completely vague reactionary utopias. This was not a matter of chance but the inevitable upshot of his proposition and its social foundation. It was, indeed, again not by chance that the leader problem was raised precisely by sociologists of those countries where there was no really advanced bourgeois democracy (Max Weber in Germany, Pareto in Italy). Max

Weber also saw clearly – in his concrete analyses – that precisely Germany's undemocratic, quasi-parliamentary development was bound to entail a defective and fateful choice of leader. Politically he called for the democratizing, the parliamentarization of Germany in view of this very point. But when he summed up his views theoretically, he again drifted into an irrationalist mysticism. As is well known, Max Weber in his sociology regarded the chosen state of the democratic leader in particular as 'charisma', a term already expressing the conceptually unfathomable and incomprehensible irrational character of leadership. For Max Weber this was not to be avoided. For if – following the Rickertian methodology of history, which only recognizes individual phenomena – we ask why it was that Pericles or Julius Caesar, Oliver Cromwell or Marat became leaders and try to find a sociological generalization covering the separate historical answers, there will arise the concept of 'charisma', which roughly pins down in a pseudo-concept our ignorant amazement, i.e., something irrational. When, on the other hand, Hegel spoke of the 'world-historical individual', he was proceeding not from the individual but from the historically allotted task of an age, a nation, and regarded as 'world-historical' that individual who could solve this task. Hegel well knew that the question of whether, among those with the potential awareness and capacity for action needed in this situation, it is the individual X or Y who does in fact become 'world-historical' conceals within it an element of irreducible chance. Max Weber posed the question precisely from the angle of this unavoidable chance element and sought an 'explanation' for it. Hence he was sure to land up with the partly abstract, partly mystical and irrational pseudo-concept of 'charisma'.

Meanwhile the problem itself had been clarified in historical materialism far beyond the insight accessible to Hegel. The very analysis of the class struggles, and of the varying composition and structure of classes, further diversified according to historical periods, countries and evolutionary stages, offered the methodological possibility of posing and

solving in full clarity that which was truly and scientifically soluble in this question. It did so by establishing that the economic and political struggle of a class was always linked with the training of a leader caste. And the nature, composition, selection, etc., of this caste could be elucidated scientifically from the conditions of the class struggle, the composition, evolutionary stage and so forth of the class, and the reciprocal relationship between the mass and its leaders etc. In content and methodology Lenin's *What Is To Be Done?* was the model of such an analysis. To bourgeois sociology, the findings and the methods of a scientific proposition of this kind were automatically inaccessible. This was not only because of its repudiation in principle of the class struggle (in spite of this stance, it could still have attained at least a Hegelian clarity). It was because bourgeois sociology posed the question – more or less consciously – as a challenge to the democratic upsurge and because, from the very start, the problem's methodological basis was not the interaction of leadership and masses, but – more or less – the antithetical enmity between them. Such class reasons gave rise to a proposition that was at once abstract and irrationalist: a reduction of the problem of democracy to the leader question. Only distortedly irrationalist, anti-democratic answers could be given to so limited and distorted a question. This is best seen in Robert Michels's book on the sociology of party political life. In order to degrade democracy and especially labour democracy, the phenomena which reformism had produced in the social democrat parties and in the trade unions they influenced were elevated to 'sociological laws'. From a specific phenomenon of one part of the labour movement in the imperialist age, Michels deduced the 'law' that it was impossible for the masses to evolve an appropriate leader caste from within their own ranks.

We have illustrated the contrast, in Max Weber, between concrete politico-historical criticism where he proved the incapacity, with regard to Wilhelmine Germany, of quasi-parliamentary absolutism to evolve a caste of leaders on the

one hand, and his irrational mystical 'charisma' sociology on the other. There is also a similar internal inconsistency in his brother. But with the latter, the criticism of Germany's democratic backwardness was merely episodic, whereas irrationalist mysticism embraced not only the choice of leader but the whole problem of democracy and leadership. Alfred Weber appealed to the country's youth, demanded a separation of personal criterion from party opinion in selecting a leader, and called for the working out of 'an intellectually aristocratic norm filled with substance, delineated in character'.[41] Of course he was unable to say what the substance of such a norm might be, for according to his theory the substance was not definable, only 'experience'. Thus the ambitious launching of his new sociology ended with the wholly unsubstantiated, suggested vision of a new change of direction, with vague hints of a total upheaval in terms of world-outlook, and with an appeal to a 'generation unthinkable without Nietzsche, its master',[42] albeit a Nietzsche minus the 'blond beast'. It was on this 'basis' that the new men were supposed to procure peaceful co-operation between nations.

Confused though these studies are, and despite the inevitable meagreness and eclecticism of their intellectual results, we must not underestimate the importance of such essays of a sociology of leadership in creating a mental climate favourable to the acceptance of the Nazi mystique of the *Führer*. A methodological foundation was now achieved inasmuch as the whole problem-complex was made the necessarily irrational object of subjective experiences. Lacking such a climate, the fascist theory of the *Führer* could never have gained credence among the intelligentsia. The experiential, irrationalist character of the choice of leader in the Hitler movement was only a facade for the corruption and tyranny which characterized this movement, and it had its own very clear-cut, rational principles of selection (trustworthiness in the eyes of monopoly capitalism accompanied by the most barbaric of means). These latter motives were

very far from the thoughts of Max and Alfred Weber. But none of this at all affects the objective connection in the development of German ideology towards fascism.

This mixture of distinctly reactionary philosophy and indistinctly liberal sociological conclusions and pseudo-democratic utopian perspectives is a clear reflection of the ideology of the Weimar 'republic without republicans'. The incoherent and eclectic character of this sociology reflects not just Alfred Weber's personal qualities, but also the changes taking place at the time that these views originated. Dating from before the war, the original conception had survived the war period and the tide of revolution to receive its literary form at the time of 'relative stabilization'. At this time the greatest of hopes and illusions were being cherished by that moderate German intelligentsia which, while going along with the reactionary trends of 'vitalism' all the way in the philosophical sphere, recoiled from the politico-social conclusions of its extreme representatives, especially the fascists. This phase of development was the time most favourable to such hazy utopias. These intellectuals were in no position – not even on an ideological basis – to enter into a real struggle against the reactionaries. They resorted, therefore, to daydreams of the permanance of 'relative stabilization' (and after this collapsed, of its return). And they accordingly adjusted their social theories with a view to absorbing as much as possible of vitalism and existentialism, while also salving something of sociology's scientific character. Simultaneously this rescue operation implied, as we have noted in Alfred Weber's case, an energetic struggle against the Left, and above all against historical materialism. And it was also intended to substantiate in theory the social importance, the leading social role of this 'floating' intelligentsia.

Of the younger generation of German sociologists, Karl Mannheim was the outstanding representative of this orientation. The effects of 'relative stabilization' played an even more decisive role in shaping his views than with the older

Alfred Weber. Hence the latter's overtly mystical, intuitionist sociology of culture was supplanted, in Mannheim, by a sceptically relativistic 'sociology of knowledge' which carried on a flirtation with existentialism. (This phase in the development of German sociology is, as we have shown in Chapter IV, represented also in the contemporaneous works of the philosopher Max Scheler.)

Like all agnosticists and relativists of the imperial period, Mannheim protested against the accusation of relativism. He solved the question with a new term and called himself a relationist. The difference between relativism and relationism is about the same as that between the yellow and the green devil in Lenin's letter to Gorky.[43] For Mannheim 'overcame' relativism by pronouncing obsolete and discarding the old epistemology, which at least put forward the demand for objective truth and termed the denial of it relativism. Modern epistemology, on the other hand, was to 'proceed from the thesis that there are areas of thought where uncommitted, unrelated cognition is quite unimaginable'.[44] Or, more radically as regards the realm of social knowledge: 'But primarily, each of us gets to see that aspect of the social whole to which he is oriented in terms of the will.'[45] Here Mannheim's source is obvious: it was historical materialism's theory of ideologies. But, like all the popularizers and popular opponents of this doctrine, he failed to observe that in it, the relative and absolute mesh in a dialectical reciprocal relationship, and that this gives rise to the approximative character of human knowledge, for which objective truth (the correct reflection of objective reality) is always an inherent element and criterion. Thus the theory involved a 'false consciousness' as a complementary pole to correct consciousness, whereas Mannheim conceived his relationism as the typification and systematizing of every possible kind of false consciousness.

But it was just through this that Mannheim intended to disprove historical materialism. After bourgeois epistemology and sociology had desperately staved off the idea that social

Being determines consciousness, it was forced to give in to historical materialism on this question. But this capitulation was, on the one hand, as we have just noted, a relativistic caricature in which, and by the agency of which, any objectivity of knowledge was repudiated. On the other hand, this capitulation to Marxism was to be instantly converted into an – avowedly irrefutable – argument against historical materialism. For to be consistent, one would have to apply the latter to itself; i.e., if the theory of ideologies was correct, then it would also apply to the ideology of the proletariat, to Marxism; if all ideologies had only a relative degree of truth in them, then Marxism too could not claim more. This 'irrefutable' reasoning was the result of simply eliminating both the dialectic of the absolute and relative, and historical development and its concrete facts, which always clearly illustrate how this dialectic of the absolute and relative works out in any given case. Thus arrived what we know as the night of thorough-going relativism, in which all cats looked grey and all perceptions relative. So this refutation of Marxism offers us only a sociological variation on the Spenglerian theory of culture cycles. Although the question of ascertaining truth did crop up again in Mannheim's book, it did so only in the form: 'which standpoint provides the biggest chances of an optimum of truth . . .'[46] And with that, according to Mannheim, the problem of relativism fell into obsolescence.

Here the connection with Max Weber is clearly visible. Only, Rickert's neo-Kantianism gave way to a sociologized existentialism à la Jaspers and Heidegger in that, as we have seen, each social perception was presented in principle as 'situation-bound' and the current crisis of thinking was made the epistemological starting-point and a basis for dismissing the obsolete demand for objectivity. Mannheim formulated his epistemological position as follows: 'There is no "thinking in general"; on the contrary a living being of a specific type thinks in a world of a specific type in order to fulfil a specified function in life.'[47] Mannheim even went so far as to see

in the call for absolute truth in thinking only an – inferior – speculation on a 'need of security'.

Mannheim thereby put himself in a somewhat awkward situation with regard to historical materialism. It was very easy for Heidegger or Jaspers to answer the Kierkegaard-influenced appeal to the 'existing man' because they saw in all social categories only a profoundly unreal 'shell'. But Mannheim was a sociologist, and a thinking bound up with Being logically meant, in his case, that social Being defines consciousness. He found an escape route by cultivating a formalistic and relativistic sophistry, by projecting irrationalism into historical materialism and – in close connection with all this – by a radical elimination of economics from sociology. Let us begin with the last of these. Mannheim stated in his later work that competition and controls were not economic but 'general sociological principles, which we just happened to locate and observe first in economics'.[48] By thus abstractly generalizing away from all concrete objectiveness and clearly defined objectivity, Mannheim enabled himself to define any economic or social category just as he pleased and to propound any amount of analyses and contrasts between such vacuous and abstract concepts. Only by this abstract distancing from objective socio-economic reality did it become possible to reveal the 'irrational' motives in historical materialism. Consequently, Mannheim regarded the method of historical materialism as a 'synthesis between intuitionism and an extreme rationalizing desire'.[49] The revolutionary situation, or as Mannheim put it, the 'passing moment' (*Augenblick*), was viewed as an irrational 'gap'. (Here the results of the neo-Hegelian corruption of the dialectic and the equation by Kroner and Glockner of dialectics and irrationalism had their sociological repercussions. To the dialectic of revolution so concrete in Marxism, Mannheim gave as strong a Kierkegaardian twist as the neo-Hegelians had given to dialectics as a whole.)

Historical materialism in this interpretation – i.e., adjusted in accordance with extreme relativism, and rendered

vitalistically irrational – had great merits in Mannheim's opinion. But it also made the mistake of 'absolutizing' the socio-economic structure of society. Moreover, as already shown, it failed to see that its unmasking of ideologies was – yet another ideology. Now we can see for what purpose Mannheim needed to reshape historical materialism as indicated above. With the disappearance of economics and the irrationalizing of the social process, a general 'situation-bound state' of thought and cognition supplanted the constantly historically concrete relation between economic foundation and ideology. So it now seemed illogical for historical materialism to distinguish between true and false consciousness. In short, it did not come up to the mark of the 'modern epistemology', relationalism. Thus historical materialism's theory of ideologies was not formulated in a sufficiently general way. This universality, Mannheim argued, could only be reached if the 'relationalistic situation-bound state' of thought was correspondingly generalized, i.e., if the relativity of all thinking was corrected by dissolving all objectivity. Then we would have that interpenetration of the various styles of thinking indispensable to a sociology of knowledge. Historical materialism would then form one of the many particularities with regard to this universality and totality.

Mannheim now went on from here to moot the problems of ideological and utopian thinking, of the possibility of scientific politics, of governmental planning, etc. The fruits of these inquiries were extremely scanty. Mannheim was abiding by an extremely formalistic standpoint from which he could obtain only a fully abstract typology of the positions possible in each event, without being able to make a factually important statement about them. Mannheim's typologizing was so abstract that his separate types embraced the most diverse and inherently contradictory directions, just in order for him to produce a synoptical, limited number of types in socio-historical reality. Thus he identified as uniform types social democracy and communism on the one hand,

liberalism and democracy on the other. In this, as we shall see, the overtly reactionary Carl Schmitt was far superior to him. Schmitt perceived in the antithesis of liberalism and democracy an important present-day problem.

The result of the 'Mannheimian sociology of knowledge' was not much more than an actualization of Max Weber's doctrine of the 'ideal type'. And Mannheim was logically obliged to adhere to a scientific agnosticism, leaving all decision to the intuition, the experience, the 'charisma' of the individual. But this is where the illusions of 'relative stabilization' set in. To the 'floating' intelligentsia was imputed the chance and the role of ascertaining the truth that met the present situation from the totality of standpoints and attitudes linked to these standpoints; This intelligentsia, according to Mannheim, stood outside social class: 'It forms a centre, *but not a centre in terms of class*.' Now why the thinking of the 'floating intelligentsia' was no longer 'situation-bound', and why relationalism did not now apply its own tenet to itself, as it was asking historical materialism to do, is known only to the sociology of knowledge. Mannheim asserted of this social group that it possessed a social sensibility enabling it to 'share the feelings of the dynamically conflicting forces', but that was a hollow claim without proof. That this group had the delusion that it was standing above social class and the class struggles is a well-known fact. Historical materialism not only repeatedly described it, but also deduced it from the social Being of this group. Here it was Mannheim's duty to point out that the bond with social Being, with the 'situation' which, in his new epistemology, defined the thinking of every man living in society was absent from this group or present in a modified way. But he did not even attempt to show this, and simply had recourse to the 'floating intelligentsia's' illusions about itself. Its situation as propounded by Mannheim now gave rise to its calling 'to locate in each event the point from which a total orientation in what is happening can be undertaken, and to act as watchmen in an otherwise all too murky night'.[50] Since, in view of

his methodological hypotheses, Mannheim could not draw upon Alfred Weber's 'vision', he was of course unable to tell us anything at all about the content of this 'total orientation'.

His experiences under Hitler's régime did not alter Mannheim's basic conception. Certainly this experience did not leave him unmarked, for his views became more decided: 'The fundamental evil of modern society does not lie in the great number but in the fact that the liberal framework has not yet succeeded in bringing about the organic structure needed for a large-scale society.'[51] The reason for this, in Mannheim's opinion, was that the nineteenth and twentieth centuries had effected a 'fundamental democratization' making it possible for the irrationalisms to function incorrectly. 'That is the condition of a mass society in which those irrationalisms as yet unformed and uncoordinated in the social framework are pressed into politics. This condition is a dangerous one because democracy's mass apparatus brings irrationality into places where rational guidance is needed.'[52] From this it would follow that a surplus of democracy, and not the lack of democracy, democratic experience and tradition, was the main cause of the fascist development in Germany. Here Mannheim was doing the same as a great many spokesmen for anti-democratic, imperialistically corrupt liberalism. Since they had always contested democracy out of a fear of its social consequences, they seized on the case of Hitler with delight and satisfaction in order to camouflage their old, unchanged rebuttal of democracy as a battle against the Right and reaction. And in so doing, they used wholly uncritically the demagogic social democrat equation of fascism and bolshevism as the collective enemy of 'true' (i.e., liberalist) democracy.

The central problem of the times, according to Mannheim, was this: we have entered the epoch of social planning, but our thinking, morality and so forth are still at more rudimentary stages of development. It was the task of sociology and of the psychology linked with it to put right this discrepancy between men and their tasks. Sociology, Mannheim

wrote, 'will pursue principles that will redirect militant energies and guide them to a sublimation'.[53] Hence there were three progressive tendencies in present-day psychology: pragmatism, behaviourism and 'depth-psychology' (Freud and Adler). 'Pioneer types' were to be trained with the assistance of these, since the role of advance parties, of élites in social events was of crucial importance. So Mannheim was reviving once more the old problem of leader selection. Alfred Weber's overt irrationalism had now vanished, but the problem had by no means become more concrete. In a society whose economic basis and social structure continued to depend on monopoly capitalism, and whose development was therefore bound to be an imperialist one as long as this basis remained unaltered, Mannheim was seeking to create an anti-imperialist leader caste through education, through the psychological sublimation of irrationalism. And such a utopia, if it were not to represent pure empty demagogy in the imperialist interest, could only be created by radically eliminating all objective categories of the life of society. Mannheim then discussed in great detail some problems of the education, morality, etc., of the new élite, its relation to the old élite, etc. But he did not make the politico-social substance of this new élite any more concrete than Alfred Weber had done.

On one point only did Mannheim visibly adopt a clearer stance. He repudiated any social solution through the use of violence, through dictatorship. And here, in a truly formalistic manner, he again treated as equivalents fascist dictatorship and the dictatorship of the proletariat, revolutionary and counter-revolutionary violence. For this is always the case with the ideologists who fear a radical democratic transformation of society, a real defusing and short-circuiting of the imperialist forces of monopoly capitalism far more than a recurrence and resurgence of fascism.

There was only one point on which Mannheim transcended pure formalism and developed something akin to a personal standpoint. That was his hope of a compromise between the

embattled parties of the individual states, between the embattled powers on an international scale. 'But such a change of mentality would be a true revolution in the history of the world . . .' To illustrate the possibility of such an answer, Mannheim suggested that an attack by the inhabitants of Mars might bring the hostile groups into agreement. Of course he himself admitted that this was impossible. He thought, however, that the annihilating character of modern warfare was becoming increasingly clear. 'Fears of a future war with its dreadful powers of destruction could increase to such an extent that they would have the same effect as fear of a concrete enemy. In this event, men would decide on compromise solutions for fear of impending general annihilation, and would submit to a central umbrella organization which would administer social planning for all.'[54] As usual with Mannheim, this lacks any indication of what economic and social character such an 'umbrella organization' might have, and of what difference the socio-economic character of such organizations would make. Obviously Mannheim regarded Anglo-Saxon imperialism – as dogmatically as he had previously regarded the intelligentsia – as 'floating' and above social conflicts and 'situation-bound' thinking. In this he becomes one of numerous forerunners of the imperialist reaction after Hitler's downfall.

The sociological movement emanating from Max Weber was profoundly sterile. Its sterility is evident from a programme of this sort for those bourgeois intellectuals who were reluctant to give in to reactionary fascist irrationalism without a struggle, but who were wholly unable to counter it with a clear and decisive democratic programme. Not to mention the fact that in their epistemological and sociological views, they were deeply implicated in those reactionary tendencies from which fascism ultimately derived on the ideological level. Their inconsistency left this part of the anti-fascist intelligentsia weak and indeed ideologically defenceless in the face of fascist demagogy. And as the example of Mannheim shows, experience of fascism did not

help to overcome this vulnerability. His views as set out in this book are as much of an ideology of helpless surrender to a reactionary wave in post-war times as his sociology of knowledge before the war.

6. Pre-Fascist and Fascist Sociology (Spann, Freyer, Carl Schmitt)

In accordance with the character and outcome of the German class struggles during the Weimar Republic, a thoroughly reactionary direction became dominant in German sociology. We have seen how Max Weber – involuntarily – paved a way for the new irrationalism methodologically, and how Alfred Weber went a long way towards existentialism, etc. But to put forward a plain and simple reactionary content, a plain and simple reactionary methodology of some sort did not suffice in this period. The outcome of the class struggles indicates the failure of all essays in established Prussian reaction (with or without the Hohenzollerns). The winner was a new barbaric form of reaction, Hitlerian 'National Socialism'. Correspondingly, it was those sociologists becoming – whether or not they were aware of this from the outset – allies of the tendencies assisting the fascist victory in advance who also gained the upper hand ideologically.

Characteristic of this situation was the episodic role which so pronounced a reactionary as Othmar Spann played in German sociology. Long before Hitler's seizure of power, Spann shared most of the social views of fascism. He saw his main enemies partly in the liberal ideas of 1789, but above all in the Marxist ideas of 1917. He anticipated those national socialist demagogics which charged with Marxism everyone who was not an avowed reactionary; Spann even levelled this charge against the German economic leaders and especially sharply against Max Weber. In anticipation of fascism he removed 'self-interest' from the 'comprehensive economy'

and turned the capitalists into 'economic leaders', the workers a 'band of followers' and a new class,[55] etc.

As will be already clear from these few indications, Spann achieved a very large measure of agreement with the subsequent national socialism; were it worth our while to go into more details, the affinity would emerge more clearly still. Nevertheless Rosenberg rejected the figure of Spann as a whole.[56] Now why was this? It was because Spann developed all his views from a philosophico-sociological system that was certainly extremely reactionary, but in a Catholic and scholastic sense (adapted to Austrian clerical fascism). It was therefore irreconcilable with the most important principles of German fascism's social demagogy. Like all the learned reactionaries of the post-war period, Spann too dismissed the category of causality, not however in order to supplant it with irrationalist myth, but to establish a static and inflexible scholastic doctrine of totality and component parts. Thus Spann originated a system of an *a priori* stable classification. While challenging all progressive scientific thinking in the same way as fascism, this 'comprehensive' study created a system analogous to medieval Catholic scholasticism. And accordingly, it had to be anchored in an ancient, hereditary, traditional authority. Spann's debt to Catholicism was therefore not fortuitous, and therein lies one of the most important reasons why he, like everything Catholic, was repudiated by the National Socialists. Moreover Spann's theory rejected every form of revolution and violent upheaval – a view which National Socialism could not afford to tolerate before its seizure of power. Spann polemicized against Hegel, for instance, because the latter's categories went from the bottom upwards and not the reverse, and because his philosophy was constructed upon the idea of progress: this the 'National Socialist world-view' could still accept. When, however, Spann replaced Hegel's 'suspension' (*Aufhebung*) with the purely conservative category of the 'preservation of innocence',[57] i.e., sought an authoritarian maintenance of the status quo, he was transgressing against

the needs of the social demagogy of National Socialism. Therefore the fascist ideologists who were polemicizing against the 'Red Front *and* reaction' on behalf of their social demagogy turned against Spann as much as Spengler. And finally, Spann's scholastic, Catholic hierarchy had room neither for racial theory nor for the irrationalist mystique of the *Führer*. Because of his general reactionary tendencies, Spann was very much in fashion among all the German obscurantists for a while, but Hitlerian fascism then swept him aside.

More important as regards the transition to fascism are Hans Freyer and Carl Schmitt. Freyer's initial work consisted partly of historical, specialist investigations, and partly of a dithyrambic, mystical philosophy. Directly after this he attempted to construct a new, up-to-date sociology out of German sociology's previous traditions chiefly by synthesizing Max Weber's typological casuistry and Dilthey's experiential philosophy. From the outset this had a strong vitalistic, indeed existentialist orientation, but with a long-lasting tendency to seek a synthesis between 'intellect' and 'life'. Hence the State stood at the centre of these treatises. In his *Prometheus* Freyer outlined a downright Leviathan-like picture of the State's irresistible violence and the intellect's total impotence in the face of power. But that was only his preamble. He sought, on the contrary, to demonstrate their reliance upon each other: 'The history of power is its dialectic; the intellect has need of power to win real recognition on Earth among men. Considered intrinsically, however, power has a still more urgent need of the intellect if it is to emerge as a real force out of a mangled and downtrodden mass of possibilities.'[58] Freyer now expounded this interaction in more detail in his book on the State. Here he indicated two dialectical paths. One of them was, in his view, concretely historical: that leading from the intellect to the State. The second, on the other hand, signified 'the timeless law of the State structure',[59] the path from the State to the intellect. But the stages along this second path (might,

law, form), Freyer claimed, were only intellectual reiterations of the real stages along the first path (faith, style, State). Both these paths represent a vitalist caricature of the *Phenomenology of the Mind*, drawing heavily on all the 'achievements' of German sociology from Toennies to Max Weber.

As for the individual stages of these 'phenomenological' paths, Freyer's stage of faith was nothing more than Toennies's community concept. Its forms were myth, cult and language. The next stage, that of style, appears more complicated and contradictory. According to Freyer it was a 'necessary episode of the intellect'. This stage differs from the preceding one in that the concrete form is now the 'it', whereas it was previously the 'you'. In this case the forms are science, art and justice. In all, this stage was a caricature of Hegel's 'absolute intellect' in the spirit of pre-fascist anti-intellectuality, depicting it as a sphere of dehumanization and also – in contrast to Hegel – as a transition to what the latter called 'objective mind'. Style, with Freyer, not only tears the community apart but also exhibits distinctly decadent features: 'The genius is the social world's most negative phenomenon. Genius needs the community as the Devil needs the Godhead: in order to deny it.'[60] (This was a seasonable variation of Max Weber's 'battle of the gods'.)

More important to Freyer's system was the concrete path to the dissolution of the community. It was expressed in the problem of rule. Here the fascist aspects of Freyer's sociology are already fairly visible. 'One is a master through birth . . . one is a bondservant by nature, not by misfortune.'[61] The replacing of ranks or stations by classes was also, for Freyer, a sign of the decay accompanying a time of transition. The history of any decline was 'the history of economization . . . When a style comes to an end, the saying comes true that world-history is the history of class struggles.'[62] This statement, as we shall see later in a more concrete form, contains a – negatively slanted – acknowledgement of historical materialism. To be sure, even this acknowledgement contains

an abundance of Spenglerian motifs. For the view of the conversion of ranks into classes as a sign of decline was modelled on the epoch of Caesars and plebeians from the *Decline of the West*. There was, though, a difference significant to the course taken by the fascist infiltration of German ideology, namely that Spengler's reactionary fatalism lost ground in Freyer and was supplanted by a counter-revolutionary activism.

The apparent recognition of historical materialism was only a means of criticizing it in an 'original' way. Above all, Freyer tackled the de-economizing of sociology far more radically than his predecessors. Carrying on the theory which Max Weber had cautiously expressed in the form of a preponderant interaction, Freyer reduced the whole genesis of capitalism to purely ideological motives. 'As we know, the theory of capitalism and its development harks back very successfully to philosophical elements ... the innermost substance of the capitalist form of life is composed of a particular morality, metaphysic and doctrine of life.'[63] Drawing a parallel between Marx and Nietzsche, Freyer's pupil Hugo Fischer voiced the same idea even more vividly: 'The category of capital is a specification of the rampant *category of decadence* in the philosophy of culture, metaphysics and sociology. Capital is the form of economic life representing its decadence. The basic error committed by Marxism and Marx himself was to regard decadence as a form of capitalism instead of capitalism as a type of decadence.'[64]

This 'critical' position left Freyer with manifold advantages. Firstly, it enabled him to adapt for his own purposes what he called the dynamics of Marxism. He could introduce into sociology a radical, and radically subjectivist existentialism without – to all outward appearances – invalidating its social objectivity, but also without being bound to the real objective dialectic of the economic process. Freyer too gave rise to a pseudo-objectivity, an irrationalist quasi-dialectic, but his way of 'accepting' Marxism into his thought more strongly reinforced the semblance of dialectics and objectivity

than was the case with his predecessors. Thus he was in a position even to acknowledge the fact of the class struggle, for in the activist abstraction through which he viewed it, the class struggle had ceased to be dangerous. To Freyer it meant 'a tension with regard to ruling power between heterogeneous party groups'.[65] This is such an abstract concept of the internal social struggle that any groupings and strategies could be redesignated 'revolutionary struggle' if the exterior form of the revolutionary forces was preserved. We shall note a similar tendency in Carl Schmitt, and this was no coincidence. As fascism increasingly armed itself for the 'revolutionary' seizure of power, there arose the need both to present this as authentic revolution and to conceal the monopoly-capitalist character of the whole movement.

A further point is that this onset of fascism occurred during a period when the economic pressure on the masses (intellectuals included) was becoming increasingly unbearable. Fascism had need of the resulting despair and bitterness, the inclination towards resistance and rebellion. In utilizing the anti-capitalist feelings the situation gave rise to, it only sought to prevent the resulting tensions and indeed explosions from being vented against capitalism, which it wanted, rather, to provide with the terrorist instrument of rule. Here pre-fascist sociology performed important preliminary work. In devaluing, in terms of world-outlook, the whole domain of economics, it was on the surface more radical than Marxism. For whereas the latter was directed only against a 'superficial' phenomenon, capitalism, this pre-fascist or fascist sociology was demanding a 'total' upheaval – without affecting the sway of monopoly capitalism in the slightest. But at the same time, it could cater for the immediate longing of the broad masses, especially the petty bourgeoisie, by having a period 'without economics' succeed the 'age of economics' and by devising a perspective of the 'taming of economics' through the intellect, State, etc. Freyer described economics (which, like most popularizers, he identified with technology) 'as the true anarchist opposing the totality of the State', and as a

force which for all its apparent power was completely without influence at bottom: 'the boundless world of mere ways and means does hold within itself the power of limitless progress, but not the power to form self-contained areas for the workings of destiny through the intellect'. Hence a dictatorship of the State over economics was needed. 'The economy is recalcitrant and must be taken more strongly in hand.'[66]

Accordingly, historical materialism, in Freyer's sociology, amounted to a mentally adequate expression of the 'age of economics', the period of decadence. Historical materialism as an intellectual expression of a decline was only capable of comprehending the decline, and not the positive side. 'A style perishes in class struggles, but it does not arise out of them. It arises out of the tension between dominant and subject races ordained by nature.'[67] In each historical instance, these class struggles now gave rise to the State. But this process seemed as yet far from complete: 'Perhaps the political change of mind in the history of mankind generally has not been accomplished in a way enabling its full meaning to come to light.'[68] This change was reserved for Hitler later. The State now developed into the *Reich*, in which all previous forms were superseded.

The reverse path leading from the State to the intellect was, as indicated, an intellectual reiteration of the concrete path. We shall pick out only the most important elements in Freyer's lines of approach. In treating of power he naturally arrived at a glorification of war and conquest: 'Not merely in accordance with reality . . . but by definition, the State is founded upon war and has its beginning in it.' The State 'must conquer in order to be'.[69] To this was added the glorification of race: 'Racial blood is the sacred stuff from which a people is formed.' Hence the most important task of political power was to 'hold sacred the race'.[70] The next stage, law, correspondingly dealt chiefly with the subjugation under the State of economics, which Freyer always identified with technology and repudiated as being an anarchic principle

and a mechanization of life. The dissolution of social classes also belonged to this process. In the last stage, in form, the leader finally appeared. The leader created 'the single classless but multi-layered, untyrannical but strictly interlocking formation of the people. To be a people means to become a people, under the guidance of the leader.'[71] Here again already, we can see how Freyer was building a fascist doctrinal system out of the elements of German sociology up to that time.

Freyer's further development amounted to a still greater reinforcement of his existential, irrationalist tendencies. His theoretical magnum opus, *Sociology as the Science of Reality*, was an attempt to create a theoretical basis for such tendencies. He offered a detailed critique of sociology to date, strongly emphasizing the merits of Dilthey, Toennies, Simmel and the Weber brothers, in order to demonstrate that if sociology remained a mere 'logos science', i.e., a theoretical science in the neo-Kantian sense, it would inevitably become formalistic and unhistorical, a mere 'morphology of the social world'. And this dismissal of formal sociology he underlined also in terms of political world-outlook by stressing that, consciously or unconsciously, 'the typically liberal view'[72] lay behind such a sociology. Real sociology was, Freyer believed, an 'ethos science'. Its epistemology was built on the Heidegger-Jaspers concept of existence. 'A live reality perceives itself.' The constructions of sociology were 'the existential situation of man'.[73] Hence Freyer rejected sociology's 'value-freedom'. He sought to lift sociology out of the condition of a specialist science: 'Even if unconsciously and involuntarily, every sociological system must carry within itself a historio-philosophical substance.'[74] It was its task intellectually to pave the way for a decision and to render it a necessary one.

There is a patent affinity between this sociology and the existentialism of Heidegger and Jaspers, but the basis of it was consciously transferred from the solitary individual into the social domain. This methodological change meant a

concomitant shifting of emphasis. With the existentialists, the essential point was a nihilistic destruction of objectivity, a devaluation of every 'shell', and the 'decision' remained – pure Kierkegaard, this – with the solitary individual. Freyer, on the other hand, instigated a struggle against what was 'dead' and 'mechanical' about economics, on behalf of the 'living life' of State, *Reich* and people. So whereas the existentialists went only so far as to destroy ideologically all the bourgeois class' intellectual defences against the impending fascism, Freyer was already constructing out of these elements the positive road to fascism. Hence he formulated the essence of sociology's 'situation' as follows: 'Sociology originates as the scientific self-consciousness of a bourgeois society which senses itself as marking a critical phase. Hence it arises as a science of the present day from the very outset . . .' We study the past, according to Freyer, 'not in order to invoke the past, but in order to deepen our perception of present reality and present decisions through an insight into their preconditions.' And he continued: 'A reality of unequivocal historical situation-value, a society which has decomposed with the State and grown self-legitimizing becomes the dialectical centre of the system.'[75] The flaw in previous interpretations of bourgeois society, above all those of Hegel and Toennies, lay in their static nature. Freyer wanted to introduce a dynamic into sociology, and in connection with this, he recognized the historical necessity of revolutions. The present world, in his opinion, was on the brink of one such revolution. The 'peripeteia' of society was, he stated, 'the existential situation in which sociology is anchored'.[76]

Freyer now drew the concrete inferences from this argumentation of sociology in individual polemical pamphlets like *Rule and Planning* and, above all, *Revolution from the Right*. Here he provided a historio-philosophical survey of European development since the French Revolution. He saw the period as one of permanent revolution, and always a revolution 'from the Left'. Summing up the nineteenth century, he wrote: 'Its states of equilibrium are specious, its nations class

struggles . . . its economy built upon crises. This epoch is sheer dialectics: dialectical materialism becomes the doctrine that has understood its law of motion the most profoundly.' Materialist philosophy, although it was 'a wild myth' and a 'wild sort of chiliasm', had 'fully grasped for the first time the revolution from the Left'. But the revolution had not occurred. The nineteenth century 'liquidates itself'.[77] Reformism, in Freyer's eyes, had brought about the great change. The change began with the emergence of social policies, but without the active participation of the proletariat this was a 'feeble conciliatory idea'. Only the victory of reformism within the labour movement had enabled the socialist movement to become a historically decisive power; for when it arrived, the nineteenth century renounced its revolution.

These polemical thoughts of Freyer contain a repudiation of historical materialism which was, in fact, 'original'. In themselves they were still relatively lucid, although in essence they were making of the nineteenth century and its history a Spenglerian 'culture cycle' with solipsistically autonomous principles. Only in the positive part does irrational obscurity set in. The proletariat's turn to reformism cleared the way, Freyer thought, for 'revolution from the Right'. The bearer of this revolution was the people, 'which is not society, not class, not interest and therefore not appeasable, but revolutionary to the roots'. The people 'is a new formation with its own will and own justice . . . it is the adversary of the industrial society'.[78] Now here Freyer was already giving tongue to a purely mystical irrationalism. One could, he argued, make no comment about popular forces: 'For the rest, one cannot measure a nothing – or an everything.' And with Heidegger's nullifying Nothing now coming into its own, Freyer refused also to comment with regard to the future, the new State that was coming into being, and the rule of the 'people'. The State that was to emerge out of the 'revolution from the Right' was, according to Freyer, the 'concentrated will of the people: not a stasis but a tension, a constructive formation of

lines of energy . . . The revolutionary principle which informs an epoch is not, in essence, a structure, order or edifice, but pure energy, pure eruption, pure protest . . . For it hinges precisely on the fact that the new principle dares to remain the active nil in the dialectic of the present, and therefore pure political energy; otherwise it will be built in overnight and never come to act.'[79] Freyer concluded his other pamphlet in an equally obscure, mystical-irrationalist manner: 'Here again (i.e., in political ethics) the only true imperative is to make the correct decision, not to know that it is correct or why.'[80]

This obscurity has, however, a meaning which is easy to scrutinize. Freyer sought to have the 'revolution from the Right' accomplished in such a way that it could give rise to the boundless, completely unrestricted dictatorship of Hitler. The 'revolution from the Right' was thus intended to cast a deliberate darkness upon the awareness of the people enacting it, a political activity aimed against the Weimar system without a fixed objective or commitment to a programme. (We recall the earlier discussion of economics and 'freedom from economics'.) To this end Freyer had, in earlier works, already revived in an up-to-date form Max Weber's theory of the charismatic leader. There already, he set the leader the task 'of forming the nation such that its *Reich* is its destiny',[81] i.e., of binding the broad masses of the German people to the imperialist objective of German monopoly capitalism come what may. Freyer saw also the ambitiousness of the leader that was inevitably linked with this. But he wanted to give just this ambitiousness, the striving for German global power, a philosophico-sociological sanction. 'The statesman does not take his bearings from the hazards but from the timetable. He does not make the possible a reality, but what is necessary a possibility.' And here, in the philosophical transfiguring of the irreality of German imperialist aggression, existentialism's obscurity recurred as a matter of course: these objectives were ones 'transcending human logic and ethics'. The irrationalist

darkness had fallen, but the meaning is plain to behold.

Even more decided, if that were possible, was the contribution of German sociology to fascism in the work of Carl Schmitt. Schmitt was a lawyer or, more accurately, a philosopher and sociologist of law. In this capacity he began by extending the programmatic ideas of Dilthey's humanistic (social) science and Max Weber's sociology. He used Max Weber's 'neutrality' to combat social causation and, like Weber, employed it as a weapon against historical materialism. 'Whether the ideal matter of radical abstraction is here the reflection of a sociological reality, or whether social reality is viewed as the result of a particular mode of thinking and hence also of acting, does not come into consideration.'[82] Sociology's task was limited, he believed, to finding parallels, analogies and so on between the various social and ideological forms. Schmitt's basic reactionary tendencies were always clearly explicit and closely related to vitalism and existentialism, but his conception had special nuances to it right from the start.

We should stress above all that Schmitt dismissed all 'restoration' ideology. And in connection with this, he had only a withering contempt for the fashionable glorifying of the Romantic thinkers; in particular he derided a man held in great esteem by Spann and others, Adam Müller. Schmitt wrote a book of his own about 'Political Romanticism' in order to prove the hollowness of this approach. Romanticism was, in his eyes, 'only the aesthetic realm's intermediate step between the moralism of the eighteenth century and the economism of the nineteenth'.[83] The starting-point of this polemic was that the reactionary core of Romantic thought was, to Schmitt's mind, outmoded, and that a new reactionary ideology was needed at present. His decidedly pre-fascist attitude is already manifest in the fact that he repudiated every outmoded and obsolete form of reaction, and that his interest was focused solely on the working out of a reactionary ideology to suit the times. Hence he discovered the significance 'for the history of the

mind' of the mid-nineteenth-century Spanish reactionary, Donoso Cortés. Cortés was important because he achieved a break with 'restoration' ideology and grasped that since there were no longer any kings, there was also no legitimacy in the traditional sense. For this reason he called outright for a dictatorship to oppose the revolutionary forces. Schmitt also quoted with approval Cortés's statement that the bourgeoisie was a 'debating class'. His sole criticism of his favourite was that Cortés aimed his polemics against Proudhon, although elements of his later confederacy were present in the latter, and failed to observe the real enemy, namely Marx.[84]

At the same time, Schmitt conducted a violent polemic against neo-Kantian jurisprudence and its idea of the norm, which transformed the whole State into a network of hollow formal relations and regarded the State as just a kind of 'accounting point'. He wrote in opposition to neo-Kantianism in law philosophy: 'All important ideas of man's intellectual sphere are existential and not normative.' In law philosophy neo-Kantianism overlooked 'the simple jurisprudential truth that norms only apply to normal situations and the hypothetical normality of the situation is a statutory component of its "validity" '.[85] This was an extension of Max Weber's conception of power on the one hand, and a criticism of the Jellinek-Kelsen 'meta-juristic' concept on the other. Here Schmitt was endeavouring to recognize as the real, authentic problem of law philosophy precisely what neo-Kantianism excluded from its domain: namely, through what power justice is laid down and revoked respectively. And here he was entirely in the right against liberal neo-Kantianism, as indeed he was in his sometimes ingenious polemic against liberal sociology. From the standpoint of a demagogic, monopoly-capitalist dictatorship he often saw clean through the unsubstantiated dogmatism masquerading as strict epistemology by which neo-Kantianism converted justice into an autonomous, self-legitimizing area, on the pattern of its epistemology or aesthetics. The neo-Kantian detaching of the validity of the 'symbolic forms' from the process of

their social genesis was also completely untenable on the epistemological and aesthetic planes. But what was truly far-fetched was the dogmatic drawing of analogies between the validity of legal precepts and this area, since they always apply in a concrete, socially determined way. That two and two make four is a truth independent of consciousness. But the laying down of five or ten years' imprisonment for some crime or other does not depend on the inner substance of the legal precept. It depends on whether the competent political authority has decided it thus or otherwise; but the character, composition, etc., of that authority are pre-determined by politico-social and ultimately economic factors.

The same difference obtains for the revocation of validity: on the one hand, proof of non-agreement with a reality existing independently of consciousness, on the other a corrective law, an amendment, and so on. Now since the neo-Kantians divorced the 'validity' of legal precepts from all social issues (sociology and jurisprudence; Being and Owing in Kelsen's terms), they could provide at best an immanent interpretation of the legal precepts applying in each instance, and never a scientific explanation of their contents, genesis and expiration. Jellinek's 'meta-juristic' conception lay precisely therein. Schmitt quoted, with justified irony, Anschütz's remarks on the budget-less condition as a 'gap in the law': 'here constitutional law ceases'.[86] He was also right to put the chief stress on the real continuity of socio-political life and to treat formal justice as only part of it.

For these methodological reasons in themselves, his interest centred on the analysis of juristic exceptions. It lay in the nature of these, he said, 'that the State stands firm, whereas justice retreats'; there 'still remains an order in the juristic sense, even in the absence of law and order'.[87] In investigating this unity – no matter, for the time being, for what motives – he went decidedly beyond the liberalism of the neo-Kantians. 'The exceptional case is more interesting than the normal one . . . in the exception, the force of real life penetrates the crust of a mechanism stiffened by repetition.'

And he summed up his argument as follows: 'He is sovereign who has power of decision over the exceptional condition.'[88]

With Schmitt, this methodological approach and this passionate interest in the theory of dictatorship were linked with the fact that he was irreconcilably hostile to the Weimar system from the outset. Initially, this hostility manifested itself as a scientific critique, as an account of the crisis of liberal ideology and, in connection with it, the crisis of the parliamentary system. In contrast to Karl Mannheim who, as we have noted, simply identified liberalism and democracy, Schmitt absorbed all the nineteenth-century anti-democratic polemics in his system in order to prove the irreconcilable antithesis of liberalism and democracy and to show the inevitable growth of mass democracy into dictatorship. Above all, Schmitt subjected the parliamentary system to a sociological analysis. He regarded social homogeneity as the precondition of parliamentary government: 'The method of establishing a will by simply ascertaining the majority view is sensible and acceptable if we can assume a substantial homogeneity of the whole people.'[89]

Naturally such a homogeneity never existed in the class societies. Schmitt was overlooking the fact that while the functioning of liberal parliamentarism he had described did, as he stated, depend on a certain parity of interests, this went only for the ruling classes, and not the people as a whole. It presupposed, moreover, the powerlessness of the rest of the people, and this was a point he ignored. Hence he could define this system's dissipative tendencies only in very abstract terms: 'As soon as the hypothesis belonging to the legality of this system of a validity equally legal on both sides ceases, there is no longer a way out.'[90] That is only the description of an external symptom, not an explanation of the matter itself which, to be sure, is only possible on the basis of concrete class analyses. In reality there corresponded to this condition as described by Schmitt a long period of English parliamentary government, Guizot's period of the *juste milieu*, which he too cited as a model example. Here

one might, with major reservations, interpret public hearings and discussion, truth arising out of exchanges of view, as ideological symptoms but not, as Schmitt did, as the intellectual foundations of the parliamentary system.

For Schmitt, this whole analysis had the purpose of proving the impossibility of the Weimar Republic's parliamentary rule, so as to demonstrate the necessity of going over to dictatorship. In it, he offered occasionally correct, albeit always largely ideological examinations of the past and of the behaviour of the liberal bourgeoisie. 'Hatred of kingship and aristocracy drives the liberal bourgeois to the Left; fears for his property when threatened by radical democracy and socialism drives him back to the Right to a powerful monarchy whose army can protect him; so he vacillates between both enemies, both of whom he would like to outwit.'[91] More important is the realization which dawned on him now and again that 'economy' (i.e., capitalism, G.L.) was 'no longer *eo ipso* liberty' (since Schmitt failed to see that it had never been so, he could only surmise the change in 'liberty' under imperialism, not grasp it precisely), and that the development of the forces of production revealed its contradictory nature[92] (here, naturally, Schmitt was referring only to technology). Schmitt used all these statements solely in order to disparage democratic parliamentary government, to stress its proneness to crises, its historical obsolescence and above all its incompatibility with mass democracy. (Let us recall at this point Max Weber's Caesaristic fits and the views of mass democracy held by Alfred Weber and Mannheim!) In Schmitt's view, mass democracy exploded that homogeneous basis of fundamentally aligned interests which had been the bedrock of liberal ideas in, for instance, the English parliamentary system.

Mass democracy, he argued, had left these idyllic states behind. But the effect of democracy was, to his way of thinking, purely negative and inherently subject to crises. Democracy today, Schmitt wrote, 'leads immediately to a crisis of democracy itself, because the general principle of human

equality cannot answer the problem of the substantive equality and homogeneity necessary to a democracy. It leads further to a crisis of parliamentarism which must be distinguished from the democratic crisis.' Schmitt also pointed out 'that a democracy of the masses, of man, is incapable of realizing any political form, even the democratic State'.[93] And in consequence of the democratic parties of the masses, democracy itself was turning into a mere mirage. Even the election process, in Schmitt's opinion, no longer existed. 'There appear five party lists, originating in a highly occult, clandestine way and dictated by five organizations. The masses proceed into five sheep-pens awaiting them, as it were, and the statistical record of this process is called an "election".' This meant that under these circumstances the will of the people could never, from now on, 'merge in a single concourse'.[94] Thus it now appeared the sole task of parliament 'to preserve an absurd status quo'.[95] On the parliamentary question, Schmitt summed up by saying that parliament was becoming 'the scene of a pluralistic division of the organized social powers'.[96] It signified a breaking up of the State as much as the growing might of the Princes had once meant the breaking up of the old German Empire. This state of decay and permanent crisis was engendering the necessity for exceptional measures, for the dictatorship of the *Reichspräsident*. Schmitt's pre-Hitlerian political activity centred mainly on this question, the justification for a dictatorship of the *Reichspräsident*.

Here we observe, despite the apparent contrast, Schmitt's fundamental affinity with the reactionary ideologists of the Bismarckian and Wilhelmine empire. Whereas these ideologists defended the status quo of their time through thick and thin, Schmitt was passionately opposed to that of his age. Hence the contrasts in terms of form and 'history of the mind'. In reality both sides contested democracy with equal vehemence in different circumstances: the despised status quo was that of the Weimar Republic and the Treaty of Versailles. Schmitt was challenging the status quo as a

reactionary imperialist just as his forerunners had defended theirs as reactionary imperialists.

In spite of the existentialist trimmings, the ceaseless flirting with 'life' and so-called historical concreteness, the positive core of Schmitt's sociology of law behind all these polemics was a very threadbare design. It was the reduction of all political and hence legal and State relations to terms of friend and foe. In line with his thinking's existentialist foundations, Schmitt eliminated from this basic schema all rationality and with it all concrete content. He stated: '. . . no programme, no ideal, no norm and no purpose confers authority over the physical life of other men . . . War, fighting men's readiness for death, the physical slaughter of fellow-men who stand on the enemy side – all that does not have a normative but only an existential sense. And it does so in the reality of a situation of real battle with a real enemy, not in any kind of ideals, programmes and normativities . . . If there really are enemies in the ontological meaning of the word, to which we are here referring, then it makes sense, but only political sense, to repulse them physically where necessary and to join battle with them.'[97]

From such thoughts Schmitt derived the essence of his political concept: 'Political thinking and political instinct are proved . . . in theory and practice by the capacity to distinguish between friend and foe.' The State's political existence rested upon 'determining itself the distinction between friend and foe'.[98] In these central concepts of law philosophy as formulated by Schmitt, we can see plainly where the existentialist conception was leading: to the union of an extremely scanty and insubstantial abstractness on the one hand and an irrationalist arbitrariness on the other. It was precisely by claiming to solve all the problems of social life that Schmitt's antithetical pairing of 'friend and enemy' revealed its hollow and arbitrary character. But this claim made it highly influential during the period of the fascist takeover of German ideology: as a methodological, abstract, purportedly scientific prolegomenon to the racial antithesis construed by Hitler and

Rosenberg. In particular the arbitrariness which was of the essence of this conceptualizing provided a 'scientific' bridge to the 'National-Socialist world-view'.

Liberalism, Schmitt explained, was systematically undermining this political foundation and the basis of the State. The nineteenth century was an age of neutralization and de-politicizing in the name of culture. It placed culture, progress, education and non-political science in this false antithesis to politics. And Schmitt saw in this tendency a hostility towards a 'strong Germany'. The centres of this ideology were, in his view, the small neutral states, Switzerland, the Netherlands and Scandinavia. But this orientation also had influential representatives in Germany in the persons of Jakob Burckhardt, Stefan George, Thomas Mann, Sigmund Freud, etc.

Schmitt now considered from this standpoint the history of Germany. In stark contrast to Max Weber he saw in the origin of constitutional rule and the road to parliamentary government the degradation of this 'strong Germany'. So his analysis of the crisis of the parliamentary system and his concept of friend and enemy – which was based on the desire to renew German imperialism – led him to unconditional approval of Hitler. Already, his earlier critique of liberalism and democracy had included the 'original' thesis that fascism did not contradict democracy. And before Hitler's seizure of power, Schmitt was already describing Italian fascism with enthusiasm as a 'heroic attempt to preserve and assert the dignity of the State and national unity against the pluralism of economic interests'.[99] Likewise, even before Hitler's time he pointed out that 'the stronger myth lies in the national sphere', and that socialism possessed a relatively 'inferior mythology'.[100]

It is no wonder that with these hypotheses, Schmitt became an ardent supporter of Hitler and found for all his atrocities a suitable theory from 'law philosophy'. Thus after the massacre of the supporters of the 'second revolution' (1934), Schmitt wrote an essay bearing the title:

'The *Führer* Protects Justice'. In it he defended the crassest form of arbitrary fascist justice and most firmly upheld the view that the *Führer* had the sole right

> to distinguish between friend and foe . . . The *Führer* is in earnest over the warnings of German history. That affords him the right and the power to found a new State and a new order . . . The *Führer* is protecting justice from the vilest misuse when, in the hour of danger, he creates justice directly as the supreme authority by virtue of his leader's office . . . The office of judge emanates from that of *Führer*. Anyone . . . wishing to separate the two is seeking to put the State out of joint with the aid of justice . . . The *Führer* himself determines the content and scope of a transgression against the law.[101]

After these statements it will not surprise us that Schmitt revived for the age of Hitler the old theme of pre-war anti-democratic propaganda, namely Germany's ideological superiority over the democratic states. 'In the Western democracies today, major twentieth-century problems are still being treated in terms of propositions from the times of Talleyrand and Louis-Philippe, and answered accordingly. In German law studies, the exposition of such problems is a relatively long way ahead. We have gained this lead through experience that was often hard and bitter, but it cannot be disputed.'[102] This superiority was that of predatory imperialism. Schmitt – expanding his old antithesis of friend and enemy in terms of global politics – now proceeded to argue the Hitlerian State philosophically as follows: 'The core of the matter is found in war. The character of total war determines the character and shape of the State's totality. But total war receives its meaning through the total enemy.'[103]

Schmitt not only supported Hitler's bestial dictatorship in home affairs. Already before the outbreak of the Second World War, during the preparations for it, he became the leading law ideologist of Hitlerian Germany's plans to conquer

the world. He resisted the 'universalist' claims of the League of Nations and called instead for the application of the Monroe doctrine to Germany and territory in which she had interests. He quoted a statement by Hitler on this subject and commented: 'That expresses the idea of a peacefully arbitrated (*schiedlich-friedlich*) demarcation of the major territories in the simplest business-like terms. It eliminates the confusion that an economic imperialism created around the Monroe doctrine by twisting its reasonable idea of territorial demarcation into an ideological claim to global intervention.'[104] This theory too rested on the fascist dogma of the 'Reich'. 'Empires in this sense are the leading and supporting powers whose political idea is radiated over a specified major territory and which fundamentally exclude the intervention of extra-territorial powers with regard to this territory.'[105] Such a division of the world, which would guarantee the appropriate 'major territories' for Germany and Japan, would, in Schmitt's view, mark the start of a new and higher condition of international justice. There would no longer be nation-states, as before, but only 'empires'. The concrete consequences of this Schmitt spelled out in another essay bearing the significant title 'Woe to the Neutrals!' Here it was argued that the concept of major territories implied the abolition of neutrality. So in 1938, Schmitt had penned in advance the 'international' apologia for Hitlerian aggression and the fascist rape of the nations. Thus German sociology contributed to the propaganda for Hitler's bestial imperialism. The German professors used to be called the intellectual bodyguard of the Hohenzollerns. Now they were the intellectual S.A. and S.S.

NOTES

1 Marx: *Capital*, Vol. I, Afterword to the 2nd edition.
2 Schmoller: *Über einige Grundfragen der Sozialpolitik und Volkswirtschaftslehre*, 2nd edition, Leipzig 1904, p. 292.

3 Ibid., p. 50.
4 Dilthey: *Introduction to the Humanistic Sciences.*
5 Toennies: *Community and Association.*
6 Ibid.
7 Ibid.
8 Ibid.
9 Marx: *Introduction to the Grundrisse* and Engels to C. Schmidt on 27.10.1890, Marx-Engels: *Ausgewählte Briefe*, Berlin 1953, p. 504.
10 Marx: *Theorien über den Mehrwert*, Vol. I, Stuttgart 1919, p. 382.
11 Toennies: Op. cit.
12 Ibid.
13 Ibid.
14 Rickert: *Science and History.*
15 Max Weber: *Gesammelte Aufsätze zur Religionssoziologie*, Tübingen 1920, Vol. I, pp. 238 and 240.
16 Ibid., pp. 252f.
17 Max Weber: *Wirtschaft und Gesellschaft*, Tübingen 1922, p. 277.
18 Max Weber: *Religionssoziologie*, p. 37.
19 Max Weber: *Collected Political Works*, Munich 1921, pp. 258f.
20 Marianne Weber: *Max Weber*, Tübingen 1926, p. 665.
21 Kelsen: *Hauptprobleme der Staatsrechtslehre*, Tübingen 1911, p. 411.
22 Preuss: *Zur Methode der juristischen Begriffsbildung*, Schmoller's Yearbook, 1900, p. 370.
23 Max Weber: *Gesammelte Aufsätze zur Wissenschaftslehre*, Tübingen 1922, p. 403.
24 Max Weber: *Wirtschaft und Gesellschaft*, p. 9.
25 Max Weber: *Wissenschaftslehre*, op. cit., p. 325.
26 Max Weber: *Gesammelte Aufsätze zur Wissenschaftslehre*, pp. 149f.
27 Ibid., p. 545.
28 Max Weber: *Religionssoziologie*, p. 14.
29 Max Weber: *Gesammelte Aufsätze zur Wissenschaftslehre*, p. 46.
30 Ibid., p. 132.
31 Ibid., pp. 545f.
32 Ibid., p. 555.
33 Walther Rathenau: *Letters*, Dresden 1927, p. 186.
34 Alfred Weber: *Ideen zur Staats- und Kultursoziologie*, Karlsruhe 1927, p. 120.
35 Ibid., p. 23.
36 Ibid., p. 84.

37 Ibid., pp. 38ff.
38 Ibid., p. 9.
39 Ibid., pp. 126 and 104.
40 Ibid., p. 113.
41 Ibid., p. 130.
42 Ibid., p. 141.
43 Lenin: *Letters*, 14.11.1913.
44 Mannheim: *Ideology and Utopia*.
45 Ibid.
46 Ibid.
47 Mannheim: *Man and Society in an Age of Reconstruction*.
48 Ibid.
49 Mannheim: *Ideology and Utopia*.
50 Ibid.
51 Mannheim: *Man and Society in an Age of Reconstruction*.
52 Ibid.
53 Ibid.
54 Ibid.
55 Spann: *Kämpfende Wissenschaft*, Jena 1934, pp. 9f.
56 Rosenberg: *The Myth of the Twentieth Century*.
57 Spann: *Geschichtsphilosophie*, Jena 1932, pp. 138f.
58 Freyer: *Prometheus*, Jena 1923, p. 25.
59 Freyer: *Der Staat*, Leipzig 1925, p. 131.
60 Ibid., p. 92.
61 Ibid., p. 86.
62 Ibid., p. 88.
63 Freyer: *Theorie des objektiven Geistes*, Leipzig 1928, p. 39.
64 Hugo Fischer: *Marx*, Jena 1932, p. 31.
65 Freyer: *Sociology as the Science of Reality*.
66 Freyer: *Der Staat*, p. 177.
67 Ibid.
68 Ibid., p. 96.
69 Ibid., p. 146.
70 Ibid., p. 153.
71 Ibid., p. 199.
72 Freyer: *Sociology as the Science of Reality*.
73 Ibid.
74 Ibid.
75 Ibid.
76 Ibid.
77 Freyer: *Revolution from the Right*.
78 Ibid.
79 Ibid.

80 Freyer: *Rule and Planning.*
81 Freyer: *Der Staat*, pp. 119 and 202f.
82 Schmitt: *Politische Theologie*, 2nd impression, Munich/Leipzig 1934, pp. 58ff.
83 Schmitt: *Der Begriff des Politischen*, Munich/Leipzig 1932, p. 70.
84 Schmitt: *Positionen und Begriffe*, Hamburg 1940, pp. 118f.
85 Ibid., p. 124.
86 Schmitt: *Politische Theologie*, p. 22.
87 Ibid., pp. 18f.
88 Ibid., pp. 11 and 22.
89 Schmitt: *Legalität und Legitimität*, Munich/Leipzig 1932, p. 31.
90 Ibid.
91 Schmitt: *Politische Theologie*, p. 77.
92 Schmitt: *Der Begriff des Politischen*, p. 62.
93 Schmitt: *Die geistesgeschichtliche Lage des heutigen Parlamentarismus*, 2nd impression, Munich/Leipzig 1926, pp. 21f.
94 Schmitt: *Positionen und Begriffe*, p. 188.
95 Ibid., p. 185.
96 Ibid., p. 156.
97 Schmitt: *Der Begriff des Politischen*, p. 37.
98 Ibid., pp. 54 and 38.
99 Schmitt: *Positionen und Begriffe*, p. 110.
100 Schmitt: *Die geistesgeschichtliche Lage des heutigen Parlamentarismus*, pp. 86f.
101 Schmitt: *Positionen und Begriffe*, pp. 200ff.
102 Ibid., p. 5.
103 Ibid., p. 236.
104 Ibid., p. 302.
105 Ibid., p. 303.

CHAPTER VII

SOCIAL DARWINISM, RACIAL THEORY AND FASCISM

1. Beginnings of Racial Theory in the Eighteenth Century

Biologism in philosophy and sociology has always been a basis for reactionary philosophical tendencies. Of course this has nothing to do with biology as a science; it stemmed rather from the conditions of the class struggle, which made pseudo-biological concepts and methods a suitable instrument of the reactionary battle against the idea of progress. During the course of history such use of disfigured and distorted biological concepts in philosophy and sociology has occurred in either a naive or a sophisticated form, depending on circumstances. However, the application of the analogy of the organism to society and the State has always tended, and not by accident, to prove the 'natural principle' behind any given social structure; this tendency is already clearly apparent in the old, anecdotal form of the fable of Menenius Agrippa. In the reactionary struggle against the French Revolution, the comparison with the organism acquired a fresh nuance, as early as Burke, in that it referred not only to a static condition, but also to dynamic development. Only 'organic growth', that is to say change through small and gradual reforms with the consent of the ruling class, was regarded as 'a natural principle', whereas every revolutionary upheaval received the dismissive tag of 'contrary to nature'. This view gained a particularly extensive form in the course of the development of reactionary German romanticism (Savigny, the historical law school, etc.). The antithesis of 'organic growth' and 'mechanical fabrication' was now elaborated: it

constituted a defence of 'naturally grown' feudal privileges against the praxis of the French Revolution and the bourgeois ideologies underlying it, which were repudiated as mechanical, highbrow and abstract.

This antithesis, which the French Revolution first heightened to an uncommon degree, goes a long way back in time. In accordance with its own class interests, the ideology of the rising bourgeois class was fighting for the equality of all men (i.e., for their equal rights as bourgeois citizens in a formal legal context). It strongly criticized the existing feudal privileges, the feudal inequality of rank of the State's citizenry. Now at the time that these struggles were intensified, the nobility's dominance was already undermined both economically and politically, so that it was losing its concrete medieval social functions and developing more and more into a purely parasitical body. And this produced an inevitable need to defend privileges ideologically.

It was out of these struggles that racial theory sprouted. The nobility's ideologists defended inequality of station with the argument that this was only the juristic expression of a natural inequality of the human species, the human races, and that as a 'fact of nature' it could not be invalidated through any kind of institutions without jeopardizing the highest values of mankind. As early as the start of the eighteenth century, Count de Boulainvilliers wrote a book (1727) in which he tried to prove that in France, the nobility represented the descendants of the old Frankish ruling class, whereas the rest of the population were heirs of the subject Gauls.[1] Therefore two qualitatively different races were confronting one another, and the only way to abolish the superiority of the Franks would be by destroying their civilization. Eighteenth-century writers already passionately contested this thesis. In 1734, for instance, Dubos declared that the Frankish conquest of France was a legend.[2]

These polemics became particularly trenchant at the time of the French Revolution. In his *Ruins*[3] Volney derided the nobility's claim to represent a superior and pure race. He

ironically demonstrated how great a part of the existing nobility was made up of *nouveaux riches*, former merchants, artisans, and so forth, who had purchased their titles with cash from the Crown and who, therefore, were pure plebeians with regard to 'race'. And the French bourgeoisie's leading ideologist in the early days of the Revolution, Sieyès, challenged in principle the founding of justice on the basis of conquests. The third estate, he said, 'needs only to transfer itself back to the year preceding the conquest, and because it is strong enough today not to succumb to the conquerors, its resistance will doubtless be more effective. Why should it not send back to the Frankish forests all these families who are foolishly claiming to be descended from the conquerors and to inherit their rights?'[4]

2. Gobineau's Racial Theory Argument

Thus racial theory – in its first rudimentary form – was already scientifically discredited at the time of the French Revolution. But the class forces behind it did not disappear in the revolution; the struggle against democracy continued and constantly took new forms. Thus racial theory was bound to flare up again in various forms. Its further vicissitudes were determined by the class struggles – partly by the varying amount of influence which feudal or semi-feudal reaction gained in the crisis-beset development of bourgeois democracy, and partly by the ideological needs of a reactionary bourgeoisie turned anti-democratic. For the latter looked to the remnants of the feudal age for political support, and in this connection appropriated elements of its ideology. Thus there came about, especially in Germany, the various 'organic' theories we have mentioned.

In the first half of the nineteenth century, however, racial theory remained without notable influence ideologically. Its representatives during that period are completely forgotten

nowadays. It was the fascist 'scholars' who gradually brought these ancestors to light; in 1855, for example, a Magdeburg professor called Karl Vollgraf published a work on racial theory which it would be hard to trace in even the largest reference books today. The reason is that in Germany, the development of reaction after the crushing of the 1848 revolution occurred in forms which did not, as yet, create any need for a racialist substantiation of noble privileges. Bismarck's Bonapartist compromise guaranteed the Prussian Junkers their politically dominant position in Germany on terms which favoured the development of capitalism without creating a bourgeois democracy. Thus the feudal Junkers were not threatened in a way necessitating any such invocation of their racial superiority.

But at about the same time as the aforementioned work, there appeared a book which – gradually – threw the racial idea into prominence on a universal scale: Gobineau's *The Inequality of the Human Races*. This book too was written during a reactionary period, that of Napoleon III, but the circumstances of its origin are markedly different from parallel phenomena in Germany. Here, the Junkers had undisputed possession of the political positions of power, and the capitalization of Germany could only be effected in a way that preserved their interests. In the Second Empire, on the other hand, the reactionaries disappointed those legitimist-feudal circles in France which, as part of the 'party of order', had enabled Louis Napoleon to come to power in the times of revolutionary crisis. The better minds among them had also learnt from the revolution a thing or two about the contradictions of bourgeois democracy. Hence the possibility of a fresh advance by feudal racial ideology, whose most influential spokesman in the long run was the aforesaid Gobineau. Granted, in France even his influence was slight at first. In his letters to Tocqueville, he complained that his book was being hushed up in France and was having a real effect only in the United States. Tocqueville, who rejected the book in spite of his friendship with Gobineau, pointed

out to him that this was because the book chimed with the slave-owners' interests in the southern states.[5] At all events, this first major instance of the influence of modern racial theory is significant on the socio-historical plane. Gobineau himself had proceeded from feudal-aristocratic class interests and considerations. Nonetheless, he had to live and proclaim his ideas in a society where the nobility's desire to return to its old hereditary ranks had long since sunk to a reactionary utopia, while the bourgeoisie's defensive struggle against the rising proletariat had shifted to the centre of events (battle of June 1848). And precisely the great planters in the southern United States were – despite the slave-holding form of their exploitation – capitalists, producers of the basic raw materials of the capitalist economy of the time. Thus under the conditions of the nineteenth/twentieth century, an effective renewal of racial theory could only be achieved if it became a battle ideology of the reactionary bourgeoisie. As we have seen, philosophical irrationalism in general from Schelling via Schopenhauer, Nietzsche, etc., followed the road of such an embourgeoisement. Racial theory from Gobineau to Rosenberg had also to go through this process.

Gobineau's starting-point and principal bias was the struggle against democracy, against the 'unscientific' and 'unnatural' idea of the equality of men. Tocqueville promptly criticized this after a single reading, pointing out that according to Gobineau, everything evil in history derived from this idea of equality. The book, said Tocqueville, was reactionary and had arisen out of a general mood of revolution-weariness. Its effect was fatalistic; it was opium handed to a sick patient. Indeed Tocqueville took the opportunity to prove – and this particularly hurt Gobineau – that his racial theory was irreconcilable with Christianity and with Catholicism.[6]

In these observations, the celebrated liberal-moderate historian Tocqueville correctly showed Gobineau's specific characteristics in terms of politics and world-view. It is already evident from these observations that Gobineau was a transitional figure in the history of racial theory. On the one

hand, he gave to old feudal-reactionary talk of the 'natural' inequality of man a new, 'seasonable', i.e., semi-bourgeois form. On the other hand, it was not yet possible for him to complete this modernization, this bourgeois version of racial theory in a really radical way. He struck the pose of a natural scientist and imitated the latter's 'sublime impartiality', but this quickly revealed its counter-revolutionary aspect. Thus Gobineau wrote: 'In the sight of this (natural-scientific observation, G.L.), the rebel will be nothing but an impatient, ambitious malefactor, *Timoleon* only an assassin, *Robespierre* a ruthless criminal.'[7]

This dichotomy of an arrogated 'natural-scientific' objectivity and feudal reactionary propaganda is manifest in Gobineau's entire *oeuvre*. He was an embattled reactionary, and his racial theory an anti-democratic battle theory. So for him, the acceptance of the equality of men was only a symptom of bastardization, of racial impurity. In 'normal times', he asserted, inequality was accepted as axiomatic. 'The majority of the citizens of a state, once that mixed blood is flowing in their veins, feel prompted by their large numbers to proclaim as a generally valid truth something which only holds good for themselves: that all men are equal.'[8]

He was, however, unable to make this combative line concrete and to indicate appropriate objectives or even methods to his supporters. He offered only the fatalistic perspective of an inevitable demise of culture as a result of racial mingling: 'The original white race has disappeared from the face of the earth . . . Thus, today, the white race is represented only through bastards.'[9] Once this mingling process is completed, there will come about a 'decline into insignificance . . . from that point the peoples, weighed down like human cattle in a gloomy stupor, will live ossified in their inconsequence, like the ruminating oxen in the stagnant pools of the Pontine marshes . . . It is not death that awakens our sorrow, but the certainty that it reaches us only stripped of dignity.'[10]

It is chiefly this fatalistic pessimism that distinguishes Gobineau from his important successors, Chamberlain, Hitler and Rosenberg. With these, racial theory was to a mounting degree the organ of an actively militant reactionary demagogy. And this demagogy, likewise, increasingly cast off the old feudal confines of reaction to become an obscurantist ideology of reactionary monopoly capitalism. Here, of course, we must not forget that Gobineau's successors preserved elements of his racialist pessimism in a specific sense, namely in the view that development always means deterioration (racial mixture is necessarily a corruption of the species). Thus the activism of later racial theory sprang from the same pessimistic, anti-evolutionary basis as with Gobineau. The only difference was that a desperate, ambitious activism supplanted fatalistic despair. This change brought to the fore two elements absent from Gobineau. One was the social demagogy of a purportedly rebellious anti-capitalism as a basis for action (for although Gobineau too nursed a profound antipathy against purely capitalist culture and its ideology, this remained feudal in substance and aesthetic-fatalistic in content). Secondly, parallel with this change, the later theorists divorced themselves from Christian-feudal reactionary ideology and made extensive concessions – again, of a demagogic kind – to the growing departure of broad masses from religion. (We shall see presently that on this point, as on many others, Chamberlain formed the bridge between Gobineau and Rosenberg.)

These differences were dictated not by personal but by historical factors. Modern social demagogy did not spring up until the imperial epoch. Its first – primitive and transitory – forms were Stöcker's anti-Semitism in Germany (from 1878) and *boulangisme* in France (1886-9). In Austria it appeared in an already more advanced form in Lueger's Christian Social anti-Semitic propaganda, which directly influenced Hitler in his youth. After the First World War it was never off the agenda. The Hitler movement was only its most advanced, unscrupulous and successful variety.

But, in addition, a quite different exacerbation of the class conflicts from that of Gobineau's time was necessary. The broad masses needed to be much more profoundly disturbed by the contradictions of bourgeois democracy and disappointed with the paths to which bourgeois democracy and reformism in the labour movement were pointing, etc. The social demagogy of racial theory, which was in essence aristocratic-reactionary and anti-democratic, now no longer made direct reference back to the feudal past as an ideal condition worthy of restoration, but masqueraded as a doctrine pointing to the future. Under Napoleon III the feudal-aristocratic opposition was still, to a large extent, overtly feudal, its face turned towards the past. And the labouring masses disappointed with the Bonapartist régime, as far as they could recover from the blow of 1848 and shake off the influence of the Decembrists' demagogy, evolved more and more strongly towards the Left, in the direction of the regaining of democracy, and indeed of the socialist struggle. It was from this situation that Gobineau derived his peculiar features, especially his fatalistic pessimism. When the prospect of democratic development was radically denied and there was a convulsive clinging to an irrevocable past feudal inequality, such a fatalistic mood of doom could be the only result.

So the following elements determined Gobineau's position in the development of racial theory. He was the first author for a long time to reintroduce the racial idea to broad circles and to bring it back into fashion among at least the decadent intelligentsia. He moreover expanded the arbitrary method that later, via Chamberlain, became an operative factor with Hitler and Rosenberg. This was a mixture of purportedly natural-scientific exactness and high-flown mysticism, intended to make the old feudal racial theory acceptable and palatable to modern readers in an atmosphere of perfect arbitrariness and a tangle of unresolved, insoluble contradictions.

The ancient racial theory was extremely simple; indeed we can hardly call it a theory at all. It proceeded from the thesis

that everyone could tell an aristocrat. For, as an aristocrat, he was of pure stock and descended from the superior race. (The Franks in contrast to the plebeian Celts of Gaul.) Modernized racial theory, in the face of scientific developments, could no longer hold this simple position. It had to start with a tactical withdrawal. It is, after all, a generally acknowledged fact of modern science that a single pure race has never existed (at least not in historical times). Secondly, it is also generally known and recognized that there are, similarly, objective distinguishing features for the various races only to a very limited extent. And these general criteria fall down completely when it comes to the racial definition of a historical people, nation or even individual.

That would suffice to destroy racial theory as an explanatory method of history. Gobineau's 'achievement' in the development of reactionary ideology lay in the fact that he opened the doors to that revival of racial theory which was later to culminate in Hitler. With regard to the first complex of ideas, the theory of racial purity, Gobineau was plainly a transitional figure. Using some pseudo-scientific phraseology which was always entirely abstract, he chose the path of purely intuitive, irrationalist, historical myth. That is to say, he proceeded to spin fantasies and built a new world-history on a so-called racial foundation. He did this wholly naively, basing his case on the feudal-aristocratic tradition, and treated races, miscegenation, etc., as something perfectly well known that required no further elucidation and analysis. (In these tendencies he was rubbing shoulders with many similarly pseudo-scientific French sociologists of his time, who also spoke of race as though the content and scope of this concept were things scientifically definite and definable. None of his colleagues, to be sure, gave racial theory this exclusive central place in their methodology. With Taine, Renan and others, their equally vague and unscientific racial concept was only one explanatory reason among many.)

Gobineau's pseudo-scientific and at the same time intuitionist apodicticity formed no small element of his influence,

although also of its limitation. The conscious, militant later racial theorists who paved the way for fascism also looked on this obviously unscientific approach as blameworthy in Gobineau. Thus Chamberlain, who tacitly appropriated a good deal from him in other respects, vehemently dismissed his work with the accusation that he had no inkling of natural science. Chamberlain wrote: 'A theory of race that is useful and can be taken seriously cannot be constructed on the tale of Sem, Cham and Japhet and such ingenious intuitions, mixed with hair-raising hypotheses, but only on a thorough and comprehensive knowledge of natural science.'[11] This criticism also expresses the antithesis that, whereas Gobineau as an orthodox Catholic believer took great trouble to harmonize his racialist view of history with the Old Testament, Chamberlain already repudiated the latter as Jewish trumpery.

Gobineau had to postulate the question of racial purity nevertheless. Purity of race was, in his view, an ideal condition and never fully realized. He stated:

> It would be false to assert that all miscegenation is a bad thing. If the three major basic types had remained strictly apart and formed no mutual links, then the upper hand would doubtless always have remained with the finest branches of the white race, and the black and yellow-skinned types would have been subject to the meanest nations of this race for all eternity. This would have been a kind of ideal condition which history has never offered. We can only gain some idea of it if we consider the indisputable superiority of those groups of our race which have remained the least adulterated . . . at all events the human races have lived in a state of miscegenation since the dawn of history.[12]

Gobineau's historical mysticism sprang from this necessary concession to the scientific developments of his time. While he did not know what race was and could not define its

characteristics, and knew that the peoples historically known to us have come about through miscegenation, he also 'knew' in very precise detail when, how and to what degree instances of miscegenation were good or bad. It would serve no useful purpose to recount here the details of Gobineau's wild and senseless history-fudging, not even so as to refute them. Let us give just one example to illustrate the speculativeness of his method. Gobineau advanced the claim that the origin of art was everywhere the result of a mingling with the black race. Granted, he described epic poetry as an achievement of the 'Aryan family of peoples'. But, he added, 'even with this popular species, it evolved its fire and its full splendour only in those nations which did not remain free of miscegenation with black people'. In arguing this thesis he went on to state: 'The negro possesses . . . a very high degree of that sensual disposition without which art is unthinkable. But his lack of intellectual talents, on the other hand, leaves him incapable of artistic refinement . . . If his natural propensities are to bear fruit, then he must enter into a union with a race whose talents are differently disposed.'[13]

We see, therefore, that for Gobineau miscegenation, the union with races of lower standing (and he considered the negro race the lowest) affected the fate of all culture; it was that bastardizing process which gave rise, in his view, to the aforementioned apocalyptic perspective of fateful universal doom. He also proclaimed, however, that so decisive a factor of culture as art could only derive from a mingling with the allegedly lowest race, the Negro race. So, on the one hand, we are told that the 'pure-blooded' heroes of Homer or the Norse sagas rank far higher 'than present-day races which are mixed a hundred times over'.[14] But, on the other hand, the *Iliad* and the *Edda* could only spring from miscegenation with negroes. And of course Gobineau 'knew' very precisely when, how, where and to what degree a given mixture would either produce the highest peaks of cultural attainment or condemn a culture to perdition.

This one example may suffice to illustrate the crass

contradictions and the arbitrariness of Gobineau's method. All the more because – in order not to find himself at odds with Christianity – he had to accept the common origin of mankind, or rather he accepted it at times and left it open at others, and then again had recourse to the biblical trinity of Noah's sons, Sem, Cham and Japhet. On the other hand, he built his whole theory – untroubled by the fact that he was thereby entering into insoluble conflicts with the above supposition – upon the dogmatic, qualitative physiological and psychological inequality of race. As propagator of this doctrinaire inequality he enthusiastically acclaimed the slave-holders of the southern United States, as we have already noted. And he also proclaimed, for instance, the incapacity for civilization, in principle, of the primitive western Asian population. 'It could not become civilized because it lacked the necessary insight . . . it had to suffice to force its members into useful labour like animated machines.'[15] Yet since Gobineau was aware that the Catholic church laid claims to universality, he had to acknowledge that Christianity was within the reach of all men. This, however, was of no consequence to racial equality: 'Hence in treating my question, one must keep Christianity completely apart.'[16] Again, Gobineau took the view, on the one hand, that Christianity was culture's supreme manifestation and that all men, irrespective of race, had the capacity to share in this cultural peak. On the other, he asserted also that all the lower races were uncivilizable in principle, that they were fit only to serve as slaves, living machines and beasts of burden for the higher races.

On such points, Gobineau proves backward in relation to the modern proponents of racial theory, and he was in fact spurned by them. This antithesis expresses very clearly the totally barbaric character of modern racial theory. It becomes plain how the theory degraded all the findings of the evolution of thought in modern times to instruments of an unprecedented obscurantism which served imperialist ends. Whereas in the eighteenth and nineteenth centuries, the ideological

struggle against Christianity was waged in the name of progress and freedom, the imperialist advocates of racial theory converted the religious critique into a tool of extreme reaction. The modern racial theorists passionately repudiated just that principle which constituted the historical progressiveness of Christianity, namely the recognition – however abstract – of the equality of all men (before God). Gobineau appeared backward in their eyes because here he sought a compromise; a compromise in which Tocqueville, to be sure, rightly perceived a hypocrisy. The later imperialist advocates of racial theory did in actual fact accomplish this break with Christianity.

Despite this backwardness in Gobineau, his successors drew more from him than they were prepared to admit. Above all he was the first to produce a really effective pseudo-scientific pamphlet contesting democracy and equality, on a racialist basis. Moreover, his book marked the first large-scale attempt to reconstruct the whole of world-history with the aid of racial theory, and to do so by tracing back to racial questions all historical crises, social conflicts and differences. With him, this was in effect tantamount to saying that every change to the social structure was 'unnatural' and led to man's downfall, and therefore could not possibly be a step forward. About this ideal condition reigning at the outset Gobineau wrote the following: 'It has been already established that every social order is founded upon three original classes, each of which represents a racial variety: the nobility, a more or less accurate reflection of the conquering race; the bourgeoisie, composed of mixed stock coming close to the chief race; and the common people, who live in servitude or at least in a very depressed position. These last belong to a lower race which came about in the south through miscegenation with negroes, and in the north with Finns.'[17] The Aryans alone, he asserted, had realized this ideal form, which one could observe in the Indian castes and in European feudalism. The Semites had never raised themselves to the same height. This exclusively backward-looking

tendency too was repudiated by later racial theorists. However, their so-called perspective of the future was only a revival of ancient barbaric conditions accomplished with all the atrocities of imperialism. Thus even in spite of their dismissive attitude, which was connected with the further development of reactionary tendencies in the imperialist epoch, the later racialists proceeded from the same basis, in many respects, as the founder of modern racial theory.

In founding the historical 'methodology' of racial theory, Gobineau again created something which was preserved in later developments. The dogmatic insistence on the inequality of men necessarily implied a rejection of the concept of mankind, and with this there vanished one of the finest achievements of modern science: the idea of the uniform and regular development of men. Attacks on this had been occurring for a very long time. We know also that even without a racialist basis, it was possible to take apart the idea of mankind's uniform development (as Spengler did). But the significance of racial theory in the history of recent reactionary thought is that in it, all the important elements in this repudiation of world-history were concentrated on attacking reason. The denial of a uniform history of man implied at the same time a denial of the equality of man, of progress and of reason. For Gobineau, there was only a history of the white race. This monstrous reactionary idea remained a staple of later racial theory. Gobineau stated:

> In the oriental world, the unremitting struggle of racial forces was only enacted between the Aryan element on the one hand, and the black and yellow principle on the other. It is superfluous to mention that where only the black races were in contest or the yellow races were moving within their own circle, or even where mixtures of black and yellow-skinned peoples were at odds with each other, no history is possible. These struggles were essentially barren, like the ethnic motoric forces which prompted them. They did not create anything, and no memory of

them has survived . . . *History results only from the mutual contact of white races.*[18]

This view of history now yielded a unique 'theory' of primitive history which was to remain a part of racial theory. For the racial theories, the differences in the stages of culture no longer signified phases of development that were completed successively by one and the same people, one and the same society. Instead, each stage was equated with specified races and placed in an eternal, metaphysical context. While specified races were permanently barbaric, others had never been savages or barbarians. Thus Gobineau thought of the transition from the Stone Age to the Bronze Age as a change – of races! He wrote of the white race: 'It strikes us above all that the white race is never manifested in the same primitive state as the other two. From the first day (!) it proved relatively cultivated and possessed the essential seeds of a superior condition. This later developed in its separate branches and created the various forms of civilization.' Gobineau asserted that from the start, the white races fought with their enemies on war chariots, and that they were able to fashion metal, wood and leather from the outset. 'The primal white races knew how to weave materials for their clothing. They lived in large villages which they decked out with pyramids, obelisks or mounds of earth or stones. They had broken in horses . . . Their wealth consisted in numerous herds of bulls and cows.'[19] Naturally Gobineau did not even raise the question of how such a culture originated; evidently he thought that such an inquiry would already be a psychological sign of the bastard state. We can set this picture of the white race against Gobineau's aforestated observations on the uncivilizable primitive peoples of western Asia.

So we see that in Gobineau the destruction of historical science was already far advanced. His view reflects not only the feudal traditions of the European colonizers but also their racial arrogance towards the 'coloured people', whom they regarded as 'lacking a history' and uncivilizable. To be

sure, as we have demonstrated, this interpretation of history logically indicated that the Aryans represented not only the climax but also the end of history. Fatalistic pessimism was inevitable for Gobineau. Several decades later, it won him a great popularity among the similarly pessimistic decadent intelligentsia of the turn of the century. And it made him redundant when the obscurantism of imperialist racial theory became militant and activist and proceeded to the crucial offensive against human culture.

3. Social Darwinism (Gumplowicz, Ratzenhofer, Woltmann)

In order for racial theory to become the ruling ideology of extreme reaction, it had to shed its overtly feudal trappings and put on the costume and mask of the very latest 'scientific thinking'. But this involved more than merely a change of dress. The latter was only a reflection of a change in the decisive class character of the new racial theory. Even in its most modern form, certainly, it was still a pseudo-biological defence of class privileges. But now the issue was no longer merely one of the historical nobility – as was largely the case with Gobineau. It concerned, on the one hand, the privileges of the European races as opposed to the coloured ones (as already with Gobineau), as also of the Germanic races – chiefly the German nation – within the other European races (which made it an ideology of German global control). On the other hand, it concerned the claim to dominance of the capitalist class within each separate nation and thus the origin of a 'new nobility', not any more the conservation of the historical feudal aristocracy.

This change came about little by little. Almost half a century elapsed before the new racial theory found in Chamberlain a leading theoretician to match Gobineau's role in propounding the old theory.

So-called Social Darwinism played a decisive part in

bridging these two stages of racial theory. Darwin's doctrine had an immense influence on the whole development of science and outlook in the second half of the nineteenth century. Progressive science was enormously enriched and stimulated by Darwin's works: major scientific advances took place wherever genuine scientists and philosophers were engaged in absorbing and digesting the real substance of Darwin's *oeuvre*. Thus Engels wrote to Marx: 'Incidentally, the Darwin I am just reading is quite a name. One side of teleology was still intact up to now, but not any longer. Moreover, never has there been a finer attempt to demonstrate historical development in Nature, and certainly none so felicitous.'[20] Marx wrote to Engels in similar terms: 'This book, although developed in the blunt English fashion, is the one that contains the natural-historical basis for our view.'[21]

Darwin, however, attained to universal influence when the social sciences were undergoing a general crisis, and his influence ran into this crisis. On the whole, the reactionary bourgeois ideologists contested Darwinism – chiefly its consequences for philosophy and world-outlook, but also its methodology and findings in the natural sciences. Above all, the struggle of reactionary bourgeois ideology was aimed against the theory of evolution, and thus against the very point in which Engels rightly saw the greatest advance which Darwin's work signified. So the basic line taken by the bourgeois sciences, bourgeois philosophy especially, was anti-Darwinist.

That, however, did not prevent a Darwinism that had become a cliché from temporarily playing no mean role in the social sciences. Reviewing a book by F.A. Lange, Marx criticized very sharply this newly emerging tendency in the social sciences:

> Herr Lange has made a great discovery. All history is to be subsumed under a single great law of nature. This law of nature is the *cliché* (for as used here, the Darwinian term becomes a mere cliché) 'struggle for life', and its substance

> is the Malthusian law of population or rather over-population. Thus instead of analysing the 'struggle for life' as it presents itself historically in various specified forms of society, all one must do is to convert that concrete struggle into the catchphrase 'struggle for life', and the latter into the Malthusian 'population fantasy'. You must admit that this is a very searching method – as far as stuck-up, pseudo-scientific, high-flown ignorance and mental laziness are concerned.[22]

Let us consider briefly the general preconditions for the emergence of so-called Darwinism in sociology. The classical economy had dissolved as a result of the class struggles, in England especially. Its transformation into a popular economy had repercussions which were not confined to economics in the narrower sense. It was not by accident that sociology became divorced from economics around this very time and thereby established itself as an independent discipline. (With Comte the divorce was from Saint-Simon's utopianism, but that does not greatly affect the situation. Comte detached sociology from its economic basis just as Spencer, for instance, was later to do in England.) And having renounced its methodologically necessary economic basis, the new sociology sought and found support for its purported objectivity and orderliness in the natural sciences. Of course this substantiation of sociology through chemistry, biology, etc., could only be effected by coining abstract clichés from the findings of the natural sciences, as Marx showed above in the case of Lange and Darwin. Comte, Spencer and so-called organic sociology in Germany all operated in this way. It is patent that, given such an orientation in sociology, the world-influence of Darwinian theory could not possibly pass it by without deeply affecting it.

It goes without saying that there were profounder reasons for this influence than the mere methodological needs of bourgeois sociology. In the last quarter of the nineteenth century, bourgeois ideology entered a new phase of capitalist

apologetics. Both the harmonist doctrine of popular economics and the theory of organic growth in quasi-biological sociology were proving inadequate, particularly with regard to the struggle against socialist ideas. They were proving ineffective among broad circles of that public to which bourgeois sociology was addressing itself. The reason for this failure of the harmonist doctrine of popular economics and organic sociology lay in a heightening of the capitalist contradictions and, in association with it, an aggravation of the class struggles. Manifesting themselves with increasing vigour, these revealed more and more clearly the worthlessness of the harmonist doctrine. Now if capitalism was to be justified as the best economic and social system conceivable, and if sociology was to lead to a reconciliation with the capitalist system and convince the undecided of its unsurpassable merit – as a bourgeois apologetic science was obliged to do, then the contradictions and above all the inhuman sides of capitalism could be excused and glossed over no longer. It was precisely with these that the apologia had to begin. In short: whereas capitalist apologetics had hitherto denied the 'bad aspects' of this system, it was precisely thence that the new apologetic proceeded. It sought to persuade the bourgeois intelligentsia to approve these 'bad aspects', or at least to come to terms with them as supposedly unalterable, nature-given and 'perennial'.

Clearly Darwinism in its hackneyed form offered an exceptionally suitable starting-point for this new form of apologetics. We have noted also that at about the same time, Nietzsche was likewise exploiting stereotyped Darwinism in this direction. In view of this strong ideological need, it is no wonder that sociological schools sprang up to execute this new form of capitalist apologetics with its pseudo-Darwinian basis. This Social Darwinism presented, moreover, the most manifold possibilities. Firstly, it engendered a 'monistic', 'natural-scientific' view of sociology. Society was presented as a completely homogeneous part of the general cosmic order. Whereas Engels welcomed Darwinism because it

required a historical interpretation of nature, this sociology used a hackneyed Darwinism in order to demolish historicism in the social sciences. Secondly, not only all economic categories but also classes disappeared from sociology. They were supplanted by the racial 'struggle for life'. In the third place, oppression, inequality, exploitation and so forth were presented as 'facts of nature' or 'laws of nature' which, as such, could not be avoided or revoked. Thus all the frightful products of capitalism were justified as being 'in accordance with nature'. Fourthly, a sociology based on 'natural laws' led men to acquiesce in a capitalist destiny. Gumplowicz formulated this side of Social Darwinism with great firmness. The last word in sociology was, for him, the interpretation 'of human history as a natural process'. This interpretation was '*the summit of all human morality* because it preaches most persuasively the self-sacrificial subordination of man to those laws of nature which alone govern history'; and because it was 'the morality of rational resignation'.[23] Finally, this doctrine presented itself as loftily objective and above party issues, though its main front was of course clearly opposed to socialism and its adherents. Thus Gumplowicz's pupil Ratzenhofer said of the various parties' attitude to sociology that men in privileged positions were hostile to it, but so too were the oppressed, 'because it has to deprive them of illusions about their chances of a complete fulfilment of their desires'.[24]

This Social Darwinism was an international phenomenon far exceeding sociology in the narrower sense. (Compare, for instance, Lombroso's theory of the 'born criminal'.) Granted, this direction never gained sole dominance in bourgeois sociology. The shrewder and better trained bourgeois sociologists soon saw through the emptiness and phrasemongering of this sensational new method. Discussions arose on an international scale. Social Darwinism was challenged not only by the representatives of old liberal thought, who tried to eliminate all violence – at least from the ideology – in the spirit of the harmonist doctrine and fulminated against

the Social Darwinists' 'Machiavellism'. Novikov,[25] for instance, contested 'banditism' both from 'above' (Bismarck) and 'from below' (Marx and the class struggle). In the latter respect he was in agreement with his Darwinist opponents, except that he attempted to refute Marxism by other methods.

But sociologists who were promoting the imperialist period's ideological development from other sides also sharply rejected Social Darwinism. Chief among these was Toennies, who wrote: 'No argument for or against free competition, for or against cartels and trusts, State concerns and monopolies, capitalism or socialism is hidden in the principles of the theory of descent as though this were a Christmas stocking – we must neither fear nor hope for something of importance as a result of applying it . . . These efforts have a strong tinge of the ridiculous, as does any nigger dressing-up with spurious arguments, and they characterize a low degree of scientific thinking.'[26]

Gumplowicz was the typical, trend-setting representative of Social Darwinism in the German-speaking realm. He – and, even more markedly, his pupil Ratzenhofer – proceeded from the absolute identity of and lack of qualitative distinction between natural and social processes. Sociology was, according to Gumplowicz, the 'natural history of mankind'. And he went on to elucidate this methodological starting-point by saying that it was the task of natural science 'to explain the processes of history through the governance of unalterable natural laws'.[27] Ratzenhofer made it plainly evident how this was to be understood. We shall quote just one or two statements illustrating his method: 'Viewed accordingly, the principal laws of chemistry must also be sociological laws . . . The relationship of the elements, the greater or lesser mutual affinity between them or their dislike of certain associations are phenomena which not merely resemble the passions in social life, love and hate, but are causally identical with them.'[28]

In all their tendencies' external manifestations, Gumplowicz

and Ratzenhofer were the polar opposite of Gobineau: sober specialist science in contrast to Gobineau's wild speculations, strictly natural-scientific monism in contrast to orthodox Catholicism, etc., etc. But they cultivated a decisive common basic feature of the 'biological' method: that of tracing social phenomena back to an apparent set of laws with the aid of specious natural-scientific analogies. Here we can see also a specific bias which later became fully evident in fascism: the apodosis of conclusions reached purely on the basis of analogies, analogies which were often extremely superficial, trivial, irrelevant and which in no respect clinched the argument.

By means of this supposedly natural-scientific method, Social Darwinism revoked history. Man, it claimed, had not changed in the course of history. Gumplowicz stated: 'Just let us rid ourselves of the vain illusion that man nowadays – civilized man!! – is any different in his nature, urges and needs, his capabilities and intellectual characteristics than he was in his primal state.'[29] Thus sociology in its Darwinist garb expelled from the observation of society not only all economics, but also all social elements. That was methodologically necessary. For if sociology is founded on biology or anthropology, then it cannot permit of any essential change, let alone progress. After all, the changes in man that have occurred in recorded history are not of a biological kind, but social. Therefore the biological proposition implies that what it takes to be the essence is subject to no further change or development. This too helped significantly in paving the way for the fascist interpretation of history.

Indeed Gumplowicz, with the aid of the similarly hackneyed law of the conservation of energy, presented this antihistorism as a 'cosmic law'. He wrote:

> In the realm of society's natural process, as in all the rest of nature, the operative forces can never go astray, and while their sum may be converted into differently operating forces, it can never be diminished. It is possible that

> the sum of the social energies operative in the realm of mankind since the earliest times will never diminish. Once, they manifested themselves in countless tribal wars and clan feuds – and with the development of the social process in individual areas, with the progress of social amalgamation and the growth of culture, these energies are not lost but are expended in different forms. The sum of mutual exploitations in each given social community will never, perhaps, be smaller, although it may at times be practised in other forms. Thus numerically fewer wars are being fought in Europe nowadays than in earlier centuries, but the size and significance of the individual wars (e.g., Franco-German, Russo-Turkish, Russo-Japanese) are a match for the numerous earlier wars.[30]

From these purported laws it followed, for Gumplowicz, that 'the *mass* of organisms on the earth must always remain constant, and that this mass is pre-determined through the cosmic conditions of our globe . . . If parts of it increase, then the others must go by the board.'[31] At this point, monist sociology successfully brought this pseudo-Darwinism to dry land in a cosmically expanded Malthusianism.

The upshot of all this for Social Darwinism was, firstly, that there was no universal human progress; at best there was progress within a specified cultural realm. Here Gumplowicz was anticipating Spengler's theory of culture cycles. He explained that progress was conceivable 'only within the development of a disjunct cultural realm, starting afresh and running its course in each instance'.[32] There was, therefore, no unified history of mankind. As we can see, that repudiation of world-history which had gained currency through Spengler and Chamberlain was deeply rooted in the ideological needs of the imperialist bourgeoisie; it originated in outwardly very dissimilar, methodologically downright contrary systems. Gumplowicz maintained 'that we cannot have any idea of human development as a unified whole because we have no self-contained idea of the subject of

such a whole'.[33] With Gumplowicz, as later with Spengler and advanced racial theory, the development within each cultural realm followed a circular pattern: '. . . each nation arrives at its highest stage of culture, ripens towards the point of decay, and the downfall is occasioned by the first barbarians to come along'.[34] It is not hard to discern that here again, we are dealing with the shaky apodosis of analogies. Gumplowicz, like Spengler after him, was simply applying the biological phases of individual life (youth, maturity, old age) by analogy to the cultural realms, or culture cycles. We see here the sharp contrast between the progressive and reactionary effects of Darwinism. Whereas Darwin's discoveries helped Marx and Engels to grasp nature and society as a great unified historical process, Social Darwinism dissolved philosophically that conception of a unified world-history of mankind attained by progressive bourgeois thought.

This fundamentally incorrect mystical method – a toying with analogies behind a monist mask – led to totally false conclusions even where the original starting-point lay in social observations which were not contrary to the facts. Thus Gumplowicz perceived that the origin of the State was very closely connected with the social inequality of men. But since he sought to explain this inequality not through economic but pseudo-scientific cosmic causes, correct observation gave rise to a reactionary mysticism. This engendered the close affinity of Social Darwinism with the most reactionary theory in that for Gumplowicz – as for Gobineau – the 'original inequality' of men formed the point of departure. Ratzenhofer stated with the same firmness as Gobineau and later racial theory: 'Inequality is . . . the natural condition, equality is unnatural and impossible.'[35]

As in Gobineau's case, this pseudo-scientific mysticizing of economic facts had its basis in a general anti-democratic tendency. The great difference was that, whereas Gobineau revived the old, feudal-aristocratic anti-democratism, Social Darwinism expressed that of the bourgeoisie and a now victorious capitalism. Understandably, it did so most strongly

in countries like Germany and Austro-Hungary where no triumphant bourgeois revolution preceded this economic dominance. So Gumplowicz examined the fate of the doctrines of equality in history, and (like later racial theory) he characteristically interpreted Judaism, Mohammedanism, the Christian church and the French Revolution as completely equal tendencies. He now established that these tendencies were doomed to failure,

> and for the simple reason that these doctrines run counter to man's nature, so that their sway is at best only *nominal* . . . What *in point of fact and perennially* rules supreme in the world is a quite different set of teachings and precepts better suited to the rudimentary nature of the masses. It is not Buddhist teachings, the words of Christ or the 'principles' of the French Revolution that reverberate in the din of embattled nations – in that din resound the cries of: here Aryan, here Semite, here Mongol; here European, here Asian; here White, here Coloured, here Christian, here Moslem, here German, here Roman, here slave, and so on in a thousand and one variations. And among battle cries of this sort *history is made*, and human blood is spilled wholesale – with a view to the fulfilment of a *world-historical law of nature* which we are still a long way from discerning.[36]

Gumplowicz was, as we can see, still far from eagerly affirming this 'natural process'; as we have noted, he advocated a response of 'rational resignation'. But with his primitive biologist view of history, his mysticizing of the facts of class struggle into a racial struggle 'ordained by nature' and the anti-democratic attitude permeating this whole conception, he was paving the way for the fascist view of history. Hence it was no accident that, with some reservations, he repeatedly lavished praise on distinct reactionaries who put forward such a concept, like Haller, Lombroso and Gobineau. His pupil Ratzenhofer voiced this anti-democratic attitude

more pungently: 'The slogans of freedom, equality and international brotherhood are lying phantoms . . . The idea of sudden revolution is unhistorical.'[37]

In the light of these hypotheses, it is easy to understand why the State formed the centre of sociology with Gumplowicz and his school. The State, on the basis of the 'natural' inequality of man, was the demiurge of the division of labour in society. This view was levelled chiefly against working class aspirations. Its aim was to demonstrate that the State, as an 'ordering of inequality', was the 'sole possible order for men'.[38] With these theories Gumplowicz not only completely divorced sociology from economics but sought to restrict the latter – which, of course, he only knew in its contemporary vulgar form – to a specific specialist discipline in contrast to sociology, which was universal. In this tendency to belittle economics, Social Darwinism was likewise anticipating imperialist reactionary ideology. According to Gumplowicz, economics could make no claim whatever to comprehend society; it was just concerned with economic phenomena. 'But', he went on, 'the essence and life of a society is by no means fully spent in its economic activity, just as the individual is not fully occupied by it. Indeed, it is far rather the case that sociology might advance the claim to consider political economy as one of its parts.'[39]

This reversal of the relation between politics and economics was connected with the central issue in Social Darwinism, namely the endeavour to grasp biologically, and thus do away with, every social distinction, class stratification and class struggle. Here a deep-seated conflict arose in Gumplowicz himself, who was subjectively honest as a scholar. It is of wider interest because it reflects the intellectual and methodological confusion of this transitional stage and also shows how helpless this German-speaking intelligentsia was with regard to mainstream reactionary development. The hypotheses we have outlined necessarily entailed substituting race for class in sociology, particularly since physical force was regarded as the primary element in the State's

development, so that class stratification was presented as the dominance of one race over another.

And in his first, widely noted book *Race and State* (1875), Gumplowicz did in fact formulate the problem such that he simply identified races with classes. But in the course of his subsequent work, he came to see more and more clearly the untenability of this postulate. He admitted as much in his second important work, *The Racial Struggle* (1883). In it he wrote of the racial issue: 'Here everything is arbitrary, subjective appearance and opinion (*Scheinen und Meinen*): nowhere is there firm ground or a firm piece of evidence, nor is there a positive result anywhere.' And since, as a scientific monist, he was seeking at least a minimum of objective characteristics of racial differences, he arrived at the following conclusions.

> The sorry role played by all anthropological *measuring of skulls* and the like can be appreciated by anyone who has ever tried to gain enlightenment through these studies of mankind's different types. Everything is higgledy-piggledy, and the 'mean' figures and measurements offer no palpable result. What one anthropologist describes as the Germanic type, another deems apposite to the slave type. We find Mongolian types among 'Aryans', and we constantly land in the position of taking 'Aryans' for Semites and vice versa if we abide by 'anthropological' categories.[40]

Even Ratzenhofer, who outstripped his teacher in many reactionary aspects and, like Gobineau, viewed the negroes for instance as born slaves, had to concede the lack of scientific substantiation in this respect. 'Racial dispositions are, indubitably, an authoritative basis for social behaviour, but only in the rarest cases is it possible to prove the same for single individuals.'[41]

Gumplowicz and his school rejected, however, the economic basis of the class struggle. Consequently, an observation of the problems of racial determining factors was bound to lead to a sorry and muddled eclecticism. And the development

of imperialist reactionary ideology, after having been fertilized by the stimuli of Social Darwinism, simply passed this by. Illustrative of the transitional nature of the figure of Gumplowicz in racial theory is a conversation with a younger advocate of Social Darwinism, Woltmann, which Gumplowicz published in a later edition of *The Racial Struggle*. Woltmann accused him of deviating from the correct path he had taken in his first book and of adulterating the correct racial concept. Gumplowicz defended himself thus:

> In my home region I was . . . already struck by the circumstance that the individual social classes represented quite heterogeneous races; there was the Polish nobility, which rightly always considered itself of different stock from the farmer; there was the German middle class and beside it the Jews – so many classes, so many races . . . But my subsequent experience and knowledgc, coupled with mature reflection, taught me that in the Western European countries, the individual classes of society have already long ceased to represent anthropological races . . . and yet they bchave to each other like races and carry on a social racial struggle . . . In my *Racial Struggle*, the anthropological concept of race has been renounced, but the racial struggle has remained the same, although the races have not been anthropological ones for a very long time. But it is the *struggle* that counts; it provides an explanation for all phenomena in the State, the genesis of justice and State development.[42]

It is typical that here Gumplowicz, objectively considered, completely abandoned the social theory of race in essence while preserving it unaltered in his terminology – and in his case that means: in its crucial philosophical consequences.

Woltmann represents a higher stage of the transition to the reactionary development of biologism. His specific position rested on the fact that as an erstwhile social democrat (he was a revisionist seeking to link Marx with Darwin

and Kant), he was able to make important advances in accommodating racial theory to imperialist needs. He extended Gumplowicz's idea that class struggles are essentially racial struggles, 'purged' it of Gumplowicz's scruples and illogicalities, and consequently adopted – in updated form – certain lines of Gobineau's thinking, as also elements of French racial theory, which had advanced in the meantime (Lapouge, etc.).

Woltmann retained from his social democrat past the terminology of social development and social structuring, but he changed all these categories into ones of biological racial theory. Thus surplus value, for instance, he treated as a biological concept. The social division of labour 'is founded ... upon the natural inequality of physical and spiritual attributes'.[43] The class antitheses were 'latent racial antitheses'.[44] On this basis he so varied the revisionist glorification of capitalism as to imply that the latter constituted the best social order for natural selection. It goes without saying that Woltmann became an ideological defender of colonial oppression as well. In his opinion it was a 'hopeless undertaking to make Negroes and Indians capable of genuine civilization'; in the colonies the Whites would 'always form the *master race* only'.[45] And on the basis of Social Darwinism he revived Gobineau's doctrine, but already as the ideology of German imperialism, by stating: 'The Nordic race is the born carrier of global civilization.'[46]

Thus behind the facade of a social doctrine, Woltmann represented the radical-reactionary, imperialist theory of race with all its consequences. And that applies to the entire methodology (let us recall the aforestated comments on equality). Like Gumplowicz he repudiated the unitarian development of mankind. It was wrong, he claimed, 'to speak of an evolution of the human race ... *what evolve are the individual races*'.[47] Of course Woltmann too saw that there are no 'pure races' in historical reality, and that all psychological distinguishing marks applied to race are highly dubious. But unlike Gumplowicz, he did not honestly admit this contradiction. Instead, he tried to evade it through

demagogic convolutions; thus he introduced – with one eye to surmounting Gobineau's fatalism – the concept of racial 'de-miscegenation' (an idea of later significance for Hitler and Rosenberg). His stress on the importance of artificial racial breeding, originating in a mixture of cross-breeding and incest, gave rise to a markedly optimistic perspective contrasting with that of Gobineau. But in spite of all his impressive sociological and biological terminology, Woltmann did not manage to be any less arbitrary than Gobineau: at times he treated miscegenation as absolutely harmful and corrupting, at others he thought that the most important elements of 'breeding' derived precisely from cross-breeding. His surmounting of Gobineau's pessimism rested upon the 'modest hope . . . of sustaining and protecting the sound and noble condition of the present generation through measures of racial hygiene and racial policy'.[48] We shall see in due course what a barbaric, despotic system Hitlerism created from this 'modest hope'.

Woltmann too attained to no decisive influence. That was not because he was 'scientifically' better or worse than earlier or later racial theorists, but because there was not yet a politico-social basis for the wider influence of applied racial theory in Germany at the time. The particular brand of racial theory that Woltmann represented confirmed this lack of effect. French racial theorists (e.g., the aforementioned Lapouge) could only daydream of Aryan mastery and outlined – exceeding Gobineau in their pessimism – horrific prospects of a Russian predominance in Europe, or of a European coalition under Jewish leadership, etc.[49] Such German theorists as Otto Ammon, meanwhile, could only grip the most extreme 'Pan-Germans' with a crude and patently unscientific propaganda of German predominance. Woltmann, on the other hand, condemned himself to ineffectiveness among reactionary circles through decided tendencies whereby he tried to achieve compromises between racial theory and his past revisionism. Like all reactionaries, he combated the idea of human equality and democracy. But

he did not, for example, join in condemning the French Revolution as a slave uprising, an inferior race's revolt against the aristocracy (the Aryans, Franks). Nor did he share the view of the whole labour movement as a revolt of racial inferiors. He wrote of the French Revolution: 'The revolution's leaders were almost entirely Germanic . . . *The revolution merely raised to power a different stratum of the Germanic race*. It would be a mistake to believe that the "third estate" came to power in France. Power was gained only by the bourgeoisie, i.e., the upper Germanic stratum of the middle class, just as the present labour movement, viewed anthropologically, reflects only the effective rise to power and liberty of the upper Germanic strata of the working class.'[50] This compound of a revisionist substantiation of the rise of the labour aristocracy and a racialist glorification of the Germanic spirit could not possibly gain wide currency in German reactionary circles at that time. No reactionary German could welcome the interpretation of the French Revolution as a 'heroic deed of the Germanic spirit', to say nothing of the 'Germanic' labour movement. Such fluctuations and inconsistencies made Woltmann's racial theory a transitory episode, although not a few of his ideas retained their influence into the fascist period.

4. H.S. Chamberlain as the Founder of Modern Racialism

The real representative advocate of racial theory in the prewar period was H.S. Chamberlain. As a thinker, he too was far from possessing any true originality. He is significant in that he united old racial theory and also the imperialist revival of it with general reactionary tendencies typical of the imperialist age, above all, vitalism. He thereby provided racial theory with just that 'philosophical' synthesis which reactionary extremism needed at the time. The authentic vitalists of this period (Dilthey, Simmel, etc.) were still too

strongly associated with old, partly liberal agnostic tendencies. Nietzsche in part was too close to an aesthetic, oppositional decadence, and in part, despite his nearness to Social Darwinism in other respects, he rejected racial theory in the narrower sense. Social Darwinism in turn lacked philosophical generalizations; inasmuch as its advocates undertook these they were scientific-monist ones, and thus of no use to reactionary extremism. Chamberlain now summed up 'philosophically' all the tendencies that mattered to the reactionary extremists. To that extent he cut an important figure: the ideological link between old reaction and the coming fascism.

Of course Chamberlain was not the only such link. An important forerunner, whom the fascists likewise revered as a direct spiritual ancestor, was Lagarde. It is certainly no accident that the German Kaiser Wilhelm II was closely associated with Lagarde and came under his intellectual influence in his youth,[51] when he also supported Stöcker's anti-Semitic demagogy. Nor was it by accident that there later arose a personal correspondence between the German Kaiser and Chamberlain. As early as 1901, the Kaiser described himself in a letter to Chamberlain as a 'fellow-combatant and ally in the struggle for Germania against Rome, Jerusalem, etc.'[52] And the Kaiser said of Chamberlain's influence on his own thinking: 'And now all the ancient Aryan Germanic elements amassed and dormant within me had gradually to emerge by strenuous effort. They came into open conflict with what was "inherited", often manifested themselves in a bizarre form and often, because they were more of an obscure inkling, stirred within me shapelessly and unconsciously, seeking an outlet. Then you appeared, and with your magic wand you brought order into confusion, light into darkness; the goals which had to be striven and toiled for; the elucidation of obscurely sensed paths which had to be followed in order to save the Germans, and thereby to save mankind.'[53]

This friendship lasted until Chamberlain's death. Chamberlain received the Iron Cross for his war-mongering

essays, and the amicable correspondence continued after the fall of the dynasty. But at the same time, Chamberlain also made contact with the new leader of extreme reaction. In 1923 there took place a meeting between him and Hitler, and Chamberlain summed up his impression of it as follows: 'My faith in the German spirit has not wavered for one moment, but my hopes – this I admit – had sunk to a low ebb. You have transformed my state of soul at a stroke. That Germany should engender a Hitler in the hour of her greatest need testifies to the life in her; the same goes for the influence that Hitler radiates; for those two things – personality and influence – go together. That the magnificent Ludendorff should openly join you and declare his sympathy with the movement emanating from you: how splendidly that confirms your worth!'[54]

Lagarde and his subsequent lesser successors (e.g., Langbehn, the author of 'Rembrandt as Educator') were still outsiders. They could ally themselves only peripherally and intermittently with current reactionary politics. Chamberlain saw in Lagarde 'the complementary political genius to Bismarck'.[55] He described Lagarde's 'German Writings' (*Deutsche Schriften*) as among 'the most valuable of books'. His special achievement was to have located in Christianity the inferior Semitic religious instincts and their harmful effect on Christian religion; that was a deed 'earning admiration and gratitude'. Lagarde wished to have the whole of the Old Testament eliminated from Christian religious teaching; for, he stated, 'the Gospel has been ruined, as far as that is possible, by its influence'.[56] Although Chamberlain criticized Lagarde for ploughing a lone furrow, which made him a solitary outsider, he nevertheless saw in him one of his most important forerunners.

Here the most significant element was the attitude to religion and Christianity. It blended the themes of the old and new forms of reactionary extremism. The old Prussian *Junker* reaction was Protestant-Pietist and thus traditional and orthodox on all religious issues. Germany's capitalist

development and the need to retain a hold on political supremacy in an aggressively imperialist State – one requiring for its aggression an ideology that would embrace and mobilize all social strata – transformed the situation within the ranks of the reactionary extremists. Admittedly the working class especially was not easy to infiltrate in this way; here reformism had a lengthy job to do before a surrender to German imperialism became a possibility. Hence the new reactionary extremism was oriented primarily to the petty-bourgeois masses, who were not directly susceptible to the *Junker* influence, and hence there sprang up various forms of demagogic ideology (Stöcker's anti-Semitism, later Naumann's nationalism, and so on).

Among the intellectuals, too, the most diverse tendencies held sway. Nietzsche, who was active at around the same time as Lagarde, likewise dissociated himself from orthodox Protestantism. But whereas he sought and announced a new religion draped with atheistic slogans, Lagarde attempted to renew Protestantism by eliminating the Semitic elements. Both of them criticized the capitalist age's lack of culture, but in such a way that the butt of their criticism was directed against democracy and the labour movement. Here they fell in with the reactionary tendencies of imperialist vitalism. But for all the extent of Nietzsche's influence on the intelligentsia, this philosophy was not calculated to form a basis for influencing the broad masses.

Now at this point Chamberlain came on the scene as the most important mind to continue Lagarde's line of thought. He expanded his racial theory into a general 'world-view' assimilating all reactionary extremist tendencies, both old and new, and combining a cultural critique at the 'highest level' with vulgar anti-Semitic agitation and propaganda for the German race's exclusive vocation as rulers. It both contested outmoded Christianity and renewed it, thus addressing itself to believers and unbelievers at one and the same time, while also converting this Christian revival into a tool of anti-democratic, world-conquering imperialist

Hohenzollern policy.

And racial theory formed the kernel of this new philosophy. As we have noted, Chamberlain rejected Gobineau's form of racialism; at the same time he stated his allegiance to a Social Darwinism. Directly after the aforestated critical comments on Gobineau he wrote: 'My master is primarily ... Charles Darwin.'[57] It must be said that the Darwin he acknowledged was Darwin minus the theory of evolution. Of evolution Chamberlain once wrote: 'My instinct tells me that the idea of man is not in agreement with nature.'[58] That, to his mind, disposed of the theory of evolution. Darwin's positive achievement, in Chamberlain's eyes, was 'the proof of the significance of race in the entire realm of living beings'.[59] Here again, it must be said, Chamberlain dismissed all questions of origin and cause. The Darwin whom he accepted was merely a colleague of the 'men of praxis'; 'I follow the great natural scientist into the stable and the chicken-run and to the nurseryman and say that here we have something which gives substance to the word "race", is unarguable and obvious to everybody.'[60]

So Chamberlain's method derived from grossly incongruous views: each of his interpretations juxtaposed the most vulgar empiricism and mystical intuitive philosophy. Certainly this dichotomy was nothing new in German reactionary philosophy. The older Schelling had already called his theory of revealed knowledge, his irrationalist philosophy of intuition a 'philosophical empiricism', and Eduard von Hartmann later endeavoured to rescue this philosophy from the past and to modernize it. It does not greatly matter whether Chamberlain was familiar with these predecessors of his or not. This, at all events, is where the essence of his successes as a philosopher lay: he was speaking for 'modern' people, and all the achievements of capitalist industry and the technology and science supporting it were therefore to be preserved and justified philosophically. Indeed, the new philosophy was to be presented as though it were, through a radical empiricism, to protect this modern natural-scientific

praxis against impermissible inroads on the part of an abstract philosophy. Yet it was from this very soil that there sprang up the racial mystique, the German race's claim to world mastery.

Chamberlain's racialism was thus suspended between a purportedly empiricist obviousness and the wildest obscurantist mysticism. On the one hand, Chamberlain cited as evidence the experience of animal breeders and horticulturists. These 'knew' what race was. And, Chamberlain added, 'why should mankind constitute an exception?'[61] Elsewhere, discussing the merits of racehorses and Newfoundland dogs, he continued: 'Here again, nobody acquainted in detail with the results of animal breeding can doubt that the history of mankind before us and around us obeys the same law.'[62] Here, too, the role of Darwinian sociology is plainly visible: it was that of removing all social elements from the theory of society as inessential to it. And yet Chamberlain knew perfectly well that the objective defining characteristics of race are quite invalid for men. When the distinguished German scholar Steinmetz put this point to him he replied: 'That is all very well . . . but life itself, which shows everywhere that race is a fact of importance to all organic existence . . ., life does not wait for scholars . . . to get to the bottom of it.'[63]

Hence the need for a leap into irrationalist intuition and into the inner life. 'The possession of "race" in our *own consciousness* carries immediate conviction as nothing else does. Any member of a decidedly pure race will sense the fact all the time.'[64] This 'argument' was of great import for the future of racialism. For here Chamberlain was reversing the issue: intuition was not intended to judge the truth or falsity of an objective set of facts, but itself determined the racial standing of the inquirer, and anyone who did not have this intuition would be proved a cross-breed, a bastard, by dint of that very fact. Thus Chamberlain proudly announced as the essence of his method: 'Without troubling myself about a definition, I have demonstrated what race is in my own breast, in the great deeds of genius, and on the

glittering pages of human history.'[65]

So here the most utterly subjective arbitrariness was laid down as a 'method'. (We can readily see how close Chamberlain's methodological efforts came to Nietzsche on the one hand, and to the intuition theory of Dilthey's 'descriptive psychology' and phenomenological 'intuition of the essence' on the other.) This obscurantist tendency was summed up in myth. Aspirations to myth were widespread in the imperialist period, especially in Germany. Agnosticism was crossing the border into mysticism, while mysticism and myth had a twofold function – this was already so with Nietzsche. Above all, mysticism helped to reduce every objective observation to the level of a mere myth. Empiriocriticism, the neo-Kantian philosophy of 'As If' and pragmatism were constantly operating in the epistemological field with a related method. Chamberlain exploited thoroughly all the achievements of this neo-Kantianism, whose major representatives such as Cohen or Simmel he repeatedly showered with praise (even though they were Jews); and he took this mythical line of thought to a radical close. Thus he said of Darwinian theory that it was 'simply a fiction, a useful and salutary figment of the imagination'.[66] So it was evident, according to Chamberlain, 'that Aristotle simply substituted one myth for another . . . and that is because no philosophy can manage without myths – myths not just as emergency aids and to fill a few gaps, but as a basic element that carries through the whole'.[67]

The really philosophical standpoint, in Chamberlain's view, consisted in an awareness of the mythical character of all thinking. The first efflorescence of philosophy, that of ancient India, was clear on that point; the Indian philosophers 'well knew that their myths were myths'.[68] Men had lost sight of this truth in the course of the later European development, and Kant was the first to regain the correct philosophical attitude: 'With Kant, man first attains to awareness about his own myth-forming.'[69] That, according to Chamberlain, was Kant's 'Copernican deed'. In this way

Chamberlain reassured his modern readers of the continuing validity of natural scientific development (in its details, in specialist research); all that needed challenging was the claim to objective truth. For, Chamberlain stated, the value of science 'is not its substance of truth – this, after all, is only symbolic – but its usefulness as a practical method and its importance in shaping imagination and character'.[70]

The appeal to praxis we have already encountered in Nietzsche and Dilthey. A real social need was at stake here. All relevance to the major problems of mankind's development, and consequently to human praxis, had vanished from standard bourgeois thinking. In view of the strict, and ever-increasing, scientific specialization forced upon academic science and philosophy by the capitalist division of labour, and in view of the agnosticism now dominating them, it was impossible for them to satisfy this concretely existing need on the basis of their own methodology. As we have noted, not even so outstanding a contemporary figure as Max Weber was able to pose these questions rationally, let alone answer them, through the insights of (bourgeois) science as it had become in the course of (capitalist) development. And at the same time, the irresistible nature of this need for solutions resulted in a transference of such propositions and answers to a fundamentally irrationalist 'faith'. Chamberlain, like Nietzsche before him, unscrupulously accomplished what Max Weber undertook with many reservations: he set up myth as the era in which these answers could emerge spontaneously. To that end, science had to be downgraded to an unconscious myth, and the imperialist age's extreme relativism offered the most varied starting-points for such an interpretation. Simmel, as we have seen, was already aiming at abolishing scientific progress relativistically, and placed myth-forming and science on a single plane. With Simmel, therefore, science was already half-aware of its mythical character, and Chamberlain had to go only one step further to interpret Kant's epistemology as this growing self-consciousness of the mythical, fictive basic character of every

view of the world. (Relativistically-minded modern liberal thinkers, while becoming very sharply opposed to the 'dogmatic' aspect of materialism, were extremely patient towards and indeed full of sympathetic understanding for the most obscurantist intellectual trends of the time. Here again we see that objectively, this relativism of theirs was assisting the birth of fascist ideology.)

It is also readily visible that the theory of myth and forming of myth appeared the most viable philosophical path to praxis on an imperialist basis. For not only was this path, as we have noted, inaccessible to the specialist scientific disciplines (and imperialist bourgeois philosophy, as long as it did not pass into the mythical sphere, was likewise a specialist science). It was also more and more evident that the old religious philosophies handed down through history were similarly unable to serve as signposts. Their philosophy and the praxis resulting from it were not intimately enough related to contemporary problems to effect the connection. Old reactionary thinking sought to unite the outlook and ethos of the traditional religions with modern philosophical needs. But recognizing the new situation, the new reactionaries sanctioned the concrete break intellectually and undertook to create through myth not only a fresh philosophy, but also a seasonable substitute for religion. This was what distinguished the new from the old reaction.

But the doctrine of myth had another positive side to it: the justification of mere inner experience, of irrationalism and intuitionism raised to a philosophy. Now this is where Chamberlain's renewal of religion came in. Its starting-point was a critique of contemporary culture. Here Chamberlain too proceeded from the fashionable antithesis between civilization and culture which played a cardinal role in imperialist vitalism. Culture was the Germanic and also the aristocratic element; civilization by itself, on the other hand, was Western European, superficial, Jewish, democratic. But for all the superiority of culture over mere civilization, and of the Germanic race over the lower ones, the Germanic

character had one crucial, dangerous failing: it lacked an indigenous religion. Chamberlain regarded it as his chief task to summon and restore to life this religion, and in this sense he was carrying on Lagarde's life-work.

The line of the 'genuine' Germanic Aryan religion traced by Chamberlain ran via ancient India to Christ, and from the latter to Kant. In this respect ancient India, before it was ruined by miscegenation, was in a far more advantageous position: 'There, religion is also the transmitter of science . . . , whereas here, all genuine science has always been in conflict with religion.'[71] The division between religion and science 'is the acknowledgement of an official lie. This lie, which is vitiating the life of the individual and society, . . . derives solely from the fact that we Indo-Europeans . . . have stooped so low as to accept Jewish history as the basis and Syro-Egyptian magic arts as the crown of our supposed "religion".'[72] The superiority of ancient Indian philosophy lay in the fact that it was 'a-logical' and 'that logic does not rule its thinking, but serves it only when needed'. Indian philosophy was an esoteric knowledge beyond 'all concern with proofs'.[73] Here we see clearly whence and whither Chamberlain's path was leading. He proceeded from that alienation from religion which formed the starting-point for the expansion of modern religious atheism. At the same time he was in league with those who proposed to overcome this alienation through a new, 'purified' religion. Thus he was continuing the thought of both Nietzsche and Lagarde. His solution was amazingly simple: that rupture with reason and science which vitalism proclaimed as a scientific or philosophical reform Chamberlain declared to be the new religion. For the pre-war period, this (simple, all too simple) solution meant too sudden a break with all scientific thinking on the one hand, and was too uncompromising with regard to the 'tragic' postures of religious atheism on the other. So Chamberlain – precisely among the intellectual élite – was still an outsider during this period. It was for that very reason that fascism proper was able to turn him into a classic:

Chamberlain raised vitalism to just that pitch the fascists required.

From what has been stated we can already perceive the connection between this issue and racialism. For Christ took the big step towards renewing Aryan philosophy, in Europe only, with the saying: The Kingdom of God is within. Christ signified 'the appearance of a new human type'; 'only with him did mankind obtain a *moral culture*'.[74] Here, to be sure, Chamberlain faced the difficulty of 'proving' that Christ had nothing to do with the Jewish race. His excuse was that Christ's teaching had been racially tainted by Judaism and by the tribal chaos of Rome in its decline. As stated, Kant was the first to adopt the Aryan Germanic standpoint again, and the first to show that religion was 'a generating of the idea of God from the depths of one's heart'.[75]

In general Chamberlain's exegesis of Kant followed the purely agnosticist line of imperial neo-Kantianism, but with an even greater dose of mysticism. Thus he wrote of the 'thing-in-itself': 'The thing cannot be dealt with apart from the subject. A thing "in itself" detached from the reason or, to put it more plainly, a thing "for no reason" is even more of a non-idea than a non-thing, for understanding and reason alone create unity in diversity. They alone, therefore, engender "thing". This is not because nothing exists outside of reason, but because the reason alone has shaping power.'[76]

Only this interpretation of Kantian doctrine could, in Chamberlain's view, provide the Germanic world with an indigenous religion, a real religious culture. A terrible backwardness was prevailing in Europe in this respect: 'With regard to religion, we Europeans are roughly at the point where the Hottentots stand in relation to science; what we call religion is an empirical mish-mash, and our theology (of all denominations) is, in Kant's judgement, "a magic lantern of chimeras".'[77] This backwardness needed dispelling. If the mystical obscurantism preached by Chamberlain were to hold sway in Europe, it would open up future prospects for the Aryan race.

But why those vast distances in time? For as we know, many centuries separate ancient India from Christ and the latter from Kant. Here was enacted precisely the essential substance of Chamberlain's philosophy, the racial struggle. The struggle was between the Aryan Germanic people of light and the powers of darkness, Judaism and Rome. With this Chamberlain's thinking, which as expounded so far differed little from ordinary imperialist vitalism, took on the 'original' slant that pointed into the fascist future. Similarly, Chamberlain repudiated world-history both in methodology and in content. He wrote: 'As soon as we speak of *mankind* in general, and fancy that we see in history a development, progress, education, etc., of "mankind", we are leaving the firm ground of facts and floating in airy abstractions. For this mankind that has been already philosophized about so much suffers from the severe weakness that it does not even exist.'[78] Only races existed. The theory of mankind 'is obstructing all correct insight into history'; it had 'to be painstakingly dug out like weed . . . before we may state the patent truth with any hope of being understood: our present civilization and culture is specifically Germanic and the exclusive work of the Germanic race'.[79]

Here Chamberlain was expressing with great candour the viewpoint that all previous ideas of mankind and humanity must be abolished so that the 'patent truth' of Germanic world mastery could become a philosophy. It is only logical that Chamberlain, like Gobineau and the Social Darwinists, acknowledged progress and decay only in the individual races. Chamberlain, however, differed from his predecessors in that he linked racial theory with a historical perspective. He thereby surmounted both the racial pessimism of Gobineau and other French adherents to racialism and also the scientific monism of the Social Darwinists, whose theory similarly yielded only a resigned insight into the ineluctable motions of the cosmos. This, of course, meant the absolute glorification of the Germanic race and an absolute rejection of everything non-Germanic. In setting up this perspective,

Chamberlain came very near to vulgar pan-German propaganda. But he differed from it on two counts. One was that he stood in a close relationship to vitalism, whereas that propaganda was much more backward and unmodern philosophically. And closely connected with this was the fact that Chamberlain's historical theory and perspective, though as reactionary and hostile to progress as the pan-Germans', were less avowedly bound to the *Junker* status quo of Prussian Germany. While this too forced something of an outsider role upon Chamberlain before the First World War, it was just this that directly linked him with the new, post-war reaction, with fascism. Thus Chamberlain wrote of contemporary culture: 'What is not Germanic in it is . . . the germ of a disease . . . , or foreign cargo sailing under a German flag . . . until, that is, we sink these pirate vessels with lead.'[80] For 'the most sacred of duties . . . is to serve the Germanic race'.[81]

Chamberlain now expressed this philosophical allegiance to German imperialism with the most brutal cynicism: 'Nobody can prove that Germanic supremacy is a blessing for all the Earth's inhabitants; from the beginning right up to the present, we have seen the Germans slaughtering whole tribes and peoples . . . so as to procure room for themselves.'[82] Here Chamberlain was perpetuating the Nietzschean line of indirect imperialist apologetics, the 'blond beast' line that so many of Nietzsche's liberal admirers would prefer to regard as non-existent or inessential to him. But at this juncture it is plain how necessary and how central this particular line was to both of them, to Nietzsche as well as Chamberlain. In other respects they may have greatly differed, and a big difference in stature may have separated Nietzsche the literary stylist and psychologist of culture from Chamberlain. But both stood out from the other vitalists and racialists in that they strove to provide a historical perspective for the imperialist age on the basis of a pessimistic cultural critique. But what kind of perspective might that be, if not an imperialist one? And if it was an imperialist one, then what else could it

contain – as its essential tenet – but the myth of imperialist aggression and inhumanity? Where this perspective was lacking, all that could emerge was a scepticism bordering on nihilism, a state of despair or of resignation as 'the final wisdom', as reflected in the history of vitalism from Dilthey and Simmel to Heidegger and Klages. Objectively considered, the imperialist period could follow one of only two courses: it could either approve imperialism along with its world wars, its subjugation and exploitation of colonial peoples and its own masses, or else imperialism could be effectively repudiated, the masses could revolt and destroy monopoly capitalism. The thinking man had to side openly and firmly, either for or against. Otherwise his life, no matter whether he sympathized with imperialism as with fascism or disliked them, could only end without prospects, in despair. (We have already repeatedly illustrated the objectively positive service to fascism of the philosophy of despair.) Nietzsche and Chamberlain, to be sure, differed not only in stature but also in their closeness to the concrete realization of imperialism. Nietzsche was merely its prophet; hence the general, abstract, 'poetic' form of his imperialist myth. Chamberlain was already more active, a direct participant in the ideological preliminaries to the First World War. Hence we can already clearly discern in him the outlines of bestial imperialism à la Rosenberg and Hitler.

With Chamberlain, racialism already served to give this bestiality a clear conscience. For those belonging to the other races, he claimed, were not human beings in the proper sense of the word. Even when speaking about abstractly epistemological issues, Chamberlain did not omit to add that truth, too, exists only for the chosen race: 'When I say "peculiarly true", I mean peculiarly true for us Germans.'[83] This exclusion of the non-Germanic remainder of mankind from all natural right and capacity for culture permeated the whole of Chamberlain's so-called philosophy. Pure racial attributes constituted a definitive, biological-aristocratic selection principle. Thus Chamberlain wrote of Indian philosophy:

'Indian philosophy is aristocratic to the core . . . it knows that the highest perceptions are accessible only to the chosen, and that the chosen individual can only be trained if he has specific physical racial qualifications.'[84] That a 'democracy of absolute equality'[85] was known to Judaism and Mohammedanism indicated their members' racial inferiority.

Thus Chamberlain originated the racialist substitute for world-history. Along with the history of mankind, the old division of antiquity, Middle Ages and the modern period was also rejected. Even the idea of the Renaissance seemed absurd to Chamberlain. For him there were only individual Aryan racial cultures (India, Persia, Greece, Rome, the medieval Teutonic empires, modern Germany), and they decayed as a result of miscegenation, of bastardization. Chamberlain's most important concept in his account of the forces opposing Aryan supremacy was the 'tribal chaos' arising in consequence of Roman territorial dominance. Here a universal miscegenation ensued and gave rise to the danger of a cultural decline. The Germanic peoples came to the rescue. Everything that was great and good and stood for high culture, whether in Italy or in Spain, was the work of descendants of the Germanic conquerors. Everything that was dangerous or bad and lacking in culture was represented, in this struggle, as the product of Judaism and tribal chaos – of which the Roman Catholic Church, according to Chamberlain, was the organized epitome and ideological guardian. Thus the whole of history since the decline of the Roman Empire amounted to a conflict between the Germanic bringers of light and Jerusalem and Rome, the powers of darkness.

This conflict determined the association of religion and racialism in Chamberlain's conception. As Chamberlain 'proved', Christ was no Jew. The religion he had founded was the strict negation of the Jewish religion. The latter was an 'abstract materialism' and a 'worship of idols'.[86] Kant's great achievement lay precisely in his having 'overthrown Nus-Jahwe for good'.[87] Therewith Chamberlain obtained a complete merger of the hitherto separate trends of imperialist

reaction: vitalistic irrationalism and racial theory. This abolition of Judaism and Jewish traditions in philosophy was here tantamount to the destruction of reason. The vitalist-irrationalist undermining and dissolution of thinking and reason thereby acquired a clear, myth-like, universally tangible shape and began to leave the narrow confines of lecture platform and literary periodical. But at the same time, racialism was shaking off its positivist-scientific sobriety: an intellectual and moral climate was originating in which it could become a religious substitute for desperate and fanatically aroused masses. Here, admittedly, Chamberlain was only the 'prophet', the herald of the man to come. But the latter had nothing new to add to Chamberlain's doctrine in content or methodology: he had only to adjust it for mass consumption.

According to this doctrine, the (Aryan) Christ's and Christianity's great achievement had been already totally distorted by the half-Jew Paul and especially by Augustine, the product of the 'tribal chaos'. As a counterpart and antithesis to Judaic abstract materialism, the Roman church allegedly gave rise to a 'magical materialism'[88] that was equally dangerous for the indigenous Germanic outlook. Again Chamberlain was a direct precursor of Hitler and Rosenberg in that he branded philosophically as materialism all that he found devilish (everything Jewish, all miscegenation). This too indicates how much all these polemics were primarily aimed against dialectical and historical materialism as the one serious adversary of imperialist ideology. It also shows, on the other hand, that this supposedly self-evident, groundless denigration was only possible on the basis of the preparatory work performed by the imperialist age's anti-Marxist agnosticism. Chamberlain wrote:

> The coupling of the Aryan with the Jewish spirit, and of both with follies of the nationless, religionless 'tribal chaos', is the major danger. The Jewish spirit, had it been adopted in its pure form, would have perpetrated far less

> damage . . . but as it is, it infiltrated the sublime world of Indo-European symbolism and freely creative, versatile formative energy. Like the South American poisoned dart, this spirit pierced and paralysed an organism which alone possesses life and beauty throughout the process of re-creation . . . At the same time, this dogmatic spirit transfixed as permanent religious components the silliest and most repugnant superstitions believed by miserable slaves. What had formerly been good for the 'common man' (in Origen's view) or for slaves (as Demosthenes jeered) had henceforth to be believed by the princes of the mind on penalty of eternal damnation.[89]

Thus the Aryan religion of Christ was twisted into the Roman church of tribal chaos. This distortion, Chamberlain asserted, determined European history from the period of the tribal migrations to the present day: it was 'the foundation of the nineteenth century'. For this struggle had not yet been fought to the very end; the Germanic North's rebellion against the tribal chaos of Southern Europe had not yet led to a real victory. Although, as the latest branch of the Aryan race, the Germanic people was the legitimate 'master of the world', it found itself in a problematic situation regarding its claims and its chances of rule. These, Chamberlain thought, could only be realized through a radical conquest of the elements of Judaism and tribal chaos in religion, through the birth of an indigenous Germanic religion. Thus with Chamberlain, racial theory became the 'universal philosophy', the ideological tool of Wilhelmine imperialism's aggressive claims to global mastery.

After what has been stated so far, we can readily understand that Chamberlain pursued a keen pan-German propaganda in the First World War and that he joined Hitler's side after Germany's defeat. His many war pamphlets contain little that is new in relation to what we have previously expounded. They emphasize the basic anti-democratic aspect of his tendencies more sharply than his theoretical writings;

even before the war he advised Wilhelm II to blow up the *Reichstag* in order to clear the road for his plans. The Germans' vocation as masters of the world was also given a more marked prominence in these pamphlets than in the previous writings, and along with the central, religio-racial problem, the elimination of democracy and establishment of rule by the chosen few was increasingly stressed as an internal obstacle to be overcome. The significance of Prussia also received a stronger affirmative note than before. Polemicizing against the contrast of Weimar and Potsdam widely drawn by Anglo-democratic circles in particular, Chamberlain wrote: 'The foreigner who professes to like a Germany without Prussia is . . . either a fool or a scoundrel.'[90] Naturally the German imperialist facets of his programmatic bias emerge from these writings nakedly, without 'philosophical' trappings. He emphasized quite openly that German world-mastery was at stake; a victory in Europe did not mean the end of the struggle, and they had to conquer and subjugate the whole world. The issue, to Chamberlain's mind, was that of global dominion or perdition: the Germany he envisaged could not be other than aggressively imperialist; 'if Germany does not rule the world . . . then she will disappear from the map; it is a matter of Either-Or'.[91] So Chamberlain's racialist philosophy logically contributed to the propaganda of the then most aggressive and reactionary group of German imperialists, the pan-Germans.

5. The 'National-Socialist Philosophy' as the Demagogic Synthesis of German Imperialist Philosophy

We now see that in the form of a so-called philosophy for decadent reactionary intellectuals, and in a war propaganda for barbarized, chauvinistic bourgeois philistines, the outlines of 'National-Socialist philosophy' were virtually complete. It only remained to convey it to the streets from the salons,

cafés and common rooms. Hitler and his henchmen accomplished this final step in the development of reactionary extremism in Germany. In doing so, they fully acknowledged the services of Chamberlain. Rosenberg himself wrote a book on him, and after the seizure of power he once stated, in order to warn fascist 'fellow-travellers' and to offer them a guideline, that National Socialism recognized only Richard Wagner, Nietzsche, Lagarde and H.S. Chamberlain as its real ancestors.[92]

But we must by no means overestimate Chamberlain's significance. He represents only a penultimate literary summing up of the most reactionary lines of thought in the German (and international) development. German fascism itself was an eclectic synthesis of all the reactionary tendencies, but because of Germany's specific development they evolved more strongly and firmly here than in other countries. In number they were unlimited, while their differences, despite the shared reactionary character, were very considerable.

Having discussed already the special conditions under which German developed, we can now refer to them again under headings (the Thirty Years' War, ducal State absolutism, capitalism's late development, Bismarck's founding of the Reich with the Prussian *Junker* class supreme, and with quasi-parliamentarism allied to the preservation of Hohenzollern 'personal rule', etc.). The result of these was that hardly one bourgeois ideological strain did not, in some form, assist an accommodation to the German reality, a reconciliation with it, and thus have a reactionary aspect. And in the imperialist period's revival of the classic philosophers (Kant, Fichte, Schelling, Hegel), bourgeois thinkers showed a sure class instinct by constantly appropriating precisely their reactionary sides. Bringing these into prominence, they 'purged' the old philosophies of their progressive foundations and tendencies.

Thus Kant was thoroughly 'purged' of his wavering between materialism and idealism (Lenin); thus Rickert's reactionary neo-Kantian school exploited the later Fichte's

irrationalism to extend neo-Kantianism; thus Eduard von Hartmann revived the later Schelling's philosophy, whose reactionary character was expressed more strongly and effectively still in the subsequent influence of Kierkegaard. Thus neo-Hegelianism used Hegel's reconciliation with the reality of Prussia to turn him into a precursor of Bismarck and to expand his philosophy in general – thoroughly 'purged' of all dialectics – into that of conserving German backwardness, into a synthesis of all reactionary trends. Then there were the thinkers whose basic tendencies were reactionary from the start, such as Schopenhauer, the Romantics (chiefly Adam Müller, Görres, etc.) and Nietzsche. Fascism, inheriting the collective legacy of Germany's reactionary development, used it in order to establish a bestial imperialism in home and foreign affairs.

National Socialism was a major appeal to the worst instincts of the German people. Above all, it appealed to those bad qualities formed in the course of centuries as a result of failed revolutions and the lack of a democratic German development and ideology. (Engels spoke of the 'servility that had penetrated the national consciousness as a result of the humiliation of the Thirty Years' War'.[93]) The modern form of this servility was a complete failure to recognize that in spite of the growth of German capitalism, and in spite of the outward military might of the Prussianized German Reich, the 'German misery' had continued to prevail at home almost unchanged. But with most ideologists, there was far more to it than simply a failure to perceive this state of affairs. On the contrary, they evolved more and more powerfully an ideology which saw in this preservation of the 'German misery', in the quasi-constitutional character of Bismarck's Reich, and in the unchallenged supremacy of reactionary Prussianism, *Junker* rule, Prussian militarism and bureaucracy, a higher form of social structure and political constitution than that evolved in the West in the train of bourgeois revolution. In the imperialist age, as we know, the Western democracies, because of the abrupt

emergence of the contradictions and limitations of bourgeois democracy, gave rise to an increasingly broad and pointed critique of democracy as a whole. But in Russia, this criticism was already growing into an ideological negation of liberalism among the revolutionary democrats, especially Chernyshevsky. And Lenin, during the imperialist period, used a consistent Marxist critique of bourgeois democracy to extend the Marxian doctrine of the dictatorship of the proletariat and proletarian democracy, thus putting in a more concrete form than Marx himself the theory of the transition from capitalism to socialism. In Western Europe, on the other hand, the critique of democracy was only operating between the extreme and erroneous poles of ultra-reaction and anarchism or syndicalism in the labour movement. Although the German imperialist ideologists enthusiastically adopted this critique, they used it only in order to pass off a Prussianized Germany as a higher, forward-looking social and political form surmounting the contradictions of democracy. The adoption of the Western critique of democracy thus engendered the ideology of aggressive German imperialism, the doctrine of the German 'mission' to signpost the future for mankind, and this on the very basis of a conserving of all the retrograde institutions of the 'German misery'.

This special form of the German 'mission' also created great confusion among all those thinkers inclined to be progressive in their aims, or who at least intended to fight against extreme reaction. A blind, slavish, uncritical obsequiousness towards the existing political authority of the day was coupled with an idealizing of the political and social forms of a backward Germany. It thwarted Germany's development into a bourgeois democracy, steered it into totally wrong channels and created (often involuntary) ideological support for those reactionary ways of thinking where a glorification of German backwardness corresponded to natural class interests. This contradictory nature of the German development was already strongly tangible in Stein's reform movement, and especially in Baron Stein himself. It

was manifested in the later Hegel's bureaucratic-patrician political theory, in his distortion of a correct view of the Reformation – as a kind of bourgeois revolution – to the effect that it already signified the completion of democratic revolutionary tasks in Germany. It even penetrated the labour movement with Lassalle's ever-influential political theory and created there an opportunistic legalism to a degree unknown elsewhere, an idolizing of the State in itself.

The ideology of extreme reaction first took shape intellectually on the Right wing of romanticism, in very close conjunction with the most retrograde circles of *Junker* reaction in Prussia. It received a powerful boost in that the democratic critical resistance opposing it, the democratic critical exposure of reactionary ideology in Germany, was far weaker than in any other country in the world. This even applied, save for the periods when Marx and Engels were exerting an immediate influence, to the German labour movement. In his critique of the Erfurt manifesto, Engels issued a serious warning to German social democracy for neglecting its most vital tasks in the struggle against reaction and for German democratization, and for even fostering illusions of the 'lackadaisical "coalescence" of the old shambles "with the socialist society" '.[94]

Engels' criticism was levelled against those German illusions which expected a 'coalescence' with socialism of the existing Germany, i.e., a country that had not yet become democratized and for which all the tasks of democratization, including the concrete realization of national unity – the central issue of Germany's transformation into a democracy – were revolutionary tasks. Such a road to socialism as that mooted at Erfurt was, in Engels's opinion, only liable to distract attention from the major tasks of the revolutionary democratization of Germany. And to fight for the latter could be the only correct preliminary – objective and subjective – to socialism in Germany.

But this criticism was not understood in the German labour movement. There arose the false extremes of a 'reconciliation'

with undemocratic, imperialist Germany on the one hand, and of an abstract proclamation of socialism abstractly bypassing the revolutionary democratic tasks on the other. Among the leading ideologists of German social democracy in the imperial age, Franz Mehring was practically the only one in whom the traditions of revolutionary struggle against Prussian reaction were really alive and kicking. Lenin observed and sharply criticized this turn of events at an early date: 'The republican tradition is greatly enfeebled among the socialists of Europe . . . , not infrequently the weakening of republican propaganda signifies the lack of a vital thrust towards the total victory of the proletariat in general. Not for nothing did Engels, in criticizing the Erfurt draft manifesto in 1891, devote all his energy to alerting the German workers to the importance of the republican struggle, the possibility that such a struggle would become a live issue in Germany as well.'[95]

Under these conditions, the whole of bourgeois ideology was completely saturated with reactionary forms and contents. Agnosticism and mysticism governed the thinking of even those bourgeois minds that favoured progress in their main political bias. Even racial theory infiltrated these circles; let us mention just Rathenau, later the victim of fascist assassins. Hand in hand with this went, as we have noted, the modernization of reactionary *Junker* ideology. It goes without saying that this process was not a uniform one either. The old forms and the old slogans ('For God, King and Fatherland'; '*Am deutschen Wesen soll die Welt genesen*'; recourse to orthodox Protestantism, etc.) survived until far into the Weimar Republic, influencing certain numerically limited petty-bourgeois circles; we may recall German nationalist propaganda, the 'steel helmets' and so on. But beside this there was an ever-growing need to mould the most extreme reactionary contents and most aggressive objectives of German imperialism into a form capable of winning over to its internal and external aims the broad masses of the petty bourgeoisie, farmers, intellectuals and also the workers.

Germany's defeat in the First World War gave rise to two closely linked problem complexes. They facilitated this reconstruction of extreme reactionary ideology, its 'modernization' and its efficacy among broad masses of the German people. The first complex was the general national resentment of the Treaty of Versailles. The social democrats' opportunism and the communists' weakness did not permit of a popular liberation from the humiliating burdens of the past, the consequences of the war, by way of a radical revolution, as happened in Russia. As a result of this failure in 1918, the masses were increasingly ensnared under imperialist reactionary leadership in their national aspirations. The campaign against the Treaty of Versailles, the watchword of national liberation miscarried as a slogan of the revolutionary democratic unification of the German nation and changed more and more into a revival of aggressive German imperialism.

The second problem complex, which was interwoven with the first at every point and reinforced its efficacy, was the disappointment of the masses over the social results of the 1918 rising. Hopes at that time – and they extended far into the petty bourgeoisie and intelligentsia – were running exceptionally high. The fact, therefore, that under the aegis of the Weimar Republic, the régime of Junkers allied with the big capitalists was just as oppressive as before was bound to cause immense disappointment. The great economic crisis in 1929, and the Weimar democracy's firmly reactionary economic and social policy during this crisis, only intensified it. At the same time, it became evident that no movement which aimed simply at harking back to the pre-war state of affairs (a Hohenzollern restoration) could gain a mass influence. So in the camp of reactionary extremism there sprang up a need for social demagogy: a camouflaging of aggressive imperialist goals as 'national and social revolution'.

The intervention of Hitler and his helpmates met these vital needs of the most reactionary members of the German Junker class and big capitalists. They fulfilled them by

conveying ultra-reactionary ideology, seasonably modernized, out of the salons and cafés on to the streets.

Hitler's ideology was nothing beyond an extremely crafty, cynically subtle exploitation of this set of problems. Their past activity had well equipped Hitler himself and his closest associates for the task. In Vienna Hitler had been a student of Lueger's anti-Semitic social demagogy, and later he became an agent for the *Reichswehr* in Germany. His chief ideologist, Rosenberg, was a pupil of the Black Hundred in Tsarist Russia and later likewise a German agent. Both of them, like the other German fascist leaders, were ruthless and unscrupulous hirelings of the most reactionary imperialism, demagogic front-runners for the Prusso-German policy of aggression and suppression. Hence they ceased to possess even the semblance of an ideological *bona fides*: they themselves regarded their own 'doctrine' with total cynicism and incredulous indifference. Playing with virtuosity on the German people's aforestated backward attributes, attributes corrupted through its historical development, they put this doctrine at the service of German imperialist capitalism, the big capitalists and ruling Junkers, the preservation of Prussianized Germany, the latter's expansion and its battle for global dominance.

In their speeches and writings, the fascist leaders poured out with a nauseating show of emotion their national and social demagogic, whose public second names were honour, loyalty, faith, sacrifice, etc. But when they came together in private, they spoke with the most cynical, knowing smiles of their own messages and manifestos. Today we still know relatively little of this intimate material concerning the fascist leaders.[96] Nevertheless, the fugitive Danzig leader Rauschning, for example, has published enough information on his personal contacts with Hitler and the others for us to obtain a fairly solid picture of the situation.

Here I shall give just a couple of characteristic examples. – Rauschning had a conversation with Hitler in which they discussed the central dogma of German fascism, racial theory.

Hitler voiced the following opinion on this subject: 'The "nation" is a political expression of democracy and liberalism. We must get rid of this false construction and replace it with the racial idea, which is not yet shopworn politically . . . I know very well . . . that there is no such thing as race in the scientific sense . . . As a politician I need a concept enabling us to abolish the previous historical foundations and replace them with a completely new, anti-historical order, and to put this on an intellectual footing.' Their task was to destroy national boundaries. 'With the racial concept, National Socialism can carry out its revolution and overturn the world.'[97] Here it is clear that for Hitler, racial theory was only a pretext for making attractive and plausible to the masses a wholesale conquest and subjugation of Europe and the destruction of the European peoples as distinct nations.

As we know, research into the first beginnings of the German people was closely linked with racial theory. The fascists proclaimed it one of the most important parts of their doctrine and even set up special scientific departments to investigate it. Their attitude to this special science of theirs is illustrated in a conversation which Rauschning had with the Gestapo leader Himmler. The latter, who had prohibited a German scholar from giving lectures in prehistory at Danzig, spoke about this ban to Rauschning as follows: 'It doesn't matter one bit whether this, that or the other is the real truth about the early history of the Germanic tribes. Hypotheses change every other year, and science goes from one to the next. So there is no real reason why the Party shouldn't stipulate a particular hypothesis as a starting point, even if it contradicts prevailing scientific opinion. The important thing – and this is why the State pays these fellows (the professors, G.L.) – is to have such thoughts on history as will confirm our people in the national pride it needs.'[98]

We know also how central a role anti-Semitism played in 'National Socialist philosophy' and Hitlerian propaganda. When, however, Rauschning was talking to Hitler about this question and naively asking him if he intended to exterminate

the Jews, Hitler replied: 'No. Otherwise we would have to invent them again. It is always important for us to have a visible enemy, not just an abstract one.' And when the notorious *Protocols of the Wise Men of Zion* that had figured centrally in the Hitlerites' pogrom agitation came up in the same discussion, Rauschning expressed doubts as to their authenticity. Hitler answered: 'I don't care a damn whether the story is true historically. Even if it isn't . . . , it sounds all the more convincing.'[99] To these we could add umpteen further examples, even from the limited material available on the fascist leaders' personal convictions. But those we have cited will more than suffice, I think, to illustrate the attitude of Hitler and his cronies to their own 'theory'. We should just add that Hitler, again in a conversation with Rauschning, described the central thesis of his own social demagogic, so-called Prussian Socialism, as stupid nonsense.[100]

All this clearly reflects the foundations of National-Socialist 'methodology'. But we can also readily round them out from Hitler's writings. Here too we shall refer only to a couple of main points that make it evident that, with Hitler and his colleagues, we are not simply dealing with a false and dangerous theory in need of refutation with intellectual arguments. What we are dealing with is a hotch-potch, concocted with unscrupulous demagogy, of the most diverse reactionary theories for which the only criterion was whether they would enable Hitler to hoodwink the masses.

This kind of propaganda derived, in Hitler, from a cavalier contempt for the people. He wrote: 'The people, in its overwhelming majority, is so feminine in temperament and attitude that emotional feeling determines its thoughts and actions far more than sober consideration.'[101] Here, as we can see, Hitler was translating the results of imperial 'aristocratic epistemology' and the social philosophy of 'mass concentration' (*Vermassung*) into the language of practical demagogy. It was from this viewpoint that he elaborated his propaganda methods. Suggestion was to be substituted for conviction, and a torrid atmosphere of blind faith, the hysterical faith of

men in despair, was to be engendered by all possible means. Here again the vitalist campaign against reason – irrespective of how much of it Hitler knew – formed the philosophical basis for a sheer demagogic technique. Hitler's 'originality' lay in the fact that he was the first to apply techniques of American advertising to German politics and propaganda. His object was to stupefy and defraud the masses. In his *magnum opus* he admitted that his goal was a demagogic one, that of breaking down men's free will and capacity to think. By what tricks this goal could be achieved was the only question to which Hitler devoted close and assiduous study. In so doing he examined all conceivable external details of the power of suggestion, of the susceptibility of the masses. Again, let us quote a single example:

> In all these instances, it is a matter of making inroads on man's freedom of will. Naturally this applies most to assemblies, where men of basically opposed wills come together and must now be won over to a new will. In the morning and even throughout the day, men's volitional powers seem to resist with the utmost energy any attempt to impose on them an alien will and opinion. In the evening, on the other hand, they will succumb more readily to the ruling force of a stronger act of will. For in truth, every such assembly represents a contest between two opposed forces. Now the outstanding eloquence of a dominating apostle-type will more easily convert to the fresh will men who themselves have already undergone a perfectly natural weakening of their powers of resistance than those who are still in full possession of their intellectual and volitional powers.[102]

Hitler expressed himself with the same cynicism with regard to his own party programme. He conceded that in the course of time, changes might become objectively necessary. But he automatically repudiated such changes on principle: 'Every attempt at this, however, has usually dire results. For

it throws open to discussion something that was supposed to be unshakeably firm . . . For how do we propose to instil blind faith in the correctness of a doctrine if we ourselves spread uncertainty and doubt through constant alterations to its outer structure?'[103]

This propaganda technique is connected with one of the few straight points of Hitler's 'philosophy'. Hitler was passionately opposed to objective truth, and he contested objectivity in every sphere of life. He regarded himself as the agent for a capitalist display whose purposes he was striving to achieve with ruthlessly crafty propaganda techniques – in conscious independence of any objective truth or accuracy. In this respect he was truly the clever pupil of American advertising. When he was discussing the techniques of propaganda, this intrinsic character of his sometimes found an unwittingly grotesque expression. Again, let us give one example: 'What, for instance, would you say to a poster which was intended to commend a new soap, but which also described other soaps as "good"? . . . Now exactly the same goes for political advertising.'[104]

This fusion of German vitalism and American advertising was no accident either. Both are manifestations of the imperialist age. Both appealed to the desolation and disorientation of the people of this age, to their imprisonment in a fetishized category system belonging to monopoly capitalism. They played on men's numb suffering under the system and their inability to break free from it. But the American system of advertising was aimed at the man in the street, appealing to his most immediate daily needs, and in these the objective standardization through monopoly capitalism was mingled with a vague desire – within this framework – to stay 'personal'. Vitalism, on the other hand, reached out via extremely circuitous routes to the intellectual élite, where the inner resistance to standardization was much more fiery, albeit – objectively speaking – equally hopeless. Hence advertising techniques were cynically demagogic from the outset, an immediate expression of monopoly capitalism,

whereas vitalism was for a long time pursued *bona fide* or at least with indirect, quasi-scientific and quasi-literary means. But for all their differences they were united – objectively considered – in distracting attention from all objectivity, in a one-sided appeal to feelings, experiences, etc., and in trying to eliminate and pour contempt on reason and independent, rational judgement. There was, therefore, a specific social necessity which explains why the products and the method of vitalism were conveyed to the streets with the tools of American advertising.

In that Hitler combined in his own person vitalism and monopoly capitalism, the latter's most advanced techniques, i.e., American techniques, were coupled with its most advanced imperialist reactionary ideology, i.e., the German ideology. The very possibility of this parallel, this unity indicates that we can only understand and criticize all the barbarity, cynicism and so forth of the Hitler period by considering the economics, social structure and social trends of monopoly capitalism. Any attempt to interpret Hitlerism as a revival of some barbarism or other will miss the most crucial specific features of German fascism.

It is only from the angle of these cynical, unscrupulous advertising techniques that we can accurately portray the Hitler fascists' so-called ideology. For all that they ever asked was: what use is this idea, what advantage does it have? – in total independence of objective truth which, indeed, they vehemently and scornfully rejected. (In this they were in complete agreement with modern philosophy from Nietzsche via pragmatism up to our own day.) Now, however, these coarse and muscular advertising techniques joined forces with the products of imperialist vitalism, the philosophy of the most 'refined' minds of this period. For that agnosticist irrationalism which had gone on developing in Germany from Nietzsche, Dilthey and Simmel to Klages, Heidegger and Jaspers had as its final outcome a repudiation of objective truth no less vehement than that which Hitler voiced from other motives and with other arguments. Thus vitalist

irrationalism's relevance to fascist 'philosophy' did not hang on individual epistemological findings; these, difficult and subtle, were only meant for small intellectual circles. It had to do with a general spiritual mood of radical doubt concerning the possibility of objective knowledge and the value of reason and understanding, as also with a blind faith in intuitive, irrational 'prophecies' contradicting reason and understanding. In short, it had to do with an atmosphere of hysterical, superstitious credulity whereby the obscurantism of the campaign against objective truth, reason and understanding appeared to be the last word in modern science and the 'most advanced' epistemology.

These affiliated tendencies helped to create an intellectual atmosphere facilitating the upsurge and infiltration of the fascist madness. Because of them Rosenberg, the leading National-Socialist ideologist, had a certain sympathy with the most Right-wing proponents of irrationalist vitalism. Spengler and Klages, for instance, he mentioned in approving tones, although he dismissed the concrete substance of their doctrine and regarded their whole activity as having been superseded through the birth of National Socialism. For while vitalist irrationalism was indispensable to the intellectual climate surrounding fascism, it was itself too refined, ethereal, subtle and too indirectly linked with the aims of German monopoly capitalism to be exploited directly for coarsely demagogic purposes. What was needed for these was precisely that association between vitalism and racialism which we have noted in Chamberlain. Here Hitler and Rosenberg found the intellectual tools directly applicable to their demagogic purposes – on the one hand, the 'philosophy' for a German intelligentsia infected by reaction, and on the other, the basis for a solid and brutal demagogy, a doctrine seemingly plain to everyone, with which to bemuse the masses wandering in a despairing search for salvation.

The Nazis took over from Chamberlain the 'inward' racial theory, the deciding of racial characteristics on an intuitive basis. Although their propaganda made much of so-called

physiological characteristics (shape of skull, colour of hair, eyes, etc.), intuition was the essential criterion nevertheless. One of the Hitler movement's official philosophers, Ernst Krieck, stated this relationship to biology quite openly: '"Biological philosophy", however, signifies something intrinsically different from laying philosophical foundations with the existing specialist science of "biology".'[105] Hence Rosenberg too, in his programmatic writings, talked much more about 'soul' than about objective racial characteristics. He argued this with the pronouncement: 'Soul . . . means race as seen from within.'[106] That was a direct continuation of Chamberlain's racial theory.

But we also find that Rosenberg was a zealous student of Chamberlain in all the other most important conditions. Like the latter he denied causality; like the latter he rejected any investigation of origins. And like his teacher he dismissed the existence of a universal history of mankind: only individual races, and notably the Aryans, the Germanic race, had any history. But even theirs was only a history in outward appearance. In reality, he claimed, the good in a race could not change. On this issue Rosenberg stated: 'In essence the first major mythical pinnacle of achievement is not further consummated, but simply assumes different forms. The *value* which inspirits a god or hero is perennial, in good as in evil . . . One form of Odin has died . . . But Odin as an eternal reflection of the primal spiritual powers of Nordic man is as much alive today as five thousand years ago.' And he summed up the conclusions to this postulate as follows: 'The latest possible "knowledge" of a race is already enclosed in its initial myth.'[107]

With this, vitalism's inner conflict reached its conclusion. It resolved the dichotomy between objectively anti-historical, anthropological typology and the attempt to argue, on this very basis, a (non-principled, irrationalist) theory of history. Naturally this conflict was resolved, as Chamberlain above all had foreshadowed in one way, and Spengler, Klages, Heidegger *et al*. in others, as a victory for anti-historicism and

a theoretical abolition of history. This brought to light in full clarity the objective-theoretical impossibility of comprehending history methodologically after excluding the idea of progress. If Rosenberg, here, was putting a drastic end to all imperialist pseudo-historicism, he was only drawing, in his mythical-demagogic manner, all the conclusions of a position already implicit in the cautious antinomies of a thinker like Dilthey.

This interpretation of race conformed not only to Chamberlain, but also to Gobineau. As its inevitable sequel, any transformation was viewed as only a corruption caused by miscegenation. Hence Rosenberg eagerly adopted Chamberlain's idea of 'tribal chaos' – with Roman Catholicism and Judaism as the two principal menaces. Hence, like Chamberlain, he regarded it as the central failing of Germanic life that it had no 'indigenous' religion. In view of Rosenberg's total insignificance as a thinker it would be tedious to examine where he copied Chamberlain word for word and where he modified him. What is important is the method whereby he turned Chamberlain's reactionary literary sentiments into an action programme for national and social demagogy. The heightening of Chamberlain's activist doctrine, in contrast to the fatalism of Gobineau and the Social Darwinists, was the most significant element here. Hitler and Rosenberg took up three of Chamberlain's main points: firstly, the concept of tribal chaos and resistance to it; secondly, the racial capacity for self-regeneration; and thirdly, racial theory as an up-to-date substitute for religion. All three points they demagogically exaggerated and simplified in the interests of German imperialist aggression.

As far as the first point is concerned, Rosenberg too placed Judaism and Rome at the centre of the struggle as the chief adversaries. But no longer was the campaign waged in a 'polite' literary manner of the kind which Chamberlain, especially at the outset, had displayed, with his constant deference to 'outstanding' individual Jews and Catholics. Instead there sprang up an overt and unscrupulous pogrom demagogy.

For Chamberlain, the Jews were already agents of the 'portentous' idea of equality. Now, capitalism and socialism were paired together as the consequences. They were taken as equivalents and challenged as current manifestations of 'tribal chaos'. Here again an old reactionary tradition was contributing to the social demagogy of the Hitler movement. As we know, during the nineteenth century the contradictions of the capitalist system produced everywhere a romantic anti-capitalist movement. Initially, this was of relatively substantial scientific merit because of its lively critique of these contradictions, and Sismondi went so far as to demonstrate the inevitability of economic crises in capitalism; the young Carlyle performed similar work in the social field. The 1848 revolution, the emergence of scientific socialism and its amalgamation with the revolutionary working class quickly changed the face of romantic anti-capitalism. It was, as an ideology of the petty bourgeoisie, backward-looking from the beginning (in Sismondi, towards the simple pre-capitalist production of goods; in Carlyle, towards the 'ordered economy' of the Middle Ages in contrast to capitalist anarchy). The purely ideological aspect of romantic anti-capitalism's development preserved this backward-looking tendency. And that was all the more so because the closely related tendency to oppose culture to civilization necessarily entailed a critique of the capitalist lack of culture from the standpoint of great bygone cultures. But the necessity of also forming a view on socialism, as a movement leading beyond capitalism, brought about a fundamental change of direction. The principle of 'order' was sought and located in capitalism itself to a mounting extent, although without relinquishing that critique of capitalist culture that drew its criteria from the past. But, from now on, the force that might lead away from anarchy was sought in big capitalism itself. That was already Carlyle's standpoint after the revolution in 1848. Nietzsche, as we have seen, provided the most vivid formulation of this contradictory twofold tendency on the eve of the imperialist age.

This social situation, and the intellectual situation it determined, had two consequences. Firstly, capitalism's 'good sides' had to be distinguished from its 'bad' ones. Proudhon had already made this point, and vulgar liberal apologetics were always at pains to depict the 'bad' sides as volatile, incidental features of capitalism. But this trend could only become a component of romantic anti-capitalism when an indirect apologetic began to defend the capitalist system precisely from the angle of its 'bad sides', the development of this apologetic being expected to surmount the anarchy of vulgar liberal capitalism, to bring a new 'order' nearer. In short, romantic anti-capitalism would have to be turned into an ideology of imperialist capitalism. Secondly, and in very close connection with this change, the rebuttal of socialism was coupled with this new attitude to capitalism: socialism was now presented as the continuation and extension of those anti-cultural tendencies, threats to human personality, that were being contested in capitalism. And it was expected of imperialism, of 'regulated' capitalism, that they would in practice vanquish those tendencies.

One factor aided this change of direction: the bourgeois intelligentsia's loss of all culture, all knowledge in the economic field since the collapse of classical economics. Thus the economic contrast between capitalism and socialism lay beyond the horizon of its awareness. And since socialism aimed at surmounting capitalism in a forward direction, i.e., progressively, via a higher development of the productive forces, and since by that the intellectuals understood only technology and division of labour, it was easy for such identifications of (the repudiated) capitalism with socialism to come about. One of the first to formulate this identification in an impressive way was Dostoievsky, in *Notes from the Underground*. Philosophically, Nietzsche once again was the successful proponent of this idea, summing up everything reprehensible about capitalism under the heading of democracy. Spengler and others followed suit. Thus, here again, Rosenberg was heir to an erroneous attitude that had been

long developing, and so he could easily employ it for his demagogic ends. Thus he declared war 'on the last anarchic offshoots of liberal commercial imperialism, whose victims in their despair became involved with Bolshevik Marxism in order to finish off what democracy began: the extermination of racial and national consciousness'.[108] And elsewhere Rosenberg wrote: 'Raceless authority demanded the anarchy of freedom. Rome and Jacobinism in its ancient forms and its later, purest formation in Babeuf and Lenin condition each other internally.'[109]

This interpretation of history formed, to Rosenberg's mind, the ideological basis for social demagogy. Marxism in its struggle against capital was, according to Rosenberg, falsifying the real proposition and working in the interests of international Jewry. Racialists, on the other hand, had to ask 'in *whose* hands this capital lies, and by what principles it is regulated, guided or supervised. This last issue is the crucial one.'[110] Racialism made it possible to simplify all romantic anti-capitalism's complicated thought processes into a question of ownership according to racial qualifications. Fascist social demagogy was bent on sustaining German reactionary monopoly capitalism, on saving it from the revolutionary danger which sparked off the great economic crisis. Hence this distinction by Rosenberg, and hence Feder's distinction between capital that is grasping (*raffend*) and capital that is creative (*schaffend*). In monetary and commercial capital, the non-proletarian masses saw their direct exploitation. By turning this point to advantage, and with the aid of racialist social demagogy, the extremely widespread mass bitterness at being exploited through monopoly capitalism was steered into anti-Semitic channels.

But at the same time, the Chamberlain concept of tribal chaos was also used as an argument for imperialist aggression. Those states against which German imperialism's greed for conquest was chiefly aimed were depicted as a 'racial chaos'. This applied above all to Russia, but also to France; the latter was 'scarcely to be considered a European state any

longer today, but rather an offshoot of Africa, led by Jews'.[111] Hitler too called France an 'African state on European soil'. Hitler and Rosenberg, we see, were 'arguing' the aggressive goals of German imperialism 'in principle' from racialist precepts. It is perhaps worth commenting that, here again, the fascists' so-called philosophy resembled an advertising poster which could have a new one of diametrically opposed content pasted over it when they had something different to sell. Thus when the Nazis were hoping to create a European coalition against the Soviet Union with the help of the 'Four Power Agreement', Rosenberg promptly 'forgot' all that he had written about the 'blackening' and 'befouling' of the French. The France he was trying to win as a temporary ally was suddenly no longer 'bastardized', but a farming country whose decisive basic feature had become a 'worship of the soil',[112] i.e., something positive in the eyes of 'National Socialist philosophy'.

As far as the second question, race regeneration, is concerned, Hitler expressly admitted it. He wrote: 'At the basis of it there lies a natural process of regeneration, albeit a slow one, which gradually eliminates racial impurities again as long as a basic supply of racially pure elements is still present and no further bastardization takes place.'[113] This view brought fascism into line with such optimistic racialists as Chamberlain and Woltmann as well. For these authors, however, all that would save racial purity was a complex of racial hygienic measures. And these fascism proceeded to adopt (marriage control, prohibition on marriage, etc.), but it handled them as tools of a terrible and arbitrary tyranny. Hitler knew full well that skull measurements, family trees and the like can be used to prove anything, and also the very opposite. Hence he applied these devices systematically as a means of pressure and extortion. As Ernst Krieck wrote: 'Race is assessed by the type and degree of potential achievement for the whole life of the race and nation.'[114] That amounts to saying that, on the one hand, racial purity in the fascist system is the precondition of all forward movement and indeed of any

moderately tolerable life. On the other hand, however, it depended entirely on the whim of the fascist men in power who was to be considered a member of the pure race, and who a non-member. For a Goebbels, the most suspicious appearance and the most dubious ancestry might be of no account in one instance, while somebody else who ventured to express a reservation on some issue could be instantly pronounced a mongrel and condemned as 'Jewified' in mind and character.

It is here evident why fascism appropriated Chamberlain's 'inward', intuitionist definition of race. When propagating racial theory in mass assemblies it was useful to operate with 'exact', visible and easily comprehensible racial characteristics. For the ruling machinery of fascist despotism, on the other hand, the 'inward' criterion as formulated by Krieck was the most suitable precisely because it was the most arbitrary. Thus the regeneration and preservation of racial purity were used as an instrument for keeping the whole German people in a condition of slavish obedience, and thus for inculcating that mindlessness, servility and lack of public-spiritedness which had always been hallmarks of the German distress, but which had never before reached the pitch it did under fascism and Hitler's racial policy.

It was typical of the way this fascist ethic developed that Chamberlain already presented loyalty as a specific moral attribute of Germanic man. As an example – and again this is very typical – Chamberlain cited the German mercenaries who had played a vile, cruel, always counter-revolutionary and anti-progressive role in return for money throughout Europe. The old German democrats stigmatized this mercenary period as a disgrace to Germany, but Chamberlain already saw it as a morally cardinal racial characteristic. And Krieck, when writing of the heroic man, formulated his essence as follows: 'Destiny demands of the heroic man the sense of honour which submits to every order.'[115]

But that does not exhaust the significance of this complex for the Hitler movement. On the one hand, it was exploited in

order to obtain and to establish unlimited rule by a minority in Germany herself. Rosenberg, paraphrasing Chamberlain, stated that no nation was racially unitarian, not even the German. From this it followed that the dominance of the higher-ranking, purer race (the Nordic) needed safeguarding by every possible means. Rosenberg maintained that there were at least five races in Germany, but that only the Nordic was 'bearing genuine cultural fruit'. He went on: 'This emphasizing of the Nordic race does not mean any sowing of racial hatred in Germany. It means the reverse, the conscious acknowledgement of a sanguine *cementing link* within our nationhood . . . The day that Nordic blood runs completely dry, Germany would fall apart and go to the wall in anonymous chaos.'[116] According to Rosenberg, the axiomatic carrier of this Nordic blood was the National Socialist movement; this was the 'new nobility'. Its stock was eighty per cent Nordic, and 'verification' in the movement signified more than a 'head-index count'.[117] Here we see at the same time the modernization of reactionary thought through racial theory. Although fascism retained the predominance of the Prussian *Junker* caste, it turned it into one part only of the new nobility. The Junkers had to share their old parasitical life with new parasites, the Nazi movement's upper crust. So that no part of this racially determined nobility should want for anything, fascism intended to extend each one's field of operation to immeasureable lengths. Thus Rosenberg planned to create a 'nobility of blood and achievement' on the basis of racial purity.

In the above sentences we have touched already on the further and intrinsic goal of German fascism, namely German dominance over the whole world. Fascism adopted all the old dreams of mastery and claims to dominion of the worst German chauvinism, but exceeded them many times over. If we consider this issue in connection with 'National-Socialist philosophy', we must first take a look at its aristocratic character and pseudo-biological foundation. Hitler said of racial theory that it proceeded from the higher or lesser value

of the different races. And it 'feels obliged by this knowledge, in accordance with the eternal will that rules this universe, to support the victory of the better and stronger, to demand the subordination of the worse and weaker. It thus honours in principle nature's aristocratic basic idea and believes in the force of this law down to the last individual being.'[118]

With Nietzsche and in Social Darwinism, the biological argument for the dominance of the exploiting classes and the colonizing nations was already an ideology of inhumanity. For it presented the oppressed person as a fundamentally different creature, as 'biologically' born to be exploited and enslaved. Hitler went further still. He wrote: 'So the presence of lower men was one of the most important prerequisites for the forming of higher cultures . . . It is certain that the first human culture was based less on the tamed animal than on the employment of lower men.'[119]

In racialist eyes the Aryan or German was a living being qualitatively different from the other human races in every respect. In no sphere of human activity did they speak a common language; understanding between them was impossible in principle – unless a corruption and sullying of racial purity ensued. The slightest humane feeling towards the enemies of fascism – who, according to 'inner' racial theory belonged *eo ipso* to lower races – was a sign of racial impurity in anyone who felt such an emotion. Thus fascism inculcated a dogmatic inhumanity in the whole German people; or rather, in view of our above statements, it subjected the whole people to a tyrannical pressure that forced a bestial inhumanity on all, offered rewards for it and threatened all who acted humanely with expulsion from the 'popular community', with ostracism.

The qualitative division of men into higher and lower races permeated the whole 'National-Socialist philosophy'. In the philosophical field we have already come across this doctrine in Chamberlain, and Rosenberg assiduously executed his germinal ideas in all spheres of epistemology, aesthetics,

and so on. This, however, was only an ideological foundation for the atrocious praxis of National Socialism, a praxis applied to the best of the German people from the outset, and to other nations from the start of the world war, to the horror, disgust and hatred of mankind. Hence Rosenberg, after stressing Chamberlain's merits, was quite justified in saying: 'World history as racial history is today's repudiation of this declining doctrine of *humanitas*.'[120]

The point of this theory was to induce the Germans to treat as animals all dissenters at home and members of alien races further afield: as beasts of burden and cattle for the slaughterhouse respectively. Thus the Hitler-Rosenberg type of German imperialist aggression constituted, in racialist form, a philosophy of modernized cannibalism. It extracted from racialism's reactionary theory of inequality all the barbaric consequences possible, and took them to bestial extremes. Hence the constant criticizing by Hitler and Rosenberg of the old type of chauvinism and nationalism. This critique was, in part, a demagogic intended to win over those masses who were dissatisfied with the old Hohenzollern régime, and who could never therefore be enlisted for the cause of its renewal. (Weakness of the German nationalists' propaganda.) This critique, however, was moving in the direction of a heightened aggressive chauvinism; in its own view, the old Hohenzollern nationalism had been insufficiently aggressive, far too humane and irresolute.

Hitler rebuffed the old Hohenzollern plans for colonization and expansion. He criticized especially sharply the aim of assimilating conquered nations by force through Germanization. What he advocated was extermination. It was not clear to people, he explained, 'that Germanization can only be practised on the land itself, never on human beings'.[121] That is to say, the German Reich ought to expand, conquer fertile lands and expel or wipe out their population. Long before seizing power, Hitler already had the following programme: 'The foreign policy of the national State must safeguard the existence, on this planet, of the race as

epitomized by the State by creating a healthy, sturdy and natural relationship between the number and the growth of the people on the one hand, and the greatness and goodness of the ground and soil on the other.'[122]

This fascist theory of *Lebensraum* was the basis for Hitlerite Germany's criminal attack on the Soviet Union. It is clear from Hitler's *Mein Kampf* that the fascist movement was founded on this plan from the very beginning. (Here it is interesting to note again how the fascist leaders stood with regard to their own theory. As we have seen, the so-called theoretical basis of both the internal construction and the outward aggression was the dominance of 'Nordic blood'. Hence Hitler and Rosenberg were perpetually flirting with the 'tribally related' Nordic peoples. But it turned out during the world war that these peoples were not prepared to join the European 'new order' of their own accord or to be made quislings. Thereupon Rosenberg, in a communiqué which he wrote with Hitler's secretary, Martin Bormann, suddenly declared that these peoples were not fully qualified Aryans but a mere national composite, a bastardized race with Finnish-Mongolian, Slav, Celtic-Gallic and other elements. The simultaneous 'axis' of Berlin-Rome-Tokyo, which involved going along with the Japanese imperialists, determined the propagation of the Japanese as the 'oriental Prussians'. Thus here too, racial theory for Hitler and Rosenberg was merely a propaganda instrument, a mere 'soap advertisement' for aggressive German imperialism.)

So Hitler and Rosenberg proclaimed with total cynicism the bestial idea of Germany's conquest of the world. Within Germany, S.A. and S.S. jackboots were to trample on anything that might obstruct these fiendish plans: above all, the labour movement, but also, every vestige of reason, science, humanity. In order to create the atmosphere needed to carry out the 'education' of the German masses in these atrocities, everything from the past was revived that smacked of the reactionary, chauvinistic and inhuman. In this context we must now consider the third problem complex, the resumption

of Chamberlain's plan of an indigenous German religion. National Socialism's despotic rule could tolerate no other ideological power beside itself. It was inevitable that 'National-Socialist philosophy' should evolve into a religious substitute.

Essential to this process, once again, was the modernizing tendency already visible in Chamberlain. Rosenberg, himself a decadently disorganized intellectual, had a flair for those ideological perplexities which, after the collapse of the world war, arose in Germany chiefly within the intelligentsia: a breaking away from the old religious beliefs and, at the same time, an immense need of a new belief or superstition which found expression in gullibility, obscurantism and confused searching. Accordingly he wrote: 'Millions are roaming at large between the armed forces of Marxist chaos and the adherents of the Church, inwardly in complete disorder and at the mercy of confusing dogmas and avaricious "prophets", but also driven for the most part by a powerful longing for new values and new forms.'[123] Even such a reactionary of the old school as the deposed Kaiser wrote to Chamberlain in 1923: 'The Church has failed.'[124]

Thus everywhere it went, the National-Socialist movement claimed that it was founding a new religion. Admittedly Hitler himself, before seizing power, was careful not to alienate the followers of historical beliefs whom he wanted to win over on this issue; he therefore proclaimed religious freedom and the neutrality of the National-Socialist movement on the religious question. But after coming to power, he clearly demonstrated how he interpreted religious freedom in practice with his suppression of Catholicism, undermining of the Protestant Church and persecution of recalcitrant Catholics and orthodox Protestant believers.

This tendency, however, was plainly evident from Rosenberg's writings even before the coup. Rosenberg adopted, as we have already stressed, the Lagarde-Chamberlain plan for the Germanization of Christianity. The Old Testament had to be abolished as a religious primer;[125] Jesus as a German was already one of the points in Chamberlain's

programme for religious renewal. With Rosenberg, Christ was already wearing S.A. jackboots: 'Jesus appears to us today as a self-aware master.'[126] And Rosenberg laid down in the same breath that this Aryanized, 'de-Judaized' Christianity must be rendered a supine agent of fascist imperial policy: 'But a German religious movement bent on developing into a national one will have to declare that the ideal of charity is at all costs to be subordinated to the idea of national honour.'[127]

What Hitler and Rosenberg understood by 'national honour' has emerged clearly enough from the aforegoing exposition. To create this fascist religious substitute, Rosenberg made his racial theory culminate in the myth of Germanic greatness, again through an eclectic summary of all the reactionary tendencies of a century, from romantic feudalism to imperialist vitalism. He cited as his objective: 'To embody the aspiration of the Nordic racial soul, as symbolized by popular myth, in the German Church – that is for me the greatest task of our century.'[128]

Hitler himself explained to Rauschning in 1932: 'One can only be either a German or a Christian. One cannot be both . . . One cannot turn Jesus into an Aryan, that is nonsense.' (Again it is interesting to note what Hitler thought of the racialist endeavours of his personal philosophers, Chamberlain and Rosenberg.) He went on: 'What can we do? The same as the Catholic Church did when it imposed its faith on the heathen: to conserve what is usable while changing its meaning.'[129]

All these German fascist tendencies, demagogic in form and wilfully despotic in content and nature, were concentrated in the country's political theory and practice. As we know, Germany in the modern age developed on lines different to those taken by Western Europe as also Russia. Whereas everywhere else, the dissolution of feudalism gave rise to unified nation-states, in Germany it led to a political fragmentation. Hence Lenin was right in saying that the central issue of the bourgeois revolution in Germany was the creation of national unity. In the development of Germany,

this situation produced various results which were peculiar to the country, but always unfavourable and connected with the reinforcement of reactionary ideas. Firstly, absolutism in Germany lacked those progressive features that were visible wherever it was the organ for establishing the political unity of a nation. Secondly, this line of development was connected with a belated and feeble development of the bourgeois class and with a long retention of relics of feudalism and the political predominance of the nobility. Thirdly, the bourgeois democratic revolution was weaker, less clear-cut and more susceptible to reactionary distractions than elsewhere, since its chief task was the setting up of a missing central power and not the progressive democratic transformation of one that already existed.

Naturally enough, these features also governed the development of German ideology. Marx stated the following about the belated class development in Germany linked with this trend: 'The necessary result was that during the epoch of absolute monarchy, which occurred here in its very lamest, semi-patriarchal form, the particular sphere into which the administration of public affairs fell through the division of labour acquired an abnormal independence, which modern bureaucracy took further still. The State thus constituted itself as a seemingly autonomous power and has preserved in Germany to this day a position – a transitional stage – which was only temporary in other countries.'[130] Thus in other countries the ideology of absolutism, even if it turned the State into a 'leviathan', distinctly reflected class struggles and class interests, as also the position and function of the State in these conflicts – albeit by no means fully or consciously. But in Germany, because of that backwardness we have outlined, there arose the theory of the State as the embodiment of the absolute idea, a theory which degenerated into a State mystique and idolatry. (This is also clearly visible in Hegel's law philosophy.)

Reactionary tendencies of both the nineteenth and the twentieth century proceeded along these lines in many

respects. Without question State idolatry was one of the ideological mainstays of that retrograde critique of the Western democracies, that glorification of German backwardness, of which we have repeatedly spoken. Exploiting and underlining the backward facets of Hegelian philosophy, imperialist neo-Hegelianism played a role of some significance in this development. Only, fascism was not simply a continuation of conventional reactionary trends but a qualitatively outstanding peak of Germany's reactionary development; Dimitrov rightly remarks that in fascism, one bourgeois government was not simply replaced by another, but that a change of system ensued.

Fascist demagogy with regard to the State question was very closely linked with this situation. Here, as in other fields, Hitler again adopted a demagogic pseudo-revolutionary stance in order to exploit for propaganda purposes the disappointment of the masses at Germany's political development so far and their alienation from the State. In attacking the existing political system and its ideological champions, he adopted a radical and even 'revolutionary' posture. Hitler wrote: 'We cannot have State authority as an end in itself, for in that case all tyranny on this earth would be unassailable and sanctioned . . . But in general we must never forget that the highest purpose of human existence is not to maintain a State or indeed a government, but to preserve the national character. Once, however, this itself is in danger of being suppressed or even eliminated, the question of legality will play a subordinate role . . . human rights can break political rights . . .'[131] Hitler now infers from these premises 'that the State represents not an end but a means. It may well be the precondition of a superior human culture, only it is not the cause of it. Rather this lies exclusively in the existence of a race with cultural potentialities.'[132]

Hitler's extreme anti-democratism also finds expression in this spuriously revolutionary demagogy. Again it does so, to be sure, in a mendaciously demagogic manner whereby Hitler exploited all the reactionary nonsense that German imperialist

ideologists had concocted to argue the superiority of a backward Germany to the Western democracies. Here, as in his definition of the State itself, Hitler naturally centred his agitation on the cunning demagogy of racialism. Democracy was, as Chamberlain had claimed, a Judaized institution: 'Only the Jew can praise an institution as grubby and false as himself.'[133] Hitler did not, however, oppose the old German monarchy to the despised western Jewish democracy, as did the common or garden reactionaries of the old school. As a banner for the despotic arbitrary government he was planning, Hitler devised a new demagogic watchword: Germanic democracy. As opposed to Jewish democracy, he stated, there was 'the true Germanic democracy of the freely elected leader, with his obligation to accept complete responsibility for his deeds and omissions. In this democracy, there is no majority poll on individual issues but only the ruling of a single person, who must then back his decision with his possessions and life.'[134] (The content of this demagogy also has a long preliminary history; here let us just recall Max Weber's conversation with Ludendorff.) In another passage Hitler gave an even clearer definition of the essence of 'Germanic democracy': '*Authority of every leader reaching downwards, and responsibility reaching upwards*.'[135] It will be plain to anyone familiar with German history that this so-called principle of Germanic democracy was nothing more than a modernized rehashing of the axiom of Prussia's King Friedrich II, *à propos* military organization, that the soldiers needed to fear their subalterns more than the enemy.

As a general point it must not be overlooked that this professedly new political theory of Hitler was deeply rooted in the Prusso-German political development and its thinking. Indeed, Hitler's idea of the leader was no more than a modernized, plebiscitary variant of the old Prussian king-concept, the theory of 'personal rule' by a king answerable only to God for his deeds. It was connected also with the Restoration theory of Haller, who viewed the State as the autocratically run private possession of the king; with the political theory

of the Prussian conservatives' theorist, Stahl, who was philosophically dependent on the later Schelling; and with the views of the romantic-reactionary Prussian King Friedrich Wilhelm IV, who was influenced by Haller and Stahl. This was the king who would not suffer 'a sheet of paper' (the Constitution) to stand between king and nation and encroach on the autonomous freedom of action of the divinely inspired king, and so forth.

'Germanic democracy' was of course a brusque denial of human equality. Hitler wrote: 'It does not dawn on this depraved bourgeois world that it is truly committing a sin against all reason; that it is a criminal folly to train a congenital semi-ape until he looks like a barrister, while millions belonging to the most highly bred race have to remain in wholly unworthy positions.'[136] Rosenberg formulated with even more brutal cynicism this racial doctrine of the inequality of men as a matter of principle. In 1932, in connection with the Potempa trial and the death sentence passed on a number of swinish Nazi butchers of working people, Nazis whom Hitler assured of his sympathy in a telegram, Rosenberg voiced his thoughts thus: 'This reveals the vast chasm which will divide for ever *our* thinking, *our* sense of justice from liberalism and reaction. It is characteristic of the "justice" prevailing today and encrusting all the people's healthy instincts of self-preservation that one man be deemed equal to another.'[137]

At first glance we are here dealing merely with a brash and hollow demagogy intended to exploit the disappointment of the masses with the Weimar Republic and to stir them into pseudo-revolutionary – in reality, counter-revolutionary – activity. But much more than this was at stake. To be sure, the Hitlerian State brought about a ghastly realization of all reactionary dreams about the 'omnipotence' of the State. Never was there a State so immeasurably powerful, never a despotism that could interfere so freely with the whole of men's lives. But here again, we are dealing not with straightforward wilful encroachments, but with the fiendishly

tyrannical nature of the fascist State. The National-Socialist régime, said Stuckart, a Secretary of State, 'embraces comprehensively the earthly existence of the German'. That is to say, the State was entitled to intervene at will in every single aspect of an individual's life. And Hitlerian fascism rejected as a matter of principle any protection of individual rights and any legal safeguard. That again would be liberalism. The liberal view of the State, Stuckart continued, 'placed the individual and society in antithesis to the State in that it thought it necessary to make provision for freeing the State citizen from the bonds of a paramount political force and for protecting his personal rights from State interference'.[138] German fascism destroyed these safeguards of the personal rights of the individual.

Thus after Hitler's coup, the pseudo-revolutionary demagogic polemic against the old political theories turned into a substantiation of the absolute, unlimited despotism of the Hitler clique. Its 'political theory' served primarily to give this unlimited and arbitrary despotism a 'theoretical' basis and to wipe out justice and the safeguarding of justice both in theory and in practice in the fascist State. Rosenberg formulated clearly the fascist theory of justice by resorting to a purportedly ancient Indian legal precept: 'Justice is that which Aryan men hold to be right.'[139]

Before seizing power, Hitler had already programmatically opposed equality before the law in a political context by distinguishing, for the benefit of the future State, between the racially pure citizen and the member of the State who enjoyed no rights at all. This principle was executed in the fascist State on the basis of 'inner' racial theory. The aforesaid Secretary of State, Stuckart, argued that the conferring of State citizenship on any individual followed 'an individual test of his worthiness', but 'who is to be regarded as having a racial affiliation of blood is not expressly stated in the laws'.[140] Decisions on this were subject to the unlimited arbitrariness of Hitler's ruling clique.

Fascism now likewise advanced this arbitrariness as a

'principle', again making a demagogic appeal to that bitterness which the democratic State's formal equality before the law had evoked in the broad masses in view of the crying material inequality. The new Reich, wrote Stuckart, 'is no longer a constitutional State . . . , but a philosophical State based on German customs'. With reference to the evolution of justice in the Hitler State, Stuckart now laid down that all the old legal categories, including those of the constitution, had lost their substance. 'The formal constitutional concept has . . . lost its meaning for the German Reich.'[141]

Thus the population was totally lacking in rights and absolutely dependent on the whims of the ruling Hitler clique. The explanation provided to account for this condition was that the National-Socialist State was breaking with the old 'bourgeois' neutrality and objectivity of the earlier State. It was again intended to use the anger of the masses at the older State's hypocritical impartiality to win credulous acceptance of this fascist despotism as marking a step forward. Another fascist Secretary of State, Roland Freisler, President of the Supreme Court, said: The State 'consciously makes itself the fighter for National-Socialist philosophy among the German people . . . The starting point and the goal of all action is not the individual but the people in its perennial sequence of generations.'[142]

'Germanic democracy' was, according to fascist propaganda, thereby realized on an institutional basis. That its substance was in reality the complete negation of any popular influence on political decisions is evident from what we have expounded so far. But Nazi propaganda aimed at presenting this enslaved condition, this institutionalized servility, as a general raising of the people's political awareness. The Reich's chief Press officer, Otto Dietrich, clearly illustrated how the Nazis envisaged this 'Germanic democracy' and politicizing of the nation. 'National Socialism', Dietrich wrote, 'does not ask of the individual that he pursue politics. This art is reserved for a few men who have a calling and mission. But it asks each single member of the German

people to think and feel politically.' This political thinking 'is not complicated, not confusing or scientifically problematic. It is simple, clear and unified.' And Dietrich also explained what he meant by that. For the *Führer* was the 'executor of the will of the people', not however through election but in consequence of 'that immanent will to self-affirmation inherent in every nation according to racial blood'.[143]

All this masquerade of 'Germanic democracy' was no more than the boundless dictatorship of the *Führer* (i.e., through his agency, the dictatorship of the most reactionary and aggressive section of German monopoly capitalism). The tremendous enslavement and mindless servility to which it gave rise is most clearly stated in the introduction to that compilation from which we have quoted Stuckart, Freisler and Dietrich. In it we read the following: All real decision rests with the *Führer*; if he decides otherwise than is set out in this – official – compilation, 'then National Socialism has not changed its views on the matter, but the author has mistaken the true attitude of National Socialism to this particular problem'.[144]

This *Führer* dictatorship could produce only lackeys and profiteers of the most reactionary and aggressive part of German imperialist reaction. Its 'Germanic democracy' reared the repulsive type of a human breed that was boundlessly servile to men of higher rank, and just as boundlessly, cruelly tyrannical towards men below it. The German *Misere* constantly produced the elements of such a type within the German people. If we look at Germany's progressive literature, we find that it takes this type as its butt time and again. (In, for instance, Heinrich Mann's novel *Man of Straw*, which portrays the Wilhelmine manifestation of the type with devastating satire.) But what had hitherto grown up spontaneously, as it were, from German backwardness and its ideological idealization now became a conscious product of Hitler's 'work of education'.

Not for nothing did Hitler and Rosenberg, in works fundamental to fascist philosophy, occupy themselves with

the questions of morality and education in great detail. Rosenberg placed honour at the centre of Aryan-Germanic morality just as Chamberlain had put loyalty at its centre. What we are to understand by Rosenberg's 'honour' is already patent from what we have discussed so far. It was an empty, high-flown cliché meant to provide a demagogic camouflage for the Hitlerites' total amorality. Hitler voiced this amorality with similar clarity in private conversation with Rauschning: 'Moralistic platitudes are essential for the masses. There could be no greater mistake for a politician than to be seen posing as the immoral superman ... Of course I shall not make it a matter of principle whether or not to act immorally in the conventional sense. I do not abide, you see, by any principles whatever – that's all.'[145]

Now how Hitler envisaged his 'work of education' in concrete terms, he also told Rauschning in no uncertain manner. The latter expressed objections to the abuses going on in the concentration camps. Hitler replied: '*Brutality is respected* ... The ordinary man in the street only respects brute force and ruthlessness ... The people need to be kept in a salutary state of fear. They *want* to fear something ... Why make a fuss over brutality and wax indignant over tortures? The masses want it. They want something that will give them shudders of terror.'[146]

This, however, was only one aspect of the 'work of education', the aspect turned towards the broad masses. For the fascist upper crust, Hitler had already the watchword of limitless corruption, 'Get rich!'. On this subject too he spoke to Rauschning candidly and cynically: 'I allow my men every liberty ... Do as you like, but don't get caught at it ... Have we pulled things out of the mire just to be sent home empty-handed?' But for Hitler, this 'Get rich!' had a further 'educational' advantage: if the crimes of unreliable Party members were known, one had greater control over them. Spying and mutual denunciation would begin in the 'Party élite': 'Each man is in everyone else's power, and nobody remains his own master. That is the desired result

of the slogan "Get rich!" '[147]

Now since the whole of the Third Reich pivoted on a hierarchy of the leader and his following, a structure reaching from caretaker to Chancellor, the cynical Hitlerian method with its mixture of corruption and brutalization was able to pervert morally the broadest sections of the German nation. It faced the choice of becoming corrupt hangmen or victims of torture, and this systematic pressure now gave rise to the barbaric type of the Hitler soldier, from whose atrocities all Europe suffered until the Allied victories put an end to his rampaging.

The Hitlerites made a principle of barbarity. Hitler spoke to Rauschning about it at the time of his conflicts with the Hugenberg German nationals: 'They regard me as an unwashed barbarian . . . Yes, we are barbarians. We want to be. The name is an honourable one. *We* shall rejuvenate the world!'[148] (As may be recalled, Nietzsche first voiced this thought, the truth of which was realized in the imperial world war.) In Germany the Hitler régime illustrated the nature of this 'rejuvenation' with its horrible deeds, as did Hitler's army in every corner of Europe. But such deeds – and we can never stress this too heavily – were not isolated excesses but the inevitable consequence of the Hitler régime; it was just what Hitler had intended. On this subject, too , he spoke to Rauschning with candour in private conversation: 'My doctrine is a tough one. Every weakness must be driven out of them (the young people trained by Hitler, G.L.). In my régime's strongholds there will grow up a youth before whom the whole world will tremble. A vehemently active, lordly, callous, brutal youth – that's what I set out to achieve. There must be neither weakness nor mildness in them. I would like to see in their eyes one day a gleam of pride and the independence of beasts of prey . . . In this way I shall wipe out the effects of a human taming process that has gone on for thousands of years. I shall then command a pure and noble human material. With it we can create our new order.' Not, of course, by way of the intellect: 'Learning

is harmful for my young men.'[149] 'They need discipline, and must never fear death.'[150] Here Hitler reveals the real content of Rosenberg's demagogic talk about 'honour'.

Hitler did in fact put into practice his real goals in this area. Although failing dismally in his ambitious plan to impose German rule on the whole civilized world, he did achieve the corruption and brutalization of a large sector of the German nation. In the process, as we have seen, he skilfully exploited with demagogic cynicism all the obscurantist and reactionary theories which had sprung up in a retarded Germany as and when he needed them. He deliberately cultivated all the instincts both servile and bestial which had flourished in the German *Misere* so as to create those hordes with which he overran Europe. 'But even if we could not conquer it, we would snatch half the world into ruin with us and permit no triumph over Germany. There will be no second 1918. We shall not capitulate.'[151]

Whether or not we view the suicide of Hitler, the world criminal, as a capitulation is irrelevant. One thing is certain: 1945 was not a repeat of 1918. The collapse of Hitler's Germany was no straightforward defeat, however crushing, no mere change of system, but the end of a whole line of development. It ended that falsely based German unity which started with the defeat of the 1848 revolution and was complete by 1870-1; it posed this central issue of the German nation entirely afresh once again. Indeed, one may say that the whole misguided history of Germany became due for revision. A hundred years before, Alexander von Humboldt – who was really not inordinately radical – had already seen that with the defeat of the Peasants' War, Germany had lost her way. She needed to retrace her steps to that date in order to find the right direction; what had happened since was the inevitable result of it. Not, however, a sequel in the sense of a timeless ontology, but in the sense of a very concrete German history. And thereupon this train of thought brings us to Franz Mehring's shrewd observation that the Battle of Jena was the German version of the storming of the Bastille. And

in 1918, we may add, events repeated themselves just as fruitlessly. And a second repetition in 1945 concretely demanded of all thinking and intellectually honest Germans that they draw from this insight all the political, social and philosophical consequences: that they complete voluntarily and internally the externally dictated uprising and radically remove the harmful legacy of the German Middle Ages from the German nation's future road.

But this was not a decline, as Hitler demagogically proclaimed, but the start of a process of rebirth. 'It would be ridiculous', said Stalin as early as 1942, 'to equate the Hitler clique with the German people and the German State. The experience of history tells us that Hitlers come and go, but the German people and State endure.'[152]

In this book we have devoted attention to the ideological or, more strictly, the philosophical side of this development. Seen from such a viewpoint, 1945 signifies primarily this: when irrationalism, the dogmatic and total destruction of reason became a major country's official world-view, and when that country went to war with its social and ideological adversary, the socialist Soviet Union, it sustained a crushing defeat. And the defeat was as total as the war had been. Hitlerism cannot be resurrected in that form in which it evolved. Nobody disputes that the imperialist forces which produced it are also operative today – even to a greater degree. (We shall discuss in our epilogue the fundamental difference in the situation notwithstanding all the continuously operative, socio-economically parallel tendencies.) At this juncture, having portrayed the passage of German irrationalism from theory into practice, and the inevitable collapse of this diabolical world-historical climax to a philosophical orientation, it only remains for us to comment on that point which this whole book undertook to demonstrate. It is that both the climax and its collapse were, historically, equally necessary, although not of course in a fatalistic sense. Just as Hitler came to political and military grief not through individual – and hence avoidable – errors of judgement, so

irrationalism as a world-outlook received a corresponding practical form in Hitlerism, and it perished in a similarly appropriate form. In revealing the nihilistic cynicism of Hitler and his henchmen and in showing that they did not themselves believe in the doctrine they demagogically proclaimed – thereby translating it into practice –, our studies do not refute these facts of the matter; on the contrary they confirm them. For it is just here that we find the perfect expression of that dialectical unity of cynical nihilism and speculative, uncritical credulity and frivolous superstition which every irrationalism contains implicitly and which simply acquired a matching figure in Hitler. We underestimate the historical significance of the German destiny (embracing that of the destiny of irrational philosophy) if, in assessing Hitler, we put the accent solely on his low intellectual and moral standards. In itself, to be sure, such an assessment is correct. But it was again historical necessity which caused the lowering of standards. It is a steep descent from Schelling and Schopenhauer – via Nietzsche, Dilthey, Spengler, etc. – to Hitler and Rosenberg. But in its very steepness, it sufficiently expresses the character of irrationalism and the necessity of its development.

Part of this necessity was the adversary against which National Socialism came to grief in practical, politico-military terms: the socialist Soviet Union. Here we are concerned only with the philosophical aspect of the question. Hitler, in bringing irrationalism to practical fulfilment, was the executor of Nietzsche's spiritual testament and of the philosophical development coming after Nietzsche and from him. We showed in the relevant chaper how inevitable it was that the irrationalism in Nietzsche should turn against socialism. We showed then that he had run up against an opponent that was unknown and, from the irrationalist viewpoint, inscrutable and inaccessible to the understanding. For all the difference in level between Nietzsche the philosopher and Hitler the demagogue in intellect and culture – and as we have stressed, this too expresses the inevitability of the historical

development –, there was precious little difference in their knowledge and understanding of the adversary on precisely this cardinal issue. It was, one may safely say, as good as non-existent. And in Hitler's politics, we can see the translation of irrationalist philosophy into practice.

The destruction or the restitution of reason is not an academic question for specialist philosophers. Throughout this book we have tried to show that the stance adopted towards reason, the bias towards affirming or denying it and the acknowledgement or dismissal of its effectualness reached from life into philosophy, and not from philosophy into life. Reason is denied or its impotence is declared (Scheler) as soon as reality itself, the life led by the thinker evinces no movement forward into a future worth affirming, no prospect of a future surpassing the present. Behind all anti-rational attitudes, therefore – objectively, in the process of the socio-historical development itself, and subjectively, in the position of the individual concerned – there lies the question of whether one sides with decline and decay or with the new and emerging. (And we have repeatedly shown that so-called impartiality, the so-called transcending of parties and the sense of sublimity always implies a siding with the decadent.)

Hence – and whether or not an individual wants it or is even aware of it – every stand for or against reason is inseparably linked with his opinion of socialism. That was not always the case. The intellectual struggles up to 1848 had as their chief content the conflict between that bourgeois-democratic progress which the French Revolution set in motion and the German feudal-absolutist status quo. After the Battle of June in 1848, more especially after the Paris Commune and most of all after the October Revolution in 1917, the fronts were quite differently aligned. Whether the individual knew it or not, the struggle between socialism and monopoly capitalism now helped to determine all his decisions. And everything expressing his general outlook – however abstractly epistemological or ontological its form –

is ultimately determined by the standpoint he adopts. It is now clear that the world-historical resolution of the Second World War cannot fail to leave a mark on anyone who takes his own questions of world-outlook seriously and does not want to deceive himself with an emotional befogging of the issues or with logical somersaults. He cannot remain blind to the fact that in this war irrationalist philosophy, put into practice after holding sway for almost a century, suffered a crushing defeat in the theoretical sense also. Nor can he overlook the fact that the socialist outlook, so often hushed up and equally often repudiated – supposedly for ever –, achieved a historic victory by virtue of the deeds of the Soviet peoples, who were inspired by it in practice as in theory. It was a victory for reason – become concrete and practical – over the ghastly and diabolical myths of irrationalism.

The philosophical controversies ineluctably ensuing from this new world situation for every honest thinker do not, of course, commit him to joining those parties which represent and are trying to realize Marxism-Leninism. We are here dealing with a question which is not so much directly political as one implying that each person find his bearings in his present life on the most universal level. Although the majority of thinkers barely grasped this during the period we have depicted – they helped, on the contrary, to obscure the problem to the best of their abilities – it deeply engaged the best artists and writers of the era. This movement has never ceased to operate since Zola's declaration that every time he tackled a concrete issue, he found himself confronting socialism. Without making any claim to comprehensiveness, we can cite such names as Courbet and William Morris, Anatole France and Romain Rolland, Shaw and Dreiser, Heinrich and Thomas Mann. The overwhelming majority of them have never been socialist in their philosophy. But what lifts their works, from Courbet's paintings to the profoundly bourgeois Thomas Mann's *Doctor Faustus*, above their contemporaries' pessimistic, nihilistic decadence and

underpins the inner soundness of their output is that they had the courage to come to terms with socialism, the major progressive force of present times, with the future facing us. And this without timidity, without succumbing in fear and hatred to truth-distorting myths or a flight from reality.

This too has been an international phenomenon. But it has a very special significance for German culture, and this is not merely so because it is precisely in Germany that this controversy has, since 1945, become a particularly urgent topical issue. Rather it is because – and this, it must be said, is intimately connected with the present intellectual situation in general – the point at issue is to resolve a chronic morbidity in German culture that reached an acutely critical peak in the age of Hitler and the foregoing period. The Germans were unable to make anything of their own distinguished past and reap the benefits for latter-day achievements like other major nations. That was because they crippled their own classical development. They thereby relegated it to a half-buried past, a fading and academic memory on the one hand, and reinforced current evil influences by distorting and falsifying it in a reactionary manner on the other.

To be brief, we are here thinking of the work of Karl Marx and Friedrich Engels as the vitally operative mainspring of a genuine German culture. From an objectively historical angle, this work was the intellectual crowning of all those progressive tendencies arising on behalf of the German people's liberation and its moulding into a nation (and none the less so for the fact that in content and method, it signifies a qualitative advance on all previous work). The intellectual spadework for the bourgeois-democratic revolution in Germany – from Lessing to Heine, from Kant to Hegel and Feuerbach – climaxed in the classic formulation of the theory of proletarian revolution. And this, from an objectively historical angle, is an achievement which every nation on Earth must admire in the German development. But subjectively, it passed German culture by unnoticed. Marx did not become an active, enriching factor in Germany's

culture. And precisely because its development was crippled in this area, Germany's great past was doomed partly to ossify and to degenerate into academic small-talk, and partly to merge with the foggy vapours of decadence in a – false and damaging – reactionary unity. Such a German line of cultural development as the oft-quoted Goethe-Schopenhauer-Wagner-Nietzsche line invokes Hitler in the name of Germany's great past.

To make the contrast clear, let us take the cultural development of Russia. Pushkin and Gogol were followed by the major democratic-revolutionary theorists, Belinsky and Herzen, Chernyshevsky and Dobrolyubov. Their activity enabled the country of Tolstoy to incorporate Lenin as a great pioneering figure in his own national culture as well as abroad. Socialism and regard for the national culture formed an organic unity for the Russians and not a painful antithesis, as for so many of the best German minds in the previous century.

We repeat: by no means does one have to be a socialist to sense the urgency of this problem and to take a vigorous part in finding a solution. Already in the twenties, Thomas Mann wrote: 'I said that things would only go well with Germany and that she would only find her feet when Karl Marx has read Friedrich Hölderlin – an encounter which, by the way, is in the process of happening. I forgot to add that a one-sided acquaintance would be bound to remain sterile.'[153] With this advice Mann already clearly sketched the answer for Germany and her culture before the catastrophe of Hitler.

Such a revision of Germany's past in the name of her future is essential if the third, externally originating 'storming of the Bastille' is to become an action undertaken by the Germans themselves in the end. Here we have been discussing only the cultural, and chiefly the philosophical aspect of this question. But we have tried to show how all such problems, even the most abstract, grow out of the life of society and become important factors in its development. There is no recognition of past events that is fruitful for the present without a perspective on the future; and no concrete national perspective

on the future without an accurately illuminated past.

The purpose of this book is a summons to that work. It is calling for a final settlement with the harmful legacy of the German *Misere* and for the construction of a real and authentic German future – through digesting critically the rich and as yet far from fully recognized progressive legacy. Demolition, clearance and a fresh start will amount to a great deal of work. With the best will in the world, the reactionary irrationalist traditions of more than a century cannot be overcome in a matter of days or months. But there is no other possible way to recovery. That reason which has been lost or destroyed can only be located in reality itself and can only be restored in interaction with it. And in order to attain to reality, the break is essential. It is difficult, but not impossible. Goethe has his Faust say:

> Hence all magnanimous persons bold
> The boundless in like trust do hold.
> (*Drum fassen Geister würdig gross zu schaun*
> *Zum Grenzenlosen grenzenlos Vertraun*.)

NOTES

1 A. Thierry: *Considérations sur l'histoire de France*, *Oeuvres*, Paris, Garnier, Vol. VII, pp. 65f.
2 Ibid., pp. 71f.
3 Volney: *The Ruins*, Chapter 15.
4 Sieyès: *Qu'est-ce que le tiers état?* Chapter 2.
5 *Correspondence entre Tocqueville et Gobineau*, Paris 1909, p. 291.
6 Ibid., pp. 194, 254 and 306.
7 Gobineau: *The Inequality of the Human Races*.
8 Ibid.
9 Ibid.
10 Ibid.
11 Chamberlain: *Wehr und Gegenwehr*, Munich 1912, p. 14.
12 Gobineau: Op. cit.
13 Ibid.

14 Ibid.
15 Ibid.
16 Ibid.
17 Ibid.
18 Ibid.
19 Ibid.
20 Engels to Marx, 12.12.1859.
21 Marx to Engels, 19.12.1860.
22 Marx to Kugelmann, 27.6.1870.
23 Gumplowicz: *Outlines of Sociology*.
24 Ratzenhofer: *Die soziologische Erkenntnis*, Leipzig 1898, p. 265.
25 Novikov: *Critique du Darwinisme social*, Paris 1910, p. 10.
26 Toennies: *Soziologische Studien und Kritiken*, Jena 1925, Vol. I, p. 204.
27 Gumplowicz: *Die soziologische Staatsidee*, Graz 1892, p. 5.
28 Ratzenhofer: Op. cit., p. 91.
29 Gumplowicz: *The Racial Struggle*.
30 Ibid.
31 Ibid.
32 Gumplowicz: *Grundriss der Soziologie*, p. 255.
33 Ibid., p. 249.
34 Ibid., p. 252.
35 Ratzenhofer: *Grundriss der Soziologie*, Leipzig 1907, pp. 165f.
36 Gumplowicz: *The Racial Struggle*.
37 Ratzenhofer: *Grundriss der Soziologie*, pp. 93 and 95.
38 Gumplowicz: *Die soziologische Staatsidee*, p. 48.
39 Gumplowicz: *Soziologische Essays*, Innsbruck 1928, pp. 180f.
40 Gumplowicz: *The Racial Struggle*.
41 Ratzenhofer: *Grundriss der Soziologie*, p. 296.
42 Gumplowicz: *The Racial Struggle*.
43 Woltmann: *Politische Anthropologie*, Eisenach-Leipzig 1903, p. 191.
44 Ibid., p. 192.
45 Ibid., p. 198.
46 Ibid., p. 287.
47 Ibid., p. 159.
48 Ibid., p. 324.
49 G. Vacher de Lapouge: *L'arien*, Paris 1899, p. 495.
50 Woltmann: Op. cit., p. 294.
51 I was unable to locate the Memoirs of Lagarde's wife. The fact is quoted from an article by Mehring, *Neue Zeit*, 13th Yr., Vol. I, pp. 225f.
52 Chamberlain: *Briefe*, Munich 1920, Vol. II, p. 143.

53 Ibid., p. 142.
54 Ibid., p. 126.
55 Chamberlain: *Politische Ideale*, 3rd impression, Munich 1926, p. 114.
56 Chamberlain: *Wehr und Gegenwehr*, pp. 61f.
57 Ibid., p. 14.
59 Chamberlain: *Briefe*, Vol. I, p. 84.
59 Ibid.
60 Chamberlain: *Wehr und Gegenwehr*, pp. 61f.
61 Chamberlain: *Die Grundlagen des 19. Jahrhunderts*, 2nd impression, Munich 1900, Vol. I, p. 265.
62 Ibid., p. 285.
63 Chamberlain: *Wehr und Gegenwehr*, p. 40.
64 Chamberlain: *Die Grundlagen des 19. Jahrhunderts*, Vol. I, pp. 271f.
65 Ibid., p. 290.
66 Chamberlain: *Briefe*, Vol. I, pp. 26f.
67 Chamberlain: *Kant*, 2nd impression, Munich 1909, pp. 282f.
68 Ibid., p. 300.
69 Ibid., p. 387.
70 Ibid., p. 751.
71 Chamberlain: *Die arische Weltanschauung*, 2nd impression, Munich 1912, p. 73.
72 Ibid., pp. 74f.
73 Ibid., p. 51.
74 Chamberlain: *Die Grundlagen des 19. Jahrhunderts*, Vol. I, p. 204.
75 Chamberlain: *Kant*, p. 746.
76 Ibid., p. 667.
77 Ibid., p. 749.
78 Chamberlain: *Die Grundlagen des 19. Jahrhunderts*, Vol. II, p. 703.
79 Ibid., Vol. II, p. 709.
80 Ibid., Vol. II, p. 725.
81 Ibid., Vol. II, p. 721.
82 Ibid., Vol. II, p. 726.
83 Ibid., Vol. II, p. 775.
84 Chamberlain: *Die arische Weltanschauung*, p. 17.
85 Ibid.
86 Chamberlain: *Die Grundlagen des 19. Jahrhunderts*, Vol. I, p. 230.
87 Chamberlain: *Kant*, p. 303.
88 Chamberlain: *Die Grundlagen des 19. Jahrhunderts*, Vol. II, p. 644.

89 Ibid., Vol. II, pp. 592f.
90 Chamberlain: *War Essays*, Munich 1915, p. 76. (Translated in 1915 as *The Ravings of a Renegade*.)
91 Chamberlain: *Politische Ideale*, p. 39.
92 Rosenberg: *Gestalten der Idee*, 2nd impression, Munich 1936, p.18.
93 Engels: *Anti-Dühring*.
94 Engels to Kautsky, 29.6.1891.
95 Lenin: *Works*, Vol. XII, pp. 151f. (Russian).
96 This was written before the end of the Second World War.
97 H. Rauschning: *The Voice of Destruction*, New York 1940, p. 232.
98 Ibid., p. 227.
99 Ibid., pp. 237f.
100 Ibid., p. 132.
101 Hitler: *Mein Kampf*.
102 Ibid.
103 Ibid.
104 Ibid.
105 E. Krieck: *Völkisch-politische Anthropologie*, Leipzig 1936, Vol. II, p. 2.
106 Rosenberg: *The Myth of the Twentieth Century*.
107 Ibid.
108 Ibid.
109 Ibid.
110 Ibid.
111 Ibid.
112 Rosenberg: *Krisis und Neubau Europas*, Berlin 1934, pp. 10f.
113 Hitler: *Mein Kampf*.
114 E. Krieck: *Völkisch-politische Anthropologie*, p. 544.
115 Ibid., p. 59.
116 Rosenberg: *The Myth of the Twentieth Century*.
117 Ibid.
118 Hitler: *Mein Kampf*.
119 Ibid.
120 Rosenberg: *The Myth of the Twentieth Century*.
121 Hitler: *Mein Kampf*.
122 Ibid.
123 Rosenberg: *The Myth of the Twentieth Century*.
124 Chamberlain: *Briefe*, Vol. II, p. 265.
125 Rosenberg: *The Myth of the Twentieth Century*.
126 Ibid.
127 Ibid.
128 Ibid.

129 Rauschning: Op. cit., pp. 49f.
130 Marx-Engels: *The German Ideology*.
131 Hitler: *Mein Kampf*.
132 Ibid.
133 Ibid.
134 Ibid.
135 Ibid.
136 Ibid.
137 Rosenberg: *Blut und Ehre*, Munich 1934, p. 71.
138 *Grundlagen, Aufbau und Wirtschaftsordnung des national-sozialistischen Staates*, edited by H.H. Lammers, Secretary of State and Chief of the Imperial Chancellery, and H. Pfundtner, Secretary of State in the Ministry of the Interior, Berlin 1936, Book 15, pp. 16f.
139 Rosenberg: *The Myth of the Twentieth Century*.
140 *Grundlagen*, Book 15, p. 25.
141 Ibid., p. 18.
142 Ibid., Book 17, pp. 6f.
143 Ibid., Book 2, p. 9.
144 Ibid., Introduction, p. 9.
145 Rauschning: Op. cit. p. 281.
146 Ibid., p. 83.
147 Ibid., pp. 94f.
148 Ibid., p. 86.
149 Ibid., p. 252.
150 Ibid., p. 121.
151 Ibid.
152 Stalin: Army order of 23 February 1942.
153 Thomas Mann: *Order of the Day*.

EPILOGUE

ON POST-WAR IRRATIONALISM

In our studies so far we have attempted to portray, in its chief elements, the course of irrationalism's development from the feudal-reactionary ideological backlash against the French Revolution to Hitlerism and its inevitable demise. We began this exposition when Hitler was still in power, the fullness of power; with his downfall, it became an essentially historical one. But only in part, we should add. For nobody today will presume to claim that either the ideology or the procedures of Hitlerism belong entirely to past history. At the war's end, admittedly, major sections of the masses just freed from the fascist nightmare cherished the illusion that a really new period of peace and liberty might be beginning. Scarcely a year later, however, Churchill's Fulton speech meant that all their dreams were cruelly shattered. And it became clear to ever-larger circles that – as the initiated had long known – the end of the war signified, rather, making ready for another war, against the Soviet Union, and that to influence the masses ideologically in favour of this formed a central problem for the imperialists. Today, therefore, in the midst of the intensified Cold War, a polemic against irrationalism as an ideology of militant reaction, albeit a polemic essentially historical in orientation, cannot possibly end with Hitler. It must attempt to outline at least the most important elements of the movement after Hitler's downfall.

That is the aim of our epilogue. As already indicated, of course, in no respect does it claim to be scientifically complete and exhaustive, either in an extensive or an intensive sense. For in the period after the end of the Second World War, the United States gained increasing prominence as the

leading power of imperialist reaction, taking Germany's place in this respect. In substance, then, we would have to write a history of that nation's philosophy as precise as that we have produced for Germany in order to show the derivation and roots, both social and intellectual, of the present ideologies of the 'American age'. It goes without saying that this would take a whole book, possibly of the size of this one, and the author considers himself by no means equipped to write such a work (or even an outline). Our concern in this epilogue can only be to give rough outlines of the most important new elements in post-war social trends and to illustrate their ideological reflections through a number of especially typical instances. And the primary object of this is to provide a link between our foregoing studies and life today. It is naturally proper that the study should finally turn to Germany again, partly because of the important role which the plans of American imperialism allot to the Germans, and partly because important figures from pre-fascism play no small part in the ideology of Western Germany today. In accordance with the design as a whole, we shall treat these subjects too not so much exhaustively as by giving typical examples. This epilogue's only claim is to indicate the chief prevailing trends in the Cold War ideologies in their most characteristic exponents.

1

If we now move on to the actual questions of substance, we are at once faced with the question of how the new features of the post-1945 period manifested themselves. The anti-fascist coalition crumbled very rapidly, and the 'crusade' against communism — the main *leitmotif* of Hitlerian propaganda — was taken up by 'democrats' with an increasing display of energy. Naturally this meant a change of orientation (and also of content and structure) in 'democratic' views.

Since they had opposed fascism during the war, they could at times rightly regard themselves as continuing the long departed heyday of bourgeois democracy -- or they could at least pose as so doing. This forward-looking direction had a great charm that explains why, even after its total reversal, it was attempted to preserve the semblance of such a continuity and to direct the struggle against 'totalitarianism', whereby fascism and communism were now reduced to this common denominator. Apart from the fact that this view was a piece of old hat from the junk-shop of social democratism and Trotskyism, it promptly and inevitably evinced a fresh piece of hypocrisy in its concrete situation. For in order to combat communism effectively on the political plane, this 'democracy' had to form an intimate alliance with the German survivors from the Nazi movement (Hjalmar Schacht, Krupp, Hitler's generals) as well as with France, etc. etc. Unavoidably, 'anti-totalitarian' ideology more and more took on distinctly fascist features.

The 'crusade' against communism and Marxism-Leninism was similarly an old legacy of bourgeois ideology turned reactionary. As we have shown, Nietzsche first set this ideological struggle in motion along every line; and as we have seen, the struggle grew more and more widespread and acute after 1917, until with Hitler it finally reached a temporary climax which coupled the lowest intellectual standards hitherto known with lying and provocation (the *Reichstag* fire) and bestial cruelty (Auschwitz, etc.). Subsequently, this temporary nadir was further exceeded by the 'Cold War' stage-managed from Washington. Here again, the ideological offensive was combined with provocations of the most diverse kinds to surpass Hitler's version of this struggle in every sphere. But in this book we shall occupy ourselves only with the ideological side of the matter.

Until now we have emphasized those features of the 'free world' ideology promoted by the U.S.A. which were also a part of fascism. This was so as to obtain a proper footing for our following exposition, which will be concerned with

the differences from Hitlerian ideology. But it would misfire and mislead if we failed to consider these differences, indeed contrasting features, within the common social and ideological context. A straightforward revival of Hitlerism is scarcely possible under existing conditions. Of course Franco's fascism went on undisturbed, and of course Adenauer's political machinery teemed with erstwhile leading fascists; of course fascist secret unions and organizations have – with American help – sprung up in Germany time and again. And of course the updated form and extension of Nazi ideology has been able to find overt expression, not only in 'careless', reluctantly disowned statements by Nazi officers and in memoirs and hagiographies of the Hitlerian leaders, but also in programmatic periodicals – quite openly. An example of the latter is 'Nation Europa, the monthly for European Renewal', which proclaims: 'The Reich, completely shattered more than once and yet always rising anew, has acquired still greater powers' etc. etc. But not even in Western Germany is all this the new ideology's principal line, at least not at the time of writing. With Hitler's collapse, international – and hence German – reaction was thrown into a new objective situation and was forced to draw the consequences on the ideological plane as well.

Hitler stupefied and conquered the German masses with his social and national demagogy. That meant that his myth, a product of extreme irrationalism, was capable of two things. First, it could channel specific national feelings, justified in themselves, into an ideology of imperialist chauvinism, imperialist aggression and the suppression and destruction of other peoples by the Germans. Secondly, the myth confirmed the unlimited sway of German monopoly capitalism, substantially in the most reactionary and barbaric style. According to its formal demagogic, however, this was a completely new, 'revolutionary' social order professedly standing above the dilemma of capitalism and socialism. We have dealt in such detail with the mendacious myth of 'German socialism' and 'Germanic democracy', both in its

genesis and its functioning, that we do not now need to discuss it at length.

These two myths, which are closely related and form an ideological unity, were both destroyed when the war was resolved, the Hitlerian form of social demagogy especially. Socialism triumphed in the Central European national democracies and in China, while powerful communist parties of the masses began to flourish, notably in France and Italy. After this every group of monopoly capitalists found it a far too hazardous ploy to risk again the slogan of the 'other' socialism as a manoeuvre to divert the masses from communism. Hitler was still able to gain power by these means, but let us remember that as soon as 1934 he was having to apply the bloodiest terrorism in order to counteract the supporters of the 'second revolution'.

There is moreover – and this is a primary theme – the economic difference between the leading power of reactionary monopoly capitalism in each case, between Hitler's Germany and the United States today. As we know, the result of capitalism's delayed development in Germany was that when she entered the imperialist period, she found a colonial world already carved up. Hence her imperialist politics were militaristically aggressive – overtly so: she was striving for a violent redistribution of territories. The defeat of these endeavours in the First World War, its economic and social effects and, in particular, the German repercussions of the economic world crisis that began in 1929 shook German capitalism to the foundations. Hitler's solution, his social demagogy, sprang from this parlous state of German capitalism. And his national demagogy, the programme for new and even more comprehensive imperialist aggression was able to blend with the social demagogy by summoning Germany, as a 'proletarian nation', to the barricades against the Western exponents of monopoly capitalism and by passing off imperialist rivalries as a national and social war of liberation against monopoly capital.

None of these motives ever played a part in either the

domestic or the foreign policy of the United States. A tottering of the capitalist system was never in question, not even in the most critical times. In contrast to Germany, the U.S.A. had a constitution which was democratic from the start. And its ruling class managed, particularly during the imperialist era, to have the democratic forms so effectively preserved that by democratically legal means, it achieved a dictatorship of monopoly capitalism at least as firm as that which Hitler set up with his tyrannic procedures. This smoothly functioning democracy, so-called, was created by the Presidential prerogative, the Supreme Court's authority in constitutional questions (and the monopoly capitalists always decided which were constitutional questions), the finance monopoly over the Press, radio, etc., electioneering costs, which successfully prevented really democratic parties from springing up beside the two parties of monopoly capitalism, and lastly the use of terroristic devices (the lynching system). And this democracy could, in substance, realize everything sought by Hitler without needing to break with democracy formally. In addition, there was the incomparably broader and more solid economic basis of monopoly capitalism. In Norman Mailer's highly interesting American war novel *The Naked and the Dead*, his General Cummings expresses the difference most vividly:

> As kinetic energy, a country is organization, co-ordinated effort, your epithet, fascism . . . Historically the purpose of this war is to translate America's potential into kinetic energy. The concept of fascism, far sounder than communism if you consider it, for it's grounded firmly in men's actual natures, merely started in the wrong country, in a country which did not have enough intrinsic potential power to develop completely. In Germany with that basic frustration of limited physical means there were bound to be excesses. But the dreams, the concept was sound enough . . . For the past century the entire historical process has been working toward greater and greater

> consolidation of power. Physical power for this century, an extension of our universe, and a political power, a political organization to make it possible. Your men of power in America, I can tell you, are becoming conscious of their real aims for the first time in our history. Watch. After the war our foreign policy is going to be far more naked, far less hypocritical than it has ever been.[1]

We can therefore readily understand that the United States' monopoly capitalists neither require nor can apply either a 'German socialism' or a 'Germanic democracy' in their home affairs. Capitalism, for them, is and will remain the ideal economic system, and 'democratic freedom' the model for every State institution and form of government. How this 'democratic freedom' develops into fascist coercion – without undergoing any formal changes – has been long recognized not only by the world at large but also by Americans of intelligence and integrity. It by no means takes a Marxist to perceive it. The profoundly bourgeois author Sinclair Lewis portrayed this development in his novel *It Can't Happen Here* – albeit with some illusions regarding the behaviour of the liberal bourgeoisie. And previously, e.g., in *Elmer Gantry*, he correctly exposed the fascist terrorism which the 'democrats' tolerated and indeed artificially cultivated.

So economic, social and political conditions in the United States were bound to give rise to an ideology whose central point became an overt defence of capitalism and capitalist 'freedom'. From the philosophical-methodological angle, then, the henceforward effectively leading role of American ideology in the reactionary camp meant a break with the method which we have described, in its German version, as an indirect apologetic for capitalism. This collapsed along with Hitler as the leading ideology of reaction; it had to yield again to the direct apologetic for capitalism.

In the interests of clarity, we shall begin with capitalism's methods of defence. For the form taken by these methods also determined the complex whose purpose was to link

national sentiments with imperialist interests. The problem of monopoly capitalism remained central to direct as well as indirect apologetics, and this is understandable. For the chief task of any apologetic is to appease the spontaneous indignation of the masses and to steer it into a direction favouring the capitalist system; but this indignation is directed precisely against monopoly organizations. The masses, having grasped already their connection with capitalist laws of motion, can in any case not be won with an apologetic propaganda. The existence, dominance and expansion of the monopolies amounts to an automatic daily advertisement for socialism. And this not only among those directly exploited, but also among the intellectuals. The Gaullist Raymond Aron once noted with deep regret the inefficacy of American propaganda on the French intelligentsia, indeed the latter's hostile rejection of it. The reason he gave was that: 'for most European intellectuals, anti-capitalism is far more than a mere economic theory, it is an article of faith'.

Hitler solved the question in a very simple fashion. He translated the German – but only the German – monopolies into the new form of 'German socialism'. (It was extreme irrationalist philosophy which engendered the spiritual atmosphere of blind faith for this claptrap.) Now since the ideologists of American monopoly capitalism were neither able nor willing to follow this road, it became necessary for them to turn monopoly capitalism into something contingent, a removable contingency moreover. Let us just quote Lippmann as an example. His was a standard method of vulgar economics: identifying technology with economics, he virtually always spoke of technology instead of economics in order to obtain his 'proof', although this in itself could carry no conviction in the light of its own postulates: the development of technology and mass production 'does not presuppose a monopoly'. 'Concentration has its origin in privilege and not in technology.' But where did such privilege come from? The answer is extremely simple: the liberals, as the result of a short-sighted and faulty application of the

laissez-faire principle, had permitted and indeed encouraged its genesis; the 'intellectual upper hand' of collectivism supposedly existed between 1848 and 1870. (Whence this superiority? Again the answer is extremely simple: it resulted from the 'intellectual climate'. A whole century earlier, Reuter's Uncle Bräsig[2] had, in a humorous parody of such 'explanations', declared that 'poverty stems from *pauvreté*'.) It was out of this liberal error, Lippmann asserted, that monopolies had arisen. And he was far from holding a monopoly in this truism. The Swiss economist Röpke explained the origin of monopolies in similar terms, professing to locate their cause in the 'cult of the colossal' which reigned at the end of the nineteenth century. Like Lippmann, he too denied the economic inevitability of the concentration of capital and with it, that of cartels, trusts, umbrella organizations, and so on. Elsewhere he saw in the monopolies a legacy of the feudal period – without noticing the contradiction to the theory just stated. The trusts, said Lippmann, had not grown organically, but were 'artificially grown'.

At all events, and however we interpret the causes of their appearance, Lippmann and Röpke were agreed that monopolies were by no means inevitable. They then blithely eliminated all the essential objective conditions from the imperialist economy; like their prototypes, the popular economists of the mid nineteenth century, they encompassed mentally just the surface aspects of capitalism. And naturally any aspects artificially isolated from the essence, from the mechanics must be distorted, even mere surface ones.

Granted, even were concentration and monopoly not manifestations of imperialist capitalism resulting inevitably from economic laws, their existence still has disturbing effects with which the apologist must somehow come to terms. In Lippmann's view, classical political economy already recognized them (modern monopolies?! G.L.) as 'frictions' and 'disturbances', but had shown by these expressions that it underestimated 'their social significance quite hugely'. That assessment had to be adjusted through the

demagogy of direct apologetics. 'Hence the exceptional importance of the question as to whether we ascribe the collapse of liberalism to the error the liberals made or, as the collectivists believe, to a kind of ineluctable historical necessity.' For only in the former case is the error a reparable one. If the legislation of bourgeois society has brought about the trusts, etc., it can also restrict and indeed entirely abolish them; it can, as Lippmann says, put an end to the concentration of capital, the 'businessmen's collectivism'. That, Lippmann maintained, was now the major task facing the liberal revival. He scornfully dismissed other liberals' compromise attempts, such as those of Stuart Chase: 'Political democracy can remain stable in *all* areas *if it only keeps its distance* from the economy.' (Lippmann's italics.) On the contrary, the mistake made by liberalism was that 'it chose to regard property and the authorities of capital-based societies as absolute and untouchable.' But a change was possible in Lippmann's view: 'Men nowadays are capable of reforming the social order by changing the laws.'

Since Lippmann saw only the subjectivistically distorted surface of capitalist society, it did not even occur to him to ask how laws come about, i.e., to examine more closely the relation between the economy and the politico-juristic superstructure. With the blank face of a parliamentary cretin he could calmly state that such a change was possible. But he ignored the one interesting question, the question of which social forces could accomplish the change in reality. He contented himself with demagogically hatching – theoretically shallow – projects to lead the naive reader astray. In Lippmann's fellow-thinker Röpke, we clearly see the extent to which any *bona fides* was lacking from such lines of thought. Röpke backed up his 'active' anti-monopoly policy, which culminated by appealing to the legislature as much as Lippmann's did, with the following arguments: 'That this last road is eminently viable has been proved by the U.S. through the Sherman Act of 1890, a law prohibiting any monopoly or monopoly agreement and still representing the basis of

American economic justice today.' The facts, of course, at once forced him to add that 'this law has proved to be ineffective to date'. This, he maintained, was due, on the one hand, to the tariff policy of the U.S., which encouraged monopolies; and the law had never been executed with real energy on the other. Now if such writers draw on all this to posit their neo-liberal line – the abolition of monopolies by law – as a concretely promising prospect (without going into the socio-economic causes of the concrete failure), we can only marvel at their boldness. They themselves could not possibly believe in such balderdash, yet they offered it to their readers.

Lippman and Röpke, of course, are just two examples. Other authors said the same but formulated their thoughts in different ways. Two elements which they all had in common need stressing particularly. Firstly, the idea of capitalism (termed 'the free market economy') as the ideal social order. Any 'disturbances' which occurred were mere side-effects which could always be eradicated through legislation; and this was a possibility because one was living in the 'freedom' of a 'democracy' where the majority vote was decisive and all-powerful. Secondly this method signified, ideally, a return to the classic economists. But what was the true nature of this return? It was the classic thinkers' great theoretical deed to have substantiated the theory of labour value, i.e., to have comprehended the principles of capitalism in real terms (albeit faultily and fragmentarily), such that the theory of surplus value (exploitation), the perception of capitalism's contradictions could be established from this angle, as already became visible in the Ricardo school's breakdown. In reality, of course, there can be no question here of such a turning back. The connection was not with the classic thinkers themselves but with their degenerate epigones, the vulgar economists, who had already erased all contradictions from the theory of capitalism and interpreted the classics as if their own shallow harmonizing at all costs constituted the classic doctrine's very essence.

Previously, Marx had clearly demonstrated this vulgarizing tendency in a by no means unimportant transitional figure, James Mill. Contrasting the master (Ricardo) with Mill he wrote: 'With the master, the new and significant evolves amid the "compost heap" of contradictions. He works the law forcibly out of the contrasting phenomena.' With Mill, on the contrary: 'Where the economic relationship – and therefore the categories expressing it also – includes antitheses, where it is contradiction and the very unity of contradictions, he emphasizes the element of their *unity* and denies the *antitheses*.' This tendency became more marked still with the outright vulgarizers.

Even now, however, we have not adequately defined modern economics. For the change in theory during the pre-imperial and imperial age, the total subjectifying of economics, from the marginal utility theory to Keynes and modern American learning, likewise claims to be a classical legacy, and Lippmann's recourse to Adam Smith, for instance, again includes an interpretation which falsifies history. In reality, even so shallow a vulgarizer and apologist as Say inevitably looks a profound thinker and uncompromising explorer of truth by comparison with modern economists. In Malthus we can discern very clearly the character of such a legacy. After what has been stated, it cannot seem surprising that he has been highly honoured in modern times and that his population theory has gained exceptional influence. But even Malthus had to be 'improved' in a reactionary direction to suit the modern purposes of apologists for the imperialist economy. He himself wrote only an 'apologetic for the misery of the working class' (Marx). Now, however, the current revival of Malthusianism has given rise to a call to exterminate whole nations, an apologetic for wars necessitating a series of mass human sacrifices (Vogt). But even more moderate thinkers, ones not inclined overtly to draw such far-reaching consequences, have been thoroughly Malthusian in regarding the rapid increase in population as causing the misery; as preventing the blessings of capitalism from ending

in universal prosperity (Röpke).

This treatise does not pretend even to suggest the problems of the modern capitalist economy. Our only goal in this analysis is to register the general ideological change of direction after Hitler's downfall. Hitlerian social demagogy was linked with an overt irrationalism and it culminated in this: contradictions in capitalism that were thought insoluble – by normal means – led to the leap into a radically irrationalistic myth. The present, directly apologetic, defence of capitalism renounces myth and irrationalism, or so it appears. With regard to form, mode of presentation, and style we are here dealing with purely conceptual, scientific deduction. But this is only so in appearance. For the content of the conceptual constructions is a pure conceptual void, a construction of non-existent connections, a denial of concrete principles and a halt at those bogus connections which the immediate surface of economic reality displays immediately (and thus non-conceptually). We are therefore dealing with a new form of irrationalism disguised as a rationalism.

But not, it must be said, with one that is fundamentally new. We have already remarked on the return of American economics (and its European adherents) to vulgar economics. At the same time we pointed out that in these modern economics, all anti-scientific tendencies have been heightened to match the conditions of direct capitalist apologetics in the imperial age. So if Marx has already proved the irrational trends immanent in the old vulgar economics, this is true of modern economics on a scale so greatly enlarged that the growth in quantity has precipitated a new quality: the irrationalism implicit in the old vulgar economics has now become an explicit one. Since Marx's statements on the subject provide a basic and comprehensive exposition of the problems arising, I think he should be quoted in detail: 'The agencies of the irrational forms, which present specific economic conditions and epitomize them in practice, do not however affect the effective carriers of these conditions in practice, in their usual dealings. And since they are used to

operating within them, their minds see nothing objectionable about it. For them there is nothing mysterious in a total contradiction. In phenomena alienated from the inner connected order and become absurd if taken in isolation, they feel as much at home as fish in water. Here it is the case that, as Hegel says with regard to certain mathematical formulae, what ordinary common sense finds irrational is the rational, and what it holds rational is irrationality itself.'

2

May we remind the reader at this point that the above allusion is to Hegel's mathematical studies, which we discussed in detail in Chapter II. Hegel showed in those writings how the emergence of genuine dialectical contradictions creates the semblance of an irrationality for metaphysical thinking. But at the same time, he showed how dialectical thought can resolve the contradictions into a higher rationality. What Hegel demonstrated on the general level through an example taken from mathematics, Marx presented on the level of a broader and deeper social generalization: he shows us the concrete circumstances that raise the problems of irrationalism and turn their intellectual reflection into methodological, philosophical problems of irrationalism. Here Marx gave convincing proof of how and why capitalism's immediate agents could move in this irrational milieu with complete freedom and lack of problems. Ideologists on the same social and intellectual level too could naively accept as truisms the 'irrationality' of social categories (their 'forms and conditions of existence', as Marx puts it). Of course the thus unacknowledged irrationality has to come to light in various ways, but it does so unrecognized at first, unconsciously and not yet crystallized into an irrationalist philosophy. Naturally this applies to the old popular economists themselves, but also to the beginnings of Machism and especially pragmatism which,

as we showed in our preface, is an ideology of capitalist agents consciously anchored in capitalist immediacy, a Babbitt philosophy. However, the growing acuteness of the social contradictions necessitated a 'deepening' of the philosophical questions. The most typical example is the development of German irrationalism in the imperial age, with Hitler as its climax.

Today, however, with the decided return of capitalist apologetics to the direct form, a new situation was bound to arise from the philosophical angle as well. It is perfectly natural for the Machist-pragmatist rather than the German type of irrationalism to reign in philosophy also. Without exception, this shift has determined socially the whole of semantics in the U.S.A., the neo-Machism of Wittgenstein and Carnap, and Dewey's extension of pragmatism. It has also dictated the fact that those philosophical trends more strongly inclined, in their methodology, to carry on as such directions the pre-fascist line of German irrationalism did not blossom into leading ideologies, but could take effect only as 'third road' theories; French Existentialism, for example. (Here, where we can only deal with the mainstream of thought, we shall not discuss this movement, especially as we have done so already in other contexts. Cf. my book *Existentialism or Marxism?*, Berlin 1951.)

It goes without saying that here again, in line with this epilogue's general aim, we do not have a detailed analysis and characterization in mind even with regard to the principal orientations. We shall confine ourselves to indicating certain decisive evolving trends in order to sketch the new aspect of the prevailing post-war imperialist philosophy. It also goes without saying that these trends had already been active in American philosophy for a very long time, throughout the imperial period; today they govern its whole ideology. In Dewey they had long been apparent as an advanced phase of pragmatism which was consciously an ideology of capitalist agents, the builders and active supporters of the 'American life-style', from the outset. And pragmatism, consciously

rejecting objective examination of a reality independent of the consciousness, studied only the practical usefulness of individual actions in surroundings taken to be immutable – immutable, that is, in essence, not in the details concerning individual action. It was only natural that the imperialist development of these surroundings found an exact reflection in the content and structure of Dewey's philosophy.

But in semantics and neo-Machism also – their dividing-lines are often blurred – there has arisen a vigorous further development of the earliest Machism in accordance with the ideological requirements of modern American imperialism. The early Machist show of 'strict scientific thinking' has been preserved unaltered, but at the same time the departure from objective reality has gone far beyond the earlier standards. Philosophy's task is now no longer an 'analysis of sensations' but only one of word-meanings and sentence-structures. And parallel with the formal-academic total loss of substance which this has entailed, overt direct apologetics have emerged far more prominently than ever before. Machism came about originally as a philosophical weapon against materialism, chiefly in the field of the epistemology of natural science. The modern agnostic forms which were elaborated in the process naturally constituted a good starting-point for many an irrationalist current, and Machism was always of philosophical assistance to irrationalism. Now, a general direct apologetic has plainly emerged. Semantics examine energetically and systematically the general concepts of social and economic life, only to find them trivial, empty word-formations. What follows? The English Marxist Maurice Cornforth tells us very clearly in a quotation from Barrows Dunham's *Man against Myth*: 'As we clearly see, there are no dogs in general, no human race, no profit system, no political parties, no fascism, no undernourished peoples, no shabby clothes, no truth, no social justice. With things standing thus there is no economic problem, no political problem, no fascist problem, no nutrition question and no social question . . . By simply breathing out,' he continues,

'they have spirited out of the world every important problem to have tormented the human race during its entire history.'

And in addition, Cornforth showed most lucidly the social consequences of such a philosophy. He stated: 'To take a simple example, let us consider the kind of discussion that occurs very frequently between workers and employers. What is the semantic prescription for solving the dispute? It is expressed very clearly in the words of the boss who says: "Let's forget all this twaddle about labour and capital and profit and exploitation, which is only the meaningless invention of political agitators who are playing on your emotions. Let's speak man to man, as Adam to Adam, and let's try and understand each other." That is actually the way in which employers very often argue. They learnt to be semanticists before semantics was even invented.' And Cornforth shows this inevitable consequence of the semantic method, the point where it fulfils the social function set by imperialist capitalism, in other cases as well, such as that of the Malthusian Vogt, who settles all agrarian issues semantically – with similar results in terms of class.

With Vogt, however, the method's other side also clearly appears: he reveals an irrational mysticism which was only latent and implicit in Machism itself. For Vogt, in applying the semantic method to the agrarian question, says that the land is 'an ineffable reality'. Here he was exceeding conventional agnosticism. For him, reality no longer simply lies outside the area of the perceptible, it is also an irrational chaos. Stuart Chase expresses this tendency more distinctly still. Examining the process of abstraction, he gives the description of a pencil as an example. Although this is a non-verbal, spatio-temporal occurrence, he tries to express it somehow or other. And the fruit of this endeavour to express the non-verbal in words is the definition of a pencil as 'a mad dance of electrons'. Here the new irrationalism amounts to a completely irrational subjectifying, anthropologizing and mythicizing of natural phenomena. For in the first place, Chase's definition is in no sense that of a pencil as

a particular part of objective reality, unequivocally definable through its attributes and functions. What Chase says of it could just as well be said of a house, a desk, etc. To describe objects from concrete reality, nature and society (since a pencil is a social object as well) solely in terms of the movement of electrons already constitutes an irrational mysticism. But in the second place, the very movement of electrons is a 'mad dance' only for the impressionism of a willed immediacy; objectively considered, it has principles of its own which science can – to an approximate degree – observe rationally. Although Stuart Chase clothes his definition in the currently fashionable cloak of modern scientific 'exactitude', a wild irrational mysticism is visible behind it.

Without committing ourselves to a detailed analysis of this new brand of irrationalism, let us attempt briefly to illustrate this orientation's general philosophical character. Wittgenstein, one of its leading figures, offers a number of statements which are central to its methodology. He wrote: 'Sentences can represent the whole reality, but they cannot represent what must be meant in them by reality for this representation to become possible – the logical form . . . Sentences cannot represent the logical form, the form is reflected in the sentences. Language cannot represent that which reflects itself in language. *We* cannot express through language that which expresses *itself* through language. Sentences *show* the logical form of reality. They exhibit it . . . That which one *can* show, *one cannot* utter.'

Here, perhaps I may remind the reader of my studies of the phenomenological method, especially Max Scheler's discussion of it, in order to give due weight both to the (socially determined) unity of the various modern irrationalist trends and to the (likewise socially determined) variety of their stages. Scheler resorted as much as Wittgenstein to this immediate irrationalist foundation as the sole bedrock, the sole content of philosophy. There was, to be sure, the difference that he regarded this irrationalist content as still utterable; only at the existentialist stage of phenomenology

did the irrationalism of the foundation manifest itself quite clearly. In stressing this parallel we by no means wish to claim that existentialism influenced Wittgenstein; such methodological issues have a social basis, and both the shared and the unlike elements of the method and conclusions reflect this basis. The same applies to the relation between Wittgenstein and the later existentialist development of phenomenology and semantics as to the epistemological affinity between Mach and Husserl, to which we referred in the appropriate place. (Certainly Scheler's *Ohnmacht der Vernunft*, 'The impotence of reason', may also be mentioned in this context.)

Wittgenstein was therefore forced to draw the consequences of this situation. He said of the relation of science (the science of semantics) to life: 'We feel that even if we have answered all the questions of science, we did not so much as touch the problems of life. For then, to be sure, not a single question will remain, and just this is the answer. We perceive the solution to the life problem in the problem's disappearance. (Is not that the reason why men to whom life's meaning became evident are incapable of saying out loud of what this meaning consists?) That is truly the ineffable. It *reveals itself*; it is the mystical.'

It is no accident that a burning admirer of Wittgenstein, José Ferrater Mora, extols him precisely as a philosopher of despair. He comments on the general characteristics of the age and its representative thinker as follows:

> Heidegger, Sartre, Kafka and Camus let us go on living with confidence in a world's existence. However awesome the break they proclaim, it is not a radical one. The ground where they find their footing holds firm. The shattering earthquake reduces our old dwellings to ruins, but even among the ruins one can go on living and can build new houses. But Wittgenstein, after these sad losses, leaves us wholly bereft of support. For if the ground disappears along with the ruins, the roots along with the felled tree,

> we shall no longer have any support. No longer, too, will we be able to resort to nothingness or face the absurd with minds that are clear. We will have to disappear altogether.

Mora also recognizes that with Wittgenstein, as with semantics in general, the chief culprit is reason and thinking: 'Thinking is the great disruptive influence, we could almost say the great temptation. The misdeed itself, the act of thinking becomes man's great guilt, his essential sin.' In the world described by Wittgenstein, the centre is 'undiluted absurdity'; in it the question has 'put itself in question'. And Chase confirms this world-view and its semantic analysis by drawing such radical conclusions that the exposition lapses into the grotesquely amusing. He envies his tomcat Hoby who 'is not subject to the hallucinations caused by wrong word-usage . . . since he has no truck with philosophy and formal logic . . . When I go astray in the language jungle I revert to Hoby's outlook as though to a magnet.'

So the irrationalism in 'strictly scientific' direct apologetics exudes from every pore. But its leading exponents were unwilling to acknowledge its connection with the movement that culminated in Hitler. Instead, they sought out and located (so they thought) a glorious ancestry for it. Just as Truman and Eisenhower wished to appear to the public not as Hitler's successors but as continuing the mission of George Washington or Abraham Lincoln, so the direct apologetics of our day, although irrationalist at heart, have preferred to seek their ancestors in the Enlightenment. This exactly matches the economists' efforts to feign a return to their classic authors: a practical impossibility, as we have shown. To them, Say and his still shallower successors as well as Malthus – seen as more reactionary and barbaric than he actually was – represented the classic authors *de facto*. The same situation obtains in philosophy. Kaufmann, for instance, sought to turn Nietzsche into a worthy successor to the great Enlightenment minds, and it is extremely typical that the present-day 'renaissance of Enlightenment' has revalued and hailed as a

great rediscovery the Marquis de Sade, etc.

It is not fortuitous that the forging of such connections has proved fruitless. True, the earlier apologists and vulgarizers suppressed economic truths, distorted the correlations and banished the genuine problems in order to substitute spurious ones. But for all their scientific *mala fides*, they honestly believed in the inviolability of capitalism and its unlimited possibilities of development. That also goes for the corresponding literary output, weak and bad as it was, of Ohnet or Gustav Freytag. But today the literary parallels to the economy of direct apologetics and the philosophy of semantics are manifest in such advocates of nihilistic despair as Kafka or Camus. (Here we are speaking of literature as a graph of social trends; questions of aesthetic merit are beside the point in this context.)

Of the phenomenon of despair we shall speak more fully later. For the moment the observation will suffice that we may note precisely in the leading ideologists a profound disbelief in their own apologetic exposition and the optimistic perspectives which are supposed to follow from it. No doubt there can exist blockheads – even masses of them – who believe Lippmann's notion that one fine day, albeit little by little, the United States legislature will really abolish the 'excessive' concentration of capital, the trusts, and so on. But naturally so experienced and well versed a publicist as Lippmann does not believe a word of it. But what, in that case, does he believe? What determines his attitude? Despair or cynicism, or both together.

There is more than one explanation for these moods among the ideological defenders of imperialism. They were founded not only on the impossibility of obtaining a satisfactory theoretical solution to the problems of monopoly capitalism, one that would preserve its reign intact as well as appease the hostile mood of the masses. They stemmed also from the current state of the struggle against the chief adversary, socialism. (Clearly, this central question also determined the philosophical situation to a decisive extent.)

For the whole of capitalist learning was bent, ideologically, on rebutting in a cogent manner the socialist alternative that was weighing on it more and more inescapably. Between the two world wars, this seemed relatively simple for the capitalist ideologists. While Soviet power was still in the process of becoming established they constantly prophesied socialism's definitive collapse for the coming week, before going over to a more long-term demonstration of the abortive 'experiment'. They pronounced each Five Year Plan unrealizable before it started, misrepresented the teething troubles of socialist reconstruction as symptoms of a definite failure, and so on. Such arguments still crop up time and again today, of course. But their success as propaganda has become increasingly dubious, for their discrepancy with the facts has been growing more and more obvious. The Soviet army's successful resistance to the strongest land power in the world, its annihilating victory over Hitler, the peaceful and monumental reconstruction of the post-war era, the ability to produce its own atomic bombs, etc. – these have given the world irrefutable proof of the socialist economy's high economic and technical standards, the ever-rising curve of its development.

All this has had a paralysing effect on the propaganda of imminent collapse. It could not, of course, be relinquished, but its persuasiveness has steadily decreased and has had to be replaced by other methods. But these new methods, at a time when the Cold War's crucial ideological battles were going on, have shown the constantly declining quality of anti-Soviet propaganda. Only outright calumny and false testimony by hired agents could carry through the attempts at a fresh offensive. If we reflect that, thirty years before Otto Bauer was the main ideologist of such theories of alarm and despondency, whereas the Americans now turned to Kravtchenko, we can measure precisely this fall in standards. And since it is the central ideological question with which we are dealing, we also obtain a precise index for the decline in standards in the less directly propagandist fields of economics,

philosophy, and so forth.

How deeply the Kravtchenko principle penetrates the most abstract-looking philosophical exchanges is best illustrated by the debate between Camus and Sartre. Camus's last book was severely but fairly criticized in Sartre's periodical by Francis Jeanson. In an indignant reply, Camus evaded all the important arguments – especially with regard to historicality, to which we shall return shortly in another context – so as to make the Kravtchenko issue, that of penal work-camps in the Soviet Union, the focal point of a philosophical discussion. This he did in a debate about Hegel and Marx, revolution, historical necessity and individual freedom. In his reply, Sartre rightly did not enter into Camus's demagogic absurdities. He refuted his arguments objectively, contenting himself on this issue with unmasking the moral *mala fides* of Camus and his ilk: 'Let us be serious, Camus,' he wrote, 'and please tell me what feelings the revelations of Rousset awaken in an anti-communist heart. Despair? Sadness? Shame at being human? Get along with you! . . . The only feeling that such news arouses in the anti-communist is – and I find it hard to say this – a feeling of *joy*. Joy at having one's *proof* to hand at last and seeing what one wanted to see!'

Such themes naturally played a decisive role in Hitlerian ideology and propaganda as well, as we have shown in detail in the chapter concerned. We have also repeatedly indicated how important, in this connection, speculating on the despair of the masses was in the capitalist countries, and how cynically Hitler used despair and delirium to consolidate the rule of monopoly capitalism. But, on the one hand, all this was concealed for a long while by the talmi-gold, the bogus glitter of social demagogy. (To illustrate the difference in the situation today, let us refer merely to the emotional power of a slogan like the 'breaking of vassalage', in contrast to Lippmann's consoling promises of a statutory elimination of monopolies.) And, on the other hand, whereas despair for Hitler was a socially given starting-point, today's direct apologetic is meant to stifle society's despair at birth. What,

therefore, was a vehicle in Hitler's case is – in this respect – a barrier today.

Again, it is not ideology that has brought this antithesis into reality. It is the social reality which determines the propaganda's starting-point and its objective. Since Hitler tricked monopoly capitalism out in a 'socialist' form, he was able to abuse for his own ends the despair and bitterness of the masses over their exploitation by capitalists. In the United States, on the other hand, the ideology of the ruling class is the maintenance of monopoly capitalism as it stands. Instead, therefore, of stirring up discontent it must calm it down.

Unquestionably many American imperial activists feel that the direct apologetic of monopoly capitalism – as compared to Hitler's indirect apologetic – has put them in a less favourable position from the propagandist angle. So inevitably, attempts have been initiated to discover new forms of indirect apologetics attuned to American conditions. But how? The contrast between direct and indirect apologetics is not simply a question of form but one of social content. The masses that are being depressed and exploited by monopoly capitalism seek a means of escape. The dry reasonableness of Lippmann, say, has great disadvantages, and these are constantly surfacing as irrationalism and despair.

The most famous and influential attempt to gain a new, more effective theoretical basis by twisting round the indirect apologetic which Hitler used so effectively is Burnham's 'managerial revolution'. This is a very clear effort to adopt and to put into practice the cardinal structure of indirect apologetics. Burnham does not want to deny monopoly capitalism's contradictions, and does not even want to trivialize them as easily removable 'disorders'. On the contrary, just like Hitler he takes them as his starting-point and aims at gaining from their analysis a new and enticing social-demagogic perspective. Since he is a renegade Trotskyite, it is a simple matter for him to use the equation of Bolshevism with fascism. He offers, moreover, a corollary borrowed

straight from the technocrats (and already present, in embryo, in Thorstein Veblen), whereby an analogous process also takes place in normal capitalism. The capitalists themselves, the legal owners of the means of production, distance themselves increasingly from production itself and take a less and less active part in its practical management, being replaced by the leading functionaries, Burnham's managers. Like all the 'insights' of contemporary apologetics, this is of course as old as the hills. As early as 1835 Andrew Ure, in his *Philosophy of Manufactures*, called the manager 'the soul of our enterprise system'. Burnham, like the nowadays 'classic' Malthus, was not only an unscrupulous sycophant but also a shameless plagiarist of economic writings that had fallen into oblivion. So the *de facto* rule of the managers, according to Burnham, is the major universal principle in the present economic development. It asserts itself equally – under politically differing forms – in socialism, fascism and the United States. Thereby Burnham, like the Hitlerian ideologists as well as the semanticists, excludes all real socio-economic differences and contrasts between the different systems. And this gives rise to a non-conceptual semantic obscurity in which the communist functionary or factory manager is presented as identical with the capitalist manager.

But at all events, Burnham arrived in this way at a programme of indirect apologetics. Like Hitler, he demagogically professes to negate capitalism. And like Hitler he denies that history poses the dilemma of choosing between capitalism or socialism; like Hitler, he claims to have found a *tertium datur*. Certainly, for all the far-reaching methodological affinity, the changing times and the difference of operational field have left their stamp on the content and form of both constructions. Hitler overrode the dilemma of capitalism versus socialism with the aid of an irrational myth which excited strong emotions. (This began with that despair and longing for relief experienced by the masses in the misery of the crisis of 1929.) Burnham too sketches the theoretical outlines of a myth, but he does so in the sober tone of dry,

objective 'scientific thinking'. Indeed, whereas with Hitler the essential substance of the ideology he proclaimed was a direct result of the mythical solution to the dilemma, Burnham wants to make a sharp, clear-cut division between scientific statement (myth) and ideology; we shall return to this question to study it in more detail. The difference of tone in itself illustrates the difference in period and relevant circumstances and so, as has become already evident, strongly affects the methodology itself. Cynical as Hitler was in the role of chief propagandist and hangman of monopoly capitalism, he could reckon with the likelihood that the proclamation of his myth would carry the desperate masses along with it. But what could Burnham expect from his myth? The indirect apologetics of monopoly capitalism, as whose prophet he figures, can only result at best in an 'élitist circulation' (Pareto). This, however, cannot be more than an ideological cushion for the bourgeoisie and bourgeois intelligentsia in the face of a really profound upheaval in society.

Both men, Hitler and Burnham, endeavoured not only to rescue but also to consolidate monopoly capitalism. Hitler, however, sought to accomplish this with the semblance of a 'revolution' that would – on the surface – transform the whole of society. Burnham too, we admit, mentions revolution, but the whole structure of capitalism, particularly in its relation to mass labour, again remains basically unaltered. The so-called revolution is patently confined solely to the leading sector. Hitler and Burnham, of course, both based their outlook on their contempt for the masses. Nevertheless Hitler sparked off a mass movement, and his demagogy retained the *appearance* of giving the masses a say even during the Nazi régime. Burnham, on the other hand – just like the liberals he heartily despised – regards 'mass concentration' (*Vermassung*) as the major danger, and hence strives openly to thwart all power in the hands of the masses. One obvious aspect of this is that Burnham equates Hitlerian and American Press propaganda with the communist

enlightenment and further education of the masses. In consequence of all this, Burnham in going over to indirect apologetics fails to produce any effective myth that would at once result in striking social-demagogic catchwords. Burnham's indirect apologetic climaxed merely in a *call* to create a corresponding ideology. This, however, was carefully separated from the (purportedly) objectively scientific theory, totally independent of it in content and method.

What, therefore, was unified with Hitler is divided with Burnham. The science, here, is 'objective' (in the sense of semantics and neo-Machism), and in itself has nothing to do with ideology or propaganda. Burnham employed this 'objectivity' to suggest to his readers the fateful inevitability of managerial evolution. The ideology, on the other hand, was determined by the concrete tasks in each instance and had not the slightest relevant to the reality of social evolution and the growth in our perception of it. Ideologies must, Burnham said, '1. express at least in rough outline what currently matches the interests of the ruling class and help to create a model of thought and sensibility salutary to the maintenance of a given social order's key institutions and relations; 2. at the same time, these must be so expressed as to be capable of appealing to mass feeling. An ideology which embraces the interests of a given ruling class would have no value at all as a social bond if it openly expressed its function, namely that of safeguarding the power of the ruling class over the rest of society. The ideology must speak ostensibly on behalf of mankind, the people, the nation, the future, God, destiny, and so on.'

It is hardly possible to imagine a higher degree of élitist cynicism than this. All the same, Burnham here sought to dissociate himself from those of his colleagues who thought that any old ideology could, with the appropriate propaganda machinery, fulfil this function. Such ideas, he said, were wrong: 'More is involved than a skilful propaganda technique. A successful ideology must – even if confused in form – appear to the masses as though it were voicing some

of their interests.' This distinction constitutes the latest acme of cynicism. Certainly we have gone through a great deal in the last decades; we have been acquainted with, among other things, the conversations between Hitler and Rauschning. But the effect of Burnham's book is the effect that Rosenberg would have made if he had included those conversations in his *Myth of the Twentieth Century* as explanatory glosses. As the exponent of the new indirect apologetics, Burnham is simultaneously his own Rauschning.

But this piling up of cynical contempt for humanity had not only the moral aspect that we have studied so far. It also exhibits some political aspects in practice. Although Hitler made similarly cynical statements from time to time (e.g., in comparing political propaganda to soap advertising), he also created a diabolically effective concrete ideology which, although or because it touched the lowest intellectual and moral level hitherto plumbed in human history, still had a mighty and dangerous power over the masses. Here Burnham contents himself with the cynically sketched prescription for an effective ideology, professedly because the 'science' for which he stood was too grand to manufacture ideologies. (To be sure, after the war he himself emerged as the chief propagandist of fresh aggression.) In reality this dualism reflects his inability to expand his indirect apologetic – which was created precisely in order to make up for and to outstrip the weak effect of direct apologetics on the masses – into an ideology that would evoke widespread mass enthusiasm. He contents himself with a methodological recipe because he could no longer find an effective ideology to go with this indirect defence of monopoly capitalism. For the working masses could never warm to the idea that shareholders were being succeeded by managers, all the less in view of Burnham's contention that working conditions were bound to remain the same. Thus Burnham's charge that the technocrats were stating their aims all too openly also applies to himself. But over and above this, his now infamous atempt to create an indirect apologetic for the purposes of American imperialism

is itself proof of the fact that the recourse to indirect apologetics did not reflect any lack of skill or experience on the ideologists' part. It was the necessary ideological consequence of the structure and potential influence of American imperialism. And Burnham himself furnishes proof of this point in that his later war propaganda, writings which tried to create an ideology for the crusade against the Soviet Union, virtually never return to this 'managerial revolution'.

3

All this leads us on to the second demagogic complex, national demagogy. As we have noted, Hitler steered German national sentiments which were well founded, and hence readily kindled into enthusiasm, into the chauvinistic ideology of aggression and global conquest. Burnham and associated direct apologists set the same target not only for the American nation, but for every nation. They were, however, unable to produce an ideology of this kind. Hitler too came to grief with the expansion of his ideology beyond Germany's frontiers into an ideology of the 'new Europe'. But the failure of Burnham and company begins much earlier than that. For how could one rouse any enthusiasm in the ordinary American for the defence of his country on the Yalu River in Korea, or in Morocco? Of course a narrow section of monopoly capitalists and their aides were wildly excited about these plans. Of course heated discussions of such subjects can spring up in clubs or cafés even among ordinary men – under the influence of neatly packaged, monopolistically handled war propaganda. But the big question is: what are we left with if these catchphrases are converted into practice, if they grow into personal issues of life and death? Realistic records of the Second World War offer a none too rosy prospect. Although Japan had been treated as the 'old enemy' for decades, and although the war started with the

Japanese attack on Pearl Harbor, the soldiers in Mailer's book talk as follows: 'What have I got against these goddam Japs? Do you think I care whether they keep this goddam jungle or not?' And the dialogue goes on to express their really deep hatred of their own superiors. Bromfield portrays the same situation, only in a more apathetic tone. If, in Stefan Heym's novel,[3] there are isolated enthusiastic combatants, that is only because they believe (naively) in the crusade to spread democracy. The substance of the novel is precisely their disappointment as a result of the actual American imperialist policy in occupied Germany, the suppression of democracy and the protection of fascists by the real military leaders. And experience of the effects of the Korean war carries one in the same direction.

For Burnham and his ilk, therefore, the central issue would be to make the man in the street grasp that the national life of the American people is threatened by the Soviet Union's 'aggressive designs'. But Burnham himself states: 'Whatever the truth about the military potential of the Red Army, it seems reasonably clear that the communist leaders regard its military role as strategic defence.' Indeed, Burnham takes this defensive character of the Soviet Union's policy so seriously that – in line with some statements by MacArthur – he draws this conclusion: 'For two or three years we are free to behave towards the Soviet Union and communism as we like, without risk of military conflict.' This voices clearly the ideology of naked open aggression. It is not, therefore, a personal propagandistic weakness in Burnham and his associates if they have failed to mobilize the masses into what purports to be national self-defence. That was all the more inevitable because the Soviet peace policy and readiness to negotiate becomes more and more plain to the masses as the Soviet Union, in all her public statements, stresses indefatigably that the peaceful coexistence of different social systems is eminently possible. The difference in practice between Hitler's indirect and American direct apologetics is manifest in the consideration that, whereas Hitler succeeded in gradually

manoeuvring the German labour force into an imperial war of aggression, the American imperialists and their ideologists are forced to begin at that very point at which Hitler finally arrived after a long period of preparation and deception.

The deeper cause of this situation lies in the fact that the American imperial ideologists, above all Burnham, do not see the Soviet Union primarily as a rival political power to the U.S.A. Indeed often, as we have noted, they are compelled to admit that such a political contest for world rule does not exist in the Soviet Union's mind. They see the real danger instead in the spread of communism, and it is this, not the socialist State as such, that they consider their real adversary. Here again we are concerned chiefly with the ideological aspects of this question complex; and for that very reason, the antithesis just stated is not new to us. For imperialist bourgeois ideology, socialism has been the main enemy since Nietzsche. To be sure, this struggle was a largely ideological one for a long while (albeit combined with bourgeois political reprisals). Only since the socialist victory in the Soviet Union has it become more and more strongly bound up with methods used in the imperialist powers' foreign policies. And it is only natural for this struggle to have become increasingly acute with the growth of Soviet power and the victory of socialism in other countries as well.

It is beyond the scope of our studies to investigate how the imperialist powers' foreign policy – from the support of a Koltshak or Denekin to the present Cold War – has absorbed more and more elements of civil war. This is of import to our theme only because the challenge to communist ideology has thereby shifted to the centre of all controversy more openly than ever before. Objectively and in point of fact this has been the case since Nietzsche; but the ensuing shifts of accent represent something qualitatively new. It was possible to say in our foregoing studies that the exacerbation of the struggle was linked with a continual drop in the intellectual and moral level of bourgeois ideology. This was already evident in Nietzsche's entry into this arena, by comparison with the

founders of modern irrationalism in combating the bourgeois concept of progress. This drop in standards eventually culminated in Hitler. Now Burnham and his ilk have long exceeded it. With Burnham, the question inevitably arises of what one can and must oppose to the communist outlook. Hitler still had the iridescent soap bubbles of his myth; Burnham has only the scum.

And Burnham did sense a weakness in his position here. That is why he strongly resisted any claim to a world-outlook. Many people, he remarked, were fascinated by this appeal to one and demanded something similar from the bourgeois side. 'Since we *cannot* have such a belief because of the nature of the situation,' said Burnham, 'we are imperceptibly cramped into a posture of sterility and passiveness.' Burnham planned to reawaken an active, attacking spirit by means of two arguments. Firstly, he identified a world-outlook with totalitarianism and defined the very lack of a philosophy in the bourgeois world today as its supreme merit, to be defended as a sacred possession. Secondly, he deemed a world-outlook to be superfluous from the practical political angle also. 'In the second place,' he stated, 'it is untrue that a war or a social conflict can only end in success if the programme and its defence take a "positive" form. Most often the opposite is true. On the whole, men understand far better what they are *against* than what they are *for*.' By way of an example he cited the French Revolution as a negation of the *ancien régime*. But it does not take a profound knowledge of history to see through the sophistry of these arguments. When the French peasants said no to feudalism, that was a verbal expression – among many others – of their striving for possession of land, for a free say in their labour and the fruits of it, for political freedom and so on, i.e., something positive. In the reality of society, the terms yes and no are inseparably linked dialectically. There does not exist a no in social reality which does not incorporate an essentially positive element. Even the machine-wreckers, through their no, were striving for something positive; that

this something was full of backward prejudices and extremely vague is another matter. But this vagueness was not present in the French Revolution as far as its bourgeois democratic aims are concerned. Only when the victory's contradictory features began to point beyond bourgeois society did any vagueness set in (as an ideological characteristic of the primitive, undeveloped state of the notion of socialism possible at the time). And here again, it did not assume the form of pure negativity for which Burnham calls.

It goes without saying that Burnham's standpoint is also inadmissible from a philosophical angle. It is an existentialist myth – whose untenability I have proved in my examination of this subject – that a particular and peculiar reality (Heidegger's 'nullifying nothing', etc.) may pertain to negation. Affirmation and negation are related to the self-same objective reality and they express – often in different forms, sometimes with certain variations in content – the same concrete substance. But despite the philosophical untenability of this fetishizing of the negation, it certainly does have real social foundations. It is the ideological self-defence of those intellectuals who have lost all social stability, who thus feel totally isolated socially, in a situation *vis à vis de rien*. (Naturally the negative character of such a situation is again something that positively exists, and when important writers like Dostoievsky describe it, their account differs only in the psychology of such figures from the psychology of normal men. Only in extreme decadence is this psychology inflated into a component in the shaping of reality itself; then a literature parallel to existentialist philosophy comes into being.) Now Burnham sought to make this nihilism the ideological starting-point of the struggle against socialism. The world which he was defending no longer had a philosophy or ideals, and out of this necessity he made a virtue – one, it must be said, which rates as such only in the eyes of decadent intellectual parasites.

Certainly it is a universal phenomenon today for the defence of the 'free world' as a basis for the supposedly

healthy development of mankind to proceed in extremely close alliance with decadent thought and morality. This alliance is not fortuitous. For, on the one hand, all decadent minds detect instinctively that their existence can have a foundation only in an objectively decayed world, even if subjectively they believe themselves to be passionately against that world. And, on the other, the political cynicism of ultra-reactionary systems can make much use of just such decadent ideologists. It is not by accident that today, Burnham more or less occupies the position of Rosenberg or Goebbels: all three represent a similar type of decadence. The ideology of the direct apologetic of monopoly capitalism has to employ the methods of a hypocritical cynicism, suppressing all popular freedom in the name of freedom and democracy, preparing for war and waging it in the name of safeguarding peace, and so on. This propaganda, moreover, not only uses downright lies (the Kravtchenko method) in its claims. It also arranges for various imperialist crimes to be depicted, with the Press monopoly's help, as non-existent (bacteria warfare, mistreatment of Korean and Chinese prisoners-of-war, etc.). It is plain that just as the cynical nihilists Rosenberg and Goebbels were Hitler's 'born' propagandists, the cynical hypocrite of Burnham's type is the 'born' ideologist for the Cold War today.

Here it is unnecessary for us to consider the political consequences and perspectives of such propaganda more closely. Let us give just one example of how this nihilism affects the ideology behind practical politics and how, in drawing the consequences from the social situation and the resulting ideology, it reveals its own nature, its negativity. Some time ago the former General Staff officer of Hitler's *Wehrmacht*, Adalbert Weinstein, published a collection of writings. In it, the essence of the German army now coming into being is defined as an 'army without emotion'. Military feeling, the argument runs, means an exaggeration of martial values; it is also the product of national consciousness, the will to fight and masculine pride. In the past, such feeling was

linked with the reality of wars. This link snapped with Hitler's propaganda, but the soldiers at the front, having relinquished all emotion, tried to wipe out the enemy wherever possible. From all this Weinstein drew the following conclusions: 'The struggle of the industrialized nations no longer knows the "pathos" of war . . . In reality the American troops constitute, in their training methods and on the battlefield, an army without emotion.'

The conclusion, here, is as interesting as the argument leading up to it. Weinstein perceived clearly that the old wars were charged with feeling (i.e., with a content inspiring the nation, the masses), and that under Hitler the feeling vanished. But since Weinstein was unable to counter Hitler's inhuman martial objectives with real socio-human ideals he made the same virtue of necessity as Burnham does in general ideological terms. He opposed Hitler's empty propaganda with a total ideational vacuum by locating the reason for this loss of 'pathos' in the industrialization of Germany and the U.S.A., and not in the reactionary turn taken by their social development.

With this, Weinstein as a war theorist arrived at the very point which Burnham reached in his general ideological formulation. Such agreement could be proved between many authors today. It shows to what extent the reality of society always dictates the proposition, method and solution. Monopoly capitalism's ideologists have only a purely negative answer to all present-day questions: at all costs no communism, anything but that; and if we have no positive ideal with which to oppose it, then let nothingness be the ideal. But however cynically authors like Burnham define the 'sociological' criteria of a purportedly effective ideology, nothing can be conjured out of nothingness that would really mobilize the masses for permanent dedication to a cause on which they would stake their lives: no ideology even in Burnham's spirit. Although the monopoly of public opinion may occasionally delude great masses through mercurial and contradictory lies, Hitler's example shows that there are severe

limits to such influence in the unceasing confrontation with reality.

By examining Weinstein's views we have already crossed beyond the U.S. frontiers. This we had to do, for the crusade proclaimed against communism by Burnham was required to mobilize not only the American people but peoples all over the world. Here lies the second weak point in the reactionary ideology prevailing today. And Burnham voices it with open cynicism: 'The U.S.A. needs allies – allies and not mercenaries. And yet it is uncertain who is or can be an ally, and to what degree.' The cynical hypocrisy of Burnham's exposition is expressed in his contrast between allies and mercenaries, since United States foreign policy actually seeks mercenaries, although to be sure it calls them allies. These doubts, which were already well founded when Burnham wrote the above words, are manifested far more distinctly and concretely in an essay published two years later by Raymond Aron. In dealing with the Franco-American relationship, Aron turns to the subject of old and new fellow-travellers, 'those people, that is, who accept American command just as quickly as, in bygone times, they bowed to the rule of the Third Reich. Sometimes, regrettably, it is the same people.' He holds it against them – again, very regretfully – 'that it is just these Western Europeans who are seemingly not in the least concerned about the threat arising through a Russian supremacy in the cultural field'. And he finds – in non-communists most markedly – an attitude which is that of neutralists; they 'deny our dependence, maintaining simply that it is in the Europeans' power to shake off the so-called supremacy of America and that the danger of war will recede, if not be completely banished, as soon as Europeans dissociate themselves for good from their influential protectors. In an extreme form this view is found above all in France, and especially among the French intellectuals.'

As a symptom all this is undoubtedly important – but what lies behind it? We have indicated the answer in commenting on Burnham's statements about allies and mercenaries.

The best definition so far of the principle behind American foreign policy has been given by Hitler's erstwhile official lawyer, the Carl Schmitt already well known to readers of this book. Schmitt is now not only endeavouring for and obtaining a full amnesty, but is in the process of rising to become the legal theorist of the 'American age'. Schmitt's formulation rivals Burnham's in cynicism but surpasses it in precision: '*cujus economia, ejus regio*'. This is a cynically candid expression of the United States' absolute claim to global dominion; and not by chance is it an up-to-date secular variant on the Augsburg Convention (*cujus regio, ejus religio*). In both cases naked power relations are stated as absolute determinants, only now of course at a more advanced stage, hence economic in substance and absolute in all political respects.

Naturally economic supremacy in the capitalist world had long been a means of intervening in the internal affairs of politically independent but economically dependent states. But as long as different groups of rival imperial powers existed, this very rivalry set specific limits to such interference. As a result of the Second World War, however, the U.S.A. was left as the sole imperial power really independent in the economic sense, at least during the time that has hitherto elapsed. That is to say: not only on colonial territory has the competition between imperial states become highly unequal (certainly it is still going on); what were imperial powers up to now have found themselves more and more dependent on America economically. Clearly this new situation was also reflected more and more strongly in the interdependence of her foreign and domestic policies, and the former became determined more and more by this new economic basis. Schmitt expresses this state of affairs – one which has existed for a very long time *de facto* – with the same candid cynicism with which, as Hitler's ideological right-hand man, he once voiced the principle 'Woe to the neutrals!'

It is clear that the qualitatively altered situation had also

to be reflected in ideology. The most important such form it took was an increasingly widespread cosmopolitanism, the view that the independence of nation-states and their political sovereignty had been overtaken by history. (The predominance of cosmopolitanism does not mean the total disappearance of chauvinist campaigns, cf. the agitation against the Oder-Neisse line in Western Germany. But on the whole it is the less significant phenomenon.) Economic, political and cultural developments, said the cosmopolitan ideologists, were driving increasingly towards an integration of individual states, the annulment of national sovereignties and ultimately towards a global State.

Here, as in Hitlerian ideology, one can observe that the bourgeois thinking of the imperial period had tacitly to concede defeat in the intellectual struggle with historical materialism. Although publicly combating the latter even more militantly where possible, it was capable of constructing a counter-ideology only with the help of (distorted and falsified) borrowings from it. And this counter-ideology is a caricature strung together from twisted scraps of historical materialism. That was already how Hitler's 'socialism' was constructed; such elements are to be found in Burnham's manager-theory (the redundancy of the capitalist in production, etc.); the priority of the economic basis over political sovereignty appears in Schmitt; and all this also applies here. The Marxian view of capitalism's historical mission, of the creation of a unified world market and world economy was now presented in a distorted, caricaturistic form, everything turning topsy-turvy and every truth becoming a lie. For, in the first place, there is less of a unified capitalist world economy today than ever before. More than 800 million people live outside the capitalist sphere of influence. In the second place – and this is particularly relevant to cosmopolitanism and the world State – it is untrue that the origin of a world economy and market would render national sovereignty and the independence of nations outmoded and do away with these constructions. The intensifying of the

economic links does not mean the end of autonomous national development. On the contrary, the evolution of socialism shows that even peoples previously living 'free of history' awoke precisely in socialism to a conscious national life. There is no dying out of national culture, of an awareness of national independence and an enthusiasm for it among any of the peoples pursuing a socialist life. On the contrary, they are gaining strength all the time.

But this movement is also found in peoples living under capitalism. Indeed the penetration by capitalism of hitherto pre-capitalist areas has given rise everywhere to national feelings, national consciousness and a striving after national independence. The historical thesis of cosmopolitanism, the world-State theory, is in glaring contradiction to the facts of present-day reality. Naturally it too is supported by specific social facts. But here, similarly, the fundamental blindness of imperialist ideology clearly emerges. Granted, it is forced to acknowledge the presence in society of the mounting awareness of the masses, and of their demand for economic and social, political and cultural recognition. But it interprets these things as a menace to culture, as wholly reprehensible, so here once again its endeavours are purely defensive. (Political measures of repression are not the concern of this book.) We have dealt repeatedly and in detail with the history of this bourgeois attitude as the problem of *Vermassung*. We have noted also how Hitler's national and social demagogy supplied for a transitional period a short-lived bogus solution.

Here again the limit to the prevailing direct apologetic of capitalism is delineated by the fact that in reverting to nineteenth-century liberal ideology, it also inherited the latter's dread of the masses and resistance to their independence; obviously it did so in a qualitatively heightened form reflecting conditions in the imperialist period. That means that this ideology took nothing into account besides the situation and perspective of the ruling class and its intellectual following; the 'cultivation' of the masses was left to

propaganda (and repression). Burnham's division of science and propaganda is thus founded on the situation of the post-war imperialist bourgeoisie.

Now as far as the national question and cosmopolitanism, the world-State and so on are concerned – in this context –, Ricardo Lombardi has rightly pointed out that all capitalist colonization is connected with a buttressing of the old ruling classes. These form an alliance with the colonizers in order to prop up their tottering power. Earlier it was the feudal classes (and it still is in, for instance, some Arab states). Now if, as today, fully developed capitalist states and indeed major powers are being 'colonized' by the United States, present-day monopoly capitalism is taking over the role which the feudal classes used to play: it becomes the 'native' prop for the betrayal of national independence. On this foundation, the ideology of cosmopolitanism acquires real, not impotent supporters. Burnham's negative catch-phrase – resistance to communism at all costs, even at the expense of national sovereignty – finds a concrete basis among this social group and the intellectuals serving it. And on this basis the cosmopolitan ideology turns into one of a doctrinaire betrayal of the homeland.

To be sure, this situation does not mean that the existing real antitheses are superseded in the national question. On the contrary, they are constantly exacerbated in point of fact. For among every people, the safeguarding of national independence and sovereignty will also mobilize those groups that otherwise would be indifferent, indeed averse to communism. Since the communists – true to Marxist-Leninist doctrine – always figure everywhere as the guardians and pioneers of national freedom and self-determination, resistance to communism in the American spirit is bound to win communism new allies all the time. Hitler fell down miserably on this issue, with his plan for the 'new European order'. The impossibility of the American plan to revive Hitler's policy on a global scale is already manifest before being fully put into practice.

It is also manifest here why such empty and automatically ineffective catchphrases as Weinstein's 'war without emotion' are bound to spring up everywhere. Inflammatory slogans, political or martial feeling can only stem from convictions and emotions which the nation really possesses; that dogmatic antithesis to popular endeavours we have outlined is a force reducing the direct apologetic of American imperialism to an insubstantial propaganda technique from the very start.

Again, to examine this more closely is not our task. We have mentioned one essential element which already enters into ideology, namely the exploitation of the press monopoly, etc., to depict non-existent things as reality and to assert the absence of facts which are plain to see, such as the aforementioned bacteria warfare. All this already happened under Hitler. The difference is merely that although – from the international angle – the American propaganda machine is far more powerful, it does not have the corrupt charm of Hitler's beguiling mysticism. It has to be drier, more sober, and for that reason the contrasts between its aims and the real wishes of the masses will come to light more quickly. Of course it would be a gross political error to underestimate the potential influence of so mighty a machine. As planned, we shall not go into a concrete assessment of the issue here. What matters in analysing the ideology is to point out the illusions produced by the pressure of the machine itself on the one hand, and arising out of the stated view of 'mass feeling' on the other – the illusion, above all, that such propaganda could really convince everybody that only 'communist fifth columns' would develop a resistance to the ideals of the 'American age'. Hitler in his time confused his quislings with nations; now many ideologists of direct apologetics are confusing the majority of nations with 'fifth columns'. The reason, in both cases, is a contempt for the masses and hence a blindness towards their real will. Besides this, and there is an inner connection here, we have the megalomania of the machinery. The American professor Henry Morgenthau calls attention to the fact that the press,

radio, etc., are by no means identical with real public opinion in America; that the false association has given rise to false crowd-pulling politics. 'The administration', he says, 'has become a prisoner of its own propaganda.'

4

This flimsiness of the direct apologetics of American imperialism is closely linked with another difference from Hitler's indirect apologetic. We refer to the public relationship to religion and the churches. Hitler's myth put forward the claim to be an immediate substitute for religion. It therefore contained an overt polemic against Catholicism; it was, as we have shown in the relevant chapter, a demagogic continuation of the religious atheism of irrationalist philosophy. All these motives are absent from present-day direct apologetics: these, on the contrary, seek support very actively from all the churches, and especially the Roman Catholic; the Vatican's propaganda machine is as close to the 'Voice of America' as the Banca di Santo Spirito to Wall Street. Here we must certainly stress that Rosenberg's hostility to Catholicism must not be taken too seriously either. For certain sections it meant an ideological shadow-boxing, but it did not stop the Hitler régime from receiving concrete support from the Vatican and the leading German Catholics.

It is self-evident that this difference did not arise primarily out of the shortcomings of ideology as a most welcome complement, but out of the socio-historical evolution of the United States themselves. There, Church and commerce were always as intimately linked as were capitalism and Protestant sects at the time of their founding. And since the United States did not go through any such crises as those experienced by European nations after the French Revolution, there was no profound shaking of religious faith either. Thus the defence of capitalist society in America did not need to

incorporate religious atheism in the systems of indirect apologetics. The so-called agnosticism of a part of the high-brow intelligentsia was something perfectly harmless in comparison to the European ideological crises. So it was organically, out of the social evolution of the United States themselves, that the alliance between the churches – above all, the Vatican – and American imperialism grew into a crusade against communism.

Again, it is not our present task to analyse and to judge the political, the practical propagandistic importance of this alliance (e.g., its influence on backward agricultural and petty bourgeois sectors). The only issue which concerns us is the ideological side: whether the alliance with religion and the Church can fill this direct apologetic's pure and empty negativity with a philosophical content, whether it can make up for the obligatory renunciation of a religious substitute à la Rosenberg. These questions too, we think, must be answered in the negative. That such philosophical trends as French Existentialism which continue the religious-atheistic line cannot attain to a leading role internationally, that they represent an intermediate stage, a 'third road' ideology, is only a negative symptom of this situation. A positive one would be provable only if it could be shown where and when a new spiritual motive arises through this alliance with religion and the Church, an element of religious (or even just pseudo-religious) enthusiasm.

But there is not a trace of this. And so profoundly counter-revolutionary a thinker as the White Russian émigré Berdyaev correctly indicates the cause. He writes, with deep sorrow, of the unreligious condition of contemporary man: 'The overwhelming majority of men, Christians included, are materialists, and they do not believe in the power of the spirit; they believe in nothing but material power, military or economic.' But this basic attitude is by no means incompatible with an allegiance to religion and even a cult of myths. In dealing with Schopenhauer and Kierkegaard, we have referred to the spiritual comfort offered to a decadent intelligentsia by the

religious atheism of the one and the emotional religiosity of the other. The more advanced the decadence, the stronger the need for such a comfort will become. It has already assumed overtly religious forms in previous ages (e.g., in the Austrian type of baroque Catholicism). Thus today, it can have the religious tint which is in vogue politically – and can do so in a candidly cynical way –, without having undergone the slightest change in basic moral attitude or the least enrichment in philosophical matters. Aldous Huxley, who has recently begun preaching mysticism, represents this attitude with uncommonly frank cynicism. He does not, of course, believe in the slightest in the real core of any genuinely mystical state, in the mystical union with God, but he adds: 'But that by no means diminishes the value of mysticism as a road to well-being. Nobody regards Swedish gymnastics or cleaning one's teeth as a direct avenue to God. If we make a habit of yoga or Pepsodent, we do it for our well-being. For the same reason we should make a habit of mysticism and moral virtue.'

It will no longer surprise the reader that such an ideological comfort should appear precisely at a time when intellectuals were invoking God in despair. The connection is clearly visible in Aldous Huxley's cynicism. With Bertrand Russell, this 'religious' despair is manifested even more cynically, pursuing – in an apparently jocular way – all the counter-revolutionary, aggressive imperialist consequences. Russell offers, on the plane of religious metaphysics, the following perspective: 'Perhaps – I sometimes imagine – God does not want us to understand the mechanism with which he steers the material universe. Perhaps nuclear physicists have come so close to the ultimate secrets that he thinks it is time to call a halt to their work. And what simpler method could he adopt than to let them carry on their inventions until mankind is wiped out? If I could imagine that deer and squirrels, nightingales and larks would survive this catastrophe, I could face it with some equanimity; man has proved, after all, that he is unworthy to be the lord of Creation.' But such

apocalyptic moods always have an exactly delineated political content: the life-and-death struggle against socialism. For people like Bertrand Russell, the demise of humanity is more bearable than the prospect of a socialist victory. And of course the apocalypse is not to be taken seriously; its real substance, that which Russell desires, is for 'the White terror to succeed the Red', and for 'a single military government (the American, naturally – G.L.) to be set up all over the world'. The 'religious renaissance', then, is nothing more than a further ideological sanction of atomic and bacteria warfare.

Lippmann once wrote: 'When the times grow out of joint, some men storm the barricades and others retire to a monastery.' We have shown the ideological difficulties of the counter-revolutionary barricades and have also intimated that ideologically, the aid of religion should not be rated too highly. As regards the monastery idea, this is a general sign of decadence in times of crisis: an ideological retreat from great conflicts and the repudiation of a standpoint. The detail of whether it is a Buddhist-atheist monastery or a Catholic one is, if we examine the ideology of withdrawal (which we cannot do here), of no great importance. All the more significant, however, is the direction taken in the escape. For even in judging the ideology, it would (precisely where the conflicts are great and decisive) be wrong to take the viewpoint 'whoever is not for it is against it', or simply to lump together all who seek a 'third road' or want to be neutral. No, in that respect every 'monastery' is still for or against one of the parties to the struggle. Mauriac or Graham Greene, when they write religious fiction in which all concretely social matter pales into insignificance beside religious themes, are standing – and we do not need to take into account Mauriac's overtly war-mongering publications – on the imperialist side of the barricade merely by staying in the 'monastery'. On the other hand, Karl Barth's rejection of any social distinctions in religion, for example, contains a rejection of imperialist warfare. Not for nothing does the imperialist press speak of

Barth, and of Niemöller in particular, as lost souls in a 'no man's land' (or even as abductors into a 'no man's land'), whereas it sees in Mauriac or Graham Greene a significant extension in depth to its mental portrait of the world. Here this Press is evincing a sound political and aesthetic instinct. In no respect – save for built-in 'miracles' – does the world shaped by these writers differ from the decadent movement's barbaric unleashing of the instincts, and such 'monasteries' may very well be suitable places of training for future collaborators or even for imperialist butchers.

Mention of these religious ideologies affords us a chance to make a few comments on the 'great history philosopher' of our day, A.J. Toynbee. Philosophically, his now famous *oeuvre* offers nothing new whatever. On all the main issues Toynbee is a straightforward epigone of the vitalist epigone Spengler, from whom he has borrowed all his important concepts, such as opposition to the unity of history, the equating of all civilizations, the denouncing of progress as illusory, and so on. His so-called originality is expressed in wholly trivial details; for however many such 'culture cycles' either one of them constructs – with equal arbitrariness – they result in as few concrete differences as exist between, to recall Lenin's joke, a red devil and a blue one, i.e., none at all.

It also matters little that Toynbee does not draw on Spengler's biological irrationalism. For to his mind, a culture's historical transition from a static to a dynamic condition is a pure irrational miracle instead. To effect this transition, Toynbee also uses purely mythological similes, and he argues this method with the following 'epistemological' considerations: 'The occurrence can be best expressed in such mythological images, for they are not affected by the contradictions arising when an observation is translated into logical terms. If God's universe is perfect, no Devil can logically exist apart from it, while if the Devil does exist, then the perfection which he comes to disrupt would necessarily be already imperfect through the mere fact of his

existence. This contradiction, which is beyond a logical solution, the imagination of the poet and prophet transcends intuitively . . .' So here, but in a far clumsier and more rudimentary form than in the later Schelling, mythology becomes the 'intuitive form to absorb and to express universal truths'. The removal of Spengler's biological irrationalism thus produces, if anything, an even wilder nonsense. Here a comparison with Spengler clearly shows the general decline in standards which we have already observed in Spengler compared to Nietzsche and Dilthey.

In view of this it is not worth examining Toynbee's writings in detail. Let us emphasize just one point, the point at which his connection with Christian allegiance is clearly manifest in the decisive part of his philosophy of history. Toynbee sees the only way out of the current crisis in an imitation of Christ: 'He who lives by the sword will perish by the sword.' But his admonition is directed exclusively at the 'internal' and 'external' proletariat (another of the discoveries which Toynbee makes for the whole of history, but again a high-flown copy of the fascist theory of 'proletarian nations'). His admonition does not apply to the ruling classes, whose use of violence he finds very compatible with Christianity.

If we now consider the overall ideological situation as outlined so far, we must immediately ask what scope it affords to originality, to profundity and influence. The answer is none at all, and we are not alone in saying this. Let us turn to so respected an ideologist of decadence and friend of America as Denis de Rougemont:

> But unfortunately this revolt by culture against the world surrounding us was denied all direct influence up to the present. It is the affair of an élite which, increasingly isolated from the general mass, becomes alienated from political, social and economic occurrences which obey their own laws, laws that are growing less and less acceptable to the human spirit. Between the businessman, the politician, the proletarian on the one hand and a Rilke or a

> Heidegger on the other, there is no longer a common language, a common visualization of the goal or the values of life and society. They are linked at best by such vague words as freedom, democracy and justice, and each man imagines something different by these. No longer is there a universally recognized authority to proclaim 'the truth' and to fix a common set of values. Almost everything that is going on in Europe today finds itself somehow at odds with what is right and proper in the view of the various orthodoxies, according to bourgeois morality or the criteria of reason.

Our illustrious author is not content with this observation. He gives a very characteristic example of the inefficacy of the one ideology he esteems, the hero of which is another prominent figure in the same movement, Arthur Koestler. After one of his anti-communist novels had appeared, Koestler received some letters from students, and Rougemont quotes the following extract: 'Your portrayal of Stalinism is in my opinion perfectly correct. That is why I am joining the Communist Party, because I was just looking for such a discipline.'

This failure and impotence are not surprising. The single word 'despair', as the substance of this ideology, does not suffice to explain matters, for as we have seen, Heidegger's despair was able directly to prepare the way for Hitlerism. Today a writer like Graham Greene is able to exert a similar influence. But now we are dealing with something different, something additional and more concrete. Not just with a general despair about all human activity; this, from Schopenhauer to Heidegger, has led into the reactionary camp or at least to collaboration with it. Rougemont, Koestler and their ilk, however, are not only despairing in general; their doubt and their despair are directed primarily towards those 'glad tidings' which they came to announce: towards the defence of the 'free world'.

Let us turn again to an authentic witness of events, Koestler

himself, speaking through a character in his novel *The Age of Longing*. One has a distinct feeling that the character, Julien, is speaking more frankly than the author would otherwise dare to speak: 'Now I happen to believe that Europe is doomed, a chapter in history which is drawing to its finish. This is so to speak my contemplative truth. Looking at the world with detachment, in the sign of eternity, I find it not even disturbing. But I also happen to believe in the ethical imperative of fighting evil, even if the fight is hopeless . . . And on this plane my contemplative truth becomes defeatist propaganda and thus an immoral influence.' And this confession closes with an observation – of some importance, coming from Koestler – about the future of art and literature in the 'free world' so zealously defended by the author: 'European art is dying out, because it can't live without truth, and its truth has become arsenic . . .'[4]

That means that Koestler is saying of his own world that it cannot bear an art which faithfully reflects reality. But that is exactly what the outstanding anti-fascists once observed about the relation of the Third Reich to true and realistic art. It is also part of the emerging picture, to be sure, that such observations by no means prevent men like Rougemont and Koestler from engaging in American war propaganda. (The same observation, therefore, which made rigorous anti-Hitlerites of honest men of letters produces in the defenders of the 'free world' only the luxury of a self-irony, a cheekily self-indulgent nuance to their imperialist propaganda.) Here we find confirmed in a new domain our earlier remarks on the hypocritical cynicism of these ideologists. Believing in what they preach no more than Lippmann, they copy Burnham in acting as their own Rauschning – even if they distribute the incongruities over different writings.

Naturally despair does not lead solely to submission or even to making common cause with imperialist reaction. It can sometimes mark a crisis giving rise to a new awareness of reason. But it may also harbour such a collapse into inactivity, an intended self-surrender reaching suicidal

proportions, that its usefulness – even its reactionary usefulness – appears to be more than questionable. The highly successful American novelist Louis Bromfield has depicted such a fate in his *Mr Smith*. From the social angle he is no doubt right when he makes his narrator draw a parallel between himself and Babbitt:

> In writing of these men, I am not writing just of Babbitts. There are no Babbitts left. They belonged to a particular phase of American life, and that phase is over. Today Babbitt, with his vanity, his easy nature, his strong extravertedness and the rowdiness covering up his lack of culture, is a misfit and in some ways an outcast. All his qualities and his true problem have been ousted to some extent by illness and perplexity, whose victims are unaware of it and seek refuge in materialism, excessive activity and alcohol. Babbitt was crude in his way, but healthy. The illness of which I am writing and which is constantly on the increase, is quite different. I know what I am talking about, and I fear for a whole nation and people.

Bromfield and his hero, to be sure, overestimate Babbitt's healthiness. Readers of both novels will know that what ruins the life of Bromfield's hero also crops up in Babbitt's life, albeit as a mere episode; the seeds of Bromfield's despair, though existing in Babbitt in embryo, are there put to rights by 'American freedom' (from a boycott to material and moral ruin). This is not to discredit Bromfield. Seen through Mr Smith's eyes, Babbitt is bound to seem healthy and robust, and it is precisely Bromfield's achievement to have portrayed accurately the turning of one type into a qualitatively different type in consequence of social developments. It is part and parcel of this heightening that Mr. Smith has even less inkling of the true determining causes of his fate than Babbitt did. In both characters, however, there is an instinctive revolt against a specifically American 'conformism', against the 'standardization' – by force if necessary – of all

thoughts and feelings. Sinclair Lewis, who was more conscious of these issues than Bromfield now is, said of such tendencies among the 'Good Citizens' League' (which liquidates Babbitt's excursion into eccentricity): 'And they confirm that American democracy may not mean equality of means but does on the other hand dictate a sound uniformity in thinking, dress, morals, painting and mode of expression.' Sinclair Lewis (though not Babbitt) even knew that this conformism in the shapes of 'democracy' and 'liberty' was a universal capitalist phenomenon, only manifesting itself far more strongly in the United States than elsewhere on earth. The idea of defending just *this* world in the name of the right to 'nonconformity' is another clear example of the Rauschning syndrome.

What is therefore at stake in this development – whether or not Bromfield knows it – is the fate of the average man under capitalism gone to seed. We can understand only too well why men of healthy vital instincts should spontaneously revolt against such a perspective of their existence. This revolt often assumes an anti-capitalist form, usually fairly vague; we have already read of Raymond Aron's indignation at the general spreading of such feelings in Europe. But he was not the only thinker to object to it by a long chalk. Professor D.W. Brogan of Cambridge, for instance, sees in the anti-capitalist sentiments of many Europeans the roots of their anti-Americanism. For us it is a matter of indifference that Professor Brogan wants to overcome these sentiments; indeed his very friendliness towards America lends to his observations a particular value. He writes: 'For if someone rejects the modern (capitalist, G.L.) world, he is perfectly entitled to reject it in its most representative form, and this is in the majority of cases the American form. Not because the Americans are especially depraved, but because they occupy a leading position in the technological field in the world today. It cannot be helped that unfavourable conclusions about America may possibly be drawn from this. At all events anyone rejecting the modern world for one reason or another is well advised to reject it in its most consummate

form.' That is exactly the fate of Mr. Smith, of which the average European and above all the intellectual has a fear amounting to panic. Already he is disoriented and driven to despair by his own monopoly capitalism, which is still relatively undeveloped – so how alarming its American consummation must seem to him!

It is Bromfield's further achievement to have shown the connection between modern decadent art (up to Surrealism) and Mr. Smith's desperate loss of his bearings: he shows us the feelings and outlook (or rather, the lack of an outlook) which give rise to the effect of this art. Mr. Smith tells of a journey he made to New Orleans to drown the memory of his domestic surroundings with a few days' drinking and whoring. 'When I look back on that trip, my whole impression of it always reminds me of one of those Surrealist paintings composed entirely of a tangle of narrow streets with lurid neon lights screaming out "The Jolly Fellow" and "The Wild Man", a tangle of disconnected hands and arms, nothing but ghostly figures reaching out from narrow alleys and entrances to pull a man off the rails. Certainly it looks like that to one who has had a lot to drink.'

Mr. Smith's experience is unconscious, elemental. But it can be readily reconciled with critical endeavours to show more precisely why abstract art has become supreme among elevated circles in the United States, and what has made it so. The Marxist Finkelstein, who gives a vivid indication of these methods in an essay, quotes an article in the *New York Times* by Aline B. Louchain: 'Humanism goes back to the anthropomorphic philosophy of the Greeks when man was at home in the world, making himself "the measure of things", and when art – in the world as it is – found expression by creating a representation of the world as man desires it to be. Such thinking presupposes a finite, calculable universe with independent, powerful man at its centre, and a reality largely accessible to man's faculties of comprehension. But with our modern scientific research, such a picture of the universe is no longer possible.' Of course what the author of the article

sets forth as a conclusion has no relevance to the findings of the natural sciences today. The telling question of why a reactionary-decadent, agnosticist-mystical journalism receives attention even from certain natural scientists exceeds the scope of these studies. The important point, for us, is that there is a direct road from the spontaneous description of the escape from an inhuman condition into the extra-human realm to a theoretical argumentation of this art from the anti-human principle. This contemporary road stretches far back into the imperial age, leading from Paul Ernst and Worringer via Ortega y Gasset to Malraux.

If this were a purely aesthetic problem, there would be scant reason for occupying ourselves with it now. But is it sheer coincidence that Paul Ernst ended his career as a supporter of Hitler, that Ortega y Gasset – as a leading combatant of *Vermassung* – became a typical anti-democrat of our times, or that Malraux turned into the Goebbels of De Gaulle? Because none of this is fortuitous, the protection of abstract, i.e., consciously anti-human and anti-realistic art by leading circles in America is likewise no accident, and only snobbery *as well* on the surface. It is no more of an accident than the persecution and suppression of realism. As Hitler has already proved, a system of this kind cannot tolerate realism. Today we receive the same picture, but from the manifestations of American 'democracy'. In itself the tendency is not new, but its present upsurge signifies something qualitatively new. The fate of Mark Twain as a writer is common knowledge. We have already referred to the 'democratic' terrorism in Babbitt. Later Sinclair Lewis described in *Arrowsmith* the 'kid-glove' and in *Elmer Gantry* and *Kingsblood Royal* the notoriously terroristic methods of the 'free world'. They sufficiently account for the great fluctuations in this highly gifted realist as well as the fate of such initially highly promising realists as John Steinbeck and others. And the relation of the 'free world' to realism can be precisely traced in the treatment of Chaplin, Howard Fast and Paul Robeson.

The persecution of artistic realism in itself is no longer just an aesthetic matter. But its socio-ideological aspects are revealed more distinctly still if we consider the human content expressed in a decadent literature protected precisely at the points where the moral consequences of a decadent outlook clearly emerge. And this is not a Marxist's 'anti-Americanism', as we see from observations which Professor H.S. Commager, an American, has made on these issues. 'The men and women who allow such frenzied rein to their natural instincts in Faulkner, Caldwell, Farrell and Hemingway, in Waldo Frank, Evelyn Scott and Eugene O'Neill are as amoral as animals . . . Nobody who has examined Ezra Pound's career can doubt that his quest for obscurity is connected with his hatred of democracy.' And he adds in conclusion that the attack on reason fomented by such writers 'is the deepest degradation of man'.

It is at this point that the problem of modern art – through the mediation of ethics – tilts over into politics. Artistic policies pursued in the United States have energetically promoted this. Whereas earlier, in Europe especially, the unleashing of the instincts as the substance of art was confined to small circles of an 'élite' among the decadent, parasitic intelligentsia, this content is now being popularized on a broad scale. The barriers between 'esoteric' art and mass kitsch are being dismantled with increasing vigour. The cinema, radio, literary digests, etc., are spreading to the widest extent exactly what in Faulkner, say, is celebrated as 'quality' literature: the uninhibited venting of even the worst instincts. The constant increase in juvenile delinquency, for instance, demonstrates the results of such 'social pedagogics'.

To seek the causes in literature would admittedly be wrong; we are simply dealing with symptoms. The Ku-Klux-Klan and other lynching organizations put the bestial release of the instincts into practice long before leading authors were drawn to the subject. (To avoid any misunderstanding: we are now talking of the approval and glorification in literature of an unleashing of the instincts. The realistic mode of

representation that 'calls a spade a spade' has no connection with this matter.) Certainly detective and gangster films, trashy literature of various types, the Superman of the comic strips and the brutalizing of sport, etc., were the pioneering forerunners of this development. But only now has a comprehensive system arisen that encompasses the top and bottom ends equally.

It was a characteristic of the Hitler régime that, by skilful manoeuvres, it led essentially and harmlessly mediocre people, sometimes even gifted ones, into becoming accomplices and indeed active participants in terrible crimes and barbaric deeds of inhumanity. Without such 'social pedagogics' Auschwitz, for example, would not have been possible. Now it is the special feature of the American development that elements of such tendencies have always existed – in the South, since the liberation of the slaves. The direct extension of a partially original accumulation of capital into the age of monopoly capitalism facilitated and encouraged the country to pursue such a social path. There is also the specifically Southern nuance whereby the most backward and anachronistic form of exploitation (slavery) had a more or less distinctly capitalist character from the outset. As the result of all this, social elements which otherwise belong entirely to the original accumulation grew, with the appropriate modifications, directly into imperialist capitalism. This further gave rise to the special peculiarity that all this evolved within forms of an exemplary bourgeois democracy; the United States are unfamiliar with any feudalism or absolute monarchy of the kind developed in Europe. And another important component of Hitlerism – racial theory and racial discrimination – was also operative there, especially in the South but later rife everywhere, at a time when racialism still constituted the personal view of reactionary extremists and outsiders in Europe. We pointed out before that Gobineau, unrecognized at home, found his first enthusiastic readers in the southern states of North America. The more American imperialism became the world's leading reactionary power,

the more widespread these tendencies grew. They were used – if anything, more deliberately and systematically than under Hitler – to pave the way for aggression, imperialist war and for the barbaric waging of wars that had already started (as in Korea). The respectable Democrats in the U.S.A. fought and are fighting a hitherto vain struggle against these tendencies.

Another aspect of the same picture is that nowhere but in the U.S.A. does there exist such a network, such a system of 'cross-links' between overt gangsters and the official State and municipal machinery. (Professor H.H. Wilson has published a poll conducted by the National Opinion Research Office in 1944, according to which five Americans out of every seven questioned thought all politicians were corrupt.) Here too we can ascertain a constant feeling of indignation on the part of ordinary decent people. But this feeling has no real power behind it, chiefly because the monopoly of public debate, the power of a press governed by the aforestated network and the machinery of the two political parties are continually combining demagogically to mislead it. It is, for instance, highly probable that the Republican election victory in 1952 was partly due to a spontaneous revolt by many ordinary people against the corruption of the Democrats. Here we can predict with a fair amount of certainty that in a few years' time, there will be a similar revolt against Republican corruption; the case of Vice-President Nixon, which was successfully covered up, sheds a glaring light on the fact that the Republicans are by nature as corrupt as the Democrats. To illustrate this with a random example, let us take the case of O'Dwyer. The following is a quotation from the *Neue Zürcher Zeitung* – which is certainly not anti-American:

> O'Dwyer's appointment as ambassador to Mexico was solely the result of a need to move the Mayor of New York out of the country before the disgraceful scandals of his hardly commendable administration were exposed. The soil of America has become so hot for this former New

York policeman that he prefers to spend the rest of his life in Mexico as 'counsellor' to a lawyer's office there. Truman only accepted O'Dwyer's resignation, as he writes in his reply, 'with reluctance and warmest thanks for services rendered'. But O'Dwyer will still be representing the United States along with several other special delegates at the inauguration in a few days' time of the new Mexican President, Ruiz Cortines.

And at the time of writing this epilogue, the exposure of MacCarran appears about to 'break'. His case is – as a symptom – perhaps even more interesting because MacCarran, who is closely associated with gangster organizations, was a veritable pioneer of the 'true American way of life' and scourge of 'anti-American tendencies'. In its way the MacCarran case symbolizes in a nutshell what is going on among the dominant sector of war-mongers as much as the (far more innocent) Captain of Köpenick could once be said to symbolize the state of things in Wilhelmine Germany.[5]

The particular blend of corruption, gangsterism, crime and political terrorism was also characteristic of the Hitler régime. We may recall Rauschning's conversation with the *Führer* in which the latter approved of the corruption of the ruling class because absolute obedience could be extorted from its members at any time, their corrupt behaviour being a well-known fact. Naturally this motive also plays a major role in the corruption prevailing today. With each public exposure it turns out that many initiates have long been informed of the matter but had their reasons for concealing it in public. But the 'cross-links' with the gangster world have the further 'political' advantage that in awkward cases, the ruling class always has at its bidding the adequate terrorist organizations to intimidate and, if need be, to liquidate troublesome elements. This is a substitute in 'normal' times of peace for what military discipline achieves in wartime. 'Fear is the condition of twentieth-century man,' says Mailer's General Cummings. And to magnify this fear still further, there is the

ever-increasing apparatus of the secret police, the legally permissible use of torture in police interrogations, etc. Of course all this finds an epitome in the Army. 'The Army functions best when each individual fears the man above him and despises his inferiors,' says the same General Cummings. The resulting general atmosphere of fear is by no means at odds with the aforestated problem of the unleashing of the instincts. On the contrary this is an absolute necessity, in combating both the internal and the external enemy. As under Hitler, it has simply to be suitably channelled, guided into the desired direction. And the relation of the ruling class to the gangster world is an important intermediate link, intellectual-moral and organizational, in this process.

To the subject complex of the release of the instincts, gangster life, intellectual and moral corruption belongs the unprecedently powerful role which renegades play in contesting communism. Of course the phenomenon itself is not entirely new. Between the two world wars, after all, we witnessed Trotsky's international propaganda activity and deeds of provocation; there were the various Eastmans, Doriots and so on. But today it is not only ordinary police agents like Kravtchenko and his ilk who stand in the forefront of world publicity. The most celebrated authors such as Dos Passos, Silone, Koestler and Malraux, leading politicians like Ernst Reuter, such publicists as Burnham and many others are apostates of communism.

Naturally this gives rise to the question: what makes the apostates of the communist movement so precious in the war-mongers' eyes precisely nowadays? As we have already mentioned, the hollowness and poverty of imperialist ideology was bound to entail a constant borrowing from Marxist precepts – in a distorted form – in an attempt to utilize details of Marxism, absurdly garbled, in the anti-Marxist struggle itself. And naturally the apostates are experts on this subject. (Cf. Burnham's treatment of monopolies in contrast to Lippmann or Röpke.) It turns out that even the most superficial study of Marxism offers immense advantages over

the most thorough bourgeois university education, especially in economics and politics. For let us remark at this point that the overwhelming majority of apostates who have now become famous only moved for a time on the periphery of the communist movement. As the renegade Borkenau observes, only Silone and Reuter were responsible Communist Party functionaries. (It is not worth examining the difference in talents in detail, although Silone, for example, was a realist to be taken seriously in his communist period, whereas Koestler remained the trivial and superficial journalist he always was in his much-acclaimed pot-boilers with their mixture of psychology and sociology.) Also to be considered is the 'authenticity' of their disclosures about communism, whose propaganda value the imperialists assess irrespective of whether the apostates concerned were, in view of their extremely peripheral place in the movement, in any position at all to be really informed about it. Since, as we have shown, anti-communist propaganda has hit upon Kravtchenko, it will find some value in every lie and calumny, however tailored to mercenary purposes. Moreover, the apostates are seen as particularly reliable because no road back is now open to them. Burnham expresses this by saying that they are more immune to the ideological poison of communism than those who have not gone through the same transitional phase; their 'no' to communism has more feeling in it than that of the rest. Their hatred, vengefulness and resentment are emotions of great value to anti-communist propaganda. Thus in spite of the extremely modest standard of their knowledge and talents, they become pioneers and leading figures in the ideological struggle against communism. This again is a precise indication of how low bourgeois ideology has sunk today.

It is from this situation, from recognizing the intellectual and moral inferiority of their present masters, that the apostates' pride and arrogance derive. Crossman records a conversation with Koestler in which the latter says: 'We, the former communists, are the only people on your side who know what is really at stake.' And Silone even goes so far as

to state 'that the final battle would be fought out between communists and ex-communists'. This, of course, is a bad joke which only goes to show that Silone has already forgotten what can be learned in any primary school. But the remark is typical of one facet of the apostates' intellectual and moral stance. The other facet is a fresh nuance, a further intensifying of a decadent psychology and morals. And herein lies the crucial motive for their importance to the contemporary bourgeoisie. The latter has a real use only for moral cripples or gangsters. Hence the apostates are its best human material. For time and again, they display the decadently warped and fragmented basis of their spiritual disposition, for which they over-compensate through arrogance. Crossman observes: 'The true ex-communist can never become an integrated personality again.' And Koestler confirms this diagnosis when he makes one of his characters, an ex-communist poet, say of himself: 'There is lyric poetry and sacred poetry, and a poetry of love and a poetry of rebellion; the poets of apostasy do not exist.'[6]

Thus although the psychology of the apostate creates, on the face of it, an extreme outsider, it nevertheless contains something which is highly typical of the whole period. The cardinal lack of inner integrity, expressed as hypocritical cynicism, permeates all life's inner and outer manifestations. It is quite impossible and impermissible to state explicitly the true substance of the ideological struggle against communism, namely the struggle to preserve exploitation against the attempt to end it. The whole foundation of the ideological dispute must therefore be mendacious: the struggle is represented as between 'freedom' and 'oppression' – once again, a cynically promulgated bare-faced lie. The whole Kravtchenko method follows from this basic mendacity of the 'free world'.

We can perceive its consequences in every cultural sphere. The administrative drive towards an American cultural hegemony is oriented not only towards directly political realms. In part American ideological leadership is regarded as a

universal question, but in part the material interests of American publishers, film manufacturers, etc., also play a crucial role. Film production units which are as highly developed artistically as the French and Italian are having to struggle desperately for their livelihood against the competition of State-supported trash from the U.S.A. The progressive French work of literature must, to survive in spite of the mass distribution of horror, detective and digest stories, safeguard itself through an organized mass movement, and so on. While American Cold War propaganda professes to rescue European culture from the 'totalitarianism of the East', true European culture is fighting an all-out battle to preserve its naked existence, a battle against the agencies of the 'American century'.

That is the external situation. And the internal one? We have mentioned already a whole series of decisive cultural problems. Here we would like to stress just one more. This problem, although only of real interest to a relatively narrow section of the intelligentsia, nonetheless constitutes the common factor uniting intellectuals otherwise far apart and linking them to philosophical tendencies of the 'free world'. We are referring to the right to nonconformity. But just here we are dealing with a sheer illusion. Monopoly capitalism's publishing, film-making, press and other machinery restricts – especially under Cold War conditions – the effective scope of this nonconformism to an extraordinary extent. It goes without saying that nuances of personal bias within the content laid down in each instance are not only allowed but expected. But should there occur a real, concrete deviation from the prescribed path in matters of intrinsic content, there ensues a hushing-up process on the part of the public apparatus (e.g., Eluard's funeral and the obituaries of him) which is wont to amount to direct persecution (Chaplin). Nonconformity's champions should therefore ask themselves what kind of nonconformism is allowed in practice in the 'free world'. Sartre, for example, was a hero of 'freedom of thought' as long as he opposed communism in his writings;

since taking part, in 1952, in the People's Congress for Peace in Vienna, he has become a subject of scorn for the 'free world'. Thus we find in the 'free world' a most unequivocal answer to the question: conformity to whom and what? One may (and should) boldly declare one's nonconformism, so-called, by making a stand against the Soviet Union and socialism in the United States, Adenauer's Germany, etc. One can even carry it out with whatever arguments one pleases. But one must conform to monopoly capitalism and its aggressive imperialist politics in order to be recognized as a proper 'nonconformist'.

But the problem of nonconformity goes deeper. In his *Empirio-Criticism* Lenin had already shown that the academics' various individual epistemological nuances, furiously attacked and defended as they were, are no longer distinguishable when considered from the angle of the really crucial epistemological question: idealism or materialism? This applies on a heightened scale to ideological problems today. Anyone giving his attention to the really decisive philosophical problems will discern an alarmingly conformist monotony in the – at first sight – incommensurable chaos of individual nuances. We have indicated, for example, the close proximity of Wittgenstein and Heidegger (between whom there was no mutual influencing) when regarded from this viewpoint. The situation is exactly the same in ethics, in the interpretation of history, in the stance taken towards society, and in aesthetics. And also, of course, in literature and art themselves.

Precisely the most individualistic, most radically nonconformist tendencies involve a radical levelling down of this kind. For objectively (and hence artistically as well) 'the real richness of the individual' depends 'wholly on the richness of his real relations' (Marx), and the more defiantly modern art focuses on the purely self-sufficient personality detached from society and from social relationships, the greater the similarity will be between figures outwardly so extraordinarily diverse, until there is no perceptible difference.

For objectively (and hence artistically as well) the world of culturally evolved human relations is incomparably more varied than the bare world of the instincts. And this is why an art concentrating on the latter with almost dogmatic insistence is careering inevitably towards monotony and levelling down. How alike Aeneas and Dido are to Romeo and Juliet in their copulation, whereas the differences in erotic feelings determined by their society and culture have created genuine and enduring individuals. The solipsistic, abstract approach of the majority of modern nonconformists has brought about an inhuman levelling in the standards of creative work. Thus an (involuntary) inner regimentation goes hand in hand with the external regimentation we have indicated above on the part of monopoly capitalism. Ernst Fischer, the distinguished Austrian thinker, rightly said at the Peace Congress in Wroclaw that modern nonconformists are as alike as peas in a pod.

The louder and rowdier the proclamation of nonconformity, the shallower, more uniform and standardized the personality will be. This structure, as reflected in artistic creation and its audience, is an objective fraud which inevitably springs up from the soil of monopoly capitalism; subjectively it is very often a case of self-deception, a delusion. This is the general character of the 'free world' today. It was already thus under Hitler. But in Hitler's day, the fraud was concealed from some people by a gaudy veil of myths, while others thought that Hitler's demagogy and tyranny (and not the character of advanced monopoly capitalism, of which Hitler was a mere tool) constituted the only obstacle, and that with its elimination, nonconformist individualism would come into its own. Now the veils have been removed, and the delirium is over. Today, everyone must see that the precondition of a tolerated nonconformity is an obligatory apologetic of the capitalist system, and this in its present aggressive and bellicose form. Room for manoeuvre in this world is becoming increasingly narrow, and the prescribed content to be promulgated increasingly meagre and fraudulent. It is hard to

believe, but true. Cold War ideology has entailed a drop in standards even in comparison with the Hitler era. One has only to compare Hans Grimm with Koestler, or Rosenberg with Burnham.

The causes we have already revealed. They stem from the collapse of indirect apologetics, which at least offered ideologists the illusory semblance of a link with the people. However much effort modern 'brains trusts' devote to the task, they are incapable of devising a form for their central content – the struggle against communism – that could really win the people's enthusiasm. The fraud is becoming bigger and bigger, its mode of appearance less and less attractive and appealing. Hitler was still able to sum up everything reactionary accruing from the irrationalist developments of a century and a half and, as we have noted, to take irrationalism out of polite society on to the streets. Today, the socially determined necessity of direct apologetics renders this too impossible.

5

It goes without saying that all these tendencies, which we have outlined so far chiefly as they occur in the prevailing American ideology, are also to be found in Western Germany. Here, admittedly, they occur with specific variations, and in view of the immediate importance of Western Germany's role, it is certainly worth at least taking a look at these. The main point to observe is that Western Germany is the seat of former Hitlerian fascists. Naturally the occupying powers have done nothing to uproot Nazism in the organizational and ideological sense. On the contrary, they did all they could to salvage and preserve for the future those elements in the Nazi movement and its mental ambit that could be used in the campaign against the Soviet Union. Nevertheless a certain mental adjustment – in both external and internal

respects – was needed in order for a henchman of Hitler to become an ideologist of Truman or Eisenhower. It will suffice to recall those differences in ideological structure we have indicated in their basic outlines, for all the affinities as regards the principal questions. This issue is of particular interest to us because we can study the present further development which has been undertaken in the American period by ideologists who played a leading part in preparing and establishing Hitler's dominion.

The situation is simplest when it comes to those who – either of their own accord or because of chance personal circumstances – did not themselves participate in Hitler's régime directly although, considered from an objectively ideological angle, as extreme developers of irrationalism they blazed an intellectual trail for Hitler and led a quiet, secure life under his rule. Jaspers is the chief representative of this type. Today the well-tried principle of his philosophizing still holds good: to go along with fashionably reactionary trends all the way, while at the same time accommodating them to the tepid *juste milieu* of a petty-bourgeois salon of intellectuals. Since Jaspers was an existentialist, irrationalist, Kierkegaardian and Nietzschean, nobody in Hitler's time could raise a concrete objection to him. Now, after Hitler's downfall, Jaspers discovers . . . reason. This is natural: today 'reason' is dedicated to refuting Marxism as irrationalism was previously. It begins in an 'original' way by alleging that Marxism is actually a pseudo-scientific kind of magic: 'The destructive element is the creative element. When nothingness is introduced, Being appears automatically. But in the process of comprehension and action this is, in fact, a rehearsal of magical dealing in the guise of a pseudo-science. Corresponding to this magic is the Marxist claim to command a higher knowledge.' Jaspers's pretended originality consists in the use of a vogue word like 'magical', which was meant to give Marxism a devastatingly compromising ring in the age of semantic logic. This apart, the same argument has been already advanced seventy-five years previously by Dühring,

and its rebuttal may be easily located in Engels's *Anti-Dühring*. Here, ignoring the ABC of Marxism, Jaspers triumphantly repudiates inventions of his own creating.

As a good remedy for the 'superstition of knowledge' that Marxism supposedly presents, Jaspers recommends his own, fashionably up-to-date irrationalism: we must revert to the 'original deed' of fashionable so-called ontology. 'Then the language of all things becomes discernible, and myth meaningful; poetry and art become the "organon of philosophy" (Schelling). But the language of myth is distinct from a cognitive content. What is perceived in contemplation and is then animating in practice may neither be extinguished nor acquire the character of cognition when reason compels the test of truth. This verification is not a test by experience but a test against one's own intrinsic nature, by whether it causes an upsurge or decline in selfhood (*Selbstsein*), by the extent of our love.'

And in association with this Jaspers now defines as follows the connection between his old and new philosophy: 'Decades ago I spoke of existential philosophy, and I added that we were dealing not with a new or a particular philosophy but with the one perennial philosophy, which may, for an instant of abandonment to the merely objective realm, be accentuated with Kierkegaard's basic idea. Today I would prefer to call philosophy rational philosophy because it seems incumbent on us to emphasize its ancient essence. If reason is lost, philosophy itself will be lost.' To stress the predominance of reason is the sole possible guarantee of the origin of genuine myth: 'Thus myth is the inescapable language of transcendent truth. The creation of genuine myth is true illumination. This myth conceals reason inside it and is controlled by reason. Through myth, image and symbol we acquire our profoundest insight at the ultimate point.' Where this safeguard is lacking, veneration will inevitably arise. The danger here, according to Jaspers, is that there then comes about not an 'impotent nothingness' but a 'potent enchantment'. Jaspers thus employs the ancient distinction between white

and black magic to introduce into philosophy the line pursued by the leaders of the Cold War. That is to say, the 'experience' of the criminal Munich policy is supposed to be a reason for rejecting as appeasement any serious negotiations with the Soviet Union. So what Jaspers had neglected to contribute to the ideological rebuttal of Nazism, he now makes up for as an anti-Marxist campaigner. The parallels are all the more valid in that Chamberlain's political proximity to Hitler was no less than the philosophical proximity of Jaspers's irrationalism to its Nazi slant.

The emphasis on myth does not affect Jaspers's contact with semantics. We can already say this because his constant invocation of Kant is just as agnosticist and irrational as the basic philosophical position of semantics; let us remember the irrationalism of Wittgenstein. Both give expression, under a flimsy mask of rationality, to a despair over reason, to the impotence and dissolution of reason. For Jaspers 'reason' is, for example, *a priori* unhistorical (because Marx recognizes the rationality of history, Jaspers calls him a relativist), and it forms an antithesis to causal perception – 'causally I recognize only the non-rational,' he writes. Thus it is bound to be completely powerless in the face of reality. What Jaspers thus understands as a philosophy of reason is the old irrationalism in a garb matching modern American needs. It is the same philosophy of no exit as before, again tailored to the spiritual and moral comfort of a self-sufficient petty-bourgeois intelligentsia.

For Heidegger, it was far harder to engineer a transition of this kind. He had not only helped ideologically to bring Nazism about but had also made a direct and active stand on Hitler's behalf. To obtain an amnesty in such circumstances as well as a leading role once more, in order to assist the renewed barbarization of philosophy, and to do so by associating with professed combatants of Hitler, but without conceding the 'achievements' gained in paving the way for Hitler intellectually – in other words, to present a public image changed and unchanged at the same time – is a more

difficult task. How does Heidegger solve it? The Kierkegaardian arsenal offers an outstanding weapon for these purposes: an incognito. This is central to Heidegger's thinking today. With Kierkegaard himself, to be sure, the situation was relatively simple. Objectively, because in his case the incognito followed logically from the anti-rationality, the anti-humanity of the relationship to God; personally, because he had nothing compromising to hide.

Heidegger – unworldly, world-despising thinkers are often very practical in the conduct of their private lives – knows very well that atheism is not a going commodity whilst there exists an alliance between the Vatican and Wall Street. He draws from this the appropriate consequences. Not, of course, in the form of an overt break with the atheism and nihilism of *Being and Time*, but simply by stating apodictically that his *chef d'oeuvre* was neither atheistic nor nihilistic. But in spite of this concession to present-day religious trends, he cannot render Kierkegaard's theology of immediate use to his personal aims. He attempts, on the contrary, to deduce a dogmatic incognito as the essence of all historicity from an extension of the familiar theory of history and time. (In its intrinsic content, it must be admitted, this is still only an up-to-date variant of Kierkegaard's thesis that there is a world-history only in the sight of God.) For Heidegger, history is now a realm of errancy (*Irre*), of the dogmatic, ontological incognito:

> Being withdraws by enclosing itself in that which-is-in-being (*das Seiende*). In this way Being confuses what-is-in-being, while clarifying it, with errancy. What-is-in-being has been realized in errancy, in which Being misleads it and thus creates . . . error. Error is the essential arena of history. In it, the essential matter of history passes its likeness by . . . From the epoch of Being comes the epochal nature of its destiny, in which authentic world-history consists. Every time that Being holds fast in its destiny, world is an abrupt, unexpected event. Every epoch in world-history is an epoch of errancy.

Here Heidegger found the ontological arguments and justification for his behaviour in the Hitler period. In his book on, or rather against humanism this idea receives a more concrete form still. He stresses – through his falsification of Hölderlin – that the latter's relation to Greek antiquity is 'essentially different from humanism'. 'Hence the young Germans who knew of Hölderlin thought and lived differently in the face of death from what was publicly proclaimed to be German opinion.' Here Heidegger discreetly refrains from saying – evidently this also belongs to the ontologically historical incognito – that those young men were not only in a 'situation confronting death' under Hitler, but took a highly active part in murder and torture, pillage and rape. Evidently he considers it superfluous to mention this, for after all the incognito covers everything up: who can tell what a pupil of Heidegger intoxicated by Hölderlin 'thought and lived' when he was pushing women and children into the gas chambers at Auschwitz? Nobody can tell, either, what Heidegger himself 'thought and lived' when he led the Freiburg students to vote for Hitler. There is nothing unequivocally knowable in history as he presents it: it is a general 'errancy'.

Here, Heidegger has a threefold aim in view. Firstly, a total denial of responsibility for what he did to give Hitler active support. Secondly, he wants to preserve his old existential standpoint. Thirdly, he wants to make it seem as if all the changes he has effected today to accommodate himself to American policies had always represented his views. Such acrobatic feats can only be accomplished by resorting to scientific dishonesty. His former pupil, Karl Löwith, has exposed a fraud of this kind in the *Neue Rundschau*.

> But a contradiction cannot be resolved either by a shift in perspective of one's view or by a dialectical correspondence. In the postface to the fourth edition of *Was ist Metaphysik?* we read with regard to the truth of Being that Being 'may well' exist without that which-is-in-being,

'but' that what-is-in-being can never exist without Being. In the fifth edition published six years later, the 'but', i.e., the stressing of an antithesis, is left out and the 'well' replaced by a 'never', i.e., the whole meaning of the sentence is turned into the opposite, without any indication of this change. What would one say to a theologian who claimed on one occasion that God may well exist without a Creation and on another that he could never exist without it? How do we account for the fact that a linguistic thinker who weighs his words as carefully as Heidegger makes such a radical change to so crucial a passage? For obviously only one of the two formulations can be the true and proper one.

Now whither is this philosophy bound? It retains from pre-fascism its extremely anti-rational character. When Heidegger now says, 'Thinking only begins when we have learnt that the reason we have glorified for centuries is thought's most stubborn antagonist,' he is only drawing the most extreme inferences from what was implicit in Husserl's 'intuitive vision' (*Wesensschau*) from the outset. And since, as we have shown, phenomenology in its origins was closely related to Machism, it is not too tricky for Heidegger – in essence – to come very near to semantics. His terminological peculiarities are well known, as is his verbal hair-splitting. Now, as the crowning of Machism, phenomenology and semantics, he succeeds in making a philosophical method of language. 'Thinking collects language into the simple telling. Thus language is the language of Being as the clouds are the clouds in the sky. With its telling, thinking makes modest furrows in language. They are more modest even that the furrows which a countryman slowly ploughs in a field.' Here we have 'poetic' semantics as a particular German nuance. But in both cases the irrationalist abyss is the same, no matter whether the immediate form of expression is deliberately 'poetic' or soberly prosaic.

The methodological approximation points to an objective

proximity. Heidegger's Being (in contrast to what-is-in-being) is not all that far removed from what, according to Wittgenstein, could only be shown and not stated. And a similar method will give rise to similar consequences. In Hitler Heidegger greeted the dawning of a new age and thereby, to put it mildly, brought eternal disgrace upon himself. Today he is more cautious, at least in expression, but he seeks to ingratiate himself with today's or tomorrow's rulers as much as with Hitler. He expresses himself with caution, with a deliberate obscurity, but he lets the idea of a new age glimmer through this twilight again.

> Are we standing indeed on the eve of the vastest transformation of the earth and the time of the historical space on which it hinges? Are we on the eve of a night that will precede a different dawn? Are we about to march off into the historical land of this global evening? Will the land of eveningtide emerge first? Is this evening land[7] to become the scene of the coming and more incipiently transmitted history, over and above Occident and Orient and passing beyond the European stage? Are we contemporaries already occidental in a sense that is only coming to light with our passage into the global dark? How are any philosophies of history that are purely historically measured to account for history if they only dazzle with what is surveyable in material historically inculcated, without ever conceiving the foundations of its explanatory causes from the essence of history, and the latter from Being itself? *Are* we the latecomers we are? But are we at the same time also attendants on the dawn of a quite different world epoch which will have left our present historical ideas of history behind?

The form of inquiry and the pessimistic impressions suggest Germany's situation today. They are indispensable, for without the pessimistic tone one cannot influence the élite, so-called, of the intellectuals – especially German intellectuals

– not even today. But we can see or at least glimpse behind this – in an intended twilight – the outlines of the 'American century', of the global State under American command. (Certainly, if a German imperialism should achieve independence at some future date and again aspire to global power, these words from Heidegger can then be applied to it too as a 'prophecy'.) Heidegger's disgrace over Hitler is not enough for him; he needs a second disgrace at all costs. This would be the suitable fulfilment of his philosophy of history – as a doctrine of 'errancy'.

Naturally the perspective we have drawn is – in immediate terms – the most important feature of these statements by Heidegger. But beside the perspective, the method must not be overlooked completely. We have noted that Heidegger posits an 'authentic' historicity in order to challenge real historicity as 'vulgar' more effectively. This tendency becomes acuter in the post-war period. Whereas his *Being and Time* was in character a single great polemic against Marxism, but without revealing this character through as much as a distinct reference, Heidegger now feels already obliged to speak of Marx openly. 'What Marx, deriving from Hegel in a substantial and significant sense, recognized as the alienation of man reaches back at root into the homelessness of man in the modern epoch . . . Because Marx, in experiencing alienation, delves into an essential dimension of history, the Marxist view of history is taken to be superior to all other versions.' Granted, he promptly reduces Marxism to technics, like all bourgeois vulgarizers of historical perception. But this statement, of course, already amounts to saying openly that Heidegger regards Marxism as the chief antagonist. On the one hand all this expresses bourgeois philosophy's universal rearguard action against Marxism: just as Nietzsche, after Schopenhauer's repudiation of all history, was forced to argu a mythical pseudo-historicism, so imperialist phenomenology proceeds from Husserl's a-historicism via Scheler to Heidegger's 'authentic' historicity. And on the other hand, the comments quoted above clearly show that he intends

thereby to discredit all real and concrete historical knowledge. For he states: 'How are any philosophies of history that are purely historically measured to account for history if they only dazzle with what is surveyable in material historically inculcated, without ever conceiving the foundations of its explanatory causes from the essence of history, and the latter from Being itself?'

We are dealing here with a universal tendency of the age. To illustrate this with a topical example, let us recall the Camus-Sartre discussion already mentioned in other contexts. How far Camus squares with Heidegger in points of detail is of no importance at all in this context. The important thing is that he bitterly resists a-historicism or indeed anti-historicism while at the same time arguing his individualistic and anarchic withdrawal from real history in the name of a 'supra-history', just as Heidegger plays off the historicity of Being against that of 'what-is-in-being'. Still more important as the sign of a salutary existentialist crisis, however, is the passionate protest by Sartre and his followers against Camus's position. Sartre says – and rightly so as a reply to Camus: 'Our freedom today is nothing but the *choice of the struggle whereby we can become free*. The paradoxical aspect of this formulation simply expresses the paradox of our *historical* condition.' As far as Sartre's philosophizing goes, the paradox is undoubtedly there, but objectively speaking it can be traced to a protest. This derives from the sound instincts of a man of our time who does not wish to share the guilt for the global catastrophe set in motion from America. Clearly seeing the role of the proletarian class struggle and the communist parties in averting this threat of war in practice, he consequently perceives the danger of the Heidegger-Camus conception of history in its real repercussions. But he fails to notice – for the time being – that he is here playing off a paradoxically contradictory existentialist standpoint against a rigorously existentialist one. For the whole paradox in his polemical comments boils down to his using the concept of freedom first in the orthodox

existentialist sense but then, in the same thesis, in a concretely historical sense. Sartre's fate as a thinker will depend on the direction in which he can and wants to resolve this 'paradox'.

Heidegger keeps his cynicism hidden behind a verbosity which flirts with obscurity and has pretensions to poetry. This cynicism is voiced quite nakedly by Hitler's former personal jurist and law theorist, Carl Schmitt. We have already given the ideological gist of his present-day theory of international law. From this formulation we can already see that Schmitt is serving American imperialism as busily as he once served Hitler. Today he is again acting as cleverly, paradoxically and cynically as before. Thus he stands every chance of a benevolent reception, of a full say at the current headquarters of international reaction and war-mongering. But he too feels (or at any rate felt) the need to 'purge' himself of his Hitlerian sins. And since he seeks – far more decidedly than Heidegger – to salvage all his earlier, aggressively reactionary endeavours for the American future (or, as the case may be, for that of a newly arisen and independent German imperialism), he too takes the incognito as the proffered ideological tool.

In his comments on a radio talk by Karl Mannheim just after the war, Schmitt gives such an innocent explanation for his role in the Hitler régime that the cynical and nihilistic character of the incognito, the philosophical claim to the most shameless lie will be evident to any intelligent person. Schmitt writes: 'There remained the old-established quiet tradition of withdrawal into a private inner life, along with the utmost readiness for a right and proper collaboration with anything decreed by any legitimate government.' He even has the temerity to accuse of superficiality anyone venturing to criticize such behaviour as his under Hitler: 'If the only thing deserving attention is what appears under the spotlight of a fully known and sanctioned public life, and if furthermore it is considered that an unqualified spiritual subjection lies in entering into this public arena,

then to be sure the scientific work of these twelve years would merit no special attention!' (We have not neglected to pay 'special attention' to Schmitt's 'scientific' activities under Hitler.) What went on in Carl Schmitt's incognito inner life during the Hitler period remains, of course, undisclosed; in places Schmitt lifts the incognito to suggest discreetly that he was one of the people who did not agree with Hitler. But it is a historical fact that at a time when, say, Niemöller, Wiechert and Niekisch – not to mention the communists – clearly voiced their opposition to Nazism, Schmitt was elaborating principles of law philosophy and international rights that vindicated Hitler's deeds, from the mass murders of 1934 to the German Army's invasion of neutral countries.

Schmitt himself senses that in his case, the incognito of a subjectivist state of abstraction à la Kierkegaard and Heidegger does not carry conviction. He therefore also invokes an important (purported) historical analogy. He writes of Hobbes: '*Hobbes*, on the other hand, had a much better grasp. After a further century of theological disputes and European civil wars, his despair is infinitely deeper than Bodin's. Hobbes belongs to the great solitary figures of the seventeenth century, who were all acquainted with one another. He grasped not only the manifold character of the modern leviathan but also how to get on with it and the behaviour commending itself to an independently-minded individual if he becomes involved in such a dangerous matter . . . He reflected, spoke and wrote on these perilous subjects, always with an inviolate intellectual freedom and always well shielded in his person, always either in flight or in inconspicuous seclusion.' The 'small' – but neither philosophically nor politico-ethically trivial – difference is that Hobbes stood for progress in his time, whereas Schmitt supported the most extreme reaction of his day. But there lies still more behind this analogy: Schmitt's avowed continuation of his activity on the farthest wing of militant reaction. His interpretation of the analogy is as follows: just as it did not matter to Hobbes whether the liquidation of feudalism, the

setting up of a modern bourgeois centralized State was carried out by the Stuarts or Cromwell, it does not matter to him – Carl Schmitt – whether it is Hitler, Eisenhower or a newly arisen German imperialism that sets up the absolute dictatorship of monopoly capitalism.

Hence now, as we have already shown, he is able to devise the best epigrammatic summary of the United States' foreign policy, just as he had formulated this for Hitler. Hence he shows today the ineluctability of the dilemma of isolation or intervention for the U.S.A.: 'The contradictions stem from the unresolved problems of a territorial development involving an obligation either to set limits to the invasion and to find other major territories beside those recognizing themselves as such, or else to turn back what has hitherto been a war of national claims into a world-wide civil war.' And hence Schmitt is now publishing old and new essays on his long-standing favourite, Donoso Cortés. What is the essential point they make? It is the antithesis of bourgeois ideology and Marxism. The latter has grasped the link with the present time of historical developments from 1848 up to the present, whereas bourgeois ideology has not. Schmitt sums up the situation as follows: 'In their awareness of continuity, the communist authors have a considerable superiority and even a monopoly over the other historians, who cannot accept the events of 1848 and thereby forfeit the right to depict the present. Bourgeois historians are in a state of great embarrassment. On the one hand they condemn the suppression of the revolution because they do not want to be reactionary, while on the other they welcome the restoration of calm and security as a victory for order.' It is now a matter of breaking this communist monopoly and of bringing to light the 'non-socialist continuities' (i.e., the successes and traditions of the counter-revolution). Donoso Cortés, according to Schmitt, is the ideologist just suited to arguing such a continuity. 'But the essential point is the accurate observation that the pseudo-religion of absolute humanity is exactly what opens the door to an inhuman reign of terror. That was a

fresh observation, profounder than de Maistre's many splendid dicta on revolution, war and bloodshed. By comparison with the Spaniard, who gazed into the abyss of the horrors of 1848, de Maistre is still an aristocrat of the restoration of the *ancien régime* who prolonged and deepened the eighteenth-century spirit.' According to Schmitt, it follows that 'the monopoly of the interpretation of the century does, however, contain something extremely important, viz., the historical legitimacy of autonomous power, the right to violence and absolution from the world-spirit for all crimes committed on its behalf'.

So Donoso Cortés becomes the forebear of an arbitrary, absolute dictatorship of monopoly capitalism to be set up at some future date. Donoso's 'great theoretical significance for the history of counter-revolutionary theory lies in the fact that he gave up the legitimist arguments and no longer propounded a political philosophy of restoration but a theory of dictatorship'. And Schmitt has such an enthusiasm for this prospect that he lays his incognito aside and openly states what makes his hero so irresistibly fascinating: 'His contempt for human beings knew no bounds; their blind understanding, their feeble wills, the derisory *élan* of their carnal desires seem so pitiful to him that all the vocabulary of all human languages is not sufficient to express the full baseness of these creatures.' Here we clearly perceive Schmitt's association with all anti-human tendencies, past and present, along with the reason for it in socio-human terms: he is an enemy of the masses grown blind with hatred, a fanatic in the campaign against *Vermassung* or mass feeling. We also see in this statement the reality behind Schmitt's claim not to have been in agreement with the Hitler régime. Evidently he regarded Hitler's social demagogy, whose falsity he certainly saw through, as a contemptible masquerade of the absolute dictatorship of monopoly capitalism. For Schmitt, as for Spengler, Ernst Jünger and others, Hitler was 'too democratic', 'too vulgar'. (This professed opposition did not of course stop Schmitt from zealously assisting Hitler

ideologically to the best of his abilities.) Today, after the collapse of social demagogy and indirect apologetics, Carl Schmitt understandably scents fresh hope.

The cynicism of this incognito ideology is, naturally enough, very widespread among West German intellectuals. It received its most overt and concentrated form in Ernst von Salomon's *Fragebogen*,[8] a fact that may account for this book's huge success. Salomon too belongs to those who, objectively considered, helped to pave the way for Hitler, who had 'reservations' about the Hitler régime, and who therefore attempted after the war to argue an ideological justification of their *J'ai vécu* standpoint. Salomon's cynicism as expressed in his book differs to his advantage from that of Heidegger, Carl Schmitt and Ernst Jünger in that he is at least upright in not glossing over his *J'ai vécu* feelings. He wanted simply to survive the Hitler régime – to be sure in the best material circumstances possible – and his so-called opposition was limited to voicing certain scruples in very private circles. In his case, therefore, the incognito has a robustly prosaic character, without existentialist mysticism: it is a straightforward mimicry under Nazi conditions.

Ernst Jünger on the other hand, whose *The Worker*, as we know, contributed far more to the origin of Nazi ideology than did Salomon's outsider writings, participated much more markedly in the Hitler régime, albeit largely as a mere figurehead. After the event, however, he portrayed his 'opposition' stance far more plainly. But this again followed the line of an aristocratic protest against the vulgarity of Hitler's demagogy and not against its social content. Jünger differs from Schmitt only in that he overtly gave prominence to the role of the hereditary Prussian *Junker* nobility in an absolute dictatorship ('Burgenland' in his novel *Heliopolis*). In addition he provides, as philosophical background, an avowal of myth and magic as tokens of the difference between the modern period and the nineteenth century. 'The special character of the nineteenth-century spirit lay in its neglect of this relation of rationality to the depths of

consciousness. In its self-sufficiency it imagined that developments were progressing on a level determined by itself, in an enclosed *juste milieu* which it had created and exercised control over, and which it defined as consciousness. Given this state of affairs, the awakening was bound to occur. It happened at the very moment that the rational roots had reached the sub-soil of myths. This can be verified in words, imagery, ideas and even in the sciences. They all became stronger than befitted human proportions, human decorum. Mythical figures now advanced upon the rational ones in a series of terrible battles, and the new worlds of myth, dream and nocturnal magic stood revealed in the glow of the conflagrations.' Jünger thus joins the ranks of ideologists like Jaspers, Heidegger and Schmitt who, as 'opponents' to Hitler, offered irrational myth as a weapon to the new imperialism, and themselves as the soldiers.

We have emphasized the outsider element in Salomon's attitude in the pre-Hitler period. As we know, he circulated among the most diverse reactionary groups, taking part in the murder of Rathenau, the *Landvolk* movement and so on; it is characteristic of his nihilistic cynicism that he calls this latter activity a 'coarse bit of fun'. He experienced the crisis preceding Hitler's seizure of power and the growing influence, during it, of the communist philosophy; his brother Bruno even became a communist. This crisis also forced Ernst himself to try and come to terms with Marxism. Of course no real understanding was gained in his case, indeed the encounter even ended with his rejection of Marxism, although Salomon states on occasion – and this is again very typical of his cynicism: 'But the communist was simply right in the matter.' It is equally typical of him, however, that such an observation had no effect at all on his subsequent attitude.

And so he fitted into the Hitler régime, leading a quiet and untroubled life. And although sometimes the Nazis' actions made him extremely angry, he remained in essence – even in his heart – entirely passive. He spoke of this passivity, this avoidance of all protest to his wife *à propos* the Jewish

pogroms in Berlin: 'Is it because we know we shall find no answering echo? It is not that. It is much worse. To tell the truth we are dead already. We cannot live by our own lights any longer at all.' Straight after this he related an episode experienced in Berlin and sums up its effects thus: 'I made my way home along the Kurfürstendamm and thought very hard indeed – there must, there just must be a third solution. And if there was not, what was better: to act like a fool, or to act like a coward?'

This plainly honest pragmatism distinguishes Salomon to his advantage from the romantically and mystically inflated nihilism of Jünger and his following. Hence he is able to sketch animated scenes from everyday life in the Hitler period; hence he is able to lay bare in a realistic way the cruelty and corruption of the American 'liberators'. But the core of the *Fragebogen* is Salomon's allegiance to a *J'ai vécu* cynicism. When he and his wife were released from their brief American imprisonment, there took place between them a dialogue which is so typical of the contemporary mood that we must quote from it at some length. Salomon says to his wife: 'You came out of it very well! You have no cause for complaint. Far less cause than everybody you know and all the millions you don't know! And the same is true of myself. We have had a good time of it, Ille, and must not feel any resentment, we are among the few who must not feel any resentment.' So Salomon adjusts himself to a *J'ai vécu* attitude for the new period as well.

But more typical still, and a stronger expression of real mass feelings as a retrospective summary of the experiences of the Hitler period, is his wife Ille's reply. She says: 'I must tell you something awful! I did not have a good time of it! I know, you were thinking all along that the main thing was that we got out alive. But I have not got out alive. I am no longer the woman I was when I married you! What was best and most precious in me is dead. They have killed it off. The last twelve years were frightful for me. I have always made an effort not to let you see it. We have had a good life,

if you like, a good life from day to day.' She tells how both of them, Salomon and herself, knew the details of all the atrocities committed under Hitler but – in order not to jeopardize a life of prosperity and relative security – never acknowledged them and were never prepared to. She now sums up her morale as a result of all this: 'I love life and I want a full life or no life at all! But dignity is one part of it! Not only a face or arms and legs, but dignity as well! And these twelve years have sought to take away my dignity! For what does living mean if not loving? I wanted to love the day and the country, the Germans among whom I was living, and you and myself! And I was not allowed to. I had to learn to despise it all, the day and the country and the Germans and you and myself!'

6

Even in Ille, of course, there are no discernible conclusions drawn from her experiences. But the concrete substance of her outburst contains more than an emotionally critical summing-up; unknown to her, it also implies the human possibilities of a way out. Millions of Illes – mostly as unconscious of it as herself – have experienced similar and often far more harrowing things under Hitler and now behold with horror the preliminaries to another war, and the sprouting of a new fascism. The spontaneous cry 'Leave us out!' roughly expresses the emotional consequences of what Ille von Salomon experienced and tried to couch in halting phrases. At present this cry expresses only a mounting fear among broad masses, fears of a fresh war, fears for one's own life, for the lives of relatives, for one's possessions. But there is also a flickering dread of another violation and spoiling of the human dignity of personal integrity. Of course there are concomitant manifestations – on a mass scale, even – of a far greater awareness; there are the public statements and the

commitment of persons who are ready to sacrifice their all to ensure that nothing akin to the Hitler régime can ever arise in Germany again. And there is also appearing, albeit slowly and paradoxically, an awareness of how much the American Cold War and its German branch office, the Adenauer government, is preparing for something similar in (seemingly) different and (purportedly) diametrically opposite forms.

For the time being – chiefly in Western Germany, but also in many other countries of the capitalist world – such voices are being drowned by the 'Voice of America'. The substance of this propaganda we have already expounded in detail; we have also revealed its inner hollowness, its worthlessness and its lies. But of course the danger inherent in such propaganda is still immense nonetheless. The mass of those capable of being led astray, of the cowardly and easily intimidated, the weak and passive spirits, of minds poisoned spiritually and morally, is still exceptionally large. The situation as a whole, however, has altered radically. Before the Second World War Hitler unfurled on the streets the flag of irrationalism and the destruction of reason. Today, reason is descending from the lecture platform, workshop or laboratory on to the streets to plead its cause before the masses, and in the vanguard of the masses. This strategic offensive by progressive philosophy, by the defence of reason is the specifically new element of the post-war period.

Around 1848 there first appeared the major, really decisive adversary of the destruction of reason: Marxism. And since 1917 it has evolved not only into the philosophy of the peoples of one-sixth of the earth, but is also manifested at a higher intellectual stage as Leninism-Marxism, as the further development of Marxism in a period of world wars and world revolutions. The *Communist Manifesto* had already been for a long time one of the most widely read and translated works in world literature. After 1917 Lenin's works joined it – along with a wider distribution of the writings of Marx and Engels. But in this respect, too, the post-1945 period signifies a qualitative change. There are few countries

where the translation and distribution of these works did not proceed by leaps and bounds. We need not even mention China, the new People's Republics or lands like France and Italy, where communist supporters constitute over one-third of the population. Even where the communists' organized strength is still relatively slight, we can observe a rapid growth in acquaintance with Marxism-Leninism, and the influence of Marxist philosophy reaches far beyond those frontiers. Regarding this matter again, we are concerned with the ideological aspect only. But it is also necessary to say that in these countries it is no longer just a question of the translation and distribution of the Marxist-Leninist classics, but of a rapid growth in native Marxist research, a scientific treatment of the country's history and present condition in the Marxist-Leninist spirit, using its intellectual weapons in the struggle against reaction.

This upsurge is taking effect far beyond party political limits. The attraction of Marxism-Leninism for leading progressive intellectuals is steadily increasing. More and more natural scientists are grasping how much help dialectical materialism can offer them, especially since this, through its very solution of concrete scientific problems, has raised both science itself and the method of dialectical materialism to a higher stage in the Soviet Union. More and more writers are experiencing the same with regard to their art. Hence the Soviet Union's discoveries and achievements are triggering off so sharp a defensive action in reactionary bourgeois science and philosophy (the Lysenko controversy). And hence such discussions are taking on more and more of a Kravtchenko flavour in the 'free world'. So as to block the increasingly irresistible appeal of progressive art and science, people are speaking far less of the actual problems than of the (alleged) persecutions to which 'nonconformist' scholars and artists are subject in the Soviet Union. To be sure, Kravtchenko affairs will always give rise to some technical hitches; it appears to be a practical impossibility adequately to brief all one's agents in opportunities for spreading lies and calumny.

Thus not long ago, a certain Senator Wiley had the misfortune indignantly to defend in the name of freedom the supporters, persecuted by Stalin, of the 'philologist Araktcheyev', evidently without knowing that this Araktcheyev was a notorious reactionary General and politician from the time of Tsar Nicholas I, and that Stalin was invoking his name and methods to bring similar contempt upon those who restricted the freedom of scientific discussion.

The other new element in the active, large-scale defence of reason is the peace movement. This too we shall now consider solely from the standpoint of our subject: the destruction or restoration of reason. It is patent that today as under Hitler, war-mongering is again the major social force working towards the destruction of reason; and today its ideological battlefield is the Cold War. It amounts to the spreading of a vague fatalism, panic and a paralysing fear among human beings the world over. An undoubtedly competent witness, Faulkner, said in his Nobel Prize speech: 'The tragedy of our age is a general dread which governs the entire world. We have already carried it inside us for so long that we can even live with it. There are no spiritual problems left, there only remains the question: when am I going to be blown up?' And the German author Zuckmayer says, in very similar terms: 'What is the reality of this world situation which confronts us at the present time? It is a nightmare for the large majority. I believe that ninety per cent of all the people alive today, all over the world, do not want or hope for what appears to be impending. But they must allow it to happen without a chance of counter-measures, just as in a nightmare one knows that one is dreaming, that one is having a nightmare, that one is being tormented and stifled by the incubus, and yet cannot shake it off, cannot move, cry out or wake up.'

This fear, this nightmare was the main ideological weapon in the Cold War as long as the U.S.A. believed it could still flaunt with the atomic bomb monopoly. If other motives –

spurious olive branches, the 'liberation' of nations 'oppressed' by socialism, etc. – now also enter into it, nonetheless to foster such feelings of panic still remains an important Cold War weapon (cf. the special issue of Collier's Magazine). To catch the masses unawares – and even governments – is still an essential part of the strategy. But nowadays it is no longer a bolt from the blue, as in 1914. A fatalistic paralysis of the human will and understanding, the constant existence of a state of tense panic constitute the preliminary tactics.

New, however, is the total difference in the reaction of the masses from what it was before the two past world wars. Everyone knows of the 600 million peace signatures. Once again, we shall look into this only as far as it relates to our subject. The peace movement as such has no philosophy, and knows no barriers in respect of political, philosophical or religious convictions. Here Christian and Moslem priests, Quakers and pacifists, liberals and neutrals, etc., are working hand in hand with socialists and communists. But little though the peace movement entails a 'conformism', its mere existence, its growth and its increasingly concrete outlines imply a raising and answering of the great philosophical question: for or against reason. Of course the questions and answers within the new entity, as regards individuals and groups, are extremely diverse and often totally opposed. But the great common principle behind such divergences is no less than the defence of human reason, and not merely its existence in general, but its actual influence and impact on history, in which we are all more or less active participants.

Everywhere, the peace movement had and has its beginnings in spontaneous emotion, manifested most clearly in the West German *Ohne uns* movement. In essence, the 500 million signatures to the Stockholm protest against atomic warfare also indicate an instinctive revolt by the masses against this criminal project. This spontaneous outburst of mass feeling, however, differs qualitatively from all previous ones. It would be wrong to gauge its proportions purely quantitatively, although such a mounting mass indignation already signifies

something that is new in itself. The essentially new feature emerges particularly sharply if we think of the moment of its eruption. Previous mass waves of anti-war feeling occurred mostly in the third or fourth year of war, were often phenomena resulting from major defeats, and were nearly always directly triggered off by the crushing burden of a war economy. Today, however, this mass movement is breaking out *before* a war, albeit also *during* the *Cold* War. Thus it has a preventive, averting character and is far more than a mere reaction to accomplished historical facts. This in itself lifts the movement out of the realm of pure spontaneity or emotionality. Every attempt at prevention implies a strong element of a rational, conscious desire to control future, forthcoming events. The experiences of two world wars have therefore accumulated in this spontaneity. It evinces a fundamentally new physiognomy: that of reason in spontaneity.

Pietro Nenni, the vice-president of the world peace movement, has underlined in a speech the important difference he sees between the peace partisans' second major campaign, the 600 million signatures demanding a pact of the five major powers, and the Stockholm appeal. Here, he says, the path leads from spontaneity to conscious awareness, from emotion to the use of reason – its use for a very concrete task decisively influencing both each individual's life and the life of mankind. The rational perception that has its origins here is twofold: perception of the objective task, and perception of one's own share in its execution. And it is just these two aspects which show that where war and peace are concerned, human reason – if humanity is not to come to grief – must take the initiative, neither leaving events to run their own immanent course nor permitting them to be swayed by criminal intentions.

How far and with what amount of subjective awareness individual relations to the whole are worked out inwardly varies very considerably, but that is not crucial here. Important is the clear, objectively discernible meaning of the 600 million signatures. In constructing a more and more concrete

defence of peace (identifying aggression, defending the nations' independence, examining the possibility of the peaceful coexistence of different social systems, a methodical approach to negotiations, etc.), the peace movement is increasingly leading to ever-higher generalizations and making an increasingly strong appeal to the independent judgement – resistant to all mendacious propaganda – and reason of many hundred millions of people.

Not only is such an intellectualization and rationalism not daunting for the masses; they actually find it highly attractive. (Contrast this with the high tide of irrationalist fascism, when the few bourgeois champions of reason were excusing themselves on account of their rationalism or were forced to look like solitary, oddly paradoxical eccentrics.) And this movement for the restoration of reason and the safeguarding of peace – the two are inseparable – is taking a hold among ever broader sections of the masses; wider and wider circles are coming together, joining forces and marching united – without, of course, so much as a suggestion of a philosophical 'conformity'.

The peace movement's practical aims and perspectives are not something we can discuss now. But its mere existence has a world-historical significance for human thought: the *protection of reason as taking the form of a mass movement*. After a century of the increasing dominance of irrationalism, the defence of reason and the restoration of subverted reason is starting on its triumphal march among the masses. Politically, the peace movement sets out to isolate from the masses and thereby to condemn to impotence the numerically small but, at present, crucially influential coterie of monopoly capitalists and militarists. Its ideological side, meanwhile, has the programmatic bias of removing the influence, on popular thinking and sensibilities, of manufacturers of decadent and irrationalist theories of any kind, of anti-rational and anti-human declarations. It is not enough by a long chalk that a writer like Denis de Rougemont should justifiably complain at his associates' lack of influence. As

long as the gap is filled by gangster films and hack literature, we cannot regard this great task as completed.

This *mass rising on behalf of reason* is the great contemporary response to the hysterical fear of *Vermassung* or mass movements and the irrationalism closely linked with that fear. This rising is therefore a counterblast, historically considered, to the Hitlerian rising of uncontrolled, anti-rational instincts. It is an active comeback and, still more, a nipping in the bud of intended future atrocities like Hitler's.

More than a hundred years ago Marx wrote: 'To be sure, the weapon of criticism cannot replace the critique of the weapon. Material violence must be overthrown with material violence, but theory too becomes material violence the moment it seizes the masses.' We Marxists know that philosophically too, the great deciding contest between reason and anti-reason, between materialist dialectics and irrationalism can – so long after this struggle has become a contest over Marxism – only be brought to a final victorious end with the proletariat's triumph over the bourgeoisie, the overthrow of capitalism and the setting up of socialism. It goes without saying that all this has to remain entirely beyond the peace movement's objectives. Hence not even on the ideological plane can its mighty effort to reinstate reason and restore it to power fight the final deciding battle. But this does not at all lessen its world-historical significance. The movement has opened its campaign by mobilizing 600 millions, and it is in the process of mobilizing further hundreds of millions. It is the first major mass rising against the madness of imperialist unreason. Fighting in reason's name, the masses have proclaimed their rights on the streets, their right to a share in determining our destiny. No longer will they forgo this right, the use of reason on their own behalf and on behalf of mankind, the right to live in a rationally guided world and not amid the chaotic madness of war.

BUDAPEST, JANUARY 1953

NOTES

1 Mailer: *The Naked and the Dead*, 26th impression, London 1971, pp. 244-5.

2 Translator's note. An invention of the Low German humorist Fritz Reuter (1810-74), author of such popular novels as *Ut de Franzosentid*.

3 *The Crusaders*.

4 Koestler: *The Age of Longing*, Danube Edition, London 1970, p. 142.

5 Translator's note. The subject of Carl Zuckmayer's satirical play *Der Hauptmann von Köpenick*, 1930.

6 Koestler: *The Age of Longing*, p. 141.

7 Translator's note. *Abendland*: Heidegger is playing on the 'evening' image in this German word for the West or Occident.

8 Translator's note. An autobiographical history covering the period from 1919 to 1945, and published in 1951.

INDEX OF PERSONS

Works mentioned in the text are listed under their author. Page references in bold type denote a detailed examination.